W9-COO-346

# COMMIT SOCIOLOGY

## Volume 1

Introduction to Sociology | University of Toronto

First Custom Edition

Christian O. Caron & Robert Brym

 NELSON EDUCATION

# NELSON / EDUCATION

COPYRIGHT © 2014 by Nelson Education Ltd.

Printed and bound in Canada
1  2  3  4  16 15  14  13

For more information contact Nelson Education Ltd., 1120 Birchmount Road, Toronto, Ontario, M1K 5G4. Or you can visit our Internet site at http://www.nelson.com

ALL RIGHTS RESERVED. No part of this work covered by the copyright herein may be reproduced, transcribed, or used in any form or by any means—graphic, electronic, or mechanical, including photocopying, recording, taping, Web distribution, or information storage and retrieval systems—without the written permission of the publisher.

For permission to use material from this text or product, submit all requests online at www.cengage.com/permissions. Further questions about permissions can be emailed to permissionrequest@cengage.com

Every effort has been made to trace ownership of all copyrighted material and to secure permission from copyright holders. In the event of any question arising as to the use of any material, we will be pleased to make the necessary corrections in future printings.

This textbook is a Nelson custom publication. Because your instructor has chosen to produce a custom publication, you pay only for material that you will use in your course.

ISBN-13: 978-0-17-656307-3
ISBN-10: 0-17-656307-5

**Consists of Selections from:**

*New Society, 7th Edition*
Robert J. Brym
ISBN 10: 0-17-650999-2, © 2013

*Seeing Sociology: Core Modules, 1st Edition*
Joan Ferrante
ISBN 10: 1-133-96316-1, © 2014

*Understanding Society: An Introductory Reader, 4th Edition*
Margaret L. Andersen | Kim A. Logio | Howard F. Taylor
ISBN 10: 1-111-18596-4, © 2011

*Sociological Footprints: Introductory Readings in Sociology, 11th Edition*
Leonard Cargan, Jeanne H. Ballantine
ISBN 10: 0-495-60128-4, © 2010

*Images of Society: Readings That Inspire and Inform Sociology, 3rd Edition*
Jerry P. White, Michael Carroll
ISBN 10: 0-17-651416-3, © 2013

*Society in Question, 7th Edition*
Robert J. Brym
ISBN 10: 0-17-650998-4, © 2014

*Race, Class, and Gender: An Anthology, 8th Edition*
Margaret L. Andersen, Patricia Hill Collins
ISBN 10: 1-111-83094-0, © 2013

*Fundamentals of Social Research, 3rd Canadian Edition*
Earl Babbie, Lucia Benaquisto
ISBN 10: 0-17-650388-9, © 2014

*Sociology in Our Times, Sixth Canadian Edition*
Jane Lothian Murray, Rick Linden, Diana Kendall
ISBN 10: 0-17-651000-1, © 2014

*Understanding Social Problems, 4th Canadian Edition*
Linda A. Mooney, M. Morgan Holmes, David Knox, Caroline Schacht
ISBN 10: 0-17-650277-7, © 2012

**Cover Credit:**

©Ted Soqui/Corbis

# Table of Contents

# Introduction to Sociology

# INTRODUCTION
# TO SOCIOLOGY

**Robert J. Brym**
UNIVERSITY OF TORONTO

SOURCE: © Lárus Sigurðarson.

4

**IN THIS CHAPTER YOU WILL LEARN THAT**

- The causes of human behaviour lie partly in the patterns of social relations that surround and penetrate people.

- Sociologists examine the connection between personal troubles and social relations.

- Sociological research is often motivated by the desire to improve the social world. At the same time, sociologists adopt scientific methods to test their ideas.

- Sociology originated at the time of the Industrial Revolution. The founders of sociology diagnosed the massive social transformations of their day. They also suggested ways of overcoming the social problems created by the Industrial Revolution.

- Today's Postindustrial Revolution similarly challenges us. The chief value of sociology is that it can help clarify the scope, direction, and significance of social change. Sociology can also suggest ways of managing change.

## INTRODUCTION

### WHY I DECIDED NOT TO STUDY SOCIOLOGY

When I started university at the age of 18, I was bewildered by the wide variety of courses I could choose from. Having now taught sociology for more than 30 years, and having met thousands of undergraduates, I am quite sure most students today feel as I did then.

One source of confusion for me was uncertainty about why I was in university in the first place. Like you, I knew higher education could improve my chance of finding good work. But, like most students, I also had a sense that higher education is supposed to provide something more than just the training necessary to embark on a career that is interesting and pays well. Several high-school teachers and guidance counsellors had told me that university was also supposed to "broaden my horizons" and teach me to "think critically." I wasn't entirely sure what they meant, but they made it sound interesting enough to make me want to know more. Thus, I decided in my first year to take mainly "practical" courses that might prepare me for a law degree (economics, political science, and psychology). I also enrolled in a couple of other courses to indulge my "intellectual" side (philosophy, drama).

One thing I knew for sure: I didn't want to study sociology. Sociology, I came to believe, was thin soup with uncertain ingredients. When I asked a second-year student what sociology is, he told me it deals mainly with why people are unequal—why some are rich and others poor, some powerful and others weak. Coming as I did from a poor immigrant family in the Maritimes, an economically depressed region, it appeared that sociology could teach me something about my own life. But it also seemed a lot like what I imagined economics and political science to be about. What, then, was unique about sociology? My growing sense that sociology had nothing special to offer was confirmed when another second-year student told me that sociologists try to describe the ideal society and figure out how to make the world a better place. That description appealed to my youthful sense of the world's injustice. However, it also sounded a lot like philosophy. A third-year student explained that sociology analyzes how and why people assume different roles in their lives. She made sociology appear similar to drama. Finally, one student reported that in her sociology class, she was learning why people commit suicide, homicide, and other deviant acts. That seemed like abnormal psychology to me. I concluded that sociology had no distinct flavour all its own. Accordingly, I decided to forgo it for tastier courses.

## A CHANGE OF MIND

Despite the opinion I'd formed, I found myself taking no fewer than four sociology courses a year after starting university. That revolution in my life was due partly to the pull of an extraordinary professor I happened to meet just before I began my second year. He set me thinking in an altogether new way about what I could and should do with my life. He exploded some of my deepest beliefs. He started me thinking sociologically.

Specifically, he first put Yorick's dilemma to me. Yorick is a character—sort of—in *Hamlet*. Toward the end of the play, Hamlet finds two gravediggers at work. They unearth the remains of the former court jester, Yorick, who used to amuse Hamlet and carry him around on his back when Hamlet was a child. Holding high his old friend's skull, Hamlet reflects on what we must all come to. Even the remains of Alexander the Great, he says, turn to dust.

This incident implies Yorick's dilemma and, indeed, the dilemma of all thinking people. Life is finite. If we want to make the most of it, we must figure out how best to live. That is no easy task. It requires study, reflection, and the selection of values and goals. Ideally, higher education is supposed to supply students with just that opportunity. Finally, I was beginning to understand what I could expect from university apart from job training.

The professor I met also convinced me that sociology in particular could open up a new and superior way of comprehending my world. Specifically, he said it could clarify my place in society, how I might best manoeuvre through it, and even, perhaps, how I might contribute to improving it, however modestly. Before beginning my study of sociology, I had

Life is finite, and if we want to make the most of it, we must figure out how best to live. Sociology offers a useful perspective for understanding our current predicament and seeing possible ways of dealing with it.

SOURCE: M.C. Escher's "Relativity" © 2012 The M.C. Escher Company-Holland. All rights reserved. www.mcescher.com.

always taken for granted that things happen in the world—and to me—because physical and emotional forces cause them. Famine, I thought, is caused by drought, war by territorial greed, economic success by hard work, marriage by love, suicide by bottomless depression, rape by depraved lust. But now, this professor repeatedly threw evidence in my face that contradicted my easy formulas. If drought causes famine, why have so many famines occurred in perfectly normal weather conditions or involved some groups hoarding or destroying food so others would starve? If hard work causes prosperity, why are so many hard workers poor? If love causes marriage, why are so many families the site of violence against women and children? And so the questions multiplied.

As if it were not enough that the professor's sociological evidence upset many of my assumptions about the way the world worked, he also challenged me to understand sociology's unique way of explaining social life. He defined **sociology** as the systematic study of human behaviour in social context. He explained that *social* causes are distinct from physical and emotional causes. Understanding social causes can help clarify otherwise inexplicable features of famine, marriage, and so on. In public school, my teachers had taught me that people are free to do what they want with their lives. However, my new professor taught me that the organization of the social world opens some opportunities and closes others, thus constraining our freedom and helping to make us what we are. By examining the operation of these powerful social forces, he said, sociology can help us to know ourselves, our capabilities and limitations. I was hooked. And so, of course, I hope you will be, too.

### THE GOALS OF THIS CHAPTER

In this chapter I aim to achieve three goals. First, I illustrate the power of sociology to dispel foggy assumptions and help us see the operation of the social world more clearly. To that end, I examine a phenomenon that at first glance appears to be solely the outcome of breakdowns in individual functioning: suicide. You will see that, in fact, *social relations* among people powerfully influence suicide rates. This exercise introduces you to what is unique about the sociological perspective.

Second, I show that, from its origins, sociological research has been motivated by a desire to improve the social world. Thus, sociology is not just a dry, academic exercise but a means of charting a better course for society. At the same time, however, sociologists adopt scientific methods to test their ideas, thus increasing the validity of the results. I illustrate these points by briefly analyzing the work of the founders of the discipline.

Third, I suggest that sociology can help you come to grips with your century, just as it helped the founders of sociology deal with theirs. Today we are witnessing massive and disorienting social changes. Entire countries are breaking up. Women are demanding equality with men in all spheres of life. New religions are emerging and old ones reviving. People's wants are increasingly governed by the mass media. Computers are radically altering the way people work and entertain themselves. There are proportionately fewer good jobs to go around. Environmental ruin threatens us all. As was the case a hundred years ago, sociologists today try to understand social phenomena and suggest credible ways of improving their societies. By promising to make sociology relevant to you, this chapter should be viewed as an open invitation to participate in sociology's challenge.

But first things first. Before showing how sociology can help us comprehend and better our world, let us briefly examine the problem of suicide. That will help to illustrate how the sociological perspective can clarify and sometimes overturn commonsense beliefs.

## THE SOCIOLOGICAL PERSPECTIVE

By analyzing suicide sociologically, you can put to a tough test my claim that sociology gives you a unique, surprising, and enlightening perspective on social events. After all, suicide appears to be the supremely antisocial and nonsocial act. It is condemned by nearly everyone in society. It is typically committed in private, far from the public's intrusive glare. It is rare. In recent years, there have been about 13 suicides annually for every 100 000 people in Canada (Statistics Canada, 2004). Canada's suicide rate places us fortieth among the 105 countries that publish suicide statistics; see Figure 1.1. And when you think about why people commit such an act, you are likely to focus on their individual states of mind rather than on the state of society. In other words, what usually interests us are the aspects of specific individuals' lives that caused them to become depressed or angry enough to do something as awful as killing themselves. We usually do not think about the patterns

## FIGURE 1.1    SUICIDE RATE BY COUNTRY, CIRCA 2011

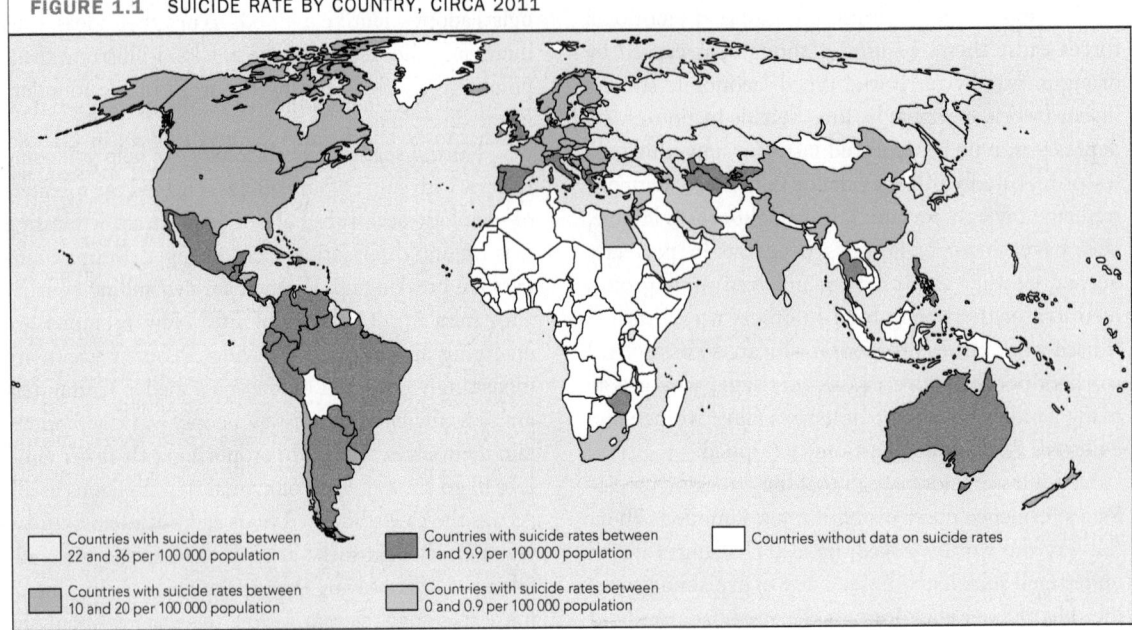

Countries with suicide rates between 22 and 36 per 100 000 population

Countries with suicide rates between 10 and 20 per 100 000 population

Countries with suicide rates between 1 and 9.9 per 100 000 population

Countries with suicide rates between 0 and 0.9 per 100 000 population

Countries without data on suicide rates

SOURCE: World Health Organization, 2011, "Suicide rates per 100,000 by country, year and sex (Table): Most recent year available; as of 2011." On the World Wide Web at http://www.who.int/mental_health/prevention/suicide_rates/en/ (retrieved 20 December 2011).

of social relations that might encourage such actions in general. If sociology can reveal the hidden social causes of such an apparently antisocial and nonsocial phenomenon, there must be something to it!

## THE SOCIOLOGICAL EXPLANATION OF SUICIDE

At the end of the nineteenth century, French sociologist Émile Durkheim (1951 [1897]), one of the pioneers of the discipline, demonstrated that suicide is more than just an individual act of desperation resulting from psychological disorder, as was commonly believed at the time. Suicide rates, he showed, are strongly influenced by social forces.

Durkheim made his case by examining the association between rates of suicide and rates of psychological disorder for different groups. The idea that psychological disorder causes suicide is supported, he reasoned, only if suicide rates tend to be high where rates of psychological disorder are high, and low where rates of psychological disorder are low. However, his analysis of European government statistics, hospital records, and other sources revealed nothing of the kind. He discovered there were slightly more women than men in insane asylums. Yet there were four male suicides for every female suicide. Jews had the highest

rate of psychological disorder among the major religious groups in France. However, they also had the lowest suicide rate. Psychological disorders occurred most frequently when a person reached maturity. Suicide rates, though, increased steadily with age.

Clearly, suicide rates and rates of psychological disorder did not vary proportionately. What then accounts for variations in suicide rates? Durkheim argued that suicide rates vary because of differences in the degree of **social solidarity** in different groups. According to Durkheim, the more a group's members share beliefs and values, and the more frequently and intensely they interact, the more social solidarity a group exhibits. In turn, the more social solidarity a group exhibits, the more firmly anchored individuals are to the social world, and the less likely they are to take their own lives if adversity strikes. In other words, Durkheim expected groups with a high degree of solidarity to have lower suicide rates than groups with a low degree of solidarity did—at least up to a certain point (see Figure 1.2).

To support his argument, Durkheim showed that married adults are half as likely as unmarried adults are to commit suicide. That is because marriage usually creates social ties and a sort of moral cement that bind the individual to society. Similarly, he argued that women are less likely to commit suicide than

**FIGURE 1.2    DURKHEIM'S THEORY OF SUICIDE**

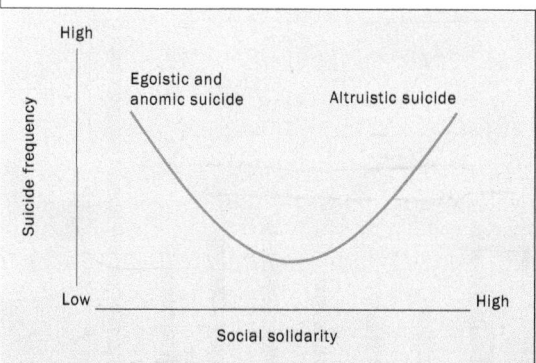

Durkheim argued that as the level of social solidarity increases, the suicide rate declines. Then, beyond a certain point, it starts to rise. Hence the U-shaped curve in this graph. Durkheim called suicides that occur in high-solidarity settings altruistic. Altruism means devotion to the interests of others. **Altruistic suicide** occurs when norms tightly govern behaviour so that individual actions are often in the group's interest. For example, when soldiers knowingly give up their lives to protect members of their unit, they commit altruistic suicide out of a deep sense of comradeship. In contrast, suicide that occurs in low-solidarity settings is egoistic or anomic, said Durkheim. **Egoistic suicide** results from a lack of integration of the individual into society because of weak social ties to others. *Anomie* means "without order." **Anomic suicide** occurs when norms governing behaviour are vaguely defined. For example, in Durkheim's view, when people live in a society that lacks a widely shared code of morality, the rate of anomic suicide is likely to be high.

men are. Why? Women are generally more involved in the intimate social relations of family life. Jews, Durkheim wrote, are less likely to commit suicide than Christians are. The reason? Centuries of persecution have turned them into a group that is more defensive and tightly knit. And seniors are more prone than the young and the middle-aged are to take their own lives in the face of misfortune. That is because they are most likely to live alone, to have lost a spouse, and to lack a job and a wide network of friends. In general, Durkheim wrote, "suicide varies with the degree of integration of the social groups of which the individual forms a part" (Durkheim, 1951 [1897]:209). Note that his generalization tells us nothing about why any particular *individual* may take his or her life. That is a question for psychology. But it does tell us that a person's likelihood of committing suicide decreases with the degree to which he or she is anchored in society. And it says something surprising and uniquely sociological about how and why the suicide rate varies from group to group.

## SUICIDE IN CANADA TODAY

Durkheim's theory is not just a historical curiosity. It sheds light on the factors that account for variations in suicide rates here and now. Consider Figure 1.3, which shows suicide rates by age and sex in Canada for 2008. Comparing rates for men and women, we immediately see that, as in Durkheim's France, men are much more likely than women are to commit suicide (3.6 times more likely, to be precise). However, looking at differences between age groups, we see a striking difference between Durkheim's France and contemporary Canada. When Durkheim wrote, youth suicide was extremely rare and suicide among working-age people was uncommon. In Canada today, suicide among people between the ages of 10 and 64 is much more common, having increased substantially since the 1960s. Suicide rates do *not* increase steadily with age in Canada today. True, the suicide rate is highest among people over the age of 89. However, it is higher for people between the ages of 40 and 59 than it is for people between the ages of 60 and 89. Moreover, the rate of suicide for people between the ages of 15 and 24, practically zero in Durkheim's France, stands at about 10 per 100 000 in Canada today.

Although the rate of suicide among young people was negligible in Durkheim's France, his theory of social solidarity helps us to understand why it has risen for this age cohort in Canada over the past half century. In brief, shared moral principles and strong social ties have eroded since the early 1960s for Canada's youth. Consider the following facts:

- Church, synagogue, mosque, and temple attendance is down, particularly for young people. Thus, more than half of Canadians attended religious services weekly in the 1960s. Today the figure is less than one-third, and it is only one-sixth for people born after 1960.
- Unemployment is up, again especially for youth. Thus, the unemployment rate was around 3 percent for most of the 1960s. It rose steadily to around 10 percent for most of the 1990s and stood at 7.4 percent in November 2011. Moreover, for Canadians between the ages of 15 and 24, the unemployment rate is about twice as high as it is for older Canadians (14.1 percent in November 2011; Statistics Canada, 2011b).
- The rate of divorce has increased sixfold since the early 1960s. Out-of-marriage births are also much more common than they used to be. As a result,

**FIGURE 1.3   SUICIDE BY AGE AND SEX, CANADA, 2008**

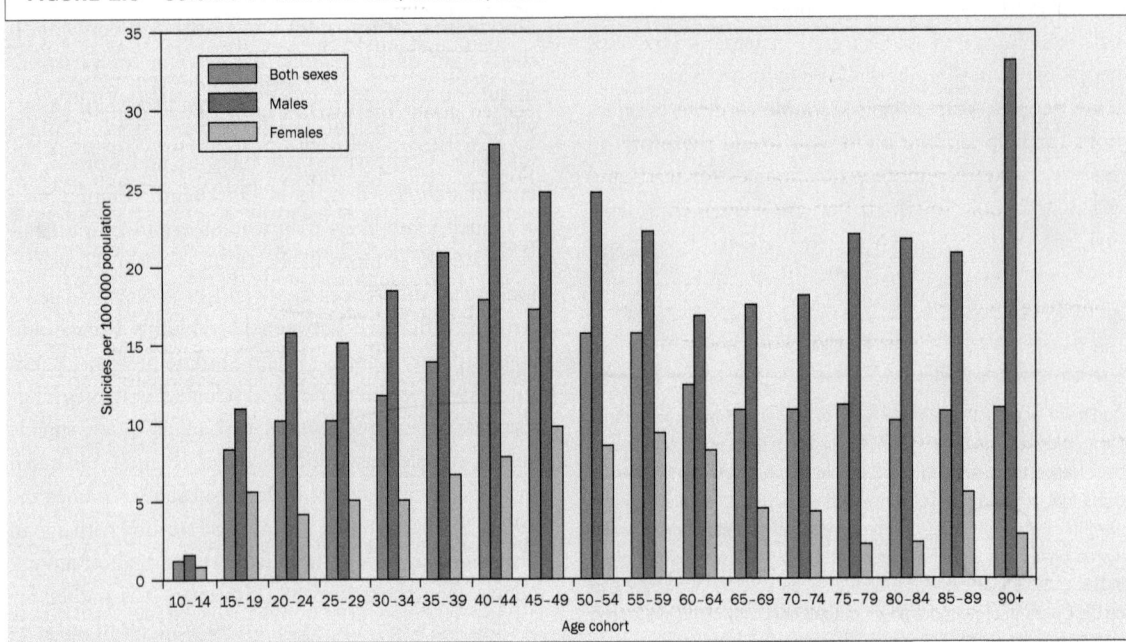

SOURCE: Statistics Canada (2011a).

children are more often brought up in single-parent families than in the past. This fact suggests that they enjoy less frequent and intimate social interaction with parents and less adult supervision.

- Since the 1960s, an increasingly large proportion of lesbians, gays, bisexuals, and transsexuals have come "out of the closet." Most Canadians accept the lifestyles of sexual minorities, but in many Canadian schools lesbians, gays, bisexuals, and transsexuals are prone to being bullied, terrorized, and socially excluded. Consequently, an alarmingly high proportion of youth suicides are committed by members of sexual minorities (Carole, 2011).

In sum, the figures cited above suggest that the level of social solidarity is now lower than it was just a few decades ago for young people. Less firmly rooted in society, and less likely to share moral standards, young people in Canada today are more likely than they were half a century ago to take their own lives if they find themselves in the midst of a personal crisis.

## FROM PERSONAL TROUBLES TO SOCIAL STRUCTURES

You have known for a long time that you live in a society. Yet until now, you may not have fully appreciated that society also lives in you. That is, patterns of social relations affect your innermost thoughts and feelings, influence your actions, and thus help shape who you are. As we have seen, one such pattern of social relations is the level of social solidarity that characterizes the various groups to which you belong.

Sociologists call relatively stable patterns of social relations **social structures.** One of the sociologist's main tasks is to identify and explain the connection between people's personal troubles and the social structures in which people are embedded. This work is harder than it may at first seem. In everyday life, we usually see things mainly from our own point of view. Our experiences appear unique to each of us. If we think about them at all, social structures may appear remote and impersonal. To see how social structures operate inside us, we require sociological training.

An important step in broadening our sociological awareness involves recognizing that three levels of social structure surround and penetrate us. Think of these structures as concentric circles radiating out from you.

**Microstructures** are patterns of intimate social relations. They are formed during face-to-face interaction. Families, friendship circles, and work associations are all examples of microstructures.

Understanding the operation of microstructures can be useful. Let's say you are looking for a job.

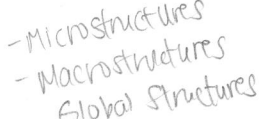

You might think you would do best to ask as many close friends and relatives as possible for leads and contacts. However, sociological research shows that people you know well are likely to know many of the same people. After asking a couple of close connections for help landing a job, you would therefore do best to ask more remote acquaintances for leads and contacts. People to whom you are weakly connected (and who are weakly connected among themselves) are more likely to know *different* groups of people. Therefore, they will give you more information about job possibilities and ensure that word about your job search spreads farther. You are more likely to find a job faster if you understand "the strength of weak ties" in microstructural settings (Granovetter, 1973).

**Macrostructures** are patterns of social relations that lie outside and above your circle of intimates and acquaintances. Macrostructures include class relations and **patriarchy,** the traditional system of economic and political inequality between women and men in most societies. Understanding the operation of macrostructures can also be useful. Consider, for example, one aspect of patriarchy. Most married women who work full-time in the paid labour force do more housework, child care, and eldercare than their husbands do. Governments and businesses support this arrangement insofar as they give little assistance to families in the form of nurseries, after-school programs for children, senior homes, and so on. Yet the unequal division of work in the household is a major source of dissatisfaction with marriage, especially in families that cannot afford to buy these services privately. Thus, sociological research shows that when spouses share domestic responsibilities equally, they are happier with their marriages and less likely to divorce (Hochschild with Machung, 1989). When a marriage is in danger of dissolving, it is common for partners to blame themselves and each other for their troubles. However, it should now be clear that forces other than incompatible personalities often put stresses on families. Understanding how the macrostructure of patriarchy crops up in everyday life, and doing something to change that structure, can thus help people lead happier lives.

The third level of society that surrounds and permeates us comprises **global structures.** International organizations, patterns of worldwide travel and communication, and the economic relations between countries are examples of global structures. Global structures are increasingly important as inexpensive travel and communication allow all parts of the world to become interconnected culturally, economically, and politically.

Understanding the operation of global structures can be useful, too. For instance, many people are concerned about the world's poor. They donate money to charities to help with famine and disaster relief. Some people also approve of the Canadian government giving foreign aid to poor countries. However, many of these same people do not appreciate that charity and foreign aid alone do not seem able to end world poverty. That is because charity and foreign aid have been unable to overcome the structure of social relations among countries that have created, and now sustain, global inequality.

As we will see in Chapter 9, Development and Underdevelopment, Britain, France, and other imperial powers locked some countries into poverty when they colonized them between the seventeenth and nineteenth centuries. In the twentieth century, the poor (or "developing") countries borrowed money from these same rich countries and Western banks to pay for airports, roads, harbours, sanitation systems, basic healthcare, and so on. Today, poor countries pay far more to rich countries and Western banks in interest on those loans than they receive in aid and charity. Foreign aid equals about one-tenth of interest payments (Jubilee Debt Campaign, 2010: 6; Organisation for Economic Co-operation and Development, 2008: 6). It thus seems that relying exclusively on foreign aid and charity can do little to help solve the problem of world poverty. Understanding how the global structure of international relations created and helps maintain global inequality suggests new policy priorities for helping the world's poor. One such priority might involve campaigning for the cancellation of foreign debt in compensation for past injustices. Some government officials in Canada and other countries have been promoting this policy for the past decade.

As these examples illustrate, personal problems are connected to social structures at the microlevel, macrolevel, and global level. Whether the personal problem involves finding a job, keeping a marriage intact, or figuring out a way to act justly to end world poverty, social-structural considerations broaden our understanding of the problem and suggest appropriate courses of action.

## THE SOCIOLOGICAL IMAGINATION

In the 1950s, the great American sociologist C. Wright Mills (1959) called the ability to see the connection between personal troubles and social structures the **sociological imagination.** He emphasized the difficulty of developing this quality of mind. His language is sexist by today's standards, but his argument is as true and inspiring today as it was in the 1950s:

> When a society becomes industrialized, a peasant becomes a worker; a feudal lord is liquidated or becomes a businessman. When classes rise or fall, a man is employed or unemployed; when the rate of investment goes up or down, a man takes new heart or goes broke. When war happens, an insurance salesman becomes a rocket launcher; a store clerk, a radar man; a wife lives alone; a child grows up without a father. Neither the life of an individual nor the history of a society can be understood without understanding both.
>
> Yet men do not usually define the troubles they endure in terms of historical change. … The well-being they enjoy, they do not usually impute to the big ups and downs of the society in which they live. Seldom aware of the intricate connection between the patterns of their own lives and the course of world history, ordinary men do not usually know what this connection means for the kind of men they are becoming and for the kind of history-making in which they might take part. They do not possess the quality of mind essential to grasp the interplay of men and society, of biography and history, of self and world. They cannot cope with their personal troubles in such a way as to control the structural transformations that usually lie behind them.
>
> What they need … is a quality of mind that will help them to [see] … what is going on in the world and … what may be happening within themselves. It is this quality … that … may be called the sociological imagination. (Mills, 1959: 3–4)

The sociological imagination is a recent addition to the human repertoire. It is only about two centuries old. True, in ancient and medieval times, some philosophers wrote about society. However, their thinking was not sociological. They believed God and nature controlled society. They spent much of their time sketching blueprints for the ideal society and urging people to follow those blueprints. They relied on speculation rather than on evidence to reach conclusions about how society works.

The sociological imagination was born when three modern revolutions pushed people to think about society in an entirely new way. First, the **Scientific Revolution** began about 1550. It encouraged the view that sound conclusions about the workings of society must be based on solid evidence, not just on speculation. Second, the **Democratic Revolution** began about 1750. It suggested that people are responsible for organizing society and that human intervention can therefore solve social problems. Third, the **Industrial Revolution** began about 1780. It created a host of new and serious social problems that attracted the attention of many social thinkers. Let us briefly consider these three sources of the sociological imagination.

## ORIGINS OF THE SOCIOLOGICAL IMAGINATION

### The Scientific Revolution

It is said that a group of medieval monks once wanted to know how many angels could dance on the head of a pin. They consulted ancient books in Hebrew, Greek, and Latin. They thought long and hard. They employed all their intellectual skills to debate the issue. They did not, however, resolve the dispute because they never considered inspecting the head of a pin and counting. Any such suggestion would have been considered heresy. We, in contrast, would call it the beginning of a scientific approach to the subject.

People often link the Scientific Revolution to specific ideas, such as Copernicus's theory that Earth revolves around the Sun and Newton's laws of motion. However, science is less a collection of ideas than a method of inquiry. For instance, in 1609, Galileo pointed his newly invented telescope at the heavens, made some careful observations, and showed that his observations fit Copernicus's theory. This is the core of the scientific method: using evidence to make a case for a particular point of view. By the mid-seventeenth century, some philosophers, such as Descartes in France and Hobbes in England, were calling for a science of society. When sociology emerged as a distinct discipline in the nineteenth century, commitment to the scientific method was one firm pillar of the sociological imagination.

## The Democratic Revolution

The second pillar of the sociological imagination is the realization that people control society and can change it. Four hundred years ago, most Europeans thought otherwise. For them, God ordained the social order.

Consider the English engraving reproduced in Figure 1.4. It shows how most educated Europeans pictured the universe in Shakespeare's time. Note the cloud at the top of the circle. The Hebrew name of God is inscribed on it. God's hand extends from the cloud. It holds a chain, which is attached to a woman representing Nature. Nature also holds a chain in her hand. It is connected to "the ape of Nature," representing humankind. The symbolism is clear: God and his intermediary, Nature, control human action. Note also that the engraving arranges everything in a linked hierarchy. The hierarchy includes the mineral, vegetable, and animal kingdoms; the elements; heavenly objects; angels; and so on. Each level of the hierarchy corresponds to and controls some aspect of the level below it. For example, people believed Archangels regulated the movements of the planet Mercury and the movements of Mercury affected human commerce. Similarly, in the medieval view, God ordained a hierarchy of people. The richest people were seen as the closest to God and therefore deserving of great privilege. Supposedly, kings and queens ruled because God wanted them to (Tillyard, 1943).

The American Revolution (1775–83) and the French Revolution (1789–99) helped to undermine these ideas. These democratic political upheavals showed that society could experience massive change in a short period. They proved that people could replace unsatisfactory rulers. And they suggested that *people* control society. The implications for social thought were profound, for if it was possible to change society by human intervention, then a science of society could play a big role. The new science could help people figure out ways of overcoming various

---

**FIGURE 1.4    THE ELIZABETHAN WORLDVIEW**

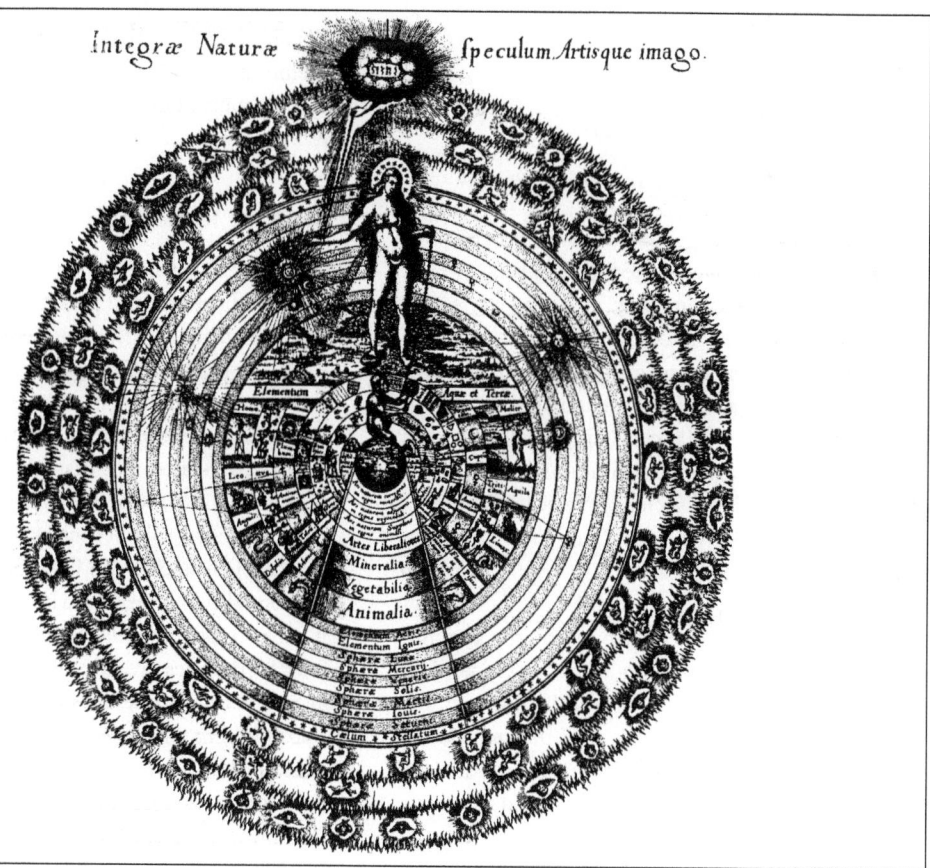

SOURCE: From Robert Fludd's *Utriusque* Cosmi *Historia* (1617–19). Photograph courtesy of Houghton Library, Harvard College Library.

social problems, improving the welfare of all citizens, and finding the most effective way to reach given goals. Much of the justification for sociology as a science arose out of the democratic revolutions that shook Europe and North America.

## The Industrial Revolution

The third pillar of the sociological imagination was the Industrial Revolution. It began in England about 1780. Because of the growth of industry, masses of people moved from countryside to city, worked agonizingly long hours in crowded and dangerous mines and factories, lost faith in their religions, confronted faceless bureaucracies, and reacted to the filth and poverty of their existence by means of strikes, crime, revolution, and war. Scholars had never seen a sociological laboratory like this. The Scientific Revolution suggested that a science of society is possible. The Democratic Revolution suggested that people can intervene to improve society. The Industrial Revolution now presented social thinkers with a host of pressing social problems crying out for solutions. They responded by giving birth to the sociological imagination.

## SOCIOLOGICAL THEORIES

### THE ORIGINS OF SOCIOLOGY

The term *sociology* was coined by the French social thinker Auguste Comte in 1838 (Thompson, 1975). Comte tried to place the study of society on scientific foundations. He wanted to understand the social world as it is, not as he or anyone else imagined it should be. This was a highly original approach to the study of society. In ancient and medieval times, philosophers from diverse civilizations had sketched blueprints for the ideal society. We see evidence of this approach in the work of Confucius in China, Ibn Khaldun in Tunisia, and Plato and Aristotle in Greece. But Comte was swept up in the scientific revolution of his time. He was inspired by the astronomers and physicists of the modern era—Copernicus in Poland, Galileo in Italy, Newton in England. He wanted to test the validity of his ideas through careful observation of the real world rather than assuming that "God" or "human nature" determined the shape of society (see Box 1.1).

Despite Comte's breakthrough, there was a tension in his work, for although he was eager to adopt the scientific method in his study of society, he was a conservative thinker, motivated [...] opposition to rapid change in French soc[...] a time not only of scientific but also of [...]d social revolution. Comte witnessed the [...]c forces unleashed by the French Revoluti[...] indus- trialization of society, and the rapi[...] of cities. What he saw shocked and angered [...]im because rapid social change was destroying many of the things he valued, especially respect for authority. He therefore urged slow change and the preservation of much that was traditional in social life. Thus, at its very origin, sociological research was motivated by adherence to scientific methods of research *and* a vision of the ideal society.

The same sort of tension is evident in the work of the most important early figures in the history of sociology: Karl Marx, Émile Durkheim, and Max Weber. These three men lived in the period from 1820 to 1920. They witnessed various phases of Europe's wrenching transition to industrial capitalism, and they wanted to understand and explain it. Like Comte, they were all committed to the scientific method of research. However, they also wanted to chart a better course for their societies. The ideas they developed are therefore not just diagnostic tools from which we can still learn much, but also, like many sociological ideas, prescriptions for combating social ills.

### THEORY, RESEARCH, AND VALUES

To clarify the tension in sociology between analysis and ideal, diagnosis and prescription, we can usefully distinguish three terms: theory, research, and values.

Sociological ideas are generally stated in the form of theories. A **theory** is a tentative explanation of some aspect of social life. It states how and why certain facts are related. For example, in his theory of suicide, Durkheim showed how facts about suicide rates are related to facts about social solidarity. This enabled him to explain suicide as a function of social solidarity. In this broad definition, even a hunch qualifies as a theory if it suggests how and why certain facts are related.

*After* theories are formulated, the sociologist can conduct research. **Research** is the process of carefully observing social reality to assess the validity of a theory. It is because research can call the validity of a theory into question that theories are said to be only "tentative" explanations. The research process is discussed in detail in Chapter 20, Research Methods.

*Before* sociologists can formulate a theory, however, they must decide which problems are important

## BOX 1.1    SCIENTIFIC VERSUS COMMONSENSE KNOWLEDGE

To better understand how scientific and non-scientific knowledge differ, consider the following statements, each of which represents a commonly accepted basis for knowing that something is "true" in our everyday lives:

1. "The proper place for women is in the home. That's the way it's always been." This statement represents knowledge based on tradition. Although some traditional knowledge is valid (sugar will rot your teeth), some is not (masturbation will not blind you). Science is required to sort out valid from invalid knowledge.

2. "Apparently, weak magnets can be used to heal many illnesses. I read all about it in the newspaper." This statement represents knowledge based on authority. We often think something is true because we read it in an authoritative source or hear it from an expert. But authoritative sources and experts can be wrong. For example, nineteenth-century Western physicians commonly "bled" their patients with leeches to draw "poisons" from their bodies, often doing more harm than good. As this example suggests, scientists should always question authority to arrive at more valid knowledge.

3. "I was driving my bike last night when I saw the car accident. The car that caused it was dark brown." This statement represents knowledge based on casual observation. However, we are usually pretty careless observers. That is why good lawyers can often trip up eyewitnesses in courtrooms; eyewitnesses are rarely certain about what they saw. In general, uncertainty can be reduced by observing in a conscious and deliberate manner and by recording observations. That is just what scientists do.

4. "If you work hard, you can get ahead. I know because several of my parents' friends started off poor but are now comfortably middle class." This statement represents knowledge based on over-generalization. For instance, if you know a few people who started off poor, worked hard, and became rich, you may think any poor person can become rich if he or she works hard enough. You may not know about the more numerous poor people who work hard and remain poor. Scientists, however, sample cases that are representative of entire populations. This enables them to avoid overgeneralization. They also avoid overgeneralization by repeating research. This ensures that research findings are not idiosyncratic.

5. "I'm right because I can't think of any contrary cases." This statement represents knowledge based on selective observation. Sometimes we ignore evidence that challenges our firmly held beliefs. Thus, you may know people who work hard but remain poor. To maintain your belief that hard work results in wealth, you will have to ignore those cases. The scientific requirement that evidence be drawn from representative samples of the population minimizes bias arising from selective observation.

6. "Mr. Smith is poor even though he works hard but that's because he has a disability. People with disabilities are the only exception to the rule that if you work hard you can get ahead." This statement represents knowledge based on qualification. Qualifications or "exceptions to the rule" are often made in everyday life—and they are in science, too. The difference is that in everyday life, qualifications are easily accepted as valid, whereas in scientific inquiry, they are typically treated as hypotheses that must be tested as rigorously as the original hypothesis.

7. "The Toronto Blue Jays won 50 percent of their baseball games last month but 80 percent of the games they played on Thursdays. Because it happened so often before, I bet they'll win next Thursday." This statement represents knowledge based on illogical reasoning. In everyday life, we may expect the recurrence of events without reasonable cause, ignoring the fact that rare sequences of events often occur just by chance. For example, it is possible to flip a coin 10 times and have it come up heads each time. On average, this will happen once every 1024 times you flip a coin 10 times. In the absence of any apparent reason for this happening, it is merely coincidental. It is illogical to believe otherwise. Scientists refrain from such illogical reasoning. They also use statistical techniques to distinguish between events that are probably due to chance and those that are not.

8. "I just can't be wrong." This statement represents knowledge based on ego-defence. Even scientists may be passionately committed to the conclusions they reach in their research because they have invested much time and energy in them. It is other scientists—more accurately, the whole institution of science, with its commitment to publishing research results and critically scrutinizing findings—that strictly limits ego-defence in scientific understanding.

*(continued)*

**BOX 1.1**      *(continued)*

9. "The matter is settled once and for all." This statement represents knowledge based on the premature closure of inquiry. It involves deciding that all the relevant evidence has been gathered on a particular subject. Science, however, is committed to the idea that all theories are only temporarily true. Matters are never settled.

10. "There must be supernatural forces at work here." This statement represents knowledge based on mystification. When we can find no rational explanation for a phenomenon, we may attribute it to forces that cannot be observed or fully understood. Although such forces may exist, scientists remain skeptical. They are committed to discovering real, observable causes of real, observable effects.

SOURCE: From Babbie, *Practice of Social Research*, 6E. © 1992 Cengage Learning.

enough to study and how the parts of society fit together. If they are going to recommend ways of improving the operation of some aspect of society, they must even have an opinion about what the ideal society ought to look like. As we will soon see, these issues are shaped in large measure by sociologists' values. **Values** are ideas about what is right and wrong, good and bad. Inevitably, values help sociologists formulate and

favour certain theories over others (Edel, 1965; Kuhn, 1970). So sociological theories may be modified and even rejected because of research, but they are often motivated by sociologists' values.

Durkheim, Marx, and Weber initiated three of the major theoretical traditions in sociology: functionalism, conflict theory, and symbolic interactionism. A fourth approach, feminism, has arisen in recent decades

Before delving into social research, a sociologist must first develop hypotheses—testable claims about the social world. Testing hypotheses by means of research helps determine the validity of theories.

SOURCE: © Davidian/iStockphoto.com.

*[handwritten: 4) Re-establishing equilibrium]*

to correct some of the deficiencies of the three long-established traditions. It will become clear as you read this book that there are many more sociological theories than just these four. However, because these four traditions have been especially influential in the development of sociology, you will find it useful to read a thumbnail sketch of each one here at the beginning.[1]

## FUNCTIONALISM

*[handwritten: 1) Social relations  2) Maintain stability  3) Based on shared values]*

Durkheim's theory of suicide is an early example of what sociologists now call **functionalist theory.** Functionalist theories incorporate four features:

1. They stress that human behaviour is governed by relatively stable patterns of social relations, or social structures. For example, Durkheim emphasized how suicide rates are influenced by patterns of social solidarity. Usually the social structures analyzed by functionalists are macrostructures.

2. Functionalism underlines how social structures maintain or undermine social stability. Typically, Durkheim analyzed how the growth of industries and cities in nineteenth-century Europe lowered the level of social solidarity and contributed to social instability. One aspect of instability, said Durkheim, is a higher suicide rate. Another is frequent strikes by workers.

3. Functionalist theories emphasize that social structures are based mainly on shared values. Thus, when Durkheim wrote about social solidarity, he sometimes meant the frequency and intensity of social interaction, but more often he thought of social solidarity as a sort of moral cement that binds people together.

4. Functionalism suggests that re-establishing equilibrium can best solve most social problems. Thus, Durkheim said that social stability could be restored in late-nineteenth-century Europe by creating new associations of employers and workers that would lower workers' expectations about what they could expect out of life. If, said Durkheim, more people could agree on wanting less, social solidarity would rise and there would be fewer strikes, fewer suicides, and so on. Functionalism, then, was a conservative response to widespread social unrest in nineteenth century France. (A more radical response would have been to argue that if people are expressing discontent because they are getting less out of life than they expect, discontent can be lowered by figuring out ways for them to get more out of life.)

Although functionalist thinking influenced North American sociology at the end of the nineteenth century, it was only during the continent's greatest economic crisis ever, the Great Depression of 1929–39, that functionalism took deep root here (Russett, 1966). With 30 percent of the paid labour force unemployed and labour unrest reaching unprecedented levels, it is not surprising that sociologists with a conservative frame of mind were attracted to a theory that focused on how social equilibrium could be restored. Functionalist theory remained popular in North America for 30 years. It experienced a minor revival in the early 1990s but never regained the dominance it enjoyed from the 1930s to the early 1960s.

Sociologist Talcott Parsons was the foremost proponent of functionalism. He is best known for identifying how various institutions must work to ensure the smooth operation of society as a whole. For instance, when the family successfully raises new generations, the military successfully defends society against external threats, schools are able to teach students the skills and values they need to function as productive adults, and religions create a shared moral code among people, then, said Parsons, society is well integrated and in equilibrium (Parsons, 1951).

Parsons was criticized for exaggerating the degree to which members of society share common values and social institutions contribute to social harmony. This led North America's other leading functionalist, Robert Merton, to propose that social structures may have different consequences for different categories of people. Merton noted that some of those consequences might be disruptive or **dysfunctional** (Merton, 1968 [1949]). Moreover, said Merton, although some functions are **manifest** (visible and intended), others are **latent** (invisible and unintended). For instance, a manifest function of schools is to transmit skills from one generation to the next. A latent function of schools is to encourage the development of a separate youth culture that often conflicts with parents' values (Coleman, 1961; Hersch, 1998).

## CONFLICT THEORY

The second major theoretical tradition in sociology emphasizes the centrality of conflict in social life. **Conflict theory** incorporates these four features:

1. It generally focuses on large, macrolevel structures, such as relations between or among classes.

2. Conflict theory shows how major patterns of inequality in society produce social stability

in some circumstances and social change in others.

3. Conflict theory stresses how members of privileged groups try to maintain their advantages while subordinate groups struggle to increase theirs. From this point of view, social conditions at a given time are the expression of an ongoing power struggle between privileged and subordinate groups.

4. Conflict theory typically leads to the suggestion that decreasing privilege will lower the level of conflict and increase the sum total of human welfare.

The conflict paradigm originated in the work of Karl Marx. A generation before Durkheim, Marx observed the destitution and discontent produced by the Industrial Revolution and proposed a sweeping argument about the way societies develop (Marx, 1904 [1859]; Marx and Engels, 1972 [1848]). Marx's theory was radically different from Durkheim's. Class conflict lies at the centre of his ideas.

Marx argued that owners of industry are eager to improve the way work is organized and to adopt new tools, machines, and production methods. These innovations allow them to produce more efficiently, earn higher profits, and drive inefficient competitors out of business. However, according to Marx, the drive for profits causes capitalists to concentrate workers in larger and larger establishments, keep wages as low as possible, and invest as little as possible in improving working conditions. Thus, in factories and in mines, a large and growing class of poor workers comes to oppose a small and shrinking class of wealthy owners.

Marx believed that workers would ultimately become aware of belonging to the same exploited class. Their sense of "class consciousness," he wrote, would encourage the growth of trade unions and labour parties. These organizations would eventually seek to put an end to private ownership of property, replacing it with a system in which everyone shared property and wealth. This was the "communist" society envisaged by Marx—a society in which there is no private property and everyone shares wealth in proportion to their need.

### Weber

Although some of Marx's ideas have been usefully adapted to the study of contemporary society, his predictions about the inevitable collapse of capitalism have been questioned. Max Weber, a German sociologist who wrote his major works a generation after Marx, was among the first to find flaws in Marx's

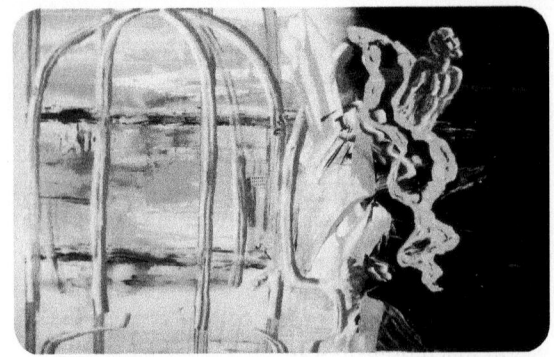

Max Weber wrote that the modern era is a bureaucratically organized "iron cage." Sociology promises to teach us both the dimensions of that cage and the possibilities for release.
SOURCE: Carol Wainio, *Untitled* (1985). Acrylic on canvas, 33" × 350". Photograph courtesy of the S.L. Simpson Gallery, Toronto. Courtesy Carol Wainio.

argument (Weber, 1946). Weber noted the rapid growth of the "service" sector of the economy with its many nonmanual workers and professionals. He argued that many members of these occupational groups stabilize society because they enjoy higher status and income than do manual workers employed in the manufacturing sector. In addition, Weber showed that class conflict is not the only driving force of history. In his view, politics and religion are also important sources of historical change (see the next section). Other writers pointed out that Marx did not understand how investing in technology would make it possible for workers to toil fewer hours under less oppressive conditions. Nor did he foresee that higher wages, better working conditions, and government benefits, such as employment insurance and medicare, would pacify manual workers. Thus, we see that many of the particulars of Marx's theory were called into question by Weber and other sociologists. Nonetheless, Marx's insights about the fundamental importance of conflict in social life were influential—and still are today.

## SYMBOLIC INTERACTIONISM

Above we noted that Weber criticized Marx's interpretation of the development of capitalism. Among other things, Weber argued that early capitalist development was caused not just by favourable *economic* circumstances. In addition, he said, certain *religious* beliefs facilitated robust capitalist growth. In particular, sixteenth- and seventeenth-century Protestants believed their religious doubts could be reduced, and a state of grace ensured, if they worked diligently and lived modestly. Weber called this belief

1) Microlevel social settings
2) Requires understanding of subj. meanings
3) Creation of circumstances
4) Tolerance of others

the **Protestant ethic.** He believed it had an unintended effect: People who adhered to the Protestant ethic saved and invested more than others did. Thus, according to Weber, capitalism developed most robustly where the Protestant ethic took hold. He concluded that capitalism did not develop because of the operation of economic forces alone, as Marx argued. Instead, it depended partly on the religious meaning individuals attached to their work (Weber, 1958 [1904–05]).

In much of his research, Weber emphasized the importance of empathetically understanding people's motives and the meanings they attach to things to gain a clear sense of the significance of their actions. He called this aspect of his approach to sociological research the method of *Verstehen* (pronounced Fer-SHTAY-en, meaning "understanding" in German).

The idea that subjective meanings must be analyzed in any complete sociological analysis was only one of Weber's contributions to early sociological theory. Weber was also an important conflict theorist, as you will learn in later chapters. At present, however, it is enough to note that his emphasis on subjective meanings found rich soil in North America, for here was an idea that resonated deeply with the individualism of North American culture. A century ago, it was widely believed that individual talent and initiative could achieve just about anything on this continent of opportunity. Small wonder, then, that much of early North American sociology focused on the individual or, more precisely, on the connection between the individual and the larger society. For example, George Herbert Mead at the University of Chicago was the driving force behind the study of how individual identity is formed in the course of interaction with other people. We discuss his contribution in Chapter 3, Socialization. Here we note only that the work of Mead and his colleagues gave birth to symbolic interactionism, a distinctively North American theoretical tradition that continues to be a major force in sociology today.

Functionalists and conflict theorists assume that people's group memberships—whether they are young or old, male or female, rich or poor—shape their behaviour. This can sometimes make people seem like balls on a pool table: They get knocked around and cannot determine their destinations. We know from our everyday experience, however, that people are not like that. You often make choices, sometimes difficult ones. You sometimes change your mind. Moreover, two people with similar social characteristics may react differently to similar social circumstances because they may interpret those circumstances differently.

Recognizing these issues, some sociologists focus on the subjective side of social life. They work in the symbolic interactionist tradition. **Symbolic interactionism** incorporates these four features:

1. It focuses on face-to-face communication or interaction in microlevel social settings. This feature distinguishes it from both the functionalist and the conflict paradigms.
2. Symbolic interactionism emphasizes that an adequate explanation of social behaviour requires understanding the subjective meanings people attach to their social circumstances.
3. Symbolic interactionism stresses that people help to create their social circumstances and do not merely react to them.[2]
4. By underscoring the subjective meanings people create in small social settings, symbolic interactionists validate unpopular and unofficial viewpoints, thus increasing our understanding and tolerance of people who may be different from us.

To understand symbolic interactionism better, let us return briefly to the problem of suicide. If a police officer discovers a dead person at the wheel of a car that has run into a tree, it may be difficult to establish with certainty whether the death was an accident or a suicide. Interviewing friends and relatives to discover the driver's state of mind just before the crash may help to rule out the possibility of suicide. But, as this example illustrates, understanding the intention or motive of the actor is critical to understanding the meaning of a social action and explaining it. Suicide, then, is not just an objective social fact but also an inferred, and therefore subjective, social fact. A state of mind must be interpreted, usually by a coroner, before the dead body becomes a suicide statistic (Douglas, 1967).

For surviving family and friends, suicide is always painful and sometimes embarrassing. Insurance companies often deny payments to beneficiaries in the case of suicide. As a result, coroners are inclined to classify deaths as accidental whenever such an interpretation is plausible. Being human, they want to minimize the family's pain after such a horrible event. Sociologists believe that, for this reason, official suicide rates are about one-third lower than actual suicide rates.

The study of the subjective side of social life reveals many such inconsistencies, helping us to go beyond the official picture, deepening our understanding of how

*[Handwritten notes at top of page:]*

*1) Focuses on male domination, patriarchy*
*2) Male > female cause of social convention*
*3) Examines operation of patriarchy in micro and macro settings.*
*4) Patterns of inequality should be changed for the benefit of all members of society.*

society works, and supplementing the insights gained from macrolevel analysis. Moreover, by stressing the importance and validity of subjective meanings, symbolic interactionists also increase respect for and tolerance of minority and deviant viewpoints.

## FEMINIST THEORY

Few women figured prominently in the early history of sociology, largely because the strict demands placed on women by the nineteenth-century household and the lack of opportunity outside the household prevented most of them from obtaining a higher education and finding work that could support sociological research. Not surprisingly, therefore, the women who did make their mark on the discipline in its early years had unusual social backgrounds. These exceptional people introduced into the discipline gender issues that were largely ignored by Marx, Durkheim, and Weber. Appreciation for the sociological contribution of these pioneer women has grown in recent years as concern with gender issues has come to form a substantial part of the modern sociological enterprise.

*[Handwritten margin note:] first feminist*

Harriet Martineau is often called the first woman sociologist. Born in England at the beginning of the nineteenth century to a prosperous family, she never married and was able to support herself comfortably from her journalistic writings. Martineau translated Comte into English. She undertook critical studies of slavery and factory laws. She also wrote about gender inequality and was a leading advocate of voting rights and higher education for women, as well as gender equality in the family. As such, Martineau was one of the first feminists (Yates, 1985).

Despite its auspicious beginnings, feminist thinking had little impact on sociology until the mid-1960s, when the rise of the modern women's movement drew attention to the many remaining inequalities between women and men. Since then, feminist theory has had such a big influence on sociology that it may now fairly be regarded as sociology's fourth major tradition. There are several variants of modern feminism (see Chapter 7, Gender Inequality: Economic and Political Aspects). However, the various strands of **feminist theory** share the following four features:

1. Feminist theory focuses on various aspects of patriarchy, the system of male domination in society. Patriarchy, feminists contend, is at least as important as class inequality in determining a person's opportunities in life, and perhaps more so.

2. The feminist paradigm holds that male domination and female subordination are determined not by biological necessity but by structures of power and social convention. From their point of view, women are subordinate to men only because men enjoy more legal, economic, political, and cultural rights.

3. The feminist paradigm examines the operation of patriarchy in both micro and macro settings.

4. The feminist paradigm contends that existing patterns of gender inequality can and should be changed for the benefit of all members of society. The main sources of gender inequality include differences in the way boys and girls are brought up; barriers to equal opportunity in education, paid work, and politics; and the unequal division of domestic responsibilities between women and men.

The theoretical traditions outlined above are summarized in Table 1.1. As you will see in the following pages, sociologists in Canada and elsewhere have applied them to all branches of the discipline (see Box 1.2). They have elaborated and refined each of them. Some sociologists work exclusively within one tradition. Others conduct research that borrows from more than one tradition. However, all sociologists are deeply indebted to the founders of the discipline.

## THEIR REVOLUTION AND OURS

In the nineteenth century, the founders of the discipline devoted their lives to solving the great sociological puzzle of their time: the causes and consequences of the Industrial Revolution. However, the ideas that stirred them did not spring fully grown from their minds. Rather, their social experiences helped to shape their ideas. There is an important lesson to be learned here. In general, sociological ideas are influenced by the social settings in which they emerge.

This lesson immediately suggests two important questions. First, what are the great sociological puzzles of *our* time? Second, how are today's sociologists responding to the challenges presented by the social settings in which *they* live? We devote the rest of the book to answering these questions in depth. In the remainder of this chapter, we offer an outline of what you can expect to learn. To provide a context for this outline, we first say a few words about how the Industrial Revolution of the nineteenth century was transformed into the Postindustrial Revolution of our day.

**TABLE 1.1**   THE MAIN THEORETICAL TRADITIONS IN SOCIOLOGY

| PARADIGM | MAIN LEVEL OF ANALYSIS | MAIN FOCUS | MAIN QUESTION | IMAGE OF IDEAL SOCIETY |
|---|---|---|---|---|
| Functionalism | Macro | Values | How do the institutions of society contribute to value consensus and, thus, to social stability? | A state of equilibrium |
| Conflict theory | Macro | Class inequality | How do privileged groups seek to maintain their advantages and subordinate groups seek to increase theirs, often causing social change in the process? | The reduction of privilege, especially class privilege |
| Symbolic interactionism | Micro | Meaning | How do individuals communicate so as to make their social settings meaningful? | Respect for the validity of minority views |
| Feminism | Micro and macro | Patriarchy | Which social structures and interaction processes maintain male dominance and female subordination? | The reduction of gender inequality |

## THE INDUSTRIAL REVOLUTION

The Industrial Revolution involved the application of science and technology to industrial processes, the construction of factories, and the formation of a large class of "blue-collar" workers. Within about a century, it took root throughout Western Europe, North America, and Japan. A century after that, industry had begun implanting itself in most of the rest of the world.

As noted in our discussion of Marx, the industrial working class protested long workdays, low pay, and dangerous working conditions. Workers went on strike, formed unions, and joined political parties. Their protests forced governments to tax citizens to provide at least minimal protection against ill health, unemployment, and poverty. Working-class protests also forced employers to limit the length of the workweek to 40 hours, improve working conditions, and raise wages. Employers were still able to increase their profits, however, by making the organization of work more efficient and introducing new technologies.

Collecting taxes, administering social services, providing healthcare, and investing heavily in technological innovation required the growth of government and business offices, hospitals, schools, universities, and research laboratories. Thus, alongside the old manufacturing sector of the economy,

the new "service" sector was born. Its employees came to be known as "white-collar" workers. Highly trained professionals stood at the peak of the service sector. Secretaries and clerks were positioned near its base. By 1980, more than half of all people working in Canada's paid labour force were in nonmanual occupations (Ornstein, 1983: 252). Sociologists call this most recent transformation of human society the **Postindustrial Revolution.** Specifically, the Postindustrial Revolution refers to the technology-driven shift from manufacturing to service industries and the consequences of that shift for virtually all human activities (Bell, 1976; Toffler, 1990).

Especially since the early 1980s, the Postindustrial Revolution has been sped up by **globalization**—the process by which formerly separate economies, states, and cultures become tied together and people become increasingly aware of their growing interdependence (Giddens, 1990: 64; Guillén, 2001). In recent decades, rapid increases in the volume of international trade, travel, and communication have broken down the isolation and independence of most countries and people. Also contributing to globalization is the growth of many institutions that bind corporations, companies, and cultures together. These processes have caused people to depend more than ever on people in other countries for products, services, ideas, and even a sense of identity.

## BOX 1.2    THE FOUR PARADIGMS IN CANADA

Each of the four major sociological paradigms has influenced research in Canada. This is evident from the following portraits of some of Canada's leading sociologists.

SOURCE: Photo courtesy of Ed Clark.

S. D. Clark (1910–2003) received his Ph.D. from the University of Toronto. He became the first chair of the Department of Sociology at that institution. Born in Lloydminster, Alberta, he is especially well known for his studies of Canadian social development as a process of disorganization and reorganization on a series of economic frontiers (Clark, 1968). The influence of functionalism on his work is apparent in his emphasis on the way society reestablishes equilibrium after experiencing disruptions caused by economic change.

SOURCE: Reprinted with permission from Carleton University Archives.

John Porter (1921–79) was Canada's premier sociologist in the 1960s and 1970s. Born in Vancouver, he received his Ph.D. from the London School of Economics. He spent his academic career at Carleton University in Ottawa. There he served as chair of the Department of Sociology and Anthropology, dean of Arts and Science, and vice-president. His major work, *The Vertical Mosaic* (1965), is a study of class and power in Canada. Firmly rooted in the conflict paradigm, it influenced a generation of Canadian sociologists in their studies on social inequality, elite groups, French-English relations, and Canadian–American relations.

SOURCE: Courtesy the American Sociological Association.

Erving Goffman (1922–82) was born in Mannville, Alberta. He studied sociology and anthropology as an undergraduate at the University of Toronto and completed his Ph.D. at the University of Chicago. He pursued his academic career at the University of California, Berkeley, and the University of Pennsylvania. Goffman developed an international reputation for his "dramaturgical" approach to symbolic interactionism. This approach highlights the way people present themselves to others, managing their identities to create desired impressions on their "audience," in much the same way as actors do on stage (Goffman, 1959).

SOURCE: Photo © Karyn Gorra. Courtesy Margrit Eichler.

Margrit Eichler (1942–) was born in Berlin, Germany. She did her Ph.D. at Duke University in the United States before beginning her academic career in Canada. She served as chair of the Department of Sociology at the Ontario Institute for Studies in Education and head of the Women's Studies Program at the University of Toronto. She is internationally known for her work on feminist methodology (Eichler, 1987). Her work on family policy in Canada has influenced students, professional sociologists, and policymakers for more than two decades (Eichler, 1988).

The causes and consequences of postindustrialism and globalization form the great sociological puzzles of our time. Much of this book is devoted to analyzing postindustrialism, globalization, and their effects. In concluding this chapter, a review of some of the sociological issues raised by the Postindustrial Revolution and globalization is therefore in order.

## POSTINDUSTRIALISM AND GLOBALIZATION: OPPORTUNITIES AND PITFALLS

At the end of the twentieth century, many observers were wildly optimistic about the benefits that postindustrialism and globalization were supposedly going to bring to humanity. One commentator proclaimed "the end of history," by which he meant that liberal capitalism had become the unrivalled socioeconomic system in the world and its dominance was bound to usher in a long era of peace, freedom, and prosperity, leaving no corner of the world untouched (Fukuyama, 1992). Similarly, in a special issue of the *New York Times Magazine* devoted to technology, one staff writer gushed:

> Individuals are acquiring more control over their lives, their minds and their bodies, even their genes, thanks to the transformations in medicine, communications, transportation and industry. At the same time, these technologies are providing social benefits and undoing some of the damage of the past. Technology helps to conserve natural resources and diminish pollution. ... The Information Revolution, besides enabling us to visit Mars at will, is fostering peaceful cooperation on Earth by decentralizing power. Political tyrants and demagogic warmongers are losing control now that their subjects have tools to communicate directly with one another. People are using the tools to do their jobs without leaving their families. They're forming new communities in cyberspace and forming new bonds with their neighbors in real space. Technology has the potential to increase individual freedom and strengthen community. (Tierney, 1997: 46–7)

This and similar outpourings of optimism were written before the stock-market crash of 2000, the terrorist attacks of September 11, 2001, the second invasion of Iraq by the United States in 2003, and heightened fears about the consequences of climate change that surrounded the 2005 hurricane season. However, even before these devastating shocks changed the minds of all but the most starry-eyed observers, sociologists were more realistic about the prospects of humanity. On the whole, they agreed that postindustrialism and globalization promise many exciting opportunities to enhance the quality of life and increase human freedom—but they also saw many social-structural barriers to the realization of that promise.

The unresolved social issues that confront us in the era of postindustrialism and globalization fall under three headings. Each issue is addressed in later chapters.

*Autonomy versus constraint.* One of the major themes that emerges from *New Society* is that many people are freer to construct their own identities than ever before. Almost everyone used to retain their religious, ethnic, racial, and sexual identities for a lifetime, even if they were not particularly comfortable with them. In the era of postindustrialism and globalization, however, various social developments and technological advances—ranging from international migration to the World Wide Web to greater acceptance of sexual diversity—free people from traditional constraints. The theme of increasing personal autonomy is taken up in Chapter 2, Culture; Chapter 3, Socialization; Chapter 4, Gender and Sexuality; Chapter 5, Communication and Mass Media; and Chapter 13, Religion.

Some chapters, however, point out that we experience increased freedom only within certain limits. For example, we can choose a far wider variety of consumer products than ever before, but consumerism itself increasingly seems a compulsory way of life (Chapter 2, Culture). Moreover, it is a way of life that threatens the natural environment (Chapter 16, Sociology and the Environment). Meanwhile, new technologies, such as surveillance cameras, cause us to modify our behaviour and act in more conformist ways (Chapter 14, Deviance and Crime). As these examples show, the autonomy promised by postindustrialism is only half the story. The other half is that postindustrialism places new constraints on us.

*Prosperity versus inequality.* The second major theme that emerges from *New Society* is that postindustrialism opens up new economic, political, and educational opportunities. It makes work less onerous for many people. It raises the average standard of living. It enables women in particular to make rapid strides in all institutional spheres.

Again, however, we must face the less rosy aspects of postindustrialism. Tremendous economic and political inequality between women and men persists (Chapter 7, Gender Inequality: Economic and Political Aspects). So does inequality between Aboriginal and other Canadians (Chapter 8, Race and Ethnic Relations). Inequality between rich and poor in Canada has increased in recent decades (Chapter 6, Social Stratification). It is maintained partly by the educational system (Chapter 12, Education). By some measures, inequality between rich and poor nations has risen sharply (Chapter 9, Development and Underdevelopment). There are more good jobs at the top of the occupational structure, but many more bad jobs at the bottom (Chapter 11, Work and Occupations). The quality of the Canadian health-care system is threatened at precisely the moment when our population is rapidly aging and most in need of healthcare (Chapter 17, Health and Aging). Although elections are regularly held throughout much of the world, it is an illusion to think that democracy has conquered the planet (Chapter 18, Politics and Social Movements). Thus, economic and political inequality persist despite growing prosperity and opportunity.

*Diversity versus uniformity.* The third major theme that emerges from *New Society* is that postindustrial society is more tolerant of diversity than any previous form of society was. Immigration policies no longer stipulate racial, ethnic, or religious criteria for entry into the country. As a result, our cities are more socially heterogeneous than ever before (Chapter 15, Population and Urbanization). The traditional nuclear family made up of mother, father, and children has given way to a wide variety of new family forms. Myriad radio stations, TV channels, newspapers, magazines, CD titles, books, and websites are now available to us.

Yet despite growing social diversity, there is a strong push to conformity in many spheres of life. For example, most of our diverse cultural consumption is governed by the tastes and the profit motive of vast media conglomerates, most of them American-owned (Chapter 5, Communication and Mass Media). Powerful interests are trying to shore up the traditional nuclear family despite its inappropriateness for many people in postindustrial society (Chapter 10, Families). The globalization of economic, political, and cultural affairs may be threatening the survival of distinct national cultures (Chapter 19, Globalization). The push to uniformity thus counters the trend toward growing social diversity.

## WHY SOCIOLOGY?

Renowned English sociologist Anthony Giddens wrote that we live in an era "suspended between extraordinary opportunity ... and global catastrophe" (Giddens, 1982: 166). Because of the collapse of the Soviet Union in 1991 and the actions of international terrorists, nuclear, chemical, and biological catastrophes are more likely now than they were just a few years ago. A whole range of environmental issues, deep inequalities in the wealth of nations and of classes, racial and ethnic violence, and unsolved problems in the relations between women and men continue to stare us in the face and profoundly affect the quality of our daily life.

Despair and apathy is one possible response to these complex issues. But it is not a response that humans have often favoured. If it were our nature to give up hope, we would still be sitting around half-naked in the mud outside a cave.

People are more inclined to look for ways of improving their lives, and this period of human history is full of opportunities to do so. We have, for example, advanced to the point where for the first time we have the means to feed and educate everyone in the world. Similarly, it now seems possible to erode some of the inequalities that have always been with us and have always been the major source of human conflict. Students of sociology pursue careers that further such goals (see Box 1.3).

Although sociology offers no easy solutions as to how the goal of improving society may be accomplished, it does promise a useful way of understanding our current predicament and seeing possible ways of dealing with it. You sampled sociology's ability to tie personal troubles to social-structural issues when we discussed suicide. You reviewed the major theoretical perspectives that enable sociologists to connect the personal with the social-structural. When I outlined the half-fulfilled promises of postindustrialism and globalization, you saw sociology's ability to provide an understanding of where we are and where we can head.

I frankly admit that the questions raised in this book are tough to answer. Sharp controversy surrounds them all. However, I am sure that if you grapple with them, you will enhance your understanding of your society's, and your own, possibilities. In brief, sociology can help you figure out where you fit into society and how you can make society fit you. That, fundamentally, is sociology's goal.

## BOX 1.3    CAREERS IN SOCIOLOGY

Students often ask, "Can I get a good job with a sociology degree?" "Exactly what kind of work could I do with a major in sociology?" "Aren't all the good jobs these days in technical areas and the natural sciences?" To answer these questions—and to help you decide whether a sociology or other social science major makes sense for you—consider the following data on the employment of Canadians with degrees in sociology and related fields.

A study based on 1988 data found that a higher percentage of Canadian sociology graduates were employed full-time than were graduates in the other social sciences (Guppy and Hedley, 1993). A study based mainly on 1996 data (Allen, 1999) showed the following in Canada:

- The unemployment rate among social science graduates was lower than among graduates in math, physics, engineering, agriculture, and biology.
- Between 1991 and 1996, there were more new jobs for people with social science degrees than for people with degrees in other fields.
- Although women earned less than men in all fields in 1996, the discrepancy between men's and women's income was smallest among social science graduates.

On the basis of these findings, it seems that sociology degrees promise more employment security for both men and women, and less income discrimination against women, than other degrees. It also seems that the postindustrial economy requires more new employees with a social science background than new employees with a background in some technical and scientific fields.

Tens of thousands of Canadians have undergraduate sociology degrees. A sociology B.A. improves your understanding of the diverse social conditions affecting men and women, people with different sexual orientations, and people from different countries, regions, classes, races, and ethnic groups. Therefore, people with a B.A. in sociology tend to be attracted to jobs requiring good "people skills" and jobs involved with managing and promoting social change (see Table 1.2). Often, people with a B.A. in sociology go on to graduate school and obtain professional degrees in other fields, including law, urban planning, industrial relations, social work, and public policy. You will therefore find many people with bachelor's degrees in sociology working as lawyers, urban planners, city managers, and healthcare and education administrators.

Most people with a graduate degree in sociology teach and conduct research in universities, with research being a more important component of the job in larger and more prestigious institutions. However, many sociologists do not teach. Instead, they conduct research and give policy advice in a wide range of settings outside the system of higher education. In many federal government agencies, for example, sociologists are employed as researchers and policy consultants. Sociologists also conduct research and policy analysis in trade unions, nongovernmental organizations, and professional and public interest associations. In the private sector, you can find sociologists practising their craft in firms specializing in public opinion polling, management consulting, market research, standardized testing, and "evaluation research," which assesses the impact of particular policies and programs before or after they go into effect.

One way of seeing the benefits of a sociological education is to compile a list of some of the famous practical idealists who studied sociology in university. That list includes several former heads of state, among them President Fernando Cardoso of Brazil, President Tomas Masaryk of Czechoslovakia, Prime Minister Edward Seaga of Jamaica, and President Ronald Reagan of the United States. The current first lady of the United States, Michelle Obama, also has a sociology degree. The former vice-president of the Liberal Party of Canada and former president and vice-chancellor of York University in Toronto, Lorna Marsden, is a sociologist. Anthony Giddens, former director of the London School of Economics and adviser to former British Prime Minister Tony Blair, earned a sociology doctorate. So do Martin Goldfarb, chairman, president, and CEO of The Goldfarb Corporation; and Donna Dasko, senior vice-president of Environics, two of Canada's leading public opinion firms with offices and affiliates around the world. Alex Himelfarb, former clerk of the Privy Council, holds a sociology Ph.D., too. So, for that matter, does British Columbia native Steve Nash of the Los Angeles Lakers, one of the best team players in professional basketball. His agent claims he is "the most colorblind person I've ever known" (Robbins, 2005). Arguably, Nash's study of sociology contributed to his team-building ability and his performance on the court by helping him to better understand the importance of groups and diverse social conditions in shaping human behaviour.

---

**TABLE 1.2**    JOBS COMMONLY HELD BY CANADIANS WITH DEGREES IN SOCIOLOGY

**Government**

community affairs officer
urban/regional planner
legislative aide
affirmative action/employment equity worker
foreign service officer
human rights officer
personnel coordinator

**Research**

social research specialist
consumer researcher
data analyst market researcher
survey researcher
census officer/analyst
demographer/population analyst
system analyst

**Community Affairs**

occupational/career counsellor
homeless/housing worker
public health/hospital administrator
child development technician
public administration assistant
social assistance advocate
resident planning aide
group home worker
rehabilitation program worker
rural health outreach worker
housing coordinator
fundraising director/assistant
caseworker/aide
community organizer
youth outreach worker

**Corrections**

corrections officer
criminology assistant
police officer
rehabilitation counsellor
criminal investigator
juvenile court worker
parole officer

**Teaching**

college/university placement worker
public health educator
teacher admissions counsellor

**Business**

market analyst
project manager
sales representative
real estate agent
journalist
public relations officer
actuary
insurance agent
human resources manager
production manager
labour relations officer
administrative assistant
quality control manager
merchandiser/purchaser
computer analyst
data entry manager
publishing officer
advertising officer
sales manager

SOURCE: Guppy and Hedley (1993). Reprinted with permission from the Canadian Sociological Association  Société canadienne de sociologie.

---

# SUMMARY

1. Durkheim showed that social structures influence even apparently nonsocial and antisocial actions. Specifically, he showed how levels of social solidarity affect suicide rates.

2. Because of the rise in youth suicide, the pattern of suicide rates in Canada today is not exactly the same as in Durkheim's France. Nevertheless, Durkheim's theory explains the contemporary Canadian pattern well.

3. Sociologists analyze the connection between personal troubles and social structures.

4. Sociologists analyze the influence of three levels of social structure on human action: microstructures, macrostructures, and global structures.

5. Values suggest which sociological research questions are worth asking and how the parts of society fit together. Values underlie sociological theories. A theory is a tentative explanation of some aspect of social life. It states how and why specific facts are connected. Research is the process of carefully observing social reality to assess the validity of a theory.

6. There are four major theoretical traditions in sociology. Functionalism analyzes how social order is supported by macrostructures. Conflict theory analyzes how social inequality is maintained and challenged. Symbolic interactionism analyzes how meaning is created when people communicate

in microlevel settings. Feminism focuses on the social sources of patriarchy in both macro and micro settings.

7. The Scientific, Industrial, and Democratic Revolutions stimulated the rise of sociology.

8. The Postindustrial Revolution is the technology-driven shift from manufacturing to service industries and the consequences of that shift for virtually all human activities. Globalization is the process by which formerly separate economies, states, and cultures become tied together and people become increasingly aware of their growing interdependence.

9. The causes and consequences of postindustrialism and globalization form the great sociological puzzle of our time. The tension between autonomy and constraint, prosperity and inequality, and diversity and uniformity are among the chief interests of sociology today.

## QUESTIONS TO CONSIDER

1. Do you think the promise of autonomy, prosperity, and diversity will be realized in the twenty-first century? Why or why not?

2. In this chapter you learned how variations in the level of social solidarity affect the suicide rate. How do you think variations in social solidarity might affect other areas of social life, such as criminal behaviour and political protest?

3. Is a science of society possible? If you agree that such a science is possible, what are its advantages over common sense? What are its limitations?

## GLOSSARY

**Altruistic suicide** (p. 7) occurs in settings that exhibit high levels of social solidarity, according to Durkheim. Altruistic suicide results from norms very tightly governing behaviour.

**Anomic suicide** (p. 7) occurs in settings that exhibit low levels of social solidarity, according to Durkheim. Anomic suicide results from vaguely defined norms governing behaviour.

**Conflict theory** (p. 15) generally focuses on large, macrolevel structures, such as the relations between or among classes. It shows how major patterns of inequality in society produce social stability in some circumstances and social change in others. It stresses how members of privileged groups try to maintain their advantages while subordinate groups struggle to increase theirs. It typically leads to the suggestion that eliminating privilege will lower the level of conflict and increase human welfare.

The **Democratic Revolution** (p. 10) began about 1750. It suggested that people are responsible for organizing society and that human intervention can therefore solve social problems.

**Dysfunctional** consequences (p. 15) are effects of social structures that create social instability.

**Egoistic suicide** (p. 7) results from a lack of integration of the individual into society because of weak social ties to others.

**Ethnomethodology** (p. 26) is the study of how people make sense of what others do and say in terms of norms that exist independently of individual social actors.

**Feminist theory** (p. 18) claims that patriarchy is at least as important as class inequality in determining a person's opportunities in life. It holds that male domination and female subordination are determined not by biological necessity but by structures of power and social convention. It examines the operation of patriarchy in both micro and macro settings. It contends that existing patterns of gender inequality can and should be changed for the benefit of all members of society.

**Functionalist theory** (p. 15) stresses that human behaviour is governed by relatively stable social structures. It underlines how social structures maintain or undermine social stability. It emphasizes that social structures are based mainly on shared values or preferences. It suggests that reestablishing equilibrium can best solve most social problems.

**Global structures** (p. 9) are patterns of social relations that lie outside and above the national level. They include international organizations, patterns of worldwide travel and communication, and the economic relations between and among countries.

**Globalization** (p. 19) is the process by which formerly separate economies, states, and cultures are becoming tied together and people are becoming increasingly aware of their growing interdependence.

The **Industrial Revolution** (p. 10) refers to the rapid economic transformation that began in Britain in the 1780s. It involved the large-scale application of science and technology to industrial processes, the creation of factories, and the formation of a working class.

**Latent functions** (p. 15) are invisible and unintended effects of social structures.

**Macrostructures** (p. 9) are overarching patterns of social relations that lie outside and above our circle of intimates and acquaintances. Macrostructures include classes, bureaucracies, and power systems, such as patriarchy.

**Manifest functions** (p. 15) are visible and intended effects of social structures.

**Microstructures** (p. 8) are the patterns of relatively intimate social relations formed during face-to-face interaction. Families, friendship circles, and work associations are all microstructures.

**Patriarchy** (p. 9) is the traditional system of economic and political inequality between women and men.

The **Postindustrial Revolution** (p. 19) refers to the technology-driven shift from manufacturing to service industries and the consequences of that shift for virtually all human activities.

The **Protestant ethic** (p. 17) is the belief, originating in the sixteenth and seventeenth centuries, that religious doubts can be reduced, and a state of grace ensured, if people work diligently and live ascetically. According to Weber, the Protestant ethic had the unintended effect of increasing savings and investment and thus stimulating capitalist growth.

**Research** (p. 12) is the process of systematically observing reality to assess the validity of a theory.

The **Scientific Revolution** (p. 10) began about 1550. It encouraged the view that sound conclusions about the workings of society must be based on solid evidence, not just on speculation.

**Social solidarity** (p. 6) refers to (1) the degree to which group members share beliefs and values, and (2) the intensity and frequency of their interaction.

**Social structures** (p. 8) are relatively stable patterns of social relations.

The **sociological imagination** (p. 10) is the quality of mind that enables a person to see the connection between personal troubles and social structures.

**Sociology** (p. 5) is the systematic study of human behaviour in social context.

**Symbolic interactionism** (p. 17) focuses on face-to-face communication or interaction in microlevel social settings. It emphasizes that an adequate explanation of social behaviour requires understanding the subjective meanings people attach to their social circumstances. It stresses that people help to create their social circumstances and do not merely react to them. By underscoring the subjective meanings people create in small social settings, symbolic interactionism validates unpopular and nonofficial viewpoints, thus increasing our understanding and tolerance of people who may be different from us.

A **theory** (p. 12) is a tentative explanation of some aspect of social life that states how and why certain facts are related.

**Values** (p. 14) are ideas about what is right and wrong.

## SUGGESTED READING

Brym, Robert J. (2011). *Sociology as a Life or Death Issue*, 2nd Canadian ed. Toronto: Nelson. A guide to the sociological craft for beginners. It focuses on the social causes of death—specifically, the social context of hip-hop, suicide bombing, "natural" disasters, and cancer—to show how sociology can help people live longer and better lives.

The *Canadian Review of Sociology* (www.csa-scs.ca/crs-home) and the *Canadian Journal of Sociology* (http://ejournals.library.ualberta.ca/index.php/

CJS/index) will give you a taste of the practice of sociology in Canada. Visit the website of the Canadian Sociological Association at www.csa-scs.ca for sociological news and conferences.

Stephens, W. Richard, Jr. (1998). *Careers in Sociology*. New York: Allyn & Bacon. In this book, 18 sociology graduates talk about the diverse and fascinating careers they have pursued. It is available online at www.abacon.com/socsite/careers.html.

## NOTES

1. You will find more detailed discussion of these theories throughout the book. For example, on functionalism, see Chapters 12 and 13. On conflict theory, see Chapters 6, 10, 13, and 18. On symbolic interactionism, see Chapters 3 and 14. On feminism, see Chapters 4, 7, 10, and 18.

2. By emphasizing how social reality is constructed during interaction, symbolic interactionists downplay the importance of norms and understandings that precede any given interaction. **Ethnomethodology** tries to correct this shortcoming. Ethnomethodologists study how people make sense of what others do and say but stress

that norms exist independently of individual social actors. Indeed, in the ethnomethodological view, everyday interactions could not take place without preexisting shared norms. Say you pass an acquaintance on the street, who offers a friendly "How are you?" If you proceed to outline in detail your financial situation, your love life, interesting developments at work, and so on, the acquaintance will quickly become annoyed. Most people expect "How are you?" to be answered with an equally brief reply. Violate the norm, and communication quickly breaks down (Garfinkel, 1967).

# Sociological Knowledge & Science

# 1

# An Idea Whose Time Has Come

EARL BABBIE

*The author claims that this is a time of both unprecedented dangers but also of real achievements. To deal with these conditions, we need to learn why people relate to one another sometimes peacefully and sometimes with hostility. This need fits into the role of sociology because it studies interaction and relations among humans, including how humans live together and how rules come into existence. For this reason Babbie claims that sociology is an idea whose time has come.*

*As you read this selection, consider the following questions as guides:*

1. *What do you consider are the dangers now existing in the world and how you would try to resolve them?*
2. *What, if anything, are our politicians doing to resolve these dangers?*
3. *Can you think of any scientific efforts or accomplishments that attempt to deal with these dangers?*
4. *Why do you agree or disagree with Babbie's assertion that sociology is an idea whose time has come?*

There is a more pressing need for sociological insights today than at any time in history....

It is no secret that this generation faces several unprecedented dangers. No sooner has the Cold War seemingly ended than we have come to recognize the danger of localized wars among ethnic groups spilling over into wider, global conflict. This danger is made worse by the possibility that relatively small, impoverished nations could gain access to nuclear weapons, giving terrorists the opportunity to spark an international conflagration. The more we learn about the prospects of a "nuclear winter"—the likely result of the first truly nuclear war—the more evident it is that there would be no real survivors of such a large-scale nuclear exchange.

If, on the other hand, we escape the threat of nuclear extinction, there is a real possibility that we will overpopulate and pollute the planet beyond its carrying capacity. As a single indicator of this problem, some 13 to 18 million people die of starvation around the world every year, three-fourths of them children. Approximately one-fifth of all humans on the planet go to bed hungry every night.

Add to this such persistent problems as crime, inflation, unemployment, prejudice, totalitarianism, and national debts, and you have sufficient grounds

*The Sociological Spirit*, Belmont: Wadsworth, 1994.

6

for understanding the ancient Chinese curse: "May you live in interesting times."

These are unquestionably interesting times. But the picture is not completely gloomy. These are also the times of great achievements in space: humans landing on the moon, a remote-controlled craft landing on Mars, and others photographing the more distant planets. These are the times when human beings, working cooperatively around the globe, eradicated smallpox—a scourge throughout history. These are the times of an awakening of awareness and commitment to ending world hunger. And the breakup of the former USSR, along with its domination of Eastern Europe, is regarded by most as a positive development....

If it were possible to make comparable lists of the positive and negative aspects of life today, my hunch is that they might be about equal in length. At any rate, both lists would be long ones, indicating that you and I and our fellow human beings face both trying challenges and promising opportunities ahead of us.

Assuming that we'd agree in favoring peace over war, prosperity over hunger and poverty, and so forth, the question you should be asking yourself is: what determines how things turn out? Specifically, what would it take for peace to triumph over the continuing specter of wars large and small? We'd all like the answer to that question.

I suggest there is a prior question you should ask. That is: where should we look for the answer to how peace can prevail over war? Before asking what the answer is, we need to ask where the answer is likely to be found. I suggest that up until now we have tended to look for the answer to how peace can prevail over war within the domain of military technology. Most simply, we have tried to create weapons that would preserve the peace....

The point of this discussion on war and peace is to suggest that what we need to know to establish peace around the world is not likely to arise from military technology. If such an answer is to be found at all, we must look elsewhere: in the study of why people relate to one another as they do—sometimes peacefully, sometimes hostilely. This, as we'll see, lies in the domain of sociology.

## THE DOMAIN OF SOCIOLOGY

Sociology involves the study of human beings. More specifically, it is the study of interactions and relations *among* human beings. Whereas psychology is the study of what goes on inside individuals, sociology addresses what goes on between them. Sociology addresses simple, face-to-face interactions such as conversations, dating behavior, and students asking a professor to delay the term paper deadline. Equally, sociology is the study of formal organizations, the functioning of whole societies, and even relations among societies.

Sociology is the study of how human beings live together—in both the good times and the bad. It is no more a matter of how we cooperate and get along than of how we compete and conflict. Both are fundamental aspects of our living together and, hence, of sociology.

You might find it useful to view sociology as the study of our *rules for living together*. Let's take a minute to look at that.

To begin, let's consider some of the things that individuals need or want out of life: food, shelter, companionship, security, satisfaction—the list could go on and on. My purpose in considering such a list is to have us see that the things you and I need or want out of life create endless possibilities for conflict and struggle. When food is scarce, for example, I can only satisfy my need at your expense. Even in the case of companionship—where both people get what they want—you and I may fight over a particular companion.

The upshot of all this is that human beings do not seem to be constructed in a way that ensures cooperation. Bees and ants, by contrast, just seem to be wired that way. As a consequence, human

1. Hiram Maxim as quoted in Martin Hellman, *A New Way of Thinking*, Palo Alto, CA: Beyond War, 1985, p. 4.

2. Orville Wright as quoted in Martin Hellman, *A New Way of Thinking*, Palo Alto, CA: Beyond War, 1985, p. 4.

- Socialization
- Sanctions
- arbitary

beings *create rules* to establish order in the face of chaos. Sometimes we agree on the rules voluntarily, and other times some people impose the rules on everyone else. In part, sociology is the study of how rules come into existence.

Sociology is also the study of how rules are *organized* and *perpetuated*. It would be worth taking a minute to reflect on the extent and complexity of the rules by which you and I live. There is a rule, for example, that Americans must pay taxes to the government. But it doesn't end there. The rule for paying taxes has been elaborated on by a great many more specific rules indicating how much, when, and to whom taxes are to be paid. In recent years, the index to the IRS tax code has run more than 1,000 pages long, which should give you some idea of the complexity of that set of rules. The much-touted tax simplification of 1986 was 1,855 pages long.

The rules governing our lives are not all legal ones. There are rules about shaking hands when you meet someone, rules about knives and forks at dinner, rules about how long to wear your hair, and rules about what to wear to class, to the symphony, and to mud-wrestling. There are rules of grammar, rules of good grooming, and rules of efficient computer programming.

Many of the rules we've been considering were here long before you and I showed up, and many will still be here after we've left. Moreover, I doubt that you have the experience of having taken part in creating any of the rules I've listed. Nobody asked you to vote on the rules of grammar, for example. But in a critical way, you *did* vote on those rules: you voted by obeying them.

Consider the rule about not going naked in public. Even though you don't recall being asked what you thought about that one, there was a public referendum on that issue this morning—and you voted in favor of clothes. So did I. If this seems silly, by the way, realize that there are other societies in which people voted to accept a different rule this morning.

Sometime today you are likely to be asked to vote on a set of rules about eating. Some of the possibilities are eating spaghetti with a knife, pouring soup on your dessert, and throwing your food against the wall. Let's see how you vote.

The persistence of our rules is largely a function of one generation teaching them to the next generation. We speak of *socialization* as the process of learning the rules, and it becomes apparent that we are all socializing each other all the time through the use of positive and negative *sanctions*—rewards and punishments.

All the rules we've been discussing are fundamentally *arbitrary*—that is, different rules would work just as well. Although Americans have a rule that cars must be driven on the right side of the road, other societies (e.g., England, Japan) manage equally well with people driving on the left side.

Once we've established a rule, however, we tend to add weight to it. We act as though it were better than the other possibilities, that it somehow represents an eternal and universal *truth*. Sociologists often use the term *reification* in reference to the pretense that things are real when they are not, and we often *reify* the rules of society. We make the right side of the road the *right* side for cars to drive on, and we think the British and Japanese strange for not knowing that.

The rules of society take their strongest hold when they are *internalized* by individuals—taken inside ourselves and made our own. Imagine this situation, which you may have actually experienced. It is three o'clock in the morning, and you are driving along a street leading out of a small town. There is no traffic on the street in any direction as you come to a red light at an intersection. You can see there are no cars coming for a mile in every direction. There is no one around. What do you do? There's a good chance that you will sit and wait for the light to change. If someone questioned you about it, you might say, "It just wouldn't feel right."

In the event you would drive through the light and generally regard yourself as above reification and internalization, think again. You have reified and internalized countless rules. How would you feel about having live ants and cockroaches for dinner tonight, for example? Are you willing to give them a try? How do you feel about murder, rape, and child abuse? Are you pretty casual about them, or do you feel they are *really wrong?* If you think about it, you'll find you feel pretty strongly about a lot of our rules.

All of this notwithstanding, sociology is also the study of how we *break* the rules. Some people use bad grammar and pour their soup on the floor, not to mention drive too fast, steal, fix prices, commit murder, and everything in between. Although this may seem like the study of "bad people," beware.

First, the rules of society are so extensive and complex that no one can possibly keep them all. For example, there is probably a street near you that is posted with a twenty-five-mile-per-hour speed limit; that's certainly a rule. And yet if you drive twenty-five miles an hour on that street during rush hour, you may discover you're breaking another rule. Your clue will be the honking horns and shaking fists.

Beyond the impossibility of obeying all the rules, you and I might agree that some of them ought to be broken. Consider the rule, in force a few years ago, that black people had to sit in the back of the bus in some parts of America. The people who finally broke that rule are considered heroes today. By the same token, you might disagree with rules that women can't fix carburetors, that men shouldn't cry, or that professors always know better than students.

The study of how people break the rules is closely related to the study of how the rules *change* over time. Although we are always living in a sea of rules, and many seem to last forever, it is also true that the rules of society are always in a process of change. Rules pertaining to hemlines, hair length, and political views operate a little like yo-yos. Others seem to change in only one direction.

Sociology, then, is an examination of the rules that govern our living together: what they are, how they arise, and how they change. Sociology, however, is a special approach to the rules of social life. As we'll see, there are other approaches.

## A SCIENCE OF SOCIETY

...Sociology is a science of social life. Like other sciences, sociology has a ***logical/empirical*** basis. This means that, to be accepted, assertions must (1) make sense and (2) correspond to the facts. In this sense,

sociology can be characterized by a current buzz-word: *critical thinking*. The simple fact is that most of us, most of the time, are uncritical in our thinking. Much of the time we simply believe what we read or hear. Or, when we disagree, we do so on the basis of ideological points of view and prejudices that are not very well thought out.

1.   Hiram Maxim as quoted in Martin Hellman, *A New Way of Thinking*, Palo Alto, CA: Beyond War, 1985, p. 4.
2.   Orville Wright as quoted in Martin Hellman, *A New Way of Thinking*, Palo Alto, CA: Beyond War, 1985, p. 4.

Suppose you were talking with a friend about the value of going to college. Your friend disagrees: "College is a waste of time. You should get a head start in the job market instead. Most of today's millionaires never went to college, and there are plenty of college graduates pumping gas or out of work altogether." That's the kind of thing people sometimes say, and it can be convincing—especially if it's said with conviction. But does it stand up to logical and empirical testing?

Logically, it doesn't seem to make much sense, since a college education would seem to give a person access to high-paying occupations not open to people with less education....

There isn't any scientific support for the assertion that education is a worthless financial investment— even though there are some individual exceptions to the rule.

It's important to recognize that human beings generally have opinions about everything...but it needs saying here that the people you deal with every day have a tendency to express opinions about the way things are—and what they say isn't always so. Consequently, you need to protect yourself from false information. That's what critical thinking is all about, and sociology provides some powerful critical-thinking tools.

I hope these few examples will indicate that sociology is not just something you might study in college and never think about again. Sociology deals with powerful issues that determine the quality of your life. Understanding sociology can empower you to be a more effective participant in the social affairs around you whether you are a conscious player or not. Marriage, employment, prejudice, crime, and politics are only a few of the areas of social life that can be importantly affected by your ability to engage in sociological reasoning.

Let's look at the twin foundations of critical thinking and of science in more detail—seeing how they apply to sociology in particular....

## SOCIOLOGICAL QUESTIONS AND ANSWERS

The common image of science is of scientists finding the answers to questions. I will conclude this chapter with a somewhat different view of science and of sociology in particular. Science is sometimes better at raising questions than at finding answers to them. It would be useful for you to regard science as an ongoing inquiry, recognizing that questions initiate new avenues of inquiry, while answers close them down.

Science makes an especially powerful contribution when it calls into question those things that "everyone knows." Everyone used to "know," for example, that blacks were inferior to whites and that women were inferior to men. As you'll see, sociological points of view very often raise questions about things everyone else thought had already been answered. Even when we discover new and seemingly better answers about something, it's important to hold them as tentative.

There is a particular *recursive* quality in human life that makes anything we know tentative. Whenever we learn something about ourselves, what we've learned may bring about changes—even to the extent of making what we learned no longer accurate.

Suppose we studied employment opportunities across the country, for example. When our study was complete, we listed the ten cities with the most jobs available. As soon as our findings became widely known, of course, a lot of unemployed people would move to those cities, and soon those cities would not have as many jobs available as before. This is the same thing that happens when a newspaper columnist identifies a local restaurant that has great food, low prices, and no waiting. The "no waiting" part probably won't last another twenty-four hours, and the other two characteristics may disappear, too. In sociology, anything we learn can change things, so no knowledge can be counted on to remain true. Thus, we need to keep asking questions.

Even more fundamentally, sociology deals with a number of questions that will never be answered fully. Who am I? What is a human being? Are we more the result of our genes or of our environment? Is order possible without restricting freedom?... and it is unlikely that they will ever be completely answered. As we'll see, however, it can be very useful to keep asking them anyway.

I point all this out to give you an appropriate context for your own inquiry into sociology. Although there are some facts about sociology that are worth learning, it is more important for you to learn to use sociology for your own ongoing critical thinking. If you were studying brain surgery or medieval history, you might not have an opportunity to use what you learned in your day-to-day life. Sociology is very different. Every day you will wake up into a sociological laboratory with a massive experiment under way. We're all subjects in the experiment, and you now have the opportunity to join the researchers.

# Chapter 1

# Human Inquiry and Science

*All of us try to understand and predict the social world. Science—and social research in particular—are designed to avoid the common pitfalls of ordinary human inquiry.*

tkachuk/Shutterstock

# Introduction

This book is about knowing things—not so much *what* we know as *how* we know it. Let's start by examining a few things you probably know already. You know the world is round. You probably also know it's cold on the dark side of the moon, and you know people speak Chinese in China. You know that vitamin C helps to prevent colds and that unprotected sex can result in AIDS.

*How* do you know? Unless you've been to the dark side of the moon lately or done experimental research on the virtues of vitamin C, you know these things because somebody told them to you, and you believed what you were told. You may have read in *National Geographic* that people speak Chinese languages in China, and that made sense to you, so you didn't question it. Perhaps your physics or astronomy instructor told you it was cold on the dark side of the moon, or maybe you read it in a magazine.

Some of the things you know seem absolutely obvious to you. If you were asked how you know the world is round, you'd probably say, "Everybody knows that." There are a lot of things everybody knows. Of course, at one time, everyone "knew" the world was flat.

Most of what you know is a matter of agreement and belief. Little of it is based on personal experience and discovery. A big part of growing up in any society, in fact, is the process of learning to accept what everybody around you "knows" is so. If you don't know those same things, you can't really be a part of the group. If you were to question seriously whether the world is really round, you'd quickly find yourself set apart from other people. You might be sent to live in a hospital with other people who question things like that.

Although it's important to realize that most of what we know is a matter of believing what we've been told, there's nothing wrong with us in that respect. It's simply the way human societies are structured. The basis of knowledge is agreement. Because we can't learn all we need to know through personal experience and discovery alone, things are set up so we can simply believe what others tell us. We know some things through tradition, some things from "experts."

There are other ways of knowing things, however. In contrast to knowing things through agreement, we can know them through direct experience—through observation. If you dive into a glacial stream flowing through the Canadian Rockies, you don't need anyone to tell you it's cold.

You notice it all by yourself. The first time you stepped on a thorn, you knew it hurt before anyone told you.

When our experience conflicts with what everyone else knows, though, there's a good chance we'll surrender our experience in favour of the agreement.

For example, imagine you've come to a party at one of our homes. It's a high-class affair, and the drinks and food are excellent. In particular, you're taken by one of the appetizers brought around on a tray: a breaded, deep-fried tidbit that's especially zesty. You have a couple—they're so delicious! You have more. Soon you find yourself subtly moving around the room so that you'll be wherever the person next arrives with a tray of these nibblies.

Finally, you can't contain yourself any more. "What are they?" you ask. "How can I get the recipe?" And you are let in on the secret: "You've been eating breaded, deep-fried worms!" Your response is dramatic: your stomach rebels, and you promptly throw up all over the living room rug. Awful! What a terrible thing to serve guests!

The point of the story is that both of your feelings about the appetizer would be quite real. Your initial liking for them, based on your own experience, was certainly real. But so was the feeling of disgust you had when you found out that you'd been eating worms. It should be evident, however, that this feeling of disgust was strictly a product of the agreement you have with those around you that worms aren't fit to eat. That's an agreement you entered into the first time your parents found you sitting in a pile of dirt with half of a wriggling worm dangling from your lips. You learned that worms are not acceptable food in our society when they pried your mouth open and reached down your throat for the other half of the worm.

agreement reality  What we "know" as part and parcel of the culture we share with those around us.

experiential reality  What we "know" from personal experience and discovery.

Aside from these agreements, what's wrong with worms? They're probably high in protein and low in calories. Bite-sized and easily packaged, they're a distributor's dream. They are also a delicacy for some people who live in societies that lack our agreement that worms are disgusting. Some people might love the worms but be turned off by the deep-fried breading.

Here's a question you might consider: "Are worms *really* good or *really* bad to eat?" And here's a more interesting question: "*How could you know* which was really so?" This book is about answering the second kind of question.

The rest of this chapter looks at how we know what is real. We'll begin by examining inquiry as a natural human activity, something we all have engaged in every day of our lives. We'll look at the source of everyday knowledge and at some kinds of errors we make in normal inquiry. We'll then examine what makes science—in particular, social science—different. After considering some of the underlying ideas of social research, we'll conclude with an initial consideration of issues in social research.

## Looking for Reality

Reality is a tricky business. You probably already suspect that some of the things you "know" may not be true, but how can you really know what's real? People have grappled with this question for thousands of years.

One answer that has arisen out of that grappling is *science*, which offers an approach to both **agreement reality** and **experiential reality**.

Scientists have certain criteria that must be met before they'll accept the reality of something they haven't personally experienced. In general, a scientific assertion must have both *logical* and *empirical* support: it must make sense, and it must not contradict actual observation. Why do earthbound scientists accept the assertion that it's cold on the dark side of the moon? First, it makes sense, because the moon's surface heat comes from the sun's rays, and the dark side of the moon is dark because it's turned away from the sun. Second, the scientific measurements made on the moon's dark side confirm this logical expectation. So, scientists accept the reality of things they don't personally experience—they accept an agreement reality—but they have special standards for doing so.

More to the point of this book, however, science offers a special approach to the discovery of reality through personal experience. In other words, it offers a special approach to the business of inquiry. *Epistemology* is the science of knowing; *methodology* (a subfield of epistemology) might be called the science of finding out. Methodology illuminates procedures for scientific investigation. This book is an examination and presentation of social science methodology, or how social scientists find out about human social life.

Why do we need social science to discover the reality of social life? To find out, let's first consider what happens in ordinary, nonscientific inquiry.

### Ordinary Human Inquiry

Practically all people, and many other animals as well, exhibit a desire to predict their future circumstances. Humans seem predisposed to undertake this task using *causal* and *probabilistic* reasoning. We generally recognize that future circumstances are somehow caused or conditioned by present ones. We learn that getting an education will affect how much money we earn later in life and that swimming beyond the reef may bring an unhappy encounter with a shark. As students, we learn that studying hard will result in better examination grades.

We also learn that such patterns of cause and effect are *probabilistic* in nature. That is, the effects occur more often when the causes occur than when the causes are absent—but not always. Thus, students learn that studying hard produces good grades in most instances, but not every time. We recognize the danger of swimming beyond the reef without believing that every such swim will be fatal. As we'll see throughout the book, science makes these concepts of causality and probability more explicit and provides techniques for dealing with them more rigorously than does casual human inquiry. It sharpens the skills we already have by making us more conscious, rigorous, and explicit in our inquiries.

In looking at ordinary human inquiry, we need to distinguish between prediction and understanding. Often, we can make predictions without understanding—perhaps you can predict rain when your trick knee aches. And often, even if we don't understand why, we're willing to act on the basis of a demonstrated predictive ability. A racetrack buff who discovers that the third-ranked horse in the third race of the day always seems to win will probably keep betting without knowing, or caring, why it works out that way. Of course, the drawback in predicting without understanding will be powerfully evident when one of the other horses wins and our buff loses a week's pay.

Whatever the primitive drives or instincts that motivate human beings and other animals, satisfying them depends heavily on the ability to predict future circumstances. For people, however, the attempt to predict is often placed in a context of knowledge and understanding. If you can understand why things are related to one another, why certain regular patterns occur, you can predict better than if you simply observe and remember those patterns. Thus, human inquiry aims at answering both "what" and "why" questions, and we pursue these goals by observing and figuring out.

As we suggested earlier in the chapter, our attempts to learn about the world are only partly linked to direct, personal inquiry or experience. Another, much larger, part comes from the agreed-upon knowledge that others give us, those things "everyone knows." This agreement reality both assists and hinders our attempts to find out for ourselves. To see how, consider two important sources of our secondhand knowledge—tradition and authority.

### Tradition

Each of us inherits a culture made up, in part, of firmly accepted knowledge about the workings of the world. We may learn from others that eating too much candy will decay our teeth, that the circumference of a circle is approximately twenty-two sevenths of its diameter, that masturbation will blind us, or even that great fortunes are primarily the result of hard work. We may test a few of these "truths" on our own, but we simply accept the great majority of them. These are things that "everybody knows."

Tradition, in this sense of the term, offers some clear advantages to human inquiry. By accepting what everybody knows, we are spared the overwhelming task of starting from scratch in our search for regularities and understanding. Knowledge is cumulative, and an inherited body of information and understanding is the jumping-off point for the development of more knowledge. We often speak of "standing on the shoulders of giants," that is, of previous generations.

At the same time, tradition may hinder human inquiry. If we seek a fresh understanding of something everybody already understands and has always understood, we may be marked as fools for our efforts. More to the point, however, it rarely occurs to most of us to seek a different understanding of something we all "know" to be true.

## Authority

Despite the power of tradition, new knowledge appears every day. Quite aside from our own personal inquiries, we benefit throughout our lives from new discoveries and understandings produced by others. Often, acceptance of these new acquisitions will depend on the status of the discoverer. You're more likely to believe the medical researcher who declares that the common cold can be transmitted through kissing, for example, than to believe your uncle Pete.

Like tradition, authority can both assist and hinder human inquiry. We do well to trust in the judgment of the person who has special training, expertise, and credentials in a given matter, especially in the face of controversy. At the same time, inquiry can be greatly hindered by the legitimate authorities that err within their own province. Biologists, after all, make mistakes in the field of biology. Moreover, biological knowledge changes over time.

Inquiry is also hindered when we depend on the authority of experts speaking outside their realm of expertise. For example, consider the political or religious leader with no medical or biochemical expertise who declares that marijuana can fry your brain. The advertising industry plays heavily on this misuse of authority by, for example, having popular athletes discuss the nutritional value of breakfast cereals or having movie actors evaluate the performance of automobiles.

Both tradition and authority, then, are double-edged swords in the search for knowledge about the world. Simply put, they provide us with a starting point for our own inquiry, but they can lead us to start at the wrong point and push us off in the wrong direction.

## Errors in Inquiry and Some Solutions

Quite aside from the potential dangers of tradition and authority, we often stumble and fall when we set out to learn for ourselves. Let's look at some of the common errors we make in our casual inquiries and look at the ways science guards against those errors.

### Inaccurate Observations

Frequently, we make mistakes in our observations. For example, what was your methodology instructor wearing on the first day of class? If you have to guess, it's because most of our daily observations are casual and semiconscious. That's why we often disagree about what really happened.

In contrast to casual human inquiry, scientific observation is a conscious activity. Simply making observation more deliberate helps reduce error. In trying to recall what your instructor was wearing on the first day of class, you'd probably make a mistake. However, if you had gone to the first class with a conscious plan to observe and record what your instructor was wearing, you'd be far more likely to be accurate.

In many cases, both simple and complex measurement devices help guard against inaccurate observations. Moreover, they add a degree of precision well beyond the capacity of the unassisted human senses. Suppose, for example, that you had taken colour photographs of your instructor that day.

## Overgeneralization

When we look for patterns among the specific things we observe around us, we often assume that a few similar events are evidence of a general pattern. That is, we overgeneralize on the basis of limited observations. (Think back to our now broke racetrack buff.)

Probably the tendency to overgeneralize is greatest when the pressure to arrive at a general understanding is high. Yet it also occurs without such pressure. Whenever overgeneralization does occur, it can misdirect or impede inquiry.

Imagine you are a reporter covering an animal-rights demonstration. You have orders to turn in your story in just two hours, and you need to know why people are demonstrating. Rushing to the scene, you start interviewing them, asking for their reasons. If the first three demonstrators you interview give you essentially the same reason, you may simply assume that the other 3,000 are also there for that reason. Unfortunately, when your story appears, your editor gets scores of letters from protesters who were there for an entirely different reason.

Scientists guard against overgeneralization by committing themselves in advance to a sufficiently large and representative sample of observations. The **replication** of inquiry provides another safeguard. Basically, replication means repeating a study and checking to see whether the same results are produced each time. Then, as a further test, the study may be repeated again under slightly varied conditions.

## Selective Observation

One danger of overgeneralization is that it may lead to selective observation. Once we have concluded that a particular pattern exists and have developed a general understanding of why it exists, we tend to focus on future events and situations that fit the pattern and ignore those that don't. Racial and ethnic prejudices depend heavily on selective observation for their persistence.

According to my (Benaquisto) recollection, every time we went on a picnic when I was a child it rained. At least that's the way I remembered it. I have since, however, been shown that this is not true—pictures taken of us on some of our picnics show that the weather on a number of those days did not correspond to my recollection. Historical almanacs record good weather on those days as well. This indicates how selective observation can work.

Sometimes, a research design will specify in advance the number and kind of observations to be made, as a basis for reaching a conclusion. If we wanted to learn whether women were more likely than men to support freedom to choose an abortion, we'd commit ourselves to making a specified number of observations on that question in a research project. We might select 1,000 carefully chosen people to be interviewed on the issue. Alternately, when making direct observations of an event, such as attending the animal-rights demonstration, social scientists make a special effort to find "deviant cases"—precisely those who do not fit into the general pattern.

## Illogical Reasoning

There are other ways in which we often deal with observations that contradict our understanding of the way things are in daily life. One example is the often heard idea that "the exception proves the rule." This idea makes no sense at all. An exception can draw attention to a rule or to a supposed rule, but in no system of logic can it prove the rule it contradicts. Yet we often use this pithy saying to brush away contradictions with a simple stroke of illogic.

What statisticians have called the *gambler's fallacy* is an illustration of illogic in day-to-day reasoning. Often we assume that a consistent run of either good or bad luck foreshadows its opposite. An evening of bad luck at poker may kindle the belief that a winning hand is just around the corner. Many a poker player has stayed in a game much too long because of that mistaken belief. Conversely, an extended period of good weather may lead you to worry that it is certain to rain on the weekend picnic.

---

**replication** Repetition of a research study in order to either confirm the findings of a previous study or bring them into question.

Although all of us sometimes fall into embarrassingly illogical reasoning, scientists try to avoid this pitfall by using systems of logic consciously and explicitly. Chapter 2 will examine the logic of science in more depth. For now, just note that logical reasoning is a conscious activity for scientists and that other scientists are always around to keep them honest.

Science, then, attempts to protect its inquiries from the common pitfalls in ordinary inquiry. Accurately observing and understanding reality is not an obvious or trivial matter, as we'll see throughout this book.

## What's Really Real?

Philosophers sometimes use the term "naïve realism" to describe the way most of us operate in our daily lives. When you sit at a table to write, you probably don't spend a lot of time thinking about whether the table is really made up of atoms, which in turn are mostly empty space. When you step into the street and see a city bus hurtling toward you, it's not the best time to reflect on methods for testing whether the bus really exists. We all live with a view that what's real is pretty obvious—and that view usually gets us through the day.

We don't want this book to interfere with your ability to deal with everyday life. We hope, however, that the preceding discussions have demonstrated that the nature of "reality" is perhaps more complex than we tend to assume in our everyday functioning. Here are three views on reality that will provide a simplistic and schematic philosophical backdrop for the discussions of science to follow. They are sometimes called *premodern, modern,* and *postmodern* views of reality (Anderson 1990).

### The Premodern View

This view of reality has guided most of human history. Our early ancestors all assumed that they saw things as they really were. In fact, this assumption was so fundamental that they didn't even see it as an assumption. No cavemom said to her cavekid, "Our tribe makes an assumption that evil spirits reside in the Old Twisted Tree." Instead, she said, *"Stay out of that tree or you'll turn into a toad!"*

As humans evolved and became aware of their diversity, they came to recognize that others did not always share their views of things. Thus, they may have discovered that another tribe didn't buy the wicked tree thing; in fact, the second tribe felt the spirits in the tree were holy and beneficial. The discovery of this diversity led members of the first tribe to conclude, "Some tribes I could name are pretty stupid." For them, the tree was still wicked, and they expected some misguided people to be moving to Toad City.

### The Modern View

What philosophers call the *modern* view accepts such diversity as legitimate, a philosophical "different strokes for different folks." As a modern thinker, you would say, "I regard the spirits in the tree as evil, but I know others regard them as good. Neither of us is right or wrong. There are simply spirits in the tree. They are neither good nor evil, but different people have different ideas about them."

It's pretty easy for many of us to adopt the modern view. Some might regard a dandelion as a beautiful flower while others see only an annoying weed. In the premodern view, a dandelion has to be either one or the other. If you think it is a weed, it is really a weed, though you may admit that some people have a warped sense of beauty. In the modern view, a dandelion is simply a dandelion. It is a plant with yellow petals and green leaves. The concepts "beautiful flower" and "annoying weed" are subjective points of view imposed on the plant by different people. Neither is a quality of the plant itself, just as "good" and "evil" were concepts imposed on the spirits in the tree.

### The Postmodern View

Another view of reality that philosophers speak of is called postmodern. In this view, the spirits don't exist. Neither does the dandelion. All that's "real" are the images we get through our points of view. Put differently, there's nothing *out there*; it's all *in here.* As Gertrude Stein said of Oakland, "There's no there, there."

No matter how bizarre the postmodern view may seem to you on first reflection, it has a

**Figure 1-1**
A Book

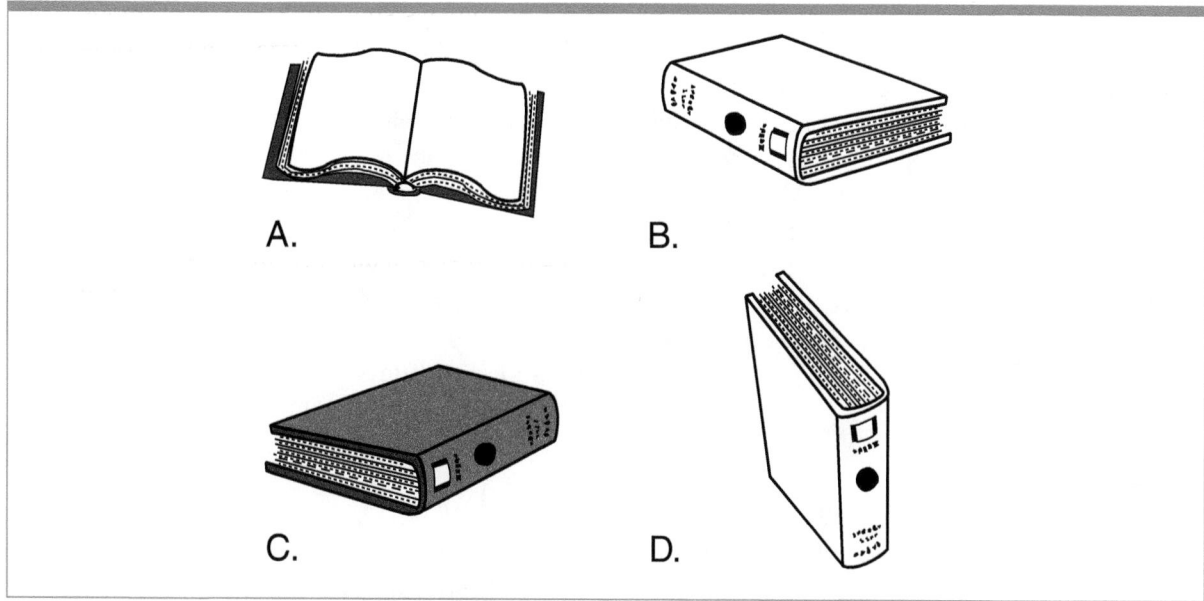

A.

B.

C.

D.

certain ironic inevitability. Take a moment to notice the book you're reading; notice specifically what it looks like. Since you're reading these words, it probably looks like Figure 1-1A.

But does Figure 1-1A represent the way your book "really" looks? Or does it merely represent what the book looks like from your current point of view? Surely Figures 1-1B, C, and D are equally valid representations. But these views of the book are very different from one another. Which is the "reality"?

As this example illustrates, there is no answer to the question "What does the book really look like?" All we can offer is the different ways it looks from different points of view. Thus, according to the postmodern view, there is no "book," only various images of it from different points of view. And all the different images are equally "true."

Now let's apply this logic to a social situation. Imagine a husband and wife arguing. When she looks over at her quarrelling husband, Figure 1-2 is what the wife sees. Take a minute to imagine what you would feel and think if you were the woman in this drawing. How would you explain later to your best friend what had happened? What solutions to the conflict would seem appropriate if you were this woman?

Of course, what the woman's husband sees is another matter altogether, as shown in Figure 1-3. Take a minute to imagine experiencing the situation from his point of view. What thoughts and feelings would you have? How would you tell your best friend what had happened? What solutions would seem appropriate for resolving the conflict?

Now, consider a third point of view. Suppose you're an outside observer, watching this interaction between a wife and husband. What would it look like to you now? Unfortunately, we can't easily portray the third point of view without knowing something about the personal feelings, beliefs, past experiences, and so forth that you would bring to your task as "outside" observer. (Though we call you an *outside* observer, you are, of course, observing from *inside* your own mental system.)

To take an extreme example, if you were a confirmed male chauvinist, you'd probably see the fight pretty much the same way the husband saw it. On the other hand, if you were committed to the view that men are generally unreasonable bums, you'd see things the way the wife saw them.

Imagine instead that you see two unreasonable people quarrelling irrationally with each other. Would you see them both as irresponsible jerks, equally responsible for the conflict? Or would you see two

**Figure 1-2**
Wife's Point of View

**Figure 1-3**
Husband's Point of View

people facing a difficult human situation, each doing the best he or she can to resolve it? Imagine feeling compassion for them and noticing how each of them attempts to end the hostility, even though the gravity of the problem keeps them fighting.

Notice how different these several views are. Which is a "true" picture of what is happening between the wife and the husband? You win the prize if you notice that the personal viewpoint you bring to the observational task will again colour your perception of what is happening.

The postmodern view represents a critical dilemma for scientists. While their task is to observe and understand what is "really" happening, they are all human and, as such, bring along personal orientations that will colour what they observe and how they explain it. There is ultimately no way people can totally step outside their humanness to see and understand the world as it "really" is—that is, independently of all human viewpoints.

Whereas the modern view acknowledges the inevitability of human subjectivity, the postmodern view suggests that there is no "objective" reality to be observed in the first place. There are only our several subjective views.

You may want to ponder these three views of reality on your own for a while. We'll return to them in Chapter 2 when we focus on more specific scientific paradigms. Ultimately, two points will emerge. First, established scientific procedures sometimes allow us to deal effectively with this dilemma—that is, we can study people without being able to view "reality" directly. Second, different philosophical stances suggest a powerful range of possibilities for structuring our research.

Let's turn now from general philosophical ideas to the foundations of the social scientific approaches to understanding. A consideration of these underpinnings of social research will prepare the way for our exploration of specific research techniques.

# The Foundations of Social Science

Science is sometimes characterized as logico-empirical. This ungainly term carries an important message. As we noted earlier, the two pillars of science are logic and observation. That is, a scientific understanding of the world must (1) make sense and (2) correspond to what we observe. Both elements are essential to science and relate to three major aspects of the social scientific enterprise: *theory, data collection,* and *data analysis.*

To oversimplify just a bit, scientific **theory** deals with the logical aspect of science, whereas data collection deals with the observational aspect. Data analysis looks for patterns in observations and, where appropriate, compares what is logically expected with what is actually observed. Although this book is primarily about data collection and data analysis—that is, how to conduct social research—the rest of Part 1 is devoted to the theoretical context of research. Parts 2 and 3 then focus on data collection, and Part 4 offers an introduction to the analysis of data.

Underlying the concepts presented in the rest of the book are some fundamental ideas that distinguish social science—theory, data collection, and analysis—from other ways of looking at social phenomena. Let's consider these ideas.

## Theory, Not Philosophy or Belief

Today social theory has to do with what is, not with what should be. For many centuries, however, social theory didn't distinguish between these two orientations. Social philosophers liberally mixed their observations of what happened around them, their speculations about why, and their ideas about how things ought to be. Although modern social scientists may do the same from time to time, as scientists they focus on how things actually are and why.

This means that scientific theory—and, more broadly, science itself—cannot settle debates about values. Science cannot determine whether capitalism is better or worse than socialism. What it can do is determine how these systems perform in terms of some set of agreed-upon criteria. For

---

**theory**  A systematic explanation for the observations that relate to a particular aspect of life: juvenile delinquency, for example, or perhaps social stratification or political revolution.

example, we could determine scientifically whether capitalism or socialism most supports human dignity and freedom only if we first agreed on some measurable definitions of dignity and freedom. Our conclusions would then be limited to the meanings specified in our definitions. They would have no general meaning beyond that.

By the same token, if we could agree that suicide rates, say, or giving to charity were good measures of the quality of a religion, then we could determine scientifically whether Buddhism or Christianity is the more effective religion. Again, our conclusion would be inextricably tied to our chosen criterion. As a practical matter, people seldom agree on precise criteria for determining issues of value, so science is seldom useful in settling such debates. In fact, questions like these are so much a matter of opinion and belief that scientific inquiry is often viewed as a threat to what is "already known."

We'll consider this issue in more detail in Chapter 12, when we look at evaluation research. As you'll see, researchers have become increasingly involved in studying programs that reflect ideological points of view, such as needle exchange or affirmative action. One of the biggest problems they face is getting people to agree on criteria of success and failure. Yet such criteria are essential if social research is to tell us anything useful about matters of value. By analogy, a stopwatch can't tell us if one sprinter is better than another unless we first agree that speed is the critical criterion.

Social science, then, can help us know only what is and why. We can use it to determine what ought to be only when people agree on the criteria for deciding what outcomes are better than others—an agreement that seldom occurs.

As we indicated earlier, even knowing "what is and why" is no simple task. Let's turn now to some of the fundamental ideas that underlie social science's efforts to describe and understand social reality.

## Social Regularities

In large part, social research aims to find patterns of regularity in social life. Although that aim is shared by all science, it is sometimes a barrier for people when they first approach social science.

Certainly at first glance the subject matter of the physical sciences seems to be more governed by regularities than does that of the social sciences. A heavy object falls to earth every time we drop it, but a person may vote for a particular candidate in one election and against that same candidate in the next. Similarly, ice always melts when heated enough, but habitually honest people sometimes steal. Despite such examples, however, social affairs do exhibit a high degree of regularity that can be revealed by research and explained by theory.

To begin, a vast number of formal norms in society create a considerable degree of regularity. For example, nearly all Canadians obey traffic laws and drive on the right side of the road rather than the left. In the Canadian military, until the 1980s only men could participate in combat. (It was not until 1989 that the Canadian Forces were directed to remove any employment restrictions that remained based on sex, with the exception of submarine duty, and in 2001 this exception was removed.) Such formal prescriptions regulate, or regularize, social behaviour.

Aside from formal prescriptions, we can observe other social norms that create more regularities. University professors tend to earn more money than do unskilled labourers. Men tend to earn more than women, and so on.

### What about Exceptions?

The objection that there are always exceptions to any social regularity does not mean that the regularity itself is unreal or unimportant. A particular woman may earn more money than most men, but that will be a small consolation to the majority of women, who earn less. The pattern still exists. Social regularities, in other words, are probabilistic patterns, and they are no less real simply because some cases don't fit the general pattern.

This point applies in physical science as well as social science. In genetics, for example, the mating of a blue-eyed person with a brown-eyed person will *probably* result in a brown-eyed offspring. The birth of a blue-eyed child does not destroy the observed regularity, because the geneticist states only that the brown-eyed offspring is more likely and, further, that brown-eyed offspring will be born in a certain percentage of the cases. The social scientist makes a similar, probabilistic prediction—that women overall are likely to earn less than men. Once a pattern like this is observed, the social scientist has grounds for asking why it exists.

## Aggregates, Not Individuals

Although social scientists often study motivations that affect individuals, the individual as such is seldom the subject of social science. Instead, social scientists create theories about the aggregate behaviour of many individuals. Similarly, the objects of their research are typically aggregates, or collections, rather than individuals.

Sometimes the collective regularities are amazing. Consider the birthrate, for example. People have babies for any number of personal reasons. Some do it because their own parents want grandchildren. Some feel it's a way of completing their womanhood or manhood. Others want to hold their marriages together, enjoy the experience of raising a child, or perpetuate their family name. Still others have babies by accident.

If you are a parent, you could probably tell a much more detailed, idiosyncratic story. Why did you have the baby when you did, rather than a year earlier or later? Maybe you lost your job and had to delay a year before you could afford to have the baby. Maybe you felt that being a family person would demonstrate maturity.

Everyone who had a baby last year had her or his own reasons for doing so. Yet, despite this vast diversity, and despite the idiosyncrasy of each individual's reasons, the overall birthrate in a society (the number of live births per 1,000 population) is remarkably consistent from year to year. Table 1-1 presents recent birthrates for Canada.

**Table 1-1**

**Birthrates, Canada (per 1,000 population)**

| | |
|---|---|
| 1997–1998 | 11.5 |
| 1998–1999 | 11.2 |
| 1999–2000 | 10.9 |
| 2000–2001 | 10.5 |
| 2001–2002 | 10.5 |
| 2002–2003 | 10.5 |
| 2003–2004 | 10.6 |
| 2004–2005 | 10.6 |
| 2005–2006 | 10.7 |
| 2006–2007 | 11.0 |
| 2007–2008 | 11.2 |
| 2008–2009 | 11.3 |
| 2009–2010 | 11.2* |

*preliminary
From July 1 of one year to June 30 of the next year.
*Source:* Adapted from Statistics Canada, 2004–2010 from http://www.statcan.gc.ca/pub/11-402-x/2011000/chap/pop/tbl/tbl08-eng.htm, data accessed April 22, 2012; 1997 -2004 from http://www40.statcan.ca/l01/cst01/demo04b.htm, data accessed on June 2007 and December 2000.

If the Canadian birthrate were 16.2, 36.5, 8.8, 24.2, and 15.9 in five successive years, demographers who study such issues would begin dropping like flies. As you can see, however, social life is far more orderly than that. Moreover, this regularity occurs without society-wide regulation. No one plans how many babies will be born or determines who will have them. You don't need a permit to have a baby; in fact, many babies are conceived unexpectedly, and some are borne unwillingly.

*Social* scientific theories, then, typically deal with aggregated, not individual, behaviour. Their purpose is to explain why aggregate patterns of behaviour are so regular even when the individuals participating in them may change over time. It could be said that social scientists don't even seek to explain *people.* They try to understand the *systems* in which people operate, the systems that explain why people do what they do. The elements in such a system are not people but *variables.*

## A Variable Language

Our most natural attempts at understanding usually take place at the level of the concrete and idiosyncratic. That's just the way we think.

Imagine that someone says to you, "Women ought to get back into the kitchen where they belong." You are likely to hear that comment in the context of what you know about the speaker. If it's your old uncle Harry who, you recall, is also strongly opposed to daylight saving time, postal codes, and personal computers, you are likely to think his latest pronouncement simply fits into his rather dated point of view about things in general.

If, on the other hand, a male politician who was trailing a female challenger in an election race made the statement, you would probably explain his comment in a completely different way.

In both examples, you're trying to understand the behaviour of a particular individual, but *social research seeks insights into classes or types of individuals*. Social researchers would want to find out about the kind of people who share that view of women's "proper" role. Do those people have other characteristics in common that may help explain their views?

Even when researchers focus their attention on a single case—such as a community or a juvenile gang—their aim is to gain insights that would help people understand other communities and other juvenile gangs. Similarly, the attempt to fully understand one individual carries the broader purpose of understanding people or types of people in general.

When this venture into understanding and explanation ends, social researchers will be able to make sense out of more than one person. In understanding what makes a group of people hostile to women who are active outside the home, they gain insight into all the individuals who share that characteristic. This is possible because, in an important sense, they have not been studying antifeminists as much as they have been studying antifeminism. It might turn out that Uncle Harry and the politician have more in common than first appeared.

Antifeminism is spoken of as a *variable* because it varies. Some people display the

attitude more than others. Social researchers are interested in understanding the system of variables that causes a particular attitude to be strong in one instance and weak in another.

The idea of a system composed of variables may seem rather strange, so let's look at an analogy. The subject of a physician's attention is the patient. If the patient is ill, the physician's purpose is to help the patient get well. By contrast, a medical researcher's subject matter is different: the variables that cause a disease, for example. The medical researcher may study the physician's patient, but for the researcher that patient is relevant only as a carrier of the disease.

That is not to say that medical researchers don't care about real people. They certainly do. Their ultimate purpose in studying diseases is to protect people from them. But in their research, they are less interested in individual patients than they are in the patterns governing the appearance of disease—in essence, the patients are relevant only for what they reveal about the disease under study. In fact, when they can study a disease meaningfully without involving actual patients, they do so.

Social research, then, involves the study of variables and their relationships. Social theories are written in a language of variables, and people get involved only as the "carriers" of those variables.

Variables, in turn, have what social researchers call attributes or values. **Attributes** are characteristics or qualities that describe an object—in this case, a person. Examples are female, Asian, alienated, conservative, dishonest, intelligent, and farmer. Anything you might say to describe yourself or someone else involves an attribute.

**Variables**, on the other hand, are logical groupings of attributes. Thus, for example, male and female are attributes, and *sex* or *gender* are the variables composed of these two attributes. The variable *occupation* is composed of attributes such as farmer, professor, and truck driver. *Social class* is a variable composed of a set of attributes such as upper class, middle class, and lower class. Sometimes it helps to think of attributes as the "categories" that make up a variable. (See Figure 1-4 for a schematic review of what social scientists mean by variables and attributes.)

---

**attributes** Characteristics of people or things.

**variables** Logical groupings of *attributes*. The variable *gender* is made up of the attributes *male* and *female*.

---

**Figure 1-4**
Variables and Attributes

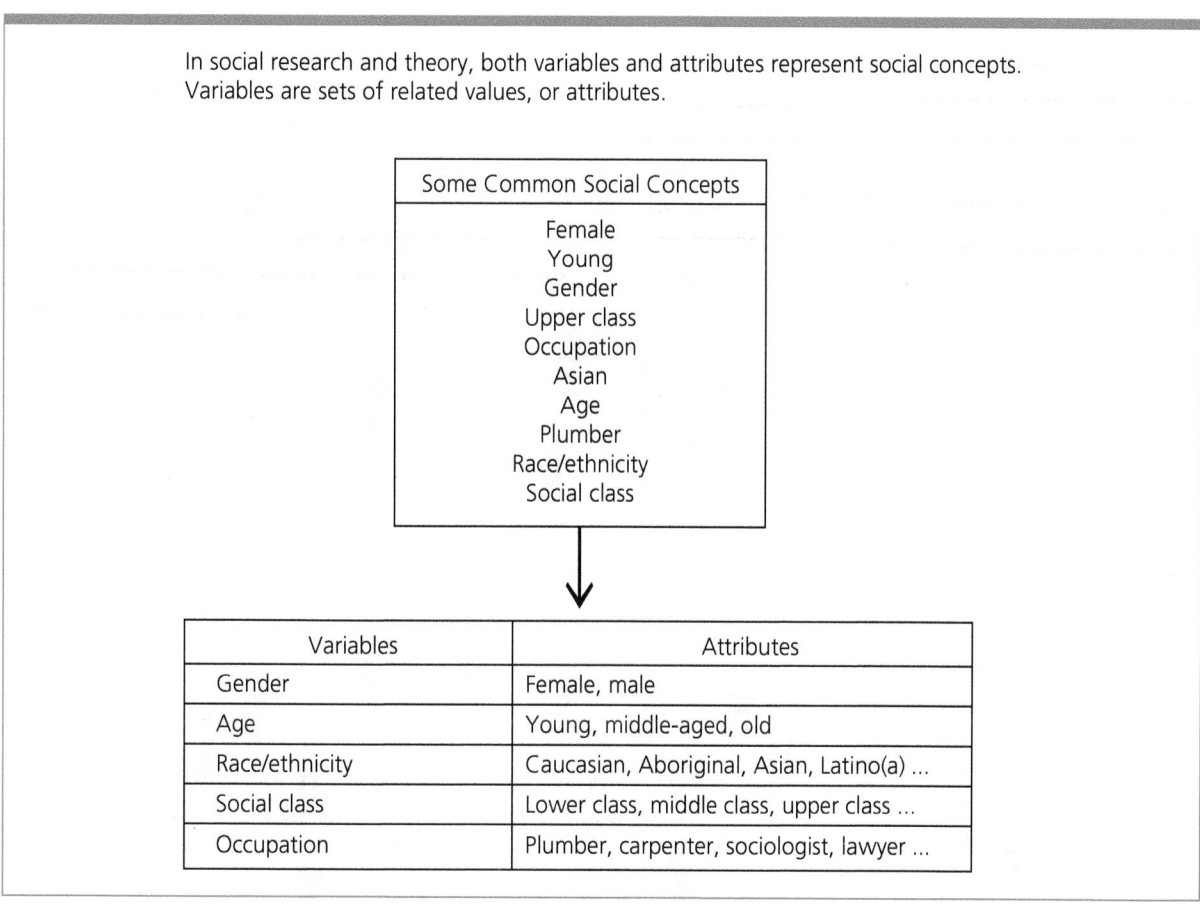

In social research and theory, both variables and attributes represent social concepts. Variables are sets of related values, or attributes.

Some Common Social Concepts

Female
Young
Gender
Upper class
Occupation
Asian
Age
Plumber
Race/ethnicity
Social class

| Variables | Attributes |
|---|---|
| Gender | Female, male |
| Age | Young, middle-aged, old |
| Race/ethnicity | Caucasian, Aboriginal, Asian, Latino(a) ... |
| Social class | Lower class, middle class, upper class ... |
| Occupation | Plumber, carpenter, sociologist, lawyer ... |

The relationship between attributes and variables lies at the heart of both description and explanation in science. For example, we might describe a university class in terms of the variable *gender* by reporting the observed frequencies of the attributes male and female: "The class is 60 percent men and 40 percent women." An unemployment rate can be thought of as a description of the variable *employment status of a labour force* in terms of the attributes employed and unemployed. Even the report of *family income for a city* is a summary of attributes composing that variable: $10,980; $35,000; $85,470; and so forth.

The relationship between attributes and variables is more complicated in the case of explanation and gets to the heart of the variable language of scientific theory. Here's a simple example involving two variables, *education* and *prejudice*. For the sake of simplicity, let's assume that the variable *education* has only two attributes: educated and uneducated. Similarly, let's give the variable *prejudice* two attributes: prejudiced and unprejudiced.

Now let's suppose that we have 20 people—10 are educated and 10 are uneducated. Let's also suppose that 90 percent of the uneducated are prejudiced, and the other 10 percent are unprejudiced, and that 30 percent of the educated people are prejudiced, and the other 70 percent are unprejudiced. This is illustrated graphically in Figure 1-5A.

Figure 1-5A illustrates a relationship or association between the variables *education* and *prejudice*. This relationship can be seen in the pairings of attributes on the two variables. There are two predominant pairings: (1) those who are educated and unprejudiced and (2) those who are uneducated and prejudiced.

**Figure 1-5**
**Illustration of Relationship between Two Variables (Two Possibilities)**

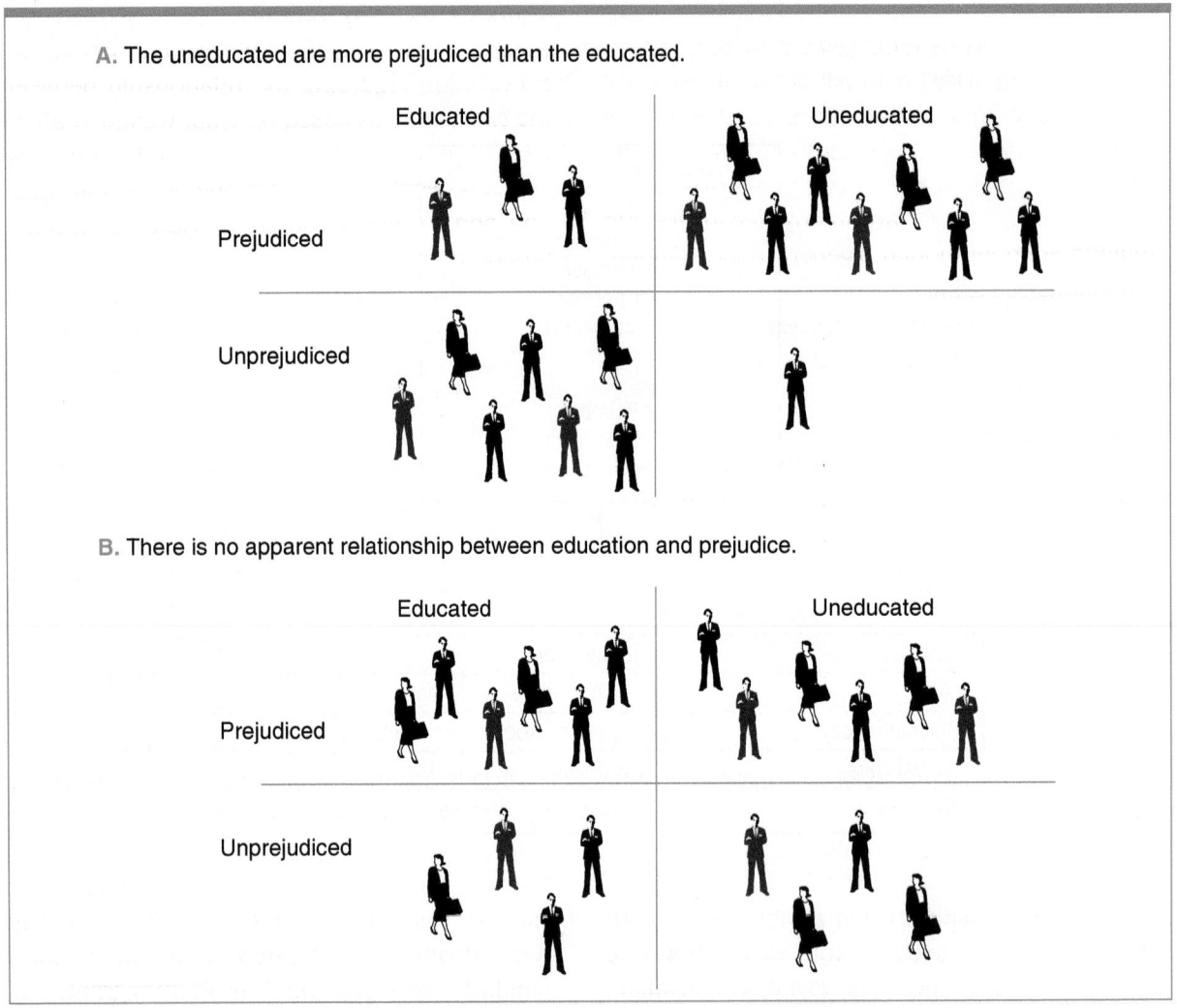

A. The uneducated are more prejudiced than the educated.

| | Educated | Uneducated |
|---|---|---|
| Prejudiced | | |
| Unprejudiced | | |

B. There is no apparent relationship between education and prejudice.

| | Educated | Uneducated |
|---|---|---|
| Prejudiced | | |
| Unprejudiced | | |

Here are two other useful ways of viewing that relationship. First, let's suppose that we play a game in which we bet on your ability to guess whether a person is prejudiced or unprejudiced. We'll pick the people one at a time (not telling you which ones we've picked), and you have to guess whether each person is prejudiced. We'll do it for all 20 people in Figure 1-5A. Your best strategy in this case would be to guess prejudiced each time, since 12 out of the 20 are categorized that way. Thus, you'll get 12 right and 8 wrong, for a net success of 4.

Now let's suppose that when we pick a person from the figure, we have to tell you whether the person is educated or uneducated. Your best strategy now would be to guess prejudiced for each uneducated person and unprejudiced for each educated person. If you followed that strategy, you'd get 16 right and 4 wrong. Your improvement in guessing prejudice by knowing education is an illustration of what it means to say that variables are related.

Second, by contrast, let's consider how the 20 people would be distributed if education and prejudice were unrelated to each other. This is illustrated in Figure 1-5B. Recall that half the people are educated, and half are uneducated. Also notice that 12 of the 20 (60 percent) are prejudiced. If 6 of the 10 people in each group were prejudiced, we would conclude that the two

*causation*

variables were unrelated to each other. Knowing a person's education would not be of any value to you in guessing whether that person was prejudiced. Those who are educated are equally as prejudiced as those who are uneducated.

We'll be looking at the nature of relationships between variables in some depth in Part 4. In particular, we'll explore some of the ways relationships can be discovered and interpreted in research analysis. For now, though, a general understanding of relationships is important so you can appreciate the logic of social scientific theories.

Theories describe the relationships we might logically expect among variables. Often, the expectation involves the idea of causation. That is, a person's attributes on one variable are expected to cause, predispose, or encourage a particular attribute on another variable. In the example just illustrated, we might theorize that a person's being educated or uneducated causes a lesser or greater likelihood of that person seeming prejudiced.

As we'll discuss in more detail later in the book, *education* and *prejudice* in this example would be regarded as **independent** and **dependent variables**, respectively. These two concepts are implicit in causal, or deterministic, models. In this example, we assume that the likelihood of being prejudiced is determined or caused by something. In other words, *prejudice* depends on something else, and so it is called the dependent variable. What the dependent variable depends on is an independent variable, in this case *education*. For the purposes of this study, *education* is an "independent" variable because it is independent of *prejudice* (that is, people's level of education is not caused by whether or not they are prejudiced).

Of course, variations in levels of education can, in turn, be found to depend on something else. People whose parents have a lot of education, for example, are more likely to get a lot of education than are people whose parents have little education. In this relationship, the subject's education is the dependent variable, and the parents' education is the independent variable. We can say the independent variable is the cause, the dependent variable the effect.

Returning to our example in Figure 1-5, we looked at the distribution of the 20 people in terms of the two variables. In constructing a social scientific theory, we would derive an expectation regarding the relationship between the two variables based on what we know about each. We know, for example, that education exposes people to a wide range of cultural variation and to diverse points of view—in short, it broadens their perspectives. Prejudice, on the other hand, represents a narrower perspective. Logically, then, we might expect education and prejudice to be somewhat incompatible. We might, therefore, arrive at an expectation that increasing education would reduce the occurrence of prejudice, an expectation that would be supported by the observations.

Since Figure 1-5 illustrates two possibilities—that education reduces the likelihood of prejudice or that it has no effect—you might be interested in seeing some real data. As one measure of prejudice, in a survey of Edmonton, Alberta students in 1992 (seven years after graduating from high school), each was asked to express how he or she felt about the opinion that "too many immigrants have been getting jobs in Canada." The students used a scale that ranged from (1) strongly disagree to (5) strongly agree (with 3 indicating a neutral position). The researchers combined question responses of 1 and 2 to create the category of positive attitudes toward immigrants and responses of 4 and 5 to create a category of negative attitudes toward immigrants. Those whose response was 3 were categorized as holding

**independent variable** A variable with values that are not problematic in an analysis but are taken as simply given. An independent variable is presumed to cause or determine a dependent variable.

**dependent variable** A variable assumed to depend on or be caused by another (called the independent variable). If you find that income is partly a function of *amount of formal education, income* is being treated as a dependent variable.

**Table 1-2**
Education and Attitudes toward Immigrants

| Educational Level of Respondents | Attitudes toward Immigrants | | | |
|---|---|---|---|---|
| | Positive | Neutral | Negative | |
| No Postsecondary Education | 19.7% | 29.5% | 50.8% | 100% (121) |
| Postsecondary Education | 44.9 | 31.7 | 23.4 | 100% (276) |

Adapted from Sorensen and Krahn, 1996:10.

neutral attitudes. About 38 percent of the sample held positive attitudes, 31 percent negative attitudes, and 31 percent neutral attitudes.

These data come from an analysis conducted by Sorensen and Krahn (1996) to test whether higher education produces more liberal attitudes toward immigrants. As we'll see later in the book, their analysis was more complex than the data we present here display. For now, however, let's look at a partial result from their report.

Table 1-2 presents an analysis of those data, grouping respondents according to their levels of educational attainment. The easiest way to read this table is to focus on the last column of percentages: those holding negative attitudes. Negative attitudes toward immigrants were held by over 50 percent of the respondents with no postsecondary education, while only about 23 percent of those with postsecondary education expressed negative attitudes toward immigrants. This finding supports the view that education reduces prejudice, as prejudice was measured here.

Notice that the theory has to do with the two variables *education* and *prejudice,* not with people as such. People are the carriers of those two variables, so the relationship between the variables can be seen only when we observe people. Ultimately, however, the theory uses a language of variables. It describes the associations that we might logically expect to exist between particular attributes of different variables.

There are often competing theories and hypotheses about what accounts most strongly for the variation in a given factor (variable), such as attitudes toward immigrants. A more recent study by Mulder and Krahn (2005) tests alternative hypotheses derived from theories that have been proposed to account for variation in attitudes toward immigrants. Their analysis of attitudes held by a more general sample of urban Albertans confirms that the more educated are more supportive and accepting of immigrants and cultural diversity than are those who are less educated. If you would like to explore for yourself the relationship between education and various indicators of prejudice in the United States, you may use the Web to examine data from the U.S. General Social Survey (GSS). See Chapter 8 (p. 263) for details on how to access and use this website.

## Some Dialectics of Social Research

There is no one way to do social research. (If there were, this would be a much shorter book.) In fact, much of the power and potential of social research lies in the many valid approaches it comprises.

Four broad and interrelated distinctions, however, underlie the variety of research approaches. Although these distinctions can be seen as competing choices, a good social researcher learns each of these orientations. What we mean by the "dialectics" of social research, therefore, is that there is a fruitful tension between the complementary concepts we are about to describe.

### Idiographic and Nomothetic Explanation

All of us go through life explaining things. We do it every day. You explain why you did poorly or well on an exam, why your favourite team is winning or losing, why you may be having trouble getting dates you enjoy. In our everyday explanations, we engage in two distinct forms of causal reasoning, though we do not ordinarily distinguish them.

Sometimes we attempt to explain a single situation exhaustively. Thus, for example, you may have done poorly on an exam because (1) you had forgotten there was an exam that day, (2) it was in your worst subject, (3) a traffic jam made you late for class, (4) your roommate had kept you up the night before the exam with loud music, (5) the police kept you until dawn demanding to know what you had done with your roommate's stereo—and what you had done with your roommate, for that matter, and (6) a wild band of coyotes ate your textbook. Given all these circumstances, it's no wonder that you did poorly.

This type of causal reasoning is called an **idiographic** explanation. *Idio* in this context means unique, separate, peculiar, or distinct, as in the word *idiosyncrasy*. When we have completed an idiographic explanation, we feel that we fully understand the causes of what happened in this particular instance. At the same time, the scope of our explanation is limited to the single case at hand. While parts of the idiographic explanation might apply to other situations, our intention is to explain one case fully.

Now consider a different kind of explanation. (1) Every time you study with a group, you do better on the exam than if you study alone. (2) Your favourite team does better at home than on the road. (3) Fraternity and sorority members get more dates than members of the biology club. Notice that this type of explanation is more general, covering a wider range of experience or observation. It speaks implicitly of the relationship between variables. For example, (a) whether or not you study in a group and (b) how well you do on the exam. This type of explanation—labelled **nomothetic**—seeks to explain a class of situations or events rather than a single one. Moreover, it seeks to explain "economically," using only one or just a few explanatory factors. Finally, it settles for a partial rather than a full explanation.

In each of these examples, you might qualify your causal statements with such words or phrases as "on the whole," "usually," or "all else being equal." Thus, you usually do better on exams when you've studied in a group, but not always. Similarly, your team has won some games on the road and lost some at home. And the attractive head of the biology club may get lots of dates, while the homely members of fraternities and sororities may spend a lot of Saturday nights alone reading. Such exceptions are accepted in the trade-off for a broader range of overall explanation. As we noted earlier, patterns are real and important even when they are not perfect.

Both the idiographic and the nomothetic approaches to understanding can be useful to you in your daily life. The nomothetic patterns you discover might offer a good guide for planning your study habits, for example, while the idiographic explanation might be more convincing to your parole officer.

By the same token, both idiographic and nomothetic reasoning are powerful tools for social research. Consider first idiographic reasoning. The researcher who seeks an exhaustive understanding of the inner workings of a particular juvenile gang, a particular criminal actor, or the particular reasons why a given region desires to secede from or join a country, engages in idiographic research: she or he tries to understand that particular group, individual, or event as fully as possible.

**idiographic** An approach to explanation in which we seek to exhaust the idiosyncratic causes of a particular condition or event. Imagine trying to list all the reasons why you chose to attend your particular university. Given all those reasons, it's difficult to imagine your making any other choice.

**nomothetic** An approach to explanation in which we seek to identify a few causal factors that influence a class of conditions or events. Imagine the two or three key factors that determine which universities students choose, such as proximity, reputation, and so forth.

David Mackenzie (1986), for example, undertook an in-depth study of the reasons behind Newfoundland's entrance into Confederation in 1949—both why Canada accepted Newfoundland and the decision of Newfoundland to join. He detailed all the intricate aspects of this specific union—for instance, the evolution of Canadian policy toward Newfoundland, the key political actors involved, and the major role that World War II played. His goal was to fully understand the history of the decision in this particular case. His was an idiographic approach to understanding.

One might also undertake a study of the specific and detailed reasons behind the actions of a single criminal actor—for example, the serial killer Paul Bernardo, who was caught and convicted in Ontario in the 1990s. An attempt to fully understand his particular behaviour would be an idiographic approach.

Often, however, researchers aim at a more generalized understanding across a class of events, even though the level of understanding is inevitably less complete with respect to any one case. In other words, they seek a nomothetic explanation. For example, researchers who seek to uncover the chief factors leading to juvenile delinquency are pursuing a nomothetic inquiry. They might discover that children from broken homes are more likely to be delinquent than those from intact families. This explanation would extend well beyond any single child, but it would do so at the expense of a complete explanation of any one child's delinquency.

In contrast to Mackenzie's idiographic approach to the study of Newfoundland, Susan Tiano (1994) sought to understand the overall impact of Third World industrialization on the status of women. Does the movement by women into the industrial labour force signify liberation or oppression? Her survey of women factory workers in Mexico illustrates the nomothetic approach to understanding.

Another example of the nomothetic approach is Anderson and Paskeviciute's (2006) study of the potential impact of heterogeneity (ethnic and linguistic diversity) on citizenship behaviour in 44 countries. Among a number of findings, they noted that in less democratic, more linguistically heterogeneous societies, people have an increased likelihood of belonging to voluntary associations and showing interest in politics. However, in societies with established democracies, linguistic heterogeneity decreases individuals' interest in politics.

Excessive attachment to any one approach to a given issue arguably limits our understanding of it. In 1989, Laxer critiqued the current level of understanding of Canadian political economy on this ground. He critiqued what he saw as two dominant approaches to understanding Canadian political economy. Each side, he said, was wedded to extreme opposite positions—"the two ends of the pole of idiographic and nomothetic inquiry" (p. 186):

> The two perspectives share few common assumptions. For many Marxists, Canada is largely a place in which to demonstrate the workings of general Marxist laws. They are the nomothetic "internationalist" theorists. On the other side, the new political economists start from nationalist and historical assumptions and emphasize the uniqueness of Canadian political and economic structures. Issues are explained by external influences and factors which are peculiar to Canada. They are the idiographic historians.
>
> (p. 179)

He ultimately argues that each approach would benefit from dialogue with the other—that a balance between these two approaches would provide a better understanding of Canadian political economy. As he said,

> There are ways to bridge the bifurcation of the uniqueness versus general laws approaches in Canadian political economy. The comparative-historical method is a promising approach. Instead of assuming that either everything in Canada is unique or else that nothing in Canada is unique, we can do comparative work on a whole range of questions to see in what ways events and patterns in Canada are similar to and different from those in other countries.*
>
> (p. 188)

---

*Gordon Laxer, 1989. "The Schizophrenic Character of Canadian Political Economy." *Canadian Review of Sociology and Anthropology,* Vol 26: Pg. 178–192.

Thus, a combination of approaches can also prove very useful in many instances.

As you've just seen, social scientists can access two distinct kinds of explanation. Just as physicists sometimes treat light as a particle and other times as a wave, so social scientists can search for broad patterns of relationships today and probe the narrowly particular tomorrow. Both are good science, both are rewarding, and both can be fun.

## Inductive and Deductive Theory

Like the idiographic and nomothetic forms of explanation, inductive and deductive thinking both play a role in our daily lives. They, too, represent an important variation in social research.

There are two routes to the conclusion that you do better on exams if you study with others. On the one hand, you might find yourself puzzling, halfway through your university career, why you do so well on exams sometimes but poorly at other times. You might list all the exams you've taken, noting how well you did on each. Then you might try to recall any circumstances shared by all the good exams and by all the poor ones. Did you do better on multiple-choice exams or essay exams? Morning exams or afternoon exams? Exams in the natural sciences, the humanities, or the social sciences? Times when you studied alone or ... SHAZAM! It occurs to you that you have almost always done best on exams when you studied with others. This mode of inquiry is known as *induction*.

Inductive reasoning, or **induction**, moves from the particular to the general, from a set of specific observations to the discovery of a pattern that represents some degree of order among all the given events. Notice, incidentally, that your discovery doesn't necessarily tell you *why* the pattern exists—just that it does.

On the other hand, you might arrive at the same conclusion about studying for exams in a very different way. Imagine approaching your first set of exams in university. You wonder about the best ways to study—how much you should review the readings, how much to focus on class notes. You learn that some students prepare by rewriting their notes in an orderly fashion. Then you consider whether to study at a measured pace or pull an all-nighter just before the exam. Among these kinds of musings, you might ask whether you should get together with other students in the class or just study on your own. You could evaluate the pros and cons of both options.

Studying with others might not be as efficient, because a lot of time might be spent on things you already understand. On the other hand, you can understand something even better when you've explained it to someone else. And other students might understand parts of the course you haven't gotten yet. Several minds can reveal perspectives that might have escaped you. Also, your commitment to study with others makes it more likely that you'll study rather than decide to watch the music video channel.

In this fashion, you might add up the pros and cons and conclude, logically, that you'd benefit from studying with others. It seems reasonable to you, the way it seems reasonable that you'll do better if you study rather than not. Sometimes, we say things like this are true "in theory." To complete the process, we test whether they're true in practice. For a complete test, you might study alone for half your exams and study with others for the other exams. This procedure would test your logical reasoning.

This second mode of inquiry, known as deductive reasoning or **deduction**, moves from the

---

**induction** The logical model in which general principles are developed from specific observations. Having noted that Jews and Catholics are more likely to vote Liberal than Protestants are, you might conclude that religious minorities in Canada are more affiliated with the Liberal Party and explain why. This would be an example of induction.

**deduction** The logical model in which specific expectations of hypotheses are developed on the basis of general principles. Starting from the general principle that all deans are meanies, you might anticipate that this one won't let you change courses. This anticipation would be the result of deduction.

general to the specific. It moves from (1) a pattern that might be logically or theoretically expected to (2) observations that test whether the expected pattern actually occurs. Notice that deduction begins with "why" and moves to "whether," while induction moves in the opposite direction.

As you'll see later in this book, these two very different approaches are both valid avenues for science. Moreover, induction and deduction often work together to provide ever more powerful and complete understandings.

Notice, by the way, that the distinction between deductive and inductive reasoning is not necessarily linked to the distinction between nomothetic and idiographic modes of explanation. These four characterizations represent four possibilities, in everyday life as much as in social research.

For example, idiographically and deductively, you might prepare for a particular date by taking into account everything you know about the person you're dating, trying to anticipate logically how you can prepare—what kinds of clothing, behaviour, hairstyle, oral hygiene, and so forth, are likely to produce a successful date. Or, idiographically and inductively, you might try to figure out what it was exactly that caused your date to call 911.

A nomothetic, deductive approach arises when you coach others on your "rules of dating," when you wisely explain why their dates will be impressed to hear them expound on the dangers of satanic messages concealed in rock and roll lyrics. When you later review your life and wonder why you didn't date more musicians, you might engage in nomothetic induction.

We'll return to induction and deduction in Chapter 2. Let's turn now to a third broad distinction that generates rich variations in social research.

## Quantitative and Qualitative Data

The distinction between quantitative and qualitative data in social research is essentially the distinction between numerical and nonnumerical data. When we say someone is attractive, we've made a qualitative assertion. When we say he or she is a 9 on a scale from 1 to 10, we are attempting to quantify that qualitative assessment. Similarly, when an ice skater's performance is evaluated as an 8 on a scale of 10, the judge is attempting to quantify her or his qualitative assessment of the performance.

Every observation is qualitative at the outset, whether it is our experience of someone's attractiveness, our assessment of someone's artistic or athletic ability, the location of a pointer on a measuring scale, or a check mark entered in a questionnaire. None of these things is inherently numerical or quantitative, but sometimes it is useful to convert them to a numerical form.

Quantification often makes our observations more explicit. It also can make it easier to aggregate, compare, and summarize data. Further, it opens up the possibility of statistical analyses, ranging from simple averages to complex formulas and mathematical models.

Quantitative data, then, offer the advantages that numbers have over words as measures of some quality. On the other hand, they also have the disadvantages that numbers have, including a potential loss of richness of meaning. For example, a social researcher might want to know whether university students aged 18 to 22 tend to date people older or younger than themselves. A quantitative answer to this question seems easily attained. The researcher asks a number of university students how old each of their dates has been, calculates an average, and compares it with the age of the subject. Case closed.

Or is it? While "age" here represents the number of years people have been alive, sometimes people use the term differently; perhaps for some, "age" really means "maturity." Though your dates may tend to be younger than you, you may date people who act more maturely and thus represent the same "age." Or someone might see "age" as how young or old your dates look or maybe the degree of variation in their life experiences and worldliness. These latter meanings would be lost in the quantitative calculation of average age. In short, qualitative data can be richer in meaning than quantified data. This is implicit in the cliché "He is older than his years."

The poetic meaning of this expression would be lost in attempts to specify *how much* older.

On the other hand, qualitative data can have the disadvantages of purely verbal descriptions. For example, the richness of meaning we just mentioned is partly a function of ambiguity. If the expression "older than his years" meant something to you when you read it, that meaning arises from your own experiences, from people you have known who might fit the description of being "older than their years" or perhaps the times you have heard others use that expression. Two things are certain: (1) the expression probably doesn't mean exactly the same thing to you as it does to someone else, and (2) you don't know exactly what someone else means by the expression and vice versa.

Earl Babbie has a friend, Ray Zhang, who was responsible for communications at the 1989 freedom demonstrations in Tiananmen Square, Beijing. Following the Army clampdown, Ray fled south, was arrested, and then was released with orders to return to Beijing. Instead, he escaped from China and made his way to Paris. Eventually, he went to the United States, where he resumed the graduate studies he had been forced to abandon in fleeing his homeland. Ray has had to deal with the difficulties of getting enrolled in school without any transcripts from China, studying in a foreign language, and meeting his financial needs, all on his own, half a world away from his family. Ray has spoken often of one day returning to China to build a system of democracy.

You'll probably agree that Ray is someone who seems to be "older than his years" and worldly in his experiences. This qualitative description, while it fleshes out the meaning of the phrase, still does not equip us to say *how much older*; neither can we compare two people in these terms without the risk of disagreeing as to which one is more "worldly."

It might be possible to quantify this concept, however. For example, we might establish a list of life experiences that would contribute to what we mean by worldliness. These might include:

- Getting married
- Getting divorced
- Losing a parent to a fatal illness
- Seeing a murder committed
- Being arrested
- Being exiled
- Being fired from a job
- Becoming homeless

We might quantify people's worldliness as the number of such experiences they've had: the more such experiences, the more worldly we'd say they were. If we thought of some experiences as more powerful than others, we could give those experiences more points. Once we had made our list and point system, scoring people and comparing their worldliness on a numerical scale would be straightforward. We would have no difficulty agreeing on who had more points than whom.

To quantify a nonnumerical concept like worldliness, then, we need to be explicit about what the concept means. By focusing specifically on what we'll include in our measurement of the concept, however, we also exclude any other meanings. Inevitably, then, we face a trade-off: any explicated, quantitative measure will be less rich in meaning than the corresponding qualitative description.

What a dilemma! Which approach should we choose? Which is better? Which is more appropriate to social research?

The good news is that we don't need to choose. In fact, we shouldn't. Both qualitative and quantitative methods are useful and legitimate in social research. Some research situations and topics are most amenable to qualitative examination, others to quantification, and still others that would be best studied by using a combination of both approaches.

Yet you'll find that these two approaches call for different skills and procedures. As a result, you may feel more comfortable with—and become more adept in—one or the other. You'll be a stronger researcher, however, to the extent that you can effectively use both approaches. Certainly, all researchers, whatever their personal inclinations, should recognize the legitimacy of both.

You may have noticed that the qualitative approach seems more aligned with idiographic explanations, while nomothetic explanations are more easily achieved through quantification. Although this is true, these relationships are not absolute. Moreover, both approaches present considerable "grey area." Recognizing the distinction between qualitative and quantitative research doesn't mean that you must identify your research activities with one to the exclusion of the other. A complete understanding of a topic often requires both techniques.

## Pure and Applied Research

From the beginning, social scientists have shown two distinct motivations: understanding and application. On the one hand, they are fascinated by the nature of human social life and are driven to explain it, to make sense out of apparent chaos. *Pure* research in all scientific fields finds justification in "knowledge for knowledge's sake."

At the same time, perhaps inspired by their subject matter, social scientists are committed to having what they learn make a difference—to seeing their knowledge of society put into action. Sometimes they focus on making things better. If one of us studies prejudice, for example, we'd like what we discover to result in a more tolerant society.

Applied social scientists, however, put their research into practice in many immediate and direct ways as well. Experiments and surveys, for example, can be used in marketing products. In-depth interviewing techniques can be especially useful in social work encounters. Chapter 12 of this book deals with evaluation research, by which social scientists determine the effectiveness of social interventions.

As with each of the other dialectics just discussed, some social scientists are more inclined toward pure research, others toward application. Ultimately, both orientations are valid and vital elements in social research as a whole.

# The Ethics of Social Research

Most of this book is devoted to the logic and skills of doing social research, the various techniques preferred by social researchers, and the reasons why researchers value them. There are, however, some vital nonscientific concerns that shape the activities of social researchers. A key concern is the matter of ethics in research.

We'll deal extensively with research ethics in Chapter 3, and other chapters will refer to ethical issues as appropriate. Here, we want to introduce two basic ethical issues to keep in mind as you read the rest of this book.

## No Harm to Subjects

The foremost ethical rule of social research is that it brings *no harm to research subjects*. This rule is one that everyone would agree with in principle; however, it's sometimes difficult to follow it absolutely.

Suppose, for example, some of the people that researchers interview about their religious views realize for the first time that they have doubts about their religion. Or suppose a study of treatment of women in a society leads some women to become unhappy with their jobs or marriages. When does investigating a subject do harm by affecting the people who take part in the study?

As you'll see, abiding by this seemingly simple ethical rule requires vigilance on the part of researchers. In designing your own studies, be sure to ask yourself whether your research could harm the people you intend to study. Since everything we do in life *could possibly* harm someone else, all researchers must weigh the relative risk against the importance and possible benefits of the research activity.

Social researchers have many ways to guard against harming people. For example, they are careful to respect the privacy of subjects. Research often requires learning private details of people's lives, and researchers are committed to maintain the *confidentiality* of what they learn. Often they collect information *anonymously*, so there is no way of identifying individuals with the information they voluntarily provide, thus preventing even the accidental release of information.

You'll see that while deception is necessary in the execution of some kinds of research projects, researchers are committed to avoiding deception except when it's inescapable. (For example, if you introduce a survey or experiment by saying, "We want to learn how prejudiced you are," the subjects will likely modify what they do and say, so as to appear unprejudiced.) When it's deemed necessary to deceive people as to our research purposes, however, we must ask whether the potential value of the research justifies the act of deception.

### Voluntary Participation

Another basic ethical rule of social research is that *participation should be voluntary.* Again, in principle, this appears to be a pretty simple rule to follow. A researcher who forced people to participate in the experiment or survey would be roundly criticized. When someone calls and asks you to participate in a telephone survey, you're free to refuse.

Yet things are not always so clear-cut. When we formally observe a campus demonstration, we do not ask for permission from all the participants. When a researcher pretends to join a religious cult to do research on it, those being observed have not volunteered for the research project. Social researchers often debate whether a particular research design did or did not violate established research ethics.

The issue of voluntary participation can arise even when you ask for and receive written permission from your participants. I (Benaquisto, 2000), for example, conducted a study concerning views on issues of crime, punishment, and sentencing. I sought full and informed consent from each participant. Each was given a sheet of paper that explained the study's purpose and a consent form to sign giving me permission to obtain some personal information about them and indicating their agreement to voluntarily participate in the study. They were also told that they were free to withdraw from the study at any time. The people I studied, however, were male prison inmates in Canadian federal institutions. Given the population I was studying, it was very important to keep in mind

a number of issues that might interfere with obtaining true voluntary participation. For instance, one central concern was the possibility that some of the inmates were illiterate, and many people who are unable to read are reluctant to admit it. With regard to the study, this not only raises ethical concerns but also could have a significant impact on the outcome. First, to what extent can someone who signs a consent form without knowing what it says be participating voluntarily? Second, unable to read the form and embarrassed to admit it, the person may refuse the study rather than sign a form he or she doesn't understand. Therefore, having gained some information about the group under study before beginning the interviews, I was aware of such potential problems and attempted to avoid them by having the forms read to the inmates as a matter of course, rather than giving them the form to read and sign on their own. In addition, the inmates were encouraged to ask questions and an attempt was made to determine that they understood what they were being told.

Another concern regarding voluntary participation that this study illustrates has to do with unsaid expectations. It's often a concern that people in controlled environments, such as prisons or mental asylums, might believe that cooperation and participation in a research study would somehow benefit them personally—or that nonparticipation will produce negative consequences for them. It was therefore very important that every inmate be told that participating in the study would in no way help him personally and that the research was completely independent of the prison administration (this helps to guarantee them confidentiality as well). It's impossible to know with certainty the reasons someone volunteers to participate in a study; however, when possible, we as researchers have a responsibility to do all we can to try to ensure true voluntary participation.

As we continue examining the many aspects of social research, you'll see the great complexity of ethical issues and the seriousness of ethical concerns. This seriousness is evident in the codes of ethics created and published by professional associations whose members engage in social research and by government agencies that fund such research. It is a topic that certainly deserves your attention and one that will be taken up at length in Chapter 3.

These, then, are some of the foundations of social research. We hope this discussion has helped to show how social science is anything but routine or boring. At its best, it is a vibrant, exciting, and important activity. All we need is an open mind and a sense of adventure.

## Main Points

- This book's subject is how we find out about social reality.
- Inquiry is a natural human activity. Much of ordinary human inquiry seeks to explain events and predict future events.
- Much of what we know, we know by agreement rather than by experience. Two important sources of agreed-upon knowledge are tradition and authority. However, these useful sources of knowledge can lead us astray.
- When we understand through direct experience, we make observations and seek patterns of regularities in what we observe.
- Science seeks to protect against mistakes we make in day-to-day inquiry.
- Whereas we often observe inaccurately, researchers seek to avoid such errors by making observation a careful and deliberate activity.
- Sometimes we jump to general conclusions on the basis of only a few observations, so scientists seek to avoid overgeneralization by committing themselves to a sufficient number of observations and by replicating studies.
- In everyday life, we sometimes reason illogically. Researchers seek to avoid illogical reasoning by being as careful and deliberate in their reasoning as in their observations. Moreover, the public nature of science means that others are always there to challenge faulty reasoning.
- Three views of "reality" are the premodern, modern, and postmodern views. In the postmodern view, there is no "objective" reality

independent of our subjective experiences. Different philosophical views suggest a range of possibilities for scientific research.
- Social theory attempts to discuss and explain what is, not what should be. Theory should not be confused with philosophy or belief.
- Social science looks for regularities in social life.
- Social scientists are interested in explaining human aggregates, not individuals.
- Theories are written in the language of variables. A variable is a logical set of attributes. An attribute is a characteristic, such as male or female. Gender, for example, is a variable made up of these attributes.
- In causal explanation, the presumed cause is the independent variable, while the affected variable is the dependent variable.
- Idiographic explanations seek to understand specific cases fully, whereas nomothetic explanations seek a generalized understanding of many cases.
- Inductive theories reason from specific observations to general patterns.
- Deductive theories start from general statements and predict specific observations.
- Quantitative data are numerical; qualitative data are not. Both types of data are useful for different research purposes.
- Both pure and applied research are valid and vital parts of the social scientific enterprise.
- Ethics is a key consideration in the design of social research. Two fundamental ethical guidelines are that participation in social research be voluntary and that no harm should come to research subjects.

## Review Questions and Exercises

1. Review the common errors of human inquiry discussed in this chapter. Find a magazine or newspaper article, or perhaps a letter to the editor, that illustrates one of these errors. Discuss how a scientist would have avoided it.

2. List five social variables and the attributes they comprise.

3. Go to one of the following websites and find examples of both qualitative and quantitative data.
   a. Library and Archives of Canada— Bibliothéque et Archives Canada http://www.collectionscanada.ca
   b. UN High Commissioner for Refugees http://www.unhcr.org
   c. National Library of Australia http://www.nla.gov.au/
   d. Inter-University Consortium for Political and Social Research (ICPSR) http://www.icpsr.umich.edu

## Continuity Project

To demonstrate the interconnections among the various elements of social research, you might want to apply the materials of each successive chapter to a single research project. We'll suggest here the topic of *gender equality/ inequality,* but your instructor may suggest something different.

In the context of this first chapter, you might consider how this topic could be approached with a qualitative or a quantitative orientation. What would be some quantitative indicators of the equality or inequality of men and women? How could you observe indicators of equality/ inequality qualitatively?

Improve your comprehension through additional practice! Go to http://www.nelson.com/babbie3ce to access the Premium Site, where you can test your understanding of the content in each chapter through quizzes and exercises.

# Culture

© CP PHOTO/Kevin Frayer

According to our ideal of culture, Canada will "prosper in diversity," and the *Multicultural Act* legislated cultural freedom. But many changes are occurring in our Canadian culture. Increasing cultural diversity can either cause long-simmering racial and ethnic antagonisms to come closer to the boiling point or result in the creation of a truly multicultural society in which diversity is respected and encouraged.

Since Canada's multiculturalism policy was first introduced more than 40 years ago, supporters and critics have debated the effects on the social, economic, and political integration of immigrants. Multiculturalism presents challenges for both new Canadians (who must fit in and succeed) and the native population (to accept and become comfortable with increasing diversity) (Environics, 2010:31). Multiculturalism remains a positive reality for the majority of Canadians. It has become a significant symbol of our Canadian identity and a source of national pride. However, it is not without its challenges. The following comments of student Kai James reflect some of these challenges:

*My name is Kai, and I'm Canadian. However, I am unlike many other Black youth in Canada whose parents emigrated from the Caribbean in that I identify as a Canadian. Yes, I was born here and I'm one hundred percent Canadian. Whether they like it or not, even the majority of those youth born in the Caribbean but raised in Canada are Canadians. They are as Canadian as our first prime minister, Sir John A. Macdonald, who was not born in Canada but in Scotland.*

*What makes Sir John A. Macdonald and millions of other citizens who have immigrated to this country Canadian is very simple. All have contributed to Canadian society to some extent, big or small, culturally, economically, and politically. And they continue to constantly reshape and redefine what we know as "Canadian," a notion that changes every day. So why do some Black youth constantly deny their Canadian identity even when they were born in Canada? . . .*

*Only one thing is for certain. The current generation of Canadian Black youth is clearly Canadian. We are educated in the Canadian school system. We've been immersed in Canadian institutions, the Canadian political climate, and the Canadian geographic environment . . . At the same time, aspects of Caribbean culture are present in our style, slang, and values. Black youth in Canada have created a cultural blend that is truly unique and truly Canadian.* (James and Shadd, 2001:17-19)

As our world appears to grow increasingly smaller because of rapid transportation, global communications, and international business transactions and political alliances—and sometimes because of hostility, terrorism, and warfare—learning about cultural diversity, within our own nation and globally, is extremely important for our individual and collective well-being. Although the world's population shares a common humanity—and perhaps some components of culture—cultural differences pose crucial barriers to our understanding of others. Sociology provides us with a framework for examining and developing a greater awareness of culture and cultural diversity, as well as how cultures change over time and place.

What is culture? Why is it so significant to our personal identities? What happens when others are intolerant of our culture? **Culture** is the knowledge, language, values, customs, and material objects that are passed from person to person and from one generation to the next in a human group or society. As previously defined, a society is a large social grouping that occupies the same geographic territory and is subject to the same political authority and dominant cultural expectations. While a society is made up of people, a culture is made up of ideas, behaviour, and material possessions. Society and culture are interdependent; neither could exist without the other. If we look across the cultures of various nations, we may see opportunities for future cooperation based on our shared beliefs, values, and attitudes, or we may see potential for lack of understanding, discord, and conflict based on divergent ideas and worldviews. Before reading on, test your knowledge of multiculturalism in Canada by answering the questions in Box 3.1 and referring to Table 3.1, both on page 63.

In this chapter, we will examine society and culture, with special attention to the components of culture and the relationship between cultural change and diversity. We will also analyze culture from functionalist, conflict, feminist, interactionist, and postmodern perspectives.

## Critical Thinking Questions

1. To what extent does our own culture keep us from understanding, accepting, or learning from other cultures?

2. Is intolerance toward "outsiders"–people who are viewed as being different from one's own group or way of life–accepted by some people in Canada? Why?

3. It has been suggested that the cultural freedom legislated by the *Multicultural Act* is more "symbolic" than real. Do you agree?

---

| CHAPTER FOCUS QUESTION | What part does culture play in shaping people and the social relations in which they participate? |

## LEARNING OBJECTIVES
### AFTER READING THIS CHAPTER, YOU SHOULD BE ABLE TO

**LO-1** Understand the importance of culture in our lives and those of others in society.

**LO-2** Identify the essential components of culture.

**LO-3** Describe what causes cultural change in societies.

**LO-4** Compare and contrast ethnocentrism and cultural relativism as approaches to examining cultural differences.

**LO-5** Explain how the various sociological perspectives view culture.

**69**

## CULTURE AND SOCIETY IN A CHANGING WORLD

**culture** The knowledge, language, values, customs, and material objects that are passed from person to person and from one generation to the next in a human group or society.

Understanding how culture affects our lives helps us develop a sociological imagination. When we meet someone from a culture vastly different from our own, or when we travel in another country, it may be easier to perceive the enormous influence of culture on people's lives. However, as our society has become more diverse and communication among members of international cultures more frequent, the need to appreciate diversity and to understand how people in other cultures view their world has also increased (Samovar and Porter, 1991b). For example, many international travellers and businesspeople have learned the importance of knowing what gestures mean in various nations (see Figure 3.1). As a comparison, in Argentina, rotating an index finger around the front of the ear means someone has a telephone call, but in North American culture, it usually suggests that a person is "crazy" (Axtell, 1991).

## LO-1    CULTURE AND SOCIETY

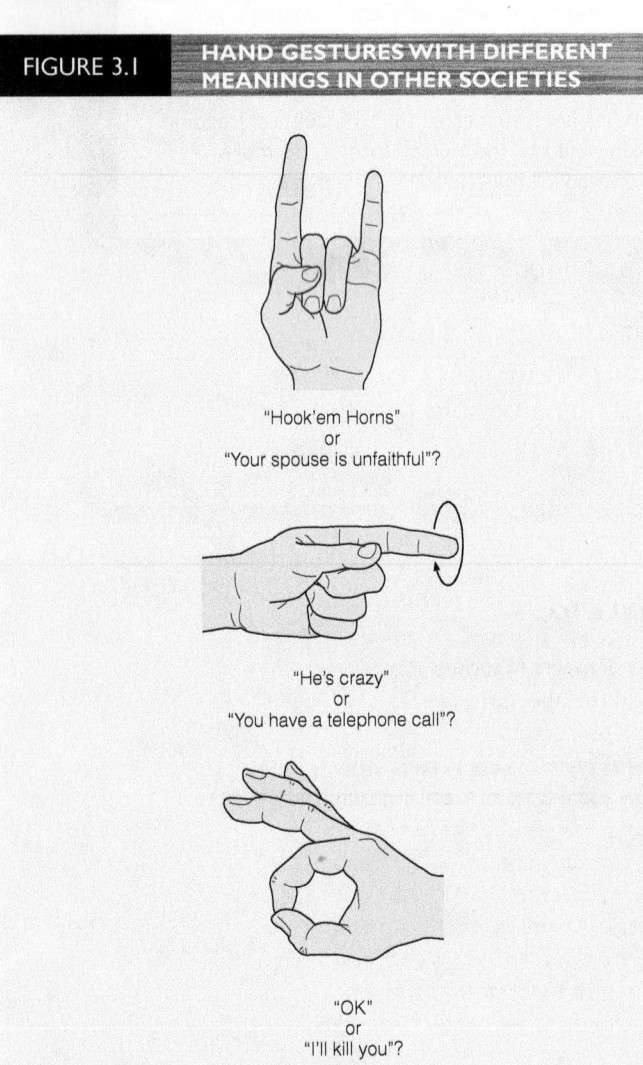

**FIGURE 3.1    HAND GESTURES WITH DIFFERENT MEANINGS IN OTHER SOCIETIES**

"Hook'em Horns"
or
"Your spouse is unfaithful"?

"He's crazy"
or
"You have a telephone call"?

"OK"
or
"I'll kill you"?

As international travellers and businesspeople have learned, hand gestures may have very different meanings in different cultures.

## The Importance of Culture

How important is culture in determining how people think and act daily? Simply stated, culture is essential for our individual survival and for our communication with other people. We rely on culture because we are not born with the information we need to survive. We do not know how to take care of ourselves, how to behave, how to dress, what to eat, which gods to worship, or how to make or spend money. We must learn about culture through interaction, observation, and imitation in order to participate as members of the group. Sharing a common culture with others simplifies day-to-day interactions. We must, however, also understand other cultures and the worldviews therein.

Just as culture is essential for individuals, it is also fundamental for the survival of societies. Culture has been described as "the common denominator that makes the actions of individuals intelligible to the group" (Haviland, 1993:30). Some system of making and enforcing rules necessarily exists in all societies. What would happen, for example, if *all* rules and laws in Canada suddenly disappeared? At a basic level, we need rules in order to navigate our bicycles and cars through traffic. At a more abstract level, we need laws to establish and protect our rights.

To survive, societies need rules about civility and tolerance toward others. We are not born knowing how to express kindness or hatred toward others, although some people may say, "Well, that's just human nature," when explaining someone's behaviour. Such a statement is built on the assumption that what we do as human beings is determined by *nature* (our biological and genetic makeup) rather than *nurture* (our social environment)—in other words, that our behaviour is

BOX 3.1 **SOCIOLOGY AND EVERYDAY LIFE**

## How Much Do You Know About Multiculturalism in Canada?

| True | False | |
|------|-------|---|
| T | F | 1. Canada is one of the most multicultural countries in the world. |
| T | F | 2. A 2010 public opinion-poll asked Canadians to describe what made them most proud of their country. Multiculturalism ranked fourth on the list. |
| T | F | 3. Recent high levels of illegal immigration have led an increasing number of Canadians to reject multiculturalism. |
| T | F | 4. The majority of Canadians regard multiculturalism as good for Canada. |
| T | F | 5. Multiculturalism and social integration are mutually exclusive goals. |

For answers to the quiz about multiculturalism in Canada, go to **www.nelson.com/sociologyinourtimes6e.**

| TABLE 3.1 | BASIS OF PRIDE IN BEING CANADIAN: TOP MENTIONS, 1994–2010 | | | |
|-----------|------|------|------|------|
| | **1994** | **2003** | **2006** | **2010** |
| Free country/freedom/democracy | 31 | 28 | 27 | 27 |
| Quality of life | 5 | 6 | 3 | 10 |
| Humanitarian/caring people | 9 | 13 | 9 | 9 |
| Multiculturalism | 3 | 6 | 11 | 6 |
| Healthcare system | 3 | 2 | 6 | — |
| Peaceful country | 7 | 5 | 6 | 4 |
| Beauty of the land | 7 | 4 | 4 | 4 |
| Born here/my country | 5 | 4 | 2 | 3 |
| Social programs | 2 | 1 | — | 3 |

*Source:* Environics Institute, "Focus Canada 2010." Found at http://www.environicsinstitute.org/institute-projects/current-projects/focus-canada.

instinctive. An *instinct* is an unlearned, biologically determined behaviour pattern common to all members of a species that predictably occurs whenever certain environmental conditions exist. For example, spiders do not learn to build webs; they build webs because of instincts that are triggered by basic biological needs, such as protection and reproduction.

Humans do not have instincts. What we most often think of as instinctive behaviour can be attributed to reflexes and drives. A *reflex* is an unlearned, biologically determined involuntary response to a physical stimulus (such as a sneeze after breathing some pepper in through the nose or the blinking of an eye when a speck of dust gets in it). *Drives* are unlearned, biologically determined impulses common to all members of a species that satisfy needs, such as for sleep, food, water, and sexual gratification. Reflexes and drives do not determine how people will behave in human societies; even the expression of these biological characteristics is channelled by culture. For example, we may be taught that the "appropriate" way to sneeze (an involuntary response) is to use a tissue or turn our head away from others (a learned response). Most contemporary sociologists agree that culture and social learning—not nature—account for virtually all of our behaviour patterns.

Since humans cannot rely on instincts to survive, culture is a "tool kit" for survival. According to the sociologist Ann Swidler, culture is a "tool kit of symbols, stories, rituals, and world

**material culture** A component of culture that consists of the physical or tangible creations—such as clothing, shelter, and art—that members of a society make, use, and share.

**technology** The knowledge, techniques, and tools that make it possible for people to transform resources into usable forms, as well as the knowledge and skills required to use them after they are developed.

views, which people may use in varying configurations to solve different kinds of problems" (1986:273). The tools we choose will vary according to our own personality and the situations we face. We are not puppets on a string; we make choices from among the items in our own "toolbox."

## Material and Nonmaterial Culture

Our cultural toolbox is divided into two major parts: *material* and *nonmaterial* culture (Ogburn, 1966/1922).

**Material culture** consists of the physical or tangible creations that members of a society make, use, and share. Initially, items of material culture begin as raw materials or resources, such as ore, trees, and oil. Through technology, these raw materials are transformed into usable items (ranging from books and computers to guns and bombs). Sociologists define **technology** as the knowledge, techniques, and tools that make it possible for people to transform resources into usable forms, as well as the knowledge and skills required to use them after they are developed. From this standpoint, technology is both concrete and abstract. For example, technology includes a pair of scissors and the knowledge and skill necessary to make

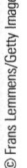

Food is a universal type of material culture, but what people eat and how they eat it vary widely, as shown in these cross-cultural examples from the United Arab Emirates (upper left), Holland (upper right), and China (bottom). What might be some of the reasons for the similarities and differences you see in these photos?

them from iron, carbon, and chromium (Westrum, 1991). At the most basic level, material culture is important because it is our buffer against the environment. For example, we create shelter to protect ourselves from the weather and provide ourselves with privacy. Beyond the survival level, we make, use, and share objects that are interesting and important to us. Why are you wearing the particular clothes you have on today? Perhaps you're communicating something about yourself, such as where you attend school, what kind of music you like, or where you went on vacation.

**Nonmaterial culture** consists of the abstract or intangible human creations of society that influence people's behaviour. Language, beliefs, values, rules of behaviour, family patterns, and political systems are examples of nonmaterial culture. A central component of nonmaterial culture is *beliefs*—the mental acceptance or conviction that certain things are true or real. Beliefs may be based on tradition, faith, experience, scientific research, or some combination of these. Faith in a supreme being, conviction that education is the key to success, and the opinion that smoking causes cancer are examples of beliefs. We also have beliefs in items of material culture. For example, most students believe that computers are the key to technological advancement and progress.

> **nonmaterial culture**
> A component of culture that consists of the abstract or intangible human creations of society—such as attitudes, beliefs, and values—that influence people's behaviour.

The customs and rituals associated with weddings are one example of non-material culture. What can you infer about beliefs and attitudes about marriage in the societies represented by these photographs?

The symbols shown here are international comparisons of road signs for elderly and disabled persons.

**cultural universals**
Customs and practices that occur across all societies.

## Cultural Universals

Because all humans face the same basic needs (such as food, clothing, and shelter), we engage in similar activities that contribute to our survival. Anthropologist George Murdock (1945:124) compiled a list of more than 70 **cultural universals**—customs and practices that occur across all societies. His categories included appearance (such as bodily adornment and hairstyles), activities (such as sports, dancing, games, joking, and visiting), social institutions (such as family, law, and religion), and customary practices (such as cooking, folklore, gift giving, and hospitality). These general customs and practices may be present in all cultures, but their specific forms vary from one group to another and from one time to another within the same group. For example, while telling jokes may be a universal practice, what is considered a joke in one society may be an insult in another.

How do sociologists view cultural universals? In terms of their functions, cultural universals are useful because they ensure the smooth and continual operation of society (Radcliffe-Brown, 1952). A society must meet basic human needs by providing food, shelter, and some degree of safety for its members so that they will survive. Children and other new members (such as immigrants) must be taught the ways of the group. A society also must settle disputes and deal with people's emotions. All the while, the self-interest of individuals must be balanced with the needs of society as a whole. Cultural universals help to fulfill these important functions of society.

From another perspective, however, cultural universals are not the result of functional necessity; these practices may have been *imposed* by members of one society on members of another. Similar customs and practices do not necessarily constitute cultural universals. They may be an indication that a conquering nation used its power to enforce certain types of behaviour on those who were defeated (Sargent, 1987). Sociologists might ask, Who determines the dominant cultural patterns? For example, although religion is a cultural universal, traditional religious practices of indigenous peoples (those who first live in an area) have often been repressed and even stamped out by subsequent settlers or conquerors who hold political and economic power over them.

### TIME TO REVIEW

- What are cultural universals?
- Explain how functionalists and conflict theorists view cultural universals.

## LO-2   COMPONENTS OF CULTURE

Even though the specifics of individual cultures vary widely, all cultures have four common nonmaterial cultural components: symbols, language, values, and norms. These components contribute to both harmony and conflict in a society.

## Symbols

A symbol is anything that meaningfully represents something else. Culture could not exist without symbols because there would be no shared meanings among people. Symbols can simultaneously produce loyalty and animosity, love and hate. They help us communicate ideas, such as love or patriotism, because they express abstract concepts with visible objects. To complicate matters, however, the interpretation of symbols varies in different cultural contexts. For some Indo-Canadians, for example, the colour green rather than white symbolizes purity or virginity Similarly, although a swastika represents hate to most Canadians, to a member of the Church of Jesus Christ Christian/Aryan Nations, a swastika represents love.

Flags can stand for patriotism, nationalism, school spirit, or religious beliefs held by members of a group or society. In our technology-oriented society, *emoticons* are a new system of symbols used to express emotions when people are communicating on their computers via chat lines or email (see Figure 3.2.)

Symbols can stand for love (a heart or a valentine), peace (a dove), or hate (a Nazi swastika), just as words can be used to convey meanings. Symbols also can transmit other types of ideas. A siren is a symbol that denotes an emergency situation and sends the message to clear the way immediately. Gestures are also a symbolic form of communication—a movement of the head, body, or hands can express ideas or feelings to others. For example, in Canada, pointing toward your chest with your thumb or finger is a symbol for *me*. We are also all aware of how useful our middle finger can be in communicating messages to inconsiderate drivers.

Symbols affect our thoughts about class. For example, how a person is dressed or the kind of car he or she drives is often at least subconsciously used as a measure of that individual's economic standing or position. With regard to clothing, although many people wear casual clothes on a daily basis, where the clothing was purchased is sometimes used as a symbol of social status. Were the items purchased at Walmart, Old Navy, Club Monaco, or Holt Renfrew? What indicators on the clothing—such as the Nike swoosh, some other logo, or a brand name—say something about the product's status? Automobiles and their logos are also symbols that have cultural meaning beyond the shopping environment in which they originate.

| FIGURE 3.2 | EMOTICONS |
| --- | --- |

```
:) = SMILE

:D = SMILE/LAUGHING/BIG GRIN

;) = WINK

:X = MY LIPS ARE SEALED

:P = STICKING OUT TONGUE

{ } = HUG

:( = FROWN

:'( = CRYING

0:) = ANGEL

}:> = DEVIL
```

The symbols shown here are examples of emoticons, or "smileys," a symbolic way to express moods in email or text messages. Turn the page sideways and the meaning of each emoticon will be clear.

## Language

**Language** is a system of symbols that expresses ideas and enables people to think and communicate with one another. Verbal (spoken) and nonverbal (written or gestured) language help us describe reality. One of our most important human attributes is the ability to use language to share our experiences, feelings, and knowledge with others. Language can create visual images in our head, such as "the kittens look like little cotton balls" (Samovar and Porter, 1991a). Language also allows people to distinguish themselves from outsiders and maintain group boundaries and solidarity (Farb, 1973).

Language is not solely a human characteristic. Other animals use sounds, gestures, touch, and smell to communicate with one another, but they use signals with fixed meanings that are limited to the immediate situation (the present) and cannot encompass past or future situations. For example, chimpanzees can use elements of Standard American Sign Language and manipulate physical objects to make "sentences," but they are not physically endowed with the vocal apparatus needed to form the consonants required for verbal language. As a result, nonhuman animals cannot transmit the more complex aspects of culture to their offspring. Humans have a unique ability to manipulate symbols to express abstract concepts and rules, and thus to create and transmit culture from one generation to the next.

**language** A system of symbols that expresses ideas and enables people to think and communicate with one another.

**LANGUAGE AND SOCIAL REALITY** One key issue in sociology is whether language *creates* or simply *communicates* reality. Consider, for example, the terms used by organizations

Notice that the sign conveys information about both wheelchair access and gender.

© Norman Chan/Shutterstock

**Sapir-Whorf hypothesis**
The proposition that language shapes its speakers' view of reality.

involved in the abortion debate: pro-life and pro-choice. Do such terms create or simply express a reality?

Anthropological linguists Edward Sapir and Benjamin Whorf have suggested that language not only expresses our thoughts and perceptions but also influences our perception of reality. According to the **Sapir–Whorf hypothesis**, language shapes its speakers' view of reality (Sapir, 1961; Whorf, 1956). If people are able to think only through language, language must precede thought. If language shapes the reality we perceive and experience, some aspects of the world are viewed as important and others are virtually neglected because people know the world only in terms of the vocabulary and grammar of their own language. For example, most Aboriginal languages focus on describing relationships between things rather than using language to judge or evaluate. One Aboriginal author explains, "No, we don't have any gender. It's a relationship . . . The woman who cares for your heart—that's your wife. Your daughters are the ones who enrich your heart. Your sons are the ones that test your heart!" (Ross, 1996:116). Consequently, many Aboriginal languages do not have any personal pronouns based on gender (such as words for *she* or *he*). As writer Rupert Ross explains:

> Because they don't exist there, searching for the correct ones often seems an artificial and unreasonable exercise. As a result, Aboriginal people are often as careless about getting them right as I am when speaking French and trying to remember whether a noun has "le" or "la" in front of it . . . On the more humorous side, my Aboriginal friends appear heartily amused by the frenzied Western debate over whether God is a "He" or a "She." (1996:117)

According to Ross, language does have a dramatic impact on our perception of the world. He describes two very different worlds experienced by English-speaking Canadians and Aboriginal peoples:

> I've struggled for some time to find a way to express how I perceive the difference between my English-speaking world and the world my Aboriginal friends tell me is given to them by their languages. I have this sense that if you decide that the first reality is constant change, if you discard your belief in the usefulness of judgmental absolutes like "good" and "bad" and choose to speak in terms of relative movement like "towards harmony" instead, then a lot of other things change as well. You start to sit in a room differently, in a car differently, everywhere differently. (1996:125)

If language does create reality, are we trapped by our language? Many social scientists agree that the Sapir–Whorf hypothesis overstates the relationship between language and our thoughts and behaviour patterns. While acknowledging that language has many subtle meanings and that the words used by people reflect their central concerns, most sociologists contend that language may *influence* our behaviour and interpretation of social reality, but it does not *determine* it.

**LANGUAGE AND GENDER** What is the relationship between language and gender? What cultural assumptions about women and men does language reflect? Scholars have suggested several ways in which language and gender are intertwined:

- The English language ignores women by using the masculine form to refer to human beings in general (Basow, 1992). For example, the word *man* is used generically in words like *chairman* and *mankind,* which allegedly include both men and women. However, *man* can mean either all human beings or a male human being (Miller and Swift, 1993:71).

- Use of the pronouns *he* and *she* affects our thinking about gender. Pronouns show the gender of the person we *expect* to be in a particular occupation. For instance, nurses, secretaries, and schoolteachers are usually referred to as *she,* while doctors, engineers, electricians, and presidents are referred to as *he* (Baron, 1986).

- Words have positive connotations when relating to male power, prestige, and leadership; when related to women, they carry negative overtones of weakness, inferiority, and immaturity (Epstein, 1988:224).

- A language-based predisposition to think about women in sexual terms reinforces the notion that women are sexual objects. Women are often described by terms such as *fox, broad, bitch, babe,* or *doll,* which ascribe childlike or even petlike characteristics to them. By contrast, performance pressures are placed on men. Words such as *dude, stud,* and *hunk* define them in terms of their sexual prowess (Baker, 1993).

Gender in language has been debated and studied extensively in recent years, and greater awareness and some changes have been the result. Many organizations and publications have established guidelines for the use of nonsexist language and have changed titles such as *chairman* to *chair* or *chairperson.* "Men Working" signs in many areas have been replaced with ones that say "People Working" (Epstein, 1988). Some occupations have been given genderless titles, such as *firefighter* and *flight attendant* (Maggio, 1988). Yet many people resist change, arguing that the English language is being ruined (Epstein, 1988). Still, many scholars suggest that a more inclusive language is needed to develop a more inclusive and equitable society (see Basow, 1992).

**LANGUAGE, RACE, AND ETHNICITY** Language may create and reinforce our perceptions about race and ethnicity by transmitting preconceived ideas about the superiority of one category of people over another. Let's look at a few images conveyed by words in the English language in regard to race and ethnicity.

Does language influence our perception of reality?

- Words may have more than one meaning and create and reinforce negative images. Terms such as *blackhearted* (malevolent) and expressions such as *a black mark* (a detrimental fact) and *a Chinaman's chance of success* (unlikely to succeed) give the words *black* and *Chinaman* negative associations and derogatory imagery. By contrast, expressions such as "That's white of you" and "The good guys wear white hats" reinforce positive associations with the colour white.

- Overtly derogatory terms, such as *nigger, kike, gook, honkey, chink, squaw,* and *savage,* as well as other racial–ethnic slurs, have been "popularized" in movies, music, comic routines, and so on. Such derogatory terms are often used in conjunction with physical threats against persons.

- Words are frequently used to create or reinforce perceptions about a group. For example, Aboriginal peoples have been referred to as *savages* and described as *primitive*, while blacks have been described as *uncivilized, cannibalistic,* and *pagan.*
- The "voice" of verbs may minimize or incorrectly identify the activities or achievements of members of various minority groups. For example, use of the passive voice in the statement "Chinese Canadians *were given* the right to vote" ignores how Chinese Canadians *fought* for that right. Active-voice verbs also may inaccurately attribute achievements to people or groups. Some historians argue that cultural bias is shown by the very notion that "Cabot discovered Canada." Canada was already inhabited by people who later became known as Aboriginal Canadians (see Stannard, 1992; Takaki, 1993).

In addition to these concerns about the English language, problems also arise when more than one language is involved.

**LANGUAGE DIVERSITY IN CANADA** Canada is a linguistically diverse society. The existence of Aboriginal languages, the presence of French- and English-speaking populations, and the increasing number of other languages commonly spoken are all evidence.

Language is the chief vehicle for understanding and experiencing one's culture. In 1969, the federal government passed the *Official Languages Act,* making both French and English the country's official languages. In doing so, Canada officially became a bilingual society. However, this action by no means resolved the complex issues regarding language in our society. According to the most recent census, 68 percent of Canadians speak English only, another 13 percent speak French only, and 17 percent are bilingual. Less than 2 percent, or 520,380 Canadians, indicated that they lacked the skills to converse in either French or English (Statistics Canada, 2006b). Although French versus English language issues have been a significant source of conflict over the years, bilingualism remains a distinct component of Canadian culture.

Canada's Aboriginal languages are many and diverse. The languages reflect distinctive histories, cultures, and identities linked to family, community, the land, and traditional knowledge. Aboriginal peoples' cultures are *oral cultures,* or cultures that are transmitted through speech rather than the written word. Many Aboriginal stories can be passed on only in the Aboriginal language in which they originated. Language is not only a means of communication, but also a link that connects people with their past and grounds their social, emotional, and spiritual vitality. For Aboriginal peoples, huge losses have already occurred as a result of the assimilationist strategies of missionaries and Jesuit priests running residential schools. At these schools, Aboriginal children were forbidden to speak their language. An Ojibwa woman from northwestern Ontario describes her experience:

> Boarding school was supposed to be a place where you forgot everything about being Anishinabe. And our language too. But I said, "I'm going to talk to myself"—and that's what I did, under my covers—talked to myself in Anishinabe. If we were caught, the nuns would make us stand in a corner and repeat over and over, "I won't speak my language." (Ross, 1996:122)

**CENSUS PROFILE**

### Language Diversity in Canada

Among the categories of information gathered in the 2006 Census are data on the languages spoken in Canadian households. As shown below, two-thirds of Canadians speak English most often at home and just over one-fifth of the population speak French most often at home.

**Language Spoken Most Often in Canadian Households as Percentage Distribution.**

- Non-official language 11.1%
- French 21.2%
- English 65.9%

*Source:* Adapted from Statistics Canada Census 2006, "Language Highlight Tables," last modified March 2009. Found at http://www12.statcan.ca/census-recensement/2006/as-sa/97-555/p1-eng.cfm

Despite the efforts of Canadian Aboriginal peoples to maintain their languages, these languages are among the most endangered in the world. Only three of the more than 50 Aboriginal languages in Canada are in a healthy state; many have already disappeared or are near extinction. In the 2006 Canadian Census, only 18 percent of Aboriginal persons reported an Aboriginal language as their first language and even fewer spoke it at home (Bougie, 2010). Loss of their languages will have a profound effect on the cultural survival of Aboriginal peoples. According to Eli Taylor, a Dakota Sioux from Manitoba:

> Our native language embodies a value system about how we ought to live and relate to each other . . . Now if you destroy our language, you not only break down these relationships, but you also destroy other aspects of our Indian way of life and culture, especially those that describe man's connection with nature, the Great Spirit, the order of things. Without our language, we will cease to exist as a separate people. (Fleras and Elliott, 1992:151)

Steps to preserve indigenous languages include the introduction of Aboriginal language courses in schools and universities, Aboriginal media programming, and the recording of elders' stories, songs, and accounts of history in Aboriginal language (Bougie, 2010).

How does the presence of all these different languages affect Canadian culture? From the functionalist perspective, a shared language is essential to a common culture; language is a stabilizing force in society and an important means of cultural transmission. Through language, children learn about their cultural heritage and develop a sense of personal identity in relation to their group.

Conflict theorists view language as a source of power and social control; it perpetuates inequalities between people and between groups because words are used (intentionally or not) to "keep people in their place." As linguist Deborah Tannen has suggested, "The devastating group hatreds that result in so much suffering in our own country and around the world are related in origin to the small intolerances in our everyday conversations—our readiness to attribute good intentions to ourselves and bad intentions to others" (1993:B5). Furthermore, different languages are associated with inequalities. Consider this Aboriginal language instructor's comments on the lure of the English language: "It's to do with the perception of power. People associate English with prestige and power. We don't have movies in [Aboriginal language], we don't have hardcover books . . . or neon signs in our language" (Martin, 1996:A8). Language, then, is a reflection of our feelings and our values.

## Values

**Values** are collective ideas about what is right or wrong, good or bad, and desirable or undesirable in a particular culture (Williams, 1970). Values do not dictate which behaviours are appropriate and which are not, but they provide us with the criteria by which we evaluate people, objects, and events. Values typically come in positive and negative pairs, such as being brave or cowardly, hardworking or lazy. Since we use values to justify our behaviour, we tend to defend them staunchly (Kluckhohn, 1961).

**values** Collective ideas about what is right or wrong, good or bad, and desirable or undesirable in a particular culture.

**VALUE CONTRADICTIONS** All societies have value contradictions. **Value contradictions** are values that conflict with one another or are mutually exclusive (achieving one makes it difficult, if not impossible, to achieve another). For example, core values of morality and humanitarianism may conflict with values of individual achievement and success. Similarly, although the majority of Canadians feel that people who are poor have a right to social assistance, they have also shown strong support for governments that have dramatically cut budgets to reduce financial deficits. Can you identify any value contradictions in the list of Canadian core values outlined previously?

**value contradiction** Values that conflict with one another or are mutually exclusive.

**IDEAL VERSUS REAL CULTURE** What is the relationship between values and human behaviour? Sociologists stress that a gap always exists between ideal culture and real culture in a society.

**Ideal culture** refers to the values and standards of behaviour that people in a society profess to hold. **Real culture** refers to the values and standards of behaviour that people actually follow. For example, we may claim to be law-abiding (ideal cultural value) but smoke marijuana (real cultural behaviour), or we may regularly drive over the speed limit but think of ourselves as "good citizens."

The degree of discrepancy between ideal and real culture is relevant to sociologists investigating social change. Large discrepancies provide a foothold for demonstrating hypocrisy (pretending to be what one is not or to feel what one does not feel). These discrepancies are often a source of social problems; if the discrepancy is perceived, leaders of social movements may use them to point out people's contradictory behaviour. For example, preserving our natural environment may be a core value, but our behaviour (such as driving energy-guzzling vehicles and polluting lakes) contributes to its degradation, as is further discussed in Chapter 22.

## Norms

Values provide ideals or beliefs about behaviour but do not state explicitly how we should behave. Norms, on the other hand, have specific behavioural expectations. **Norms** are established rules of behaviour or standards of conduct. *Prescriptive norms* state what behaviour is appropriate or acceptable. For example, persons making a certain amount of money are expected to file a tax return and pay any taxes they owe. Norms based on custom direct us to open a door for a person carrying a heavy load. By contrast, *proscriptive norms* state what behaviour is inappropriate or unacceptable. Laws that prohibit us from driving over the speed limit and "good manners" that preclude texting or reading a newspaper during class are examples. Prescriptive and proscriptive norms operate at all levels of society, from our everyday actions to the formulation of laws.

**FORMAL AND INFORMAL NORMS** Not all norms are of equal importance; those that are most crucial are formalized. *Formal norms* are written down and involve specific punishments for violators. Laws are the most common type of formal norms; they have been codified and may be enforced by sanctions. **Sanctions** are rewards for appropriate behaviour or penalties for inappropriate behaviour. Examples of *positive sanctions* include praise, honours, or medals for conformity to specific norms. *Negative sanctions* range from mild disapproval to life imprisonment. In the case of law, formal sanctions are clearly defined and can be administered only by persons in certain official positions (such as police officers and judges). These people have the authority to impose the sanctions.

Less important norms are referred to as *informal norms*—unwritten standards of behaviour understood by people who share a common identity. When individuals violate informal norms, other people may apply informal sanctions. *Informal sanctions* are not clearly defined and can be applied by any member of a group. Examples are frowning at someone or making a negative comment or gesture.

**FOLKWAYS** Norms are also classified according to their relative social importance. **Folkways** are informal norms or everyday customs that may be violated without serious consequences within a particular culture (Sumner, 1959/1906). They provide rules for conduct but are not considered essential to society's survival. In Canada, folkways include using underarm deodorant, brushing one's teeth, and wearing appropriate clothing for a specific occasion. Folkways are not often enforced, and when they are, the resulting sanctions tend to be informal and relatively mild.

---

**ideal culture** The values and standards of behaviour that people in a society profess to hold.

**real culture** The values and standards of behaviour that people actually follow (as contrasted with *ideal culture*).

**norms** Established rules of behaviour or standards of conduct.

**sanctions** Rewards for appropriate behaviour or penalties for inappropriate behaviour.

**folkways** Informal norms or everyday customs that may be violated without serious consequences within a particular culture.

Folkways are culture-specific; they are learned patterns of behaviour that can vary markedly from one society to another. In Japan, for example, where the walls of restroom stalls reach to the floor, folkways dictate that a person should knock on the door before entering a stall (you cannot tell if anyone is inside without knocking). People in Canada find it disconcerting, however, when someone knocks on the door of a stall (Collins, 1991).

MORES Other norms are considered highly essential to the stability of society. **Mores** (pronounced MOR-ays) are strongly held norms with moral and ethical connotations that may not be violated without serious consequences in a particular culture. Since mores are based on cultural values and are considered crucial for the well-being of the group, violators are subject to more severe negative sanctions (such as ridicule, loss of employment, or imprisonment) than are those who fail to adhere to folkways. The strongest mores are referred to as taboos. **Taboos** are mores so strong that their violation is considered extremely offensive and even unmentionable. Violation of taboos is punishable by the group or even, according to certain belief systems, by a supernatural force. The incest taboo, which prohibits sexual or marital relations between certain categories of kin, is an example of a nearly universal taboo.

Folkways and mores provide structure and security in a society. They make everyday life more predictable and provide people with some guidelines for appearance and behaviour. As individuals travel in countries other than their own, they become aware of cross-cultural differences in folkways and mores. For example, women from Canada travelling in Muslim nations quickly become aware of mores, based on the *sharia* (the edicts of the Koran), that prescribe the dominance of men over women. In Saudi Arabia, for instance, women are not allowed to mix with men in public. Banks have branches with only women tellers—and only women customers. In hospitals, female doctors are supposed to tend only to children and other women (Alireza, 1990; Ibrahim, 1990).

LAWS **Laws** are formal, standardized norms that have been enacted by legislatures and are enforced by formal sanctions. Laws may be either civil or criminal. *Civil law* deals with disputes among persons or groups. Persons who lose civil suits may encounter negative sanctions, such as having to pay compensation to the other party or being ordered to stop certain conduct. *Criminal law,* on the other hand, deals with public safety and well-being. When criminal laws are violated, fines and prison sentences are the most likely negative sanctions.

As with material objects, all of the nonmaterial components of culture—symbols, language, values, and norms—are reflected in the popular culture of contemporary society.

**mores** Strongly held norms with moral and ethical connotations that may not be violated without serious consequences in a particular culture.

**taboos** Mores so strong that their violation is considered extremely offensive and even unmentionable.

**laws** Formal, standardized norms that have been enacted by legislatures and are enforced by formal sanctions.

---

## TIME TO REVIEW

- What are the main types of norms?

---

## TECHNOLOGY, CULTURAL CHANGE, AND DIVERSITY    LO-3

Cultures do not generally remain static. There are many forces working toward change and diversity. Some societies and individuals adapt to this change, whereas others suffer culture shock and succumb to ethnocentrism.

## Cultural Change

Societies continually experience cultural change at both material and nonmaterial levels. Changes in technology continue to shape the material culture of society. Although most technological changes are primarily modifications of existing technology, *new technologies* are changes that make a significant difference in many people's lives. Examples of new technologies include the introduction of the printing press more than 500 years ago and the advent of computers and electronic communications in the 20th century. The pace of technological change has increased rapidly in the past 150 years, as contrasted with the 4000 years before that, during which humans advanced from digging sticks and hoes to the plow.

All parts of a culture do not change at the same pace. When a change occurs in the material culture of a society, nonmaterial culture must adapt to that change. Frequently, this rate of change is uneven, resulting in a gap between the two. Sociologist William F. Ogburn (1966/1922) referred to this disparity as **cultural lag**—a gap between the technical development of a society and its moral and legal institutions. In other words, cultural lag occurs when material culture changes faster than nonmaterial culture, thus creating a lag between the two cultural components. For example, at the material cultural level, the personal computer and electronic coding have made it possible to create a unique health identifier for each person in Canada. Based on available technology (material culture), it would be possible to create a national data bank that includes everyone's individual medical records from birth to death. Using this identifier, health providers and insurance companies could rapidly transfer medical records around the globe and researchers could access unlimited data on people's diseases, test results, and treatments. The availability of this technology, however, does not mean that it will be used because, from a nonmaterial culture perspective, people may believe that such a national data bank would constitute an invasion of privacy and could easily be abused by others. Social conflict may arise between nonmaterial culture and the capabilities of material culture, often set in motion by discovery, invention, and diffusion.

**Discovery** is the process of learning about something previously unknown or unrecognized. Historically, discovery involved unearthing natural elements or existing realities, such as "discovering" fire or the true shape of the earth. Today, discovery most often results from scientific research. For example, the discovery of a polio vaccine virtually eliminated one of the major childhood diseases. A future discovery of a cure for cancer or the common cold could result in longer and more productive lives for many people.

As more discoveries have occurred, people have been able to reconfigure existing material and nonmaterial cultural items through invention. **Invention** is the process of reshaping existing cultural items into a new form. Guns, video games, airplanes, and the *Charter of Rights and Freedoms* are examples of inventions that positively or negatively affect our lives today.

When diverse groups of people come into contact, they begin to adapt one another's discoveries, inventions, and ideas for their own use. **Diffusion** is the transmission of cultural items or social practices from one group or society to another through such means as exploration, military endeavours, the media, tourism, and immigration. To illustrate, piñatas can be traced back to the 12th century, when Marco Polo brought them back from China, where they were used to celebrate the springtime harvest, to Italy, where they were filled with costly gifts in a game played by the nobility. When the piñata travelled to Spain, it became part of Lenten traditions. In Mexico, it was used to celebrate the birth of the Aztec god Huitzilopochtli (Burciaga, 1993). Today, children in many countries squeal with excitement at parties as they swing a stick at a piñata. In our "shrinking globe," cultural diffusion moves at a rapid pace as countries continually seek new markets for their products (see Box 3.2 on page 77).

## Cultural Diversity

*Cultural diversity* refers to the wide range of cultural differences found between and within nations. Cultural diversity between countries may be the result of natural circumstances

**cultural lag** William Ogburn's term for a gap between the technical development of a society (material culture) and its moral and legal institutions (nonmaterial culture).

**discovery** The process of learning about something previously unknown or unrecognized.

**invention** The process of reshaping existing cultural items into a new form.

**diffusion** The transmission of cultural items or social practices from one group or society to another.

(such as climate and geography) or social circumstances (such as level of technology and composition of the population). Some countries—such as Sweden—are referred to as *homogeneous societies,* meaning they include people who share a common culture and are typically from similar social, religious, political, and economic backgrounds. By contrast, other countries—including Canada—are referred to as *heterogeneous societies,* meaning they include people who are dissimilar in regard to social characteristics, such as nationality, race, ethnicity, class, occupation, or education (see Figure 3.3).

Canada has always been characterized by at least three main cultures. Although cultural diversity in our country is not only the result of immigration, immigration has certainly had a significant impact on the development of our culturally diverse society. Over the past 150 years, more than 13 million "documented," or legal, immigrants have arrived here; innumerable people have also entered the country as undocumented immigrants. Immigration can cause feelings of frustration and hostility, especially in people who feel threatened by the changes that large numbers of immigrants may produce. Often, people are intolerant of those who are different from themselves. When societal tensions rise, people may look for others they can blame—or single out persons because they are the "other," the "outsider," the one who does not belong. Sociologist Adrienne Shadd described her experience of being singled out as an "other":

With the widespread accessibility of television and the Internet, popular culture is increasingly accessible for both children and adults in their own homes. Studies show that many children spend more time watching television than they spend attending school.

> Routinely I am asked, "Where are you from?" or "What nationality are you?" as if to be Black, you have to come from somewhere else. I respond that I'm "Canadian" . . . I play along. The scenario usually unfolds as follows:
>
> "But where are you *originally* from?"
>
> "Canada."
>
> "Oh, *you* were born here. But where are your parents from?"
>
> "Canada."
>
> "But what about your grandparents?"
>
>   As individuals delve further into my genealogy to find out where I'm "really" from, their frustration levels rise.
>
> "No, uh, I mean . . . your *people.* Where do your *people* come from?"
>
>   At this point, questioners are totally annoyed and/or frustrated. After all, Black people in Canada are supposed to come from "the islands," aren't they? For those of us living in large urban centres, there are constant reminders that we are not regarded as truly "Canadian." (1994:11)

Have you ever been made to feel like an "outsider"? Each of us receives cultural messages that may make us feel good or bad about ourselves or may give us the perception that we belong or do not belong. However, in heterogeneous societies such as Canada, cultural diversity is inevitable. In Canada, this diversity has created some unique problems in terms of defining and maintaining our distinct Canadian culture. In fact, what is unique to Canada is the number of distinct subcultures that together make up our Canadian culture.

It has been suggested that complex societies are more likely to produce subcultures. This is certainly the case in Canada, where regional, ethnic, class, language, and religious subcultures combine to produce a highly diverse society.

**subculture** A group of people who share a distinctive set of cultural beliefs and behaviours that differ in some significant way from those of the larger society.

**SUBCULTURES** A **subculture** is a group of people who share a distinctive set of cultural beliefs and behaviours that differ in some significant way from those of the larger society. Emerging from the functionalist tradition, this concept has been applied to categories ranging from ethnic, religious, regional, and age-based categories to those categories presumed to be "deviant" or marginalized from the larger society. In the broadest use of the concept, thousands of categories of people residing in Canada might be classified as belonging to one or more subcultures, including Muslims, Italian Canadians, Orthodox Jews, Generation Xers, and bikers. However, many sociological studies of subcultures have limited the scope of inquiry to more visible distinct subcultures, such as the Hutterites, to see how subcultural participants interact with the dominant culture.

*The Hutterites*  As a subculture, the Hutterities have fought for many years to maintain their distinct identity. The Hutterites are the largest family-type communal grouping in the Western world, with close to 30,000 members living in approximately 300 settlements. They live in colonies of about 15 families, but each family usually has its own home or apartment. Colonies range in size from about 60 to 150 people (CBC, 2006b).

The Hutterites are considered a subculture because their values, norms, and appearance differ significantly from those of members of the dominant culture. They have a strong faith in God and reject worldly concerns. Their core values include the joy of work, the

---

**FIGURE 3.3    HETEROGENEITY OF CANADIAN SOCIETY**

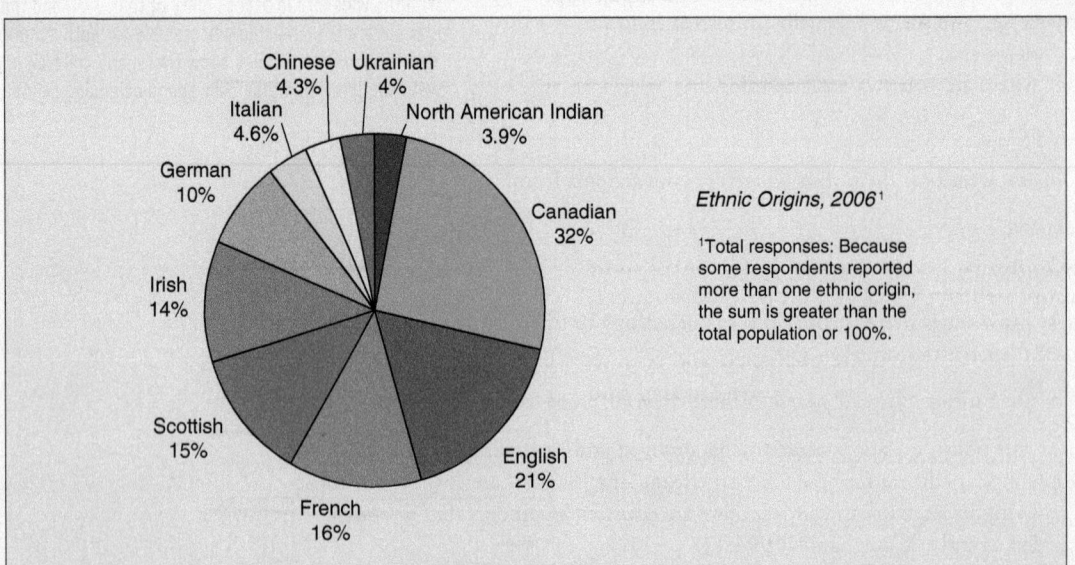

Throughout history, Canada has been heterogeneous. Today, Canada is represented by a wide variety of social categories, including our religious affiliations and ethnic origins.

*Source:* Statistics Canada, "2006 Census: Ethnic Origin, Visible Minorities, Place of Work and Mode of Transportation," The Daily, April 2, 2008.

BOX 3.2

## POINT/COUNTERPOINT

### Cultural Diffusion or Cultural Confusion: Advertising—The Global Market

Selling a product in a foreign culture requires that attention be paid to cultural differences. The world's smartest advertising minds have sometimes forgotten to do so and, as the examples below demonstrate, they have consequently come off as village idiots. Costly—often amusing—mistakes have been made by advertisers who have misread cultural attitudes, sensitivities, or superstitions, or something has simply been lost in the translation to the global marketplace. Here are a few examples:

- When the makers of Coca-Cola were launching their drink in China, they found a phrase that sounded perfect: "Ko-kou-ke-la." After printing thousands of signs, the Coke masterminds discovered that they had christened their drink "Bite the wax tadpole."
- When Colgate introduced a toothpaste called Cue in France, it turned out to be the same name as a well-known pornographic magazine.
- Most North Americans know the slogan for Kentucky Fried Chicken as "Finger-lickin' good." In China, after translation, the slogan became "Eat your fingers off."
- The American Dairy Council ran a "Got milk?" campaign that featured celebrities sporting milk moustaches. In converting the message to Spanish for its Mexican consumers, the council ended up asking, "Are you lactating?"
- "Come alive with the Pepsi Generation" was a perfectly good slogan—until it got translated into Taiwanese as "Pepsi will bring your ancestors back from the dead."

- The makers of Coors Light beer hired an agency to develop promotional materials aimed at Hispanics in the United States. In trying to translate the ad's catchphrase "Turn it loose" into Spanish, a copywriter ended up inviting customers to "Drink Coors and get diarrhea."

The lack of cultural awareness of corporate North America is obvious in the following blunders:

- When Coca-Cola introduced its two-litre bottles in Japan, it was unaware of the fact that few Japanese refrigerators are roomy enough to store such a large bottle.
- When trying to market its cake mixes in Japan in the 1960s, Betty Crocker discovered that most Japanese homes were missing a necessary ingredient: an oven.
- When McDonald's ventured into China, corporate mascot Ronald McDonald was there to clown around at the launch. Talk about a bozo move: To the Chinese, the clown is a symbol of death.
- A toothpaste company ran a commercial in Southeast Asia proclaiming that its product helped whiten teeth. The problem was that the people in the local target market were in the habit of chewing betel nut to achieve darkly stained teeth—a social sign of prestige.

*Source:* Reprinted by permission from Trish Snyder and Terri Foxman, authors of "The Global Marketing Hall of Shame" published in *Canadian Inflight Magazine* (July, 1998), 42–50.

primacy of the home, faithfulness, thriftiness, tradition, and humility. Hutterites hold conservative views of the family, believing that women are subordinate to men, birth control is unacceptable, and wives should remain at home. Children are cherished and seen as an economic asset: They help with the farming and other work.

Hutterite life is centred on the community rather than on the individual. All aspects of day-to-day life are based on sharing, right down to eating every meal in a community hall. Members of this group also have communal rather than private property; nobody is permitted to own as much as a pair of shoes (Curtis and Lambert, 1994). They have a "community of goods."

A predominant tenet of Hutterite faith is *nonassimilation*; that is, the Hutterites wish to maintain their separate status and not be absorbed into the dominant

© Winnipeg Free Press, June 7, 1998. Reproduced with permission.

**Technology and tradition meet at the Fairholme Hutterite Colony as these young women try out a new digital camera at school.**

culture. The fact that their colonies are usually located far from towns, cities, and highways emphasizes this. However, the Hutterites do not seek complete social isolation from the wider society. Although they strictly adhere to centuries-old traditions, the Hutterites do not hesitate to take advantage of 21st-century advancements (Lyons, 1998). They are successful farmers who trade with people in the surrounding communities, and they buy modern farm machinery. They also read newspapers, use home computers and telephones, and utilize the services of non-Hutterite professionals.

Applying the concept of subculture to our study of social life helps us understand how cultural differences may influence people; however, subcultural theory and research have been criticized for overstating the within-category similarities and making the assumption that most people primarily identify with others who are similar to themselves in ethnicity, religion, age, or other categories. Until recently, most studies of subcultures did not acknowledge that the experiences of women might be quite different from those of men in the same subcultural setting. Finally, some contemporary theorists argue that information technologies and the plurality and fragmentation of life in the 21st century have contributed to the creation of new subcultures in cyberspace and in the larger global community; subcultures need not be geographically specific or limited by time and space.

> **counterculture** A group that strongly rejects dominant societal values and norms and seeks alternative lifestyles.

**COUNTERCULTURES** Some subcultures actively oppose the larger society. A **counterculture** is a group that strongly rejects dominant societal values and norms and seeks alternative lifestyles (Yinger, 1960, 1982). Young people are most likely to join countercultural groups, perhaps because younger persons generally have less invested in the existing culture. Examples of countercultures include the beatniks of the 1950s, the flower children of the 1960s, the drug enthusiasts of the 1970s, and members of non-mainstream religious sects, or cults.

---

### TIME TO REVIEW

● How is cultural diversity reflected in society?

---

## Culture Shock

> **culture shock** The disorientation that people feel when they encounter cultures radically different from their own.

**Culture shock** is the disorientation that people feel when they encounter cultures radically different from their own and believe they cannot depend on their own taken-for-granted assumptions about life. When people travel to another society, they may not know how to respond to that setting. For example, Napoleon Chagnon (1992) was initially shocked at the sight of the Yanomamö (pronounced yah-noh-MAH-mah) tribe of South America in 1964.

The Yanomamö (also referred as the Yanomami) are a tribe of about 20,000 South American Indians who live in the rain forest. Although Chagnon travelled in a small aluminum motorboat for three days to reach these people, he was not prepared for the sight that met his eyes when he arrived:

> I looked up and gasped to see a dozen burly, naked, sweaty, hideous men staring at us down the shafts of their drawn arrows. Immense wads of green

tobacco were stuck between their lower teeth and lips, making them look even more hideous, and strands of dark-green slime dripped from their nostrils—strands so long that they reached down to their pectoral muscles or drizzled down their chins and stuck to their chests and bellies. We arrived as the men were blowing *ebene*, a hallucinogenic drug, up their noses. As I soon learned, one side effect of the drug is a runny nose. The mucus becomes saturated with the drug's green powder, and the Yanomamö usually just let it dangle freely from their nostrils to plop off when the strands become too heavy.

Then the stench of decaying vegetation and filth hit me, and I was almost sick to my stomach. I was horrified. What kind of welcome was this for someone who had come to live with these people and learn their way of life? (1992:12–14)

The Yanomamö have no written language, system of numbers, or calendar. They lead a nomadic lifestyle, carrying everything they own on their backs. They wear no clothes and paint their bodies; the women insert slender sticks through holes in the lower lip and the pierced nasal septum. In other words, the Yanomamö—like the members of thousands of other cultures around the world—live in a culture very different from that of Canada.

© Corbis Sygma

Even as global travel and the media make us more aware of people around the world, the distinctiveness of the Yanomamö in South America remains apparent.

## LO-4  ETHNOCENTRISM AND CULTURAL RELATIVISM

**ethnocentrism** The tendency to regard one's own culture and group as the standard—and thus superior—whereas all other groups are seen as inferior.

**cultural relativism** The belief that the behaviours and customs of any culture must be viewed and analyzed by the culture's own standards.

When observing people from other cultures, many of us use our own culture as the yardstick by which we judge the behaviour of others. Sociologists refer to this approach as **ethnocentrism**—the tendency to regard one's own culture and group as the standard, and thus superior, whereas all other groups are seen as inferior. Ethnocentrism is based on the assumption that one's own way of life is superior to all others. For example, most schoolchildren are taught that their own school and country are the best. The school song and the national anthem are forms of *positive ethnocentrism*. However, *negative ethnocentrism* can also result from constant emphasis on the superiority of one's own group or nation. Negative ethnocentrism is manifested in derogatory stereotypes that ridicule recent immigrants whose customs, dress, eating habits, or religious beliefs are markedly different from those of dominant group members. Long-term Canadian residents who are members of racial and ethnic minority groups, such as First Nations and Indo-Canadians, have also been the target of ethnocentric practices by other groups.

An alternative to ethnocentrism is **cultural relativism**—the belief that the behaviours and customs of any culture must be viewed and analyzed by the culture's own standards. For example, the anthropologist Marvin Harris (1974, 1985) uses cultural relativism to explain why cattle, which are viewed as sacred, are not killed and eaten in India, where widespread hunger and malnutrition exist. From an ethnocentric viewpoint, we might conclude that cow worship is the cause of the hunger and poverty in India. However, according to Harris, the Hindu taboo against killing cattle is very important to their economic system. Live cows are more valuable than dead ones because they have more important uses than as a direct source of food. As part of the ecological system, cows consume grasses of little value to humans. Then they produce two valuable resources—oxen (the neutered offspring of cows), to power the plows, and manure, for fuel and fertilizer—as well as milk, floor covering, and leather. As Harris's study reveals, culture must be viewed from the standpoint of those who live in a particular society.

Cultural relativism also has a downside. It may be used to excuse customs and behaviour (such as cannibalism) that may violate basic human rights. Cultural relativism is a part of the sociological imagination; researchers must be aware of the customs and norms of the society they are studying and then spell out their background assumptions so that others can spot possible biases in their studies. According to some social scientists, however, issues surrounding ethnocentrism and cultural relativism may become less distinct in the future as people around the globe increasingly share a common popular culture.

## HIGH CULTURE AND POPULAR CULTURE

What is the difference between high culture and popular culture? *High culture* consists of classical music, opera, ballet, live theatre, and other activities usually patronized by elite audiences, composed primarily of members of the upper-middle and upper classes, who have the time, money, and knowledge assumed to be necessary for its appreciation. *Popular culture* consists of activities, products, and services that are assumed to appeal primarily to members of the middle and working classes. These include rock concerts, spectator sports, movies, television soap operas, situation comedies, and, more recently, the Internet. Although we will distinguish between "high" and "popular" culture, some social analysts believe that high culture and popular culture have melded together with the rise of a consumer society in which luxury items have become more widely accessible to the masses. In a consumer society, the huge divide between the activities and possessions of wealthy elites may be indistinguishable from those of the middle and working classes.

Overall, most sociologists believe that culture and social class are intricately related. French sociologist Pierre Bourdieu's (1984) *cultural capital theory* views high culture as a device used by the dominant class to exclude the subordinate classes. According to Bourdieu, people must be trained to appreciate and understand high culture. Individuals learn about high culture in upper-middle and upper-class families and in elite education systems, especially higher education (university). Once they acquire this trained capacity, they possess a form of symbolic currency, or "cultural capital," that can be exchanged for employment and promotional opportunities in the workplace. The knowledge and skills acquired while earning a university degree (e.g., reading, writing, communication skills, logical reasoning) are valued resources on the job market, and people who possess this form of cultural capital are more likely to secure employment than people who do not. Persons from poor and working-class backgrounds typically do not acquire this cultural capital. Since knowledge and appreciation of high culture is considered a prerequisite for access to the dominant class, its members can use their cultural capital to deny access to subordinate group members and thus preserve and reproduce the existing class structure. Unlike high culture, popular culture is presumed to be available to everyone.

Activity fads, such as moshing, are particularly popular with young people. Why are such fads often short-lived?

## Forms of Popular Culture

Three prevalent forms of popular culture are fads, fashions, and leisure activities.

A *fad* is a temporary but widely copied activity followed enthusiastically by large numbers of people. Most fads are short-lived novelties (Garreau, 1993). According to the sociologist John Lofland (1993), fads can be divided into four major categories. First, *object fads* are items that people purchase even though they have little use or intrinsic value. Past and present examples include Webkinz, Harry Potter wands, SpongeBob SquarePants items, and Silly Bandz. Second, *activity fads* include everyone you know playing games of Angry Birds on their cellphones, posting Facebook pictures of celebrity look-alikes (a "doppelganger") in place of their own photo, and 24/7 texting or Tweeting friends. Third are *idea fads*, such as New Age ideologies, the "Go Green" movement, and various eat local food movements and the resurgence of farmers' markets. Fourth are *personality fads*—for example, Lady Gaga, Beyoncé, Justin Bieber, and Matthew Morrison or other characters on *Glee*, a hit Fox television series about an unusual high school glee club. A *fashion* is a currently valued style of behaviour, thinking, or appearance that is longer lasting and more widespread than a fad. Examples of fashion are found in many areas, including child rearing, education, arts, clothing, music, and sports. Soccer is an example of a fashion in sports. Until recently, only schoolchildren played soccer in Canada, but now soccer has become a really popular sport, perhaps in part because of immigration from European countries and other areas of the world where soccer is widely played.

Like soccer, other forms of popular culture move across nations. In Canada, we often assess the quality of popular culture on the basis of whether it is a Canadian or American product. Canadian artists, musicians, and entertainers often believe they have "made it" only when they become part of American popular culture. Music, television shows, novels, and street fashions from the United States have become a part of our Canadian culture. People in this country continue to be strongly influenced by popular culture from nations other than the United States, too. For example, Canada's contemporary music and clothing reflect African, Caribbean, and Asian cultural influences, among others.

Will the spread of popular culture produce a homogeneous global culture? Critics argue that the world is not developing a global culture; rather, other cultures are becoming Westernized. Political and religious leaders in some nations oppose this process, which they view as **cultural imperialism**—the extensive infusion of one nation's culture into other nations. As discussed in Chapter 17, powerful countries often use the media to spread values and ideas that dominate and even destroy other cultures. For example, some view the widespread infusion of the English

**cultural imperialism**
The extensive infusion of one nation's culture into other nations.

© REUTERS/China Daily China Daily Information Corp - CDIC

Is the proliferation of massive shopping malls in China—containing stores from the United States and Western Europe as well as local entities—an example of cultural diffusion? Or is the malling of China an example of cultural imperialism? Can "culture" be sold?

language into countries that speak other languages as a form of cultural imperialism. On the other hand, the concept of cultural imperialism may fail to take into account various cross-cultural influences. For example, cultural diffusion of literature, music, clothing, and food has occurred on a global scale. A global culture, if it comes into existence, will most likely include components from many societies and cultures.

> **TIME TO REVIEW**
>
> • To what degree are we shaped by popular culture?

## LO-5  SOCIOLOGICAL ANALYSIS OF CULTURE

Sociologists regard culture as a central ingredient in human behaviour. Although all sociologists share a similar purpose, they typically see culture through somewhat different lenses because they are guided by different theoretical perspectives in their research. What do these perspectives tell us about culture?

### Functionalist Perspectives

As previously discussed, functionalist perspectives are based on the assumption that society is a stable, orderly system with interrelated parts that serve specific functions. Anthropologist Bronislaw Malinowski (1922) suggested that culture helps people meet their *biological needs* (including food and procreation), *instrumental needs* (including law and education), and *integrative needs* (including religion and art). Societies in which people share a common language and core values are more likely to have consensus and harmony.

How might functionalist analysts view popular culture? According to many functionalist theorists, popular culture serves a significant function in society in that it may be the "glue" that holds society together. Regardless of race, class, sex, age, or other characteristics, many people are brought together (at least in spirit) to cheer teams competing in major sporting events, such as the Grey Cup or the Olympic Games. Television and the Internet help integrate recent immigrants into the mainstream culture, whereas longer-term residents may become more homogenized as a result of seeing the same images and being exposed to the same beliefs and values (Gerbner et al., 1987).

Functionalists acknowledge, however, that all societies have dysfunctions that produce a variety of societal problems. When many subcultures are present within a society, discord results from a lack of consensus about core values. In fact, popular culture may undermine core cultural values rather than reinforce them (Christians, Rotzoll, and Fackler, 1987). For example, movies may glorify crime rather than hard work as the quickest way to get ahead. According to some analysts, excessive violence in music videos, movies, and television programs may be harmful to children and young people (Medved, 1992). From this perspective, popular culture may be a factor in antisocial behaviour as seemingly diverse as hate crimes and fatal shootings in public schools.

The functionalist perspective on culture has both strength and shortcomings. On the one hand, it focuses on the needs of society and the fact that stability is essential for society's continued survival. On the other hand, it overemphasizes harmony and cooperation. This approach also fails to fully account for factors embedded in the structure of society—such as class-based inequalities, racism, and sexism—that may contribute to conflict strife.

## Conflict Perspectives

Conflict perspectives are based on the assumption that social life is a continuous struggle in which members of powerful groups seek to control scarce resources. According to this approach, values and norms help to create and sustain the privileged position of the powerful in society while excluding others. As early conflict theorist Karl Marx stressed, ideas are *cultural creations* of a society's most powerful members. Thus, it is possible for political, economic, and social leaders to use *ideology*—an integrated system of ideas that is external to, and coercive of, people—to maintain their positions of dominance in a society. As Marx stated:

> The ideas of the ruling class are in every epoch the ruling ideas, i.e., the class which is the ruling material force in society, is at the same time, its ruling intellectual force. The class, which has the means of material production at its disposal, has control at the same time over the means of mental production . . . The ruling ideas are nothing more than the ideal expression of the dominant material relationships, the dominant material relationships grasped as ideas. (Marx and Engels, 1970/1845–1846:64)

Many contemporary conflict theorists agree with Marx's assertion that ideas, a nonmaterial component of culture, are used by agents of the ruling class to affect the thoughts and actions of members of other classes.

How might conflict theorists view popular culture? Some conflict theorists believe that popular culture, which originated with everyday people, has been largely removed from their domain and has become nothing more than a part of the North American capitalist economy (Cantor, 1980, 1987; Gans, 1974). From this approach, U.S. media conglomerates, such as Time Warner, Disney, and Viacom, create popular culture, such as films, television shows, and amusement parks, in the same way that they would produce any other product or service. Creating new popular culture also promotes consumption of *commodities*—objects outside ourselves that we purchase to satisfy our human needs or wants (Fjellman, 1992). Recent studies have shown that moviegoers spend more money on popcorn, drinks, candy, and other concession stand food than they do on tickets to get into the theatre. Similarly, parkgoers at Disneyland and Walt Disney World spend as much money on merchandise—such as Magic Kingdom pencils, Mickey Mouse

Is this Japanese amusement park a sign of a homogeneous global culture or of cultural imperialism? Discuss.

hats, kitchen accessories, and clothing—as they do on admission tickets and rides (Fjellman, 1992).

From this perspective, people come to believe that they *need* things they ordinarily would not purchase. Their desire is intensified by marketing techniques that promote public trust in products and services provided by a corporation, such as the Walt Disney Company. Sociologist Pierre Bourdieu refers to this public trust as *symbolic capital:* "the acquisition of a reputation for competence and an image of respectability and honourability" (1984:291). Symbolic capital consists of culturally approved intangibles—such as honour, integrity, esteem, trust, and goodwill—that may be accumulated and used for tangible (economic) gain. Thus, people buy products at Walt Disney World (and Disney stores throughout the world) because they believe in the value of the items ("These children's pajamas are bound to be flame retardant—they came from the Disney store") and the integrity of the company ("I can trust Disney; it's been around for a long time").

Other conflict theorists examine the intertwining relationship among race, gender, and popular culture. According to sociologist K. Sue Jewell (1993), popular cultural images are often linked to negative stereotypes of people of colour, particularly black women. Jewell believes that cultural images depicting black women as mammies or domestics—such as those previously used in Aunt Jemima Pancake ads and recent resurrections of films like *Gone with the Wind*—affect contemporary black women's economic prospects in profound ways.

Conflict perspectives have two main strengths. The first is that they stress how cultural values and norms may perpetuate social inequalities. The second is that they highlight the inevitability of change and the constant tension between those who want to maintain the status quo and those who desire change.

A limitation is their focus on societal discord and the divisiveness of culture.

## Symbolic Interactionist Perspectives

Unlike functionalists and conflict theorists, who focus primarily on macrolevel concerns, symbolic interactionists engage in a microlevel analysis that views society as the sum of all people's interactions. From this perspective, symbols make communication with others possible because they provide people with shared meanings and people create, maintain, and modify culture as they go about their everyday activities.

According to some symbolic interactionists, people continually negotiate their social realities. Values and norms are not independent realities that automatically determine our behaviour; instead, we reinterpret them in each social situation we encounter. However, the classical sociologist Georg Simmel warned that the larger cultural world—including both material and nonmaterial culture—eventually takes on a life of its own apart from the actors who daily recreate social life. As a result, individuals may be more controlled by culture than they realize.

Simmel (1990/1907) suggested that money is an example of how people may be controlled by their culture. According to Simmel, people initially create money as a means of exchange, but then money acquires a social meaning that extends beyond its purely economic function. Money becomes an end in itself, rather than a means to an end. Today, we are aware of the relative "worth" not only of objects but also of individuals. Many people revere wealthy entrepreneurs and highly paid celebrities, entertainers, and sports figures for how much money they make, not for their intrinsic qualities. According to Simmel, money makes it possible for us to *relativize* everything, including our relationships with other people. When social life can be reduced to money, people become cynical, believing that anything—including people, objects, beauty, and truth—can be bought if we can pay the price.

Although Simmel acknowledged the positive functions of money, he believed that the social interpretations people give to money often produce individual feelings of cynicism and isolation.

A symbolic interactionist approach highlights how people maintain and change culture through their interactions with others. However, interactionism does not provide a systematic framework for analyzing how we shape culture and how it, in turn, shapes us. It also does not provide insight into how shared meanings are developed among people, and it does not take into account the many situations in which there is disagreement on meanings. Whereas the functional and conflict approaches tend to overemphasize the macrolevel workings of society, the interactionist viewpoint often fails to take these larger social structures into account.

## Postmodern Perspectives

Postmodern theorists believe that much of what has been written about culture in the Western world is Eurocentric—that it is based on the uncritical assumption that European culture (including its dispersed versions in countries such as Canada, the United States, Australia, and South Africa) is the true, universal culture in which all the world's people ought to believe (Lemert, 1997). By contrast, postmodernists believe that we should speak of *cultures* rather than *culture*.

However, Jean Baudrillard, one of the best-known French social theorists, believes that the world of culture today is based on *simulation,* not reality. According to Baudrillard, social life is much more a spectacle that simulates reality than reality itself. Many people gain "reality" from the media or cyberspace. For example, consider the many North American children who, upon entering school for the first time, have already watched more hours of television than the total number of classroom instruction hours they will encounter in their entire school careers (Lemert, 1997). Add to this the number of hours that some will have spent playing computer games or surfing the Internet. Baudrillard refers to this social creation as *hyperreality*—a situation in which the *simulation* of reality is more real than the thing itself. For Baudrillard, everyday life has been captured by the signs and symbols generated to represent it, and we ultimately relate to simulations and models as if they were reality.

Baudrillard (1983) uses Disneyland as an example of a simulation that conceals the reality that exists outside rather than inside the boundaries of the artificial perimeter. According to Baudrillard, Disney-like theme parks constitute a form of seduction that substitutes symbolic (seductive) power for real power, particularly the ability to bring about social change. From this perspective, amusement park "guests" may feel like "survivors" after enduring the rapid speed and gravity-defying movements of the roller coaster rides, or see themselves as "winners" after surviving fights with hideous cartoon villains on the "dark rides," when they have actually experienced the substitution of an *appearance* of power over their lives for the *absence* of real power.

In their examination of culture, postmodern social theorists make us aware of the fact that no single perspective can grasp the complexity and diversity of the social world. They also make us aware that reality may not be what it seems. According to the postmodern view, no one authority can claim to know social reality and we should *deconstruct*—take apart and subject to intense critical scrutiny—existing beliefs and theories about culture in hopes of gaining new insights (Ritzer, 1997).

Although postmodern theories of culture have been criticized on a number of grounds, we will mention only three. One criticism is postmodernism's lack of a clear conceptualization of ideas. Another is the tendency to critique other perspectives as being "grand narratives," whereas postmodernists offer their own varieties of such narratives. Finally, some analysts believe that postmodern analyses of culture lead to profound pessimism about the future.

New technologies have made educational opportunities available to a wider diversity of students, including persons with disabilities.

## CONCEPT SNAPSHOT

### COMPONENTS OF CULTURE

**Symbol:** Anything that meaningfully represents anything else.
**Language:** A set of symbols that express ideas and enable people to think and communicate with one another.
**Values:** Collective ideas about what is right or wrong, good or bad, and desirable or undesirable in a particular culture.
**Norms:** Established rules of behaviour or standards of conduct.

### FUNCTIONALIST PERSPECTIVES

A functionalist analysis of culture assumes that a common language and shared values help produce consensus and harmony. Conversely, in a society that contains numerous subcultures, discord results from a lack of consensus and shared core values.

### CONFLICT PERSPECTIVES

Conflict theorists suggest that values and norms help create and sustain a position of privilege for those in power in a society. Ideas are a cultural creation of society's most powerful members and can be used by the ruling class to affect the thoughts and actions of members of other classes.

### SYMBOLIC INTERACTIONIST PERSPECTIVES

According to symbolic interactionists, people create, maintain, and modify culture during their everyday activities. Symbols assist in our communication with others by providing shared meanings.

### POSTMODERN PERSPECTIVES

Postmodern theorists believe that culture today is based on a simulation of reality (e.g., what we see on television) rather than reality itself. According to the postmodern perspective, we should deconstruct existing beliefs and theories about culture in order to gain new insights.

## LO-1 Understand the importance of culture in our lives and those of others in society.

Culture encompasses the knowledge, language, values, and customs passed from one generation to the next in a human group or society. Culture is essential for our individual survival because, unlike nonhuman animals, we are not born with instinctive information about how to behave and how to care for ourselves and others.

Culture can be a stabilizing force for society, providing a sense of continuity; however, culture also can be a force that generates discord, conflict, and violence.

There are both material and nonmaterial expressions of culture. Material culture consists of the physical creations of society. Nonmaterial culture is more abstract and reflects the ideas, values, and beliefs of a society.

© CP PHOTO/Kevin Frayer

© Stephen Finn/Shutterstock

## LO-2 Identify the essential components of culture.

These components are symbols, language, values, and norms. Symbols express shared meanings; through them, groups communicate cultural ideas and abstract concepts. Language is a set of symbols through which groups communicate. Values are a culture's collective ideas about what is or is not acceptable. Norms are the specific behavioural expectations within a culture.

## LO-3 Describe what causes cultural change in societies.

Cultural change takes place in all societies. Change occurs through discovery and invention and through diffusion, which is the transmission of culture from one society or group to another.

© Winnipeg Free Press, June 7, 1998. Reproduced with permission.

## KEY TERMS

**counterculture** A group that strongly rejects dominant societal values and norms and seeks alternative lifestyles (p. 78).

**cultural imperialism** The extensive infusion of one nation's culture into other nations (p. 81).

**cultural lag** William Ogburn's term for a gap between the technical development of a society (material culture) and its moral and legal institutions (nonmaterial culture) (p. 74).

**cultural relativism** The belief that the behaviours and customs of any culture must be viewed and analyzed by the culture's own standards (p. 80).

**cultural universals** Customs and practices that occur across all societies (p. 66).

**culture** The knowledge, language, values, customs, and material objects that are passed from person to person and from one generation to the next in a human group or society (p. 62).

**culture shock** The disorientation that people feel when they encounter cultures radically different from their own (p. 78).

**diffusion** The transmission of cultural items or social practices from one group or society to another (p. 74).

**discovery** The process of learning about something previously unknown or unrecognized (p. 74).

**ethnocentrism** The tendency to regard one's own culture and group as the standard—and thus superior—whereas all other groups are seen as inferior (p. 80).

**folkways** Informal norms or everyday customs that may be violated without serious consequences within a particular culture (p. 72).

**ideal culture** The values and standards of behaviour that people in a society profess to hold (p. 72).

**invention** The process of reshaping existing cultural items into a new form (p. 74).

**language** A system of symbols that expresses ideas and enables people to think and communicate with one another (p. 67).

**laws** Formal, standardized norms that have been enacted by legislatures and are enforced by formal sanctions (p. 73).

**material culture** A component of culture that consists of the physical or tangible creations—such as clothing, shelter, and art—that members of a society make, use, and share (p. 64).

**mores** Strongly held norms with moral and ethical connotations that may not be violated without serious consequences in a particular culture (p. 73).

**nonmaterial culture** A component of culture that consists of the abstract or intangible human creations of society—such as attitudes, beliefs, and values—that influence people's behaviour (p. 65).

**norms** Established rules of behaviour or standards of conduct (p. 72).

**real culture** The values and standards of behaviour that people actually follow (as contrasted with *ideal culture*) (p. 72).

**sanctions** Rewards for appropriate behaviour or penalties for inappropriate behaviour (p. 72).

**LO-4**  Compare and contrast ethnocentrism and cultural relativism as approaches to examining cultural differences.

Ethnocentrism is the assumption that one's own culture is superior to other cultures. Cultural relativism counters culture shock and ethnocentrism by viewing and analyzing another culture in terms of its own values and standards.

© Corbis Sygma

© Scott Larson/Splash News/Newscom

**LO-5**  Explain how the various sociological perspectives view culture.

A functional analysis of culture assumes that a common language and shared values help produce consensus and harmony. According to some conflict theorists, culture may be used by certain groups to maintain their privilege and exclude others from society's benefits. Symbolic interactionists suggest that people create, maintain, and modify culture as they go about their everyday activities. Postmodern thinkers believe that there are many cultures in Canada alone. To gain a better understanding of how popular culture may simulate reality rather than being reality, postmodernists believe that we need a new way of conceptualizing culture and society.

## APPLICATION QUESTIONS

1. Would it be possible today to live in a totally separate culture in Canada? In what ways could you avoid all influences from the mainstream popular culture or from the values and norms of other cultures? How would you avoid any change in your culture?

2. Do fads and fashions in popular culture reflect and reinforce or challenge and change the values and norms of a society? Consider a wide variety of fads and fashions: musical styles; computer and video games and other technologies; literature; and political, social, and religious ideas.

3. Make a list of three or four uniquely Canadian symbols. Then identify examples of symbols that represent other countries.

4. In what ways do we see cultural differences in our everyday life situations and experiences? Which different cultural groups are you a part of, and how do they intersect or interact?

# KEY FIGURES

**Jean Baudrillard (1929-2007)** One of the best-known French social theorists, Baudrillard views social life as more like a spectacle that simulates reality than a reality itself.

© Steve Pyke/Getty Images

**Sapir-Whorf hypothesis** The proposition that language shapes its speakers' view of reality (p. 68).

**subculture** A group of people who share a distinctive set of cultural beliefs and behaviours that differ in some significant way from those of the larger society (p. 76).

**taboos** Mores so strong that their violation is considered extremely offensive and even unmentionable (p. 73).

**technology** The knowledge, techniques, and tools that make it possible for people to transform resources into usable forms, as well as the knowledge and skills required to use them after they are developed (p. 64).

**value contradiction** Values that conflict with one another or are mutually exclusive (p. 71).

**values** Collective ideas about what is right or wrong, good or bad, and desirable or undesirable in a particular culture (p. 71).

 CourseMate

 Test your comprehension and assess what you've learned with **CourseMate's** online quizzes.

 For other interesting Lived Experiences, watch the video clips on **CourseMate.**

 Practise what you've learned with flashcards containing key terms and definitions on **CourseMate.**

# 9

# Global Culture

## Sameness or Difference?

MANFRED B. STEGER

*Steger enters a debate here about the impact of globalization on local cultures. He shows some of the impact of global capitalism on local cultures, but also argues that local contexts have a role in whether or not cultures become the same or remain different.*

Does globalization make people around the world more alike or more different? This is the question most frequently raised in discussions on the subject of cultural globalization. A group of commentators we all might call "pessimistic hyperglobalizers" argue in favour of the former. They suggest that we are not moving towards a cultural rainbow that reflects the diversity of the world's existing cultures. Rather, we are witnessing the rise of an increasingly homogenized popular culture underwritten by a Western "culture industry" based in New York, Hollywood, London, and Milan. As evidence for their interpretation, these commentators point to Amazonian Indians wearing Nike training shoes, denizens of the Southern Sahara purchasing Texaco baseball caps, and Palestinian youths proudly displaying their Chicago Bulls sweatshirts in downtown Ramallah. Referring to the diffusion of Anglo-American values and consumer goods as the "Americanization of the world," the proponents of this cultural homogenization thesis argue that Western norms and lifestyles are overwhelming more vulnerable cultures. Although there have been serious attempts by some countries to resist these forces of "cultural imperialism"—for example, a ban on satellite dishes in Iran, and the French imposition of tariffs and quotas on imported film and television—the spread of American popular culture seems to be unstoppable.

But these manifestations of sameness are also evident inside the dominant countries of the global North. American sociologist George Ritzer coined the term "McDonaldization" to describe the wide-ranging sociocultural processes by which the principles of the fast-food restaurant are coming to dominate more and more sectors of American society as well as the rest of the world. On the surface, these principles appear to be rational in their attempts to offer

SOURCE: "Global Culture: Sameness or Difference?" by Manfred B. Steger from *Globalization—A Very Short Introduction*. 2003. New York: Oxford University Press.

efficient and predictable ways of serving people's needs. However, looking behind the façade of repetitive TV commercials that claim to "love to see you smile," we can identify a number of serious problems. For one, the generally low nutritional value of fast-food meals—and particularly their high fat content—has been implicated in the rise of serious health problems such as heart disease, diabetes, cancer, and juvenile obesity. Moreover, the impersonal, routine operations of "rational" fast-service establishments actually undermine expressions of forms of cultural diversity. In the long run, the McDonaldization of the world amounts to the imposition of uniform standards that eclipse human creativity and dehumanize social relations.

Perhaps the most thoughtful analyst in this group of pessimistic hyperglobalizers is American political theorist Benjamin Barber. In his popular book on the subject, he warns his readers against the cultural imperialism of what he calls "McWorld"—a soulless consumer capitalism that is rapidly transforming the world's diverse populations into a blandly uniform market. For Barber, McWorld is a product of a superficial American popular culture assembled in the 1950s and 1960s, driven by expansionist commercial interests. Music, video, theatre, books, and theme parks are all constructed as American image exports that create common tastes around common logos, advertising slogans, stars, songs, brand names, jingles, and trademarks.

Barber's insightful account of cultural globalization also contains the important recognition that the colonizing tendencies of McWorld provoke cultural and political resistance in the form of "Jihad"—the parochial impulse to reject and repel the homogenizing forces of the West wherever they can be found.… Jihad draws on the furies of religious fundamentalism and ethnonationalism which constitute the dark side of cultural particularism. Fuelled by opposing universal aspirations, Jihad and McWorld are locked in a bitter cultural struggle for popular allegiance. Barber asserts that both forces ultimately work against a participatory form of democracy, for they are equally prone to undermine civil liberties and thus thwart the possibility of a global democratic future.

Optimistic hyperglobalizers agree with their pessimistic colleagues that cultural globalization generates more sameness, but they consider this outcome to be a good thing. For example, American social theorist Francis Fukuyama explicitly welcomes the global spread of Anglo-American values and lifestyles, equating the Americanization of the world with the expansion of democracy and free markets. But optimistic hyperglobalizers do not just come in the form of American chauvinists who apply the old theme of manifest destiny to the global arena. Some representatives of this camp consider themselves staunch cosmopolitans who celebrate the Internet as the harbinger of a homogenized "techno-culture." Others are free-market enthusiasts who embrace the values of global consumer capitalism.

It is one thing to acknowledge the existence of powerful homogenizing tendencies in the world, but it is quite another to assert that the cultural diversity existing on our planet is destined to vanish. In fact, several influential commentators offer a contrary assessment that links globalization to new forms of cultural expression. Sociologist Roland Robertson, for example, contends that global

## The American Way Of Life

| | |
|---|---|
| Number of types of packaged bread available at a Safeway in Lake Ridge, Virginia | 104 |
| Number of those breads containing no hydrogenated fat or diglycerides | 0 |
| Amount of money spent by the fast-food industry on television advertising per year | $3 billion |
| Amount of money spent promoting the National Cancer Institute's "Five A Day" programme, which encourages the consumption of fruits and vegetables to prevent cancer and other diseases | $1 million |
| Number of "coffee drinks" available at Starbucks, whose stores accommodate a stream of over 5 million customer per week, most of whom hurry in and out | 26 |
| Number of "coffee drinks" in the 1950s coffee houses of Greenwich Village, New York City | 2 |
| Number of new models of cars available to suburban residents in 2001 | 197 |
| Number of convenient alternatives to the car available to most such residents | 0 |
| Number of U.S. daily newspapers in 2000 | 1,483 |
| Number of companies that control the majority of those newspapers | 6 |
| Number of leisure hours the average American has per week | 35 |
| Number of hours the average American spends watching television per week | 28 |

Sources: Eric Schossier, *Fast Food Nation* (Houghton & Mifflin, 2001), p. 47; www.naa.org/info/facts00/11.htm; *Consumer Reports Buying Guide 2001* (Consumers Union, 2001), pp. 147–163; Laurie Garrett, *Betrayal of Trust* (Hyperion, 2000), p. 353; www.roper.com/news/content/news169.htm; *The World Almanac and Book of Facts 2001* (World Almanac Books, 2001), p. 315; www.starbucks.com.

cultural flows often reinvigorate local cultural niches. Hence, rather than being totally obliterated by the Western consumerist forces of sameness, local difference and particularity still play an important role in creating unique local contexts. Robertson rejects the cultural homogenization thesis and speaks instead of "glocalization"—a complex interaction of the global and local characterized by cultural borrowing. The resulting expressions of cultural "hybridity" cannot be reduced to clear-cut manifestations of "sameness" or "difference." [S]uch processes of hybridization have become most visible in fashion, music, dance, film, food, and language.

In my view, the respective arguments of hyperglobalizers and sceptics are not necessarily incompatible. The contemporary experience of living and acting across cultural borders means both the loss of traditional meanings and the creation of new symbolic expressions. Reconstructed feelings of belonging coexist in uneasy tension with a sense of placelessness. Cultural globalization has contributed to a remarkable shift in people's consciousness. In fact, it appears that the old structures of modernity are slowly giving way to a new "postmodern" framework characterized by a less stable sense of identity and knowledge.

Given the complexity of global cultural flows, one would actually expect to see uneven and contradictory effects. In certain contexts, these flows might change traditional manifestations of national identity in the direction of a popular culture characterized by sameness; in others they might foster new expressions of cultural particularism; in still others they might encourage forms of cultural hybridity. Those commentators who summarily denounce the homogenizing effects of Americanization must not forget that hardly any society in the world today possesses an "authentic," self-contained culture. Those who despair at the flourishing of cultural hybridity ought to listen to exciting Indian rock songs, admire the intricacy of Hawaiian pidgin, or enjoy the culinary delights of Cuban-Chinese cuisine. Finally, those who applaud the spread of consumerist capitalism need to pay attention to its negative consequences, such as the dramatic decline of communal sentiments as well as the commodification of society and nature.

## KEY CONCEPTS

cultural imperialism          global culture          homogenization
dominant culture              globalization

## DISCUSSION QUESTIONS

1. How would you answer Steger's central question, "Does globalization make people around the world more alike?"

2. What impacts does global capitalism have on diversity in world cultures? How do you see this in your particular environment?

# Socialization & Social Interaction

# SOCIALIZATION

**William Shaffir**

**Dorothy Pawluch**
McMASTER UNIVERSITY

SOURCE: © Mark Richards/PhotoEdit.

**IN THIS CHAPTER YOU WILL LEARN THAT**

- Socialization is the social process that allow people to become members of society, develop a sense of self, and learn to participate in social relationships with others.

- Socialization takes place at all stages of the life cycle and in a variety of settings: families, schools, peer groups, the mass media, and occupational groups.

- Among the major contributors to socialization theory are Charles Cooley (who argued that individuals develop a sense of self as they interact with others), and George Herbert Mead (who focused on the way we create a sense of self by taking the roles of others).

- Socialization is a never-ending process. As people work, marry, divorce, raise children, and retire, they enter new relationships with others, learn new behaviour, and adopt new roles.

- Sometimes our self-concept undergoes abrupt change as we learn new role identities and negotiate a new self-image. Such "resocialization" occurs when we replace our way of life with a radically different one. It is most evident in jails, psychiatric hospitals, and boot camps, and in religious and political conversions.

## WHAT IS SOCIALIZATION?

As well-entrenched members of society, most of us take for granted what we need to know to function easily in a variety of social contexts. A common language that allows us to communicate with others is essential, as is knowledge about norms, laws, attitudes, beliefs, and values. What we need to know ranges from the mundane to the serious. In an elevator, people typically face forward. Murder is outlawed. Picking your teeth in public is considered ill mannered, as are most acts of self-grooming. Diversity is valued. "Shouting" or using only capital letters in computer communications will likely upset those on the receiving end. Women and men are considered equal. Wear mismatched socks and people will wonder about you.

Even more basic to functioning in society, however, is some sense of ourselves as separate from others. In other words, to interact with others we need a **self,** a sense of individual identity that allows us to understand who we are in relation to others and to differentiate ourselves from them. This sense of self allows us to react to what we learn so that once we know what is expected of us in any given situation, we can choose whether or not to behave in ways consistent with those expectations. We are constrained by societal norms and values (shared ideas about right and wrong). At the same time, we are free to decide how to behave.

Nobody comes into the world pre-programmed with a sense of self and the knowledge necessary to act and interact appropriately with others. To learn the way of life in our society and develop an identity, we undergo a process of social interaction known as **socialization.** Socialization is the vital link between individuals and society. Neither can exist without the other. We would have no sense of ourselves as distinct and autonomous human beings without interaction with others. We would not be able to function without the tools that society provides to solve the problems of survival. Chapter 2, Culture describes symbols, norms, values, and everyday practices as examples of such tools. Their use allows us to master nature and build orderly societies. However, these tools must be acquired. They must become a part of us—internalized through socialization. At the same time, society would not be possible without human beings able to interact effectively with one another and to transmit the stock of knowledge that ensures continuity from one generation to the next. Socialization thus makes social interaction, social organization, and social order possible.

Since socialization occurs in a cultural context, the content of socialization differs from one society to the next. People in a particular society learn the norms, values, and lifestyles specific to their social environment. At the same time, in every society individuals differ in significant ways from one another. Individual differences, too, are to some extent the product of socialization. Each person is influenced by distinctive subcultures of family, friends, class, race, religion, and gender. (A subculture is a group within the larger culture that has distinctive values, norms, and practices.) Our unique personal histories permit us not only to share in the larger society, but also to participate in specific parts of it. Socialization helps to explain both similarities and differences among people in a particular society.

**Primary socialization** is the crucial learning process that occurs in childhood and initiates our entry into society. Since primary socialization is so important to becoming who and what we are, it is the focus of the first part of this chapter. However, we all know that we change over time as we encounter new situations and groups. Learning to be a student, spouse or parent; learning a job; making new friends; taking on new hobbies; joining new clubs; moving to another country; and if we are lucky, growing old—all involve socialization. This kind of learning is called **secondary socialization** because it occurs after people have already undergone primary socialization. However, it is not secondary in importance. We address the ongoing nature of socialization in considering socialization through the life cycle.

## NATURE AND NURTURE

If we are products of socialization, does that mean that we are born as blank slates? Aren't we to some extent pre-programmed? Don't we have **instincts**? What about natural differences among people? Aren't some of us *naturally* more charismatic, brighter, and more compliant, while others are more aggressive or quieter?

The debate over whether biological inheritance ("nature") or social environment ("nurture") is more important in shaping our beliefs and behaviour is an old one. We can't deny that some human behaviour is the outcome of biological factors or that we seem to have certain predispositions from the moment we are born. Nor can we deny that whatever inclinations we might be born with as infants are developed in a social setting and influenced greatly by our social

experiences. Someone who is aggressive might well become gentle—or at least less aggressive—if raised in a society that places great value on pacifism or under circumstances in which aggression is discouraged. Someone with intellectual potential is not likely to realize that potential without a stimulating environment or the appropriate educational experiences. It is apparent that the old nature versus nurture debate is futile because it sets up a false opposition. Nature and nurture are inseparable. The human brain provides the physiological apparatus required for interpreting experiences, but unless children have the opportunity to learn, reason, and solve problems in early life, the brain itself may not fully develop (Begley, 1995). Attempts to determine the relative importance of nature and nurture in human development are much like trying to establish whether width or height is more significant in determining area.

The evidence for just how critical social interaction and intimate relations with others are to our development as human beings is dramatic. Some evidence comes from studies of "feral" children—children who grow up alone in the wilderness or are raised by wild animals. While most accounts of feral children are either fictional (Tarzan and Peter Pan) or the stuff of legends (Rome is said to have been founded by Romulus and Remus, twins raised by wolves), there are cases that appear to be authentic (Newton, 2002). Among them is the story of Victor, the "wild boy of Aveyron." Victor was a young boy about 11 or 12 years of age whom villagers in southern France first noticed foraging for food in the local woods in 1797. He was

Most socialization takes place informally, with the participants unaware that they are being socialized. These little girls are unconsciously learning gender roles by playing dress-up.
SOURCE: Photo courtesy of Nurit Bodemann and Shira Brym.

caught several times but escaped each time, until his final capture in 1799. Victor was dirty, walked on all fours, and had no language. His hair was matted and a clean scar across his neck led to speculation that his throat had been cut while he was a young child and he had been left to die. He was eventually brought to Paris, where interest in the boy was intense and where great efforts were made to teach and "civilize" him. These efforts were largely unsuccessful. Victor never learned to speak and was largely apathetic to others. He died in 1828. His story was dramatized by French director François Truffaut in the 1970 film *The Wild Child*.

Studies of children raised in isolation by their families also provide convincing evidence for the need for interaction. One much-publicized case of long-term isolation involved a 13-year-old girl, referred to as "Genie," who came to the attention of authorities in 1970 in California. From the age of two until she was discovered, Genie was kept in a small room in the back of her family home, unclothed and strapped most of the time to a potty chair. Her father would not allow anyone, including Genie's mother, to communicate with her. The only sounds he used with Genie were menacing growls and barks. When she was found, Genie weighed just 27 kilograms (60 pounds) and was unable to talk. She had a strange bunny walk, spat constantly, sniffed, and clawed. She hardly made any sounds; she had learned to keep quiet because her father would beat her when she made noise. One of her caretakers described Genie as "unsocialized, primitive, hardly human" (Curtiss, 1977). As Genie was cared for and began to interact with others, she made slow but steady progress. She developed a considerable vocabulary, although she was never able to speak grammatically. Her years of social isolation also left their mark on her ability to relate to others. She was withdrawn and unable to form deep attachments. Genie is now living in an adult group home somewhere in Los Angeles.

The importance of social contact in the development of human infants is evident as well in research on institutionalized children. When the repressive regime of Nicolae Ceauçescu was toppled in 1989, the media was awash with images of Romanian children who had been raised in orphanages. They were in the third to tenth percentile for physical growth and grossly delayed in motor and mental development. As they grew, many of the orphans displayed clumsy and inappropriate social behaviours. Those who were adopted by families in the West, including Canada, fared better, but many of these children, too, displayed adjustment problems.

These examples raise the question of what it means to be human. It appears that people have a basic biological need for social interaction, communication, and intimate relations with others. In other words, we need each other. Without human contact, socialization is impaired, the individual is but a shell of a human being, and irreversible damage may be done to the person's sense of self.

## THE SELF AND SOCIALIZATION

If socialization begins with the development of a self, what does that process look like? In this section, we first examine the ideas of Austrian psychoanalyst Sigmund Freud (1856–1939) because he was among the first scholars to emphasize the strong social roots of the emergence of the self. We then turn to the ideas of two American sociologists—Charles Horton Cooley (1864–1929) and George Herbert Mead (1863–1931)—whose work continues to influence how sociologists think about and study the self. We then briefly discuss the work of Paul Willis, who has extended Mead's ideas about the self in the 1990s.

### SIGMUND FREUD

Sigmund Freud proposed one of the first social-scientific interpretations of the process by which the self emerges (Freud, 1962 [1930], 1973 [1915–17]). He noted that infants demand immediate gratification but begin to form a self-image when their demands are denied—when, for example, parents decide not to feed and comfort them every time they wake up in the middle of the night. The parents' refusal at first incites howls of protest. However, infants soon learn to eat more before going to bed, sleep for longer periods, and go back to sleep if they wake up. Equally important, the infant begins to sense that its needs differ from those of its parents, it has an existence independent of others, and it must somehow balance its needs with the realities of life. Because of many such lessons in self-control, the child eventually develops a sense of what constitutes appropriate behaviour and a moral sense of right and wrong. Soon a personal conscience crystallizes. It is a storehouse of cultural standards. In addition, a psychological mechanism develops that normally balances the pleasure-seeking and restraining components of the self. Earlier thinkers believed that the self emerges naturally, the way a seed germinates. In a revolutionary departure from previous thinking on the subject, Freud argued that only social interaction allows the self to emerge.

## CHARLES HORTON COOLEY

In the early twentieth century, few scholars paid attention to the role of interaction in the development of a sense of self. In this respect, Cooley's work was groundbreaking. Cooley (1902) introduced the idea of the **looking-glass self,** suggesting that the gestures and reactions of others are a mirror or "looking glass" in which we see ourselves. Just as we look in a mirror to see a reflection of our physical body, we look to others to see a reflection of our social self. Cooley's emphasis was less on the actual responses of others than on our perception or interpretation of those responses. Just as we may be pleased or displeased with what we see when we look at ourselves physically in a mirror, so too are our conceptions about ourselves—our feelings about who and what we are—socially organized around our evaluation of how we believe ourselves to be judged by others.

This means that without the social mirror, there can be no sense of self. For Cooley, self-image emerges as a product of involvement in groups and communication with others. The first images of the self are received from **significant others**—those closest to children during the early stages of their lives, especially parents. Later, other images complement or supplant those first images, especially as the child's interaction network expands. Particularly important is the role played by an individual's **primary group,** the small group around us in which interaction is characterized by intimate, face-to-face association and cooperation. Typically, the primary group is a family.

## GEORGE HERBERT MEAD

Following Cooley, Mead (1934) explored the interplay between the individual and society. His ideas became the foundation of symbolic interactionism (see Chapter 1, Introducing Sociology).

For Mead, society is essential to human development. That is because thinking is possible only if we can communicate symbolically, and we learn to do so by interacting with others. Symbols are gestures, objects, and sounds that stand for something else and whose meaning depends on shared understanding. A dove is a bird, but when we see a dove in a poster, we know it represents peace. Such symbols come from society and they enable us to think.

Our selves derive from society, too. The key to socialization, Mead wrote, is the ability to take the role of the other. **Taking the role of the other** involves anticipating how others will see and react to

you. It is an essential skill that children must develop to be effective members of society. However, we are not born with this capacity; it must be acquired in three stages.

### Three Stages in Taking the Role of the Other

The **imitative stage** comes first. Children younger than two years old have no real conception of themselves as separate social beings, and their language skills are insufficiently developed to allow them to communicate effectively. When they play, they often act out the behaviour associated with certain roles, such as mother, father, dancer, or firefighter—but what they are doing is not true role-playing, only mimicking or imitation.

In the second stage, the **play stage,** children begin to adopt the roles of significant others—a parent, a sports celebrity, a storybook hero—and their play shifts from imitative to imaginative. They learn to imagine how people will respond without actually having to act out the situation. Through language, children can now manipulate various roles without physical action. At this stage, the role need not be firmly rooted in reality, but can be defined according to the children's wishes or their desire to please significant others. Children do not yet see role-playing as a social necessity—they merely play at the social roles of life.

Moreover, children at this stage often experience difficulty coordinating their actions with others. If you've ever seen a group of four- or five-year-olds playing soccer, you know that a child at this age rarely pays much attention to the rest of the team. Each player cares only about getting the ball and kicking it. Four- or five-year-olds have a poorly developed concept of playing a particular position and cooperating with other team members according to defined rules in order to maximize the number of goals the team scores and minimize the number of goals scored by the opposing team. This capacity develops only in stage three.

The final stage in learning to take the role of the other is the **game stage,** during which children develop a generalized impression of the behaviour people expect and awareness of their own importance to the group and vice-versa. Mead used the metaphor of a game to describe the complex behaviour required at this stage. In an organized game, such as baseball, a player must continually adjust behaviour to the needs of the team as a whole and to the specific situations that arise in the game. If the batter is running to first base, the outfielder does not throw the ball to the second baseman because she likes him better than the first baseman. Instead, her actions are oriented to the general rules and practices that make up the game. At this point, Mead held, children are responding to the **generalized other,** a conception of how people in general—not someone specific—will respond. This generalized other is internalized. It comprises the values, attitudes, and beliefs that the individual understands to be a part of society and in terms of which the individual assumes others will react. In effect, taking the role of the generalized other means that we respond to our idea of the organized group or community of which we are a part. In any given situation, we observe the conduct and reactions of other people, ascertain their points of view, anticipate what is expected of us, and then plan, rehearse, modify, and perfect our own behaviour accordingly.

### The "I" and the "Me"

In a way, then, we are not only subjects—thinking, knowing, and feeling beings—but also objects to ourselves—social and cultural beings whom we can evaluate, respond to, have feelings about, and try to modify. Mead called the subjective part of the self the "**I**" and the objective part of the self the "**me.**" The "I" acts. The "me" reflects on our actions through the lens of social norms, values, and expectations. Thus, the self is both spontaneous (I) and conformist (me), active (I) and reflective (me), experiencing (I) and experienced (me). The two aspects of our selves engage in what Mead described as an "internal conversation." This internal conversation continues throughout our lives, which means that our sense of self continues to develop as we encounter new contexts and contacts.

### PAUL WILLIS

While Mead focused on childhood socialization, British sociologist Paul Willis (1990) has emphasized the degree to which identity formation continues among teens and young adults. He also pays more attention than Mead did to variations in the social contexts within which teens and young adults forge, maintain, and transform their identities.

For Willis, class, racial, ethnic, gender, and regional differences are associated with differences in socialization patterns. In addition, the different institutions to which people belong provide them with relatively distinct symbolic resources that influence how they can express themselves and how others see them. These facts do *not* mean that people *automatically* learn the norms and values of the social contexts in which they happen to find themselves. They learn norms and values, but they also experiment and make choices from the variety of socialization opportunities they confront, and they are often helped by cultural industries, which seek to profit from the desire of young people to have fun, express themselves, and be stylish. Sometimes, young people even choose to push up against "the oppressive limits of established order and power" (Willis, 1990: 12). Yes, they may "consume" television but not necessarily passively. They shout out obscenities at politicians, insult people, and make rude comments about dress sense and personal mannerisms. Similarly with popular and rock music, young people read about and selectively excavate the history of pop and rock to control and produce their own collections. In the realm of style and fashion, Willis describes shopping as extremely hard work for young people. It is not a matter of simply going into a store and picking out an entire outfit. Great creativity is involved in selecting, combining, and recombining different clothing elements and achieving certain looks. Style and fashion are about experimenting with identity and making personal (and sometimes political) statements. Consider for example, the effect of wearing a Che Guevara shirt or a kaffiyeh (Arab headscarf)

In stressing the links among creativity, identity, and social context, Willis suggests that young people take advantage of every opportunity to make the everyday world around them meaningful. Like Mead, he reminds us that human beings are creative and strategic social actors, not pawns of vast, impersonal forces. Still, Willis acknowledges that social categories make a difference. The character of your socialization depends on the groups and institutions to which you belong and your **statuses** within those groups and institutions, that is, the culturally and socially defined positions you occupy in your social interactions.

### GENDER SOCIALIZATION

**Gender socialization** is "the process through which individuals learn to become feminine and masculine according to expectations current in their society" (Mackie, 1991: 75). It has been the subject of much sociological attention in recent decades. Gender seems to most people to be such a natural part of everyday life that we typically take it for granted. We assume that people are either male or female. However, as we show here, and as discussed in Chapter 4, Gender and Sexuality, gender identity is learned.

To the extent that a culture defines male and female roles as sharply different, parents raise boys and girls so that they *will* be sharply different (for an exception, see Box 3.1). Moreover, boys and girls grow up *wanting* to be different, believing that gender role differences are normal and necessary. Patterns of gender role socialization reveal that, from the first days of life, an infant is not simply a child but a boy or a girl. Infant boys are usually addressed differently than infant girls are, the blankets in which they are covered are usually different colours, and the rooms in which they sleep are usually decorated to show their gender. One of the first things that a child learns is whether he or she is a "he" or a "she." From an early age, children show marked gender-specific preferences for certain toys and activities (Davies, 1990). These preferences are reinforced in later years. For example, among preteens femininity is constructed partly by means of shopping. Specialty stores and specialized departments in large department stories define (and, every season, redefine) certain clothing, hairstyling products, cosmetics, and accessories as appropriate and fashionable for girls. In this way, the meaning of becoming a woman is tied to various aspects of consumer culture (Russell and Tyler, 2002).

Parents are usually the first source of children's gender learning, and indications are that parents hold and communicate different expectations for males and females. One study of children's assigned household tasks found a clear gender division of labour (Cohen, 2004): Boys were expected to mow the lawn, shovel snow, take out the garbage, and do yardwork, while the girls were expected to clean house, wash dishes, cook, and babysit younger children. Although couples today enter parenthood with a stronger commitment to sharing household responsibilities than couples did in the past, most nevertheless develop a gendered division of labour (Fox, 1998, 2001).

The mass media, too, present idealized images and stereotypes of appropriate masculine and feminine characteristics. To the degree that females were portrayed in a narrow and biased way by the media for years, the impact of gender-role stereotypes negatively affected how children perceived

---

**BOX 3.1    RAISING A GENDERLESS CHILD**

Is Storm a boy or a girl? Storm's parents are not saying.
SOURCE: Steve Russell/The Canadian Press.

Is it possible to avoid gender socialization? A Canadian family has decided to find out. When their third child, Storm, came along, Kathy Witterick and her husband, David Stocker, made the decision to raise a genderless baby. They aren't telling anyone whether Storm is a boy or a girl. The only ones who know are Storm's two brothers, a close family friend, and the two midwives who helped with Storm's delivery. Instead, Witterick and Stocker sent an email to family and friends announcing Storm's birth: "We've decided not to share Storm's sex for now—a tribute to freedom and choice in place of limitation, a stand up to what the world could become in Storm's lifetime (a more progressive place?)."

This isn't the family's first experience challenging gender stereotypes. Storm's two brothers, aged five and two, have been encouraged to pick out their own clothing since they were 18 months old. Just last week, their Dad recounts, one of them found a pink dress at Value Village that he loved because "it really poofs out at the bottom." The boys also decide whether to cut their hair or let it grow. One of them prefers his long hair in three braids, two in the front and one in the back. The boys are encouraged to challenge how they're expected to look and act based on their sex.

Witterick and Stocker are receiving a lot of criticism. "Everyone keeps asking us, 'When will this end?'" says Witterick. "And we always turn the question back. Yeah, when will this end? When will we live in a world where people can make choices to be whoever they are?"

SOURCE: Poisson, Jayme. (2011). "Parents Keep Child's Gender Secret," *Toronto Star*, 21 May. On the World Wide Web at http://www.thestar.com /article/995112.

themselves (Adams and Bettis, 2003; Massoni, 2004). Oversimplified gender-role stereotypes affected children's self-concept and interaction with peers and adults (Kortenhaus and Demarest, 1993). When in 2001 researchers examined 83 leading children's books over the preceding 30 years in terms of the gender of the main character, illustrations, and title, they found that although gender stereotyping had decreased, it was still prevalent (Gooden and Gooden, 2001). Moreover, in recent decades, specifically sexualized forms of gender socialization have become more prevalent in the mass media (Box 3.2).

Stereotyping contributes to the streaming of males and females into traditional "male" and "female" jobs. More often than not, teachers and guidance counsellors wittingly or unwittingly encourage boys and girls to pursue occupational goals that are perceived as appropriate to their gender. This phenomenon becomes a self-fulfilling prophecy: Girls develop a self-image consistent with others' perceptions of them. Thus, one study of 150 Canadian teenagers found a tendency for girls to make traditionally feminine occupational choices and to express less confidence than boys do that they would realize their occupational goals (Baker, 1985). About three-quarters of the girls planned to hold paying jobs as adults. However, they tended to see responsibility for the household and for childcare as primarily theirs and to assume that paid work must fit in with these duties. Their expectations about the future fit the actual division of household tasks (Barber and Allen, 1992; Blau and Ferber, 1992; South and Spitze, 1994). Although more women are choosing

---

BOX 3.2 **SEXUALIZING CHILDREN**

A documentary film released by Canada's National Film Board raises the question of whether children are being pushed prematurely into adulthood by the media messages around them. A guide to the film *Sexy Inc.: Our Children Under Influence* refers to "the worrying phenomenon of the hypersexualization of our environment and its noxious effect on young people." The guide goes on to say,

> Marketing and advertising are targeting younger and younger audiences and bombarding them with sexual images.... [G]irls are being represented in a sexualized and sexist way, reducing children to mere consumers and conveying dispiriting stereotypes. From a young age, girls are treated as sexual objects, their development is not respected, and the lines between childhood and adulthood are blurred. (National Film Board of Canada, 2007)

Similar questions were raised when a controversy erupted in the summer of 2011 around an issue of *French Vogue*. Thylane Loubry Blondeau, a 10-year-old much in demand as a child model, appeared on the cover. She was lying on a tiger-skin rug and was heavily made up and seductively dressed in a red dress and leopard-print stilettos. Inside the magazine, another photo showed her draped across a bed dressed in a low-cut gold lamé gown and gold stilettos.

Other examples of the hypersexualization of girls by the mass media could be listed at will, illustrating that a type of socialization that would have been considered taboo just a few decades ago has now become widespread ("French Vogue Slammed," 2011).

How does this photo of Dakota Fanning contribute to the sexualization of children?

SOURCE: © Agencia el Universal/El Universal de Mexico/Newscom.

---

SOURCE: National Film Board of Canada. 2007. *Sexy Inc. Our Children Under Influence*. A Film by Sophie Bissonnette.

careers that are not traditionally feminine, women still tend to be concentrated in certain types of work and are underrepresented in other types. In Canada, as in most other parts of the world, women are more likely to take on clerical and service jobs, such as office work, nursing, and the care of young children, and are less likely to be involved in administration and management (Brooks, Jarman, and Blackburn, 2003).

The study of gender shows us that children and adults are socialized to respond to their social world by developing certain potentials and inhibiting others. It is certainly true that biological differences between the sexes have an impact on behaviour. For example, only men can impregnate; only women can produce an ovum, carry and nurture the developing fetus, and give birth. However, sociological findings have shown increasingly and convincingly that biological differences alone are insufficient to explain biological differences. Symbolic interactionists, in particular, have shown that gender is also acquired through interactions with parents, teachers, and peers as these unfold within the larger context of a society's cultural organization (Buysse and Embser-Herbert, 2004).

The importance of gender socialization, especially as men and women cross gender lines in work and leisure and participate more fully in previously gender-segregated activities, is examined in a recent study of how traditional gender roles are reproduced in modern wedding showers (Montemurro, 2005). Showers are ideal areas of social life in which to investigate shifts in gender socialization because they involve well-defined gender "scripts" and rituals that tend to celebrate heterosexuality. Based on in-depth interviews with 51 young women and participant observation at five bridal showers, the author concludes that men's presence at wedding showers does not reflect gender convergence or alterations in traditional marriage roles: "Rather, the fact that the co-ed shower was a supplement, that women still had traditional bridal showers, and that jokes were often made that reinforced traditional notions of husband and wife roles during the gift opening at co-ed showers all suggest a lack of change" (Montemurro, 2005: 33). Hence, the author concludes that bridal and co-ed showers perpetuate traditional gender roles in marriage.

## SOCIALIZATION THROUGH THE LIFE COURSE

Sociologists refer to childhood socialization as primary socialization because it lays a foundation that influences our self-concept and involvement in social life for as long as we live. However, socialization continues throughout life, as we now show.

## ADOLESCENCE AND YOUTH

Dramatic transformations of identity, status, and social relationships occur in adolescence. We enter adolescence as children and exit as young adults.

Socialization during adolescence requires that we find some balance between autonomy and conformity, freedom and constraint. As Brym and Lie (2003) have observed, adolescence in North America is characterized by a decline in adult supervision and guidance, the increasing influence of the mass media and peer groups, and the greater assumption of adult responsibilities. In fact, pointing to the experiences encountered by adolescents, analysts have long been wondering whether the adolescence stage in the life cycle is not in the process of vanishing altogether (Friedenberg, 1959; Wolf, 1977).

Unlike children, however, most adolescents are aware of the demands being placed on them by others and of the demands they place on themselves. This makes adolescence a challenging time of life, not only for adolescents, but also for parents, friends, and teachers. Adolescence is generally associated with emotional and social turmoil. Young people experience conflict with their parents and other adults as they attempt to develop their own identity, act on their own preferences, and form their own relationships. Much turmoil at this stage is attributed to physiological changes linked to the onset of puberty. "Raging hormones" no doubt play a part. But, as we emphasized in our discussion of gender roles, hormones and biology can only explain so much. A fuller appreciation of these phenomena requires that we think sociologically about what might be going on. In the case of teen angst, inconsistencies in the socialization process also play a part. For example, adolescents are repeatedly told by adults to "grow up" but are often treated as if they are still children. Sexuality is a case in point. Adolescents typically receive messages of encouragement from the mass media and restraint from parents. Although adolescents associate adulthood with freedom, they get the confusing message from adults that in order to "act like an adult," they must not decide for themselves but rather do exactly what adults tell them to do.

This predicament would not be such a problem if most adolescents did not live at home and under the authority of adults. Tellingly, adolescent identity crises are unknown in premodern societies, where adolescence does not exist as a separate and prolonged stage of life, and young people often marry by the age of 16 and either establish independent households or remain at home yet assume adult responsibilities.

Adolescence as a distinct period of life is a product of industrialization and the extension of education that it introduced. Mass education and compulsory school attendance altered the role of the family and helped give rise to adolescence. Because young people were required to remain in school, they were not expected to assume economic responsibilities as soon as they reached sexual maturity. Instead, they continued to live at home. It was in the modern high school, where students became educated in skills and knowledge that the family was not equipped to impart, that the distinctiveness of adolescence as a stage of life first crystallized (Burgess and Richardson, 1984; see Box 3.3).

Although many families subscribe to the ideal of democracy, the reality is different (Solomon, Warin, Lewis, and Langford, 2002). Parents and teenagers often claim that openness is the route to intimacy, but in practice young people experience rules imposed by parents who are often unwilling to compromise. Parents, in turn, exercise control and seek to monitor the adolescent's behaviour. This situation causes resentment among adolescents, who realize that parent-teenager relationships often lack open communication. As parents demand more and more information, the relationship moves further away from friendship.

We should not exaggerate adults' impact on adolescents. Although, on average, the family exerts more of an influence than peer groups do regarding such fundamental matters as religious orientation, political preferences, and career aspirations, occasions also arise when young people are less influenced by their families or teachers than by their peers. Peer influence promotes youthful autonomy. It is not that adults give young people freedom, but that the conflicting and confusing messages they receive from adults, peers, the media, and their own experience require them to make up their own minds. For those who are unable to reconcile the demands of the new and the old, adolescence may be a time of considerable confusion and turmoil (Hogan and Astone, 1986). Yet for all the turbulence and rebellion generally associated with adolescence, evidence suggests that most teenagers have good experiences of adolescence and believe they have positive relationships with their parents (Coleman and Hendry, 1990).

---

## BOX 3.3  SOCIALIZATION INTO STUDENT ROLES

Research by University of Manitoba sociologists Cheryl Albas and Dan Albas (1994) explored how university students learn to perform a seemingly natural activity: studying. Based on data derived from their own observations, interviews, and logs obtained from students in their classes, Albas and Albas focused on the drama surrounding exam preparation. They described three types of students:

1. The diligently planning, high-achieving "Aces" recognized the importance of keeping their nose to the grindstone, were never satisfied with a grade lower than A, and planned their schedule to allow for adequate exam preparation.
2. The procrastinating, low-achieving "Bombers" made use of "wise nostrums, self-lulling mantras, and numerous convenient distractions, all of which are directed toward delaying serious study until the very last moment when guilt and fright force them into it" (Albas and Albas, 1994: 281).

3. The "Moderates" formed the largest category of students. They were most likely to have to juggle multiple roles (student, employee, member of a sports team, caregiver, and so on), so they had to ration their time and energy among roles.

Students seemed to fall into one of these three categories. Moreover, once they categorized themselves, or were categorized by others, as Aces, Moderates, or Bombers, their identity played an important role in structuring action. Students who viewed themselves as Aces and discovered their grades were faltering typically studied more or consulted with the professor. Bombers concluded they have little to lose by weak performance. "Give me a C and let me be free" was their motto. The authors observed that students who shared similar identities tended to be attracted to one another. They found that studying was easier if they interacted with others like themselves.

SOURCE: Albas, Daniel and Cheryl Albas. (1994). "Studying Students Studying: Perspectives, Identities and Activities." In Mary Lorenz Dietz, Robert Prus, and William Shaffir, eds., *Doing Everyday Life: Ethnography as Human Lived Experience* (pp. 273–89). Toronto: Copp Clark Longman Ltd.

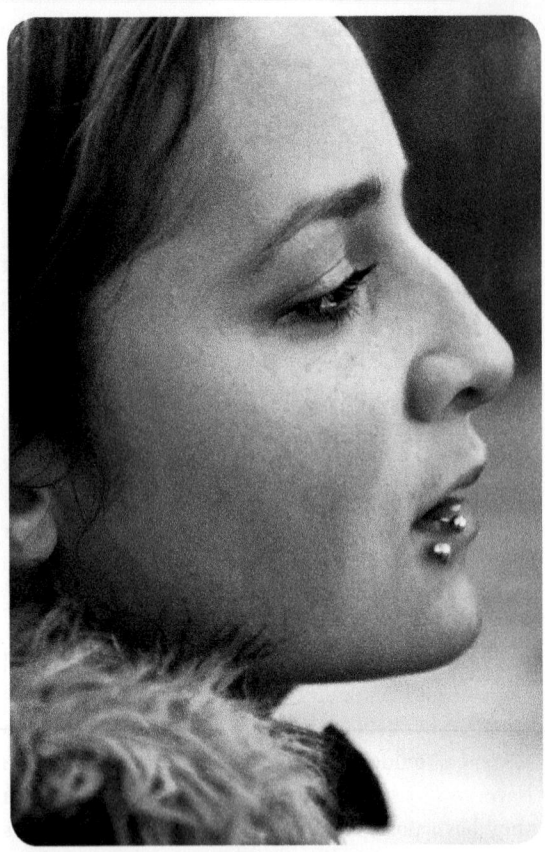

During adolescence, the most dramatic transformations of identity, status, and social relationships tend to occur.
SOURCE: © .shock/Shutterstock.

Why is this so? Adolescents may experience adolescence positively because much of it is exciting and fun. Friendships, for example, take on a different character in adolescence than in childhood. They often become intense, and people develop attachments that often last a lifetime. Many new interests arise in music, art, and fashion that adolescents use as symbols of group membership and indicators of personal taste and status. This allows them to develop passionate commitments and a sense of satisfaction and achievement when, for example, a favourite musical group has a number one song on the charts. Then, of course, there is the excitement of dating, the thrill of romance and sex, and the intense involvement in all of the accompanying activities, such as gossiping with friends, showing off a boyfriend or girlfriend, travelling together, and so on.

Finally, adolescence is also a period of **anticipatory socialization,** "the process by which aspirants to a particular social role begin to discern what it will be like to function in that position" (Stebbins, 1990: 99). Through interaction with people

who act out various roles, and by observing how roles are portrayed in the mass media, adolescents learn to incorporate the perspectives and expectations of the larger society and imagine what it would be like to enact the roles to which they aspire (Stryker, 1980: 63). In effect, the individual "rehearses" for future positions, social relationships, and even occupations. For example, students intending to enter the legal profession try imagining how this experience, in its many aspects, will affect their next few years; and successful applicants for immigration to Canada try anticipating how this experience will influence the organization of family life, gender relations, occupational choice, and the like. Many young people experience anticipatory socialization as fun. Ahead of them, though, lie an uncertain future and the responsibilities of adulthood.

## ADULT SOCIALIZATION

**Adult socialization** is the process by which adults take on new statuses and acquire new and different social identities. Adults frequently find themselves in new situations at work or in private life, meeting new people and taking on new responsibilities. To participate effectively in their society, adults must continuously undergo socialization (Clausen, 1986; Hogan and Astone, 1986; see Box 3.4).

Adult socialization differs from adolescent socialization in several important respects (Brim, 1968). Whereas adolescents seek to achieve autonomy, adults generally have control over the content and direction of their socialization. Although adolescents often have little choice but to participate in various activities, adults usually engage in socializing activities voluntarily. Because adults can often choose roles of their own free will, they can better understand and articulate their motives for new undertakings.

When we assume new statuses as adults, we need to become familiar with the expectations associated with them, learning how the statuses are best performed. Frequently such learning occurs over a considerable period as individuals interact with others in a similar situation.

Marriage constitutes one of the most important changes in anyone's life and is therefore perhaps the most important example of adult socialization. Although many of the traditional role expectations of marriage are no longer accepted uncritically, most people still choose to get married. In contrast to an

| **BOX 3.4** | **THE BOOMERANG GENERATION** |
| --- | --- |

Today, 51 percent of Canadians between the ages of 20 and 29 still live at home (Statistics Canada, 2011). That figure is double what it was 25 years ago. If we look at those between 20 and 24 years of age, the number jumps to 60 percent. Grown-up children leaving home to go to school or work, only to return to live with their parents, are sometimes called the boomerang generation or the failure-to-launch generation. Adult children living at home appear to be the new

normal not only in Canada but also in much of the Western world, raising questions about whether typical patterns of transition to adulthood are changing.

Why do you think an increasingly large proportion of young adults live at home? Can you think of economic and noneconomic forces compelling them to do so? What implications does prolonging the time that young people live at home have for their adult socialization?

earlier period when tradition largely determined the choices new couples made, newlyweds and live-in partners are now more likely to chart their own course. This independence is highly valued by most people, but it can lead to strain in relationships with friends, family, and partners. There are no courses on how to adapt to married life. Most socialization consists of a couple learning, through trial and error, how to get along with each other and with members of the extended family.

A hugely important decision during adulthood is whether to become a parent, which, of course, involves acquiring a new set of skills and statuses. The statuses are conferred automatically, but the roles and expectations accompanying them must be learned. As parents inevitably discover, relationships with children require much negotiation and adjustment. Moreover, because children grow and change, adults cannot simply adjust to their new role as parents and then relax. They must continually adapt and accommodate to changing circumstances. No wonder many parents try to take control in rigid ways; they are simply trying to achieve some measure of stability in their lives and that of their family.

Socialization during adulthood also may involve the development of a career. As many postsecondary graduates discover, the difficulty of meeting this challenge successfully increases if employment prospects are uncertain. A set of "R words" serve as signposts of the changes taking place in the workplace—restructuring, reorganization, rationalizing, and reengineering—that strike fear in the hearts of employees and postsecondary students (Lawson, 1996). In addition, the type of employment offered to graduates is in flux. Many positions are now contracted for set periods, making employment less secure and stable (see Chapter 11, Work and

Occupations). People can now expect to undergo career changes, with accompanying retraining, several times in their lives.

## SOCIALIZATION AMONG OLDER ADULTS

Some of the most difficult socialization occurs in the later years of life. Our society extends little dignity to aging. Although medical advances have prolonged lives, there are relatively few meaningful roles and valued statuses for seniors. The mass media tends to present seniors as dependent if not helpless. Such portrayals reinforce **ageism,** or discriminatory practices based on age. Just as racists think of members of particular racial groups in stereotypical terms—as, say, inherently lazy or stingy or prone to crime—ageists emphasize the declining abilities of older adults rather than their talents. Such treatment can lead seniors to develop a diminished sense of self and in the extreme case can be devastating.

Ellie Berger (2009) explored how a group of Canadian workers between 45 and 65 years of age adapted to ageism in the workplace. Employers valued their experience and knowledge but also assumed that they were less flexible, in poorer health, less creative, less interested in technological change, and less trainable than younger workers were. In response to these attitudes, older workers develop strategies aimed at countering stereotypes, including changing their résumés to make their age less obvious, taking courses to keep their skills up, and using buzzwords to show that they are current with the jargon in their field.

Other transitions in later life also require adjustment. Although many people spend a good part of their working life looking forward to retirement from the paid labour force, the realities of retirement may create identity problems for the retiree. Many older people, particularly women, face the loss of a spouse. This period involves stress as the widow or widower seeks to accommodate a new status, identity, and set of life problems. Few norms govern when the survivor should resume normal functioning or how this should come about.

Finally, socialization in old age also involves facing death and dying. In our society, people talk little about death, making it difficult to prepare for the end of life (Kellehear, 1984). As one sociologist commented, "The status of a dying person is, like retirement and widowhood, a status almost devoid of roles" (Shepard, 1993: 153)

## AGENTS OF SOCIALIZATION

Certain categories of people are especially likely to act as **agents of socialization**—individuals, groups, and institutions that impart the range of information we require to interact effectively and participate in society. In addition to parents and peers are social institutions, such as schools and the mass media, that have a significant impact on us. While we cannot interact with such institutions directly, we do interact with people, such as teachers and classmates, inside these institutions. Since they provide distinct contexts within which we take on new ideas and roles, institutions can thus serve as agents of socialization.

You may note that some agents of socialization, such as the family and the school, receive a mandate from society to "train" the next generation of members. In contrast, the peer group and the mass media do much of their "teaching" less formally and directly. Nonetheless, they profoundly influence how individuals perceive and respond to the people and the world around them.

### FAMILIES

For young children in most societies, the family is virtually their entire world for the first few years of life. Parents are in a powerful position to influence their child. After all, the newborn is helpless, and his or her survival, physical and emotional, depends on the parents, who are the source of all rewards: security, love, affection, food, and approval. Through close interaction with parents and a small number of other people, the child learns to think and speak; internalizes norms, beliefs, and values; forms basic attitudes; develops a capacity for intimate and personal relationships; and begins to develop a self-image (Handel, 1990). Later experiences

modify what children learn in the family, but it is not unusual for people to bring into adult life habits and expectations that characterized their childhood. Often, young people who rebelled against their parents' way of life and values as adolescents adopt the very same way of life and values when they become parents.

In some ways, the family is well suited to the task of socialization. It is a small group in which members typically enjoy frequent face-to-face contact. As a result, children's progress can be closely observed and adjustments made as necessary. Also, parents are usually well motivated. They have a strong emotional bond to their children, and the most meaningful and effective kind of social interaction for the purpose of socialization is fused with emotion.

However, the family is not always an effective agent of socialization. Some parents are negative role models. For instance, highly career-oriented parents may be surprised when their son opts to drop out of university "to enjoy life," rejecting a lifestyle requiring that enormous sacrifices be made for career success. Some parents have little understanding of parenting. They may be unprepared for it emotionally, and their dedication and commitment to the task may be offset by competing considerations. Some parents neglect, abuse, or even abandon their children. Some evidence suggests that parents may reproduce in their children the negative modelling they experienced in their own upbringing.

### FAMILIES AND SOCIAL CLASS

At the same time, however, families bestow statuses on us that may significantly affect our lives and sense of self. Consider, for instance, how class status affects socialization styles. Research shows that middle-class parents tend to rear children differently from the way working-class parents do (Kohn, Naoi, Schooler, and Slomczynski, 1990). Middle-class parents are likely to instill in their children the desire to think independently and become high achievers, encouraging curiosity and initiative, while working-class and poor families are more likely to stress the need for obedience and authority. Often, children in poor and low-income families are socialized to believe that lofty educational and occupational ambitions are unrealistic in light of the family's economic situation. For that reason, children from such families are often inclined to think there is little point in heeding the advice of the educational establishment to study hard. Middle- and upper-income families tend to instill in their children a strong belief in the importance of economic success and professional careers (Ballantine 1997; Lareau, 1987). In this manner, the socialization styles characteristic of different classes strongly influence children's aspirations, educational attainments, and occupational trajectories.

## FAMILIES AND ETHNICITY

Just as social class can influence how parents socialize their children, so too can ethnicity. Recently, a book titled *Battle Hymn of the Tiger Mother*, by Amy Chua, generated considerable controversy. A Yale law school professor, Chua maintains that the values of Chinese mothers—and Asian mothers more generally—are better for raising kids than "Western" parenting styles. The book begins as follows:

> A lot of people wonder how Chinese parents raise such stereotypically successful kids. They wonder what these parents do to produce so many math whizzes and music prodigies, what it's like inside the family, and whether they could do it too. Well, I can tell them, because I've done it. Here are some things my daughters, Sophia and Louisa, were never allowed to do: attend a sleepover, have a play date, be in a school play, complain about not being in a school play, watch TV or play computer games, choose their own extracurricular activities, get any grade less than an A, not be the No. 1 student in every subject except gym and drama, play any instrument other than the piano or violin. (Chua, 2011: 1–2).*

She explains that Asian culture and Western culture have completely different approaches to child rearing. As she points out,

> In one study of 50 Western American mothers and 48 Chinese immigrant mothers, almost 70% of the Western mothers said either that "stressing academic success is not good for children" or that "parents need to foster the idea that learning is fun." By contrast, roughly 0% of the Chinese mothers felt the same way. Instead, the vast majority of the Chinese mothers said that they believe their children can be "the best" students, that "academic achievement reflects successful parenting" and that if children did not excel at school then

*Chinese*

there was "a problem" and parents "were not doing their job." (Chua, 2011:2)[†]

Chua overgeneralizes about both Asian and Western culture. Within the same social class, few differences can be detected between families of Asian and Western origin in terms of educational achievement and economic attainment. Many differences between families of Asian and Western origin have to do with selective immigration: Immigration policy in Canada and other Western countries tends to select immigrants with higher education and the highest potential for economic success. Attributing ethnic differences exclusively to "culture" and "values" ignores such facts (Steinberg, 1981).

Still, the part played by ethnic culture, while difficult to tease out, should not be ignored. As we have seen, socialization unfolds against a cultural backdrop and the cultures of ethnic groups can and do shape socialization experiences. The issue of occupational choice offers an example. Few Jewish youth in Canada aspire to become police officers or firefighters. Why? It is surely not because they lack the physical stamina that such occupations demand. A more probable explanation lies elsewhere: For a variety of reasons, Jewish parents, and their parents and grandparents before them, did not encourage their offspring to consider these occupations as desirable, either economically or socially.

*Jews*

A study of Canadian Filipino youth (Salazar et al., 2001) provides interesting insights into the mechanisms by which ethnicity can affect school performance and educational attainment. Family, the study points out, is central in Filipino culture and provides the basis for both personal identity and a sense of self-worth. Most Filipinos are strongly linked to their families, which from their perspective extend beyond the nuclear family to a larger group of kin. A high value is also placed among the Filipino community on education. Moreover, education is understood not as a solitary, individual effort, but as a project or investment for the whole family. Everyone pitches in to provide help, encouragement, and as far as they can, financial support. Finally, Filipino culture understands success in school as the product of commitment and hard work, not just ability. These understandings and values come together to encourage Filipino adolescents to involve themselves in school activities and put effort into their studies. They are motivated in part by not wanting to jeopardize the

*Filipino*

---

*†SOURCE: From *Battle Hymn of the Tiger Mother* by Amy Chua, copyright © 2011 by Amy Chua and Bloomsbury Publishing Plc. Used by permission of The Penguin Press, a division of Penguin Group (USA) Inc. and Bloomsbury Publishing Plc.

family's reputation or to let down those who believe in them and support them. Ethnic cultures, then, do not determine educational and occupational success, but they do influence the range of possibilities that individuals are encouraged to consider (Dyson, 2005).

Of course, the degree to which an individual, or a family as a whole, is assimilated into the larger culture is important in the unfolding socialization drama. Thus it is not surprising that differences in socialization practices are gradually extinguished as individuals and families integrate and assimilate into the surrounding society. Yet considerable data indicate that ethnic culture frames socialization practices of day-to-day life even among individuals identifying minimally along ethnic lines.

## DIVERSE FAMILY FORMS

Finally, it is important to note the ever-increasing diversity of forms taken by the family. Families today come in all shapes and sizes. Adoption, remarriage, and the growing availability of new reproductive technologies mean that children may not be biologically related to one or any of the adults who are raising them. Children may be raised by married or unmarried heterosexual couples, married or unmarried same-sex couples, single parents, either same sex or heterosexual, extended families, or grandparents. Researchers who have studied the impact of this increasing diversity on how well adjusted the kids grow up to be have concluded that the form a family takes is less important for the development of a healthy self than having adequate resources to raise and socialize children, including both financial resources and social support (Patterson and Hastings, 2007).

Dependence on parents declines as children grow up and start interacting with peers and adults other than their parents. Peers and other adults offer approval, emotional support, and views of reality that may differ from those of one's parents. This circumstance sets up new challenges in the socialization process, as we will now see.

## SCHOOLS

Traditionally, schools have been seen as settings where social learning (cooperation, self-discipline, patriotism, and so on) is just as important as learning skills (reading, writing, arithmetic, and the like). The facade of one Canadian high school proclaims its mission in large letters carved above its main entrance, "To Build Character." One reason parents send their children to school is to be socialized, and schools are deliberately organized to achieve that goal.

Accompanying the formal curriculum of the school is a **hidden curriculum**—the informal teaching that helps ensure students' integration into society (Richer, 1988). School is usually the first setting in which children are supervised by adults who are not relatives or friends of the family. Moving from an environment of personal and intimate relationships to one that is impersonal is difficult for many children and something of a shock to almost all of them. Whereas parents often praise their children regardless of the talent they display, teachers typically seek to evaluate all students by a set of common standards. As a place where children are taught indirectly to be less emotionally dependent, the school serves as a model of much of the adult world, where many relationships are impersonal and defined by society with little emotional regard for the particular individuals who enter them. Of all the functions of the school, adjusting children to its social order—which offers a preview of what will be expected of them as they negotiate their way among the institutions of adult society—may be the most important (Bodine, 2003; Devine, 2002; Raby, 2005).

In a classic sociological paper on socialization titled "Learning the Student Role: Kindergarten as Academic Boot Camp," Harry Gracey (1967) emphasized the role schools play in teaching children how to fit into the social system, follow rules (even those that don't seem to make sense), respect authority, obey, compete, and achieve success. He compared kindergarten to military boot camps, which provide basic training for anyone entering the military. He quoted one teacher who said that she hated September because "everything has to be done rigidly, and repeatedly, until [the children] know exactly what they're supposed to do." However, by January, she said, "they know exactly what to do and I don't have to be after them all the time" (Gracey, 1967: 290). Routines are introduced from the first day of school and children are drilled in them for as long as it takes to achieve compliance. Kindergarten, Gracey concluded, is a training ground for not just the student role, but for life.

## PEER GROUPS

Although the family is the most important socializing agent in the early years, peers often begin to influence even young children. Children eventually disengage from the family as their cast of significant others begins to shift to those of similar age and interests. A

**peer group** comprises individuals who are usually of the same age and enjoy approximately equal status. The earliest peer contacts often occur under the watchful eye of parents or adults, such as teachers in a nursery school or daycare centre. In time, however, the influence of the peer group may supersede, and even conflict with, parents and familial expectations.

In childhood, peer groups are formed largely by the accident of association. Members of the same peer group are not necessarily friends. For instance, all children in a given classroom constitute a peer group but rarely form a single friendship circle. Later in life, however, we *choose* peer groups based on such criteria as common interests and activities, and similar income level or occupation.

Significantly, the peer group is the only agent of socialization in childhood and youth that is not controlled mainly by adults (Corsaro, 1992). Although parents typically play the initial leading roles in the inculcation of basic values, peers seem to have the greatest influence in lifestyle issues, such as appearance, social activities, and dating (Sebald, 1992). Research shows that, especially during adolescence, peers can strongly shape the individual's aspirations and behaviour with respect to both acceptable and criminal behaviour (Giordano, Cernkovich, and DeMaris, 1993). Certainly, the peer group contributes to socialization by enabling children to engage in experiences that the family may not provide. Here they can interact in give-and-take relationships— relationships involving conflict, competition, and cooperation—that are not always possible at home. In this manner, children find many opportunities for self-direction and self-expression in peer groups (Adler and Adler, 1998). Peer groups allow young people to examine feelings, beliefs, and ideas that are unacceptable to the family. Peers share a vision of the world and allow young people to discuss sexual and emotional relationships and developments within their school and friendship circle.

Often, peer group socialization is harsh. Peers may pressure one another to conform to a standard deemed appropriate by the group. They may tolerate little deviation from group norms concerning speech, attitudes, and dress. Paradoxically, adolescents, preoccupied with gaining autonomy from their parents, and anxious about gaining acceptance from others like themselves, may find such demands for conformity difficult to resist (Thorne, 1993). In fact, by the teenage years, the peer group may demand behaviour that conflicts sharply with the norms and values of the parental generation.

The student's values are strongly influenced by his or her peer group, which consists of people of similar age and status, regardless of whether they are friends.
SOURCE: © Stockbyte Platinum/Alamy.

In this regard, it is understandable that parents often express concern about their children's friends, particularly during the teenage years.

If peer groups often reject the norms and values of their parents, where do the group norms and values come from? In large part, from the mass media. The mass media fascinate young people, who look to media heroes as symbols of identity. Taste in music, movies, television shows, and fashion express not only common preferences but also a common style that sets the group apart, both from parents and from other sets of peers (Hebdige, 1979). In fact, a "generation gap" may characterize relations between the peer group and parents, and the peer group's influence can rival that of parents.

For example, the structure and dynamics of the peer group may help us better understand bullying both in school contexts and online. Research shows that bullying does not happen in a social void. While the bully chooses who to target, peer groups consciously or unconsciously support bullying behaviour. Bullying typically starts with teasing. The bully initiates the teasing and others join in. One high school student describes the process as follows:

> There's a big crowd, "the gang," and then there's this one boy/girl on their own. Someone from the crowd starts to spout mean shit. That's when the bullying starts. There's more bullying going on in the crowd, because the gang also wants to show off to each other a bit. (Hamarus and Kaikkonen, 2008: 338)

The desire to be a part of the group can pressure others to participate, leading to the silencing and

*Effects of ↓ risk taking*

isolation of the victim. Bullying becomes a way to show status, power, or popularity within the school community. Once a bullying dynamic is established, the peer group is forced to adapt to the norms and values set up by the bully or they risk becoming targets themselves. As the bullying escalates, those participating in it become entangled in a collusive relationship, keeping what is going on a secret from teachers and parents.

During adolescence, peer groups take on particular significance. Adolescence is often a time of physical and emotional turmoil, but also of social turbulence as individuals develop new interests, new friendships, and a new identity. Given the dramatic and sometimes traumatic changes going on within and around them, adolescents often turn to peers for support since adults often have difficulty empathizing with adolescent concerns and are often likely to respond with anxiety of their own.

We often use the term *peer pressure* to emphasize the influence peers have on adolescents, but research by Cynthia Lightfoot (1997) suggests that the impact of peers is more complex than the concept of peer pressure implies. Lightfoot did research on risk-taking among adolescents and found that the impact of peers is less a case of pressure and more a matter of example. As one of her research subjects commented, "the idea of peer pressure is a lot of bunk. ... You go somewhere and everyone else is doing it and you'd think ... they seem to be having a good time—now why wouldn't I do this?" (Lightfoot, 1997: 36).

More generally, Lightfoot found that adolescent risk-taking may have multiple effects during adolescent development. It may generate a sense of individuality and self through opposition to others or established authority. It may create a bond among people who act together and share the thrill, sense of accomplishment, or feeling of relief that comes from engaging in reckless behaviour. It may generate a sense of pride or raise one's status with peers. Or it may just be fun to do. Telling someone not to do something because it is dangerous or reckless will not be effective, Lightfoot suggests, if the perceived benefits of the action are only possible because it is dangerous or reckless.

## MASS MEDIA AND NEW COMMUNICATIONS TECHNOLOGY

Like the school and peer groups, the mass media have become important agents of socialization. The mass media include television, radio, movies, videos, CDs, the Internet, newspapers, magazines, and books. While the fastest growing mass medium is the Internet, TV viewing still consumes more of the average Canadian's time than any other mass medium. Indeed, television exhibits certain characteristics that distinguish it from the other socialization agents. Specifically, it permits imitation and role-playing. It is common for critics to express alarm about the TV shows children watch (and also about the content of popular music, especially rap, music videos, video games, and Internet websites; see Box 3.5). Depictions of violence and sex

---

**BOX 3.5    THE TENDER CUT: SELF-INJURING AS LEARNED BEHAVIOUR**

A study by Patricia Adler and Peter Adler (2011) on self-injurers showed the role that both the media and peers play in the rise of such behaviours as cutting, burning, branding, and bone-breaking. Although individuals have been self-injuring for centuries, up until the mid-1990s the behaviour was relatively rare and practised in isolation. Since then, however, self-injury has become much more common and has taken on a new meaning. Individuals are more likely to practise self-injury through what the Adlers call copycatting. They hear about these behaviours, see others engaging in them, and become curious. In some cases, they self-injure to be cool or to feel like they belong. In other cases, they turn to self-injury as a way of dealing with teenage anxiety or depression. For example, in Adler and Adler's study, Dana

reported struggling with mood swings since she was a child. Asked why she started cutting herself, she recalled seeing a *Dateline* program on self-injury and reading about it in teen magazines. On a particularly difficult day, she decided to try it:

> I was like, other people have done it; I'll try it. Maybe I'll feel better. And like, I'll know what these people are talking about, because whenever I've heard these stories, these people have sounded like me, and so, maybe if I try something like them, it will feel better. I'd completely ignore the last part of the story where they'd be like, "Oh, I've recovered," you know, the happy ending. I was concerned with how they are feeling now and how they fixed it. (Adler and Adler, 2011: 58)

SOURCE: Adler, P. A. and P. Adler. (2011). *The Tender Cut: Inside the World of Self-Injury.* New York: New York University Press.

often worry them. However, the mass media are not always a negative influence. Thus, television viewing can make people more tolerant of unfamiliar and alternative lifestyles and cultures, while violent video games can help them let off steam, and popular music can help them cope with emotional problems.

In recent years, sociologists and other social scientists have invested considerable effort trying to understand the impact of new communications technology on socialization, particularly its influences on family life. In an era where vast distances may separate family members, new communication technologies—cellphones and the Internet—allow them to keep together in ways that were not possible just a few years ago. However, the technologies have both benefits and disadvantages. While they create new opportunities for family members to interact, they also create new opportunities for family members to live in isolation from one another (see Box 3.6).

A key feature of the mass media, particularly those offering access to the Internet, is that they offer adolescents in particular more say over which information will influence them. As sociologist Jeffrey Jansen Arnett (1995) observed, the mass media enable adolescents to engage in self-socialization by selecting socialization influences from a wide array of mass-media offerings. Accordingly, some ultra-orthodox and fundamentalist religious groups, fearing the erosion of their strict ideals of conduct, have challenged the intrusion of the mass media into the lives of their children and adolescents (Lapidus, 2006).

The degree to which cellphone technology can be used to bring together and influence otherwise largely unaffiliated youth to marshal resources toward common goals was apparent during riots that broke out in London, England, in 2011. Many of the rioters were angry about racism and social inequality in the United Kingdom, while others were simply trying to take advantage of the chaos for personal gain. Whatever their motives, their text messages helped them act collectively. For instance, "If you're down for making money, we're about to go hard in east London," one looter messaged (Yelaja, 2011). Other text messages directed looters to areas of untapped riches—stores selling expensive stereo equipment, designer clothes, alcohol, and bicycles. Messages were sent through regular texts and on Facebook. At the same time, social media provided information to fearful residents and shop owners. Twitter helped them pinpoint areas of violence, organize community clean-up groups, and alert people to alternative travel routes.

## OTHER SOCIALIZING AGENTS

The family, school, peer group, and mass media are the main socializing agents, but other agents of socialization are important, too. Religious institutions, for example, may deeply affect the moral outlook of young people even in highly secular societies, such as Canada. Athletic teams may teach young people to compete, cooperate with others, follow rules, and make friends. Youth groups may be instrumental in teaching young people about group rules and expectations about conformity, and even about deviance.

| BOX 3.6 | TECHNOLOGY AND IDENTITY |
|---------|------------------------|

Sociologist Sherry Turkle (2011) explored the impact of new communication technologies on social life in a book tellingly titled *Alone Together*. She argues that the new communication technologies—email messages, text messages, Facebook postings, Skype exchanges, role-playing games, and Internet bulletin boards—have made convenience and control a priority while diminishing the expectations we have of other human beings. Instead of real friends, we "friend" strangers on Facebook. Instead of meeting for coffee, we text message. Technology, she writes, makes it easy to communicate when we want and to disengage at will. The gains come in the greater connectivity that we enjoy. We can do anything with anyone, anywhere. At the same time, we can feel overwhelmed and isolated. Relentless technological connection can lead to a new kind of solitude. However, Turkle also sees reason for optimism, ironically, among those who are the greatest users of these technologies—the young. Young people, she insists, are increasingly raising fundamental questions about what authenticity and real human connection look like in an increasingly technological age, and how true connections can be achieved.

SOURCE: Turkle, Sherry. (2011). *Alone Together: Why We Expect More From Technology and Less from Each Other.* New York: Basic Books.

In such complex societies as ours, conflict among the agencies of socialization is almost inevitable.

Some socialization takes place in so-called people-processing institutions, whose primary goal is to change the lives of the clients they serve (Goffman, 1961). People-processing institutions include hospitals, correctional facilities, and organizations that provide programs for everyone from battered women and drug addicts to "at risk" children and people with cancer. While the services they provide are framed as help, support, or rehabilitation, these institutions also socialize clients to behave, think, and feel as prescribed by the institutions.

For example, Elizabeth Armstrong (2000) showed how hospital-based prenatal programs aimed specifically at poor, black, and immigrant women, try to teach women how to comply with the hospitals' white, middle-class values, as well as their institutional needs. For example, the programs expect that women will be accompanied by a "birth partner" or "labour coach"—someone who will support them through the birthing process. However, many women find the idea of having anyone but medical professionals present culturally alien. Others prefer "not to be seen like that," or think that their partners "couldn't handle it." There are also those for whom it would be difficult to count on the support of a partner or relative since those closest to them depend on jobs from which it would be difficult to take time off of. What many of the women would really like from the hospitals is to be able to come in as soon as they think they may be going into labour. Instead, the prenatal classes teach them how to time their contractions and estimate their stage of labour so as to avoid cluttering up the labour ward with false alarms. Women are made to feel bad about misjudging.

Other sociologists have investigated socialization into the world of the deaf. The claim that the deaf must be socialized may appear strange. A person does not, after all, learn to be deaf. Children who are deaf do, however, learn the behaviours and attitudes associated with being deaf, not so much at home as in institutions devoted to their education. Specifically, in schools for the deaf, the hearing world typically serves as the yardstick for what is considered normative. Thus, chewing gum may be forbidden because the sound of smacking lips, which children who are deaf cannot hear, may offend people who can hear: "The message is always the same: hearing people must not be offended or intruded upon by the noises of the deaf" (Evans and Falk, 1986: 157). In this sense,

institutions created to educate deaf people often teach them to act in ways that suit those who can hear.

## IDENTITY AND SOCIAL CHANGE

Are we free to become whomever we want, however we want? Of course not. Socialization is an active process in which we transform our identity as we take on new roles, but we do not always do so in conditions of our own choosing. It is important to remember that social circumstances powerfully influence identity. Premodern societies formed relatively cohesive groups in which most people could find solidarity and meaning in the family, the clan, and the community. Although such groups limited the range of personal experience, they conferred a strong sense of identity and purpose. Modernity expanded the range of personal choice and permitted a greater diversity of beliefs. Still, although modernization has emancipated people from the tyranny of tradition, it often leaves them without the comfort and security of heritage and roots. Modern societies, in general, offer more autonomy but less sense of purpose and fewer enduring social ties than did past societies. Not surprisingly, many people have difficulty establishing a stable and coherent sense of who they are in modern and postmodern societies.

The result is that some people shuttle from one identity to another, changing their lifestyle in search of an elusive "true self." They may join various social groups in search of purpose and belonging, and even experiment with various religions in the hope of finding a system of beliefs that "fits" them (Wuthnow, 1998). In sociological terms, the difficulty in developing a stable and coherent identity is rooted in the individual's social surroundings. The problem of answering the question "Who am I?" reflects not only a personal crisis but also the complexity and instability of modern and postmodern societies (Giddens, 1991).

Understanding the connection between personal development and social conditions calls for a view of human development that recognizes the constant possibility of change—even radical change. Some changes are minor or inconsequential, such as developing a new taste in clothes or exercising or "buffing up." However, there are also more profound life-altering experiences over which we may exercise relatively little control. A life-threatening illness, imprisonment, and severe depression that requires institutionalization are examples. In each instance, people must learn to adapt to fundamental alterations in daily routines. Although these changes may be temporary, they nevertheless strongly influence the individual's identity.

## RESOCIALIZATION

A significant change in how we live, in the kinds of people with whom we interact, or in the way we understand others or ourselves often requires **resocialization.** Resocialization involves deliberately trying to instill particular values and behaviours in people who are members of tightly knit groups, such as fraternities or sports teams, or of **total institutions.** In total institutions, such as the military, convents, prisons, boarding schools, and psychiatric hospitals, people are isolated from the rest of society for a set period. All aspects of a person's life are strictly regulated. Authorities impose regimented routines on inmates with the goal of resocializing them into a new identity. The total institution attempts to achieve this objective by completely controlling and manipulating the environment, thus depriving its inmates of contradictory forms of social experience. Total institutions, in sociologist Erving Goffman's words, are "the forcing houses for changing persons; each is a natural experiment in what can be done to the self" (Goffman, 1961: 11–12).

People may at first join an organization willingly and then be subjected to resocialization against their will. For example, people who have joined religious cults have often found that cult leaders exercise a powerful hold over their everyday lives. Many followers develop blind obedience to their leaders, while others wanting to depart may be prevented from doing so, either by emotional pressure or in some cases by force. For most followers, however, the mental transformation they undergo suffices to keep them in the group (Beckford, 1985).

Resocialization in total institutions is a two-part process. First, the staff attempts to strip away the new inmate's established identity. This is accompanied by a series of experiences that include humiliations, degradations, and "mortification rituals," which may include physical pain. Second, efforts are made to reconstitute the inmate's sense of self by imposing a new identity and a new way of life on him or her. In a childlike condition of heightened ambiguity and stress created by degradation and humiliation, the person is ripe for conversion to the expectations of the more powerful group. The desire for security and acceptance often leads to imitation or adoption of the behaviour of authority figures (Light, 1980). The resocialized

person often undergoes a symbolic ritual death and rebirth, shedding the old identity and taking on a new one.

A particularly shameful example of how total institutions function is the experience of Canadian Aboriginal peoples in residential schools. The residential school system started in Canada in the late nineteenth century and continued until the 1960s. At their height, 80 such schools operated across the country, with a peak enrolment in 1953 of more than 11 000 students. The students were often removed involuntarily from their homes. The schools were located in isolated areas, which typically did not allow for any contact with their families or communities. The children were subjected to strict discipline and intensive surveillance. They were punished for speaking their own languages and practising their cultural traditions. Many were physically and sexually abused (Kirmayer, Simpson, and Cargo, 2003). Aboriginal communities continue to struggle today with the legacy of these experiences in the form of high rates of substance abuse, suicide, depression, and other mental health problems.

Much less dramatic but often anxiety-provoking resocialization occurs outside total institutions when newcomers are inducted into professions, such as law, the ministry, and medicine. The transformative experience of medical students en route to becoming doctors is a case in point. Professionalization involves the moral and symbolic transformation of a layperson into an individual who can assume the special role and status claimed by a professional (Haas and Shaffir, 1987). The would-be professional must undergo public initiations involving testing and ritual ordeal before being elevated to the special status and role afforded by the profession (see Box 3.7).

A classroom in a residential school
SOURCE: Library and Archives Canada.

| BOX 3.7 | THE CLOAK OF COMPETENCE |

A good example of socialization into a professional role is provided in research that Haas and Shaffir (1977) conducted on medical students at McMaster University. Haas and Shaffir found that medical students feel pressured to act as if they are in total command of what they are doing. They realize that the extent of their medical knowledge can easily be called into question by fellow students, tutors, interns, residents, faculty, and even patients. To reduce the possibility of embarrassment and humiliation, which at this stage in their medical career is easily their fate, students attempt to reduce the unpredictability of their situation by manipulating an impression of themselves as enthusiastic, interested, and eager to learn. At the same time, students seize opportunities that allow them to impress others.

The general strategy that students adopt is to mask their uncertainty and anxiety with an image of self-confidence. Image making becomes recognized as being as important as technical competence. As one student remarks: "We have to be good actors, put across the image of self-confidence, that you know it all." Referring to the importance of creating the right impression, another student said,

Dr. Jones, who was my adviser or boss for medicine, he always came and did rounds on Wednesday mornings. Well, he didn't have very many patients on the service, but we always knew that his interest was in endocrinology, and ... if he had an endocrine patient ... we knew ... that he was going to pick that endocrine patient to talk about. And so, of course, ... any dummy can read up Tuesday night like hell on the new American Diabetic Association standards for diabetes or hyperglycemia ... and you can handle general medicine. So the next day you seem fairly knowledgeable.... That afternoon you forget about it because you figure Thursday morning hematology people make their rounds and, of course, you have to read up on hematology.

Students learn that to be a good student-physician is either to be or appear to be competent. They observe that others react to their role-playing. A student describes the self-fulfilling nature of this process when he says,

To be a good GP you've got to be a good actor, you've got to respond to a situation. You have to be quick, pick up the dynamics of what is going on at the time and try to make the person leave the office thinking that you know something. And a lot of people, the way they handle that is by letting the patient know that they know it all, and only letting out a little bit at a time, and as little as possible. I think that they eventually reach a plateau where they start thinking themselves they are really great and they know it all, because they have these people who are worshipping at their feet.

SOURCE: From Hass, Jack and William Shaffir, "The Professionalization of Medical Students: Developing Competence and a Clock of Competence," *Symbolic Interaction 1* (Nov. 1977). Reprinted by permission of John Wiley and Sons.

The image of society Goffman (1961) presents in his research on total institutions is one in which large, impersonal institutions are gaining more and more control over people—over their actions, experience of the world, and sense of self. Resistance is possible in Goffman's view, and it is often successful, but only in the small events of everyday life, such as forming personal relationships with others or exchanging gifts and services. Yet today, with the advent of new forms of communication and technology, we find that new forms of autonomy and new sources of freedom and creativity have also emerged. Active, malleable, and innovative, human beings are not content to accept the world as they find it. They look for ways to transform the world and adapt it to their social needs and personal desires. Nothing better exemplifies this creative aspect of social life than the process of socialization.

## SUMMARY

1. Socialization is an active process through which human beings become members of society, develop a sense of self, and learn to participate in social relationships with others. Through socialization we acquire knowledge, skills, and motivations for participation in society.

2. Each of us is born with a set of human potentials. Nature and nurture interact in contributing to human development.

3. Socialization is lifelong, typically involving relationships with family, school, peer groups, mass media, and occupational groups. Ours is an

age-graded society as well, and early childhood, adolescence, adulthood, and old age or retirement are significant stages; different roles and responsibilities are associated with each stage.

4. Because of the importance of socialization, many scholars have focused on examining it as an active, interactional process. Charles Horton Cooley was noteworthy for his concept of the "looking-glass self," which stressed that we view ourselves as we think others view us. George Herbert Mead emphasized how people assume roles by imagining themselves in the roles of others. Paul Willis, looking at the ways in which young people do not merely accept the world around them but transform it into a symbolic expression of their particular identity and their meaningful culture, has shown the intimate links connecting the acting individual and the broader social context.

5. Gender socialization is the learning of masculine and feminine behaviour and roles. From birth, and in every area of social life, the socialization of the sexes in terms of content and expectations makes the socially constructed gender role more significant than the biological role of male or female. Assumptions about appropriate male and female attributes limit the range of acceptable behaviour and options for both sexes.

6. The most important agent of socialization is the family. Initial warmth and nurturing are essential to healthy development. The self-concept formed during childhood has lasting consequences.

7. The central function of schools in industrial society is the teaching of skills and knowledge, but they also transmit society's central cultural values and ideologies. Schools expose children to situations in which the same rules, regulations, and authority patterns apply to everyone.

8. Peer groups provide young people with a looking glass unclouded by love or duty, and an opportunity to learn roles and values that adults do not teach.

9. The traditional mass media are impersonal and large-scale socializers. New forms of media are more interactive and allow people to play with and try out different identities.

10. During adulthood, individuals are socialized as they get jobs, marry, divorce, raise children, retire, and prepare for death. These many roles involve new and different relationships with others and guidelines for behaviour.

11. Sometimes there are abrupt changes in our self-concept, and we must learn new role identities and negotiate a new self-image. Resocialization occurs when we abandon or are forced to abandon our way of life and self-concept for a radically different one. This is most efficiently done in total institutions—for example, jails, psychiatric hospitals, and boot camps—or in religious and political conversions.

## QUESTIONS TO CONSIDER

1. Consider the significant others in your life. Have they always been important to you? How have they shaped and influenced your sense of self?

2. Goffman's approach implies that "all the world's a stage" and all of us are merely "players." Do you agree with Goffman? Cite examples of impression management that you rely on and encounter in your life.

3. Prisons and psychiatric hospitals are socialization institutions organized to change, test, or "correct" people. How effective are these institutions and why are they not more successful in meeting their goals?

4. Think of any job you have had and consider the socialization that was required. Distinguish the formal and informal components of the socialization process.

5. What, if any, are the possible effects on personal identity of the use of the Internet? Could the consequences be greater separation and alienation from reality, others, and ourselves, or might the outcome for the user be a heightened sense of belonging, integration, and shared understanding? Are both extremes possible?

## GLOSSARY

**Adult socialization** (p. 60) is the process by which adults take on new statuses and acquire new and different social identities.

**Ageism** (p. 61) refers to discriminatory practices based on age.

**Agents of socialization** (p. 62) are the individuals, groups, and institutions that impart, and from which

we acquire, the range of information required to interact effectively and participate in society.

**Anticipatory socialization** (p. 60) involves beginning to take on the norms and behaviours of a role you aspire to but do not yet occupy.

In the **game stage** (p. 54) of development, children have developed a generalized impression of the behaviour people expect as well as awareness of their own importance to the group and vice-versa. This is the third and final developmental stage described by Mead.

**Gender socialization** (p. 55) is the process by which individuals learn to become feminine and masculine according to expectations current in their society.

The **generalized other** (p. 55) is a conception of how people in general will respond in a situation. It is internalized.

The **hidden curriculum** (p. 64) consists of informal teaching that helps ensure students' integration into society.

The **I** (p. 55) is the subjective or active part of the self, according to Mead.

In the **imitative stage** (p. 54) of development, children two years old and under do not interact effectively with others because they cannot take the role of the other. They merely imitate the behaviour of others. This is the first developmental stage described by Mead.

**Instincts** (p. 52) are inborn patterns of behaviour that are often responses to specific stimuli.

The idea of the **looking-glass self** (p. 54) suggests that the gestures and reactions of others are a mirror in which we see ourselves.

The **me** (p. 55) is the objective element of the self, according to Mead.

A **peer group** (p. 65) comprises individuals who are usually of the same age and enjoy approximately equal status.

In the **play stage** (p. 54), children begin to adopt the roles of significant others—a parent, a sports celebrity, a storybook hero—and their play shifts from imitative to imaginative. This is the second developmental stage described by Mead.

A **primary group** (p. 54) is a small group (especially the family) that is characterized by intimate, face-to-face association and cooperation.

**Primary socialization** (p. 52) is the crucial learning process that occurs in childhood and makes us members of society.

**Resocialization** (p. 69) is the deliberate attempt to correct or instill particular values and behaviours in an individual or group.

**Secondary socialization** (p. 52) is learning that occurs after people have undergone primary socialization.

The **self** (p. 51), a sense of individual identity, allows us to understand ourselves and differentiate ourselves from others.

**Significant others** (p. 54) are people, such as parents, who are of central importance in the development of the self.

**Socialization** (p. 51) is the social process whereby people undergo development by interacting with the people around them.

**Status** (p. 55) refers to the culturally and socially defined position a person occupies in an interaction.

**Taking the role of the other** (p. 54) involves anticipating in advance how others will see and react to you. It is an essential skill that children must develop to be effective members of society.

**Total institutions** (p. 69) are settings in which people are isolated from the rest of society for a set period and in which all aspects of a person's life are regulated under one authority.

## SUGGESTED READING

Adler, Patricia A., and Peter Adler. (1998). *Peer Power: Preadolescent Culture and Identity.* New Brunswick, NJ: Rutgers University Press. Based on eight years of observation research, this is a first-rate sociological study of the role of peer groups in preadolescent socialization.

Becker, Howard S., Blanche Geer, Everett C. Hughes, and Anselm L. Strauss. (1961). *Boys in White: Student Culture in Medical School.* Chicago: University of Chicago Press. This is the classic study of professional socialization. It examines how medical students negotiate their transition into the medical profession and are transformed into physicians.

Ebaugh, Helen Rose Fuchs. (1988). *Becoming an Ex: The Process of Role Exit.* Chicago: University of Chicago Press. This excellent study examines the process whereby people learn to disengage themselves from previous roles and claims to identity.

Goffman, Erving. (1961). *Asylums: Essays on the Social Situation of Mental Patients and Other Inmates.* Garden City, NY: Anchor Books. This account analyzes life in total institutions and describes what such institutions make of inmates and how the latter organize their life inside them.

All activities in life—including scavenging in garbage bins and living "on the streets"—are social in nature. Here, Lars Eighner recalls his experiences as a Dumpster diver while he was living under a shower curtain in a stand of bamboo in a public park. Eighner became homeless when he was evicted from his "shack" after being unemployed for about a year.

*I began Dumpster diving [scavenging in a large garbage bin] about a year before I became homeless . . . The area I frequent is inhabited by many affluent college students. I am not here by chance; the Dumpsters in this area are very rich. Students throw out many good things, including food. In particular they tend to throw everything out when they move at the end of a semester, before and after breaks, and around midterm, when many of them despair of college. So I find it advantageous to keep an eye on the academic calendar. I learned to scavenge gradually, on my own. Since then I have initiated several companions into the trade. I have learned that there is a predictable series of stages a person goes through in learning to scavenge. At first the new scavenger is filled with disgust and self-loathing. He is ashamed of being seen and may lurk around, trying to duck behind things, or he may dive at night . . . That stage passes with experience. The scavenger finds a pair of running shoes that fit and look and smell brand-new . . . He begins to understand: People throw away perfectly good stuff, a lot of perfectly good stuff. At this stage, Dumpster shyness begins to dissipate. The diver, after all, has the last laugh. He is finding all manner of good*

© Bob Collins/The Image Works

All activities in life—including panhandling and living on the streets—are social. What types of interaction are normalized or made unusual and why?

*things that are his for the taking. Those who disparage his profession are the fools, not he.* (1993: 111–119)

Eighner's "diving" activities reflect a specific pattern of social behaviour. Homeless persons and domiciled persons (those with homes) live in social worlds that have predictable patterns of social interaction. **Social interaction** is the process by which people act toward or respond to other people and is the foundation for all relationships and groups in society. In this chapter, we will look at the relationship between social structure and social interaction. Homelessness is used as an example of how social problems occur and may be perpetuated within social structures and patterns of interaction.

**Social structure** is the stable pattern of social relationships that exist within a particular group or society. This structure is essential for the survival of society and for the well-being of individuals because it provides a social web of familial support and social relationships that connects each of us to the larger society. Many homeless people have lost this vital linkage. As a result, they often experience a loss of personal dignity and sense of moral worth because of their "homeless" condition (Neal, 2004). Although there have always been homeless people, there has been a significant increase in the number of Canadians without homes. The homeless category now includes people who have never before had to depend on social assistance for food, clothing, and a roof over their head. Before reading on, take the quiz on homelessness in Box 5.1 on page 119.

**Critical Thinking Questions**

1. Sociologists suggest that all activities are social in nature. Do you agree?

2. Identify predictable patterns of social interaction with a homeless person. How do you interact with a homeless person you may encounter in your day-to-day life?

3. It was suggested above that homeless persons may not have stable familial and social relationships that are vital to well-being. What are the stable familial and social relationships in your life?

| CHAPTER FOCUS QUESTION | How is homelessness related to the social structure of a society? |

## LEARNING OBJECTIVES
### AFTER READING THIS CHAPTER, YOU SHOULD BE ABLE TO

**LO-1** Identify the key components of social structure.

**LO-2** Compare and contrast functionalist and conflict perspectives on social institutions.

**LO-3** Explain how societies maintain stability in times of social change.

**LO-4** Define and distinguish between *Gemeinschaft* and *Gesellschaft* societies.

**LO-5** Understand Erving Goffman's dramaturgical perspective and the concepts of impression management, and front stage/back stage behaviours.

# SOCIAL STRUCTURE: THE MACROLEVEL PERSPECTIVE

**social interaction**
The process by which people act toward or respond to other people.

**social structure** The stable pattern of social relationships that exist within a particular group or society.

**social marginality**
The state of being part insider and part outsider in the social structure.

Why do we need to know about social structure? Social structure provides the framework within which we interact with others. This framework is an orderly, fixed arrangement of parts that together comprise the whole group or society (see Figure 5.1). As defined in Chapter 1, a *society* is a large social grouping that shares the same geographical territory and is subject to the same political authority and dominant cultural expectations. At the macrolevel, the social structure of a society has several essential elements: social institutions, groups, statuses, roles, and norms.

Do social scientists agree about how social structure operates? No. Diverse theoretical approaches have different interpretations of how structure operates. For example, functional theorists emphasize that social structure creates order and predictability in a society (Parsons, 1951). Social structure is also important for human development: You and I develop a self-concept as each of us learns the attitudes, values, and behaviours of the people around us. When these attitudes and values are part of a predictable structure, it is easier for us to develop a positive self-concept.

By contrast, conflict theorists maintain that social structure helps determine social relations in a society and may be the source of inequality and injustice. For example, Karl Marx suggested that how economic production is organized is the most important structural aspect of society. In capitalistic societies, few people control the labour of many and the social structure helps create a system of domination and subordination that affects certain categories of people, including owners and workers, landlords and tenants, and rich celebrities and poor "nobodies."

Whether we look at social structure through the lens of functionalist or conflict theories, this structure creates boundaries that define persons and groups as "insiders," "outsiders," or "marginals." **Social marginality** is the state of being part insider and part outsider in the social

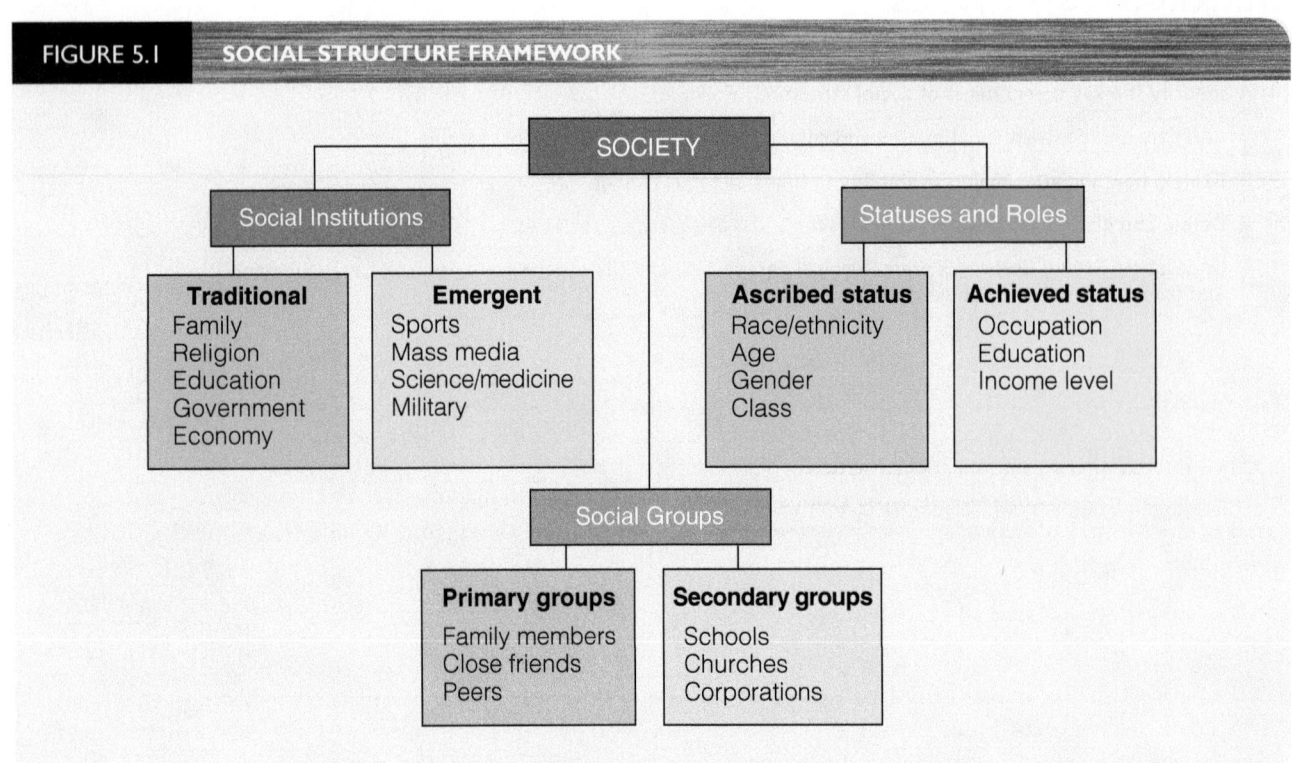

FIGURE 5.1    SOCIAL STRUCTURE FRAMEWORK

## BOX 5.1   SOCIOLOGY AND EVERYDAY LIFE

### How Much Do You Know About Homelessness?

| True | False | |
|------|-------|---|
| T | F | 1. Most homeless people choose to be homeless. |
| T | F | 2. The number of homeless persons in Canada has gradually declined over the past 30 years. |
| T | F | 3. Most homeless people are mentally ill. |
| T | F | 4. The number of homeless adolescents has increased in the past decade. |
| T | F | 5. One out of every four homeless people is a child. |

For answers to the quiz about homelessness, go to **www.nelson.com/sociologyinourtimes6e.**

structure. Sociologist Robert Park (1928) coined this term to refer to persons (such as immigrants) who simultaneously share the life and traditions of two distinct groups. Social marginality is an important concern for people because it often results in stigmatization. A **stigma** is any physical or social attribute or sign that so devalues a person's social identity that it disqualifies that person from full social acceptance (Goffman, 1963b). A convicted criminal wearing a prison uniform is an example of a person who has been stigmatized; the uniform says that the person has done something wrong and should not be allowed unsupervised outside the prison walls. The stigmatization of homelessness is discussed later in this chapter.

Why is social structure important to you? Social structure gives us the ability to interpret the social situations we encounter. For example, we expect our families to care for us, our schools to educate us, and our police to protect us. When our circumstances change dramatically, most of us feel an acute sense of anxiety because we do not know what to expect or what is expected of us. Consider, for instance, why newly homeless individuals may feel disoriented when they do not know how to function in their new situation. These persons are likely to ask questions such as "How will I survive on the streets?" "Where do I go to get help?" "Should I stay at a shelter?" and "Where can I get a job?" Social structure helps people make sense out of their social setting even when they find themselves on the streets.

> **stigma** According to Erving Goffman, any physical or social attribute or sign that so devalues a person's social identity that it disqualifies that person from full social acceptance.

## COMPONENTS OF SOCIAL STRUCTURE   LO-1

What is included in the social structure of a society? The social structure of a society includes its social positions, the relationships among those positions, and the kinds of resources attached to each of the positions. Social structure also includes all of the groups that make up society and the relationships among those groups (Smelser, 1988). Let's start our study of the components of social structure by examining the social positions that are closest to us—the individual.

### Status

No doubt you have heard the word *status* for many years. Sometimes we describe a person as "high status" or "low status," but sociologically speaking, what does the term really mean? A **status** is a socially defined position in a group or society characterized by certain expectations,

> **status** A socially defined position in a group or society characterized by certain expectations, rights, and duties.

rights, and duties. Statuses exist independently of the specific people occupying them (Linton, 1936); the statuses of professional athlete, rock musician, professor, university student, and homeless person all exist exclusive of the specific individuals who occupy these social positions. For example, although thousands of new students arrive on university campuses each year to occupy the status of first-year student, the status of university student and the expectations attached to that position have remained relatively unchanged.

As we previously mentioned, the term *status* does *not* refer to high-level positions only. Sociologists use it to refer to all socially defined positions—high rank and low rank. For example, both the position of director of Health Canada in Ottawa and that of a homeless person who is paid about five dollars a week (plus bed and board) to clean up the dining room at a homeless shelter are social statuses.

Take a moment to answer this question: Who am I? To determine who you are, you must think about your social identity, which is derived from the statuses you occupy and is based on your status set. A **status set** is made up of all the statuses that a person occupies at a given time. For example, Marie may be a psychologist, a professor, a wife, a mother, a Roman Catholic, a school volunteer, an Alberta resident, and a French Canadian. All of these socially defined positions constitute her status set.

**ASCRIBED AND ACHIEVED STATUS** Statuses are distinguished by the manner in which we acquire them. An **ascribed status** is a social position conferred on a person at birth or received involuntarily later in life, based on attributes over which the individual has little or no control, such as ethnicity, age, and gender. Marie, for example, is a female born to French Canadian parents; she was assigned these statuses at birth. An **achieved status** is a social position a person assumes voluntarily as a result of personal choice, merit, or direct effort. Achieved statuses (such as occupation, education, and income) are thought to be gained as a result of personal ability or successful competition. Most occupational positions in modern societies are achieved statuses. For instance, Marie voluntarily assumed the statuses of psychologist, professor, wife, mother, and school volunteer. However, not all achieved statuses are positions most people would want to attain: Being a criminal, a drug addict, or a homeless person, for example, is a negative achieved status.

Ascribed statuses have a significant influence on the achieved statuses we occupy. Ethnicity, gender, and age affect each person's opportunity to acquire certain achieved statuses. Those who are privileged by their positive ascribed statuses are more likely to achieve the more prestigious positions in a society. Those who are disadvantaged by their ascribed statuses may more easily acquire negative achieved statuses.

**MASTER STATUS** If we occupy many different statuses, how can we determine which is the most important? Sociologist Everett Hughes has stated that societies resolve this ambiguity by determining master statuses. A **master status** is the most important status a person occupies; it dominates all the individual's other statuses and is the overriding ingredient in determining a person's general social position (Hughes, 1945). Being poor or rich is a master status that influences many other areas of life, including health, education, and life opportunities. Historically, the most common master statuses for women have related to positions in the family, such as daughter, wife, and mother. For men, occupation has usually been the most important status, although occupation is increasingly a master status for many women as well. "What do you do?" is one of the first questions many people ask when first meeting someone. Occupation provides important clues to a person's educational level, income, and family background. An individual's ethnicity may also constitute a master status in a society in which dominant group members single out members of other groups as "inferior" on the basis of real or alleged physical, cultural, or nationality characteristics (see Feagin and Feagin, 2003).

**status set** A term used to describe all the statuses that a person occupies at a given time.

**ascribed status** A social position conferred on a person at birth or received involuntarily later in life.

**achieved status** A social position a person assumes voluntarily as a result of personal choice, merit, or direct effort.

**master status** A term used to describe the most important status a person occupies.

Master statuses confer high or low levels of personal worth and dignity on people. These are not characteristics that we inherently possess; they are derived from the statuses we occupy. For someone who has no residence, being a homeless person readily becomes a master status regardless of the person's other attributes. Homelessness is a stigmatized master status; it confers disrepute on its occupant because domiciled people often believe a homeless person has a "character flaw." The circumstances under which someone becomes homeless determine the extent to which that person is stigmatized.

STATUS SYMBOLS When people are proud of a particular social status they occupy, they often choose to use visible means to let others know about their position. A **status symbol** is a material sign that informs others of a person's specific status. For example, just as wearing a wedding ring proclaims that a person is married, owning a Rolls-Royce announces that one has "made it." In North American society, people who have "made it" frequently want symbols to inform others of their accomplishments.

In the past, a person's status was primarily linked to his or her family background, education, occupation, and other sociological attributes. Today, some sociologists suggest that celebrity status has overtaken the more traditional status indicators.

Status symbols for the domiciled and the homeless may have different meanings. Among affluent persons, a full shopping cart in the grocery store and bags of merchandise from expensive department stores indicate a lofty financial position. By contrast, among the homeless, bulging shopping bags and overloaded grocery carts suggest a completely different status.

> **status symbol** A material sign that informs others of a person's specific status.

### TIME TO REVIEW

- Define ascribed status, achieved status, and master status.
- Is being unemployed an ascribed or achieved status?
- When does unemployment become a master status?

> **role** A set of behavioural expectations associated with a given status.

## Roles

A role is the dynamic aspect of a status. Whereas we *occupy* a status, we *play* a role (Linton, 1936). A **role** is a set of behavioural expectations associated with a given status. For example, a carpenter (employee) hired to remodel a kitchen is not expected to sit down uninvited and join the family (employer) for dinner.

**Role expectation** is a group's or society's definition of the way a specific role ought to be played. By contrast, **role performance** is how a person plays the role. Role performance does not always match role expectation. Some statuses have role expectations that are highly specific, such as that of surgeon or university professor. Other statuses, such as friend or significant other, have less structured expectations. The role expectations tied to the status of student are

> **role expectation** A group's or society's definition of the way a specific role ought to be played.

> **role performance** How a person plays a role.

more specific than those for being a friend. Role expectations are typically based on a range of acceptable behaviour rather than on strictly defined standards.

Our roles are relational (or complementary); that is, they are defined in the context of roles performed by others. We can play the role of student because someone else fulfills the role of professor. Conversely, to perform the role of professor, the teacher must have one or more students.

*Role ambiguity* occurs when the expectations associated with a role are unclear. For example, it is not always clear when the provider–dependant aspect of the parent–child relationship ends. Should it end at age 18 or 21? When a person is no longer in school? Different people will answer these questions differently depending on their experiences and socialization, as well as on the parents' financial capability and willingness to continue contributing to the welfare of their adult children.

**role conflict** A situation in which incompatible role demands are placed on a person by two or more statuses held at the same time.

**role strain** The strain experienced by a person when incompatible demands are built into a single status that the person occupies.

ROLE CONFLICT AND ROLE STRAIN    Most people occupy a number of statuses, each of which has numerous role expectations attached. For example, Charles is a student who attends morning classes at the university and he is an employee at a fast-food restaurant where he works from 3 p.m. to 10 p.m. He is also Stephanie's boyfriend, and she would like to see him more often. On December 7, Charles has a final exam at 7 p.m., when he is supposed to be working. Meanwhile, Stephanie is pressuring him to take her to a movie. To top it off, his mother calls, asking him to fly home because his father is going to have emergency surgery. How can Charles be in all of these places at once? Such experiences of role conflict can be overwhelming.

**Role conflict** occurs when incompatible role demands are placed on a person by two or more statuses held at the same time. When role conflict occurs, we may feel pulled in different directions. To deal with this problem, we may prioritize our roles and first complete the one we consider to be most important. Or we may compartmentalize our lives and "insulate" our various roles (Merton, 1968); that is, we may perform the activities linked to one role for part of the day and then engage in the activities associated with another role in some other time period or elsewhere. For example, under routine circumstances, Charles would fulfill his student role for part of the day and his employee role for another part of the day. In his current situation, however, he is unable to compartmentalize his roles.

What are the competing demands of working parents in contemporary societies? What sociological term best describes this situation?

Whereas role conflict occurs between two or more statuses (such as being homeless and being a temporary employee of a social services agency), role strain takes place within one status. **Role strain** occurs when incompatible demands are built into a single status that a person occupies (Goode, 1960). For example, parents may experience role strain because of the demands of managing their time, unclear expectations, unequal division of unpaid work in the home, and lack of emotional support from the other parent. The concepts of role expectation, role performance, role conflict, and role strain are illustrated in Figure 5.2.

Parents often experience role conflict when they are trying to balance making a living and having a successful career with fulfilling their role as a good parent.

## FIGURE 5.2    ROLE EXPECTATION, PERFORMANCE, CONFLICT, AND STRAIN

**The Role of "Student"**

**Role Expectation:** a group's or society's definition of the way a specific role *ought* to be played.

**Role Performance:** how a person does play a role.

**Role Conflict:** what occurs when incompatible demands are put on a person by two or more statuses held at the same time.

**Role Strain:** what occurs when incompatible demands are built into a single status that the person holds.

When playing the role of "student," do you sometimes personally encounter these concepts?

Individuals frequently distance themselves from a role they find extremely stressful or otherwise problematic. *Role distancing* occurs when people consciously foster the impression of a lack of commitment or attachment to a particular role and merely go through the motions of role performance (Goffman, 1961b). People use distancing techniques when they do not want others to take them as the "self" implied in a particular role, especially if they think the role is "beneath them." While Charles is working in the fast-food restaurant, for example, he does not want people to think of him as a "loser in a dead-end job." He wants them to view him as a university student who is working there just to "pick up a few bucks" until he graduates. When customers from the university come in, Charles talks to them about what courses they are taking, what they are majoring in, and what professors they have. He does not discuss whether the bacon cheeseburger is better than the chili burger. When Charles is really involved in role distancing, he tells his friends that he "works there but wouldn't eat there." Role distancing is most likely to occur when people find themselves in roles in which the social identities implied are inconsistent with how they think of themselves or how they want to be viewed by others.

**ROLE EXIT** **Role exit** occurs when people disengage from social roles that have been central to their self-identity (Ebaugh, 1988). Sociologist Helen Rose Fuchs Ebaugh studied this

**role exit** A situation in which people disengage from social roles that have been central to their self-identity.

*Los Angeles Times* columnist Steve Lopez met a homeless man, Nathaniel Ayers (above), and learned that he had been a promising musician studying at the Juilliard School who had dropped out because of his struggle with mental illness. In his 2008 book, *The Soloist*, Lopez chronicles the relationship that he developed with Ayers and how he eventually helped get Ayers off the street and treated for his schizophrenia. This story is an example of role exit, and you can see it in the movie version of *The Soloist*, released in 2009.

process by interviewing ex-convicts, ex-nuns, retirees, divorced men and women, and others who had exited voluntarily from significant social roles. According to Ebaugh, role exit occurs in four stages. The first stage is doubt, in which people experience frustration or burnout when they reflect on their existing roles. The second stage involves a search for alternatives; here, people may take a leave of absence from their work or temporarily separate from their marriage partner. The third stage is the turning point at which people realize that they must take some final action, such as quitting their job or getting a divorce. The fourth and final stage involves the creation of a new identity.

Exiting the "homeless" role is often very difficult. The longer a person remains on the streets, the more difficult it becomes to exit this role. Personal resources diminish over time. Personal possessions are often stolen, lost, sold, or pawned. Work experience and skills become outdated, and physical disabilities that prevent individuals from working are likely to develop on the streets. As 21-year-old Chris describes, breaking the ties with their street families and communities was often the most challenging aspect to their role exit:

> I found my biggest one [obstacle] was leaving the crowd that I was with, like my friends, the situation with my friends, 'cause they are all like, "No, don't go, stay down here and hang with us, go do that," and that was probably my biggest crutch, was getting away from my friends because I'd been friends with them my whole life and for me to just push them away and say, "No, I'm getting away from this, I'm getting out of this." It was a big step for me (Karabanow, 2008:783).

## Groups

Groups are another important component of social structure. To sociologists, a **social group** consists of two or more people who interact frequently and share a common identity and a feeling of interdependence. Throughout our lives, most of us participate in groups, from our families and childhood friends, to our university classes, to our work and community organizations, and even to society.

Primary and secondary groups are the two basic types of social groups. A **primary group** is a small, less specialized group in which members engage in face-to-face, emotion-based interactions over an extended time. Typically, primary groups include our family, close friends, and school- or work-related peer groups. By contrast, a **secondary group** is a larger, more specialized group in which members engage in more impersonal, goal-oriented relationships for a limited time. Schools, churches, and corporations are examples of secondary groups. In secondary groups, people have few, if any, emotional ties to one another. Instead, they come together for some specific, practical purpose, such as getting a degree or a paycheque. Secondary groups are more specialized than primary ones; individuals relate to one another in terms of specific roles (such as professor and student) and more limited activities (such as course-related endeavours).

**social group** A group that consists of two or more people who interact frequently and share a common identity and a feeling of interdependence.

**primary group** A small, less specialized group in which members engage in face-to-face, emotion-based interactions over an extended time.

**secondary group** A larger, more specialized group in which the members engage in more impersonal, goal-oriented relationships for a limited time.

As discussed in Chapter 1, *social solidarity,* or cohesion, relates to a group's ability to maintain itself in the face of obstacles. Social solidarity exists when social bonds, attractions, or other forces hold members of a group in interaction over a period of time (Jary and Jary, 1991). For example, if a local church is destroyed by fire and congregation members still worship together in a makeshift setting, then they have a high degree of social solidarity.

Many of us build social networks from our personal friends in primary groups and our acquaintances in secondary groups. A **social network** is a series of social relationships that link an individual to others. Social networks work differently for men and women, for different ethnic groups, and for

For many years, capitalism has been dominated by powerful "old-boy" social networks.

members of different social classes. Research on homeless youth in Toronto and Vancouver revealed that informal social networks that the youth described as "street families" tended to form around issues of survival and support (Hagan and McCarthy, 1998). Individuals within these groups often assumed specialized roles that were defined in family terms, including references to street brothers and sisters, and even fathers and mothers.

A **formal organization** is a highly structured group formed for the purpose of completing certain tasks or achieving specific goals. Many of us spend most of our time in formal organizations, such as universities, corporations, or the government. Chapter 6 ("Groups and Organizations") analyzes the characteristics of bureaucratic organizations; however, at this point, we should note that these organizations are an important component of social structure in all industrialized societies. We expect such organizations to educate us, solve our social problems (such as crime and homelessness), and provide work opportunities.

**social network** A series of social relationships that link an individual to others.

**formal organization** A highly structured group formed for the purpose of completing certain tasks or achieving specific goals.

## LO-2 Social Institutions

At the macrolevel of all societies, certain basic activities routinely occur—children are born and socialized, goods and services are produced and distributed, order is preserved, and a sense of purpose is maintained (Aberle et al., 1950; Mack and Bradford, 1979). Social institutions are the means by which these basic needs are met. A **social institution** is a set of organized beliefs and rules that establish how a society will strive to meet its basic social needs. In the past, these needs have centred around five basic social institutions: the family, religion, education, the economy, and the government or politics. Today, mass media, sports, science and medicine, and the military are also considered social institutions.

**social institution** A set of organized beliefs and rules that establish how a society will attempt to meet its basic social needs.

*Difference*

What is the difference between a group and a social institution? A group is composed of specific, identifiable people; an institution is a standardized way of doing something. The concept of family helps distinguish between the two. When we talk about your family or my family, we are referring to a specific family. When we refer to the family as a social institution, we are talking about ideologies and standardized patterns of behaviour that organize family life. For example, the family as a social institution contains certain statuses organized into well-defined relationships, such as husband–wife, parent–child, brother–sister, and so forth. Specific families do not always conform to these ideologies and behaviour patterns.

Functional theorists emphasize that social institutions exist because they perform five essential tasks:

1. *Replacing members.* Societies and groups must have socially approved ways of replacing members who move away or die.
2. *Teaching new members.* People who are born into a society or move into it must learn the group's values and customs.
3. *Producing, distributing, and consuming goods and services.* All societies must provide and distribute goods and services for their members
4. *Preserving order.* Every group or society must preserve order within its boundaries and protect itself from attack by outsiders.
5. *Providing and maintaining a sense of purpose.* To motivate people to cooperate with one another, a sense of purpose is needed.

Although this list of functional prerequisites is shared by all societies, the institutions in each society perform these tasks in somewhat different ways depending on their specific cultural values and norms.

Conflict theorists agree with functionalists that social institutions are originally organized to meet basic social needs; however, they do not agree that social institutions work for the common good of everyone in society. For example, the homeless lack the power and resources to promote their own interests when they are opposed by dominant social groups. This problem for homeless people, especially children and youth, exists not only in Canada, but throughout the world (see Box 5.2 on page 128). From the conflict perspective, social institutions, such as the government, maintain the privileges of the wealthy and powerful while contributing to the powerlessness of others (see Domhoff, 2002).

## LO-3    STABILITY AND CHANGE IN SOCIETIES

Changes in social structure have a dramatic impact on individuals, groups, and societies. Social arrangements in contemporary societies have grown more complex with the introduction of new technology, changes in values and norms, and the rapidly shrinking "global village." How do societies maintain some degree of social solidarity in the face of such changes? Sociologists Émile Durkheim and Ferdinand Tönnies developed typologies to explain the processes of stability and change in the social structure of societies. A *typology* is a classification scheme containing two or more mutually exclusive categories that are used to compare different kinds of behaviour or types of societies.

### Durkheim: Mechanical and Organic Solidarity

Émile Durkheim (1933/1893) was concerned with this question: How do societies manage to hold together? Durkheim asserted that preindustrial societies were held together by strong traditions and by the members' shared moral beliefs and values. As societies industrialized and developed more specialized economic activities, social solidarity came to be rooted in the members' shared dependence on one another. From Durkheim's perspective, social solidarity derives from a society's social structure, which, in turn, is based on the society's division of labour. *Division of labour* refers to how the various tasks of a society are divided up and performed.

People in diverse societies (or in the same society at different points in time) divide their tasks somewhat differently, however, based on their own history, physical environment, and level of technological development.

To explain social change, Durkheim developed a typology that categorized societies as having either mechanical or organic solidarity. **Mechanical solidarity** refers to the social cohesion in preindustrial societies, in which there is minimal division of labour and people feel united by shared values and common social bonds. Durkheim used the term *mechanical solidarity* because he believed that people in such preindustrial societies feel a more or less automatic sense of belonging. Social interaction is characterized by face-to-face, intimate, primary-group relationships. Everyone is engaged in similar work, and little specialization is found in the division of labour.

**Organic solidarity** refers to the social cohesion found in industrial (and perhaps postindustrial) societies, in which people perform specialized tasks and feel united by their mutual dependence. Durkheim chose the term *organic solidarity* because he believed that individuals in industrial societies come to rely on one another in much the same way that the organs of the human body function interdependently. Social interaction is less personal, more status-oriented, and more focused on specific goals and objectives. People no longer rely on morality or shared values for social solidarity; instead, they are bound together by practical considerations.

> **mechanical solidarity**
> Émile Durkheim's term for the social cohesion that exists in preindustrial societies, in which there is a minimal division of labour and people feel united by shared values and common social bonds.

> **organic solidarity**
> Émile Durkheim's term for the social cohesion that exists in industrial (and perhaps postindustrial) societies, in which people perform specialized tasks and feel united by their mutual dependence.

## LO-4 Tönnies: *Gemeinschaft* and *Gesellschaft*

Sociologist Ferdinand Tönnies (1855–1936) used the terms *Gemeinschaft* and *Gesellschaft* to characterize the degree of social solidarity and social control found in societies. He was especially concerned about what happens to social solidarity in a society when a "loss of community" occurs.

The *Gemeinschaft* (guh-MINE-shoft) is a traditional society in which social relationships are based on personal bonds of friendship and kinship and on intergenerational stability. These relationships are based on ascribed rather than achieved status. In such societies, people have a commitment to the entire group and feel a sense of togetherness. Tönnies used the German term *Gemeinschaft* because it means commune or community; social solidarity and social control are maintained by the community. Members have a strong sense of belonging, but they also have limited privacy.

By contrast, the *Gesellschaft* (guh-ZELL-shoft) is a large, urban society in which social bonds are based on impersonal and specialized relationships, with little long-term commitment to the group or consensus on values. In such societies, most people are "strangers" who perceive that they have little in common with most other people. Consequently, self-interest dominates and little consensus exists regarding values. Tönnies selected the German term *Gesellschaft* because it means association; relationships are based on achieved statuses, and interactions among people are both rational and calculated.

> *Gemeinschaft*
> (guh-MINE-shoft) A traditional society in which social relationships are based on personal bonds of friendship and kinship and on intergenerational stability.

> *Gesellschaft*
> (guh-ZELL-shoft) A large, urban society in which social bonds are based on impersonal and specialized relationships, with little long-term commitment to the group or consensus on values.

## Social Structure and Homelessness

In *Gesellschaft* societies, such as Canada, a prevailing core value is that people should be able to take care of themselves. Thus, many people view the homeless as "throwaways"— as beyond help or as having already had enough done for them by society. Some argue that the homeless made their own bad decisions, which led them into alcoholism or drug addiction, and should be held responsible for the consequences of their actions. In this

BOX 5.2

# POINT/COUNTERPOINT

## Homeless Rights versus Public Space

I had a bit of a disturbing experience yesterday as I was running errands downtown. First, I was glad to see the south Queen sidewalk east of University open. (Months of construction on the new opera house had blocked it off.) As I continued walking eastward past the acclaimed new structure (where I have enjoyed a performance or two), I wondered why the sidewalk was so narrow. It seems this stretch of Queen should feel a bit grander. When I reached the corner of Queen and Bay, I saw some police officers and city workers "taking action on sidewalk clearance." They were clearing a homeless person's worldly belongings off the sidewalk. Using shovels. And a pickup truck . . .

I think what I saw yesterday is unacceptable. Sure, the situation is complicated. Yes, there are a lot of stakeholders and stories to appreciate. But it's unfairness I want to see shovelled out of public space. Not people. Not blankets. Not kindness. And I hope I'm not alone. (Sandals, 2007)

"Protection of public space" has become an issue in many cities. Record numbers of homeless individuals and families seek refuge on the streets and in public parks because they have nowhere else to go. However, this seemingly individualistic problem is actually linked to larger social concerns, including long-term unemployment, lack of education and affordable housing, and cutbacks in government and social service budgets. The problem of homelessness also raises significant social policy issues, including the extent to which cities can make it illegal for people to remain for extended periods of time in public spaces.

Should homeless persons be allowed to sleep on sidewalks, in parks, and in other public areas? This issue has been the source of controversy. As cities have sought to improve their downtown areas and public spaces, they have taken measures to enforce city ordinances controlling loitering (standing around or sleeping in public spaces), "aggressive panhandling," and disorderly conduct. Advocates for the homeless and civil liberties groups have filed lawsuits claiming that the rights of the homeless are being violated by the enforcement of these laws. The lawsuits assert that the homeless have a right to sleep in parks because no affordable housing is available for them. Advocates also argue that panhandling is a legitimate livelihood for some of the homeless and is protected speech under the *Charter of Rights and Freedoms*. In addition, they accuse public and law enforcement officials of seeking to punish the

homeless on the basis of their "status." According to ethics professor Arthur Schafer, punishing panhandlers is the wrong way to go about the issue:

> Do we, as a society, really want to rely upon still more laws to deal with the serious social problems of poverty, homelessness, and panhandling? Are we convinced that legal coercion, with its use of physical force backed by weapons, lawyers, courts and jails, will be effective in addressing what is essentially a social problem? Are we prepared to violate fundamental rights to freedom of expression and add further burdens to the least advantaged members of our society? (1998:1)

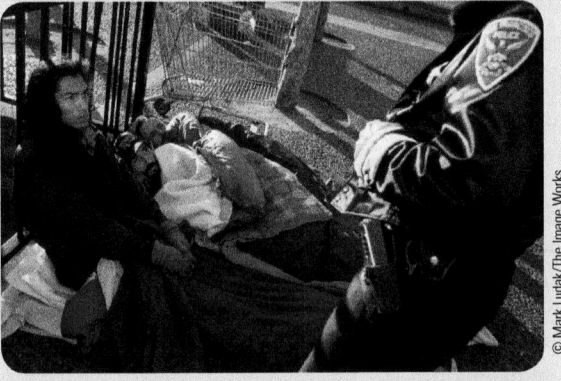

The "homeless problem" is not a new one for city governments. Of the limited public funding that is designated for the homeless, most has been spent on shelters that are frequently overcrowded and otherwise inadequate. Officials in some cities have given homeless people a one-way ticket to another city. Still others have routinely run them out of public spaces.

What responsibility does society have to the homeless? Are laws restricting the hours that public areas or parks are open to the public unfair to homeless persons? Some critics have argued that if the homeless and their advocates win these lawsuits, what they have won (at best) is the right for the homeless to live on the street under extremely adverse conditions. Others have disputed this assertion and note that if society does not make affordable housing and job opportunities available, the least it can do is stop harassing homeless people who are getting by as best they can.

© Mark Ludak/The Image Works

Contrary to a popular myth that most homeless people are single drifters, an increasing number of families are now homeless.

What do you think? What rights are involved? Whose rights should prevail?

© Bruce Ayres/Stone/Getty Images

*Sources:* Based on Kaufman, 1996; Sandals, 2007; Wood, 2002.

sense, homeless people serve as a visible example to others to "follow the rules" lest they experience a similar fate.

Alternative explanations for homelessness in *Gesellschaft* societies have been suggested. Elliot Liebow (1993) notes that homelessness is rooted in poverty; homeless people overwhelmingly are poor people who come from poor families. Homelessness is a "social class phenomenon, the direct result of a steady, across-the-board lowering of the standard of living of the working class and lower class" (1993:224). The problem is exacerbated by a lack of jobs and adequate housing. Clearly, there is no simple answer to the question about what should be done to help the homeless. Nor, as discussed in Box 5.2, is there any consensus on what legal rights the homeless have in public areas. The answers we derive as a society and as individuals are often based on our social construction of this reality of life.

## SOCIAL INTERACTION: THE MICROLEVEL PERSPECTIVE

So far in this chapter, we have focused on society and social structure from a macrolevel perspective. We have seen how the structure of society affects the statuses we occupy, the roles we play, and the groups and organizations to which we belong. Functionalist and conflict perspectives provide a macrosociological overview because they concentrate on large-scale events and broad social features. By contrast, the symbolic interactionist perspective takes a microsociological approach, asking how social institutions affect our daily lives. We will now look at society from the microlevel perspective, which focuses on social interaction among individuals, especially face-to-face encounters.

### Social Interaction and Meaning

When you are with other people, do you often wonder what they think of you? If so, you are not alone! Because most of us are concerned about the meanings others ascribe to our behaviour, we try to interpret their words and actions so that we can plan how we will react (Blumer, 1969).

These people are displaying what Goffman referred to as "civil inattention."

We know that others have expectations of us. We also have certain expectations about them. For example, if we enter an elevator that has only one other person in it, we do not expect that individual to confront us and stare into our eyes. As a matter of fact, we would be quite upset if the person did so.

Social interaction within a given society has certain shared meanings across situations. For instance, our reaction would be the same regardless of *which* elevator we rode in *which* building. Sociologist Erving Goffman (1963b) described these shared meanings in his observations about two pedestrians approaching each other on a public sidewalk. He noted that each will tend to look at the other just long enough to acknowledge the other's presence. By the time they are about two and a half metres away from each other, both individuals will tend to look downward. Goffman referred to this behaviour as *civil inattention*—the ways in which an individual shows awareness that others are present without making them the object of particular attention. The fact that people engage in civil inattention demonstrates that interaction does have a pattern, or *interaction order,* that regulates the form and processes (but not the content) of social interaction.

Does everyone interpret social interaction rituals in the same way? No. Ethnicity, gender, and social class play a part in the meanings we give to our interactions with others, including chance encounters on elevators or the street. Our perceptions about the meaning of a situation vary widely based on the statuses we occupy and our unique personal experiences.

Social encounters have different meanings for men and women, and for individuals from different social classes and ethnic groups. For example, sociologist Carol Brooks Gardner (1989) found that women frequently do not perceive street encounters to be "routine" rituals. They fear for their personal safety and try to avoid comments and propositions that are sexual in nature when they walk down the street. In another example, members of the dominant classes regard the poor, unemployed, and working class as less worthy of attention, frequently subjecting them to subtle yet systematic "attention deprivation" (Derber, 1983).

**social construction of reality** The process by which our perception of reality is shaped largely by the subjective meaning that we give to an experience.

## The Social Construction of Reality

If we interpret other people's actions so subjectively, can we have a shared social reality? Some interaction theorists believe that there is little shared reality beyond that which is socially created. Interactionists refer to this as the **social construction of reality**—the process by which our perception of reality is shaped largely by the subjective meaning that we give to an experience (Berger and Luckmann, 1967). This meaning strongly influences what we "see" and how we respond to situations.

**self-fulfilling prophecy** A situation in which a false belief or prediction produces behaviour that makes the originally false belief come true.

Our perceptions and behaviour are influenced by how we initially define situations: We act on reality as we see it. Sociologists describe this process as the *definition of the situation,* meaning that we analyze a social context in which we find ourselves, determine what is in our best interest, and adjust our attitudes and actions accordingly. This can result in a **self-fulfilling prophecy**—a false belief or prediction that produces behaviour that makes the originally false belief come true (Thomas and Thomas, 1928:72). An example would be a person who has been told repeatedly that she or he is not a good student; eventually, this person might come

**144**

to believe it to be true, stop studying, and receive failing grades.

People may define a given situation in very different ways. Consider sociologist Lesley Harman's initial reaction to her field research site, a facility for homeless women in an Ontario city: "The initial shock of facing the world of the homeless told me much about what I took for granted . . . The first day I lasted two very long hours. I went home and woke up severely depressed, weeping uncontrollably" (1989:42). In contrast, a resident typical of many of the women who lived there defined living in a hostel in this way: "This is home to me because I feel so comfortable. I can do what I really want, the staff are very nice to me, everybody is good to me, it's home, you know?" (1989:91). As these two examples show, we define situations from our own frame of reference, based on the statuses we occupy and the roles we play.

Dominant group members with prestigious statuses may have the ability to establish how other people define "reality" (Berger and Luckmann, 1967:109). Some sociologists have suggested that dominant groups, particularly high-income white males in powerful economic and political statuses, perpetuate a dominant worldview that is frequently seen as "social reality."

## Ethnomethodology

How do we know how to interact in a given situation? What rules do we follow? Ethnomethodologists are interested in the answers to these questions. **Ethnomethodology** is the study of the commonsense knowledge that people use to understand the situations in which they find themselves (Heritage, 1984:4). Sociologist Harold Garfinkel (1967) initiated this approach and coined the term: *ethno* for "people" or "folk" and *methodology* for "a system of methods." Garfinkel was critical of mainstream sociology for not recognizing the ongoing ways in which people create reality and produce their own world. Consequently, ethnomethodologists examine existing patterns of conventional behaviour in order to uncover people's *background expectancies*; that is, their shared interpretation of objects and events, as well as their resulting actions. According to ethnomethodologists, interaction is based on assumptions of shared expectancies. For example, when you are talking with someone, what are your expectations about taking turns? Based on your background expectancies, would you be surprised if the other person talked for an hour and never gave you a chance to speak?

Sharply contrasting perceptions of the same reality are evident in these people's views on the war in Iraq.

To uncover people's background expectancies, ethnomethodologists frequently break "rules" or act as though they do not understand some basic rule of social life so that they can observe other people's responses. In a series of *breaching experiments,* Garfinkel (1967) assigned different activities to his students to see how breaking the unspoken rules of behaviour created confusion.

**ethnomethodology**
The study of the commonsense knowledge that people use to understand the situations in which they find themselves.

In one experiment, when students were asked, "How are you?" they threw their questioners off balance by responding with detailed accounts rather than polite nothings.

The ethnomethodological approach contributes to our knowledge of social interaction by making us aware of subconscious social realities in our daily lives.

## LO-5   Dramaturgical Analysis

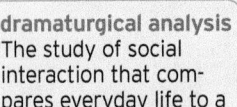

**dramaturgical analysis**
The study of social interaction that compares everyday life to a theatrical presentation.

**impression management (or presentation of self)**
A term for people's efforts to present themselves to others in ways that are most favourable to their own interests or image.

Erving Goffman suggested that day-to-day interactions have much in common with being on stage or in a dramatic production. **Dramaturgical analysis** is the study of social interaction that compares everyday life to a theatrical presentation. Members of our "audience" judge our performance and are aware that we may slip and reveal our true character (Goffman, 1959, 1963a). Consequently, most of us attempt to play our role as well as possible and to control the impressions we give to others. **Impression management, or presentation of self**, refers to people's efforts to present themselves to others in ways that are most favourable to their own interests or image.

For example, suppose that a professor has returned graded exams to your class. Will you discuss the exam and your grade with others in the class? If you are like most people, you probably play your student role differently depending on whom you are talking to and what grade you received on the exam. In a study, researchers analyzed how students "presented themselves" or "managed impressions" when exam grades were returned. Students who all received high grades ("Ace–Ace encounters") willingly talked with one another about their grades and sometimes engaged in a little bragging about how they had "aced" the test. However, encounters between students who had received high grades and those who had received low or failing grades ("Ace–Bomber encounters")

According to Erving Goffman, our day-to-day interactions have much in common with a dramatic production.

© keith morris/Alamy

**146**

were uncomfortable. The Aces felt as if they had to minimize their own grades. Consequently, they tended to attribute their success to "luck" and were quick to offer the Bombers words of encouragement. On the other hand, the Bombers believed that they had to praise the Aces and hide their own feelings of frustration and disappointment. Students who received low or failing grades ("Bomber–Bomber encounters") were more comfortable when they talked with one another because they could share their negative emotions. They often indulged in self-pity and relied on face-saving excuses (such as an illness or an unfair exam) for their poor performances (Albas and Albas, 1988).

In Goffman's terminology, *face-saving behaviour* refers to the strategies we use to rescue our performance when we experience a potential or actual loss of face. When the Bombers made excuses for their low scores, they were engaged in face-saving; the Aces attempted to help them save face by asserting that the test was unfair or that it was only a small part of the final grade. Why would the Aces and Bombers both participate in face-saving behaviour? In most social interactions, all role players have an interest in keeping the "play" going so that they can maintain their overall definition of the situation in which they perform their roles.

Goffman noted that people consciously participate in *studied nonobservance,* a face-saving technique in which one role player ignores the flaws in another's performance to avoid embarrassment for everyone involved. Most of us remember times when we have failed in our role and know that it is likely to happen again; thus, we may be more forgiving of the role failures of others.

Social interaction, like a theatre, has a front stage and a back stage. The *front stage* is the area where a player performs a specific role before an audience. The *back stage* is the area where a player is not required to perform a specific role because it is out of view of a given audience. For example, when the Aces and Bombers were talking with each other at school, they were on the "front stage." When they were in the privacy of their own residences, they were in "back stage" settings—they no longer had to perform the Ace and Bomber roles and could be themselves.

The need for impression management is most intense when role players have widely divergent or devalued statuses. As we have seen with the Aces and Bombers, the participants often play different roles under different circumstances and keep their various audiences separated from one another. If one audience becomes aware of other roles that a person plays, the impression being given at that time may be ruined. For example, homeless people may lose jobs or the opportunity to get them when their homelessness becomes known. One woman, Kim, had worked as a receptionist in a doctor's office for several weeks but was fired when the doctor learned that she was living in a shelter. According to Kim, the doctor told her, "If I had known you lived in a shelter, I would never have hired you. Shelters are places of disease" (Liebow, 1993:53–54). The homeless do not passively accept the roles into which they are cast. For the most part, they attempt—as we all do—to engage in impression management in their everyday lives.

The dramaturgical approach helps us think about the roles we play and the audiences who judge our presentation of self; however, this perspective has also been criticized for focusing on appearances and not the underlying substance. This approach may not place enough emphasis on the ways in which our everyday interactions with other people are influenced by occurrences within the larger society. For example, if some political leaders or social elites in a community deride homeless people by saying they are "lazy" or "unwilling to work," it may become easier for everyday people walking down a street to treat homeless individuals poorly. Overall, however, Goffman's dramaturgical analysis has been highly influential in the development of the sociology of emotions, an important area of contemporary theory and research.

## TIME TO REVIEW

- Provide three examples of self-fulfilling prophecies you have experienced in your interactions with others.
- Describe how daily interactions are similar to being onstage.

## The Sociology of Emotions

Why do we laugh, cry, or become angry? Are these emotional expressions biological or social? To some extent, emotions are a biologically given sense (like hearing, smell, and touch), but they also are social in origin. We are socialized to feel certain emotions, and we learn how and when to express (or not express) those emotions (Hochschild, 1983).

How do we know which emotions are appropriate for a given role? Sociologist Arlie Hochschild (1983) suggests that we acquire a set of *feeling rules,* which shape the appropriate emotions for a given role or specific situation. These rules include how, where, when, and with whom an emotion should be expressed. For example, for the role of a mourner at a funeral, feeling rules tell us which emotions are required (sadness and grief, for example), which are acceptable (a sense of relief that the deceased no longer has to suffer), and which are unacceptable (enjoyment of the occasion expressed by laughing out loud) (see Hochschild, 1983:63–68).

Feeling rules also apply to our occupational roles. For example, the truck driver who handles explosive cargos must be able to suppress fear. Although all jobs place some burden on our feelings, *emotional labour* occurs only in jobs that require personal contact with the public or the production of a state of mind (such as hope, desire, or fear) in others (Hochschild, 1983). With emotional labour, employees must display only certain carefully selected emotions. For example, flight attendants are required to act friendly toward passengers, to be helpful and open to requests, and to maintain an "omnipresent smile" to enhance the customers' status. By contrast, bill collectors are encouraged to show anger and make threats to customers, thereby supposedly deflating the customers' status and wearing down their presumed resistance to paying past-due bills. In both jobs, the employees are expected to show feelings that are often not their true ones (Hochschild, 1983).

Social class and race are determinants in managed expression and emotion management. Emotional labour is emphasized in middle- and upper-class families. Because middle- and upper-class parents often work with people, they are more likely to teach their children the importance of emotional labour in their own careers than are working-class parents, many of whom work with things, not people (Hochschild, 1983). Race is also an important factor in emotional labour. Members of visible minorities spend much of their life engaged in emotional labour because racist attitudes and discrimination make it continually necessary to manage one's feelings.

Emotional labour may produce feelings of estrangement from one's "true" self. C. Wright Mills (1956) suggested that when we "sell our personality" in the course of selling goods or services, we engage in a seriously self-alienating process. In other words, the "commercialization" of our feelings may dehumanize our work role performance and create alienation and contempt that spill over into other aspects of our life (Hochschild, 1983; Smith and Kleinman, 1989).

Clearly, the sociology of emotions helps us understand the social context of our feelings and the relationship between the roles we play and the emotions we experience. However, it may overemphasize the cost of emotional labour and the emotional controls that exist outside the individual (Wouters, 1989).

## Nonverbal Communication

**nonverbal communication** The transfer of information between persons without the use of speech.

In a typical stage drama, the players not only speak their lines but also convey information by nonverbal communication. In Chapter 3, we discussed the importance of language; now we will look at the messages we communicate without speaking. **Nonverbal communication** is the transfer of information between persons without the use of speech. It includes not only visual cues (gestures, appearances) but also vocal features (inflection, volume, pitch) and environmental factors (use of space, position) that affect meanings (Wood, 1999). Facial expressions, head movements, body positions, and other gestures carry as much of the total meaning of our communication with others as our spoken words do (Wood, 1999).

**FUNCTIONS OF NONVERBAL COMMUNICATION** Why is nonverbal communication important to you? We obtain first impressions of others from various kinds of nonverbal communication, such as the clothing they wear and their body positions. Head and facial movements may provide us with information about other people's emotional states, and others receive similar information from us (Samovar and Porter, 1991a). Through our body posture and eye contact, we signal that we do or do not wish to speak to someone. For example, we may look down at the sidewalk or off into the distance when we pass homeless persons who look as if they are going to ask for money.

Nonverbal communication establishes the relationship among people in terms of their responsiveness to and power over one another (Wood, 1999). For example, we show that we are responsive toward or like another person by maintaining eye contact and attentive body posture, and perhaps by touching and standing close. We can even express power or control over others through nonverbal communication. Goffman (1956) suggested that *demeanour* (how we behave or conduct ourselves) is relative to social power. People in positions of dominance are allowed a wider range of permissible actions than are their subordinates, who are expected to show deference. *Deference* is the symbolic means by which subordinates give a required permissive response to those in power; it confirms the existence of inequality and reaffirms each person's relationship to the other (Rollins, 1985).

---

**TIME TO REVIEW**

- Evaluate your nonverbal communication in an encounter with a police officer. What role would demeanour and deference play in this interaction having a positive or negative outcome?

---

**FACIAL EXPRESSION, EYE CONTACT, AND TOUCHING** Nonverbal communication is symbolic of our relationships with others. Who smiles? Who stares? Who makes and sustains eye contact? Who touches whom? All of these questions relate to demeanour and deference; the key issue is the status of the person who is *doing* the smiling, staring, or touching relative to the status of the recipient (Goffman, 1967).

Facial expressions, especially smiles, also reflect gender-based patterns of dominance and subordination in society. Women typically have been socialized to smile and frequently do so even when they are not happy (Halberstadt and Saitta, 1987). Jobs held predominantly by women (including flight attendant, secretary, elementary school teacher, and nurse) are more closely associated with being pleasant and smiling than are "men's jobs." In addition to smiling more frequently, many women tend to tilt their heads in deferential positions when they are talking or listening to others. By contrast, men tend to display less emotion through smiles or other facial expressions and instead seek to show that they are reserved and in control (Wood, 1999).

Women and men use eye contact differently during conversations. Women are more likely to sustain eye contact during conversations (but not otherwise) as a way of showing their interest in and involvement with others. By contrast, men are less likely to maintain prolonged eye contact during conversations but are more likely to stare at other people (especially other men) to challenge them and assert their own status (Pearson, 1985).

Eye contact can be a sign of domination or deference. For example, in a participant observation study of domestic (household) workers and their employers, sociologist Judith Rollins (1985) found that the domestics were supposed to show deference by averting their eyes when they talked to their employers. Deference also required that they present an "exaggeratedly subservient demeanour" by standing less erect and walking tentatively.

Touching is another form of nonverbal behaviour that has many different shades of meaning. Gender and power differences are evident in tactile communication from birth. Studies have shown that touching has variable meanings to parents: Boys are touched more roughly and playfully, while girls are handled more gently and protectively (Condry, Condry, and Pogatshnik, 1983). This pattern continues into adulthood, with women touched more frequently than men. Sociologist Nancy Henley (1977) attributed this pattern to power differentials between men and women and to the nature of women's roles as mothers, nurses, teachers, and secretaries. Clearly, touching has a different meaning to women than to men (Stier and Hall, 1984). Women may hug and touch others to indicate affection and emotional support, while men are more likely to touch others to give directions, assert power, and express sexual interest (Wood, 1999).

**PERSONAL SPACE** How much space do you like between yourself and other people? Anthropologist Edward Hall (1966) analyzed the physical distance between people speaking to one another and found that the amount of personal space people prefer varies from one culture to another. **Personal space** is the immediate area surrounding a person that the person claims as private. Our personal space is contained within an invisible boundary surrounding our body, much like a snail's shell. When others invade our space, we may retreat, stand our ground, or even lash out, depending on our cultural background (Samovar and Porter, 1991a).

Age, gender, kind of relationship, and social class also have an impact on the allocation of personal space. Power differentials are reflected in personal space and privacy issues. With regard to age, adults generally do not hesitate to enter the personal space of a child (Thorne, Kramarae, and Henley, 1983). Similarly, young children who invade the personal space of an adult tend to elicit a more favourable response than do older uninvited visitors (Dean, Willis, and la Rocco, 1976). The need for personal space appears to increase with age (Aiello and Jones, 1971; Baxter, 1970), although it may begin to decrease at about age 40 (Heshka and Nelson, 1972).

For some people, the idea of privacy or personal space is an unheard of luxury afforded only to those in the middle and upper classes. As we have seen in this chapter, the homeless may

> **personal space** The immediate area surrounding a person that the person claims as private.

Nonverbal communication can be thought of as an international language. What message do you receive from the facial expression and gestures of each of these people? Is it possible to misinterpret their messages?

have no space to call their own. Some may try to "stake a claim" on a heat grate or on the same bed in a shelter for more than one night, but such claims have dubious authenticity in a society in which the homeless are assumed to own nothing and have no right to lay claim to anything in the public domain.

In sum, all forms of nonverbal communication are influenced by gender, ethnicity, social class, and the personal contexts in which they occur. While it is difficult to generalize about people's nonverbal behaviour, we still need to think about our own nonverbal communication patterns. Recognizing that differences in social interaction exist is important. We should be wary of making value judgments—the differences are simply differences. Learning to understand and respect alternative styles of social interaction enhances our personal effectiveness by increasing the range of options we have for communicating with different people in diverse contexts and for varied reasons (Wood, 1999).

## KEY TERMS

**achieved status** A social position a person assumes voluntarily as a result of personal choice, merit, or direct effort (p. 120).

**ascribed status** A social position conferred on a person at birth or received involuntarily later in life (p. 120).

**dramaturgical analysis** The study of social interaction that compares everyday life to a theatrical presentation (p. 132).

**ethnomethodology** The study of the commonsense knowledge that people use to understand the situations in which they find themselves (p. 131).

**formal organization** A highly structured group formed for the purpose of completing certain tasks or achieving specific goals (p. 125).

**Gemeinschaft** (guh-MINE-shoft) A traditional society in which social relationships are based on personal bonds of friendship and kinship and on intergenerational stability (p. 127).

**Gesellschaft** (guh-ZELL-shoft) A large, urban society in which social bonds are based on impersonal and specialized relationships, with little long-term commitment to the group or consensus on values (p. 127).

**impression management (or presentation of self)** A term for people's efforts to present themselves to others in ways that are most favourable to their own interests or image (p. 132).

**master status** A term used to describe the most important status a person occupies (p. 120).

**LO-1** Identify the key components of social structure.

Social structure comprises statuses, roles, groups, and social institutions. A status is a specific position in a group or society and is characterized by certain expectations, rights, and duties. Ascribed statuses, such as gender, class, and ethnicity, are acquired at birth or involuntarily later in life. Achieved statuses, such as education and occupation, are assumed voluntarily as a result of personal choice, merit, or direct effort. We occupy a status, but a role is a set of behavioural expectations associated with a given status. A social group consists of two or more people who interact frequently and share a common identity and sense of interdependence. A formal organization is a highly structured group formed to complete certain tasks or achieve specific goals. A social institution is a set of organized beliefs and rules that establish how a society attempts to meet its basic needs.

**LO-2** Compare and contrast functionalist and conflict perspectives on social institutions.

According to functionalist theorists, social institutions perform several prerequisites of all societies: to replace members; teach new members; produce, distribute, and consume goods and services; preserve order; and provide and maintain a sense of purpose. Conflict theorists, however, note that social institutions do not work for the common good of all individuals. Institutions may enhance and uphold the power of some groups but exclude others, such as the homeless.

**LO-3** Explain how societies maintain stability in times of social change.

According to Durkheim, although changes in social structure may dramatically affect individuals and groups, societies manage to maintain some degree of stability. Mechanical solidarity refers to social cohesion in preindustrial societies, in which people are united by shared values and common social bonds. Organic solidarity refers to the cohesion in industrial societies, in which people perform specialized tasks and are united by mutual dependence.

**L0-4**  Define and distinguish between *Gemeinschaft* and *Gesellschaft* societies.

According to Ferdinand Tönnies, the *Gemeinschaft* is a traditional society in which relationships are based on personal bonds of friendship and kinship and on intergenerational stability. The *Gesellschaft* is an urban society in which social bonds are based on impersonal and specialized relationships, with little group commitment or consensus on values.

**mechanical solidarity** Émile Durkheim's term for the social cohesion that exists in preindustrial societies, in which there is a minimal division of labour and people feel united by shared values and common social bonds (p. 127).

**nonverbal communication** The transfer of information between persons without the use of speech (p. 134).

**organic solidarity** Émile Durkheim's term for the social cohesion that exists in industrial (and perhaps post-industrial) societies, in which people perform specialized tasks and feel united by their mutual dependence (p. 127).

**personal space** The immediate area surrounding a person that the person claims as private (p. 136).

**primary group** A small, less specialized group in which members engage in face-to-face, emotion-based interactions over an extended time (p. 124).

**L0-5**  Understand Erving Goffman's dramaturgical perspective and the concepts of impression management, and front stage/back stage behaviours.

According to Erving Goffman's dramaturgical analysis, our daily interactions are similar to dramatic productions. *Impression management* refers to efforts to present our self to others in ways that are most favourable to our own interests or self-image. The *front stage* is the area where a player performs a specific role before an audience. The *back stage* is the area where a player is not required to perform a specific role because it is out of view of a given audience.

**role** A set of behavioural expectations associated with a given status (p. 121).

**role conflict** A situation in which incompatible role demands are placed on a person by two or more statuses held at the same time (p. 122).

**role exit** A situation in which people disengage from social roles that have been central to their self-identity (p. 123).

**role expectation** A group's or society's definition of the way a specific role ought to be played (p. 121).

**role performance** How a person plays a role (p. 121).

**role strain** The strain experienced by a person when incompatible demands are built into a single status that the person occupies (p. 122).

**secondary group** A larger, more specialized group in which the members engage in more impersonal, goal-oriented relationships for a limited time (p. 124).

## APPLICATION QUESTIONS

1. Think of a person you know well who often irritates you or whose behaviour grates on your nerves (it could be a parent, friend, relative, or teacher). First, list that person's statuses and roles. Then analyze his or her possible role expectations, role performance, role conflicts, and role strains. Does anything you find in your analysis help to explain the irritating behaviour? (If not, change your method of analysis!) How helpful are the concepts of social structure in analyzing individual behaviour?

2. How does the structure of Canadian society influence the way in which we understand and respond to homelessness, both individually and collectively?

3. You are conducting field research on gender differences in nonverbal communication styles. How are you going to account for variations in age, ethnicity, and social class?

4. When communicating with other genders, ethnic groups, and ages, is it better to express and acknowledge different styles or to develop a common, uniform style? Why?

**self-fulfilling prophecy** A situation in which a false belief or prediction produces behaviour that makes the originally false belief come true (p. 130).

**social construction of reality** The process by which our perception of reality is shaped largely by the subjective meaning that we give to an experience (p. 130).

**social group** A group that consists of two or more people who interact frequently and share a common identity and a feeling of interdependence (p. 124).

**social institution** A set of organized beliefs and rules that establish how a society will attempt to meet its basic social needs (p. 125).

**social interaction** The process by which people act toward or respond to other people (p. 118).

**social marginality** The state of being part insider and part outsider in the social structure (p. 118).

**social network** A series of social relationships that link an individual to others (p. 125).

**social structure** The stable pattern of social relationships that exist within a particular group or society (p. 118).

**status** A socially defined position in a group or society characterized by certain expectations, rights, and duties (p. 119).

**status set** A term used to describe all the statuses that a person occupies at a given time (p. 120).

**status symbol** A material sign that informs others of a person's specific status (p. 121).

**stigma** According to Erving Goffman, any physical or social attribute or sign that so devalues a person's social identity that it disqualifies that person from full social acceptance (p. 119).

# KEY FIGURES

**Ferdinand Tönnies (1855-1936)** German sociologist Ferdinand Tonnies used the terms *Gemeinschaft* (traditional societies) and *Gesellschaft* (large urban societies) to describe the degree of social solidarity and social control in different societies.

**Erving Goffman (1922-1982)** Canadian-born sociologist Erving Goffman, author of *The Presentation of Self in Everyday Life*, used a theatre metaphor in his study of social interaction. According to Goffman day-to-day interactions are similar to a theatre production—we have a front stage and a back stage and we use "impression management" to ensure that our audience judges our performance favourably.

© American Sociological Association

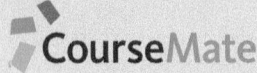

 Test your comprehension and assess what you've learned with **CourseMate's** online quizzes.

 For other interesting Lived Experiences, watch the video clips on **CourseMate.**

 Practise what you've learned with flashcards containing key terms and definitions on **CourseMate.**

# Groups & Organizations

**KENNETH PAYNE DESCRIBES HIS JOURNEY THROUGH A BUREAUCRATIC MAZE:**

*Since November, I have spent six to eight hours a day trying to persuade the authorities to accommodate me, but it just goes around in a circle... It's George Orwell's Big Brother... The bureaucracy is making me prove a negative and it turns "innocent until proven guilty" on its head... There's no common sense here. It's an inflexible bureaucracy where nobody takes any responsibility.* (Reed, 1998:A11)

What is Mr. Payne's problem? The former carpenter wants to be a schoolteacher. He has a degree in education and teaching experience. However, he is unable to get a permanent job teaching because he has a skin disease that causes the skin on his hands to blister and peel.

Why should this disqualify Mr. Payne from teaching? California legislators passed a law requiring that all teachers be fingerprinted so that they could be checked for criminal records. Because of Mr. Payne's disease, he has never had proper fingerprints, so there is no file to check against. Mr. Payne has appealed to the state and offered to prove in other ways that he has no criminal record, but he has been unable to get an exemption from the rule.

Why do people in organizations behave so inflexibly? Some rules are necessary. Even in small groups, such as families or friendship groups, informal rules help to ensure that people interact smoothly. In a large bureaucracy, an explicit system of rules and regulations means that employees and clients know what is expected of them. These rules help to ensure that everyone receives equal treatment from the organization. Unfortunately, adherence to the rules can stifle individual judgment, and some bureaucrats become so inflexible that they hurt the organization and its clients. In Mr. Payne's case, it made sense for the school system to do its best to protect children by establishing background checks for prospective teachers. However, in this case, the bureaucrats focused on fingerprinting, which is just one way of ensuring that people with criminal records are not hired as teachers. An official who was concerned with the *goal* of the policy (protecting children) rather than with one of the *means* of achieving that goal (fingerprinting) would have accepted the other ways in which Mr. Payne could have proven that he was not an offender.

While Mr. Payne suffered personal hardship, the consequences of bureaucratic inflexibility can be much more severe. In August 2005, Hurricane Katrina devastated the city of New Orleans. Tens of thousands of evacuees were not properly cared for and law and order broke down. There were massive failures in planning for the disaster and in coordinating the response after the city was flooded. While the most serious flaw was probably a lack of coordination among the local, state, and federal agencies responsible for the emergency, bureaucratic inflexibility was also pervasive.

Several incidents show that even in the face of the largest natural disaster ever to hit North America, some bureaucrats were focused more on rules and regulations than on saving lives. Despite the desperate need for water for hurricane survivors, there were occasions where truckloads of water were turned back because the drivers didn't have the proper paperwork (Lipton et al., 2005). A group of doctors were evacuated from their hospital and taken to the New Orleans airport. They offered to help tend the many sick people who had also been taken to the airport, but federal authorities were worried about liability issues and told them they could best help by mopping floors (CNN, 2005). While the doctors cleaned floors, patients died because of the lack of medical care. Another example of goal displacement occurred when hundreds of firefighters from around the United States were forced by the U.S. Federal Emergency Management Agency to delay their deployment into the emergency zone to take several days of community relations and sexual harassment training.

Much of our time is spent dealing with bureaucratic organizations. Most of us are born in hospitals, educated in schools, fed by restaurants and supermarket chains, entertained by communications companies, employed by corporations, and buried by funeral companies. Some people think of bureaucracies in a negative way because of their red tape and impersonality. While they can be inflexible and inhumane, bureaucracies are essential to modern life. Bureaucracies have been the best way of managing large numbers of people who must accomplish a common task. They are an essential part of our industrialized society.

In this chapter, you will learn about different types of groups and organizations, including bureaucracies. We live our lives in groups and they constantly affect our behaviour. Before reading on, test your knowledge about bureaucracies by taking the quiz in Box 6.1 on page 145.

**Critical Thinking Questions**

1. What bureaucracies have you recently encountered? What do you think are the benefits and shortcomings of this form of social organization?

2. Have you ever run into the kind of bureaucratic inflexibility we have described above? If you have, how did that make you feel about the organization that behaved unreasonably?

3. How do you think bureaucracies could be changed so they treat people more like individuals than is now the case?

| CHAPTER FOCUS QUESTION | How can we explain the behaviour of people who work in bureaucracies? |

## LEARNING OBJECTIVES
### AFTER READING THIS CHAPTER, YOU SHOULD BE ABLE TO

**LO-1** Identify the differences among social groups, aggregates, and categories.

**LO-2** Understand the effect that size has on the functioning of groups.

**LO-3** Explain the impact of groups on people's behaviour.

**LO-4** Identify the characteristics that define a bureaucracy and the "other face" of bureaucracies.

**LO-5** Discuss the form large organizations may take in the future.

© Lebrecht Music and Arts Photo Library/Alamy

Napoleon's defeat at Waterloo in 1815 showed that massive armies could not be led in the traditional way, by a single commander responsible for everything. Subsequently, armies developed more effective organizational structures.

## LO-1   SOCIAL GROUPS

We spend most of our lives in groups, including families, friends, and school and work groups, so it is important to understand the characteristics and dynamics of groups ranging from small, informal groups to large bureaucracies.

Consider these situations. Three strangers are standing at a street corner waiting for a traffic light to change. Do they constitute a group? Five hundred people are first-year students at a university. Do they constitute a group? In everyday usage, we use the word *group* to mean any collection of people. According to sociologists, however, the answer to these questions is no; individuals who happen to share a common feature or to be in the same place at the same time do not constitute social groups.

### Groups, Aggregates, and Categories

**aggregate** A collection of people who happen to be in the same place at the same time but have little else in common.

A *social group* is a collection of two or more people who interact frequently with one another, share a sense of belonging, and have a feeling of interdependence. Several people waiting for a traffic light to change constitute an **aggregate**—a collection of people who happen to be in the same place at the same time but have little else in common. Shoppers in a department store and passengers on an airplane are also examples of aggregates. People in aggregates share a common purpose (such as purchasing items or arriving at their destination) but generally do not interact with one another. The first-year students, at least initially, constitute a **category**—a number of people who may never have met one another but who share a similar characteristic (such as education level, age, ethnicity, and gender). Men and women make up categories, as do First Nations peoples and victims of sexual harassment. Categories are not social groups because the people in them usually do not create a social structure or have anything in common other than a particular trait.

**category** A number of people who may never have met one another but who share a similar characteristic.

Occasionally, people in aggregates and in categories form social groups. People within the category of "students" become an aggregate when they meet for an orientation. Some of them may form social groups as they interact with one another in classes, find that they have mutual interests and concerns, and develop a sense of belonging to the group.

Social groups can change over time. For example, an aggregate or category of people may become a formal organization with a specific structure and clear-cut goals. A *formal organization* is a structured group formed to achieve specific goals in the most efficient manner. Universities, factories, corporations, and the military are examples of formal organizations. Before we examine formal organizations, we need to know more about groups in general and about how they function.

## Types of Groups

Groups have varying degrees of social solidarity and structure. This structure is flexible in some groups and more rigid in others. Some groups are small and personal; others are large and impersonal. We more closely identify with the members of some groups than we do others.

**PRIMARY AND SECONDARY GROUPS** Sociologist Charles H. Cooley (1962/1909) used the term *primary group* to describe a small, less specialized group in which members engage in face-to-face, emotion-based interactions over an extended time. We have primary relationships with other individuals in our primary groups—that is, with our *significant others*.

In contrast, a *secondary group* is a larger, more specialized group in which members engage in more impersonal, goal-oriented relationships for a limited time. The size of a secondary group may vary. Twelve students in a university seminar may start out as a secondary group but eventually become a primary group as they get to know one another and communicate on a more personal basis. Formal organizations are secondary groups, but they also contain many primary groups within them. There are many thousands of primary groups within the secondary group setting of your university.

---

**BOX 6.1 SOCIOLOGY AND EVERYDAY LIFE**

### How Much Do You Know About Bureaucracy?

| True | False | |
|------|-------|---|
| T | F | 1. Large bureaucracies have existed for about a thousand years. |
| T | F | 2. Because of the efficiency and profitability of the new factory bureaucracies, people were eager to leave farms to work in the factories. |
| T | F | 3. Bureaucracies are deliberately impersonal. |
| T | F | 4. The organizational principles used by McDonald's restaurants are being adopted by other sectors of the global economy. |
| T | F | 5. The rise of Protestantism helped create the social conditions favourable to the rise of modern bureaucracies. |

For answers to the quiz about bureaucracy, go to **www.nelson.com/sociologyinourtimes6e**.

Visiting spectators to the game form an outgroup in relation to the home team fans.

**INGROUPS AND OUTGROUPS**
Groups set boundaries by distinguishing between insiders, who are members, and outsiders, who are not. William Graham Sumner (1959/1906) coined the terms *ingroup* and *outgroup* to describe people's feelings toward members of their own and other groups. An **ingroup** is a group to which a person belongs and with which the person feels a sense of identity. An **outgroup** is a group to which a person does not belong and toward which the person may feel a sense of competitiveness or hostility. Distinguishing between our ingroups and our outgroups helps us establish our individual identity.

Group boundaries may be formal, with clearly defined criteria for membership. For example, a country club that requires applicants for membership to be recommended by four current members and pay a $25,000 initiation fee and $1000 per month membership dues has set requirements for its members. The club may even post an entrance sign that states "Members Only" and use security personnel to ensure that nonmembers do not encroach on its grounds. Boundary distinctions are often reflected in symbols, such as emblems or clothing. Country club members are given membership cards to gain access to the club's facilities.. They may wear shirts with the country club's logo on them. These symbols denote that the individual is a member of the ingroup.

Group boundaries are not always as formal as they are in a private club. Friendship groups, for example, usually do not have clear guidelines for membership. Rather, the boundaries tend to be informal and vaguely defined.

Ingroup and outgroup distinctions may encourage social cohesion among members, but they also may promote classism, racism, sexism, and ageism. Ingroup members typically view themselves positively and may view members of outgroups negatively. These feelings of group superiority, or *ethnocentrism,* can be detrimental to groups and individuals not part of the ingroup. Sexual harassment and racial discrimination are two negative consequences of ethnocentrism.

**REFERENCE GROUPS** Ingroups provide us not only with a source of identity but also with a point of reference. A **reference group** is a group that strongly influences a person's behaviour and social attitudes, regardless of whether that individual is an actual member. When we evaluate our appearance, ideas, or goals, we automatically refer to the standards of a group. Sometimes, we will refer to our membership groups, such as family or friends. Other times, we will rely on groups to which we do not belong but that we might wish to join in the future, such as a social club or a profession.

**NETWORKS** A **network** is a web of social relationships that link one person with other people and, through them, with more people that those people know. Frequently, networks connect people who share common interests but who otherwise might not interact with one another. For example, if A is tied to B and B is tied to C, then a network may be formed among individuals A, B, and C. Think of the experiences that you and your friends have had looking for summer jobs. If your friend works at a company that needs more people, he or she may recommend you to the potential employer. This recommendation helps you get a job and gives the

**ingroup** A group to which a person belongs and with which the person feels a sense of identity.

**outgroup** A group to which a person does not belong and toward which the person may feel a sense of competitiveness or hostility.

**reference group** A group that strongly influences a person's behaviour and social attitudes, regardless of whether that individual is an actual member.

**network** A web of social relationships that link one person with other people and, through them, with more people that those people know.

employer the assurance that you are likely to be a good employee. Research shows that networks play a very important role for graduating students in finding employment (Granovetter, 1994).

*It's a Small World: Networks of Acquaintances*  On September 11, 2001, nearly 3000 people died when terrorists crashed two planes into New York City's World Trade Center and a third into the Pentagon. Many people around the world were surprised to learn that they, or some of their acquaintances, knew someone who had been personally touched by the tragedy. Social scientists were not surprised by this because of a fascinating research project done more than 40 years ago by psychologist Stanley Milgram (1967).

Milgram sent packages of letters to people in the Midwestern United States. The objective was to get the letters to one of two target recipients in Boston using personal contacts. Those originating the chain were given the name of the target recipient and told that the person was either a Boston stockbroker or the wife of a Harvard divinity student. They were asked to mail the letter to an acquaintance who they felt would be able to pass it on to another acquaintance even closer to the intended target. Milgram found that it took an average of five contacts to get the letters to the intended recipient.

The research was popularized through the play and movie *Six Degrees of Separation,* and the popular trivia game *Six Degrees of Kevin Bacon,* in which the objective is to link actors to other actors who have appeared in films with Kevin Bacon. Thus, Nicole Kidman has a Kevin Bacon number of 2, as she appeared in *Eyes Wide Shut* with Tom Cruise, who worked with Kevin Bacon in the film *A Few Good Men.* Since virtually no American actor has a Bacon number larger than 4, the challenge for movie trivia experts is to figure out the linkages. (See the Oracle of Bacon website at oracleofbacon.org.)

The "small world" research has important implications. Strogatz and Watts (1998) have studied the mathematics behind the phenomenon and have documented the importance of "bridges"—people who bridge very different social worlds. For example, in Milgram's study, the Boston stockbroker received 64 letters, 16 of which were delivered by the owner of a clothing store in Boston. Perhaps you can think of friends or acquaintances who come from other countries or who have unusual interests, hobbies, or jobs that would enable them to bridge vast distances or widely different social groups. The study of networks and of the role of bridges has important implications for researchers in many fields, including *epidemiology,* which is the study of the spread of disease. For example, the spread of HIV/AIDS was hastened by a Canadian flight attendant (Patient X) whose travels meant that he bridged several different networks of gay males (Saulnier, 1998).

While Milgram's research was influential, Kleinfeld (2002) found that most of Milgram's letters never reached their intended destination. We do not know if the connections failed because the participants could not think of anyone who could act as the next link in the chain, or simply because they did not bother moving the letter along toward the intended recipient. However, a study using email contacts had lower failure rates and had similar results to Milgram's. Dodds and his colleagues (2003) found that those who continued the chain needed an average of five to seven contacts to reach their targets, even when in another country. A recent study found that there was an average of just under four degrees of separation among Facebook users around the world, so social media may be bringing people closer together (Backstrom et al., 2011).

Research points out an interesting aspect of social networks. Korte and Milgram (1970) found a significantly higher number of completed chains when both the sender and the recipient were the same race, and Dodds et al. (2003) found that people most frequently contacted persons of the same gender. They found that workplace and educational contacts were most likely to be used in completing chains. These findings imply that members of groups that are less powerful and less educated may be disadvantaged in a world that is increasingly dependent upon geographically dispersed social networks.

Why is this important? We live in a world where many things get done through networks. Granovetter (1995) showed that social networks are important for employers and for people looking for work. Most people get their jobs through personal contacts rather than through formal job-search mechanisms. Those with good networks will have the advantage in their search for work, while those without extensive networks or those whose networks are not oriented to the labour market will be at a great disadvantage. If most of your friends are unemployed, they cannot help you find a job. This can perpetuate unemployment among groups, including some visible minorities and women, who may not have had the opportunity to build up strong networks.

Network analysis is becoming more important in sociology. For example, email patterns may tell us a great deal about the way in which organizations work. How do ideas spread within an organization? Do email messages frequently pass between different levels of an organization, or are communications restricted to one level? Do women and visible minorities have the same interaction patterns as white males, and are they able to bridge different parts of their organizations? On a broader level, can genuine communities flourish in cyberspace, or does the Internet reduce community by reducing the personal contact between people?

## LO-2    GROUP CHARACTERISTICS AND DYNAMICS

Our most intense relationships occur in dyads—groups composed of two members. How might the interaction of these two people differ if they were with several other people?

© Ray Morsch/zefa/Corbis

What purpose do groups serve? Why do individuals give up some of their freedom to participate in groups? According to functionalists, groups meet peoples' instrumental and expressive needs. *Instrumental*, or task-oriented, needs cannot always be met by one person, so the group works cooperatively to fulfill a specific goal. For example, you could not function as a one-person football team or single-handedly build a skyscraper. Groups help members do jobs that are difficult or impossible to do alone. They also help people meet their *expressive*, or emotional, needs, especially for self-expression and support from family, friends, and peers.

Conflict theorists and symbolic interactionists, of course, have a different understanding of groups. While not disputing that groups ideally perform positive functions, conflict theorists suggest that groups also involve power relationships whereby the needs of individual members may not be equally served. Symbolic interactionists focus on how the size of a group influences the kind of interaction that takes place among members.

To many postmodernists, groups and organizations—like other aspects of postmodern societies—are generally characterized by superficiality and by shallow social relationships. One postmodern thinker who focuses on this issue is the literary theorist Fredric Jameson, whose works have had a significant influence on contemporary sociology. According to Jameson (1984), postmodern organizations (and societies as a whole) are characterized not only by superficial relations and lack of depth but also by people experiencing a waning of emotion because the world and the people in it have become more fragmented (Ritzer, 1997). For example, Ritzer (1997) examined fast-food restaurants and concluded that both restaurant employees and customers interact in extremely superficial ways that are largely scripted by large-scale organizations: The employees learn to follow scripts in taking and filling customers' orders ("Would you like fries with that?"), while customers respond with their own "recipied" action.

## Group Size

The size of a group is important. Interactions are more personal and intense in a **small group**, in which all members are acquainted with one another and interact simultaneously.

Simmel (1950/1902–1917) suggested that small groups have distinctive interaction patterns. According to Simmel, in a **dyad**—a group composed of two members—the active participation of both members is crucial for the group's survival. If one member withdraws from interaction, or "quits," the group ceases to exist. Examples of dyads include two people who are best friends, and married couples. Dyads provide an intense bond and a sense of unity not found in most larger groups.

Adding a third person forms a **triad**. The nature of the relationship and interaction patterns change with the addition of the third person. In a triad, even if one member ignores another or declines to participate, the group can still function. In addition, two members may unite to create a coalition that can subject the third member to group pressure to conform. A *coalition* is an alliance created in an attempt to reach a shared objective or goal. If two members form a coalition, the other member may be seen as an outsider or intruder.

As group size increases beyond three, members tend to specialize in different tasks and communication patterns change. In groups of more than six or seven people, it becomes increasingly difficult for everyone to participate in the same conversation, so several conversations will likely take place simultaneously. In groups of more than 10 or 12 people, it becomes virtually impossible for all members to participate in a single conversation unless one person serves as moderator and facilitates the discussion. Figure 6.1 shows that when the size of the group increases, the number of possible social interactions increases dramatically.

**small group** A collectivity small enough for all members to be acquainted with one another and to interact simultaneously.

**dyad** A group consisting of two members.

**triad** A group composed of three members.

---

### FIGURE 6.1   GROWTH OF POSSIBLE SOCIAL INTERACTIONS BASED ON GROUP SIZE

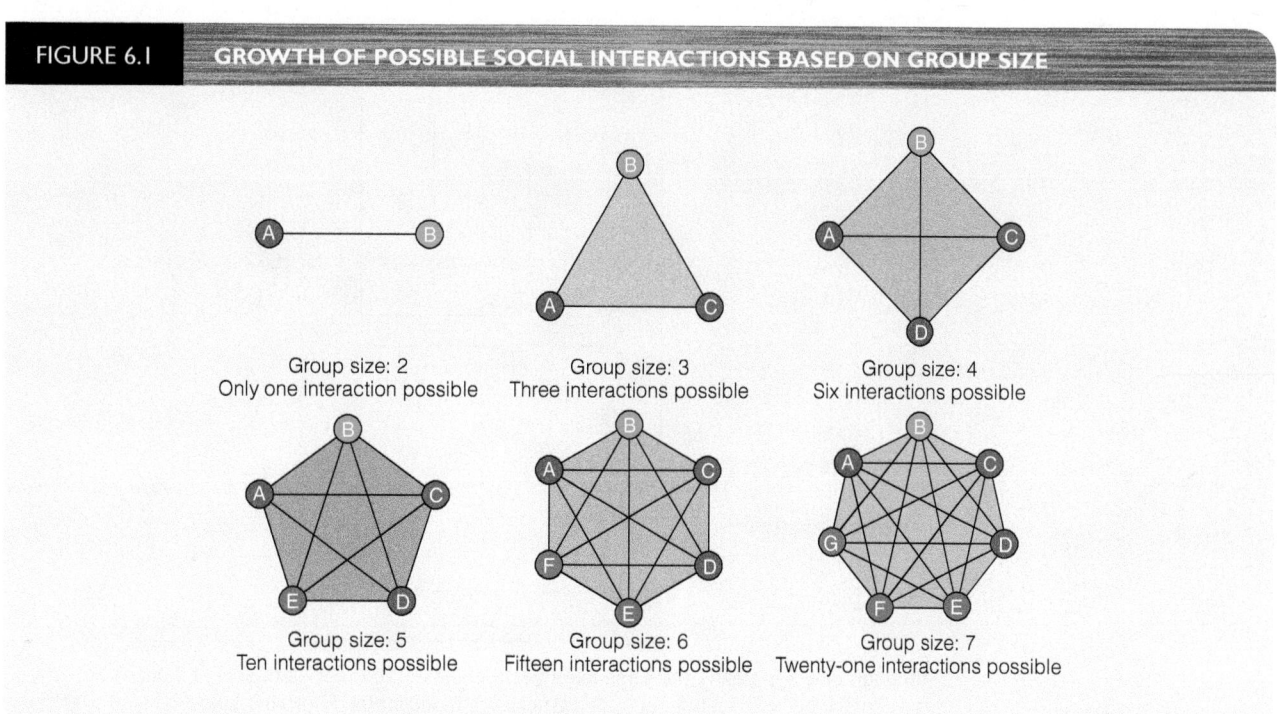

Group size: 2
Only one interaction possible

Group size: 3
Three interactions possible

Group size: 4
Six interactions possible

Group size: 5
Ten interactions possible

Group size: 6
Fifteen interactions possible

Group size: 7
Twenty-one interactions possible

### LO-3　Group Conformity

Groups exert a powerful influence in our lives. To gain and then retain our membership in groups, most of us are willing to exhibit a high level of conformity to the wishes of other group members. **Conformity** is the process of maintaining or changing behaviour to comply with the norms established by a society, subculture, or other group. We often experience powerful pressure from other group members to conform. In some situations, this pressure may be almost overwhelming.

Several researchers have found that the pressure to conform can cause group members to say they see something they don't see or to do something they otherwise would be unwilling to do. As we look at two of these studies, ask yourself what you might have done if you had been involved in this research.

**ASCH'S RESEARCH** Pressure to conform is especially strong in small groups. In a series of experiments conducted by Solomon Asch (1955, 1956), the pressure toward group conformity was so great that participants were willing to contradict their own best judgment rather than disagree with other group members.

One of Asch's experiments involved groups of undergraduate men (seven in each group) who supposedly were recruited for a study of visual perception. All the men were seated in chairs. However, the person in the sixth chair did not know that he was the only actual subject; all of the others were assisting the researcher. The participants were first shown a large card with a vertical line on it and then a second card with three vertical lines (see Figure 6.2). Each of the seven participants was asked to indicate which of the three lines on the second card was identical in length to the "standard line" on the first card.

> **conformity** The process of maintaining or changing behaviour to comply with the norms established by a society, subculture, or other group.

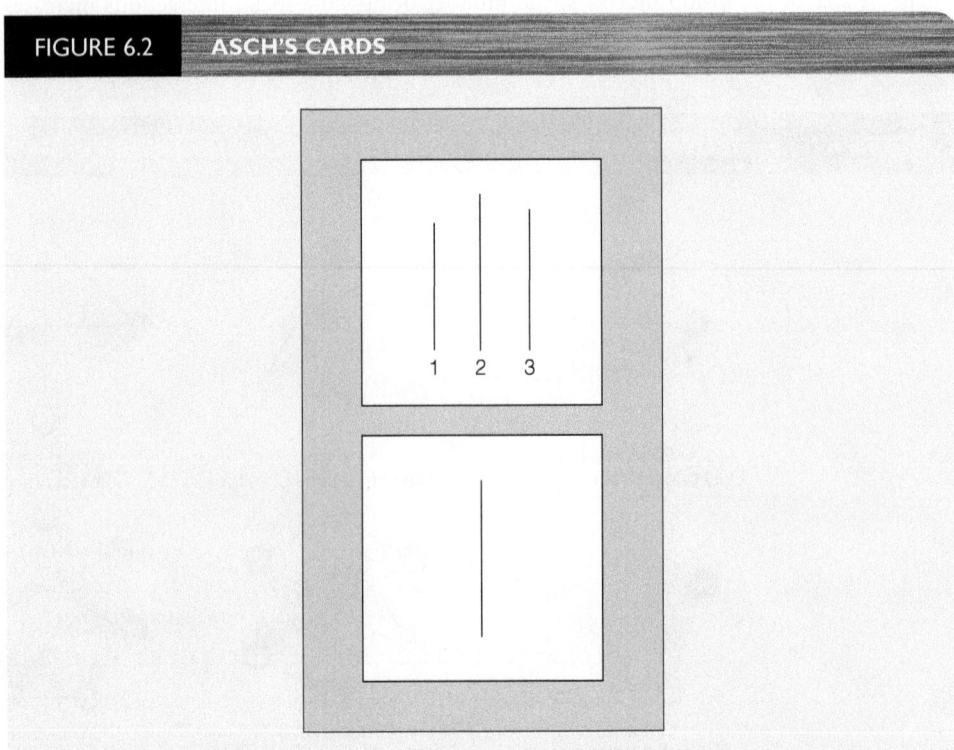

**FIGURE 6.2　ASCH'S CARDS**

Although Line 2 is clearly the same length as the line in the lower card, Solomon Asch's research assistants tried to influence "actual" participants by deliberately picking Line 1 or Line 3 as the correct match. Many of the participants went along rather than risk the opposition of the "group."

In the first test with each group, all seven men selected the correct matching line. In the second trial, all seven still answered correctly. In the third trial, however, the subject became very uncomfortable when all of the others selected the incorrect line. The subject could not understand what was happening and became even more confused as the others continued to give incorrect responses on 11 out of the next 15 trials.

If you had been in the position of the subject, how would you have responded? Would you have continued to give the correct answer, or would you have been swayed by the others? When Asch (1955) averaged the responses of the 50 actual subjects who participated in the study, he found that about 33 percent routinely chose to conform to the group by giving the same (incorrect) responses as Asch's assistants. Another 40 percent gave incorrect responses in about half of the trials. Although 25 percent always gave correct responses, even they felt very uneasy and "knew that something was wrong." In discussing the experiment afterward, most of the subjects who gave incorrect responses indicated that they had known the answers were wrong but decided to go along with the group to avoid ridicule or ostracism.

In later studies, Asch found that if even a single assistant did not agree with the others, the subject was reassured by hearing someone else question the accuracy of incorrect responses and was much less likely to give a wrong answer. Figure 6.3 shows how group size was related to conformity. This shows the power that groups have to produce conformity among members.

**MILGRAM'S RESEARCH ON OBEDIENCE** How willing are we to do something because someone in a position of authority has told us to do it? How far are we willing to go in following that individual's demands? Stanley Milgram (1963, 1974) conducted a series of controversial experiments to answer these questions about people's obedience to authority. Milgram wanted to understand atrocities, such as the Holocaust, where ordinary citizens behaved brutally when they were ordered to do so.

| FIGURE 6.3 | EFFECT OF GROUP SIZE IN THE ASCH CONFORMITY STUDIES |

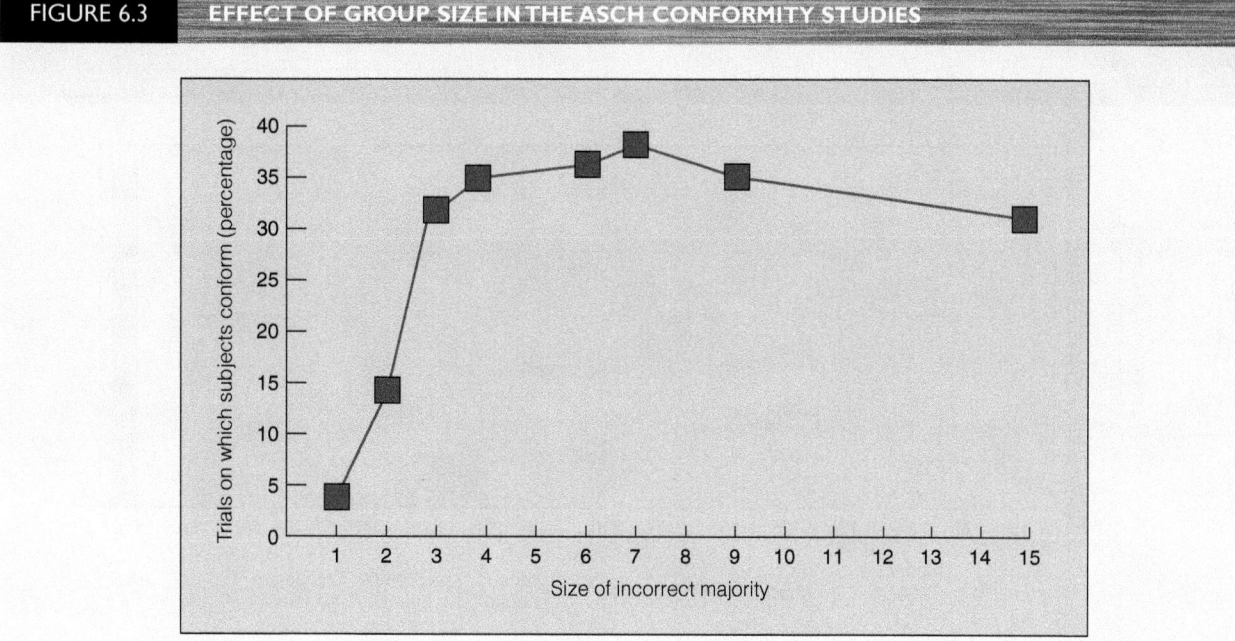

As more people are added to the "incorrect" majority, subjects' tendency to conform by giving wrong answers increases—but only up to a point. Adding more than seven people to the incorrect majority does not further increase subjects' tendency to conform—perhaps because subjects are suspicious about why so many people agree with one another.

*Source:* Asch, 1955.

Milgram's subjects were men who had responded to an advertisement for participants in an experiment. When the first (actual) subject arrived, he was told that the study concerned the effects of punishment on learning. After the second subject (an assistant of Milgram's) arrived, the two men were directed to draw slips of paper from a hat to get their assignments as either the "teacher" or the "learner." Because the drawing was rigged, the actual subject always became the teacher and the assistant the learner. Next, the learner was strapped into a chair with protruding electrodes that looked something like an electric chair. The teacher was placed in an adjoining room and given a realistic-looking but nonoperative shock generator. The "generator's" control panel showed levels that went from "Slight Shock" (15 volts) on the left, to "Intense Shock" (255 volts) in the middle, to "DANGER: SEVERE SHOCK" (375 volts), and finally "XXX" (450 volts) on the right.

The teacher was instructed to read aloud a pair of words and then repeat the first of the two words. At that time, the learner was supposed to respond with the second of the two words. If the learner could not provide the second word, the teacher was instructed to press the lever on the shock generator so that the learner would be punished for forgetting the word. Each time the learner gave an incorrect response, the teacher was supposed to increase the shock level by 15 volts. The alleged purpose of the shock was to determine whether punishment improves a person's memory.

What was the maximum level of shock that a "teacher" was willing to inflict on a "learner"? The learner had been instructed (in advance) to beat on the wall between himself and the teacher as the experiment continued, pretending that he was in intense pain. The teacher was told that the shocks might be "extremely painful" but would cause no permanent damage. At about 300 volts, when the learner quit responding to questions, the teacher often turned to the experimenter to see what he should do next. When the experimenter indicated that the teacher should give increasingly painful shocks, 65 percent of the teachers administered shocks all the way up to the "XXX" (450 volt) level (see Figure 6.4). By this point in the process, the teachers were frequently sweating, stuttering, or biting on their lip.

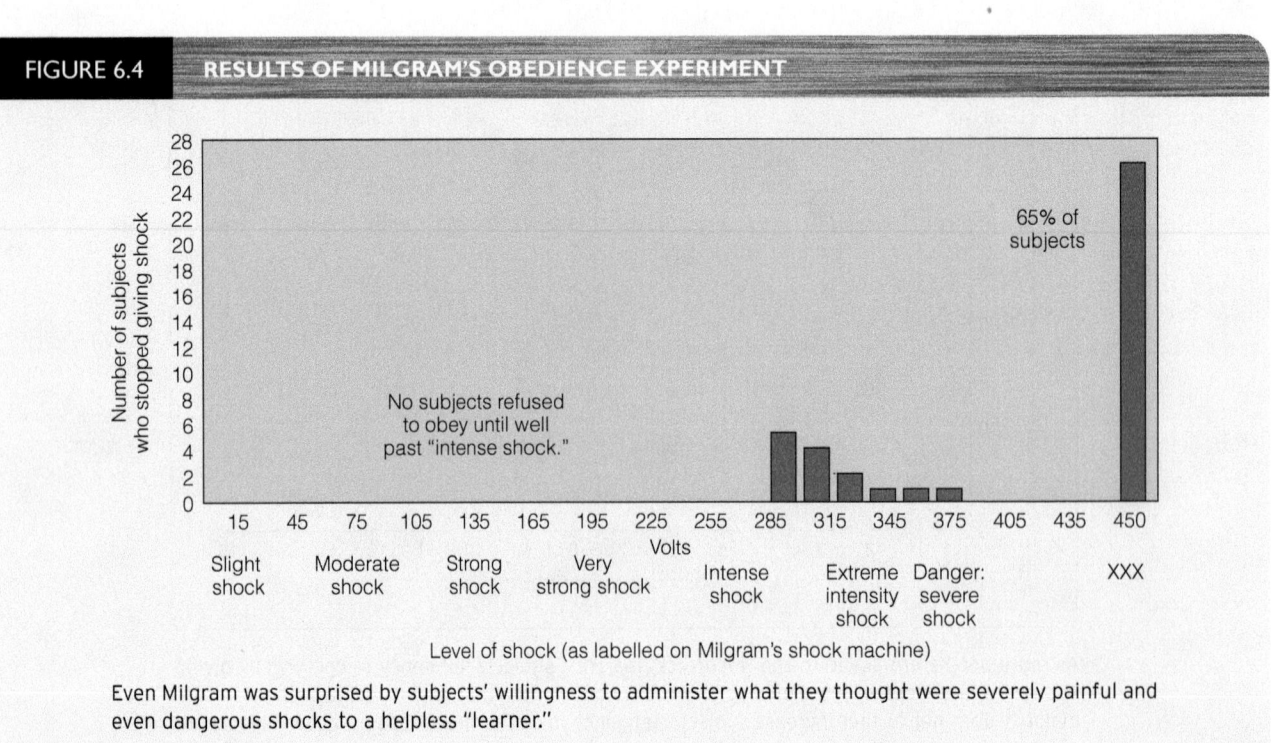

| FIGURE 6.4 | RESULTS OF MILGRAM'S OBEDIENCE EXPERIMENT |

Even Milgram was surprised by subjects' willingness to administer what they thought were severely painful and even dangerous shocks to a helpless "learner."

*Source:* Graph is based on Table 2 in Milgram, 1963: 376.

According to Milgram, the teachers—who were free to leave whenever they wanted to—continued in the experiment because they were being given directions by a person in a position of authority (a scientist wearing a white coat).

What can we learn from Milgram's study? The study suggests that obedience to authority may be more common than most of us would like to believe. None of the "teachers" challenged the process before they had applied 300 volts. Almost two-thirds went all the way to what could have been a painful jolt of electricity if the shock generator had been real. Burger (2009) has recently conducted a partial replication of Milgram's work and found that rates of obedience were similar to those of the earlier study. Most people went to the end of the experiment, and women were as likely to obey as men.

This research raises ethical questions. Milgram's subjects were deceived about the nature of the study. Many found the experiment extremely stressful, and some suffered anxiety so severe that the experimental sessions had to be ended (Milgram, 1963). It would be impossible today to obtain permission to replicate this experiment in a university setting, though such studies were common in the 1960s. Burger's partial replication of the study made a number of changes, including stopping the experiment at the 150-volt level, to obtain ethics approval. Burger felt this was justified because in Milgram's work, most people who went past this level continued all the way to the end.

In addition to ethical problems, some critics feel that Milgram's study was also methodologically flawed. Brannigan (2004) has raised the issue of whether the subjects actually believed that they were hurting people. The more realistic Milgram made the experiment, the more likely the subjects were to refuse to proceed. One critic explains why he does not take the results of Milgram's study seriously:

> Every experiment was basically preposterous . . . the entire experimental procedure from beginning to end could make no sense at all, even to the laymen. A person is strapped to a chair and immobilized and is explicitly told he is going to be exposed to extremely painful electric shocks . . . The task the student is to learn is evidently impossible. He can't learn it in a short time . . . No one could learn it . . . This experiment becomes more incredulous and senseless the further it is carried. (Mantell, 1971:110–111)

Because of the artificiality of the laboratory situation, Brannigan is very doubtful that this experiment tells us anything about why German citizens were willing to participate in the atrocities of the Holocaust. The issue of artificiality means that we should always be cautious when we consider the findings of laboratory experiments involving human behaviour.

GROUPTHINK As we have seen, individuals often respond differently in a group context than if they were alone. Janis (1972, 1989) examined group decision making and found that major blunders may be attributed to pressure toward group conformity. To describe this phenomenon, he coined the term **groupthink**—the process by which members of a cohesive group arrive at a decision that many individual members privately believe is unwise. Why not speak up at the time? Members usually want to be "team players." They may not want to be the ones who undermine the group's consensus or who challenge the leadership. Consequently, members often withhold their opinions and focus on consensus rather than on exploring all the options and making the best decision. Figure 6.5 summarizes the dynamics and results of groupthink.

Similarly, in 1986, the launch of the space shuttle Challenger, which exploded 73 seconds into its flight, killing all seven crew members, provides an example of groupthink. On the day preceding the launch, engineers at the company that designed and manufactured the shuttle's rocket boosters became concerned that freezing temperatures at the launch site would interfere with the proper functioning of the O-ring seals in the boosters. When they expressed their misgivings, they were overruled by higher officials at the company and with NASA (the government agency that administers the U.S. space program), where executives were impatient because of earlier delays. A presidential commission that investigated the tragedy concluded that neither the manufacturer nor NASA responded adequately to warnings about the seals (Lippa, 1994).

groupthink The process by which members of a cohesive group arrive at a decision that many individual members privately believe is unwise.

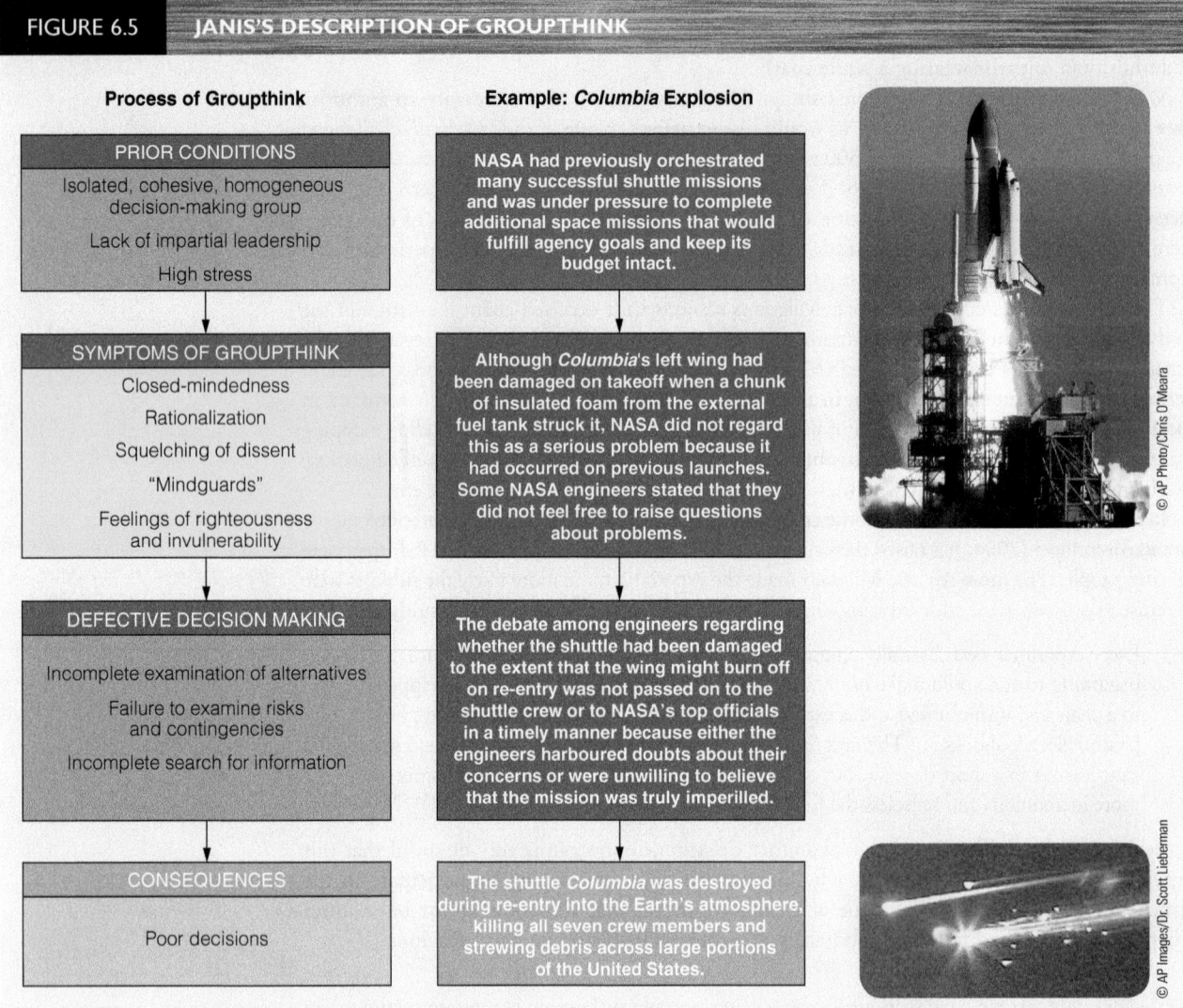

| FIGURE 6.5 | JANIS'S DESCRIPTION OF GROUPTHINK |

**Process of Groupthink**

**PRIOR CONDITIONS**

Isolated, cohesive, homogeneous decision-making group

Lack of impartial leadership

High stress

**SYMPTOMS OF GROUPTHINK**

Closed-mindedness

Rationalization

Squelching of dissent

"Mindguards"

Feelings of righteousness and invulnerability

**DEFECTIVE DECISION MAKING**

Incomplete examination of alternatives

Failure to examine risks and contingencies

Incomplete search for information

**CONSEQUENCES**

Poor decisions

**Example: *Columbia* Explosion**

NASA had previously orchestrated many successful shuttle missions and was under pressure to complete additional space missions that would fulfill agency goals and keep its budget intact.

Although *Columbia*'s left wing had been damaged on takeoff when a chunk of insulated foam from the external fuel tank struck it, NASA did not regard this as a serious problem because it had occurred on previous launches. Some NASA engineers stated that they did not feel free to raise questions about problems.

The debate among engineers regarding whether the shuttle had been damaged to the extent that the wing might burn off on re-entry was not passed on to the shuttle crew or to NASA's top officials in a timely manner because either the engineers harboured doubts about their concerns or were unwilling to believe that the mission was truly imperilled.

The shuttle *Columbia* was destroyed during re-entry into the Earth's atmosphere, killing all seven crew members and strewing debris across large portions of the United States.

© AP Photo/Chris O'Meara

© AP Images/Dr. Scott Lieberman

In Janis's model, prior conditions, such as a highly homogeneous group with committed leadership, can lead to potentially disastrous "groupthink," which short-circuits careful and impartial deliberation. Events leading up to the tragic 2003 launch of the space shuttle *Columbia* provide an example of this process.

Why did people agree to the launch despite these safety concerns? It is one thing to doubt your judgment about the length of a line, as in the Asch experiments, and quite another to send seven people to their deaths. The engineers closest to the situation almost unanimously opposed the launch. The decision, however, was ultimately made by managers more focused on the schedule than on safety concerns. NASA managers were under great pressure to keep the shuttle flights on schedule because they feared budget cuts. When the contractor suggested delaying the launch until air temperatures were above 53°F (11.7°C), NASA managers responded angrily. One said, "My God . . . when do you want me to launch, next April?" (President's Commission, 1986:96). Another said, "I'm appalled by your recommendation" (President's Commission, 1986:94). Faced with this pressure, the contractor, who was about to begin negotiating a new billion-dollar agreement with NASA, had second thoughts. Senior managers overruled the recommendations of their engineers and recommended launch. NASA managers and the contractor managers risked other people's lives to accomplish their own bureaucratic goals.

Groupthink can be hard to eliminate. Despite the clear analysis of NASA's errors in the *Challenger* case, groupthink may also have contributed to the 2003 crash of the space shuttle *Columbia*, as administrators did not listen to engineers' concerns about foam that had broken from a fuel tank on seven previous flights. Damage caused by this foam led to the destruction of the shuttle. One of the investigation board members concluded that dissent was still not welcome at NASA, even when safety was involved.

Although telephone- and computer-based procedures have streamlined registration at many schools, for many students registration exemplifies the worst aspects of academic bureaucracy. Yet students and other members of the academic community depend upon the bureaucracy to establish and administer procedures that enable the complex university system to operate smoothly.

## TIME TO REVIEW

- Discuss the differences between groups, aggregates, and categories.
- Explain the importance of the difference between primary and secondary groups.
- Discuss how people interact though networks.
- Explain how groups can lead people to make bad decisions. How does "groupthink" affect peoples' behaviour?
- Discuss the impact of group size on interaction patterns within groups.

## FORMAL ORGANIZATIONS LO-4

In earlier times, life was centred in small, informal groups, such as the family and the village. With the advent of industrialization and urbanization (as discussed in Chapter 1), people's lives became increasingly dominated by large, formal organizations. A formal organization is a highly structured group formed for the purpose of completing certain tasks or achieving specific goals. Formal organizations (such as corporations, schools, and government agencies) usually keep their basic structure for many years.

### Bureaucracies

The bureaucratic model of organization is the most universal organizational form in government, business, education, and religion. A **bureaucracy** is an organizational model characterized by a hierarchy of authority, a clear division of labour, explicit rules and procedures, and impersonality in personnel matters.

When we think of a bureaucracy, we may think of "buck-passing," such as occurs when we are directed from one office to the next without receiving an answer to our question or a solution to our problem. We also may view a bureaucracy in terms of red tape because of

> **bureaucracy** An organizational model characterized by a hierarchy of authority, a clear division of labour, explicit rules and procedures, and impersonality in personnel matters.

the situations in which there is so much paperwork and so many incomprehensible rules that no one really understands what to do. However, bureaucracy originally was not intended to be this way; it was seen as a way to make organizations *more* productive and efficient. Weber (1968/1922) was interested in the historical trend toward bureaucratization that accelerated during the Industrial Revolution. To Weber, the bureaucracy was the most efficient means of attaining organizational goals because of its coordination and control.

**WHY BUREAUCRACY?** While much of the rest of this chapter focuses on how bureaucracies work, it is also important to understand why they exist. The simple answer is that they exist because organizations grew too large to be managed in any other way. However, large organizations existed for thousands of years before the birth of bureaucracy, so we must also consider social conditions to explain why the modern bureaucratic form of social organization arose in the 19th century in Europe and North America. Weber suggested that this growth required both cultural and structural changes that did not occur until then.

The cultural change was the rejection of *traditional authority* and the acceptance of *rational-legal authority* as the basis of conduct. This means that people were less willing to accept rules based on tradition and more willing to grant legitimacy to a set of rules intended to achieve certain ends (Weber, 1947). Weber's influential work on the relationship between the rise of Protestantism and the development of capitalism (Weber, 1976) analyzes the factors that led to this change.

The social conditions for factory bureaucracies were established during the Industrial Revolution, when peasants were forced off the farms. These former peasants became the first large labour pool for the factories, as they had no alternative but to work for whatever wages the owners would pay them. The system of wage employment gave the profits from the workers' labour to the factory owner, while the workers were paid only a subsistence wage. This cheap labour provided a tremendous incentive for the factory owners to expand their enterprises. Owners used the capital their factories generated to mechanize the factories; they also developed the systems of specialization and standardization that most efficiently achieved productivity and profitability. Of course, breaking down production into specialized tasks required managers to coordinate activities, so the factories quickly became hierarchical organizations.

The success of the factory bureaucracy was important because it encouraged other organizations to adopt the same principles. The bureaucratic form quickly spread to governments, schools, and churches. Even today, we find pressure for other organizations to follow the lead of industry. Governments are continually urged to become more "businesslike," and universities face pressure to become more efficient and to meet the specialized needs of industry rather than providing students with a broader education.

**FORMAL CHARACTERISTICS OF BUREAUCRACY** Weber set forth several characteristics of bureaucratic organizations. Although real bureaucracies may not feature all of these ideal characteristics, Weber's model highlights the organizational efficiency and productivity that bureaucracies strive for.

*Division of Labour* Bureaucracies are characterized by specialization, and each member has a specific status with certain assigned tasks to fulfill. This division of labour requires the employment of specialized experts. In a university, for example, a distinct division of labour exists between the faculty and the administration.

*Hierarchy of Authority* Hierarchy of authority, or chain of command, includes each lower office being under the control of a higher one. Hierarchical authority takes the form of a pyramid. Those few individuals at the top have more power and exercise more control than do the many at the lower levels. Hierarchy inevitably influences social interaction. People lower in the hierarchy report to (and often take orders from) those above them. Persons at the upper levels are responsible not only for their own actions but also for those of the individuals they supervise.

*Rules and Regulations*  Weber asserted that rules and regulations establish authority within an organization. These rules are typically standardized and provided to members in a written format. In theory, written rules and regulations offer clear-cut standards for determining satisfactory performance. They also provide continuity so that each new member does not have to reinvent the rules and regulations.

*Qualification-Based Employment*  Bureaucracies hire staff members and professional employees based on specific qualifications. Favouritism, family connections, and other subjective factors not relevant to organizational efficiency are not acceptable criteria for employment. Individual performance is evaluated against specific standards, and promotions are based on merit as spelled out in personnel policies.

*Impersonality*  A detached approach should prevail toward clients so that personal feelings do not interfere with organizational decisions. Officials must interact with subordinates based on their  status in the organization, not on the officials' personal feelings.

**INFORMAL STRUCTURE IN BUREAUCRACIES**  An organizational chart makes the official, formal structure of a bureaucracy readily apparent. In practice, however, bureaucracies have patterns of activities and interactions that cannot be accounted for by organizational charts and formal rules. In addition to its formal structure, every bureaucracy has an informal structure, which has been called "bureaucracy's other face" (Page, 1946).

An organization's **informal structure** comprises those aspects of participants' day-to-day activities and interactions that ignore, bypass, or do not correspond with the official rules and procedures of the bureaucracy. An example is an informal "grapevine" that spreads information (with varying degrees of accuracy) much faster than do official channels of communication, which tend to be slow and unresponsive. The informal structure also includes the ideology and practices of workers on the job. Workers create a work culture to help deal with the constraints of their jobs and to guide their interactions with co-workers.

**informal structure**
Those aspects of participants' day-to-day activities and interactions that ignore, bypass, or do not correspond with the official rules and procedures of the bureaucracy.

**HAWTHORNE STUDIES AND INFORMAL NETWORKS**  The Hawthorne studies first made social scientists aware of the effect of informal networks on workers' productivity.

Researchers observed 14 men in the "bank wiring room" who were responsible for making parts of switches for telephone equipment. Although management had offered financial incentives to encourage the men to work harder, the men persisted in working according to their own informal rules. They tended to work rapidly in the morning and to ease off in the afternoon. They frequently stopped their own work to help another person who had fallen behind. When they got bored, they swapped tasks so their work was more varied. They played games and bet on horse races and baseball.

Why did these men insist on lagging behind even when they had been offered financial incentives to work harder? Perhaps they feared that the required productivity levels would increase if they showed that they could do more. Some of them also may have feared that they would lose their jobs if the work was finished more rapidly. One finding stood out: The men's productivity level was clearly related to the pressure they received from other members of their informal networks. Those who worked too hard were called "speed kings" and "rate busters"; individuals who worked too slowly were referred to as "chiselers." Those who broke the informal norm against telling a supervisor about someone else's shortcomings were called "squealers." Negative sanctions such as striking a person on the shoulder made the workers adhere to the informal norms of their work group. Ultimately, the level of productivity was determined by the workers' informal networks, not by the levels set by management (Blau and Meyer, 1987; Roethlisberger and Dickson, 1939).

Corporal Catherine Galliford is one of a number of members and former members who have launched sexual harassment suits against the RCMP. Sociologists have found that women in male-dominated fields are less likely than men to be included in informal networks and more likely to be harassed on the job. Are these two factors related? What steps could be taken to reduce the problems of harassment and lack of networks?

**POSITIVE AND NEGATIVE ASPECTS OF INFORMAL STRUCTURE** Is informal structure good or bad? Should it be controlled or encouraged? Two schools of thought have emerged with regard to these questions. One approach emphasizes control of informal groups; the other suggests that they should be nurtured.

Traditional management theories are based on the assumption that people are basically lazy and motivated by greed. Consequently, informal groups must be controlled (or eliminated) to ensure greater worker productivity. Proponents of this view cite the bank wiring room study to demonstrate the importance of controlling informal networks.

The other school of thought asserts that people are capable of cooperation. Thus, organizations should foster informal groups that permit people to work more efficiently toward organizational goals. Barnard (1938) discussed the functional aspects of informal groups. He suggested that informal groups help organizations by providing understanding and motivation for participants. Research on soldiers in combat has shown that bonds with other soldiers in each small squad or platoon have much more impact on performance than abstract notions of patriotism and love for one's country (Marshall, 1947). Even in huge organizations, close interpersonal relationships provide meaning and a sense of belonging to individual workers.

Informal groups can have a negative impact on employees who are excluded from them. While some scholars have argued that women and visible minorities receive fairer treatment in larger bureaucracies than they do in smaller organizations, others feel that they may be excluded from networks that are important for survival and advancement in the organization (Benokraitis and Feagin, 1986; Kanter, 1977; South et al., 1982). Women and visible minorities who are employed in positions traditionally held by white men (such as firefighters, police officers, and construction workers) are often excluded from the informal structure. Not only do they lack an informal network to "grease the wheels," they also may be harassed and endangered by their co-workers. For example, in 2012, many female RCMP members and ex-members sued the RCMP, claiming they had suffered sexual harassment, gender discrimination, and exposure to pornography throughout their careers. In sum, the informal structure is critical for employees—whether they are allowed to participate in it or not.

## Shortcomings of Bureaucracies

Weber's description of bureaucracy was intentionally an idealized model of a rationally organized institution. However, the characteristics that make up this "rational" model have a dark side that has frequently given bureaucracies a bad name (see Figure 6.6). Three of the major problems of bureaucracies are inefficiency and rigidity; resistance to change; and perpetuation of gender, race, and class inequalities.

**INEFFICIENCY AND RIGIDITY** Bureaucracies experience inefficiency and rigidity throughout the organization. The self-protective behaviour of officials at the top may render

FIGURE 6.6    CHARACTERISTICS AND EFFECTS OF BUREAUCRACY

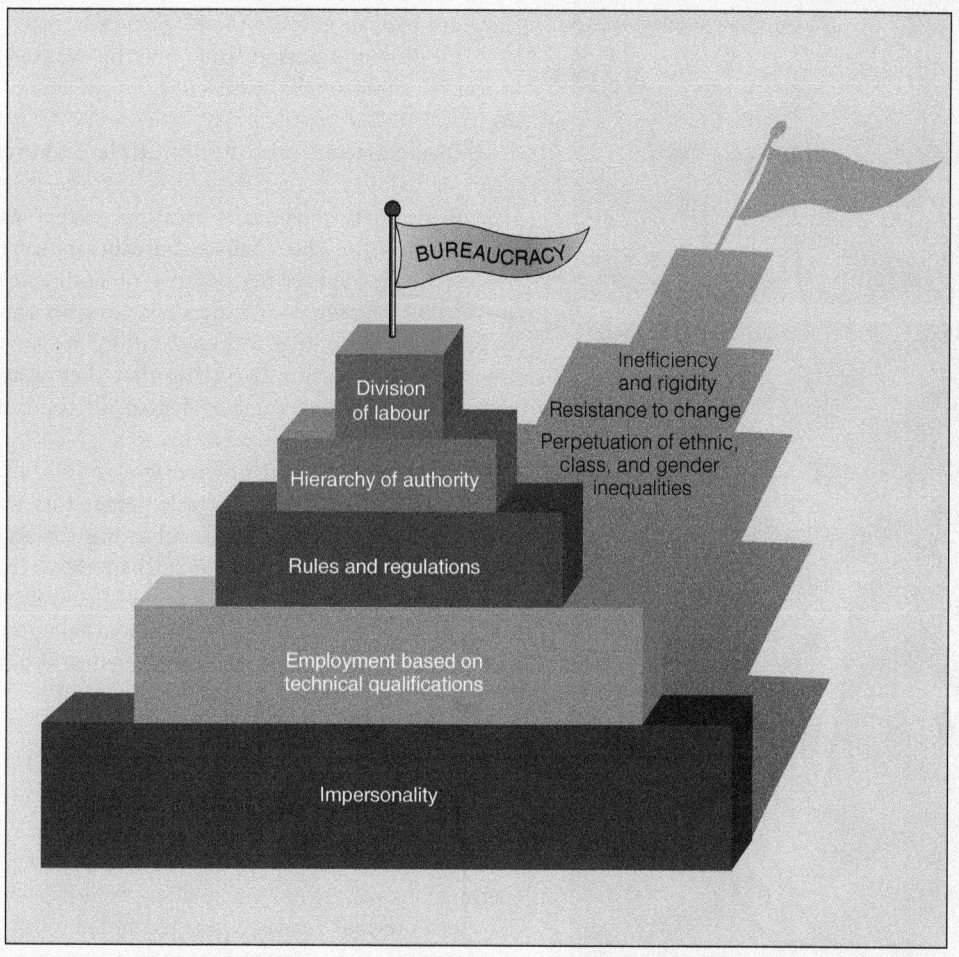

The very characteristics that define Weber's idealized bureaucracy can create or worsen the problems that many people associate with this type of organization.

the organization inefficient. One type of self-protective behaviour is the monopolization of information. Information is crucial for decision making at all levels of an organization. However, those in positions of authority may guard information because it is a source of power for them—others cannot second-guess their decisions without access to relevant (and often confidential) information (Blau and Meyer, 1987).

This information blockage is intensified by the hierarchical arrangement of officials and workers. While those at the top may use their power and authority to monopolize information, they may also fail to communicate with workers at the lower levels. As a result, they are often unaware of potential problems facing the organization. Meanwhile, those at the bottom of the structure hide their mistakes from supervisors, a practice that ultimately may result in problems for the organization.

Policies and procedures also contribute to inefficiency and rigidity. Bureaucratic regulations are often written out in great detail to ensure that almost all conceivable situations are covered (Blau and Meyer, 1987). **Goal displacement** occurs when the rules

**goal displacement** A process that occurs in organizations when the rules become an end in themselves rather than a means to an end.

The "organization man" of the computer age varies widely in manner and appearance, as shown in the contrast between the top photo of a casually clad employee at Apple Computer and the one of Bill Gates, the formally dressed chairman of Microsoft.

**bureaucratic personality** A psychological construct that describes those workers who are more concerned with following correct procedures than they are with doing the job correctly.

become an end in themselves rather than a means to an end (Merton, 1968). Administrators tend to overconform to the rules because their expertise is knowledge of the regulations and they are paid to enforce them. They also fear that if they bend the rules for one person, they may be accused of violating the norm of impersonality and engaging in favouritism (Blau and Meyer, 1987).

Bureaucrats may also be inflexible because they fear criticism or liability if they do not follow the rules closely. In the case of Kenneth Payne, the aspiring teacher you read about at the beginning of this chapter, bureaucrats were afraid to waive the need for fingerprints because of public concern about the possibility of sexual offenders working in the schools. These bureaucrats were able to avoid taking responsibility for their unreasonable decision by saying that they were "just following the rules." Mistakes can be blamed on the bureaucracy rather than on the individuals who run it.

Rigidity can also occur at lower levels of the bureaucracy. Merton (1968) used the term **bureaucratic personality** to describe workers who are more concerned with following correct procedures than they are with getting the job done correctly. Such workers are usually able to handle routine situations effectively but may be incapable of handling a unique problem or an emergency. Box 6.2 shows how bureaucratic inefficiency contributed to serious terrorist attacks in Canada and the United States.

**RESISTANCE TO CHANGE** Resistance to change occurs in all bureaucratic organizations. This resistance can make it difficult for organizations to adapt to new circumstances. Many workers are reluctant to change because they have adapted their professional and personal lives to the old way of doing their jobs. Some workers have also seen previous change efforts fail and do not want to commit to the latest effort at transforming their organization. Those trying to implement change can have a difficult task breaking through this resistance.

The hierarchical structure of bureaucracies can make this situation worse. Management is separated from labour, clerical workers from professional workers, and people doing one function from those doing another. This creates structural barriers to communication and to joint problem solving. Information is restricted and problems are dealt with in a segmented way. People are rewarded for not taking risks and punished when they try to make changes. Often, people have no structural way of getting innovative ideas from the bottom to the top, so they give up trying. Kanter provides an example of this kind of blockage in a textile company that had been dealing with frequent and costly yarn breakages for decades:

> A new plant manager interested in improving employee communication and involvement discovered a foreign-born worker with an ultimately successful idea for modifying the machine to reduce breakage—and was shocked to learn that the man had wondered about the machine modification for thirty-two years. "Why didn't you say something before?" the manager asked. The reply: "My supervisor wasn't interested and I had no one else to tell it to." (Kanter, 1983:70)

**176**

BOX 6.2    **POINT/COUNTERPOINT**

## How Bureaucratic Inefficiency Contributed to Terrorist Attacks

Bureaucratic inefficiency can impede information flow within and between large-scale organizations. Failures of governmental organizations to properly utilize information have contributed to the success of major terrorist strikes in Canada and the United States.

In 1985, an explosion destroyed Air India Flight 182, killing 329 people. The flight had originated in Vancouver and most of the victims were Canadians. After nearly two decades of investigation, two Sikh militants were tried for the crime, but they were acquitted in 2005.

Following the trial, an inquiry into the bombing was critical of the work of the RCMP and the Canadian Security and Intelligence Service (CSIS). The investigation into the bombing was seriously flawed and there was little cooperation between the RCMP and CSIS. Both the RCMP and CSIS had information that could have prevented the attack but took no action. Bureaucratic inefficiencies facilitated the attack and hindered the subsequent investigation.

One specific problem is that CSIS and the RCMP have different roles. CSIS is responsible for collecting intelligence on possible terrorist activity, while the RCMP is responsible for investigating criminal matters and assisting in the prosecution of accused persons. There has been a history of poor relationships between these agencies, and information collected by one agency has not always been made available to the other. CSIS did not process information on the prime suspect, prematurely erased wiretap evidence, and did not share evidence with the RCMP. The RCMP did not provide CSIS with intelligence information that would have allowed them to correctly assess the threat: "Unforgivably, the RCMP did not forward to CSIS the June 1st Telex that set out Air India's own intelligence, forecasting a June terrorist attempt to bomb an Air India flight by means of explosives hidden in checked baggage" (Commission of Inquiry into the Investigation of the Bombing of Air India Flight 182, 2010:23). The failure of these agencies to properly assess and share evidence contributed to the murder of hundreds of people.

These problems are not unique. Following the 2001 terrorist attacks on the United States, the Federal Bureau of Investigation (FBI), the Central Intelligence Agency (CIA), and other U.S. governmental organizations faced similar criticism about how they used and shared information before these attacks. The U.S. Senate Judiciary Committee conducted hearings in an effort to learn what information about terrorist activities and possible U.S. targets had been available to federal agencies before September 11 and why the government had not acted on this information to prevent the attacks. The judiciary committee interviewed FBI agent Coleen Rowley, who testified that she believed the culture of the FBI had prevented the organization from acting on what it knew before the attacks (*New York Times*, 2002b):

> Agent Rowley: We have a culture in the FBI that there's a certain pecking order, and it's pretty strong. And it's very rare that someone picks up the phone and calls a rank or two above themselves. It would have to be only on the strongest reasons. Typically, you would have to . . . pick up the phone and talk to somebody who is at your rank. So when you have an item that requires review by a higher level, it's incumbent for you to go to a higher-level person in your office and then for that person to make a call . . .

> Senator Grassley: In your letter [to the FBI director], you mention a culture of fear, especially a fear of taking action, and the problem of careerism. Could you talk about how this hurts investigations in the field, what the causes are, and what you think might fix these problems?

> Agent Rowley: [W]hen I looked up the definition [of careerism], I really said [it's] unbelievable how appropriate that is. I think the FBI does have a problem with that. And if I remember right, it means, "promoting one's career over integrity." So, when people make decisions, and it's basically so that [they] can get to the next level and not rock–either it's not rock the boat or do what a boss says without question. And either way that works, if you're making a decision to try to get to the next level, but you're not making that decision for the real right reason, that's a problem . . .

Organizations that resist change, rather than adapt to it, may not survive and certainly will not flourish. Thus leaders of many different organizations face the task of developing new organizational models that are better suited to today's environment. Consider the challenges faced by leaders of corporations such as those discussed in Box 6.3, "Organizations and New Media" (see Box 6.3 at **www.nelson.com/sociologyinourtimes6e**).

**PERPETUATION OF GENDER, RACE, AND CLASS INEQUALITIES** Bureaucracies can perpetuate inequalities of gender, race, and class. Power at the top of most North American bureaucracies still remains in the hands of affluent white men. These divisions can be perpetuated by the "dual labour market" in which bureaucracies provide different career paths for different categories of workers. Middle- and upper-class employees are more likely to have careers characterized by higher wages, job security, and opportunities for advancement. By contrast, poor and working-class employees (who are more likely to be women and members of racial minorities) work in occupations characterized by low wages, lack of job security, and few opportunities for promotion. This dual labour market not only reflects class, race, and gender inequities but also perpetuates them. See Box 6.4 on page 164.

While the situation has improved over the past several decades, women and members of racial minorities may also find themselves excluded from informal networks. Kanter (1977) conducted an important study of the difficulties faced by workers who did not fit the white male stereotype. There are enormous pressures on "tokens"—group members who were different from the dominant group members. Tokens were singled out and were often viewed as representatives of their group rather than as individual workers. These pressures led to higher turnover rates and to reduced performance by those in the token groups.

To counteract these pressures, organizations must establish policies that ensure supportive environments for members of disadvantaged groups. Pryor and McKinney (1991) showed how people respond to environments that condone sexist behaviour. Their experiments examined the dynamics of sexual harassment on university campuses. In one experiment, a graduate student (a member of the research team) led research subjects to believe that they would be training undergraduate women to use a computer. The actual purpose of the experiment was to observe whether the trainers (subjects) would harass the women if given the opportunity and encouraged to do so. By design, the graduate student purposely harassed the women (who were also part of the research team), setting an example for the subjects to follow.

Pryor and McKinney found that when the "trainers" were led to believe that sexual harassment was condoned and were then left alone with the women, they took full advantage of the situation in 90 percent of the experiments. One of the women on the research team felt vulnerable because of the permissive environment created by the men in charge:

> So it kind of made me feel a little bit powerless as far as that goes because there was nothing I could do about it. But I also realized that in a business setting, if this person really was my boss, that it would be harder for me to send out the negative signals or whatever to try to fend off that type of thing. (1995)

## TIME TO REVIEW

- Why have bureaucracies become the most universal organizational form in modern society?
- Describe the five characteristics that Weber believed characterized bureaucracies.
- How can the informal structure affect the way bureaucracies operate?
- Why do bureaucracies sometimes become rigid, inefficient and resistant to change?
- How do bureaucracies perpetuate inequalities of gender, race, and class?

## McDonaldization

Weber's work on bureaucracy was based on his view that rationalization was an inevitable part of the social world. George Ritzer has updated Weber's work by looking at what he calls *McDonaldization*—"the process by which the principles of the fast-food restaurant are coming to dominate more and more sectors of American society, as well as of the rest of the world" (2004:1). Ritzer believes that McDonald's restaurants embody the principles of rationalization and establish a model that is emulated by many other types of organizations. To Ritzer, fast-food restaurants go beyond Weber's model of bureaucracy. The basic elements of McDonaldization are as follows:

- *Efficiency.* Fast-food restaurants operate like an assembly line. Food is cooked, assembled, and served according to a standardized procedure. Customers line up or move quickly past a drive-through window. Despite the McDonald's slogan "We do it all for you," it is the customer who picks up the food, takes it to the table, and cleans up the garbage at the end of the meal.
- *Calculability.* The emphasis is on speed and quantity rather than quality. Cooking and serving operations are precisely timed, and the emphasis on speed often results in poor employee morale and high turnover rates. Restaurants are designed to encourage customers to leave quickly.
- *Predictability.* Standard menus and scripted encounters with staff make the experience predictable for customers. The food is supposed to taste the same wherever it is served.
- *Control.* Fast-food restaurants have never allowed individual employees much discretion; instead, employees must follow detailed procedures. The degree of control has been enhanced through technology. For example, automatic french fry cookers and other devices ensure a standardized product. Nobody claims to be a chef in a fast-food restaurant.
- *Irrationalities of rationality.* Fast-food restaurants are dehumanizing for both customers and employees. The examples of bureaucratic inflexibility used at the beginning of this chapter demonstrate this dehumanization, or **rationality**—the process by which traditional methods of social organization, characterized by informality and spontaneity, are gradually replaced by efficiently administered formal rules and procedures (bureaucracy). Kenneth Payne was denied a teaching career because of an inflexible interpretation of the rules, and the real human concerns of the victims of the New Orleans hurricane were subordinated to organizational rules.

**rationality** The process by which traditional methods of social organization, characterized by informality and spontaneity, are gradually replaced by efficiently administered formal rules and procedures (bureaucracy).

Ritzer feels that McDonaldization is expanding to other parts of our lives and to other parts of the world. Many universities process huge numbers of students by giving them classes in large lecture theatres and testing them using machine-graded, multiple-choice exams. The questions on these examinations are often taken from test banks provided by the textbook publishers, who also provide instructors with many of their teaching aids. Students who are more interested in efficiency than in learning can purchase their term papers online so they don't have to spend time writing them.

Recent increases in the number of babies born via surgery, using cesarean sections rather than waiting for a natural birth, show that even the birth process is being rationalized. Families and doctors may welcome the predictability associated with scheduling birth on a specific day during normal working hours rather than waiting for nature to take its course.

## ORGANIZATIONS OF THE FUTURE: THE NETWORK ORGANIZATION  LO-5

The form of organizations has changed over time. While we can never be certain about the future, broad social trends, such as globalization, technological innovation, and the increased prevalence of an economy based on services, make it likely that *networks* will become the dominant organization of the future. Social theorist Manuel Castells argues that "the old order, governed by discrete individual units in the pursuit of money, efficiency, happiness, or power,

BOX 6.4    **POINT/COUNTERPOINT**

## *Dilbert* and the Bureaucracy

Our experiences with red tape and other bureaucratic inefficiencies have been satirized by cartoonist (and disillusioned bureaucrat) Scott Adams. In the late 1980s, Adams began passing his cartoons around the office at Pacific Bell. Since then, *Dilbert* has become a phenomenal success and is read in more than 2000 papers in 70 countries. *Dilbert* ridicules many of the worst features of bureaucracy, including stupid bosses, cubicles, management consultants, pointless meetings, and inflexibility. (For examples of the cartoon, go to www.unitedmedia.com/comics/dilbert).

Workers enjoy *Dilbert*. The cartoons are posted on office doors, walls, and desks, and many of Adams's ideas come from readers' suggestions. The British magazine *The Economist* attributes *Dilbert's* popularity to the fact that the comic strip taps into three trends that are troubling workers:

1. Employees are forced to labour harder to compensate for the effects of downsizing.
2. Workers are afraid of being laid off and see their wage increases falling far behind those of their managers.
3. New management fads have led to constant reorganization but have had little impact on efficiency or on job satisfaction.

Ironically, while many workers feel *Dilbert* says what they are thinking about ineffective and uncaring managers, the leaders of many of North America's largest corporations have used the cartoons for training and corporate communications.

*Sources: The Economist, 1997; Merton, 1968; Whitaker, 1997.*

is being replaced by a novel one in which motives, decisions, and actions flow from ever more fluid, yet ever-present networks. It is networks, not the firm, bureaucracy, or the family, that gets things done" (Esping Anderson, 2000:68).

You can learn how global networks operate by reading about the structure of terrorist organizations in Box 6.5, or by thinking about the ways in which illicit drugs get from the coca fields of Colombia and the poppy fields of Afghanistan to users on the streets of Halifax, Toronto, and Victoria. Large bureaucracies are not involved in either of these complex global enterprises, as terrorists and drug dealers operate very effectively through decentralized global networks. One reason that drug suppression strategies have not succeeded is because there is no company called Global Drugs Inc. that can be easily located and destroyed by law enforcement agencies. Instead, there are shifting, fluid networks of people who are difficult to identify and who are easily replaced when the legal system takes them out of the network. Similar problems face those who are trying to deal with the threat of terrorism.

Another example of the operation of a flexible global network is the production of open source software, such as the Linux operating system and the Firefox Internet browser. This software was not produced by a large profit-making corporation, but by networks of people working together with no expectation of profit. The product is available freely to anyone who wishes to download it, and programmers all over the world can make improvements in the software. While some coordination is necessary to develop a product that can be used by the public, no large bureaucracy is required and individual users are free to modify programs to suit their own needs.

Networks have always had an advantage over other organizational forms because they are agile and can quickly adapt to new circumstances. However, the ability to coordinate network activities has been weak compared to hierarchical bureaucratic organizations that

---

**BOX 6.5    SOCIOLOGY IN GLOBAL PERSPECTIVE**

## The Structure of Terrorist Networks

The growth of large armies, such as the Prussian army, contributed to the development of the bureaucratic form of organization. These large armies represented the governments of established countries; however, many of today's wars are not between two countries.

Terrorist attacks around the globe and the difficulties in fighting the insurgency in Afghanistan have drawn attention to what military planners refer to as *asymmetrical warfare*. This term refers to attacks by small groups of people, who usually do not represent states or governments, upon much larger and stronger opponents. Terrorists do not directly confront their opponents, since they would be quickly defeated in such a confrontation. Rather, they use covert tactics, such as car bombs and suicide bombings, which are difficult to prevent.

To fight successfully against larger and more powerful opponents, terrorist groups must develop organizational structures that are difficult to identify and to fight against. Rather than forming large hierarchical armies, terrorist groups such as al-Qaeda have evolved sophisticated network structures. These networks are made up of loosely coupled cells, each of which has only a few members. This structure allows for a high level of secrecy, flexibility, and innovation. Participants in the network operate in a coordinated way because they have relationships with other members of the network, with whom they share a common vision of the future, not because of bureaucratic control. Al-Qaeda network members are linked by a common religious background and philosophy and through the leadership of now-deceased Osama bin Laden and his associates. Figure 6.7 is a simplified diagram of the al-Qaeda network. This structure is very different from the hierarchical organization charts of the military and security organizations that are trying

to defeat al-Qaeda. This loose and flexible network structure makes it difficult to defeat terrorist organizations. For example, the network has roots in many different countries, and information and funds can flow relatively freely from one jurisdiction to another. On the other hand, security and intelligence agencies are based in individual countries and for a variety of reasons find it difficult to work cooperatively (Arquilla and Ronfeldt, 2001). The fluid network of al-Qaeda shown in the figure contrasts with the hierarchical, vertical structure of the armies and governments opposing it. Using modern communications technology, including the Internet, information can flow to all parts of the network much more easily than can information that must be filtered through national governments and their internal bureaucracies (see Box 6.2).

Krebs (2002) analyzed the relationships between the hijackers responsible for the September 11 attacks on the United States. Mohamed Atta, who was the leader of the attacks, had contacts with each of the teams of hijackers. However, most of the others had no contact with teams other than their own. The strategy of minimizing ties among members of the network is deliberate—if security personnel identify or apprehend one or two members of the network, they can provide only limited information about other members so the entire network would not be jeopardized. In a videotape that was found at an al-Qaeda training camp in Afghanistan, Osama bin Laden said, "Those who were trained to fly didn't know the others. One group of people did not know the other group" (Department of Defense, 2001, cited in Krebs, 2002:46). It is very difficult for those opposing such networks to be able to target more than a limited part of the terrorist organization.

*Sources:* Arquilla and Ronfeldt, 2001; Krebs, 2002.

(continued)

---

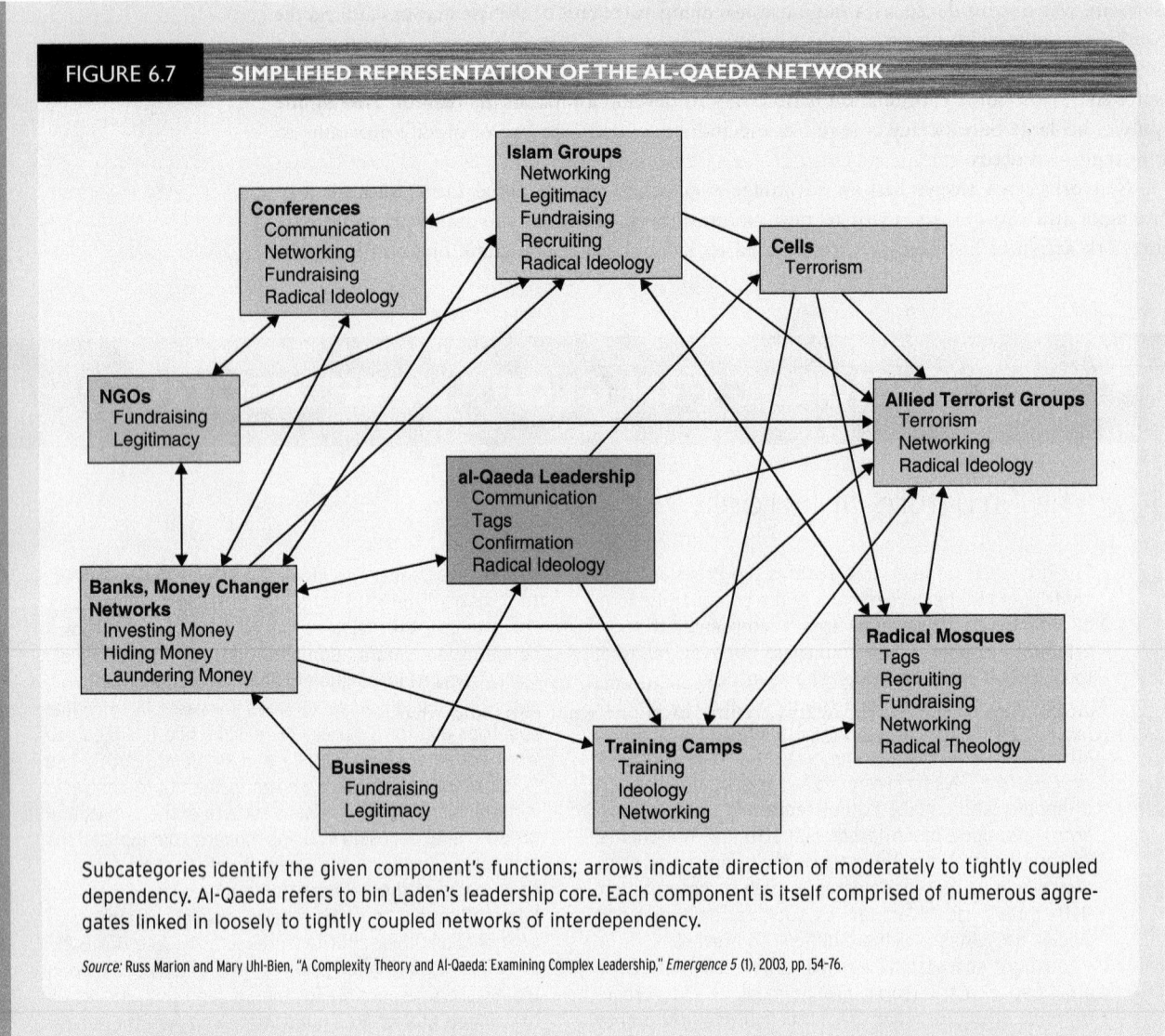

**FIGURE 6.7    SIMPLIFIED REPRESENTATION OF THE AL-QAEDA NETWORK**

Subcategories identify the given component's functions; arrows indicate direction of moderately to tightly coupled dependency. Al-Qaeda refers to bin Laden's leadership core. Each component is itself comprised of numerous aggregates linked in loosely to tightly coupled networks of interdependency.

*Source:* Russ Marion and Mary Uhl-Bien, "A Complexity Theory and Al-Qaeda: Examining Complex Leadership," *Emergence 5* (1), 2003, pp. 54-76.

have well-specified lines of communication and means of coordination. This has meant that bureaucracies have had a competitive advantage in handling complex tasks (Castells, 2000b). Modern information and communication technology has now provided networks with a competitive advantage. Each part of a network can communicate instantly with other parts, and those responsible for the network can constantly monitor performance even if the network is globally distributed. With this technology, the network can quickly shift and change, as pieces can be eliminated if they are no longer useful or can be temporarily set aside if they are not needed for a particular project (Castells, 2000b).

It is more difficult to centrally control a network than a traditional hierarchical organization because, once the network has been programmed and set in motion, it may be difficult for anyone, even those who started the network, to shut it down. With no central communication and control system, parts of the network can continue to operate even if the central core is eliminated. Thus, opponents of al-Qaeda could not shut down the network by simply closing down some of its pieces. Even Osama bin Laden would have had difficulty closing down the network or changing its goals if other members of al-Qaeda and its affiliated groups around the world wanted to continue with their activities.

Castells (2000a, 2000b) speaks of a new type of economic organization called the **network enterprise**, in which separate businesses, which may be companies or parts of companies, join together for specific projects that become the focus of the network. This structure gives those responsible for the network a great deal of flexibility, as they can select and change network partners based upon factors such as cost, efficiency, and technological innovation. The Dell laptop computer that you may be working on is the product of a network enterprise (Friedman, 2005). Dell sells its products over the Internet and by telephone rather than in stores, so your order may be taken by a person in Bangalore, India, rather than a clerk in your own city. The hardware that makes up the computer was manufactured by companies in Israel, the Philippines, Malaysia, Costa Rica, China, Taiwan, South Korea, Germany, Japan, Mexico, Singapore, Indonesia, India, and Thailand. The computers are assembled in Dell factories located in Ireland, China, Brazil, Malaysia, and the United States. Thomas Friedman describes how the company fills its orders:

> "In an average day, we sell 140,000 to 150,000 computers," explained Dick Hunter, one of Dell's three global production managers. "Those orders come over Dell.com or over the telephone. As soon as these orders come in, our suppliers know about it. They get a signal based on every component in the machine you ordered, so the supplier knows just what he has to deliver. If you are supplying power cords for desktops, you can see minute by minute how many power cords you are going to have to deliver." Every two hours, the Dell factory in Penang [Malaysia] sends an email to the various SLCs [supplier logistics centres] nearby, telling each one what parts and what quantities of those parts it wants delivered within the next 90 minutes—and not one minute later. Within 90 minutes, trucks from the various SLCs around Penang pull up to the Dell manufacturing plant and unload the parts needed for all those notebooks ordered in the last two hours. This goes on all day, every two hours," said Hunter. (2005:415)

This system is a major reason why Dell helped to dramatically reduce computer prices during the 1990s and early 2000s. A critical factor in the development of widely dispersed network organizations has been the development of modern communications technology. Networks are held together by the rapid flow of information rather than by bricks and mortar and a rigid organizational chart like that of the industrial organization. The globalized production processes used by Dell and many other large companies would not be possible without instant global communication. The Internet itself is a decentralized and loosely coupled structure. The Internet was originally designed as way of ensuring that communications systems would survive an attack targeted at the central hubs of information systems. Instead of flowing from a central hub, information on the Internet is transmitted in small packets that can follow a wide range of electronic routes and are put together at the destination computer (Castells, 2000a). Nobody owns the Internet, so it is universally accessible to anyone who has a computer and a connection. While the Internet is vulnerable to a variety of threats, including computer hacking, it would be almost impossible to completely shut it down. Flexibility and resilience are what make the Internet such a valuable tool for networks.

Castells (2004) points out that it is not simply the technology that is critical, but also the cultural and organizational means of using the technology. This means that just having computers is not enough to guarantee access to the networked global economy. Countries with ineffective systems of government, few trained workers, and no entrepreneurial culture that supports innovation will be excluded from these networks. India has been successful in getting involved in network enterprises because of an entrepreneurial culture, a democratic government, and the presence of a well-educated workforce with English language skills, while many parts of Africa and Latin America have less involvement in the new economy.

**network enterprise**
Separate businesses, which may be companies or parts of companies, join together for specific projects that become the focus of the network.

Sociologists are also concerned with assessing the impact of network enterprises on people. While this network structure can help corporations to become more profitable, the impact on workers has not always been as positive. For example, unions lose much of their bargaining power when production at one plant can be quickly moved to another part of the network in a different country. Thus a strike may result in the permanent closure of a factory and the movement of jobs offshore. It is likely that the future work lives of today's university students will be affected in many ways—some positive but others negative—by the shift to networked organizations. Because network enterprises are fluid and can quickly transform themselves, you should anticipate that your working lives may also change rapidly after you enter the labour market.

Finally, there are inherent dangers in networked organizations. These dangers were illustrated in August 2003 when the power went off for several days in much of Ontario because of a power outage in Ohio that cascaded through the transmission networks covering the northeastern U.S. and Ontario. A similar network failure led to the global financial crisis in 2008 in which lax U.S. mortgage practices affected the global economy and billions of people who had not even invested in these mortgages (Watts, 2009). Our reliance on complex physical and social networks places us at risk, and these risks are not always predictable. Global transportation networks facilitate the spread of disease; email viruses threaten our computers; a moment of indiscretion can be spread around the globe through YouTube; and any disruption of traffic between Detroit and Windsor would have a serious impact on North American automobile production and food distribution because of the system of parts manufacture and supply. Governments will be challenged in the future to determine ways of minimizing this risk.

## TIME TO REVIEW

- Explain Ritzer's theory that the principles that guide McDonald's operations are expanding to other parts of our lives and to other parts of the world.
- How does the network structure increase the effectiveness of terrorist groups?
- According to Castells, what are the advantages of network enterprises over traditional businesses?
- How is the Internet changing the way businesses operate?

## LO-1  Identify the differences among social groups, aggregates, and categories.

A social group is a collection of two or more people who interact frequently, share a sense of belonging, and depend on one another. People who happen to be in the same place at the same time are considered an aggregate. Those who share a similar characteristic are considered a category. Neither aggregates nor categories are considered social groups.

© Gari Wyn Williams/Alamy

## LO-2  Understand the effect that size has on the functioning of groups.

In small groups, all members know one another and interact simultaneously. In groups with more than three members, the dynamics of communication change and members tend to assume specialized tasks. As groups grow larger, keeping them operating effectively becomes increasingly challenging.

© Roy Morsch/zefa/Corbis

## LO-3  Explain the impact of groups on people's behaviour.

Groups have a significant influence on our values, attitudes and behaviour. Most of us our willing to exhibit a high level of conformity to the wishes of other group members. This sometimes leads to groupthink—the process by which members of a cohesive group arrive at a decision that many individual members privately believe is unwise.

© AP Photo/Chris O'Meara

## KEY TERMS

**aggregate** A collection of people who happen to be in the same place at the same time but have little else in common (p. 144).

**bureaucracy** An organizational model characterized by a hierarchy of authority, a clear division of labour, explicit rules and procedures, and impersonality in personnel matters (p. 155).

**bureaucratic personality** A psychological construct that describes those workers who are more concerned with following correct procedures than they are with doing the job correctly (p. 160).

**category** A number of people who may never have met one another but who share a similar characteristic (p. 144).

**conformity** The process of maintaining or changing behaviour to comply with the norms established by a society, subculture, or other group (p. 150).

**dyad** A group consisting of two members (p. 149).

**goal displacement** A process that occurs in organizations when the rules become an end in themselves rather than a means to an end (p. 159).

**groupthink** The process by which members of a cohesive group arrive at a decision that many individual members privately believe is unwise (p. 153).

**informal structure** Those aspects of participants' day-to-day activities and interactions that ignore, bypass, or do not correspond with the official rules and procedures of the bureaucracy (p. 157).

**ingroup** A group to which a person belongs and with which the person feels a sense of identity (p. 146).

**network** A web of social relationships that link one person with other people and, through them, with more people that those people know (p. 146).

**network enterprise** Separate businesses, which may be companies or parts of companies, join together for specific projects that become the focus of the network (p. 167).

**outgroup** A group to which a person does not belong and toward which the person may feel a sense of competitiveness or hostility (p. 146).

**rationality** The process by which traditional methods of social organization, characterized by informality and spontaneity, are gradually replaced by efficiently administered formal rules and procedures (bureaucracy) (p. 163).

**reference group** A group that strongly influences a person's behaviour and social attitudes, regardless of whether that individual is a member (p. 146).

**small group** A collectivity small enough for all members to be acquainted with one another and to interact simultaneously (p. 149).

**triad** A group composed of three members (p. 149).

**LO-4** Identify the characteristics that define a bureaucracy and the "other face" of bureaucracies.

A bureaucracy is a formal organization characterized by hierarchical authority, division of labour, explicit procedures, and impersonality. Bureaucracy's "other face" is the informal structure of daily activities and interactions that bypass the official rules and procedures. Informal networks may enhance productivity or may be counterproductive to the organization. They also may be detrimental to those who are excluded from them.

**LO-5** Discuss the form large organizations may take in the future.

While we can never be certain about the future, broad social trends, such as globalization, technological innovation, and the increased prevalence of a service economy, make it likely that networks will be the dominant organization of the future. Networked organizations, which are made possible by modern communications technology, are flexible and can respond quickly to social change.

## APPLICATION QUESTIONS

1. Do you think the insights gained from Milgram's research on obedience outweigh the elements of deception and stress that were forced on his subjects?

2. Many students have worked at a McDonald's or at some other fast-food restaurant. Relate your experience (or that of your friends) to George Ritzer's analysis of "McDonaldization."

3. Technology is changing the way organizations have to operate. Consider the entertainment industry. Downloading music and movies from the Internet has become very popular, and the film and music industries are trying hard to convince the Canadian government to pass new legislation to combat this downloading. What are the arguments of those who think that this material should be widely available on the Internet? What are the counterarguments of those who wish to see downloading regulated? Which side do you support in this debate?

4. What happens to people when they violate bureaucratic regulations? What range of sanctions do bureaucracies have to enforce these regulations?

5. Networks are important organizational forms. How have social networking sites changed the way in which people stay connected with their personal and professional networks?

# KEY FIGURES

Used courtesy of George Ritzer

**George Ritzer (b. 1940)** Ritzer is a prolific social theorist who is perhaps best known for his work on the concept of "McDonaldization." This work is a contemporary extension of Weber's study of rationalization.

Used courtesy of Manuel Castells

**Manuel Castells (b. 1942)** One of the foremost theorists of network theory, Castells is a Spanish sociologist who has taught for many years in the U.S. His other work has focused on the influence of the media, globalization, and the processes of urban life.

Photo by Eric Kroll

**Stanley Milgram (1933-1984)** Milgram was a social psychologist whose work contributed to the study of social organization. His best-known research involves his study of the "small world" and his controversial obedience studies.

**Rosabeth Moss Kanter (b. 1943)** A professor at Harvard Business School, much of Kanter's work has focused on change management. One of her best-known books, *Men and Women of the Corporation* (1977), examined the difficulties faced by members of token groups, including women, in formal organizations.

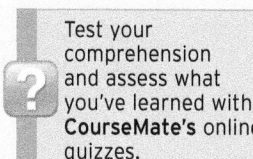
Test your comprehension and assess what you've learned with **CourseMate's** online quizzes.

For other interesting Lived Experiences, watch the video clips on **CourseMate.**

Practise what you've learned with flashcards containing key terms and definitions on **CourseMate.**

# Chapter 28

## McJobs: McDonaldization and Its Relationship to the Labor Process

GEORGE RITZER

In this selection, Ritzer wants to expand on his core arguments regarding **McDonaldization** (where society adopts the features of a fast-food restaurant and becomes a highly rationalized division of de-skilled labour). For example, while it is easy to understand how, say, the process by which food is produced in fast-food restaurants has been shaped by an emphasis on efficiency, calculability, predictability, and control, what is less obvious, but nevertheless true, is that even the interactions between workers and customers are also shaped by these emphases. In some cases, as Ritzer points out, these emphases function to blur the line between "worker" and "customer" so that customers become unpaid workers. Finally, he confronts what might be a puzzle: Why is there so little discontent among the workers whose lives have been affected by McDonaldization? Ritzer's answer is that any discontent that might arise in some particular organization is blunted by the fact that we live in a society that is being McDonaldized on so many different levels. Do you agree that McDonaldization produces little discontent? Isn't the popularity of Ritzer's argument itself some evidence to the contrary?

1. Who takes McJobs, and how are they exploited by the McDondaldized system?

In recent years the spread of McDonaldized systems has led to the creation of an enormous number of jobs. Unfortunately, the majority of them can be thought of as McDonaldized jobs, or "**McJobs.**" While we usually associate these types of positions with fast-food restaurants, and in fact there are many jobs in that setting, McJobs have spread throughout much of the economy. . . .

It is worth outlining some of the basic realities of employment in the fast-food industry in the United States since those jobs serve as a model for employment in other McDonaldized settings. The large number of people employed in fast-food restaurants accounts for over 40 percent of the approximately 6 million people employed in restaurants of all types. Fast-food restaurants rely heavily on teenage employees—almost 70 percent of their employees are 20 years of age or younger. For many, the fast-food restaurant is likely to be their first employer. It is estimated that the first job for one of every 15 workers was at McDonald's; one of every eight Americans has worked at McDonald's at some time in his or her life. The vast majority of employees are part-time workers: the average

**PART 11**

Source: Republished with permission of SAGE Publications, from *McDonaldization: The Reader*, George Ritzer, Thousand Oaks: Pine Forge Press, 2002; permission conveyed through Copyright Clearance Center, Inc.

workweek in the fast-food industry is 29.5 hours. There is a high turnover rate: Only slightly more than half the employees remain on the job for a year or more. Minorities are overrepresented in these jobs—almost two-thirds of employees are women and nearly a quarter are non-white. These are low-paid occupations, with many earning the minimum wage or slightly more. As a result, these jobs are greatly affected by changes in the minimum wage: An upward revision has an important effect on the income of these workers. However, there is a real danger that many workers would lose their positions as a result of such increases, especially in economically marginal fast-food restaurants. . . .

McJobs are characterized by the...dimensions of McDonaldization. The jobs tend to involve a series of simple tasks in which the emphasis is on performing each as efficiently as possible. Second, the time associated with many of the tasks is carefully calculated and the emphasis on the quantity of time a task should take tends to diminish the quality of the work from the point of view of the worker. That is, tasks are so simplified and streamlined that they provide little or no meaning to the worker. Third, the work is predictable; employees do and say essentially the same things hour after hour, day after day. Fourth, many nonhuman technologies are employed to control workers and reduce them to robot-like actions. Some technologies are in place, and others are in development, that will lead to the eventual replacement of many of these "human robots" with computerized robots. Finally, the rationalized McJobs lead to a variety of irrationalities, especially the dehumanization of work. The result is the extraordinarily high turnover rate described above and difficulty in maintaining an adequate supply of replacements.

The claim is usually made by spokespeople for McDonaldized systems that they are offering a large number of entry-level positions that help give employees basic skills they will need in order to move up the occupational ladder within such systems (and many of them do). This is likely to be true in the instances in which the middle-level jobs to which they move—for example, shift leader in or assistant manager or manager of a fast-food restaurant—are also routinized and scripted. . . . However, the skills acquired in McJobs are not likely to prepare one for, help one to acquire, or help one to function well in, the far more desirable postindustrial occupations which are highly complex and require high levels of skill and education. Experience in routinized actions and scripted interactions do not help much when occupations require thought and creativity. . . .

McJobs are not simply the de-skilled jobs of our industrial past in new settings; they are jobs that have a variety of new and distinctive characteristics. . . . There have also emerged many distinctive aspects of the control of these workers. Industrial and McDonaldized jobs both tend to be highly routinized in terms of what people do on the job. However, one of the things that is distinctive about McDonaldized jobs, especially since so many of them involve work that requires interaction and communication, especially with consumers, is that what people *say* on the job is also highly routinized. To put this another way, McDonaldized jobs are tightly scripted: They are characterized by *both* routinized actions . . . and scripted interactions (examples include "May I help you?"; "Would you like a dessert to go with your meal?"; and "Have a nice day!"). Scripts are crucial because many of the workers in McDonaldized systems are interactive service workers. This means that they not only produce goods and provide services, but they often do so in interaction with customers.

The scripting of interaction leads to new depths in the **de-skilling of workers**. Not only have employee actions been de-skilled; employees' ability to speak and interact with customers is now being limited and controlled. There are not only scripts to handle general situations but also a range of subscripts to deal with a variety of contingencies. Verbal and interactive skills are being taken away from employees and built into the scripts in much the same way that manual skills were taken and built into various technologies. At one time distrusted in their ability to *do* the right thing, workers now find themselves no longer trusted to *say* the right thing. Once able to create distinctive interactive styles, and to adjust them to different circumstances, employees are now asked to follow scripts as mindlessly as possible. . . .

McDonaldized systems have little interest in how their mainly part-time, short-time employees feel about and see themselves. These systems are merely interested in controlling their employees' overt behavior for as long as they work in such a system.

One very important, but rarely noted, aspect of the labor process in the fast-food restaurant and other McDonaldized systems is the extent to which customers are being led, perhaps even almost required, to perform a number of tasks without pay that were formerly performed by paid employees. For example, in the modern gasoline station the driver now does various things for free (pumps gas, cleans windows, checks oil, and even pays through a computerized credit card system built into the pump) that were formerly done by paid attendants. In these and many other settings, McDonaldization has brought the customer *into* the labor process: The customer *is* the laborer! This has several advantages for employers, such as lower (even nonexistent) labor costs, the need for fewer employers, and less trouble with personnel problems: Customers are far less likely to complain about a few seconds or minutes of tedious work than employees who devote a full workday to such tasks. Because of its advantages, as well as because customers are growing accustomed to and accepting of it, I think customers are likely to become even more involved in the labor process.

This is the most revolutionary development, at least as far as the labor process is concerned, associated with McDonaldization. . . . The analysis of the labor process must be extended to what customers do in McDonaldized systems.

The distinction between customer and employee is eroding, or in postmodern terms "imploding," and one can envision more and more work settings in which customers are asked to do an increasing amount of "work." More dramatically, it is also likely that we will see more work settings in which there are no employees at all! In such settings, customers, in interaction with non-human technologies, will do *all* of the human labor. A widespread example is the ATM in which customers (and the technology) do all of the work formerly done by bank tellers.

In a sense, a key to the success of McDonaldized systems is that they have been able to supplement the exploitation of employees with the exploitation of customers. In Marxian terms, customers create value in the tasks they perform for McDonaldized systems. And they are not simply paid less than the value they produce, they are paid *nothing at all*. In this way, customers are exploited to an even greater degree than workers. As is true of the exploitation of workers, owners are unaware of the fact that they are exploiting customers. But knowledge of exploitation is not a prerequisite to its practice.

While we have been focusing on the exploitation of customers in McDonaldized systems, this is not to say that employers have lost sight of the need to exploit workers. Beyond the usual exploitation of being paid less than the value of what they produce, McDonald's employees are often not guaranteed that they will work the number of hours they are supposed to on a given day. If business is slow, they may be sent home early in order that the employer can economize on labor costs: This reduces their take-home pay. As a result, employees often find it hard to count on a given level of income, meager as it might be, each week. In this way, and many others, employees of McDonaldized systems are even more exploited than their industrial counterparts.

This discussion brings together the two great theories in the history of sociology— Weber's theory of rationalization and Marx's

**PART 11**

theory of capitalist expansion and exploitation. **Rationalization** is a process that serves the interest of capitalists. They push it forward (largely unconsciously) because it heightens the level of exploitation of workers, allows new agents (e.g., customers) to be exploited and brings with it greater surplus value and higher profits. . . .We can see here how rationalization not only enhances control but also heightens the level and expands the reach of exploitation.

In various ways, McDonaldization is imposed on employees and even customers. They often have no choice but to conform, even if they would prefer things to be done in other ways. However, it would be a mistake to look at McDonaldization as simply being imposed on workers and customers. As discussed above, the basic ideas associated with McDonaldization are part of the value system. Many workers and customers have internalized them and conform to them of their own accord.

The emphasis on the McDonaldization of work (like that on de-skilling) tends to emphasize only one side of the dialectic between structural changes, especially those imposed by management, and the significance of the responses of employees, which are consistently downplayed. But . . . the employees of McDonaldized systems often exhibit a considerable amount of independence, perhaps even creativity, on the job. . . . Also, . . . in our rush to condemn, we must not ignore the advantages to both employees and customers of the routinization, even the scripting, of work. . . .

There is also a dialectic between living one's life in a McDonaldized society and working in a McDonaldized job. These are mutually reinforcing, and the net result is that if most of one's life is spent in one McDonaldized system or another, then one is less likely to feel dissatisfied with either one's life or one's job. This helps to account for . . . [the] finding that McDonald's workers do not evidence a high level of dissatisfaction with their work. This, perhaps, is one of the most disturbing implications of the McDonaldization thesis. If most of one's life is spent in McDonaldized

systems, then there is little or no basis for rebellion against one's McDonaldized job since one lacks a standard against which to compare, and to judge, such a job.

This also undermines one of Marx's fundamental assumptions that when all is said and done workers remain at odds with the kind of work that is being imposed on them and are a threat to those who are imposing the work. To Marx, there is a creative core (species being, for example) lying just below the surface that is ever-ready to protest, or rebel against, the rationalized and exploitative character of work. However, can that creative core survive intact, or even at all, in the face of growing up in a McDonaldized world, being bombarded by media messages from McDonaldized systems, and being socialized by and educated in McDonaldized schools?

It has been argued that the kinds of trends discussed above and in Marx's work are occurring not only among the lower layers in the occupational hierarchy but also among the middle layers. McDonaldization is something that those at the top of any hierarchy seek to avoid for themselves but are willing and eager to impose on those who rank below them in the system. Initially, it is the lowest level employees who have their work McDonaldized, but it . . . eventually creeps into those middle layers.

While guilty of exploiting and controlling employees, franchise operators are, in turn, controlled and exploited by franchise companies. Many franchise operators have done well, even becoming multimillionaires controlling perhaps hundreds of franchises, but many others have staggered or failed as a result of high start-up costs and continuing fees to the franchise companies. (The inducement to the franchisor to open as many outlets as possible threatens the profitability and even the continued existence of extant franchise owners.) The operators take much of the financial risk, while the franchise companies sit back and (often) rake in the profits. In addition, the franchise companies frequently have detailed rules, regulations, and even inspectors that they use to control the operators.

While no class within society is immune to McDonaldization, the lower classes are the most affected. They are the ones who are most likely to go to McDonaldized schools; live in inexpensive, mass-produced tract houses; and work in McDonaldized jobs. Those in the upper classes have much more of a chance of sending their children to non-McDonaldized schools, living in custom-built homes, and working in occupations in which they impose McDonaldization on others while avoiding it to a large degree themselves.

Also related to the social class issue is the fact that the McDonaldization of a significant portion of the labor force does not mean that all, or even most, of the labor force is undergoing this process. In fact, the McDonaldization of some of the labor force is occurring at the same time that another large segment is moving in a postindustrial, that is, more highly skilled, direction. Being created in this sector of society are relatively high-status, well-paid occupations requiring high levels of education and training.

McDonaldization and postindustrialization tend to occur in different sectors of the labor market. However, the spread of McJobs leads us to be dubious of the idea that we have moved into a new postindustrial era and have left behind the kind of de-skilled jobs we associated with industrial society.

It could be argued, as many have, that the focus in modern capitalism has shifted from the control and exploitation of consumption. While that may well be true, the fact is that capitalists do not, and will not, ignore the realm of production. . . . The nature of work is changing and capitalists are fully involved in finding new ways of controlling and exploiting workers. Further, they have discovered that they can even replace paid employees not only with machines, temporary workers, and so on but also with customers who are seemingly glad do the work for nothing! Here, clearly, is a new gift to the capitalist. Surplus value is now not only to be derived from the labor time of the employee but also from the leisure time of the customer. McDonaldization is helping to open a whole new world of exploitation and growth to the contemporary capitalist.

## Critical Thinking Questions

1. Are there any ties between the discussion of exploitation in this article and the discussion of exploitation in the Tuskeegee (Chapter 6) and Eugenics (Chapter 7) articles?
2. Can you draw a link between the "powerlessness" and "depersonalization" of patients mentioned in the Rosenhan article ("On Being Sane in Insane Places," Chapter 23) and the experience of people in McJobs?

**PART 11**

# Stratification

# CHAPTER 6

# SOCIAL STRATIFICATION

Sorry!
The lifestyle you
ordered is currently
out of stock

**Harvey Krahn**
UNIVERSITY OF ALBERTA

SOURCE: © BEN STANSALL/AFP/Getty Images/Newscom.

NEL

IN THIS CHAPTER YOU WILL LEARN THAT

- Persistent patterns of social inequality are based on statuses assigned to individuals at birth and on how well individuals perform certain roles. Societies vary in the degree to which mobility up and down the stratification system occurs.

- Explanations of the origins and impact of social stratification include the theory of Karl Marx, which emphasizes the exploitation of the working class by owners of land and industry as the main source of inequality and change; the theory of Max Weber, which emphasizes the power that derives from property ownership, prestige, and politics; functionalist theory, which holds that stratification is both inevitable and necessary; and several revisions of Marx's and Weber's ideas that render them more relevant to today's society.

- Although there has been considerable opportunity for upward occupational mobility in Canada, wealth and property are concentrated in relatively few hands, and one in seven Canadians is a low-income earner. Because of labour-market changes, income and wealth inequality have been increasing. Thus, the stratification structure of the future will probably not resemble the pattern that emerged in the affluent middle of the twentieth century.

- A person's position in society's stratification system has important consequences, both for lifestyle and for the quality of life. Those who are situated higher in the economic hierarchy tend to live better and longer.

# INTRODUCTION

While bundling up old newspapers for recycling, I flip through them quickly. Although the news writers don't use the term, I find myself reading about **social stratification**—that is, persistent patterns of social inequality within society.

A headline catches my attention: "20,000 more Alberta children living in poverty." The reporter writes that, between 2008 and 2009, the number of Alberta children living below the poverty line (a measurement we will discuss later in this chapter) increased by almost 40 percent, from 53 000 to 73 000 (Kleiss, 2011). The Canadian economy went into recession during 2008–09, so an increase in poverty rates is understandable. But how is it possible for 73 000 children to be living in poverty in a province with the highest average income in Canada? Perhaps their parents are unemployed or unable to work? The reporter notes, however, that more than half of these children have at least one parent who is employed full-time for the whole year. While, on average, Albertans have high incomes, some of the province's residents earn little although they work hard.

Another article reports that immigrant Canadians are more likely than other Canadians to be earning low incomes and to be unemployed even though they enjoy higher-than-average education (Hansen, 2011). In fact, while the education level of immigrants has been increasing over the past three decades because Canada gives priority to applicants who are highly educated, immigrants have been falling further behind in terms of income and unemployment rates. This seems odd since, after all, one of the reasons you attend university is to obtain an education that, you expect, will lead to a good job.

A third article about awful housing conditions in the northern Ontario community of Attawapiskat—many residents live in unheated houses without any running water—highlights another irony (Mackrael, 2011). It quotes a United Nations official who compares the poverty and poor living conditions in many First Nations communities in Canada to the situation in developing countries, the very countries emigrants are leaving to come to Canada for a better life!

However, not all of Canada's poor and unemployed are immigrants or First Nations. Some have seen their previous financial security disappear quickly because of economic restructuring. A newspaper story describes how the closing of a paper mill in Point Tupper, Nova Scotia, after 49 years of operation will lead to six hundred employees being laid off (Canadian Press, 2011). In addition, many retired mill workers are worried that their pensions will shrink if a new company does not buy and re-open the mill. I find another example of how economic restructuring is affecting workers (Hagerty and van Hasselt, 2012). In London, Ontario, 420 unionized employees of Caterpillar Inc. were "locked out" of their factory. Their employer wouldn't let them return to work unless they accepted a new contract that will cut their hourly wages from $34 to $16.50.

Although the very poor catch our attention, so do the very rich. A news item reminds me of just how rich some people are. By noon of the first working day in 2010, the one hundred most highly paid chief executive officers (CEOs) of companies operating in Canada had already earned as much as the typical Canadian worker earns in the whole year (Abma, 2012). Imagine working for half a day to earn an average $44 366 and then going on vacation for the rest of the year! However, these one hundred very rich individuals worked all year and reported average incomes of more than $8 million in 2010. The article goes on to observe that the gap between the earnings of the average Canadian worker and the earnings of the top Canadian CEOs was almost twice as high in 2010 as it was in 1998.

It's time to take the newspapers out to the curb, but one more headline can't be ignored: "Baby boomers living good life, while their children struggle." The author notes that, taking inflation into account, young couples today are earning only 5 percent more than their counterparts earned in 1976 (Pratt, 2011). In contrast, those aged 55 to 64 are earning 33 percent more than they did 35 years ago. In the meantime, housing prices in Canada have soared, and it now typically takes two earners per household to earn a decent living compared with only one earner three decades ago. The reporter quotes a University of British Columbia professor who is studying this shifting pattern of intergenerational inequality: "While the boomers retire richer than any generation before, their grandchildren are growing up in families that are poorer than [the baby boomers] were."

The common theme in these quite different stories is the existence of groups—the unemployed and low-income workers, First Nations, immigrants, young adults—that rank lower than others in the social stratification system. A low position in this ranking typically means having little power, little wealth, and little prestige, whereas a higher position generally implies the opposite. In this chapter, I begin

Caterpillar employees protest proposed wage cuts in London, Ontario, 2012. In reaction to the protests, Caterpillar shut down the plant permanently. It was widely expected that the plant's jobs would be moved to comparatively low-wage Indiana, where Caterpillar's head office is located; Caterpillar announced the plant closing just 36 hours after Indiana governor Mitch Daniels signed legislation making it more difficult for unions to organize in that state.
SOURCE: © Dave Chidley/The Canadian Press.

by discussing some of the ways in which sociologists study social stratification. I then examine a variety of theories of social stratification that attempt to explain its origins and impacts. The last section focuses on occupational and class structures and material inequality in Canada, and concludes by asking whether social inequality has been increasing.

## STRATIFICATION: A CORNERSTONE OF SOCIOLOGY

Sociologists have four basic areas of inquiry. We study social structure, or the way in which society is organized, both formally and informally. We ask questions about social order. What is it that holds together a society comprising individuals with different interests, and when and why does social order break down? Inquiries about social change form a third key area in the discipline. How and why do societies, the institutions and power structures within them, and the values and beliefs held by individual members change? Finally, sociologists spend a lot of time studying social stratification, the manner in which valued resources—that is, wealth, power, and prestige—are distributed, and the way in which advantages are passed from generation to generation.

It could easily be argued that the study of social stratification is the cornerstone of sociology. Descriptions of social structure that ignore the stratification system are clearly inadequate. Imagine describing Canadian society to someone from another country without referring to some features of stratification. Would the listener really understand our society if she or he did not know that most large corporations are run by men, that the working poor continue to struggle to make ends meet even though the majority of employed Canadians earn a decent living, that First Nations are much more likely than most others to be living in poverty, and that immigrants are doing less well today than they were several decades ago, even though they are better educated?

Furthermore, inequalities in wealth can threaten social stability (the poor resenting the wealthy, for example, and demanding more equality), and inequalities in power can be used to maintain social order. For example, powerful corporations might lobby provincial or territorial governments for changes in the labour laws that would make it more difficult for unions to organize company employees. In less democratic countries, direct control of the police and military by a powerful political minority can lead to the quick and violent suppression of unrest among the masses. We have seen many examples in the past few years in the Middle East as the Arab Spring uprisings, fuelled by high levels of social inequality, were sometimes brutally suppressed (Al-Momani, 2011).

An understanding of social stratification is also essential for studying social change, since, frequently, it is the stratification system that is undergoing change. For example, changing gender roles and the slow movement of women into positions of power and authority in North America in the past few decades are really features of a changing stratification system. The massive social, economic, and political changes that began in the former Soviet Union in the late 1980s and in China a decade earlier are, among other things, changes in stratification systems, as the main sources of power come to include both the political system and the emerging capitalist economy.

## SOCIAL HIERARCHIES IN STRATIFIED SOCIETIES

Imagine a society in which stratification did not exist, in which all things of value were distributed equally. Even if you picture a very small group, perhaps a preindustrial society with only a few hundred members, living on some isolated island where the necessities of life are easily obtained, it is still difficult to imagine a nonstratified society. A social hierarchy might emerge as a result of skill differences in fishing, in nursing the ill back to health, or in communicating with the spirits, for example. Inequalities in wealth might develop simply because some families were fortunate enough to have a larger number of children, providing more of the labour needed to accumulate valued possessions. And once accumulations of wealth began to be passed from generation to generation, a structured and relatively permanent pattern of inequality would emerge.

Perhaps you imagined some contemporary society comprising adults who, believing strongly in equality, decided to live and work together in some kind of urban or rural commune, sharing all their possessions. Again, it is easy to imagine how a social hierarchy could emerge, as those with more useful skills found themselves playing a more central role in this small-scale society. No doubt, when important decisions needed to be made, these individuals would be more likely to influence the outcome.

We do not need to repeat this mental exercise too many times before we see that social stratification in one form or another exists in all societies. However, our hypothetical examples are far from typical. In most societies, stratification is much more pronounced, and basic skills are seldom the foundation of primary social hierarchies. Nevertheless, cross-cultural variations exist in the criteria by which individuals and groups are ranked, the degree to which they can move from one position to another within the hierarchy, and the extent of inequality in wealth and power that exists within the hierarchy.

## ASCRIBED AND ACHIEVED STATUS

Let's begin by defining the rank or position that a person has within a social hierarchy as that person's **status.** We can further distinguish between an **ascribed status** and an **achieved status.** The former is assigned to individuals, typically at birth. An ascribed status can be a function of race, gender, age, and other factors that are not chosen or earned and that cannot be changed (a few people do choose their gender status, but they are rare exceptions). In contrast, an achieved status is precisely that—a position in a hierarchy that has been achieved by virtue of how well someone performs in some role. The most obvious example is that of occupational status—for instance, individuals who have performed well in law school are entitled to become lawyers, and high-performance athletes strive to achieve the status of "professional athlete." By the same logic, someone could achieve the status of "bum" by performing poorly in educational, employment, family, and other social roles.

Although we may accept that a completely non-stratified society is impossible, most of us would probably agree that a stratification system in which higher positions were achieved, not ascribed, would be preferable. In a **meritocracy,** everyone would have equal chances to compete for higher status positions and, presumably, those most capable would be awarded the highest rank. Such a society would exhibit a considerable degree of **social mobility,** as those who were more qualified moved up the social hierarchy to replace those who were less competent and who were consequently compelled to move down.

## OPEN AND CLOSED STRATIFICATION SYSTEMS

When we compare Canada with other societies, or look back at our history, we find that this country has what appears to be a fairly **open stratification system,** in which merit, rather than inheritance (or ascribed characteristics), determines social rank and in which social change is therefore possible. For example, dramatic changes in the status of various groups have occurred in this country over time. Although the

practice was not nearly as widespread in Canada as in the United States, slaves (most of them black people from Africa but also some First Nations) were bought and sold in Canada from the 1630s till the 1830s (Derreck, 2003). Chinese labourers, brought into the country to help build the railways, were kept out of most "white" jobs by law until well into the twentieth century (Li, 1982). Similarly, it was not until the 1960s that black Canadians were allowed to compete for much more than the lowest-level positions in the Canadian railway industry (Calliste, 1987). However, by the 1830s, slavery had disappeared in Canada, and we now have laws against racial discrimination.

Comparing ourselves with other contemporary societies, we note that Canada does not have an aristocracy, such as the one that exists in Britain, where children of wealthy and powerful families of long standing inherit positions and titles. The degree to which Canadians compete for higher status occupations (in the education system and, later, within the workplace) stands in clear contrast to the situation in India, for example, where the caste into which an individual is born largely determines the type of work that he or she will be allowed to do. Although discrimination on the basis of caste membership has been illegal in India for many decades, the **caste system** continues to underpin a relatively **closed stratification system.** Compared with India, Canada offers many more chances for upward social mobility, an indication of a more open stratification system.

Ascribed and achieved statuses

SOURCES: © Gouhier-Guibbaud-JMP/ABACAPRESS.COM/Newscom (l); © Ronald Martinez/Getty Images (r).

It is all too easy, however, to overlook the extent to which ascribed statuses continue to limit opportunities for many Canadians as well. Discrimination against members of First Nations and visible-minority groups continues to occur in Canada today. So, too, does discrimination against members of the gay community, against seniors and people with disabilities, and against women. These people are in lower status positions not because they competed poorly for some higher ranking in the social hierarchy, but because they are gay, are old, have disabilities, or are female.

These are fairly obvious examples of the ways in which ascribed statuses continue to play a prominent role in Canada's social stratification system. But what about the child from a wealthy family who graduates from an excellent high school in a wealthy neighbourhood, completes a degree or two in a prestigious and costly university, and then begins a career in a high-status, well-paying profession? Is this simply an example of someone achieving a deserved high-status position, or did the advantages of birth (ascribed status) play some part in this success story? Similarly, when we hear of large companies laying off hundreds of workers, does their sudden downward mobility reflect their failure to compete in an open, merit-based stratification system, or were they simply unfortunate enough to be employed in a corporation that was being downsized?

As these examples illustrate, the social stratification system consists of a number of different hierarchies, some based on ascribed characteristics, others on achievement. Elsewhere in this book, you will read chapters devoted to various dimensions of stratification and inequality, such as gender, race, and ethnicity. Other chapters address activities (for example, work) and institutions (for example, education) in which stratification processes are extremely important, and still others focus on inequalities among regions and countries. Once you have read all these chapters, you will, I expect, be convinced of the central importance of social stratification in the discipline of sociology.

## SOCIAL CLASS

You will also notice that, even though studies of gender, race, ethnicity, and work take you in quite different directions, all frequently share an emphasis on inequalities in income, wealth, or property, and on resulting inequalities in power. On average, women earn about 75 percent of what men earn. Older women are much more likely than are older men to be living in poverty. Immigrants and, particularly, First Nations are more likely to be unemployed or, if they are employed, to be in low-paying jobs. Owners of large workplaces are wealthier than most other members of society, and employees in professional and managerial occupations typically earn much more than lower-level employees. Recognizing, then, the extent to which such material inequality (that is, differences in income and wealth or property) parallels and overlaps with other social hierarchies, the rest of this chapter will focus primarily on material inequality or, after we define the terms, on social class and class structure.

Definitions of the concept of **class** vary considerably, as we will see in the next section, which outlines different theories of social stratification. I prefer to use the term in a general sense to indicate the position of an individual or a family within an economic hierarchy, along with others who have roughly the same amount of control over or access to economic or material resources. For example, an individual can be said to be a member of a class of large landowners, a class of wage-labourers and salaried workers (that is, the "working class"), or a "professional/managerial class." It is their similar economic situation and opportunities, a result of their shared position within a society's system of economic production, that makes these individuals members of the same class. In turn, we can use the term **class structure** to refer to the overall economic hierarchy comprising all such classes, choosing the word *structure* deliberately to indicate the relative stability and permanence of this social ranking.

Do you think of yourself as a member of a specific social class? Probably not very often, if at all. Like most North Americans, you probably have a reasonably good idea of how well off you are compared with others in your community. You probably have some sense of where your education, occupation, and income (or the education, occupation, and income of your parents) fit in some general hierarchy of **socioeconomic status.** "Class," however, is unlikely to be part of your everyday vocabulary. Nor is it typically part of the media's vocabulary. The newspaper stories I examined earlier, for example, identified a number of different dimensions of stratification, but social class was not among them.

This, however, does not make class a useless concept. As I have already suggested, pronounced patterns of material inequality exist in our society and overlap with most other dimensions of social stratification. The economic hierarchy is obviously not completely closed, but it is relatively stable and permanent, and it comprises some fairly distinct categories of individuals with similar amounts of control over material resources. Hence, it is useful to try to identify the classes that make up the stratification system (or class structure), to seek to understand their origin, and to examine the effects of membership in them on individuals and families. Rather than discarding the concept of class because few people think in these terms, we should perhaps ask why few people think about social classes despite their prominence. This is one of the topics discussed in the next section.

# EXPLANATIONS OF SOCIAL STRATIFICATION

Now that you have considered some examples of social stratification and learned some new concepts, it is time to examine theories (or explanations) of social stratification elaborated by a number of important social thinkers, including some who were analyzing society many decades ago and others who have written about it more recently. As you will see, it is important to take into account the time and place in which a social theory was developed, since theorists construct their social explanations on the basis of what they see around them and expect to see in the future.

## KARL MARX: CAPITALISM, EXPLOITATION, AND CLASS CONFLICT

Karl Marx had an immense impact on how we think about social stratification. He was born in Germany in 1818 but lived in England from 1849 until he died in 1883. His writings about the social and economic forces that brought about economic change look back over history but focus particularly on the rapidly changing European world that he observed during his lifetime. This was a time when industrial capitalism was transforming the economy and society. Large, mechanized, factory-based systems of production were emerging; cities were growing rapidly as peasants were being forced off the land or attracted to the city by the possibility of jobs in factories; and material inequality was extreme, as factory owners and merchants made huge profits while labourers lived in poverty. Trade unions, labour laws, and other arrangements that offer some protection to

workers did not yet exist. Thus, as Marx observed, the Industrial Revolution was a time when both the level of economic production and the degree of inequality in society increased tremendously.

## Modes of Production and Social Classes

Marx called the system of economic activity in a society its **mode of production.** In turn, its major components were the **means of production** (technology, capital investments, and raw materials) and the **social relations of production** (the relationships between the main classes involved in production). Slavery had been the primary mode of production in some societies in earlier times, and feudalism, an economic system in which peasants worked for landowners, not for a wage but for some share of the produce, was the mode of production that gave way to industrial capitalism in Europe.

Within industrial capitalism, Marx identified two major classes: the capitalist class, or **bourgeoisie,** which owned the means of production; and the **proletariat,** or working class, which exchanged its labour for wages. He also described a middle class—the **petite bourgeoisie**—comprising independent owners/producers (farmers, for example) and small-business owners. Marx expected this middle class largely to disappear as capitalism matured and drew some of its members up into the bourgeoisie but pushed most down into the proletariat. Of much greater importance in his theory of class inequality and social change was the relationship between workers and owners.

Marx reasoned that the value of a product sold was directly proportional to the average amount of labour needed to produce it. Thus, for example, an elegant piece of furniture was more valuable than its component pieces mainly because of the labour invested in it by the worker(s) who built it. Marx argued that the value of goods produced by wage-labourers far exceeded the amount needed to pay their wages and the cost of raw materials, technology, and other factors of production. Marx referred to this excess as **surplus value.** According to Marx, when commodities were sold, their surplus value was turned into profits for the owner. Marx viewed this as an exploitive relationship but one that differed from the exploitive relationships that characterized slavery or feudalism. After all, factory workers were paid a wage for their labour and were not legally forced to stay with the job. However, because most workers had few other options for making a living, and because owners controlled all aspects of the work, the legal freedom of wage-labourers to change jobs was, in practical terms, an illusion.

## Class Conflict and Class Consciousness

The idea of **class conflict** among the major classes in a society was the driving force behind Marx's theory of social change. He argued that previous modes of production had collapsed and been replaced because of class conflict. Feudalism in Europe had given way to capitalism as a result of the growing power of the merchant class relative to the traditional alliance of landowners and the aristocracy, and the deteriorating relationship between landowners and peasants. Furthermore, Marx argued, capitalism would eventually be replaced by a socialist mode of production, in which private ownership of property would disappear, along with the exploitation and inequality it produced. The impetus for this massive change would again be widespread class conflict, this time between wage-labourers and the owners of the means of production, as inequality between these two classes became more pronounced.

Marx held that this revolution would take place only when members of the working class began to recognize that they were being exploited. In other words, Marx did not take it for granted that members of a class would see how their interests were similar. Whereas capitalists might be conscious of their group interests, wage-labourers needed to become aware of their common enemy. They needed to be transformed from a "class in itself" to a "class for itself." Thus, **class consciousness** was an important social-psychological component of Marx's theory of social inequality and social change. His vision of the future was that of a revolutionary upheaval in which the oppressed working class would recognize its enemy, destroy the institutions of capitalism, and replace them with a classless society based on collective ownership of the means of production.

## Responses to Marx

During much of the twentieth century, critics of Marx's ideas pointed to the communist countries, with their apparently socialist system of government and absence of private property, and noted that inequality had not disappeared there. Instead, a new hierarchy had emerged, in which control of the political and bureaucratic apparatus was the main basis of power. These observations were largely correct. As a Russian joke from the 1970s noted, under capitalism man exploits man, but under communism it is the other way around.

In fact, I expect that Marx himself would have been highly critical of the Soviet communist system, given the degree to which individual citizens were exploited and harshly treated by a powerful minority. However, it is slowly becoming apparent that the emergence of a capitalist economy in Eastern Europe over the past two decades is leading to increased material inequality but from a different source (Silverman and Yanowitch, 2000). Today, individuals with control over some form of production or access to some marketing system are accumulating wealth while the majority of citizens appear to be no better off than before—indeed, many are worse off. The same pattern of growing social inequality has been observed in China where, despite the continued control of the economy by the Communist Party, some forms of free enterprise have been encouraged (Wu and Xie, 2002). In other words, while Marx's predictions about the inevitable emergence of a classless society have not been borne out, his type of class analysis still has considerable relevance for understanding the changing stratification system in North America, Eastern Europe, and even communist China.

Most theories of social stratification developed after Marx's were essentially a "debate with Marx's ghost" (Zeitlin with Brym, 1991: 117). Some social philosophers and sociologists elaborated on Marx's ideas, while others attempted to refute them. Among the critics, some focused on the absence of widespread class conflict, the growth of the middle class, and the relative decline in material inequality in Western Europe and North America in the twentieth century. I will examine some of these theories below, along with others that tried to develop more complex models of the contemporary class structure while basically following Marx's form of class-based analysis.

## MAX WEBER: CLASS AND OTHER DIMENSIONS OF INEQUALITY

Max Weber was born in Germany half a century after Marx—in 1864. Like Marx, he built his analysis of social stratification on a careful reading of history and a thorough analysis of the economic and political events of his day. But because he was only beginning his university studies about the time Marx died, Weber had the advantage of seeing the direction in which a more mature industrial capitalism was taking European society. He continued to write about many aspects of social stratification and social change until his death in 1920.

## Class, Status, and Party

Weber shared with Marx a belief that economic inequalities were central to the social stratification system and that the ownership of property was a primary determinant of **power,** or the ability to get others to do what you want them to do. However, he argued that power could lie in controlling other types of resources as well (Weber, 1948 [1922]). Specifically, he proposed that structures of social stratification could be better understood by looking at economic inequalities, hierarchies of prestige (or social honour), and political inequalities (control of power blocs, such as political parties or other organizations)—or, in his words, at "class, status, and party." Although these different hierarchies often overlap, they need not. For example, suddenly wealthy individuals might not receive the prestige they desire, being rejected in "high society" by those with "old money." Similarly, a politician might have considerable power through control of government resources, but might not be very wealthy or, for that matter, have much prestige.

Since Weber lived to see the emergence of white-collar workers, the growth of large private- and public-sector bureaucracies, and the growing power of trade unions, he was able to write about these alternative sources of power in a stratified capitalist society. He provided an insightful analysis of how power resided in the control of top positions in large bureaucratic organizations, even if the officeholder was not an owner of the organization. He recognized that well-educated wage-labourers might not be as powerless as were the factory workers of an earlier era. He also saw that a new class of middle-level, educated workers might not necessarily align themselves with blue-collar workers, and he was less inclined to conclude, as had Marx, that the middle class would disappear (Zeitlin with Brym, 1991: 118–19). In fact, he expected that the number of educated technical and professional workers in bureaucratic capitalist society would increase.

What Weber saw, compared with what Marx saw, was considerably more complexity in the social stratification system because of the growing diversity of the occupational structure and of capitalist enterprises. And although Weber was sometimes pessimistic in his writings about the future of democracy in a bureaucratic capitalist society, he did not link inequality and class conflict to the ultimate demise of capitalism itself, as did Marx. Similarly, although Weber, like Marx, commented on how members of a class might or might not recognize their shared interests, he did not conclude that it was the inevitable destiny of the working class to become a "class for itself."

## Social Class and Life-Chances

Despite these divergences in their thinking, Weber, like Marx, placed primary emphasis on the economic underpinnings of social stratification. However, he defined class more broadly than Marx did. Rather than insisting that a limited number of class positions were based on an individual's relationship to the means of production, Weber saw a larger variety of class positions based both on ownership of property and on other labour-market statuses, such as occupation and education. Furthermore, he emphasized the **life-chances** that class positions offer, noting that a higher position in the economic hierarchy, however obtained, provides more power and allows an individual and his or her family to enjoy more of the good things in life.

Thus, the general approach to studying stratification that I outlined earlier, one that recognizes the central importance of class while acknowledging that

Mark Carney, Governor of the Bank of Canada. Weber believed that power resided in the control of top positions in large bureaucratic organizations, even if the officeholder was not an owner of the organization.
SOURCE: © REUTERS/Chris Wattie.

gender, race, and other dimensions of social inequality can also be very important, is in the Weberian tradition. Similarly, my general definition of class as a relatively stable position within an economic hierarchy held by an individual or a family, along with others with roughly the same amount of control over or access to material resources, follows Weber's use of the term.

## DAVIS AND MOORE: A FUNCTIONAL THEORY OF STRATIFICATION

### Twentieth-Century Affluence and Functionalist Theory

Although a number of other social theorists in Europe and North America wrote about social stratification in the early decades of the twentieth century, I will skip ahead to 1945, when Kingsley Davis and Wilbert Moore published their short but much-debated "principles of social stratification." In Chapter 1, Introducing Sociology, you read about **functionalist theory**, which emphasizes consensus over conflict and seeks to explain the function, for society as a whole, of social institutions and various aspects of social structure. Davis and Moore were part of this intellectual tradition, which arose in reaction to the conflict-oriented and socially radical theories of Marx (and, to a lesser extent, of Weber).

The emergence of functionalism as an alternative theoretical approach can be better understood if we view it as reflecting the highly optimistic view in mid-twentieth-century North America that, because World War II was over and the economy was expanding rapidly, affluence was increasing, social conflict was decreasing, and a harmonious future for society was dawning. Thus, during the several decades following World War II, an era some describe as the golden era of North American capitalism (Marglin and Schor, 1990), many social scientists were attracted to theories that downplayed conflict and emphasized the benefits to all of what seemed like an ever-expanding economy.

### The Functional Necessity of Stratification

Davis and Moore (1945) argued that, because inequality exists in all societies, it must be a necessary part of society. All societies, they noted, have a variety of occupational roles that need to be filled, some requiring more training than do others, some having more functional importance, and some being less pleasant and more difficult to perform. To get people to fill important roles and to perform critical tasks well, and to spend time training for high-skill occupations, societies must ensure that the rewards for performance are greater. Thus, for example, doctors and school teachers need to be paid more than factory workers and truck drivers, and thus also rank higher than the latter in terms of social honour and prestige.

In short, according to Davis and Moore, social inequality is both inevitable and functionally necessary for society. But theirs was not a class-based and conflict-prone stratification system. Rather, Davis and Moore described a much more fluid socioeconomic hierarchy, with many different occupational statuses into which individuals are slotted on the basis of their effort and ability. The system is held together by consensus and shared values (not torn apart by conflict, as Marx theorized) because members of society generally agree that the hierarchy is fair and just. It follows that efforts to reduce social inequality will be ineffective and might even be harmful to society.

### Criticisms of Davis and Moore

Many criticisms have been levelled against Davis and Moore's theory. For example, although some differences in pay might be justified to reimburse those who spend more years in school preparing for a specific occupation, are the huge income and wealth inequalities we see in our society really necessary? Why do women often earn less than men do, even if they are equally educated and do the same type of work? Are movie stars, professional athletes, and chief executive officers with multimillion-dollar annual incomes really so much more important to society than nurses, day-care workers, prison guards, and most other low-paid workers? And how does a theory like this account for inherited wealth and for the fact that wealth leads to power and the ability to accumulate still more wealth?

Given these criticisms, what accounts for the appeal of this theory? Perhaps it is the kernel of truth at its core that is so attractive—namely, the recognition that, to some extent, differences in income and prestige are based on different amounts of effort and ability. After all, we can easily think of examples of better-paying occupations that require long years of education and training. Nevertheless, this is far from the complete story about inequality in our society, which is much more pronounced than what such differences in effort and ability might lead us to expect. In fact, the theory's appeal probably lies more in its apparent justification of these large inequalities. You might test this hypothesis by explaining the theory, first to someone with a high income or inherited wealth, and then to someone who is unemployed or earning very little. Chances are that the functionalist explanation of stratification would sound much more plausible to the wealthier person.

## GERHARD LENSKI: TECHNOLOGY AND STRATIFICATION SYSTEMS

Writing in the 1960s, a time of economic expansion and growing prosperity in North America, Gerhard Lenski (1966) developed a theory of "power and privilege" that attempted to explain the extent of material inequality in both contemporary and past societies. Lenski's explanation recognized power and conflict much more explicitly than had the Davis and Moore functionalist explanation of stratification. And, like Weber, he identified a number of different dimensions of social stratification, such as education and ethnicity, while emphasizing the centrality of economic inequalities. Although he used the term *class*, Lenski did not define it precisely, choosing instead to talk about the ruling elites in society in general terms and about how they managed to maintain their wealth and power at the expense of the masses.

Lenski reasoned that a society's technological base largely determines the degree of inequality within it. In simple hunting-and-gathering societies, he argued, the few resources of the society were distributed primarily on the basis of need. But as societies became more technologically complex, resources in excess of those required to fulfill basic needs were produced. Control of those surplus resources, or privilege, came to be based on power, allowing ruling elites to take a much larger share of these resources for themselves. Thus, the more complex agricultural societies, such as that of precolonial India, developed highly structured governing and tax-collecting systems, through which the privileged ruling elites accumulated immense amounts of wealth, while the masses lived in poverty.

As a result of industrialization and the complexity of modern technology, this "age-old evolutionary trend toward ever-increasing inequality" (Lenski, 1966: 308) was reversed. Owners of the means of production could no longer control the production process directly and had to rely instead on well-educated managerial and technical workers to keep the complex system operating. Education broadened the horizons of these middle-level employees, introducing them

to ideas of democracy, encouraging them to demand a larger share of the profits they were helping to produce, and making them more articulate in their demands for equality.

Thus, Lenski's theory proposed a causal link among complex industrial technology, the higher education of workers, and workers' insistence on sharing the growing wealth of an industrial society. But why would employers give in to such demands? Because, argued Lenski, the industrial elite needed educated workers—they could not produce wealth without them. Equally important, the much greater productivity of industrial societies compared with pre-industrial societies meant that the elite could "make economic concessions in relative terms without necessarily suffering any loss in absolute terms" (Lenski, 1966: 314). Because the economic pie was so much bigger, everyone could have a larger slice.

In one obvious sense, Lenski's theory resembled the functional theory of stratification—both noted that better-educated and more highly skilled workers are paid more. However, unlike the functionalist approach, Lenski's theory clearly took power differences into account, emphasizing how the extent of accumulation of wealth by elites, or the degree of material inequality, depends on the power and bargaining ability of middle-level workers. In fact, Lenski placed material inequality at the centre of his theory of stratification. But in contrast to Marx's nineteenth-century predictions of growing inequality as industrial capitalism matured, Lenski, writing in the middle of the twentieth century, saw a movement toward a more equal distribution of society's wealth.

## ERIK OLIN WRIGHT: A NEO-MARXIST APPROACH

In reaction against functionalism, Lenski (1966) brought power and conflict back into his explanation of social inequality. He placed material inequalities resulting from one group's domination of another at the centre of his model, thus coming closer to the approach taken by Marx and Weber. But he did not carry through with a traditional Marxist analysis built around the relationships of different classes to the means of production. In contrast, a number of neo-Marxist scholars, writing in the 1970s and 1980s, attempted to update the original Marxist model so it could be applied to the late twentieth century. We will discuss only one theorist from the neo-Marxist camp, Erik Olin Wright.

Although Marx acknowledged the existence of a middle class comprising several distinct groups, including independent producers and small-business owners, he predicted that this middle class would disappear and so spent much more time writing about the relationship between the two primary classes (capitalists and workers). Wright's contribution lies in recognizing that as industrial capitalism matured, the middle class had grown and become more diverse, and in trying to understand the class dynamics of our more complex capitalist system of production. Of particular importance in Wright's theory is his notion of **contradictory class locations**—that is, occupational groupings that have divided loyalties within a class structure. For example, although managers work for capitalists, supervising lower-level employees and trying to get them to produce as much as possible, managers are themselves employees, potentially exploited by owners. Considering the substantial numbers of people in such contradictory locations, we can begin to understand why the widespread class conflict envisioned by Marx has seldom emerged.

Wright (1985) also argued that exploitation of one class by another can occur through control of property or the means of production (as Marx had insisted), as well as through ownership of skill or credential assets and control of high positions within organizations. Thus, he identified three classes of owners (the bourgeoisie, small employers, and the petite bourgeoisie with no employees), and nine classes of wage-labourers (nonowners), differentiated on two dimensions: the possession of organizational assets and of skill/credential assets (Wright, 1985: 88). For example, "expert managers" (such as engineers or lawyers in senior management positions within large companies) fill a class location characterized by extensive organizational assets and high skill/credential assets, in contrast to basic "proletarians," who have no specific skill/credential assets and no management or supervisory responsibilities (see Figure 6.1).

Despite his intention of developing a neo-Marxist theoretical model updated to the late twentieth century, Wright's theory is similar to Weber's view of class structure in some ways (Grabb, 2007). Specifically, the different class locations created by the intersection of organizational and skill/credential assets remind us of the different classes Weber described as he commented on how similar educational and occupational statuses resulted in similar control over and access to material resources. Even so, Wright's theory of class structure and his observations about contradictory locations within it are useful, because he deliberately attempted to incorporate the complexities of modern capitalist society into his explanation of social inequality.

**FIGURE 6.1**    ERIC OLIN WRIGHT'S TYPOLOGY OF CLASS LOCATION IN CAPITALIST SOCIETY

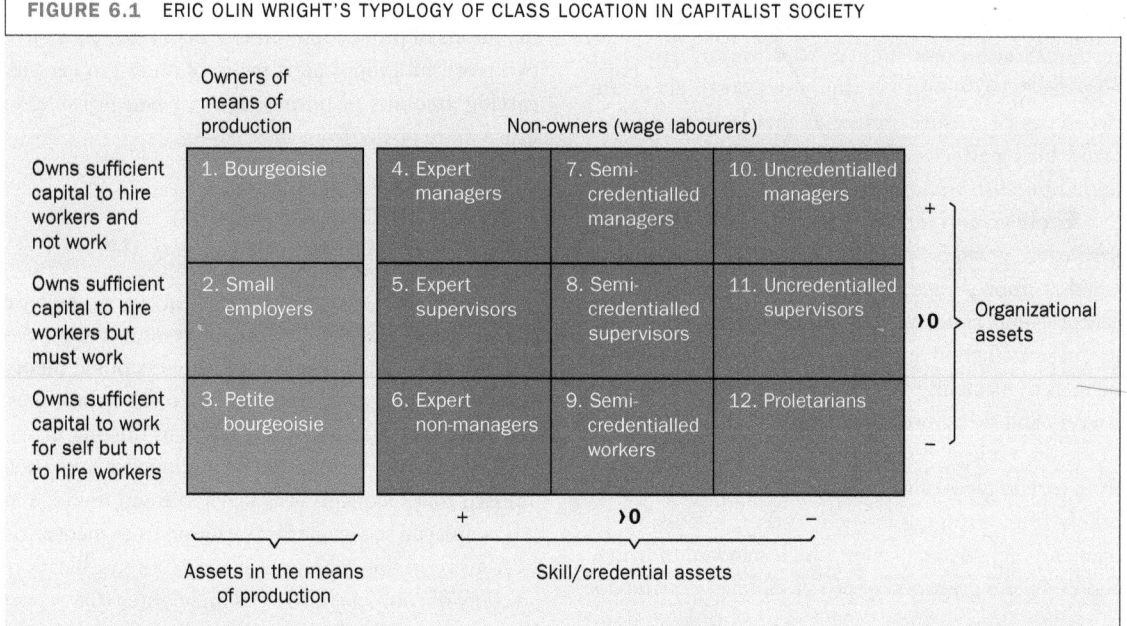

SOURCE: From Erik Olin Wright, *Classes*. 1985, p. 88. Reprinted with permission from Verso Books.

## FRANK PARKIN: A NEO-WEBERIAN APPROACH

Wright attempted to bring Marx's class analysis back into the discussion of contemporary forms of social stratification. Frank Parkin (1972, 1979) was equally explicit in stating his intellectual debts to Max Weber's discussions of power, class, and social stratification (Grabb, 2007). In fact, Parkin went so far as to argue that neo-Marxist scholars, espousing what he calls "professorial Marxism" (1979: x), were merely putting forth dressed-up Weberian arguments. As a neo-Weberian, Parkin criticized traditional Marxist and contemporary neo-Marxist analyses for failing to take into account gender, race, religious, and other forms of social stratification that do not grow out of the relations of production in capitalist society but clearly have an origin and a permanency all of their own (1979: 4–5). Nevertheless, like both Weber and Marx before him, Parkin continued to emphasize the importance of property relations in contemporary stratification systems (Grabb, 2007).

Among Parkin's most useful contributions to stratification theory is his explanation of how patterns of structured inequality, whether based on class, gender, race, or some other ascribed or achieved status, are maintained or changed. To do so, Parkin returned to a concept introduced by Weber, that of **social closure**. Parkin defines this term as "the process by which social collectivities seek to maximize rewards by restricting access to resources and opportunities to a limited circle of eligibles" (1979: 44). He then goes on to elaborate two types of closure strategies that help us understand how patterns of social inequality are maintained but also sometimes altered.

**Exclusion** refers to the organized efforts of privileged, powerful groups to maintain their advantaged position. Processes of exclusion can range from centuries-old caste systems in closed societies to the use, in contemporary open societies, of educational credentials to maintain power and privilege. For example, lawyers and other professional groups have managed to ensure, via legal restrictions, that only they can perform certain types of work in our society. By excluding others from engaging in such work, it is possible to maintain high income, enjoy a high standard of living, and exercise a great deal of power. Similarly, members of trade unions can use legal sanctions to keep non-members, who might have the same skills, from taking on some well-paying jobs.

In contrast, **usurpation** refers to the efforts of excluded groups in a stratification system to gain advantages and power. As Parkin put it, all such actions have as their goal "biting into the resources and benefits accruing to dominant groups in society" (1979: 74). As with exclusionary practices, usurpation efforts range from lobbying and voting for social change to outright revolt against groups in power. Thus, over the past several decades, we have seen successful efforts by women's groups, First Nations groups, and other disadvantaged groups to change the balance of power and privilege in Canada. Going back further, labour unions took even stronger, sometimes illegal, actions to gain new powers and a more equitable distribution of resources for their members.

Thus, like Lenski, Parkin took a keen interest in the power struggles in society between groups with more and less power (Grabb, 2007). However, Parkin's neo-Weberian theory does not contain a premise of inevitability, either one of increased inequality and eventual social revolution as Marx predicted, or one of reduced inequality resulting from technological change and economic growth as Lenski predicted. Parkin did see a clear trend with respect to processes of social closure. With the growing emphasis on education in modern society, the use of educational credentials to maintain power and privilege has become more widespread. As a result, well-educated professionals have become a powerful class grouping, sometimes almost as powerful as wealthy capitalists who control the means of production (Grabb, 2007). Beneath these two powerful groups are a range of other groups with varying amounts of power, trying, when possible, to usurp more power from those above.

## EXPLANATIONS OF SOCIAL STRATIFICATION: SUMMING UP

There are other theories of social inequality we have not discussed (Grabb, 2007). However, having been introduced to Marx and Weber, the functional theory of stratification, and several more recent approaches, you now have a sense of the range of existing explanations. Davis and Moore's functionalist approach stressed that inequality was inevitable and useful, and it downplayed social conflict resulting from inequality. In contrast to this consensus approach to stratification, a variety of conflict approaches highlighted differences in power resulting from and contributing to material inequality, the exploitation of some groups by others, and the social conflict that could result.

The theories we have reviewed differ in the assumptions they make and the conclusions they draw about the future of material inequality. Marx clearly saw inequality and exploitation of the working class increasing, and he predicted that class conflict would lead to the death of capitalism. Although Weber was not convinced that a socialist society would eventually emerge, neither did he argue that inequalities would gradually decrease (Grabb, 2007). As a neo-Weberian, Parkin takes a similar stance. Wright's emphasis on the growing number of middle-class locations also does not suggest an increasing level of material inequality, but neither does it imply the opposite. However, the functionalists and Lenski, writing in an era of economic growth and widespread optimism about the ability of capitalism to raise the overall standard of living, clearly felt that material inequalities were shrinking in Western industrial societies.

The various explanations also differ in the degree to which they emphasize class differences in access to and control of material resources. For Marx, class was the primary determining factor in this regard. Weber, using the term *class* somewhat more broadly, emphasized its central role but recognized other important dimensions of social stratification. So, too, did Parkin, who explicitly discussed the independent effects of gender, race, and religion. Davis and Moore basically ignored the concept of class. Although Lenski again focused more directly on economic inequality, he did not really describe society in terms of distinct classes, as Wright, in his neo-Marxist approach, did. Thus, if you view these theories in temporal order, it appears that social class, at least as defined in the Weberian sense, has made a comeback as an explanatory concept. In the following section, we turn from theories of social inequality to data on occupations and material inequality in Canada to see if the concept of social class still has relevance in contemporary society.

## OCCUPATIONS, SOCIAL CLASS, AND INEQUALITY IN CANADA

### OCCUPATIONAL SHIFTS OVER TIME

Some of the explanations of social stratification we reviewed above, such as Lenski's, focus directly on occupations while others, such as Wright's, rely on occupational data to discuss social class. Consequently,

it would be useful to begin this section by examining occupational shifts in Canada over the past century. Table 6.1 displays the types of occupations most common near the beginning (1911) and in the middle (1951) of the last century, and near the beginning of the twenty-first century (2006). The biggest change was the decline in agricultural occupations, from 34 percent of all labour force participants in 1911 to only 2 percent in 2006. Other natural resource-based occupations (forestry, fishing, mining) also declined, but not as steeply. Manufacturing occupations increased in relative terms (from 14 to 17 percent) between the beginning and middle of the last century, but by 2006 had dropped to only 7 percent of the total labour force. The decline in manufacturing jobs has continued since then, intensifying in 2009 as the Canadian economy shrank as a result of global financial and economic instability (Usalcas, 2010).

Manufacturing, construction, transportation, and resource-based occupations are typically called blue-collar occupations, in contrast to white-collar occupations in the managerial, professional, clerical, sales, and service categories. Table 6.1 shows that white-collar occupations have come to greatly outnumber blue-collar occupations as industrial capitalism has matured. In 2006, 13 percent of Canadian labour force participants were in managerial/administrative occupations, up from only 5 percent in 1911.

Professional/technical occupations had multiplied by almost six times in relative terms, from 4 to 23 percent. Clerical, sales, and service occupations also had become much more common, from a total of only 17 percent in 1911 to 37 percent of all occupations in 2006.

What do these occupational changes tell us with respect to our previous discussion of the bases of social stratification? First, as various theories have indicated, the proportion of occupations requiring higher education has increased, while the proportion of traditional blue-collar, "working-class" occupations has declined. With the expansion in white-collar occupations, average incomes rose, at least until the early 1980s. Thus, to the extent that occupational data can inform us about class structure in the Weberian sense, occupational shifts over the past century suggest greater class diversity, rather than a polarization of classes, as a strict reading of Marx's theory would predict, and a rising standard of living for Canadian workers, rather than increasing poverty and exploitation.

And what do the numbers in Table 6.1 not tell us? First, they do not distinguish between the

TABLE 6.1  OCCUPATIONAL DISTRIBUTION OF LABOUR FORCE PARTICIPANTS,* CANADA, 1911, 1951, 2006

| OCCUPATION TYPE | 1911 | 1951 | 2006 |
|---|---|---|---|
| Managerial/ administrative | 5% | 8% | 13% |
| Professional/ technical | 4 | 7 | 23 |
| Clerical | 4 | 11 | 12 |
| Sales | 5 | 7 | 11 |
| Service | 8 | 10 | 14 |
| Manufacturing | 14 | 17 | 7 |
| Transportation | 6 | 8 | 9 |
| Construction | 5 | 6 | 6 |
| Agriculture | 34 | 16 | 2 |
| Forestry/ fishing/mining | 5 | 4 | 2 |
| Other occupations | 10 | 6 | 1 |
| **Total** | **100** | **100** | **100** |

*Labour force participants include both the employed (paid employees and the self-employed) and the unemployed (those who want a paid job but who are unable to find one). These data are based on the population aged 15 and older.

SOURCES: 1911 and 1951 data adapted from 1911 and 1951 Census results, presented by O'Neill (1991); 2006 data adapted from 2006 Census results, Statistics Canada (2006).

occupations typically held by women and those typically held by men. Since the middle of the last century, a rising proportion of women have been entering the labour force and moving into better jobs. But, as you will see (Chapter 7, Gender Inequality), women are still more likely to be employed in clerical, sales, and service occupations (what might be called a "pink-collar sector") than in blue-collar occupations or in higher-status and better-paying managerial and professional occupations. Thus, gender-based labour-market stratification continues to exist, intersecting with class-based stratification.

Second, the data in Table 6.1 do not directly describe workers' relationships to the means of production, in Marx's terms. Statistics Canada has never collected and categorized national data along these lines, but since the early 1980s a series of Ontario-wide surveys have used Erik Olin Wright's typology (Figure 6.1) to profile the class composition of that province (Livingstone, 1999: 158). In 1996, the Ontario employed labour force comprised corporate capitalists (1 percent), small employers (8 percent), the own-account self-employed or petite bourgeoisie (14 percent), managers (8 percent), supervisors (4 percent), professional/semi-professional employees (19 percent), and service and industrial workers (46 percent). The small sample size in this study (about six hundred respondents) means that these estimates are not precise, and the single-province focus does not allow for generalizations to all of Canada. Even so, this study clearly shows that the large class of paid workers contains several distinct types with varying amounts of decision-making authority and substantial differences in income, status, and occupational power.

Third, neither Table 6.1 (which displays occupational change over time) nor the 1996 Ontario study (which uses class data from only one point in time) can show how the Canadian class structure might be changing. But we can get one indication of change from other data on self-employment. Between 1946 and 1981, a period of significant decline in the number of people employed in agriculture, the proportion of self-employed Canadians dropped dramatically, from 33 percent to 10 percent. However, beginning in the 1980s, a slow reversal of the trend began in Canada, the United States, and other Western industrialized countries. By 2008, 10 percent of employed Canadians were own-account self-employed (without any employees) and 5 percent employed others (Krahn, Lowe, and Hughes, 2011: ch. 2). Researchers are uncertain whether more Canadians are voluntarily choosing self-employment or are being pushed into it as a result of higher levels of unemployment and growing corporate and public-sector downsizing. Nevertheless, the reversal of the decline in self-employment—the increase in the size of the petite bourgeoisie—is something theorists are trying to explain as they attempt to further update Marx's ideas of class-based stratification (Myles and Turegun, 1994).

Finally, the data in Table 6.1 do not reflect some of the dramatic changes in employment opportunities and outcomes that have been occurring in the past four decades. I will return to this topic later, but for now I will simply note that unemployment rates have risen and fallen and are now rising again, part-time and temporary work have become much more common, and income growth appears to have stopped, while income and wealth inequality have increased. Consequently, the higher standard of living that accompanied occupational changes in the second half of the twentieth century is no longer guaranteed for all those in middle-status occupations. Thus we need to look carefully at the distributional side of the occupation and class structures, at "who gets what" in return for their employment (Westergaard, 1995). But before examining changing patterns of material inequality in Canada, I will first discuss another important feature of stratification systems in modern societies—opportunities for occupational mobility and status attainment.

## OCCUPATIONAL MOBILITY AND STATUS ATTAINMENT

Many people move up the occupational and income ladders during their careers, frequently after investing in higher education of some kind. Some move down, often because of economic circumstances beyond their control. Sociologists have conducted a great deal of research on such **intragenerational occupational mobility** (mobility within an individual's lifetime) and on **intergenerational occupational mobility,** the process of reaching an occupational location higher or lower than the location your parents held. Such research is interesting in itself, since we all like to compare how well we have done relative to others. It is also theoretically important since it tests hypotheses derived from theories of inequality (the functionalist perspective, for example) that propose that higher positions in society are generally filled by those most qualified.

If the only intergenerational occupational mobility we observed was a result of better-qualified people moving up to replace those who were less qualified, we should also see an equivalent amount of downward mobility. Such a scenario of "musical jobs" or, to use the technical term, **circulatory mobility,** does not really describe the Canadian situation over the past half-century, however, because of the pronounced parallel process of **structural mobility** resulting from a significant change in the shape of Canada's overall occupational structure. As noted earlier, over the past half-century, industrial societies, including Canada, experienced a great deal of growth in white-collar occupations (clerical, managerial, and professional positions) as traditional

agricultural and blue-collar industrial jobs declined in relative importance. Hence, with an increase in the number of higher-status jobs, each generation had more chances than the preceding one to improve the status of their jobs.

Even so, Canadian studies conducted over the past several decades indicate that Canada, like the United States, has a relatively open stratification system, more so than countries like Sweden, the United Kingdom, France, and the Netherlands (Wanner, 2009). In other words, in Canada relatively more people have been able to move up the occupational ladder relative to their parents. During the second half of the last century, the Canadian occupational structure opened up for women and men in different ways. The steep decline in agricultural employment meant that many men moved out of the agricultural occupations held by their fathers. For women, the major shift was away from the housework that had been the main female occupation for their mothers' generation. For both sexes, expansion of postsecondary educational opportunities, leading to higher status occupations, played an important role (Wanner, 2009). However, most of this opening of the stratification system occurred between 1973 and 1986. Little changed in terms of mobility opportunities in the following decades.

Thus, overall, Canadian mobility studies find only a limited amount of direct occupational inheritance across generations. Yet those at or near the top of the occupational hierarchy are still more likely to pass their advantages on to their children. As Richard Wanner (2009: 129) concludes, "Canada is still a stratified society characterized by a considerable amount of inheritance of privilege." This intergenerational transfer of advantage takes place primarily through different levels of access to the postsecondary education system.

Research in Canada and other Western countries examining the process of **occupational status attainment** has shown, not surprisingly, that the most important influence on the status of an individual's current job is the status of that person's first job. Individuals who enter the labour market as articling lawyers, for example, typically make their way higher up the occupational ladder than do those who began as unskilled labourers. In turn, the status of that first job is heavily influenced by the level of education completed. Such findings obviously lend some support to theories suggesting that more-qualified people, as indicated by higher education, end up in higher-status and better-paying occupations.

However, many studies have also traced education-job linkages back to the previous generation, showing that those who obtain more education and hence better jobs are more likely to come from families with better-educated parents. For example, a 14-year longitudinal study of high-school graduates in Edmonton, Alberta, showed that young people from families in which one or both parents had completed university were almost three times more likely than others were to complete university themselves (Krahn, 2009). For a variety of reasons (for example, more money for higher education, more well-educated role models), children from more advantaged backgrounds can build on their initial advantages.

## THE DISTRIBUTION OF WEALTH

Evidence from various sources demonstrates that a small number of people continue to own or control a very large portion of the wealth in Canada. For example, in 2011, 54-year-old David Thomson and his family were estimated to be worth $23 billion. While only number 17 on the *Forbes Magazine* list of "The World's Billionaires" (2011), they were Canada's wealthiest family. In contrast, in 2009, the median net worth (the difference between the total assets owned by a family, including a home, and its debt) for Canadian low-income families (excluding seniors) in which at least one person was employed was only $19 000, compared with $257 700 for non-low-income families in which someone was employed (Luong, 2011).

These statistics highlight the wealth gap between low-income and average-income families, and the wealth chasm between these two groups and very rich Canadian families, such as the Thomsons, the Westons, and the Irvings, who have business holdings spread around the globe as well as in Canada. Together with highly paid CEOs and corporate directors, these wealthy families clearly form a distinct upper class, the haute (or high) bourgeoisie in Marx's terms. By way of example, in 2010, the CEOs of the top one hundred companies listed on the Toronto Stock Exchange received a median compensation package (earnings, bonuses, and stock options) of $8.38 million (Mackenzie, 2012). It would take the average Canadian worker (employed full-time and year-round), with annual earnings of about $44 300 in 2010, 189 years to earn as much money as any of these one hundred CEOs receive in one year.

At the other end of the wealth scale are the 7 percent of Canadian families (excluding seniors) with low income and no wage earners who reported a median net worth in 2009 of only $1000. These families (about 1.2 million people in total) typically relied on government transfer payments (for example, employment, welfare, or disability support payments) and had trouble making ends meet. Three out of 10 (29 percent) were at least two months behind in paying bills, and almost one in 10 (8 percent) was at least two months behind on loan payments (Luong, 2011).

Over the long term, the economic growth experienced in Western industrialized countries, along with some income redistribution efforts by governments, have had an equalizing effect on the distribution of household wealth. Wolff (1991), for example, showed that inequality in household wealth decreased between 1920 and the 1970s in Sweden, Britain, and the United States. Although comparable data are not available for Canada for the same period, it is likely that a similar decline occurred here as well. However, Wolff also noted that, in the mid-1970s, wealth inequality began to increase again in the United States and Sweden (it remained constant in Britain). What about Canada?

A recent study reveals that, on average, Canadian families were considerably wealthier in 2005 than they were in 1970 (Morissette and Zhang, 2007). However, there is more to this story. Wealth inequality declined between 1970 and 1977, remained steady until 1984,

SOURCE: © Artizans Entertainment.

and then increased considerably in the next 20 years. Thus, back in 1984, the top 10 percent of Canadian families owned 51.8 percent of total family wealth. By 2005, this figure had increased to 58.2 percent (Morissette and Zhang, 2007). In other words, the wealth gap between rich and poor families has been growing over the past two decades in Canada.

## INCOME DISTRIBUTION

### High-Paying and Low-Paying Occupations

Although most people have virtually no contact with the wealthiest families in Canada, we are much more aware of, or perhaps are even members of, a larger, not quite as wealthy but still very affluent group of households containing one or more individuals in high-paying occupations. By way of example, 2006 census data for individuals working full-time year-round revealed Canadian dentists earned an average of $142 100 (in 2005), while medical specialists earned even more ($201 847). Judges earned almost as much ($192 448) while lawyers had to be content with average yearly earnings of $142 345 (Statistics Canada, 2006). In contrast, cashiers working full-time year-round earned only a fraction of this ($20 140), as did hotel clerks ($23 790), hair stylists and barbers ($19 746), and pet groomers and other animal-care workers ($20 898).

Using the term *class* in the Weberian sense, you could label individuals in well-paid managerial and professional occupations as members of an upper-middle class, given their high incomes and their access to and control of material resources through their employment positions. In contrast, retail workers and those employed in some service occupations (for example, food and beverage services, child-care and home-support services) work in the low-paying, insecure occupations that we might describe as the lower working class.

These occupational earning patterns hide large gender differences. Thus, among people working full-time and full-year, women's earnings were 71 percent of men's in 2007, a figure that has not changed significantly since 1995 (Krahn, Lowe, and Hughes, 2011: ch. 4). Female dentists earned, on average, 63 percent of what their male counterparts earned in 2005 ($100 047 and $158 094, respectively). Among senior managers, women earned 60 percent of what men earned. Female university professors, however, reported 2005 earnings of $78 798, more than 80 percent of the earnings of male professors ($96 281). Among the lower-paid occupations, male janitors reported annual 2005 earnings of $35 439, considerably higher than the earnings of their female counterparts ($26 980). Similar gender differences are observed in all occupational groupings (Statistics Canada, 2006) but, as these examples demonstrate, the female–male earnings ratio does vary considerably by occupation.

### Income Inequality

The 2006 census data discussed above give some indication of the distribution in Canada of employment earnings, the largest component of total income, which also includes income from investments, government assistance, and all other sources. Studies of income tax data show that the level of total income inequality in Canada has increased dramatically over the past seven decades. In 1945, at the end of World War II, the most advantaged 10 percent of Canadians (the top decile) received 37 percent of all income (Yalnizyan, 2010). While this figure fluctuated over the next four decades, income inequality in Canada slowly declined. In 1985, the top decile received 35 percent of all income. However, the long-term trend then reversed, and income inequality increased steadily during the next two decades—in 2007, the top 10 percent received 41 percent of all income (Yalnizyan, 2010; see Box 6.1).

## THE POOR

### Defining and Measuring Poverty

Poverty can be defined in different ways. We could talk about **absolute poverty,** arguing that the poor are those who have barely enough to stay alive, like many of the inhabitants of poor countries. Or we could conclude, as most Canadians do, that **relative poverty** is really what matters. If your neighbours own their homes, drive cars, eat in nice restaurants, put money into pension plans, and take vacations outside the country, while you rent a small apartment, ride the bus, look forward to a meal at McDonald's, have no savings, and read about foreign countries in the public library, you probably consider yourself poor. According to this definition, Canada does have a considerable number of poor people.

Most discussions of poverty in Canada rely on the **low-income cutoff** or **LICO** (commonly, though unofficially, known as the "poverty line"),

## BOX 6.1    CANADA'S RICHEST 1 PERCENT

In 2007, a Canadian in the richest 1 percent of tax filers made a minimum of $169 300. The average income of this class was $404 500.

Tax records for Canada's richest 1 percent go back to 1920. They show that the top 1 percent of tax filers increased their share of total income from the mid-1920s to the mid-1930s. Their share declined only after Canada went to war. From the beginning of World War II to 1977, the income share of the richest 1 percent was cut almost in half, falling from 14 percent in 1941 to 7.7 percent in 1977. Then the trend reversed direction. The share of all income going to the richest 1 percent almost doubled between 1982 and 2007, rising from 7.9 percent to 13.8 percent. By 2007, the 246 000 Canadians lucky enough to be among the richest 1 percent claimed a bigger piece of the income pie than at any time since 1941 (see Figure 6.2).

A recent study shows that, in the early 1990s, the average income of the top 10 percent was eight times as high as the average income of the bottom 10 percent (Organisation for Economic Co-operation and Development [OECD], 2011). By 2008, the top decile reported 10 times as much income as

the lowest decile. Income inequality has increased in most rich countries over the past two decades, but income inequality in Canada has been above average. Inequality was lower in Sweden, Norway, and Switzerland than in Canada, and higher in the United States and the United Kingdom.

What accounts for increasing income inequality since the mid-1970s? As in most other Western industrialized countries, part-time and temporary work became much more common in Canada, leading to lower total income for a larger proportion of workers in many industries (Fuller and Vosko, 2008). At the same time, the most highly paid corporate CEOs and managers were given ever-larger compensation packages while the Canadian income tax system was altered so that the highest earners paid a lower rate of income tax than they had paid in the past. Back in 1948, the super-rich could expect to pay 80 percent income tax on annual earnings over $2.37 million (in today's dollars). Today, the top marginal tax rate is 43 percent (Yasnizyan, 2010: 4). With less money collected through income taxes, there has also been less money for the government to redistribute to the poor.

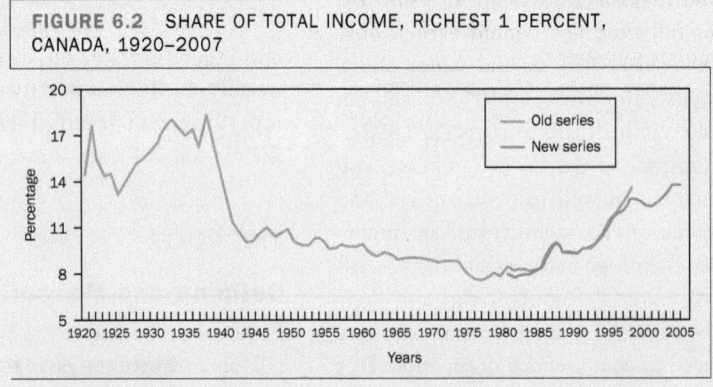

**FIGURE 6.2**    SHARE OF TOTAL INCOME, RICHEST 1 PERCENT, CANADA, 1920–2007

SOURCE: Yalnizyan, Armine. (2010). *The Rise of Canada's Richest 1%*. Ottawa: Canadian Centre for Policy Alternatives, pp. 11–12.

estimated by Statistics Canada on the basis of data obtained from its ongoing *Survey of Labour and Income Dynamics*. According to this survey, the average Canadian spends about 43 percent of after-tax income on the basic necessities (food, shelter, and clothing). To establish the LICO, Statistics Canada adds 20 percent to this figure (Statistics Canada, 2011). Hence, anyone spending more than 63 percent of after-tax income on the basic necessities is considered a low-income earner (see Box 6.2). Obviously, some

people budget better than others do, so these are average cost estimates. However, there is no denying that the cost of living is higher in larger urban centres and that it takes more money to feed and clothe additional people, so different LICOs are calculated for communities of various sizes and for families of various sizes within those communities (National Council of Welfare, 2010). For example, based on 2009 income data, Statistics Canada sets the after-tax LICO for a single person living in a city with more

| BOX 6.2 | MEASURING POVERTY: A CHALLENGE FOR CANADA |

Who is poor in Canada? It depends on the measure used, and that depends on who is measuring. Different researchers use different criteria. If poverty is defined as including only those whose physical existence is endangered, then a very small percentage of Canadians are poor—about 5% according to the Fraser Institute. If poverty is considered in relation to community norms and standards and being poor means that a person cannot fully participate in society, then the poverty rate is around 12% to 15%. This definition is used by anti-poverty organizations.

Canada does not have an official poverty line—an income level below which someone is considered poor, depending on family size and where they live—adopted by federal and provincial/territorial governments. The closest thing to an official poverty measure [is] ... the Low-Income Cut-off or LICO (before and after taxes).

LICOs set an income threshold based on spending on necessities as a percentage of income (people on low incomes spend a higher percentage of income on necessities than people with higher incomes). LICOs have a long history, but they are increasingly out-of-date because Statistics Canada has not updated them and no longer collects the data that would allow them to be updated. LICOs reflect 1992 spending patterns. ...

There are two other measures of poverty levels that have been used widely in Canada. Low-Income Measures (LIMs) set an income threshold relative to median family income. The median means half of family incomes are above it and half are below it. A poverty level of 50% or half that median income is commonly used for the LIMs (before and after tax).

Market Basket Measure (MBMs) are based on the cost of a basket of goods. What is in the basket was developed by officials at the federal department of Human Resources and Social Development Canada. The basket includes food, shelter, clothing, transportation, and other necessary household goods or services. The cost of a basket of goods varies depending on where you live. The cost of a basket of goods is compared to disposable income to determine low income.

The LIM is relatively straightforward and is useful for comparisons with other countries. An assumption behind this kind of comparison is that being poor is relative to a nation's standard of living. Half the median income in a developing country will be much lower than half the median income in Canada. The Market Basket has the advantage of clarity in describing a basket of goods, but the validity of what is in the basket is arguable (e.g., five pairs of long underwear, but no computer access). ...

These poverty measures (LICO, LIM, and MBM) do not lead to dramatically different poverty rates at the national level. But there can be important differences between these measures when considering geography (by municipality or province, for example) and family composition (single individuals, families with children, etc.).

SOURCE: Shillington, Richard and John Stapleton. (2010). *Cutting Through the Fog: Why Is It So Hard to Make Sense of Poverty Measures?* Toronto: Metcalf Foundation. On the World Wide Web at http://metcalffoundation.com/wp-content/uploads/2011/05/cutting-through-the-fog.pdf (retrieved 12 July 2012).

than half a million residents at $18 421, compared with $12 050 for a single person living in a rural area. The low-income line for a family of four in a large city was $34 829, substantially higher than that for a similar-sized family in a rural area ($22 783).

## Who Are the Poor?

Rising unemployment causes the number and proportion of people living below the poverty line to increase. In 1980, for example, 11.6 percent of all Canadians were below the after-tax poverty line but, with the recession of the early 1980s, that figure climbed to 13.7 percent by 1984. As the economy recovered, the proportion of poor Canadians dropped again to 10.2 percent in 1989 but then rose steeply to 15.2 percent in 1996 following the recession in the early 1990s. Over the next decade, the proportion of poor Canadians rose and fell. In 2009, the most recent year for which data are available, 9.6 percent of Canadians were living below the after-tax LICO (National Council of Welfare, 2011).

Although poverty rates tend to follow unemployment rates, not all of Canada's poor are unemployed or out of the labour force. Using the market basket measure (MBM) of low income (see Box 6.2), which provides slightly higher estimates than the LICO measure (10.1 percent versus 9.2 percent in 2007, for example), more than half a million Canadians (34 percent of all low-income Canadians) were supported mainly by someone who held a job (Human Resources and Skills

Development Canada [HRSDC], 2012). More than 75 percent of these **working poor** Canadians worked full-time for the full year. They were poor not because they were not working but because they earned so little. Overall, as part-time and temporary work have become more common in Canada, the working poor have come to make up a much larger proportion of Canada's poor (Sauvé, 2006).

First Nations are among the poorest citizens of our country (see Box 6.3). The most recent census data (Statistics Canada, 2008b) show unemployment rates among 25- to 54-year-old First Nations Canadians that are more than twice as high as among non-First Nations in the same age category (13 percent versus 5 percent, respectively, in 2006). First Nations living on reserves have the highest unemployment rates (23 percent in 2006). Consequently, the pov-erty rate (LICO) for First Nations living off-reserve in 2007 was 13.7 percent, compared with 9.9 percent for all Canadians (HRSDC, 2012). The comparable rate for First Nations living on reserves, if available, would be much higher (see Box 6.3).

On average, recent immigrants are younger and more educated than are native-born Canadians (see Chapter 8, Race and Ethnic Relations). Even so, in 2007, 16.4 percent of immigrants who had arrived in Canada in the previous decade were living below the LICO. Over the past decades, immigrants have come to be significantly over-represented among Canada's working poor (Wallis and Kwok, 2008). Between 1980 and 2005, the earnings (in 2005 dollars) of recent immigrants declined 21 percent, while the earnings of Canadians in general stayed roughly the same (Statistics Canada, 2008a: 40).

---

### BOX 6.3    AFTER ATTAWAPISKAT, WHAT?

When Canadians first saw the news about Attawapiskat they knew that no matter who is at fault, nobody in Canada should be using a plastic bucket for a toilet and have to dump it outside on a regular basis. Nobody should be calling a shack with mould on the walls home. And nobody in Ontario should be paying $23.50 for six apples and four small bottles of juice. ...

No one's hands are clean on this issue. The federal government has woefully underfunded the housing, educational and health needs of First Nations for years. The First Nations leadership has not been aggressive and honest enough about the conditions on many reserves. The provincial government has not ensured that the economic benefits from development on traditional lands flowed more equitably to First Nations. And the news media have ignored the reality of Third World conditions in Canada for far too long. ... This is not the first time there has been a crisis at Attawapiskat.

In 1979, 30,000 gallons of diesel fuel (the largest spill in Northern Ontario) leaked under the elementary school. The school was finally closed in 2001 because of ongoing health problems suffered by students and teachers. Ten years later, the federal government pledged (for the third time) to fund a new school. Meantime, the children remain in inadequate portables.

In May 2008, hundreds of people were evacuated from the community because of flooding caused by ice jams in the Attawapiskat River. In July 2009, a massive sewage flood dumped waste into eight buildings that housed 90 people. As a stopgap measure, De Beers (the diamond mine is 60 kilometres away) donated and retrofitted two construction trailers to house 90 people until the damaged homes could be fixed or replaced. Two years later, this "short-term solution" still houses the 90 people—who share six washrooms and four stoves. ...

Some may ask, "Why don't the people of Attawapiskat just move?" That's like asking: Why don't the people of Vancouver, Los Angeles and San Francisco move out of the San Andreas/Queen Charlotte Fault zone where earthquakes can occur? Why don't people in the Caribbean move out of the hurricane zones?

The people of Attawapiskat happen to live on inhospitable land on the fault line between advancing western civilization in pursuit of mineral wealth (mainly diamonds and chromite) and their own hunter/gatherer civilization. Many do not live in Third World conditions. About a third of them do actually get a real living and cultural identity from trapping and harvesting caribou, geese and fish. Another hundred work at the nearby De Beers diamond mine. Many still live on the land, coming into the settlement only at Christmas or other "gathering times." They don't move because it's their land. It's home.

---

SOURCE: Excerpt from J. F. (Jim) Foulds (2011), "After Attawakispat, What?" From http://www.thestar.com/opinion/editorialopinion/article/1108609-after-attawapiskat-what.

Several decades ago, senior citizens were more likely than younger Canadians were to be living below the poverty line. However, higher proportions of recent cohorts of retirees have had employer-provided pensions and personal retirement funds (Gougeon, 2009), and the federal government has maintained old-age pension levels, even though they are quite small. Consequently, in contrast to the working poor, among whom poverty rates have risen, the poverty rate for seniors has declined. In 2007, only 4.8 percent of seniors were living below the LICO, compared with 9.9 percent of the total Canadian population (HRSDC, 2012). In contrast, 21.3 percent of Canadian single parents were living below the LICO in 2007. Four out of five (82 percent) of these single parents were female. Many of these young women were completely dependent on social assistance, since it is almost impossible for a single young mother to look after children and hold down a job.

## Social Assistance for the Poor

Many people believe that "welfare" (social assistance) and employment insurance are too easy to obtain and that the amount of money received is enough to encourage people to avoid seeking work (Swanson, 2001). Is this true? Because welfare regulations vary across provinces and territories, we will examine data from Ontario, the largest province and among the provinces with the highest welfare incomes, for 1992 and 2009.

Figure 6.3 shows that, in 1992, a single, employable adult (an adult who did not have a disability, was not a senior, and was not considered unable to seek work because of family responsibilities) who was eligible for Ontario social assistance received 62 percent of the after-tax poverty line (LICO). Almost two decades later, in 2009, the same type of person receiving welfare would have received only 41 percent of the poverty line. Recall that the poverty line is lower than the median income. Thus, the $7501 this single employable adult would have received from welfare in 2009 was exactly one-third of the median income for single adults in the province (National Council of Welfare, 2010).

People with disabilities who are receiving welfare have generally been treated a bit more generously by provincial governments. Thus, in 1992, such an individual would have received total annual transfer payments that were 86 percent of the poverty line. Here again we see that welfare payments have been

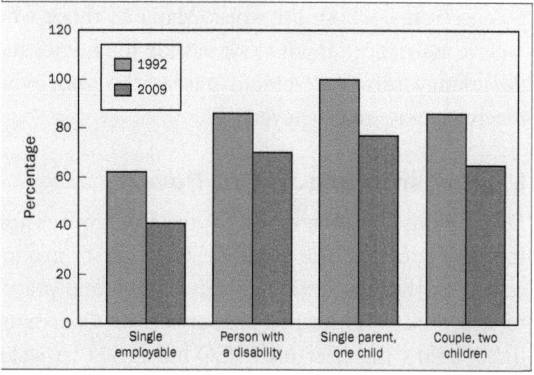

**FIGURE 6.3**   TOTAL WELFARE INCOME AS A PERCENTAGE OF (AFTER TAX) POVERTY LINE (LICO), ONTARIO, 1992 AND 2009

SOURCE: Data reported in National Council of Welfare. (2010). *Welfare Incomes: 2009*, specifically Table 13: Welfare Incomes as a Percentage of the After-Tax LICOs, 1992–2000, p. A-46; and Table 13: Welfare Incomes as a Percentage of the After-Tax LICOs, 2001–2009, p. A-47. Reproduced with the permission of the Minister of Public Works and Government Services Canada, 2012.

reduced. In 2009, the $12 905 that a person with a disability would have received from the provincial government was only 70 percent of the poverty line and only 57 percent of the median income for all single adults in Ontario.

Single parents and couples with children, like adults with disabilities, have also been treated somewhat better by the welfare system, compared to single, employable adults. However, for both groups, we see in Figure 6.3 that their total annual welfare payments, as a percentage of the appropriate low-income line for their family type, declined over the past two decades. In 2009, a single parent with one child would have received $17 372, exactly half the median income for a two-person family in Ontario that year. The $22 695 that a couple with two children would have received from welfare that year was only 29 percent of the Ontario median income for four-person families (National Council of Welfare, 2010).

Summing up, in Ontario, and also across Canada, the amount of welfare assistance is very low. Furthermore, in every province and territory, welfare incomes have been cut over the past two decades, sometimes substantially, for almost all types of recipients. As the National Council of Welfare (2010: vii) concluded, after reviewing similar data for all provinces and territories, "[r]egardless of the measure used, welfare incomes were consistently far below most socially accepted measures of adequacy." Consequently, it is difficult to accept the argument that overly generous welfare systems discourage people from looking for work. Many of those who receive assistance cannot work outside the home, and the money provided seldom pushes the poor who receive it close to the poverty line.

## Moving Into and Out of Poverty

Discussions of poverty can leave the impression that the poor and the nonpoor are separate groups and that there is little mobility from one status to the other. While the proportion of Canadians living below the after-tax LICO has varied between 9 and 15 percent over the past two decades, Statistics Canada data show that, between 1993 and 1998, one in four Canadians (24 percent) lived in a low-income family for at least one year (Morissette and Zhang, 2001). A similar but more recent analysis, also using pre-tax LICO calculations, showed that, even with a strong economy, this picture had not changed: Between 1996 and 2001, 25 percent of all Canadians lived below the poverty line for at least one year (Statistics Canada, 2005: 122).

The earlier study provided a more detailed multi-year analysis, showing that 8 percent of the total population experienced poverty (were in the low-income group) for four or more years out of a possible six. However, among Canadians living in lone-parent families, 38 percent experienced poverty for at least four years between 1993 and 1998. More recent data show that, for a single year (2003–04), about 4 percent of all Canadians slide below the poverty line while a similar proportion move above it (National Council of Welfare, 2008b). Thus, poverty is not a static

status. Individuals and families move into and out of poverty each year. Nevertheless, a sizable minority remain stuck in poverty year after year. Losing a job, having to take a lower-paying job, becoming a single parent, or being widowed can drastically increase the chance of falling into, and remaining stuck in, poverty. In addition, welfare regulations in many provinces "claw back" social assistance benefits as soon as welfare recipients start earning even a small income (National Council of Welfare, 2008a). This predicament creates a "welfare trap" that further increases the chances of poor Canadians, particularly single-parent families, remaining poor (see Box 6.4)

## MATERIAL INEQUALITY IN CANADA: SUMMING UP

### Is Inequality Increasing in Canada?

Compared with some other countries, and compared with the situation in Canada a century ago, the level of material inequality in this country today is relatively low. Even so, you have seen evidence of a great deal of inequality in wealth and income. Furthermore, there are indications that, for at least several decades, the level of inequality has been slowly rising. Corporate concentration has been increasing as a small number of huge business enterprises, many of them family owned or family run, have gained control over a larger share of the assets of Canada's biggest corporations. Wealth inequality in general appears to be increasing, income inequality has risen, and the number of working poor in Canada has increased.

Looking more closely at the labour market, we see that unemployment rates have been rising slowly but steadily for several decades. Although these rates

---

| BOX 6.4 | ONE STEP FORWARD, ONE STEP BACK: WELFARE "CLAWBACKS" |
| --- | --- |

A single mother with two children aged 15 and 19 living in subsidized housing gets $13 873 annually from welfare, GST credit, and federal child benefits. The mother takes a part-time job that pays $14 000 a year and her 19-year-old enrolls in university part-time and gets a part-time job that pays $2400. Both must now take public transit. The son has a $1000 bursary. On paper, the family's income per year is $31 273. The mother's and student's earnings reduce their welfare by $8200 (half of her pay and half of his). Their earnings also cause their subsidized rent to rise by $2268 per year. Payroll taxes eat up another $815. TTC and GO Transit passes for both cost $4728 and work-related clothing another $1000. The family is now left with $14 262 ($31 273 minus $17 011) or just $389 more before taxes than they had at the start.

SOURCE: "Case Study: Why A Job Doesn't Pay." *Toronto Star* 6 December 2007: A1. Reprinted with permission—Torstar Syndication Services.

have gone up and down a number of times, and are lower now than they were in the 1990s, the long-term trend since the mid-twentieth century has been upward. Hence, in 2011, the average annual unemployment rate was 7.4 percent, representing 1.12 million unemployed Canadians (HRSDC, 2012), a number almost equal to the populations of Saskatchewan and Prince Edward Island combined. With increasing global financial and economic uncertainty, we can expect the national unemployment rate to stay at this level over the next several years. Comparisons across provinces in 2011 reveal the extent of regional inequality in Canada, with unemployment rates of 12.7 percent in Newfoundland and Labrador, 9.5 percent in New Brunswick, 7.8 percent in Ontario, and only 5.0 percent in Saskatchewan.

Part-time employment rates have also been rising over the past few decades. Forty years ago, fewer than 4 percent of employed Canadians worked part-time. In 2008, 18.4 percent had a part-time job. Since the 1980s, the number of temporary jobs has significantly increased, as employers have begun to cut long-term wage costs by offering more limited-term contract positions. By 2008, one in eight working Canadians had a job with a specific end date (Krahn, Lowe, and Hughes, 2011: ch. 2). Real wages are no longer increasing, and inequality in earnings has been rising as a result of these part-time and temporary employment trends, as well as declines in employment in traditionally higher-paying industries and occupations.

### A More Polarized Society?

It is difficult to avoid the conclusion that, in Canada, the gap between the advantaged (those with full-time, permanent jobs) and the disadvantaged (those with part-time, temporary, or no jobs) is slowly increasing (Fuller and Vosko, 2008). A similar pattern has been observed in Britain (Dorling et al., 2007) and in the United States (Cavanagh and Collins, 2008). This is not to suggest that a new era of massive inequalities is dawning. However, the evidence is clear that material inequalities are rising, not declining, and that society is becoming more polarized in terms of access to and control over economic resources (OECD, 2011; Yalnizyan, 2010). Using Weber's definition of class, I conclude that class differences in Canada and many other countries are becoming more pronounced.

Obviously, many interrelated factors have contributed to the growth in material inequality (Krahn, Lowe, and Hughes, 2011). Although some new high-skill and well-paying jobs emerged over the past

several decades in Canada, the overall outcome has still been a net reduction in employment opportunities. Globalization, the process whereby goods and services are produced by business enterprises operating in many different countries, has led to a more competitive and cost-cutting economic environment. Business enterprises have responded by shifting many of their activities to countries in which lower wages and less rigorous environmental and labour laws allow them to earn higher profits. In North America, layoffs and downsizing were a frequent response, along with the replacement of full-time permanent jobs with part-time and temporary positions. Labour unions, which traditionally resisted attempts to cut wages and jobs, have lost some of their power. At the political level, an ideology emphasizing that "the market knows best," and that people need less rather than more government intervention in the economy and the labour market, has led to fewer government efforts to reduce material inequalities and reduced transfer payments to the poor (National Council of Welfare, 2008a). Tax cuts for the highest income groups have exacerbated patterns of income and wealth inequality (Yalnizyan, 2010; OECD, 2011). It remains to be seen how the global financial and economic uncertainties that arose in late 2008, which had significant impacts on Canada's political, economic, and financial institutions, will further affect long-term patterns of social inequality in Canada.

## CONSEQUENCES OF MATERIAL INEQUALITY

Other chapters in this textbook will go into more detail about the many consequences of material inequality for individuals and families. You will see that position in the class structure has an effect on belief systems, behaviours, and lifestyles, and that the poor, the middle classes, and the very wealthy frequently hold different opinions on various subjects, may vote differently, and certainly enjoy different lifestyles. But, much more important, people in different positions in society's economic hierarchy experience different life-chances, to use Weber's term.

### Consequences for Individuals and Families

Children from poorer families typically do not do as well in school as children from more affluent families do (Davies and Guppy, 2006). They are more likely to be enrolled in nonuniversity academic streams (Taylor and Krahn, 2009) and to drop out before completing high school (Tanner, Krahn, and Hartnagel, 1995). They are also much less likely to go to university (Krahn, 2009). As noted earlier in the discussion of occupational mobility, such effects of poverty are largely responsible for the perpetuation of class inequalities from one generation to the next.

For a variety of reasons, including better nutrition, access to better health care, and less hazardous working conditions, those who are situated higher in the economic hierarchy are typically healthier than are poor people (Raphael, 2011). Consequently, on average, the poor do not live as long as those who are better off (Wilkinson and Pickett, 2010). Similarly, when dealing with the criminal justice system, those with greater access to and control over economic resources tend to fare better (King and Winterdyk, 2010). As a result, the poor are overrepresented in jails. First Nations and visible-minority Canadians with low incomes are particularly disadvantaged when dealing with the criminal justice system (Fitzgerald and Carrington, 2008). I could go on, but these examples are probably sufficient to make the point that life-chances are a function of position in the class structure and that those higher up in the economic hierarchy enjoy a better quality of and, often, a longer life.

## Consequences for Society

In addition to these substantial consequences of material inequality for individuals and families, can material inequality have other broader social outcomes? Specifically, given the relatively high and increasing level of inequality in Canada, can we expect more social unrest? Will conflict between the "haves" and the "have-nots" increase? Those committed to a classical Marxist theory of social change might welcome such conflict; for them, it would indicate that capitalism was finally beginning to give way to a socialist society. Others might view such conflict much more negatively. Whatever the response to such a possibility, it is clear that values and beliefs directly influence the way the people respond to evidence of inequality and its consequences.

But returning to the question, can we expect an increase in social unrest and conflict as a result of higher levels of inequality? During the early 1980s, for example, the solidarity movement in British Columbia brought together members of trade unions, social-welfare organizations, and various community-based groups in opposition to the Social Credit government's cutbacks in government programs and attempts to change labour legislation. Bryan Palmer (1986) described the protests and rallies that took place as evidence of growing class conflict. However, these events were exceptional. Much more often, the poor and the near-poor put up with their less advantaged position because they have few of the resources (for example, money, education, organizations) that make it possible to fight for social change (Brym, 1979). In fact, in the past decade, we have seen more opposition from a better-organized middle class, in response to government cutbacks in health and education funding, and in support for the seniors, than from the poor in response to welfare cutbacks. And we have seen intensified negative stereotyping of the poor and those on welfare, a process that Jean Swanson (2001) calls "poor-bashing."

However, we have also seen the emergence of a remarkable new social movement, Occupy Wall Street, that brought together a wide range of individuals and groups, including middle-class, university-educated social activists, and the homeless, all concerned about the growing level of social inequality in North America. It remains to be seen whether this movement, sparked by an online suggestion from a Vancouver-based nonprofit organization (Adbusters), will have an impact on patterns of social inequality in Canada and elsewhere (see Box 6.5).

Thus, while it is unlikely that growing social inequality and fewer opportunities for upward mobility will translate into widespread social unrest in Canada, it remains possible that coalitions of concerned citizens will have an impact on this long-term trend. As for the long-term consequences for global peace and security as a result of a growing gap between rich and poor countries, they are difficult to predict. Even so, as Paul Krugman, an influential American economist, noted, "The ultimate effects of growing economic disparities on our social and political health may be hard to predict, but they are unlikely to be pleasant" (Krugman, 1994: F9).

## RESPONDING TO INEQUALITY

Some people believe that more equal distribution of society's resources would be preferable to the current level of inequality. They believe that existing differences in life-chances are unjust and look for ways in which social institutions, laws, and tax systems might be

**BOX 6.5**   **THE PROCESS IS THE POINT: THE OCCUPY MOVEMENT IN CANADA**

Since the Occupy movement arrived in Canada, pundits and media commentators have been scratching their heads, asking the same question in different ways: what is the point? Critics of the nascent movement highlight a lack of coherent goals, the apparent disorganization of those involved, and the pointlessness of camping out to create more equity. ...

The reason that public commentators are having such trouble with the Occupy movement is because it defies conventional categories. "Social movement" is the best descriptor that can be applied, but it also looks different than other social movements that Canada has seen. ... [I]t involves people setting stakes in the ground, both metaphorically and literally, indicating through that act of claiming space that they plan to stay put for the long haul. It involves experiments in direct and radical democracy. In short, it involves trying out things that are neither familiar nor widespread under our current system.

Theorists of democracy have long understood that democracy itself is a process, not an end.

Hannah Arendt famously described the public sphere as a shared table, around which we gather in order to relate to one another and find our common ground. This involves much more than going to the ballot box every four years; it requires human relationships, wrought through time spent together struggling over dilemmas and finding solutions to the problems that collectively face us. As the pressure mounts on individuals—not just young people but perhaps felt more keenly by young people—to seek out scarce jobs, pay off mounting debt, and struggle to survive under increasingly unforgiving economic circumstances, the opportunity to come together so as to share frustrations and seek solutions within the public realm is one that is rarely offered. The Occupy movement offers just such an opportunity: a genuine moment of democratic engagement not mediated through the interests of pre-existing political parties or NGOs. It represents a chance to experience the actual human relationships that lie at the root of democracy.

SOURCE: Kennelly, Jacqueline. (2011). "The Process is the Point: The Occupy Movement in Canada." This article first appeared in Carleton University's monthly online publication, *Carleton Now.* On the World Wide Web at http://carletonnow.carleton.ca/november-2011/the-process-is-the-point-the-occupy-movement-in-canada (retrieved November 2011).

SOURCE: © Tomas Abad/Alamy.

changed to reduce material inequality. Others, equally offended by inequality and its consequences, reject this reformist approach in favour of a more radical position, advocating the replacement of capitalist society by some kind of socialist or social-democratic alternative. Still others respond to evidence of extensive inequality with little ambition to change it, believing, simply, that this is "the way things are." Although perhaps bothered by its consequences, members of this group might still conclude that the existing level of inequality is inevitable and that well-intentioned efforts to reduce it will, in the long run, have little effect. They might even conclude that inequality is functional, as Davis and Moore (1945) argued nearly 70 years ago, and that efforts to reduce it will be counterproductive. In short, reactions to inequality, and recommendations about what, if anything, should be done about it, reflect personal values and political orientations.

Assuming that a lower level of inequality is a goal worth striving for, it is clear that the government has a role to play in trying to reach that goal. The Canadian state has a significant impact on the distribution of wealth and income through tax systems that redistribute wealth from the rich to the poor (Yalnizyan, 2010); through minimum-wage and other types of legislation; and through transfer payments, such as pensions for seniors and those with disabilities, social assistance for low-income individuals and families, and employment insurance. Even so, compared with some other industrialized countries, Canada spends considerably less on attempts to reduce poverty (Raphael, 2011).

Canada's welfare policies place more faith in the power of a free market, unregulated by government legislation and policies, to produce wealth and jobs that should, it is expected, trickle down to the poor (Esping-Andersen, 1990). Unfortunately, as my review of labour-market trends indicates, there is little evidence that the free market has performed successfully in this regard. Instead, unemployment rates have risen, precarious employment has become more common, and social inequality has increased. Furthermore, during the past several decades, the political mood has changed, and concerns about reducing government deficits, streamlining government, and making Canada more competitive in the global marketplace appear to have been influencing government policy more than concerns about reducing inequality. In fact, some deficit-reducing initiatives (for example, reductions in social-assistance payments) have led to increases in material inequality in Canada, as have tax reform initiatives that have favoured the very rich.

But twenty-first-century government policies do not necessarily require this trade-off. For example, government-funded job-creation strategies may continue to be useful in the future, as they were during the aftermath of the global financial crisis of 2008–09. Revised tax policies that would raise corporate income taxes, increase the marginal tax rate for Canada's highest paid citizens, and eliminate some of the tax write-offs enjoyed by the upper and middle classes could also be useful.

A large part of the problem lies, of course, in the fact that any serious effort to redistribute the wealth and income from the well-off to the poor would probably be opposed by the former. If we really want to do something about material inequality in Canada, and globally, if we want a different kind of society and a different kind of world, many of us—and that would include me—have to be willing to accept less so that others can have more.

## SUMMARY

1. Social stratification refers to persistent patterns of social inequality. Some social hierarchies are based on ascribed statuses, such as gender, race, and age, which are typically assigned to an individual at birth. Other social hierarchies are based on achieved statuses, which index how well an individual has performed in some role. A society in which considerable social mobility between statuses is possible is said to have an open stratification system.

2. Social theorists have proposed a variety of explanations of the origins and effects of social stratification systems. In his class-based theory of social stratification, Karl Marx emphasized the exploitation of the working class by the owners of the means of production and the potential for class conflict to generate social change. Max Weber also put considerable emphasis on the power that resides in ownership of property but argued that hierarchies of prestige and political power are influential as well.

3. The functional theory of social stratification suggests that inequality is both inevitable and necessary insofar as it ensures that the most qualified individuals are selected to fill the most important and rewarding roles. Power differences are downplayed in this theory, as is conflict between social classes. A number of more recent theories of social stratification, including those put forward by Gerhard Lenski, Frank Parkin, and Erik Olin Wright, have placed more emphasis on power and conflict. Wright developed a class-based theory of stratification that adapts many of Marx's ideas to contemporary circumstances. Parkin's approach follows in the footsteps of Weber.

4. Occupational shifts in Canada over the past century reveal some of the changing features of Canada's stratification system. Studies of occupational mobility show that Canada is a relatively open society. Even so, there is strong evidence that class-based advantages are often passed from one generation to the next.

5. Ownership of wealth and property in Canada is highly concentrated, and income inequality is relatively high and growing. Statistics Canada's low-income cutoff line (LICO) reveals that about one in ten Canadians is currently living below the "poverty line." There is considerable evidence that the poor and others near the bottom of the social hierarchies in our society enjoy fewer life-chances than do the well-off. The poor are less likely to do well in school and to continue on to higher education. They are also less healthy and have a shorter life expectancy, and they do not fare as well when dealing with the criminal justice system. Because of their limited access to social and material resources, the poor have seldom become an active force for social change.

6. Some theories of social stratification developed in the middle of the twentieth century suggested that material inequality was declining as the North American economy expanded. However, the period of rapid economic growth that characterized the middle decades of that century appears to have ended. As unemployment rates have risen, as part-time and temporary work become more common, and as governments cut back on social-assistance programs while reducing taxes for the very wealthy, evidence accumulates that material inequality is slowly increasing in Canada.

## QUESTIONS TO CONSIDER

1. Does social class play a more or less significant role than do ascribed statuses (such as race, gender, and age) in determining patterns of inequality in Canadian society?

2. How are social and material advantages passed from one generation to the next, resulting in persistent patterns of social inequality?

3. What role, if any, should governments play in addressing persistent patterns of social inequality?

4. What does *poverty* mean, and how should we measure it?

5. As Canada becomes a more culturally diverse country, what are the implications of high levels of poverty among immigrants and First Nations?

6. The 2011 Occupy Wall Street movement involved extended public protests about social inequality in many North American cities and around the world. Did this social movement have a lasting effect?

## GLOSSARY

**Absolute poverty** (p. 143) is the state of existence of those who have so little income that they can barely stay alive.

**Achieved status** (p. 129) is a changeable status that is acquired on the basis of how well an individual performs a particular role.

**Ascribed status** (p. 129) is a status, such as age, gender, or race, that is assigned to an individual, typically at birth, and is not chosen by the individual.

**The bourgeoisie** (p. 132), according to Marx, is one of the two main classes in the capitalist mode of production. It comprises the owners of the means of production.

A **caste system** (p. 130) is a closed stratification system, most common in India, with strict rules regarding the type of work that members of different castes (the strata of Indian society into which people are born) can do.

**Circulatory mobility** (p. 141) is the occupational mobility that occurs within a society when better-qualified individuals move upward to replace those who are less qualified and who must consequently move downward.

**Class** (p. 131) is a position in an economic hierarchy occupied by individuals or families with similar access to, or control over, material resources.

**Class conflict** (p. 133), according to Marx, is conflict between major classes within a mode of production. It eventually leads to the evolution of a new mode of production.

**Class consciousness** (p. 133), according to Marx, is the recognition by members of a class of their shared interests in opposition to members of another class.

**Class structure** (p. 131) is the relatively permanent economic hierarchy comprising different social classes.

A **closed stratification system** (p. 130) is a stratification system in which little or no social mobility occurs, because most or all statuses are ascribed.

**Contradictory class locations** (p. 137), according to Erik Olin Wright, are the locations within a class structure populated by occupational groupings with divided loyalties (for example, managers who supervise others yet report to owners).

**Exclusion** (p. 138), according to Frank Parkin, is the organized effort by privileged, more powerful groups to maintain their advantaged position.

The **functionalist theory of stratification** (p. 135) views social organization as analogous to a biological organism in which the parts (or organs) exist because of the functions they perform in maintaining the whole. In this theory, stratification exists because of vital functions it presumably performs in maintaining social equilibrium.

**Intergenerational occupational mobility** (p. 141) refers to an individual's occupational mobility, either upward or downward, in relation to her or his parents' occupational status.

**Intragenerational occupational mobility** (p. 141) refers to an individual's occupational mobility, either upward or downward, within his or her own lifetime.

**Life-chances** (p. 134), according to Weber, are the opportunities (or lack thereof) for a higher standard of living and a better quality of life that are available to members of a given class.

The **low-income cutoff (LICO)** (p. 143), known unofficially as the "poverty line," is an estimate of the income level below which a person or family might be considered to be living in relative poverty. It is defined by Statistics Canada as the level of income at which more than 63 percent of income is spent on basic necessities.

The **means of production** (p. 132), according to Marx, are one of the main components of a mode of production, consisting of the technology, capital investments, and raw materials used in production.

A **meritocracy** (p. 130) is a society in which most or all statuses are achieved on the basis of merit (how well a person performs in a given role).

The **mode of production** (p. 132), according to Marx, is the system of economic activity in a society, comprising the means of production and the social relations of production (the class system).

**Occupational status attainment** (p. 141) refers to the process whereby an individual attains a particular occupational status and the factors that influence that process.

An **open stratification system** (p. 130) is a stratification system in which merit, rather than inheritance (or ascribed characteristics), determines social rank.

The **petite bourgeoisie** (p. 132), according to Marx, is a secondary class within the capitalist mode of production, including independent owners/producers (for example, farmers) and small-business owners.

**Power** (p. 134) is the ability to impose one's will on others.

The **proletariat** (p. 132), according to Marx, is one of the two main classes in a capitalist mode of production, comprising workers who exchange their labour for a wage.

**Relative poverty** (p. 143) is a state of existence in which individuals have significantly less income than do most others in their society, causing their lifestyle to be more restricted and their life-chances to be substantially curtailed.

**Social closure** (p. 138), according to Max Weber and Frank Parkin, refers to the methods used by relatively powerful groups to maintain their unequal access to status and resources, and to exclude others from such access.

**Social mobility** (p. 130) is the process whereby individuals, families, or other groups move up or down a status hierarchy.

**Social relations of production** (p. 132), according to Marx, are one of the main components of a given mode of production—specifically, the relationships between the main classes involved in production.

**Social stratification** (p. 127) refers to persistent patterns of social inequality perpetuated by the way wealth, power, and prestige are distributed and passed from one generation to the next.

**Socioeconomic status** (p. 131) refers to a person's general status within an economic hierarchy, based on income, education, and occupation.

**Status** (p. 129) is a culturally and socially defined position that a person occupies in a group.

**Structural mobility** (p. 141) refers to the occupational mobility in a society resulting from changes in the occupational structure (for example, the upward mobility of many individuals resulting from the creation of more middle- and upper-level jobs in the economy).

**Surplus value** (p. 132), according to Marx, is the value of goods in excess of the cost of production, which takes the form of profit when the product is sold.

**Usurpation** (p. 138), according to Frank Parkin, is the effort of excluded groups within a stratification system to gain advantages and power at the expense of more powerful groups.

The **working poor** (p. 146) are individuals who work but whose income leaves them below a designated low-income, or poverty, line.

## SUGGESTED READING

Grabb, Edward and Neil Guppy, eds. (2009). *Social Inequality in Canada: Patterns, Problems, and Policies*, 5th ed. Toronto: Pearson. A comprehensive collection of readings on various dimensions of stratification in Canada.

McQuaig, Linda and Neil Brooks. (2010). *The Trouble with Billionaires*. Toronto: Penguin Canada. Have the super-rich really earned their wealth and esteem? Read this fascinating book and draw your own conclusion.

Raphael, Dennis. (2011). *Poverty in Canada: Implications for Health and Quality of Life*, 2nd ed. Toronto: Canadian Scholars' Press. An excellent interdisciplinary examination of the causes and extent of poverty in Canada, what it feels like to live in poverty, and what might be done to alleviate it.

Swanson, Jean. (2001). *Poor-Bashing: The Politics of Exclusion*. Toronto: Between the Lines. A social activist takes a critical look at how the poor and people receiving welfare in Canada are stereotyped and mistreated by the media and government, and offers useful suggestions for social change.

Wallis, Maria A. and Siu-ming Kwok, eds. (2008). *Daily Struggles: The Deepening Racialization and Feminization of Poverty in Canada*. Toronto: Canadian Scholars' Press. A collection of research papers examining the impact of race, gender, and immigrant status on poverty and social exclusion in Canada.

# Race & Ethnicity

# 10 Ethnic Relations and Race

Keisha, a student of South Asian background, tells the story of the racism she experienced when she first went to university in southern Ontario. She describes her first "big shock":

*I came to university with a big mind and an open mind and I was here to learn and it was an environment where my fellow peers, I had hoped, would have the same stand or the same understanding of a lot of things. So walking into lecture one day, I was a little bit late, so I just turned around to one of the girls and asked what was happening, and she turned to me and said something that was very awful and I will quote. She said: "Don't talk to me, filthy Paki." She was pretty loud, and the girls in front of me and behind me kind of heard and there were a couple of guys who heard and they turned around . . . I was so shocked that I couldn't respond because I couldn't fathom that someone my age, someone in the same society that I grew up in or at least at the level of education system that we were in, would not have an open mind and would say some thing like that . . . I couldn't respond because I'm a person who is very naïve . . . I didn't say anything. But I was hoping, I guess, that the people who were sitting in front of me or behind me would've said something.* (James, 2010:235)

Canada is a diverse and complex society composed of racially and ethnically different groups. Our country has a reputation as a tolerant and compassionate country whose success in race and ethnic relations has received worldwide admiration (Fleras and Elliott, 2003). Canada is widely renowned for its "cultural democracy"

© CP/Kevin Frayer

and "harmonious" ethnic diversity (James, 2005). Without question, significant gains have been made in the past 50 years for "visible" and "non-visible" minority groups in Canada (Hier and Singh Bolaria, 2007).

From a distance, Canada maintains its enviable status. However, upon closer examination, we see evidence of a more complex picture in terms of race and ethnic relations. Despite our claims that Canadians are "colour-blind," racist ideas and practices affect individuals and groups in very real ways. Racism is something that is not only part of Canada's history, but also an important aspect of current circumstances (Satzewich and Liodakis, 2007).

In this chapter, racism will be central to the discussion of race and ethnicity. One of the most important and reliable sources of information on racism is the individuals who have experienced it directly. Therefore, we will explore the subjective impact of race and ethnicity on people's lives—and examine whether those effects are changing. Before reading on, test your knowledge about race and ethnic relations in Canada by taking the quiz in Box 10.1 on page 275.

(*Source:* James, Carl E. *Seeing Ourselves: Exploring Race, Ethnicity and Culture*, 4th edition (2010). Thompson Books.)

**Critical Thinking Questions**

1. How do you think you would have responded if you had witnessed the racist incident outlined earlier?

2. How might you have responded if you, like Keisha, were the target of such racial hatred?

3. To what extent do you think race plays a part in Canadian society? In global societies?

| CHAPTER FOCUS QUESTION | What is the significance of race in Canadian society? |
|---|---|

## LEARNING OBJECTIVES
### AFTER READING THIS CHAPTER, YOU SHOULD BE ABLE TO

**LO-1** Distinguish between race and ethnicity.

**LO-2** Define and explain prejudice, discrimination, and racism.

**LO-3** Explain the major sociological perspectives on race and ethnic relations.

**LO-4** Discuss the unique historical experiences of the racial and ethnic groups in Canada.

**LO-5** Describe how Canada's immigration policies have affected the composition of Canada's racial and ethnic population today.

## LO-1    RACE AND ETHNICITY

March 21 is recognized annually as the International Day for the Elimination of Racial Discrimination because on that day, in 1960, police opened fire and killed 69 people at a peaceful demonstration against apartheid in South Africa.

**race** A term used by many people to specify groups of people distinguished by physical characteristics, such as skin colour; also, a category of people who have been singled out as inferior or superior, often on the basis of real or alleged physical characteristics, such as skin colour, hair texture, eye shape, or other subjectively selected attributes.

**ethnic group** A collection of people distinguished, by others or by themselves, primarily on the basis of cultural or nationality characteristics.

What is "race"? Some people think it refers to skin colour (the Caucasian "race"); others use it to refer to a religion (the Jewish "race"), nationality (the British "race"), or the entire human species (the human "race") (Marger, 2009). Popular usages of *race* have been based on the assumption that a race is a grouping or classification based on *genetic* variations in physical appearance, particularly skin colour. However, social scientists and biologists dispute the idea that biological race is a meaningful concept (Johnson, 1995). In fact, the idea of race has little meaning in a biological sense because of the enormous amount of interbreeding that has taken place within the human population. For these reasons, sociologists sometimes place "race" in quotation marks to show that categorizing individuals and population groups on biological characteristics is neither accurate nor based on valid distinctions between the genetic makeup of differently identified "races" (Marshall, 1998).

Race is a *socially constructed reality*, not a biological one. Understanding what we mean when we say that race is a social construct is important to our understanding of how race affects all aspects of social life and society. Race as a *social construct* means that races as such do not actually exist, but some groups are still racially defined because the *idea* persists in many people's minds that races are distinct biological categories with physically distinguishable characteristics and a shared common cultural heritage. However, research on the human genome has been unable to identify any racially based genetic differences in human beings, and fossil and DNA evidence also point to humans all being of one race. Race continues to be an important concern in the 21st century, however, not because it is a biological reality but because it takes on a life of its own when it is socially defined and shapes how we see others and ourselves. Race also has significant social consequences, such as which individuals experience prejudice and discrimination and which have the best life chances and opportunities. When we look at race in this way, the *social significance* that people accord to race is more important than any biological differences that might exist among people who are placed in arbitrary racial categories (Frankenberg, 1993).

A **race** is a category of people who have been singled out as inferior or superior, often on the basis of real or alleged physical characteristics, such as skin colour, hair texture, eye shape, or other subjectively selected attributes (Feagin and Feagin, 2011). Categories of people frequently thought of as racial groups include Asian Canadians, African Canadians, and Native or Aboriginal peoples.

How do you classify yourself with regard to race? For an increasing number of people, this is a difficult question to answer. What if you were asked about your ethnic origin or your ethnicity? The Canadian census, unlike that of the United States, collects information on ethnic origin rather than race. Whereas race refers only to *physical* characteristics, the concept of ethnicity refers to *cultural* features. An **ethnic group** is a collection of people distinguished, by others or by themselves, primarily on the basis of cultural or nationality characteristics (Feagin and Feagin, 2011). Ethnic groups share five main characteristics:

1. Unique cultural traits, such as language, clothing, holidays, or religious practices.
2. A sense of community.
3. A feeling of ethnocentrism.
4. Ascribed membership from birth.
5. Territoriality, or the tendency to occupy a distinct geographic area.

BOX 10.1    SOCIOLOGY AND EVERYDAY LIFE

## How Much Do You Know About Racial and Ethnic Relations in Canada?

| True | False | |
|------|-------|---|
| T | F | 1. Canadians are significantly less racist than Americans. |
| T | F | 2. Racism occurs only in times of economic decline and recession. |
| T | F | 3. Canada continues to employ racial criteria in the selection of new immigrants. |
| T | F | 4. No civil rights movement has ever existed in Canada. |
| T | F | 5. Slavery has never existed in Canada. |

For answers to the quiz about racial and ethnic relations in Canada, go to **www.nelson.com/ sociologyinourtimes6e**.

Although some people do not identify with any ethnic group, others participate in social interaction with the individuals in their group and feel a sense of common identity based on cultural characteristics, such as language, religion, or politics. Ethnicity provides individuals with a sense of identity and belonging based not only on their perception of being different but also on others' recognition of their uniqueness. Consider the comments from this university student:

> My ethnic identity is Polish. My parents were born in Poland and came to Canada in 1967 . . . I saw my ethnicity as an advantage and disadvantage during my life-time. When I was younger, I didn't want to admit that I was Polish. Even though I was born here, I felt that admitting my ethnicity would be a barrier to joining the "in crowd" or the "cool group" at school . . . As I became older, I realized I couldn't change my ethnicity. I was who I was. I became more proud of my Polish back-ground. It felt good to be a part of a Polish community where I was able to partici-pate in ceremonies and activities based on my Polish background. It gave me a sense of belonging to a group, a sense of identity, a sense of security. (James, 2010:62)*

## The Social Significance of Race and Ethnicity

Race and ethnicity take on great social significance because how people act in regard to these terms drastically affects other people's lives, including what opportunities they have, how they are treated, and even how long they live. It matters because it provides privilege and power for some. Fleras and Elliott discuss the significance of being white and enjoying what has some-times been referred to as *white privilege*:

> Think for a moment about the privileges associated with whiteness, many of which are taken for granted and unearned by accident of birth. Being white means you can purchase a home in any part of town and expect cordial treatment rather than community grumblings about a plummeting in real estate values. Being white saves you the embarrassment of going into a shopping mall with fears of being fol-lowed, frisked, monitored, or finger printed. Being white means you can comment on a variety of topics without having someone question your objectivity or second-guess your motives. Being white provides a peace of mind in that your actions are judged not as a betrayal of or a credit to your race, but in terms of individual idiosyncracies . . . Finally, being white ensures one the satisfaction of socializing at night, without being pulled over by the police or patted down. (2003:35)

*Source: James, Carl E. *Seeing Ourselves: Exploring Race, Ethnicity and Culture*, 4th edition (2010). Thompson Books.

Ethnicity, like race, is a basis of hierarchical ranking in society. John Porter (1965) described Canada as a "vertical mosaic," made up of different ethnic groups wielding varying degrees of social and economic power, status, and prestige. Porter's analysis of ethnic groups in Canada revealed a significant degree of ethnic stratification, with some ethnic groups heavily represented in the upper strata, or elite, and other groups heavily represented in the lower strata. The dominant group holds power over other (subordinate) ethnic groups. To what extent does a "vertical mosaic" still exist in Canada? A 2009 study by Philip Oreopoulos found that, despite the fact that immigrants to Canada are selected on the basis of their optimal skills, education, and professional qualifications, immigrants and ethnic minority Canadians still have significantly lower incomes and higher rates of unemployment. Oreopoulis constructed "mock" resumés representative of recent immigrants from the three largest countries of origin (China, India, and Pakistan) and Britain, as well as nonimmigrants with and without ethnic-sounding names. Six thousand resumés were sent out to apply to online job postings in the Toronto area. The findings indicated that applicants with English-sounding names with Canadian education and experience received callbacks 40 percent more often than did applicants with Chinese, Indian, or Pakistani names who had similar Canadian education and experience (Oreopoulos, 2009). This study provides evidence of continued ethnic stratification based on what Oreopoulos described as "substantial discrimination" by employers. Ethnic stratification is one dimension of a larger system of structured social inequality, as examined in Chapter 8.

## Majority and Minority Groups

The terms *majority group* and *minority group* are widely used, but what do they actually mean? To sociologists, a **majority** (or **dominant**) **group** is one that is advantaged and has superior resources and rights in a society (Feagin and Feagin, 2011). In Canada, whites with northern European ancestry (often referred to as Euro-Canadians or white Anglo-Saxon Protestants, or WASPs) are considered the majority group. A **minority** (or **subordinate**) **group** is one whose members, because of physical or cultural characteristics, are disadvantaged and subjected to unequal treatment by the dominant group and who regard themselves as objects of collective discrimination. All visible minorities and white women are considered minority group members in Canada. The term **visible minority** refers to an official government category of nonwhite, non-Caucasian individuals. Included in this category are Chinese, Japanese, Koreans, Filipinos, Asians, South Asians, Arabs, Southeast Asians, blacks, Latin Americans, and Pacific Islanders (Statistics Canada, 2008). Aboriginal people form a separate category of individuals with minority group status.

Today, more than five million Canadians—close to one in six—identified themselves as members of a visible minority, and, it is estimated that 20 years from now, Canada could be home to more than 14 million people belonging to a visible minority group. South Asians and Chinese will still comprise the largest visible minority groups (Statistics Canada, 2011).

Although the terms *majority group* and *minority group* are widely used, their actual meanings are not clear. In the sociological sense, *group* is misleading because people who merely share ascribed racial or ethnic characteristics do not constitute a group. Further, *majority* and *minority* have meanings associated with both numbers and domination. Numerically speaking, *minority* means that a group is smaller in number than a dominant group. In countries such as South Africa and India, however, this has not historically been true.

**majority (dominant) group** An advantaged group that is advantaged and has superior resources and rights in a society.

**minority (subordinate) group** A group whose members, because of physical or cultural characteristics, are disadvantaged and subjected to unequal treatment by the dominant group and who regard themselves as objects of collective discrimination.

**visible minority** An official government category of nonwhite, non-Caucasian individuals.

### TIME TO REVIEW

- Explain the statement "Race is a social construct."
- How significant do you think this social construct is in the lives of visible minority group members?
- What is the significance of race in the lives of majority group members?

**Prejudice** is a negative attitude based on preconceived notions about members of selected groups. The term *prejudice* comes from the Latin words *prae* ("before") and *judicium* ("judgment"), which means that people may be biased either for or against members of other groups before they have had any contact with them. Although prejudice can be either *positive* (bias in favour of a group—often our own) or *negative* (bias against a group—one we deem less worthy than our own), it most often refers to the negative attitudes people may have about members of other racial or ethnic groups. **Racial prejudice** involves beliefs that certain racial groups are innately inferior to others or have a disproportionate number of negative traits.

**prejudice** A negative attitude based on preconceived notions about members of selected groups.

**racial prejudice** Beliefs that certain racial groups are innately inferior to others or have a disproportionate number of negative traits.

## Stereotypes

Prejudice is rooted in stereotypes and ethnocentrism. When used in the context of racial and ethnic relations, ethnocentrism refers to the tendency to regard one's own culture and group as the standard—and thus superior—whereas all other groups are seen as inferior. Ethnocentrism is maintained and perpetuated by **stereotypes**—overgeneralizations about the appearance, behaviour, or other characteristics of members of particular groups. The term *stereotype* comes from the Greek word *stereos* ("solid") and refers to a fixed mental impression. Although all stereotypes are hurtful, negative stereotypes are particularly harmful to members of minority groups. Consider for example, Naomi's experience:

**stereotype** An overgeneralization about the appearance, behaviour, or other characteristics of members of particular groups.

> People whom I meet frequently ask, "What are you?" as a way of determining my racial background. I then proceed to tell them that I am Canadian. Then they ask me, "Where are your parents from?" I tell them Poland and they then look confused . . . And then when they learn that I am Jewish, their responses always amaze me. People express surprise and say, "You are Jewish!" as if I had a disease or something. And some people think they are paying me a compliment by saying, "We do not think of you as Jewish; you are different than most Jewish people we know." This is an outright insult to my ethnicity, of which I am proud. Another typical comment is that I "do not look Jewish." I do not understand what it means to "look Jewish" considering that there are Jewish people from all over the world. (James, 2010:216)*

How do people develop these stereotypes? The media are a major source of racial and ethnic stereotypes. Another source is ethnic jokes that portray minorities in a derogatory manner. Take a moment and think of an ethnic joke you have heard recently. Do you think this joke is harmful? Would you tell the joke to the member of the ethnic group that the joke is about? Paul, a student in a race and ethnic relations course at a Canadian university, discusses this issue:

> I laugh at a joke that uses a Black . . . because I associate a stereotype with what has been said, I am a bigot. For example, what do you call a Black guy in a new car? A thief. Funny, eh? No, the joke itself is not funny, but it makes reference to a stereotype about Blacks that they're all thieves, which I do not find funny . . . That kind of joke is not funny. It does not point out a funny stereotype of a certain race . . . it is pure malice and cruelty against a specific group. (James, 2001:107)†

*†*Source:* James, Carl E. *Seeing Ourselves: Exploring Race, Ethnicity and Culture,* 4th edition (2010). Thompson Books.

## Theories of Prejudice

Are some people more prejudiced than others? To answer this question, some theories focus on how individuals may transfer their internal psychological problems onto an external object or person. Others look at factors such as social learning and personality types.

The frustration-aggression hypothesis states that people who are frustrated in their efforts to achieve a highly desired goal will respond with a pattern of aggression toward others (Dollard et al., 1939). The object of their aggression becomes the **scapegoat**—a person or group that is incapable of offering resistance to the hostility or aggression of others (Marger, 2009). Scapegoats are often used as substitutes for the actual source of the frustration. For example, members of subordinate racial and ethnic groups are often blamed for societal problems (such as unemployment or an economic recession) over which they have no control.

According to some symbolic interactionists, prejudice results from social learning; in other words, it is learned from observing and imitating significant others, such as parents and peers. Initially, children do not have a frame of reference from which to question the prejudices of their relatives and friends. When they are rewarded with smiles or laughs for telling derogatory jokes or making negative comments about outgroup members, children's prejudiced attitudes may be reinforced.

Psychologist Theodor W. Adorno and his colleagues concluded that highly prejudiced individuals tend to have an **authoritarian personality**, which is characterized by excessive conformity, submissiveness to authority, intolerance, insecurity, a high level of superstition, and rigid, stereotypic thinking (Adorno et al., 1950). It is most likely to develop in a family environment in which dominating parents who are anxious about status use physical discipline but show very little love in raising their children (Adorno et al., 1950). Other scholars have linked prejudiced attitudes to traits such as submissiveness to authority, extreme anger toward outgroups, and conservative religious and political beliefs (Altemeyer, 1981, 1988; Weigel and Howes, 1985).

**scapegoat** A person or group that is incapable of offering resistance to the hostility or aggression of others.

**authoritarian personality** A personality type characterized by excessive conformity, submissiveness to authority, intolerance, insecurity, a high level of superstition, and rigid, stereotypic thinking.

## DISCRIMINATION

**discrimination** Actions or practices of dominant group members (or their representatives) that have a harmful impact on members of a subordinate group.

Whereas prejudice is an attitude, **discrimination** involves actions or practices of dominant group members (or their representatives) that have a harmful impact on members of a subordinate group (Feagin and Feagin, 2011). For example, people who are prejudiced toward South Asian, Jewish, or Aboriginal people may refuse to hire them, rent an apartment to them, or allow their children to play with them. In these instances, discrimination involves the differential treatment of minority group members not because of their ability or merit but because of irrelevant characteristics, such as skin colour or language preference. Discriminatory actions vary in severity from the use of derogatory labels to violence against individuals and groups.

Discrimination takes two basic forms: *de jure,* or legal discrimination, which is encoded in laws; and *de facto,* or informal discrimination, which is entrenched in social customs and institutions. *De jure* discrimination has been supported with explicitly discriminatory laws, such as the *Chinese Exclusionary Act,* which restricted immigration to Canada on the basis of race, or the Nuremberg laws passed in Nazi Germany, which imposed restrictions on Jews. The *Indian Act* provides other examples of *de jure* discrimination. According to the act, a Native woman who married a non-Native man automatically lost her Indian status rights and was no longer allowed to live on a reserve. Native men had no such problem. The *Indian Act* also specified that Native people who graduated from university, or who became doctors, lawyers, or ministers before 1920, were forced to give up their status rights. An amendment to the *Indian Act* in 1985 ended this legalized discrimination. The *Charter of Rights and Freedoms* prohibits discrimination on the basis of race, ethnicity, or religion. As a result, many cases of *de jure* discrimination have been eliminated. *De facto* discrimination is more subtle and less visible to public scrutiny and therefore much more difficult to eradicate.

Prejudiced attitudes do not always lead to discriminatory behaviour. Sociologist Robert Merton (1949) identified four combinations of attitudes and responses. *Unprejudiced nondiscriminators* are not personally prejudiced and do not discriminate against others. These are individuals who believe in equality for all. *Unprejudiced discriminators* may have no personal prejudices but still engage in discriminatory behaviour because of peer group pressure or economic, political, or social interests—for example, an employee who has no personal hostility toward members of certain groups but is encouraged by senior management not to hire them. *Prejudiced nondiscriminators* hold personal prejudices but do not discriminate due to peer pressure, legal demands, or a desire for profits. Such individuals are often referred to as "timid bigots" because they are reluctant to translate their attitudes into action (especially when prejudice is considered to be "politically incorrect"). Finally, *prejudiced discriminators* hold personal prejudices and actively discriminate against others—for example, the landlord who refuses to rent an apartment to an Aboriginal couple and then readily justifies his actions on the basis of racist stereotypes.

Merton's typology shows that some people may be prejudiced but not discriminate against others. Do you think it is possible for a person to discriminate against some people without holding a prejudiced attitude toward them? Why or why not?

## RACISM

**Racism** is a set of ideas that implies the superiority of one social group over another on the basis of biological or cultural characteristics, together with the power to put these beliefs into practice in a way that denies or excludes minority women and men.

Racism involves elements of prejudice, ethnocentrism, stereotyping, and discrimination. For example, racism is present in the belief that some racial or ethnic groups are superior while others are inferior—this belief is a prejudice. Racism may be the basis for unfair treatment toward members of a racial or ethnic group. In this case, the racism involves discrimination.

Fleras and Elliott (2003) make distinctions among a number of diverse types of racism (see Table 10.1). **Overt racism (or redneck or hate racism)** may take the form of deliberate and highly personal attacks, including derogatory slurs and name-calling toward members of a racial or ethnic group who are perceived to be "inferior" (James, 2010). Examples of overt racism, although rare, are available in Canada. In 2009, a Winnipeg case made national headlines when family service agencies removed two children from their parents' home and sought permanent custody because their parents were teaching the children racist views. Social workers became involved when the young girl attended school with white supremist symbols and slogans drawn all over her skin. The girl told social workers that she watched violent racist videos in her home and her parents regularly discussed killing minorities. Overt racism is also demonstrated in the racist violence perpetuated by members of white supremacist groups, including the Heritage Front, White Aryan Nation, and Western Guard, that are active in Canada. These groups are committed to an ideology of racial supremacy in which the white "race" is seen as superior to other races. This type of overt racism is becoming increasingly unacceptable in Canadian society, and few people today will tolerate the open expression of racism. In fact, overt acts of discrimination are now illegal. *The Criminal Code*, the *Charter of Rights and Freedoms*, and human rights legislation have served to limit the expression of overt racist ideology.

While blatant forms of racism have dissipated to some extent, less obvious expressions of bigotry and stereotyping that allow people to discuss their dislike of certain groups in "coded language" remain in our society. **Polite racism** is an attempt to disguise a dislike of others through behaviour that is outwardly nonprejudicial. This type of racism may be operating when members of visible minority groups are ignored or turned down for jobs or promotions on a regular basis. Polite racism may consist of subtle remarks or looks that result in members of visible minority groups feeling inferior or out of place (Fleras and Elliott, 2003). A number of studies have examined the extent to which this type of racism manifests itself in the workplace (Henry, 2006; Kunz, Milan, and Schetagne, 2000; Oreopoulis, 2009). Researchers have found that members of particular visible minority groups are often ignored; assigned unpleasant tasks at work; turned down for interviews, jobs, and promotions; or excluded from the inner circle of their workplace.

**racism** A set of ideas that implies the superiority of one social group over another on the basis of biological or cultural characteristics, together with the power to put these beliefs into practice in a way that denies or excludes minority women and men.

**overt racism (or redneck or hate racism)** Racism that may take the form of deliberate and highly personal attacks, including derogatory slurs and name-calling toward members of a racial or ethnic group who are perceived to be "inferior."

**polite racism** A term used to describe an attempt to disguise a dislike of others through behaviour that is outwardly nonprejudicial.

| | WHAT:<br>CORE SLOGAN | WHY:<br>DEGREE OF INTENT | HOW:<br>STYLE OF EXPRESSION | WHERE:<br>MAGNITUDE AND SCOPE |
|---|---|---|---|---|
| Overt racism | "X, get out." | Conscious | Personal and explicit | Interpersonal |
| Polite racism | "Sorry, the job is taken." | Moderate | Discreet and subtle | Personal |
| Subliminal racism | "I'm not racist, but . . ." | Ambivalent | Oblique | Cultural |
| Institutionalized racism | "We treat everyone the same here." | Unintentional or intentional | Impersonal | Institutional and societal |

**TABLE 10.1    THE FACTS OF RACISM**

Sources: Fleras and Elliott, 1996, 2003.

**subliminal racism** A term used to describe an unconscious racism that occurs when there is a conflict of values.

Polite racism may be largely hidden in our "politically correct" society, but the effects on victims are similar to the more obvious forms of the past—control, exclusion, and exploitation (Fleras and Elliott, 2003:70).

**Subliminal racism** is a form of subconscious racism that occurs when there is a conflict of values. Subliminal racism is not directly expressed but is demonstrated in opposition to progressive minority policies (such as Canada's immigration policy) or programs (such as employment equity or affirmative action). For example, after the 9/11 terrorist attacks, there were insinuations that Canada's "weak" immigration policies allowed the terrorists to enter the United States. Subliminal racism allows us to understand how mainstream whites can simultaneously demonstrate nearly universal support for principles of equality and at the same time undermine progressive policies and strategies directed at achieving that equality. As Fleras and Elliott highlight:

> Refugee claimants are not condemned in blunt racist terminology; rather their landed entry into Canada is criticized on procedural grounds ("jumping the queue"). Or they are belittled for taking unfair advantage of Canada's generosity or ability to shoulder the processing costs . . . Minority peoples have rights, but minority demands that fall outside conventional channels are criticized as a threat to national identity or social harmony . . . Employment equity initiatives are endorsed in principle but rejected in practice as unfair to the majority. (2003:73)

Subliminal racism, more than any other type, demonstrates the ambiguity concerning racism. Values that support racial equality are publicly supported while, at the same time, resentment at the prospect of moving over and making space for newcomers is also present. Subliminal racism enables individuals to maintain two apparently conflicting values—one

© AP/Getty Images

Recent anti-Semitic attacks on Jewish synagogues are an unfortunate indicator that some forms of overt racism still exist.

NEL

rooted in the egalitarian virtues of justice and fairness, the other in beliefs that result in resentment and selfishness (Fleras and Elliott, 2003).

**Institutionalized racism** occurs where the established rules, policies, and practices within an institution or organization produce differential treatment of various groups based on race. Although institutions can no longer openly discriminate against minorities without attracting legal sanctions, negative publicity, or consumer resistance, this type of racism nevertheless continues to exist (Fleras and Kunz, 2001). The practice of word-of-mouth recruitment is an example of an institutional practice that has the result of excluding racial minorities from the hiring selection process.

Institutional racism may also be reflected in organizational practices, rules, and procedures that have the unintended consequence of excluding minority group members. For example, occupations such as police officer and firefighter historically had minimum weight, height, and educational requirements for job applicants. These criteria resulted in discrimination because they favoured white applicants over members of many minority groups, as well as males over females. Other examples of this type of institutional racism include the requirement of a college or university degree for nonspecialized jobs, employment regulations that require people to work on their Sabbath, and the lack of recognition of foreign credentials. Institutional racism is normally reflected in statistical underrepresentation of certain groups within an institution or organization. For example, a given group may represent 15 percent of the general population but only 2 percent of those promoted to upper-management positions in a large company.

Efforts to eliminate this kind of disproportionate representation are the focus of employment equity legislation. The target groups for employment equity in Canada are visible minorities, women, persons with disabilities, and Aboriginal peoples. Strategies include modified admissions tests and requirements, enhanced recruitment of certain target groups, establishment of hiring quotas for particular minority groups, or specialized training or employment programs for specific target groups. Consideration of affirmative action strategies inevitably leads to claims of reverse discrimination by some individuals who enjoy majority group status. (For a more detailed discussion of reverse discrimination, see Box 10.2.) Consider the comments from this white male student:

> I am a white male and I am discriminated against all the time. Faced with trying to get jobs that have been reserved for minorities and not the best candidate. There is racism in Canada and as a white male I feel lots of it is aimed at myself. There was an article not long ago that Toronto Police want to hire more minority police. I think that comment in itself is racist. We don't want the best person for the job anymore? (James, 2010:243)*

The most recent analysis of employment equity programs indicates that these programs have had the most significant effect on women and Aboriginal peoples, while people with disabilities have made the fewest gains. As for members of visible minorities, although they have higher levels of education, on average, than other Canadians and very high labour-force participation rates, they continue to be concentrated in low-status, low-paying occupations (Henry and Tator, 2006, Oreopoulos, 2009).

**institutionalized racism** A situation where the established rules, policies, and practices within an institution or organization produce differential treatment of various groups based on race.

---

### TIME TO REVIEW

- Identify all the types of racism that exist in our society.
- In considering all of these, which type do you think is the most difficult to control? Which type does the most damage?

---

*Source: James, Carl E. *Seeing Ourselves: Exploring Race, Ethnicity and Culture*, 4th edition (2010). Thompson Books.

BOX 10.2 **POINT/COUNTERPOINT**

## The Myth of Reverse Racism

Is reverse racism possible? According to race relations scholars Augie Fleras and Jean Leonard Elliott, the answer is no. In the following excerpt from *Unequal Relations* (2003), they explain why:

> Are affirmative actions policies that favour visible minority group members and Aboriginal persons racist? Can minority women and men express racism ("reverse racism") against the majority sector? Can ethnic minorities be racist toward other ethnic minorities? Is it racist for Aboriginal peoples to accuse all whites of complicity in the destruction of Indigenous societies? Answers to these questions may never be settled to everyone's satisfaction, given the politics or intellectual dishonesty at play, but their very asking provides a sharper understanding of racism.
>
> Responses depend on how one defines racism—as biology or power. A reading of racism as biology suggests that anyone who approaches, defines, or treats someone else on the basis of race is a racist. Thus, minorities can be racist if they criticize or deny whites because of their whiteness ("reverse racism").
>
> But reference to racism as power points to a different conclusion. Accusations of minority ("reverse") racism must go beyond superficial appearances. There is a world of difference in using race to create equality (employment equity) versus its use to limit opportunity (discrimination), even if the rhetoric sounds the same. Emphasis must be placed instead on the context of the actions and their social consequences. Racism is not about treating others differently because they are different. Rather, it involves different treatment in colour-conscious contexts of power that limit opportunity or privileges (Blauner 1972).

> In short, racism is about the politics of difference within the context of power. Statements made by a minority group, however distasteful or bigoted, may not qualify as racist in the conventional sense of outcomes. They are largely preferences or prejudices without the capacity for harm, since minorities lack the institutional power to put bigotry into practice in a way that "stings."
>
> To be sure, minorities are not entirely powerless; after all, there is recourse to alternative sources of power-brokering, such as boycotts, civil disobedience, lobby groups, and moral suasion. And even though they may not have institutional power, minorities may have other ways to put bigotry into practice (e.g., stealing from a store owned by a member of another minority or threatening others on the basis of appearance).
>
> Still, the power that minority individuals wield in certain contexts rarely has the potential to deny or exclude. Those without access to institutionalized power or resources cannot racialize the other in ways that demean, control, or exploit. Minorities do not have the power to dominate and enforce prejudices, oppression, or subdomination. They have neither the resources to topple the dominant sector nor the critical mass to harass, exclude, exploit, persecute, dominate, or undermine the empowered. Conditions of relative powerlessness reduce minority hostility to the level of rhetoric or a protective shell in defence of minority interests. In other words, reverse racism may be a contradiction in terms. Racism is not a two-way street; more accurately, it resembles an expressway with controlled access points for those privileged enough to control the switches.

*Source:* Fleras & Elliot 2003.

LO-3 ## SOCIOLOGICAL PERSPECTIVES ON RACE AND ETHNIC RELATIONS

Symbolic interactionist, functionalist, conflict, and feminist perspectives examine race and ethnic relations in different ways. Symbolic interactionists examine how microlevel contacts between people may produce either greater racial tolerance or increased levels of hostility. Functionalists focus on the macrolevel intergroup processes that occur among members of majority and minority groups in society. Conflict theorists analyze power and economic differentials between the dominant group and subordinate groups. Feminists highlight the interactive effects of racism and sexism on the exploitation of women, who are members of a visible minority.

## Symbolic Interactionist Perspectives

What happens when people from different racial and ethnic groups come into contact with one another? In the *contact hypothesis,* symbolic interactionists point out that contact between people from divergent groups should lead to favourable attitudes and behaviour when certain factors are present. Members of each group must (1) have equal status, (2) pursue the same goals, (3) cooperate with one another to achieve their goals, and (4) receive positive feedback when they interact with one another in positive, nondiscriminatory ways (Allport, 1958; Coakley, 2004).

What happens when individuals meet someone who does not conform to their existing stereotype? Frequently, they will ignore anything that contradicts the stereotype or will interpret the situation to support their prejudices (Coakley, 2004). For example, a person who does not fit the stereotype may be seen as an exception—"You're not like other [persons of a particular race]."

When a person is seen as conforming to a stereotype, he or she may be treated simply as one of "you people." Former Los Angeles Lakers basketball star Earvin "Magic" Johnson described how he was categorized along with all other African Americans when he was bused to a predominantly white school:

> On the first day of [basketball] practice, my teammates froze me out. Time after time I was wide open, but nobody threw me the ball. At first I thought they just didn't see me. But I woke up after a kid named Danny Parks looked right at me and then took a long jumper. Which he missed.
>
> I was furious, but I didn't say a word. Shortly after that, I grabbed a defensive rebound and took the ball all the way down for a basket. I did it again and a third time, too.
>
> Finally Parks got angry and said, "Hey, pass the [bleeping] ball."
>
> That did it. I slammed down the ball and glared at him. Then I exploded. "I *knew* this would happen!" I said. "That's why I didn't want to come to this [bleeping] school in the first place!"
>
> "Oh, yeah? Well, you people are all the same," he said. "You think you're gonna come in here and do whatever you want? Look, hotshot, your job is to get the rebound. Let us do the shooting." (1992:31–32)

The interaction between Johnson and Parks demonstrates that when people from different racial and ethnic groups come into contact with one another, they may treat one another as stereotypes, not as individuals. Symbolic interactionist perspectives make us aware of the importance of intergroup contact and the fact that it may either intensify or reduce racial and ethnic stereotyping and prejudice.

## Functionalist Perspectives

How do members of subordinate racial and ethnic groups become part of the dominant group? To answer this question, early functionalists studied immigration and patterns of majority and minority group interaction.

ASSIMILATION **Assimilation** is a process by which members of subordinate racial and ethnic groups become absorbed into the dominant culture. To some analysts, assimilation is functional because it contributes to the stability of society by minimizing group differences that otherwise might result in hostility and violence.

**assimilation** A process by which members of subordinate racial and ethnic groups become absorbed into the dominant culture.

Assimilation occurs at several distinct levels, including the cultural, structural, biological, and psychological stages. *Cultural assimilation,* or *acculturation,* occurs when members of an ethnic group adopt dominant group traits, such as language, dress, values, religion, and food preferences. Cultural assimilation in this country initially followed an "Anglo-conformity" model; members of subordinate ethnic groups were expected to conform to the culture of the dominant white Anglo-Saxon population (Gordon, 1964). However, members of some groups, such as Aboriginal peoples and Québécois, refused to be assimilated and sought to maintain their unique cultural identity.

*Structural assimilation,* or *integration,* occurs when members of subordinate racial or ethnic groups gain acceptance in everyday social interaction with members of the dominant group. This type of assimilation typically starts in large, impersonal settings, such as schools and workplaces, and only later (if at all) results in close friendships and intermarriage.

*Biological assimilation,* or *amalgamation,* occurs when members of one group marry those of other social or ethnic groups. Biological assimilation has been more complete in some other countries, such as Mexico and Brazil, than in Canada.

*Psychological assimilation* involves a change in racial or ethnic self-identification on the part of an individual. Rejection by the dominant group may prevent psychological assimilation by members of some subordinate racial and ethnic groups, especially those with visible characteristics, such as skin colour or facial features that differ from those of the dominant group.

**ETHNIC PLURALISM** Instead of complete assimilation, many groups share elements of the mainstream culture while remaining culturally distinct from both the dominant group and other social and ethnic groups. **Ethnic pluralism** is the coexistence of a variety of distinct racial and ethnic groups within one society.

*Equalitarian pluralism,* or *accommodation,* is a situation in which ethnic groups coexist in equality with one another. Switzerland has been described as a model of equalitarian pluralism; more than six million people with French, German, and Italian cultural heritages peacefully coexist there.

Has Canada achieved equalitarian pluralism? The *Canadian Multiculturalism Act* of 1988 stated that "All Canadians are full and equal partners in Canadian society." The Department of Multiculturalism and Citizenship was established in 1991 with the goal of encouraging ethnic minorities to participate fully in all aspects of Canadian life while at the same time maintaining their distinct ethnic identities and cultural practices. The objective of multiculturalism is to "promote unity through diversity." Under multiculturalism, citizens are accepted as racially or ethnically different yet no less Canadian, with a corresponding package of citizen rights and entitlement, regardless of origin, creed, or colour (Fleras and Elliott, 2003:280). Multiculturalism programs provide funding for education, consultative support, and a range of activities, including heritage language training, race relations training, ethnic policing and justice, and ethnic celebrations. In implementing this pluralistic strategy, Canada gained international respect and admiration as a society

> **ethnic pluralism**
> The coexistence of a variety of distinct racial and ethnic groups within one society.

The members of this adult education class are learning English as their second language. What type of assimilation does this represent?

NEL

that is both united and distinct, where citizens are valued as "different" yet recognized as "equal."

In recent years, multiculturalism policies have been under increasing attack. For example, multiculturalism has been described as a policy that creates and maintains an "illusion" of respect for racial and ethnic differences when in reality the pressures toward conformity and the experiences with exclusion and discrimination are very similar for Canadian "multicultural minorities" and racial and ethnic minorities living in the American "melting pot" (Reitz and Breton, 1994). Neil Bissoondath, author of *Selling Illusions: The Cult of Multiculturalism in Canada* (1994), suggests that multiculturalism does not promote equalitarian pluralism. Rather, he argues, multiculturalism serves to discourage immigrants from thinking of themselves as Canadian; it exaggerates differences, which fosters racial animosity; and it alienates people from the mainstream society, which detracts from national unity. Bissoondath argues:

> Whatever policy follows multiculturalism it should support a new vision of Canadianness. A Canada where no-one is alienated with hyphenation. A nation of cultural hybrids, where every individual is unique and every individual is a Canadian, undiluted and undivided. A nation where the following conversation, so familiar— and so enervating—to many of us will no longer take place: "What nationality are you?" "Canadian." "No, I mean, what nationality are you *really?*" (1998:1)

The challenge for a pluralistic society such as Canada lies in attaining some degree of balance between the equally important values of racial and ethnic equality and national unity. To date, any consensus on multiculturalism in terms of definition, policy, or practice remains illusive.

**INEQUALITARIAN PLURALISM, OR SEGREGATION** *Inequalitarian pluralism,* or *segregation,* exists when specific ethnic groups are set apart from the dominant group and have unequal access to power and privilege (Marger, 2000). **Segregation** is the spatial and social separation of categories of people by race, ethnicity, class, gender, and/or religion. Segregation may be enforced by law (*de jure*) or by custom (*de facto*).

An example of *de jure* segregation was the Jim Crow laws, which legalized the separation of the races in all public accommodations (including hotels, restaurants, transportation, hospitals, jails, schools, churches, and cemeteries) in the Southern United States after the Civil War (Feagin and Feagin, 2011).

*De jure* segregation of blacks is also part of the history of Canada. Blacks in Canada lived in largely segregated communities in Nova Scotia, New Brunswick, and Ontario, where racial segregation was evident in the schools, government, the workplace, residential housing, and elsewhere. Segregated schools continued in Nova Scotia until the 1960s. Residential segregation was legally enforced through the use of

**segregation** A term used to describe the spatial and social separation of categories of people by race/ethnicity, class, gender, and/or religion.

Segregation laws existed and were enforced with signs such as these in both Canada and the United States until the 1960s.

racially restrictive covenants attached to deeds and leases. Separation and refusal of service were common in restaurants, theatres, and recreational facilities (Henry and Tator, 2006). Sociologist Adrienne Shadd describes her experiences growing up in North Buxton, Ontario, in the 1950s and 1960s:

> When we would go into the local ice cream parlour, the man behind the counter would serve us last, after all the Whites had been served, even if they came into the shop after us. Southwestern Ontario may as well have been below the Mason-Dixon line in those days. Dresden, home of the historic Uncle Tom's cabin, made national headlines in 1954 when Blacks tested the local restaurants after the passage of the *Fair Accommodation Practices Act* and found that two openly refused to serve them. This came as no surprise, given that for years certain eateries, hotels, and recreational clubs were restricted to us, and at one time Blacks could only sit in designated sections of movie theatres (usually the balcony) if admitted at all. (1991:11)

One of the most blatant examples of segregation in Canada is the federal government's reserve system for status Indians, which resulted in segregation of Aboriginal peoples on reserves in remote areas across the country.

With that exception, legally sanctioned forms of racial segregation have been all but eliminated, but *de facto* segregation, which is enforced by custom, still exists. Although functionalist explanations provide a description of how some early white ethnic immigrants assimilated into the cultural mainstream, they do not adequately account for the persistent racial segregation and economic inequality experienced by some minority group members.

## TIME TO REVIEW

- Compare and contrast assimilation, ethnic pluralism, and segregation.

## Conflict Perspectives

Why do some ethnic groups continue to experience subjugation after many years? Conflict theorists focus on economic stratification and access to power in their analysis of race and ethnic relations.

**internal colonialism**
According to conflict theorists, a situation in which members of a racial or ethnic group are conquered or colonized and forcibly placed under the economic and political control of the dominant group.

**INTERNAL COLONIALISM** Conflict theorists use the term **internal colonialism** to refer to a situation in which members of a racial or ethnic group are conquered or colonized and forcibly placed under the economic and political control of the dominant group. Groups that have been subjected to internal colonialism often remain in subordinate positions longer than groups that voluntarily migrated to North America.

Aboriginal peoples in Canada were colonized by Europeans and others who invaded their lands and conquered them. In the process, Aboriginal peoples lost property, political rights, aspects of their culture, and often their lives (Frideres and Gadacz, 2005). The capitalist class acquired cheap labour and land through this government-sanctioned racial exploitation. The effects of past internal colonialism are reflected today in the number of Aboriginal people who live in extreme poverty on government reserves (Frideres and Gadacz, 2005).

The experiences of internally colonized groups are unique in three ways: (1) They have been forced to exist in a society other than their own; (2) they have been kept out of the economic and political mainstream, so it is difficult for them to compete with dominant group members; and (3) they have been subjected to severe attacks on their own culture, which may lead to its extinction (Blauner, 1972).

The internal colonialism model is rooted in historical foundations of racial and ethnic inequality in North America. However, it tends to view all voluntary immigrants as having many more opportunities than do members of colonized groups. Thus, this model does not explain the continued exploitation of some immigrant groups, such as Chinese, Filipinos, and Vietnamese, and the greater acceptance of others, primarily those from Northern Europe (Cashmore, 1996).

**THE SPLIT LABOUR MARKET THEORY** Who benefits from the exploitation of visible minorities? The split labour market theory states that both white workers and members of the capitalist class benefit from the exploitation of visible minorities. **Split labour market** refers to the division of the economy into two areas of employment: a primary sector, or upper tier, composed of higher-paid (usually dominant group) workers in more secure jobs, and a secondary sector, or lower tier, made up of lower-paid (often subordinate group) workers in jobs with little security and hazardous working conditions (Bonacich, 1972, 1976). According to this perspective, white workers in the upper tier may use racial discrimination against nonwhites to protect their positions. These actions most often occur when upper-tier workers feel threatened by lower-tier workers hired by capitalists to reduce labour costs and maximize corporate profits. In the past, immigrants were a source of cheap labour that employers could use to break strikes and keep wages down. Agnes Calliste (1987) applied the split labour market theory in her study of sleeping-car porters in Canada. Calliste found a doubly submerged split labour market with three levels of stratification in this area of employment. While "white" trade unions were unable to

> **split labour market** A term used to describe the division of the economy into two areas of employment: a primary sector, or upper tier, composed of higher-paid (usually dominant group) workers in more secure jobs; and a secondary sector, or lower tier, composed of lower-paid (often subordinate group) workers in jobs with little security and hazardous working conditions.

© Charla Jones/GetStock.com

The effects of past colonialism are reflected in the poor housing conditions of many Aboriginal persons living on reserves today.

restrict access to porter positions on the basis of race, they were able to impose differential pay scales. Consequently, black porters received less pay than white porters, even though they were doing the same work. Furthermore, the labour market was doubly submerged because black immigrant workers from the United States received even less pay than both black and white Canadian porters. Throughout history, higher-paid workers have responded with racial hostility and joined movements to curtail immigration and thus do away with the source of cheap labour (Marger, 2009).

Proponents of the split labour market theory suggest that white workers benefit from racial and ethnic antagonisms. However, these analysts typically do not examine the interactive effects of race, class, and gender in the workplace.

## Feminist Perspectives

Minority women (women of colour, immigrant women, and Aboriginal women) are doubly disadvantaged as a result of their gender. The term *gendered racism* refers to the interactive effect of racism and sexism in the exploitation of women of colour. According to social psychologist Philomena Essed (1991), women's particular position must be explored within each racial or ethnic group, because their experiences will not have been the same as the men's in each grouping. For example, university-educated immigrant women have a more difficult time finding a job than university-educated male immigrants.

Capitalists do not equally exploit all workers. Gender and race or ethnicity are important in this exploitation. Historically, the high-paying primary labour market has been monopolized by white men. People of colour and most white women more often hold lower-tier jobs (Arat-Koc, 1999). Below that tier is the underground sector of the economy, characterized by illegal or quasi-legal activities, such as drug trafficking, prostitution, and working in sweatshops that do not meet minimum wage and safety standards. Many undocumented workers and some white women and people of colour attempt to earn a living in this sector (Amott and Matthaei, 1991).

## Postmodern Perspectives

Conventional theories of race and ethnicity tend to see racial or ethnic identities as organized around social structures that are fixed and closed, such as nations, tribes, bands, and communities. As such, there is little movement in or out of these groups. Postmodern perspectives, in contrast, view ethnic and racial identities as largely a consequence of personal choice and subjective definition. Ethnic and racial identities are socially constructed and given meaning by our fragmented society. These identities are constantly evolving and subject to the continuous interplay of history, power, and culture.

A postmodernist framework may ask how social actors come to understand who they are in "race" terms. Central to a postmodern perspective on race is the concept of *discourse.* Based on the work of Michael Foucault, *discourse* is used to refer to "different ways of structuring knowledge and social practice" (Fiske, 1994, cited in Henry and Tator, 2006). Postmodernists view reality as constructed through a broad range of discourses, which includes all that is written, spoken, or otherwise represented through language and communication systems (Anderson, 2006:394). Analysts using this perspective focus on *deconstructing*, which means analyzing the assumptions and meanings embedded in scientific works (Anderson, 2006).

Postmodernist scholars use this perspective to shift the frame of analysis away from race relations to an examination (deconstruction) of racist discourse. *Racist discourse,* or *racialized discourse,* is defined as a collection of words, images, and practices through which racial power is directed against ethnic and racial minority groups. An analysis of racist discourse is central to understanding the ways in which a particular society gives a voice to racism and advances the interests of whites.

Frances Henry and Carol Tator (2006) have identified examples of racist discourse that serve to sustain or perpetuate racism in our society. For example, the *discourse of denial* suggests that racism does not exist in our Canadian democratic society. When racism is shown to exist, the discourse of denial will explain it away as an isolated incident rather than an indication of systemic racism. There are numerous examples of the discourse of denial in policing agencies across the country. Despite numerous complaints of racism directed at visible minority groups and Aboriginal persons, police agencies continue to respond to allegations with, "We don't have a problem with racism within our organization," or "I have never witnessed a racist incident."

A second, related, discourse identified by Henry and Tator is "the discourse of colour-blindness," in which white people insist that they do not notice the skin colour of a racial minority. In doing so, white people also fail to "recognize that race is a part of the 'baggage' that people of colour carry with them, and the refusal to recognize racism as part of everyday values, policies, programs, and practices is part of the psychological power of racial constructions" (2006:25). By claiming to be colour-blind, members of the dominant white majority are allowed to ignore the power differentials they experience as a result of their "whiteness," as well as negating the racialized experiences of visible minority persons.

A postmodern perspective not only examines how identities of racial and ethnic minorities are formed, but also asks the same question about white identities. For example:

> [W]hite people are "raced" just as men are "gendered." And in a social context where white people have too often viewed themselves as nonracial or racially neutral, it is crucial to look at the "racialness" of the white experience . . . Whiteness is first a location of structural advantage of race privilege. Second, a "standpoint," a place from which white people look at ourselves, at others, at society. Third, "whiteness" refers to a set of cultural practices that are usually unmarked and unnamed.
> (Frankenberg, 1993, cited in Gann, 2000)

## An Alternative Perspective: Critical Race Theory

Emerging out of scholarly law studies on racial and ethnic inequality, critical race theory derives its foundation from the U.S. civil rights tradition and the writing of people like Martin Luther King, Jr., W.E.B. Du Bois, Malcolm X, and Cesar Chavez. The growth of critical race theory began in Canada during the 1980s, and it is based on the same theoretical foundation as its American counterpart; that is, a growing dissatisfaction with the failure to acknowledge and recognize the critical roles that race and racism have played in the political and legal structures of Canadian society (Aylward, 1999).

Critical race theory has several major premises, including the belief that racism is such an ingrained feature of North American society that it appears to be ordinary and natural to many people (Delgado, 1995). As a result, civil rights legislation and affirmative action laws (formal equality) may remedy some of the more overt, blatant forms of racial injustice but have little effect on subtle, business-as-usual forms of racism that people of colour experience as they go about their everyday lives. According to this approach, the best way to document racism and ongoing inequality in society is to listen to the lived experiences of people who have experienced such discrimination. In this way, we can learn what actually happens in regard to racial oppression and the many effects it has on people, including alienation, depression, and certain physical illnesses (Razack, 1998).

Central to this argument is the belief that *interest convergence* is a crucial factor in bringing about social change. According to the legal scholar Derrick Bell, white elites tolerate or encourage racial advances for people of colour *only* if the dominant-group members believe that their own self-interest will be served in so doing (cited in Delgado, 1995). From this approach, civil rights laws have typically benefited white North Americans as much as (or more than) people of colour because these laws have been used as mechanisms to ensure that "racial progress occurs at just the right pace: change that is too rapid would be unsettling to society at large; change that is too slow could prove destabilizing" (Delgado, 1995:xiv).

Critical race theory is similar to postmodernist approaches in that it calls our attention to the fact that things are not always as they seem. Formal equality under the law does not necessarily equate to actual equality in society.

## LO-4    ETHNIC GROUPS IN CANADA

How do racial and ethnic groups come into contact with one another? How do they adjust to one another and to the dominant group over time? Sociologists have explored these questions extensively; however, a detailed historical account of each group is beyond the scope of this chapter. Given the diversity of our population, imposing any kind of conceptual order on a discussion of ethnic groups in Canada is difficult. We will look briefly at some of the predominant ethnic groups in Canada. In the process, we will examine a brief history of racism with respect to each group.

## CONCEPT SNAPSHOT

| | |
|---|---|
| **SYMBOLIC INTERACTIONIST PERSPECTIVES** | Symbolic interactionists examine how microlevel contacts between individuals may produce greater racial tolerance or increase levels of hostility. According to the contact hypothesis, when members of divergent groups have equal status, shared goals, cooperation, and positive feedback, favourable attitudes and behaviour between groups can result. |
| **FUNCTIONALIST PERSPECTIVES** | Early functionalists examined immigration and patterns of majority and minority group interaction Intergroup processes include cultural, biological, structural, and psychological assimilation and ethnic pluralism—equalitarian and inequalitarian pluralism (segregation). |
| **CONFLICT PERSPECTIVES** | Conflict theorists focus on power and economic differentials between dominant and subordinate groups. Internal colonialism occurs when members of racial or ethnic groups are conquered or colonized and forcibly controlled by the dominant group. Split labour market theory examines the division of the economy into two unequal areas of employment. |
| **FEMINIST PERSPECTIVES** | Feminist perspectives highlight the fact that minority women are doubly disadvantaged as a result of their gender. *Gendered racism* describes the interactive effect of racism and sexism in the exploitation of visible minority women. |
| **POSTMODERN PERSPECTIVES** | Postmodern perspectives view racial and ethnic identities as socially constructed through a range of discourses. Postmodern perspectives focus is deconstructing racialized and racist discourse that serves to sustain and reinforce patterns of discrimination against racial and ethnic minorities. |
| **CRITICAL RACE THEORY** | Critical race theorists believe that racism is such an ingrained feature of society that it appears to be ordinary and natural to many. According to critical race theorists, human rights legislation and employment equity strategies may remedy overt discrimination but have little effect on subtle racism. Interest convergence is required to effect positive change for visible minority group members. |

## Aboriginal Peoples

Canada's Aboriginal peoples are believed to have migrated to North America from Asia about 14,000 years ago. The term *Aboriginal* itself refers to the "first," or indigenous, occupants of this country (Fleras and Elliott, 2003). Aboriginal peoples are an extremely diverse group with varying access to resources, development levels, and social health. Today, the terms *Native, First Nations,* or *Aboriginal* refer to over 600 bands across the country with approximately 50 Aboriginal languages, including Inuktitut, Cree, Ojibway, Wakashan, and Haida. Other categories of Aboriginal peoples are status Indians (those Indians with legal rights under the *Indian Act),* nonstatus Indians (those without legal rights), Métis, and Inuit. Those who settled in the southern part of Canada, Yukon, and the Mackenzie Valley can be termed *North American Indians.* Those located in the eastern Arctic and northern islands, who were formerly referred to as Eskimos, are now referred to as *Inuit.* A third category, *Métis,* who live mostly on the Prairies, are descendants of Indian and non-Indian unions (primarily French settlers and Indian women) (Dyck, 2008).

When European settlers arrived on this continent, the Aboriginal inhabitants' way of life was changed forever. Experts estimate that approximately two million Aboriginal people lived in North America at the time of contact; by 1900, however, their numbers had been reduced to under 240,000. What factors led to this drastic depopulation?

GENOCIDE, FORCED MIGRATION, AND FORCED ASSIMILATION Aboriginal people have been the victims of genocide and forced migration. Many Native Americans were either massacred or died from European diseases (such as typhoid, smallpox, and measles) and starvation (Cook, 1973; Wagner and Stearn, 1945). In battle, Aboriginal people often were no match for the Europeans, who had the latest weaponry (Amott and Matthaei, 1991). Europeans justified their aggression by stereotyping Aboriginals as "savages" and "heathens" (Frideres and Gadacz, 2004).

Aboriginal nations were forced to move in order to accommodate the white settlers. The "Trail of Tears" was one of the most disastrous of the forced migrations to occur in North America. In the coldest part of the winter of 1832, more than half of the Cherokee Nation died during or as a result of their forced relocation from the southeastern United States to the Indian Territory in Oklahoma (Thornton, 1984).

First Nations rights were clearly defined in the *Royal Proclamation* of 1763, which divided up the territory acquired by Britain. In the large area called the Indian Territory, the purchase or settlement of land was forbidden without a treaty (Dyck, 1996:154). The government broke treaty after treaty as it engaged in a policy of wholesale removal of Indigenous nations to clear the land for settlement by Anglo-Saxon "pioneers" (Green, 1977). The Canadian government then passed the *Indian Act* of 1876, which provided for federal government control of almost every aspect of Indian life. The regulations under the act included prohibitions against owning land, voting, purchasing and consuming alcohol, and leaving reserves without permission and a ticket from the government's agent (Frideres and Gadacz, 2005).

Aboriginal children were placed in residential boarding schools to facilitate their assimilation into the dominant culture. The Jesuits and other missionaries who ran these schools believed that Aboriginal peoples should not be left in their "inferior" natural state and considered it their mission to replace Aboriginal culture with Christian beliefs, values, rituals, and practices (Bolaria and Li, 1988). Many Aboriginal children who attended these schools were sexually, physically, and emotionally abused. They were not allowed to speak their language or engage in any of their traditional cultural practices. The coercive and oppressive nature of this educational experience is one of the most blatant examples of institutionalized racism (Henry et al., 1996:62). It was not until 2008 that Prime Minister Stephen Harper offered a formal apology acknowledging that the policy of forced assimilation "was wrong, has caused great harm, and has no place in our country" and that the treatment of children in residential schools "is a sad chapter in our history" (CBC News, 2008).

**ABORIGINAL PEOPLES TODAY** According to the 2006 Census, more than one million people reported they were Aboriginal, including 698,025 First Nations (North American Indian), 389,785 Métis, and 50,485 Inuit. These numbers represent approximately 4 percent of Canada's total population (Statistics Canada, 2008b). Figure 10.1 displays the composition of the Aboriginal population. Although the majority of registered Indians live on reserves, the majority of all Aboriginal people live off reserves. The Aboriginal population is unevenly distributed across Canada, with the heaviest concentrations in western and northern Canada.

The results of government assimilationist policies, forced segregation, and discrimination continue to be experienced by First Nations children, youth and families across the country. In terms of income, employment, housing, nutrition, and health, Aboriginal peoples are the most disadvantaged racial or ethnic group in Canada (Frideres, 2007). The life chances of Aboriginal peoples who live on reserves are especially limited. According to a United Nations report, First Nations children in Western countries live in Third World conditions, with an estimated 80 percent of urban Aboriginal children under the age of six living in poverty. Aboriginal people living in urban areas were more than twice as likely as non-Aboriginal people to live in poverty. And the number of Aboriginal children involved with the child welfare system across Canada continues to grow. In some provinces, over 95 percent of children involved with family services are Aboriginal. Aboriginal peoples have the highest rates of infant mortality and death by exposure and malnutrition, as well as high rates of tuberculosis, alcoholism, and suicide (Frideres, 2007). The overall life expectancy of Aboriginal people in Canada is five years less than that of non-Aboriginals, largely due to poor health services and inadequate housing on reserves. Aboriginal peoples also have had limited educational opportunities (the functional illiteracy rate for Aboriginal peoples is 45 percent, compared with the overall Canadian rate of 17 percent).

Economic disadvantage is reflected in both employment and income inequality among First Nations populations. Their rate of unemployment is twice that for non-Aboriginal Canadians. On reserves, the unemployment rate is about 29 percent, nearly three times the Canadian rate (Frideres, 2007). Finally, incomes for Aboriginal persons are about two-thirds the level of non-Aboriginals. For First Nations people on reserves, average incomes are less than half the rest of the population's incomes (National Aboriginal Economic Development Board, 2012).

Despite the state's efforts to assimilate Aboriginal peoples into Canadian culture and society, many Aboriginal people have been successful in resisting oppression. National organizations like the Assembly of First Nations, Inuit Tapiriit Kanatami, the Native Council of Canada, and the Métis National Council have been instrumental in bringing the demands of those they represent into the political and

| FIGURE 10.1 | ABORIGINAL IDENTITY POPULATION, 2006 |

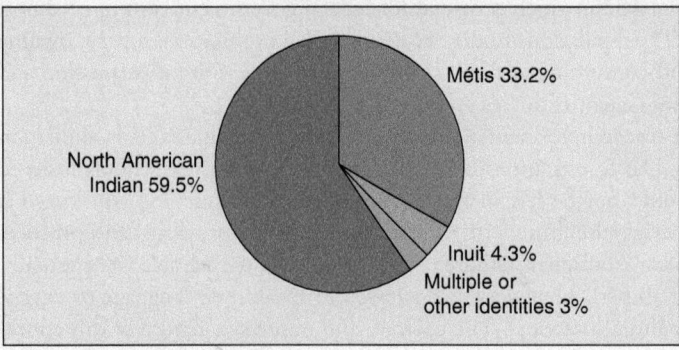

*Note:* Some respondents indicated they consider themselves members of more than one Aboriginal group.

*Source:* Statistics Canada, Census of Population, 2006, found at: http://www12.statcan.ca/english/census06/data/highlights/Aboriginal/index.cfm?Lang=E

constitutional arenas. Of these demands, the major ones have been—and still are—self-government, Aboriginal rights, and the resolution of land claims (see Frideres and Gadacz, 2005).

Aboriginal peoples today are in a period of transition from a long history marked by racism, exploitation, and domination to a contemporary life in which they are regaining control of programs directed at protecting their children, delivering education, and promoting and restoring health and commerce in Aboriginal communities. Many see the challenge for Aboriginal peoples today as being to erase negative stereotypes while maintaining their heritage and obtaining recognition for their contribution to this country's development and growth. A report released in 2012 indicated that Aboriginal Canadians are making some measurable progress toward improving their economic outcomes. However, as Chief Clarence Louie comments:

> Significant gaps remain between Aboriginal and non-Aboriginal Canadians. Clearly, much of our economic potential remains unrealized, and there is still much work to be done before Aboriginal Canadians are in the same position as other Canadians to contribute to and benefit from one of the world's wealthiest economies. (National Aboriginal Economic Development Board, 2012:5)

© CP PHOTO/Winnipeg Free Press - Jeff de Booy

The North American Indigenous Games, held on Vancouver Island in 2008, are a reflection of Aboriginal peoples' sustained efforts to maintain their unique cultures. For thousands of years before European contact, Aboriginal peoples held games throughout North America.

## The Québécois

The French were the first Europeans to immigrate to Canada in large numbers, establishing settlements in what was then known as Acadia and along the St. Lawrence River. In 1608, the first permanent settlement in New France was established at Quebec City. At this time, France's North American empire extended from Hudson Bay to Louisiana.

Following the British conquest of the French in Canada in the Seven Years' War (1756–1763), Canada became a British dominion and the French found themselves in an inferior position (Weinfeld, 1995). However, given the numerical dominance of the French, their links to the fur trade, and the fact that the French colony shared a border with the United States, the British felt it advantageous to accommodate the French. What emerged was a plural, or segmented, society in which the French were able to maintain French civil law, language, and religion; however, the overall economic, social, and political power passed to English Canada (Breton, 1988).

*The British North America Act* (1867) formally acknowledged the rights and privileges of the French and British as the founding, or charter, groups of Canadian society. French was recognized as an official language in Quebec and the provincial government in Quebec was able to maintain significant authority over culture and education. The Catholic Church was also able to retain control over educational and religious matters and many other aspects of Quebec society. During this time, it was assumed that in the future, French- and English-speaking groups would coexist and complement one another. However, during the period between Confederation and World War II, the French struggled for cultural survival because English-speaking Canadians controlled the major economic institutions in both English Canada and Quebec. During the early 1960s, the Catholic Church's control began to erode and the old elite consensus began to break down, laying the foundation for what was described as the Quiet Revolution (Satzewich and Liodakis, 2007).

During the Quiet Revolution (1960–1966), Quebec nationalism grew sharply. Under the leadership of Premier Jean Lesage, Quebec began undergoing a rapid process of modernization. During this time, the authority of the Catholic Church over the educational system was reduced as the Quebec government established a department of education. More French Canadians began pursuing higher education, particularly in business and science. The Church also lost some of its influence over moral issues, which was reflected in a declining birth rate and an increase in common-law marriages. Finally, nonfrancophone immigrants were challenging French culture by choosing to learn English and having their children learn English rather than French. Francophones came to view their language and culture as endangered, and as a result, many rejected their Canadian identity and adopted a distinctly Québécois identity.

In the 1970s, the separatist Parti Québécois was elected under the leadership of Premier René Lévesque. During this time, the controversial Bill 101 was introduced and established French as the sole official language in Quebec. In 1980, the Parti Québécois held a referendum on the question of pursuing a more independent relationship with Canada called *sovereignty association*. The proposal was narrowly rejected, but the matter was once again addressed in a second referendum in 1995 (Dyck, 2000). Although Quebeckers once again rejected sovereignty (this time by a narrow margin of 1 percent) the issue remains controversial (see Chapter 20).

**FRENCH CANADIANS TODAY** Today, almost 23 percent of the Canadian population is francophone, of which 85 percent is located in Quebec; 81 percent of Quebeckers are French-speaking and over 90 percent of French-speaking Canadians live in Quebec (Dyck, 2008). Many Quebec nationalists now see independence or separation as the ultimate protection against cultural and linguistic assimilation, as well as the route to economic power. As political scientist Rand Dyck comments:

> Given their historic constitutional rights, given their geographic concentration in
> Quebec and majority control of such a large province, and given their modern-day
> self-consciousness and self-confidence, the French fact in Canada cannot be ignored. If
> English Canada wants Quebec to remain a part of the country, it cannot go back to the
> easy days of pre-1960 unilingualism and federal government centralization. (2008:116)

French Canadians have at least forced Canada to take its second language and culture seriously, which is an important step toward attaining cultural pluralism.

## Canada's Multicultural Minorities

Home to approximately six million foreign-born immigrants, Canada is well described as a land of immigrants. Approximately 75 percent of immigrants arriving in Canada today are members of a visible minority group (Statistics Canada, 2008). But Canada's policies toward some of these groups have been far from exemplary. In fact, initial Canadian immigration policies have been described as essentially racist in orientation, assimilationist in intent, and exclusionary in outcome. For example, the *Immigration Act* of 1869 excluded certain types of undesirables, such as criminals and the diseased, and imposed strict limitations on the Japanese, Chinese, and East Asians. A "racial pecking order" was established to select potential immigrants on the basis of race and perceived ability for assimilation (Lupul, 1988; Walker, 1997, cited in Fleras and Elliott, 2003). As much energy was expended in keeping out certain "types" as was put into encouraging others to settle.

A preferred category was that of *white ethnics*—a term coined to identify immigrants who came from European countries other than England, such as Scotland, Ireland, Poland, Italy, Greece, Germany, Yugoslavia, and Russia and other former Soviet republics. Immigration from "white" countries was encouraged to ensure the British character of Canada. With the exception of visa formalities, this category of "preferred" immigrants was virtually exempt from entry restrictions (Fleras and Elliott, 2003:253). On the other hand, Jews and other Mediterranean populations required special permits for entry, and Asian populations were admitted only because they could serve as cheap labour for Canadian capitalist expansion. The restrictions regarding the Chinese, Japanese, and Jews highlighted the racist dimension of Canada's early immigration policies (Satzewich, 1998).

**CHINESE CANADIANS** The initial wave of Chinese migrants came to Canada in the 1850s, when Chinese men were attracted to emigrate by the British Columbia gold rush and by employment opportunities created by the expansion of a national railroad. Nearly 17,000 Chinese were brought to Canada at this time to lay track for the Canadian Pacific Railway. The work was brutally hard and dangerous, living conditions were appalling, food and shelter were insufficient, and due to scurvy and smallpox the fatality rate was high. These immigrants were "welcomed" only as long as there was a shortage of white workers. However, they were not permitted to bring their wives and children with them or to have sexual relations with white women, because of the fear they would spread the "yellow menace" (Henry and Tator, 2006).

As more Chinese Canadians have made gains in education and employment, many have also made a conscious effort to increase awareness of Chinese culture and develop a sense of unity and cooperation. This Chinese dragon parade exemplifies the desire to maintain traditional celebrations.

The Chinese were subjected to extreme prejudice and were referred to by derogatory terms, such as *coolies, heathens,* and *Chinks.* Some were attacked by working-class whites who feared they would lose their jobs to Chinese immigrants. In 1885, the federal government passed its first anti-Chinese bill, the purpose of which was to limit Chinese immigration, and a $50 head tax was imposed on all Chinese males arriving in Canada. In 1903, the tax was raised to $500 in a further attempt to restrict entry to Canada (Satzewich and Loidakis, 2007). Other hostile legislation included a range of racist exclusionary policies, such as prohibiting the Chinese from voting, serving in public office, serving on juries, participating in white labour unions, and working in the professions of law and pharmacy. Not until after World War II were these discriminatory policies removed from the *Immigration Act.* After immigration laws were further relaxed in the 1960s, the second and largest wave of Chinese immigration occurred, with immigrants coming primarily from Hong Kong and Taiwan (Henry and Tator, 2006).

**JAPANESE CANADIANS** When Japanese Canadians first arrived in British Columbia in the 1870s, they experienced similar discriminatory policies and practices. Like Chinese immigrants two decades earlier, the Japanese were viewed as a threat by white workers and became victims of racism and discrimination. They were paid lower wages than white labourers, had restrictions placed on their fishing licences, and were segregated in schools and public places.

In 1907, an organization known as the Asiatic Exclusion League was formed with the goal of restricting admission of Asians to Canada. Following the arrival of a ship carrying more than a thousand Japanese and a few hundred Sikhs, the league carried out a demonstration that precipitated a race riot. After the riot, the Canadian government negotiated a "gentlemen's agreement" that permitted entry only of certain categories of Japanese persons. In this agreement, the government further allowed only 400 Japanese to immigrate to Canada in a given year (Henry and Tator, 2006).

Japanese Canadians also experienced one of the most vicious forms of discrimination ever sanctioned by Canadian law. During World War II, when Canada was at war with Japan, nearly 23,000 people of Japanese ancestry—13,300 of whom were Canadian-born—were placed in jails and internment camps, forced to work, and had their property confiscated. Those interned in camp were not released until two years after the war was over (Miki and Kobayashi, 1991). German immigrants avoided this fate even though Canada was at war with both Japan and Germany. Four decades after these events, the Canadian government issued an apology for its actions and agreed to pay $20,000 to each person who had been placed in an internment camp (Henry and Tator, 2006).

**SOUTH ASIANS** Immigrants from India were also subjected to widespread anti-immigration sentiments in the early 20th century. One of the first discriminatory immigration laws was the "continuous passage" rule of 1908, which specified that South Asians could immigrate only if they came directly from India and did not stop at any ports on the way. This law made it almost impossible for them to enter the country, since no ships made direct journeys from India. For example, in 1914, a Sikh businessman chartered a ship in Hong Kong to transport more than 300 Indian passengers to Canada. On arrival in Vancouver, the passengers were refused entry. After a two-month standoff, the ship was forced to return to India (Satzewich and Liodakis, 2007).

South Asians who did manage to immigrate to Canada were subject to ongoing exclusion and hostility. Their property and businesses were frequently attacked, and they were denied citizenship and the right to vote in British Columbia until 1947 (Henry and Tator, 2006). Because they were denied their political rights, they were also precluded from entering the more prestigious professions of law, medicine, education, and pharmacy.

**JEWISH CANADIANS** Between 1933 and 1945, many Jews sought refuge from the persecution of the Nazis. During this time, Canada admitted fewer Jewish refugees as a percentage of its population than any other Western country. In 1942, a ship carrying Jewish refugees from Europe attempted to land in Halifax and was denied entrance. Jews who did immigrate experienced widespread discrimination in employment, business, and education. Other indicators of anti-Semitism included restrictions on where Jews could live, buy property, and attend university. Signs posted along Toronto's beaches warned, "No dogs or Jews allowed." Many hotels and resorts had policies prohibiting Jews as guests (Abella and Troper, 1982, quoted in Henry and Tator, 2000:80).

## IMMIGRATION TRENDS POST WORLD WAR II TO THE PRESENT  LO-5

Although the more blatantly racist aspects of immigration policy were moderated after World War II, the underlying philosophy behind immigration to Canada retained its discriminatory agenda—immigration needed to be carefully controlled, the encouragement of nonwhite immigration was not in the best interests of the country, and any economic benefits of immigration needed to be measured against the potential "social costs" of unrestrained immigration of visible minority immigrants. This philosophy was clearly articulated by Prime Minister William Lyon Mackenzie King in a 1947 speech to the House of Commons:

> The people of Canada do not wish, as a result of mass immigration, to make a fundamental alteration in the character of our population. Large scale immigration from the Orient would change the fundamental composition of the Canadian population. Any considerable oriental immigration would, moreover, be certain to give rise to social and economic problems. (Canada, 1947: Debates of the House of Commons, cited in Satzewich and Liodakis, 2007)

After the war, some of the more overtly racist immigration legislation, such as the *Chinese Immigration Act* and the continuous journey stipulations, were repealed and immigration from India was permitted on a fixed quota basis of 300 persons per year. However, the focus of postwar immigration continued to be on the "preferred" white immigrants from Europe and the United States (Satzewich and Liodakis, 2007:54).

Changes to the *Immigration Act* in 1962 opened the door to immigration on a nonracial basis. Canada became one of the first countries in the world to announce that "any suitable qualified person from anywhere in the world" would be considered for immigration, based solely on the criteria of personal merit. Education, occupation, and language skills replaced ethnicity and nationality as criteria for admission (Fleras and Elliott, 2003). The criteria for immigration underwent further reform in 1967 when a *points system* was introduced. All applicants, regardless of origin or colour, were rated according to the total of points given for the following: job training, experience, skills, level of education, knowledge of English or French, degree of demand for the applicant's occupation, and job offers (Henry and Tator, 2006). Although, as shown in Figure 10.2, this act opened the doors to those from previously excluded countries, critics have suggested that it maintained some of the same racist policies. In 2002, in response to the numerous concerns of continued exclusionary and racist immigration practices, the *Immigration and Refugee Protection Act* was implemented. This act recognizes three classes of immigrants—economic, family class, and refugee—and reflects a more open policy with selection criteria based on language skills, education, age, employment experience, and a category called "adaptability" (Henry and Tator, 2006:78).

### Growing Racial and Ethnic Diversity in Canada

Racial and ethnic diversity is increasing in Canada. This changing demographic pattern is largely the result of the elimination of overtly racist immigration policies and the opening up of immigration to low-income countries. Canada has evolved from a country largely inhabited

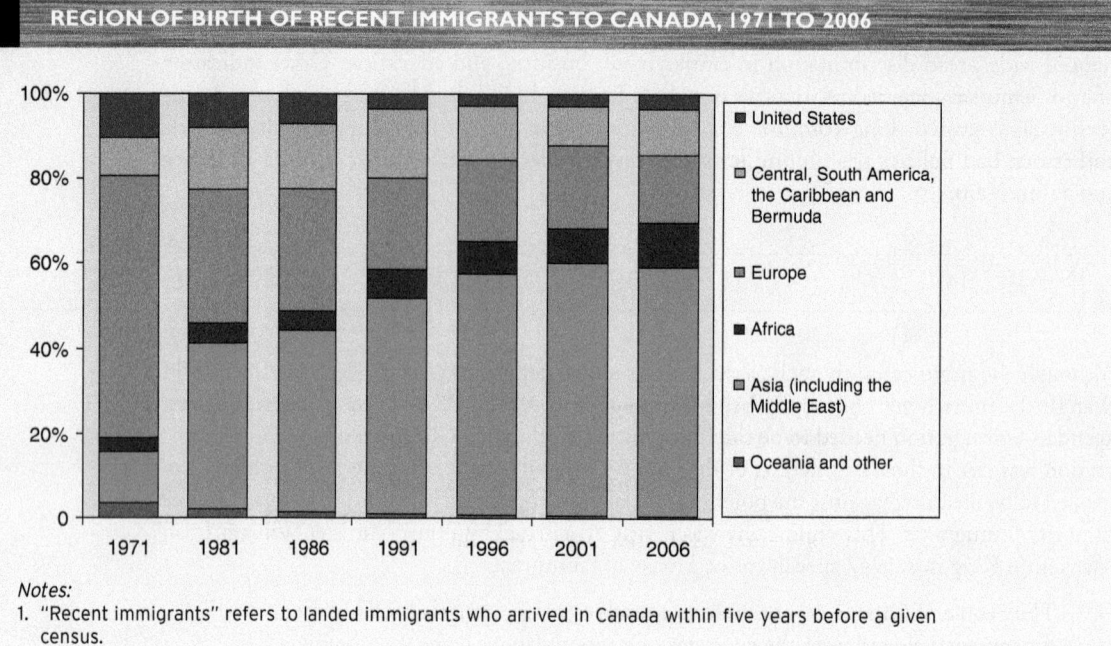

FIGURE 10.2    REGION OF BIRTH OF RECENT IMMIGRANTS TO CANADA, 1971 TO 2006

*Notes:*
1. "Recent immigrants" refers to landed immigrants who arrived in Canada within five years before a given census.
2. "Other" includes Greenland, St. Pierre and Miquelon, and the category "other country," as well as a small number of immigrants born in Canada.

*Source:* Chui, Tran, and Maheux, 2007.

by whites and Aboriginal peoples to a country made up of people from more than 70 countries. Today, people born outside of Canada make up more than 20 percent of the total population of Canada (see Figure 10.3). Newcomers from Asia make up the largest proportion of immigrants, followed by newcomers from Europe (Chui, Tran, and Maheux, 2007).

Almost all immigrants to Canada live in cities. Recent immigrants are especially attracted to Canada's three largest cities. The majority of recent immigrants have chosen to live in Toronto, Montreal, or Vancouver. Today, nearly half of the population of Toronto and nearly two-fifths of the population of Vancouver is composed of immigrants. As author Neil Bissoondath explains:

> In the new millennium Toronto, Canada's largest city, will mark an unusual milestone. In a city of three million, the words "minorities" and "majority" will be turned on their heads and the former will become the latter. Reputed to be the most ethnically diverse city in the world, Toronto has been utterly remade by immigration, just as Canada has been remade by a quarter of a century of multiculturalism. (1998:1)

What effect will these changes have on racial and ethnic relations? Several possibilities exist. On the one hand, conflict between whites and racial and ethnic minorities may become more overt and confrontational. Certainly, the concentration of visible minorities will mean that these groups will become more visible than ever in some Canadian cities. Increasing contact may lead to increased intergroup cohesion and understanding, or it may bring on racism or prejudice. Rapid political changes and the global economy have made people fearful about their future and may cause some to blame "foreigners" for their problems People may continue to use *discourses of denial* —personal beliefs that reflect larger societal mythologies, such as "I am not racist" or "I have never discriminated against anyone"—even when these are inaccurate perceptions (Henry and Tator, 2006).

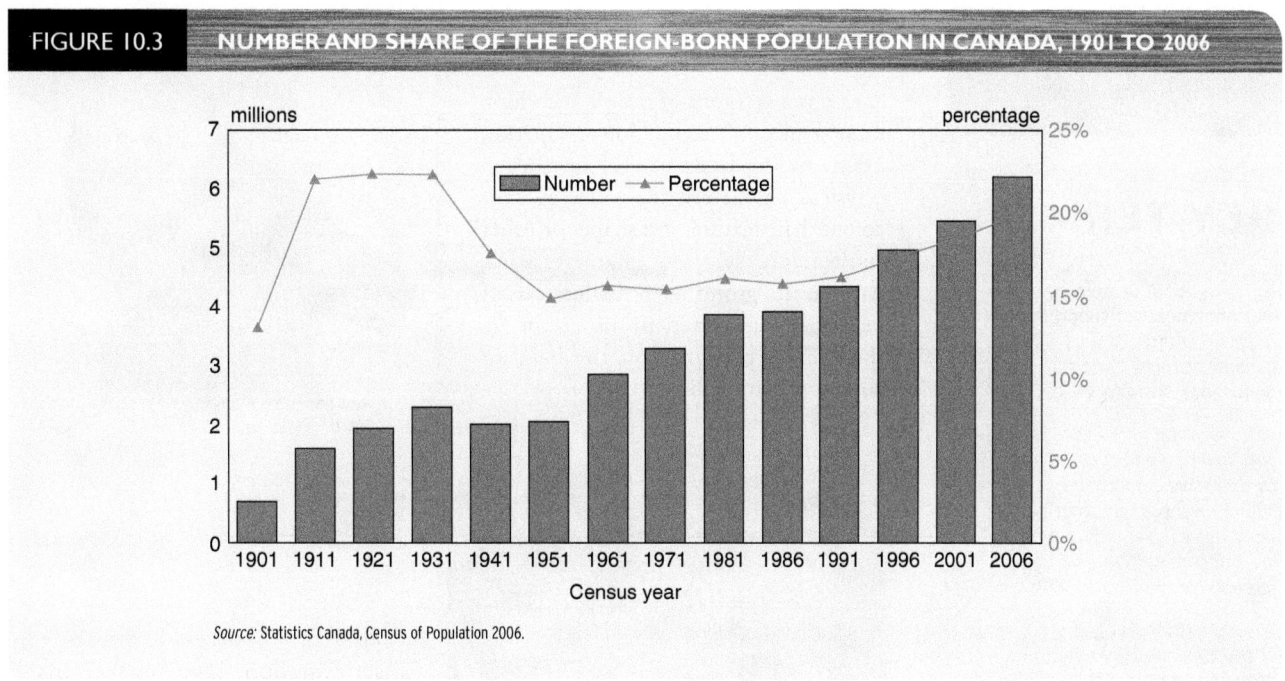

FIGURE 10.3  NUMBER AND SHARE OF THE FOREIGN-BORN POPULATION IN CANADA, 1901 TO 2006

Source: Statistics Canada, Census of Population 2006.

On the other hand, there is reason for cautious optimism. Throughout Canadian history, subordinate racial and ethnic groups have struggled to gain the freedom and rights that were previously withheld from them. Today, employment equity programs are alleviating some of the effects of past discrimination against minority groups, as well as addressing systemic and institutional forms of racism that exist in employment. Movements made up of both whites and visible minorities continue to oppose racism in everyday life, to seek to heal divisions among racial groups, and to teach children about racial tolerance (Rutstein, 1993). Many groups hope not only to affect their own countries but also to contribute to worldwide efforts to end racism (Ford, 1994).

**10**

## KEY TERMS

**assimilation** A process by which members of subordinate racial and ethnic groups become absorbed into the dominant culture (p. 283).

**authoritarian personality** A personality type characterized by excessive conformity, submissiveness to authority, intolerance, insecurity, a high level of superstition, and rigid, stereotypic thinking (p. 278).

**discrimination** Actions or practices of dominant group members (or their representatives) that have a harmful impact on members of a subordinate group (p. 278).

**ethnic group** A collection of people distinguished, by others or by themselves, primarily on the basis of cultural or nationality characteristics (p. 274).

**ethnic pluralism** The coexistence of a variety of distinct racial and ethnic groups within one society (p. 284).

**institutionalized racism** A situation where the established rules, policies, and practices within an institution or organization produce differential treatment of various groups based on race (p. 281).

**internal colonialism** According to conflict theorists, a situation in which members of a racial or ethnic group are conquered or colonized and forcibly placed under the economic and political control of the dominant group (p. 286).

**majority (dominant) group** An advantaged group that is advantaged and has superior resources and rights in a society (p. 276).

**LO-1** Distinguish between race and ethnicity.

A race is a category of people who have been singled out as inferior or superior, often on the basis of real or alleged physical characteristics, such as skin colour, hair texture, eye shape, or other subjectively selected characteristics. An ethnic group is a collection of people distinguished by others or by themselves, primarily on the basis of culture or nationality.

**LO-2** Define and explain prejudice, discrimination, and racism.

Prejudice involves attitudes, but discrimination involves actions or practices of dominant group members that have a harmful impact on members of a subordinate group. Discriminatory actions range from name-calling to violent actions and can be either *de jure* (encoded in law) or *de facto* (informal). *Racism* refers to an organized set of beliefs about the innate inferiority of some racial groups, combined with the power to discriminate on the basis of race. There are many different ways in which racism may manifest itself, including overt racism, polite racism, subliminal racism, and institutionalized racism.

**LO-3** Explain the major sociological perspectives on race and ethnic relations.

Interactionists suggest that increased contact between people from divergent groups should lead to favourable attitudes and behaviour when members of each group (1) have equal status, (2) pursue the same goals, (3) cooperate with one another to achieve goals, and

(4) receive positive feedback when they interact with one another. Functionalists stress that members of subordinate groups become absorbed into the dominant culture. Conflict theorists focus on economic stratification and access to power in race and ethnic relations. Feminist analysts highlight the fact that women who are members of racial and ethnic minorities are doubly disadvantaged as a result of their gender. There is an interactive effect of racism and sexism on the exploitation of women of colour. Postmodern theorists view racial and ethnic identities as fluid and examine how these concepts are socially constructed. Critical race theorists emphasize the significant role that race and racism have played in legal and political structures in society.

## LO-4 Discuss the unique historical experiences of the racial and ethnic groups in Canada.

When European settlers arrived on this continent, the Aboriginal inhabitants' were the victims of genocide and forced migration. Aboriginal children were placed in residential boarding schools to facilitate their assimilation into the dominant culture. Although the French were the first Europeans to immigrant to Canada in large numbers when they were defeated by the English following the seven years war they found themselves in an inferior position. Although the French were able to maintain French civil law, language, and religion; however, the overall economic, social, and political power passed to English Canada. Non-white immigrants (including Chinese, Japanese, and South Asians) were only welcomed into Canada as a source of cheap labour and were subject to racist laws and immigration policies.

## LO-5 Describe how Canada's immigration policies have affected the composition of Canada's racial and ethnic population today.

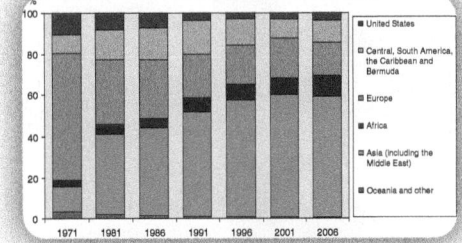

Canada's early immigration policies were described as racist and included exclusionary policies directed at Asian populations, including Chinese, Japanese, and South Asians, as well as Jews. "White ethnics" who came from European countries comprised the preferred category of immigrants. Changes to the *Immigration Act* in 1962 involving the implementation of a points system opened the door to immigration on a nonracial basis. In 2002, the *Immigration and Refugee Protection Act* was implemented, with selection criteria based on attributes of human capital and the skills of potential immigrants.

---

**minority (subordinate) group** A group whose members, because of physical or cultural characteristics, are disadvantaged and subjected to unequal treatment by the dominant group and who regard themselves as objects of collective discrimination (p. 276).

**overt racism (or redneck or hate racism)** Racism that may take the form of deliberate and highly personal attacks, including derogatory slurs and name-calling toward members of a racial or ethnic group who are perceived to be "inferior" (p. 279).

**polite racism** A term used to describe an attempt to disguise a dislike of others through behaviour that is outwardly nonprejudicial (p. 279).

**prejudice** A negative attitude based on preconceived notions about members of selected groups (p. 277).

**race** A term used by many people to specify groups of people distinguished by physical characteristics, such as skin colour; also, a category of people who have been singled out as inferior or superior, often on the basis of real or alleged physical characteristics, such as skin colour, hair texture, eye shape, or other subjectively selected attributes (p. 274).

**racial prejudice** Beliefs that certain racial groups are innately inferior to others or have a disproportionate number of negative traits (p. 277).

**racism** A set of ideas that implies the superiority of one social group over another on the basis of biological or cultural characteristics, together with the power to put these beliefs into practice in a way that denies or excludes minority women and men (p. 279).

**scapegoat** A person or group that is incapable of offering resistance to the hostility or aggression of others (p. 278).

segregation A term used to describe the spatial and social separation of categories of people by race/ethnicity, class, gender, and/or religion (p. 285).

split labour market A term used to describe the division of the economy into two areas of employment: a primary sector, or upper tier, composed of higher-paid (usually dominant group) workers in more secure jobs; and a secondary sector, or lower tier, composed of lower-paid (often subordinate group) workers in jobs with little security and hazardous working conditions (p. 287).

stereotype An overgeneralization about the appearance, behaviour, or other characteristics of members of particular groups (p. 277).

subliminal racism A term used to describe an unconscious racism that occurs when there is a conflict of values (p. 280).

visible minority An official government category of nonwhite, non-Caucasian individuals (p. 276).

# KEY FIGURES

**W.E.B. Du Bois (1868-1963)** Born in Massachusetts, Du Bois was both a race relations scholar and a civil rights activist. Du Bois was the first African American to earn a PhD at Harvard University. Over the years, he became frustrated with the lack of progress in race relations and became a co-founder of the National Association for the Advancement of Colored People (NAACP).

**Frances Henry** Now retired as a professor emerita from York University, Henry is one of Canada's leading experts in the study of racism and antiracism. Since the mid-1970s, when she published the first study of attitudes toward people of colour, she has consistently pioneered research in this field. She is co-author with Carol Tator of *The Colour of Democracy: Racism in Canadian Society* and more recently *Racism in the Canadian University*.

**Carol Tator** Tator is the author of numerous books on racism in Canada, including *Racism in the Canadian University* and *Racial Profiling in Canada: Challenging the Myth of "A Few Bad Apples."* For more than three decades, she has worked on the front lines of the antiracism and equity movement in the areas of the development and implementation of antiracism policies and programs, strategic planning, training, and research.

## APPLICATION QUESTIONS

1. Do you consider yourself defined more by your race, your ethnicity, or neither of these concepts? Explain.

2. Given that minority groups have some common experiences, why is there such deep conflict between certain minority groups?

3. What would need to happen in Canada, both individually and institutionally, for a positive form of ethnic pluralism to flourish in the 21st century?

4. Is it possible for members of racial minorities to be racist? Discuss.

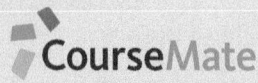

 Test your comprehension and assess what you've learned with **CourseMate's** online quizzes.

 For other interesting Lived Experiences, watch the video clips on **CourseMate.**

 Practise what you've learned with flashcards containing key terms and definitions on **CourseMate.**

NEL

# Chapter 12

# Multiculturalism or Vertical Mosaic?

## OCCUPATIONAL STRATIFICATION AMONG CANADIAN ETHNIC GROUPS

HUGH LAUTARD, University of New Brunswick
and NEIL GUPPY, University of British Columbia

## INTRODUCTION

Canada is primarily a land of immigrants. Most Canadians trace ancestral roots to Europe or Asia. This has meant, from the origin of the nation, a mixing of people with diverse ethnic roots. How well this mixing has occurred is the focus of this chapter.

The government policy of multiculturalism implies a wholesome mixing of ethnic groups, an equality among peoples of distinct cultural heritages. Canada's diverse cultural heritages are supported through many institutions, including ethnic media outlets, churches, schools, and restaurants. The equality among these diverse cultures is most actively promoted by governments but also by, for example, schools. Multicultural curricula now permeate the school system, in social studies courses, in recognizing different religious holidays, and in celebrating ethnic heritage days (Guppy and Lyon, 2012). Different cultural traditions provide separate ethnic identities within a common, egalitarian framework. Multiculturalism highlights cultural blending and ethnic equality.

A contrasting vision of Canada was proposed by sociologist John Porter (1965). Writing in the 1960s, he championed the imagery of a "vertical mosaic." "Mosaic" highlights distinct ethnic identities, but Porter saw little mixing or blending. He argued that Canada's ethnic groups were vertically arranged. According to Porter, Canada was composed of distinct social groups defined principally by social class and ethnicity. Furthermore, these social groups were vertically ranked according to income, power, and prestige. The vertical mosaic, Porter argued, accentuates distinct cultures and ethnic inequality.

---

Source: Reprinted by permission of the authors.

How useful are the contrasting images of the vertical mosaic and multiculturalism in understanding modern Canada? Canada's population has grown and diversified since 1965, when Porter published *The Vertical Mosaic*, and since 1971, when Canada adopted multiculturalism as federal government policy.

Section 12.1 of the Canadian Charter of Rights and Freedoms (1985) proclaims: "Every individual is equal before and under the law and has the right to the equal protection and equal benefit of the law without discrimination and, in particular, without discrimination based on race, national or ethnic origin, [and] colour. ..." However, despite the Charter's grounding in multicultural language, the legacy of the vertical mosaic has required additional legislation to help enhance the Charter's equality provisions. So, for example, the Employment Equity Act (1986) seeks to erase the subordinate positions of women, people with disabilities, Aboriginal peoples, and visible-minority groups. The act requires employers to hire according to equity targets to overcome ethnic inequality in the labour force. While proclaiming multiculturalism as official policy, the federal government has had to enact laws simultaneously in an attempt to erode the vertical mosaic. If the key proposition of *The Vertical Mosaic* still holds—that ethnicity shapes inequality—then such legislation as the Employment Equity Act remains important. This implies, though, that multiculturalism remains more ideology than fact, more rhetoric than reality. Is there a causal link between your ethnicity and your socioeconomic fortunes or misfortunes? We present new data that, when compared with trends published earlier, afford the longest historical perspective available on the association between ethnicity and occupation, based on 75 years of census data, from 1931 to 2006. As did Porter before us, we stress both social differences (multiple ethnic groups in a mosaic) and social stratification (vertical alignment of ethnic groups).

## IS THE SIGNIFICANCE OF ETHNICITY FOR INEQUALITY DECLINING?

In *The Vertical Mosaic*, Porter described Canada as a nation fractured by ethnicity. He saw the French and the British as two "charter status" groups, commanding greater power and privilege than "entrance status" groups (other immigrants). He analyzed the asymmetry of power favouring the British over the French and claimed that this asymmetry characterized noncharter immigrant groups, too. For Porter, "immigration and ethnic affiliation ... [were] important factors in the formation of social classes" (1965: 73).

Porter focused especially on the economic elite, in which he claimed "economic power belong[ed] almost exclusively to [White Protestants] of British origin" (Porter, 1965: 286). More recent analyses of the wealthiest Canadians show less British dominance. While the Thomson family, with its strong British roots, continues to be the wealthiest Canadian family, the corridors of power are now less WASPish (Nakhaie, 1997; Ogmundson and Doyle, 2001; Ogmundson and McLaughlin, 1990). At one time almost exclusively British, the Canadian elite, almost no matter how it is defined, now contains more people from other ethnic backgrounds. Among current Canadian billionaires are people with ethnic surnames that are very non-British, including Emanuel Saputo (food), David Azrieli (real estate), and Paul Desmarais (finance).

Porter (1965) also used census data from 1931, 1951, and 1961 to make his case. By tabulating ethnic origin and occupation, he showed which ethnic groups dominated which job categories. For example, in the 1931 census, he found British and Jewish groups were overrepresented in professional and financial occupations. Conversely, they were underrepresented in unskilled and primary jobs (fishing, logging, mining). He wrote that the "French, German, and Dutch would probably rank next, followed by Scandinavian, Eastern European, Italian, Japanese, 'Other Central European', Chinese, and Native Indian" (p. 81). His 1961 census data showed that, save for the French who had slid down a little, "the rough rank order [had] persisted over time" (p. 90).

Why were different ethnic groups represented at higher and lower occupational levels? Porter proposed two complementary explanations. First, newcomers to Canada often brought with them different educational and occupational experiences. People of British heritage frequently came with professional qualifications that were officially recognized in Canada, whereas people from other ethnic backgrounds often arrived with little education and no recognized professional skills. New entrants to Canada thus reinforced the link between ethnic ancestry and social class (Porter, 1965: 86, 1985: 40–51).[1]

Second, Porter argued that social mobility was correlated with ethnicity. Ethnic groups, he argued, either varied in how much they valued economic achievement and upward mobility or found that discrimination dampened their labour market success (Pineo and Porter, 1985: 360–61). Indeed, Porter felt that multiculturalism would impede ethnic assimilation and perpetuate the link between social class and ethnicity (Heath and Yu, 2005).

Much social science research has assessed the adequacy of Porter's vertical mosaic imagery. No doubt insightful in his era, is it an accurate portrayal of ethnic inequality through the last half century? Since the end of World War II, the sources of Canadian immigrants have shifted dramatically away from Europe and toward other continents, especially Asia. As well, Canada has changed its immigration policy. Now, greater priority is given to the skills new entrants have, as opposed to their place of birth. For example, more emphasis is now placed on education and fluency in at least one of the two official languages. Occupational experience is more valued than birthplace.

Some researchers have concluded that the vertical mosaic imagery simply needs revising to note its "colour coding." They argue that for people of visible minority background, the association between ethnicity and social class has been retained. Now we have a "new ethnic mosaic ... redrafted along lines of race and colour" (Agocs and Boyd, 1993: 333; Hou, Balakrishnan, and Jurdi, 2009; Pendakur and Pendakur, 2011).

Other research traditions have followed Porter's original lead and compared patterns of association between ethnicity and social class in successive census years. For example, Lautard and Loree (1984: 342) used detailed ethnicity and occupation data from 1931 to 1971 and concluded that "occupational inequality is still substantial enough to justify the use of the concept 'vertical mosaic' to characterize ... ethnic relations in Canada" (Darroch, 1979; Pendakur, 2002). The census data used by Porter and by Lautard and Loree combine both the foreign born and the native born, thus allowing researchers to examine social change by focusing on trends over time. However, the census data that they used provide no test for the two explanations Porter offered about the association of ethnicity and class.

Monica Boyd's (1985) research on the influence of birthplace on occupational attainment offers a test of the immigration interpretation. For foreign-born women and men, Boyd demonstrated that ethnic ancestry was correlated with occupational attainment. Even when immigrants with the same age, education, social origin, and place of residence were compared, the correlation existed. For women who were foreign-born, Boyd found a "double negative" that reinforced the vertical mosaic. She concluded that birthplace and sex are important factors underlying the Canadian mosaic (Boyd, 1985: 441).

The exact nature of the link between ethnicity and inequality turns, at least in part, on issues of definition and methodology. Porter used the best data available to him, but his approach had weaknesses despite his best efforts. The sections that follow describe the three main problems that any analyst must confront in trying to sort out whether the idea of multiculturalism or the image of a vertical mosaic best characterizes modern Canada.

## ETHNICITY

Definitions matter. How broadly or finely we choose to define ethnicity is critical in these debates. Historically, male ancestral lineage was the defining feature of ethnicity, at least as used by Statistics Canada for measurement purposes. However, this definition is problematic, not only because it privileges male descent lines. Interethnic marriages occur across generations. National borders change. An increasing number of people consider themselves to be of "Canadian" ancestry since they are descendants of people who arrived in Canada generations ago.

Porter's view of the charter status groups, the French and the British, drew no distinction among the English, the Irish, the Scottish, and the Welsh. Likewise, Statistics Canada for a long time was unable to publish distinct numbers for members of different Asian ethnic groups. That is because the number of Koreans and Cambodians, for example, was too small. Typically, the following ethnic categories have been used in the census, with older census years having even fewer distinct groups: British (English, Irish, Scottish, Welsh), French, German, Italian, Jewish, Dutch, Scandinavian, Eastern European (Polish, Ukrainian), Other European, Asian, and Native Indian.

## OCCUPATIONS

Porter originally used five broad occupational categories (professional and financial, clerical, personal service, primary and unskilled, and agriculture). Lautard and Loree (1984) used a more detailed occupational categorization with hundreds of separate job categories for each census.

Occupations are, in important ways, just jobs. To show that members of different ethnic groups concentrate in some jobs and not others says nothing about inequality; it is only a comment about different jobs. Only if those jobs have different rewards attached to them does inequality become an issue. But, what are the most salient rewards—income, working conditions, prestige, authority? The vertical mosaic clearly implies some hierarchy, but what defines that hierarchy is not specified.

## HISTORICAL COMPARABILITY

The number and kinds of occupations in Canada have changed over time. Should researchers use older census categories that tend to be broader, or the full range of jobs characterizing the modern division of labour? Likewise, the detail on ethnicity has changed historically, as has the way Statistics Canada collects this information.[2] Should only broad ethnic categories that are strictly comparable over time be used?

## MEASURING OCCUPATIONAL STRATIFICATION BY ETHNICITY

With the above limitations in mind, you might conclude that using census data to track labour market changes for members of ethnic groups is highly problematic. Our response to this is fourfold. First, these problems must be recognized and the results interpreted cautiously in light of them. Second, even partial insight is better than ignorance. Third, if the findings of this research complement the findings of other researchers who used different research methods, then the entire body of research is self-reinforcing. Fourth, if better methods exist to answer the question we are pursuing, then we encourage others to do the research.

We use census information for 1971 and 2006 and compare our results to earlier findings, beginning either in 1931 or 1951. Depending on the availability of data, we discuss changes over a period of up to 75 years. The 2006 analysis involves examining the distribution of the members of 17 ethnic groups, by gender, across about five hundred different occupations. This provides enormous detail that we need to summarize. To do so, we measure occupational differentiation by calculating an *index of dissimilarity*, and we examine occupational stratification by using an *index of net difference*.

Here first, by way of analogy, is how to understand the index of dissimilarity. In your college or university, consider the overall percentages of women and men enrolled (assume it is 55 percent and 45 percent, respectively). Now think of the percentage of women and men in each of your classes. How well is the overall gender balance of 55/45 reflected in your individual courses? Extend this to all the courses offered at your institution.

To summarize this detail, begin by calculating, for each course, any difference in the percentage of women (or men) from the overall 55/45 average. This tells you how dissimilar each course is from the overall gender balance. Totalling across all courses provides a

Index of dissimilarity

convenient summary—the higher the index number, the greater the dissimilarity. Comparing the index of dissimilarity across different faculties or different universities would tell you which has the better gender balance.

In our case, we add the percentage differences between the occupational distribution of each ethnic group and that of the rest of the labour force. Separate calculations are done for women and men. The resulting indexes are the percentages of women and men in each ethnic group who would have to be in a different occupation for there to be no occupational differences among ethnic groups.

For example, say the index of dissimilarity for women of British origin is 11 percent. This means that barely one in ten British women in the labour force would have to be in a different occupation for there to be no difference between their occupational distribution and that of women of other ethnic origins. If the index of dissimilarity for men of Aboriginal origin is 28 percent, this indicates 2.5 times as much difference, with well over one in four Aboriginal men having to be in a different occupation for them to have the same occupational distribution as non-Aboriginal men. Averaging dissimilarity indexes for ethnic groups in two different census years indicates changes in occupational differentiation among ethnic groups. We present such results for 1971 and 2006, and compare them with earlier findings for 1931, 1951, and 1961, for a combined span of 75 years.

Dissimilarity, however, does not necessarily mean disadvantage or inequality. As a method of capturing *stratification*, sociologists have adopted other methods. In this chapter, we use two separate methods to examine stratification among occupations. For 1971, we array occupations on a socioeconomic index that measures the prestige of occupations. These prestige ratings are based on the typical education and income of people in particular occupations. For 2006, where such an index is not available, we use a measure constructed by Statistics Canada to rank the occupational skill requirements of distinct jobs. Occupation data collected from the 2006 census are ranked into one of four skill groups, with the groups arrayed by estimates of educational requirements (university, college, apprenticeship training, and high school or less). To this, Statistics Canada added a "manager" category, which is unranked since the education levels of managers are diverse.

As a way of summarizing occupational inequality, we use the index of net difference. This measure (unlike the index of dissimilarity, which is always positive) may be either negative or positive. An index of net difference with a minus sign indicates the group for which it was calculated is generally lower on the occupational "ladder" relative to the rest of the labour force, while a positive index indicates higher relative position. The greater the absolute size of the index, whether positive or negative, the greater the degree of stratification, while a net difference of zero would indicate overall equality of occupational status. We use this measure to analyze occupational inequality for 1971 and 2006, and compare our results with earlier findings for 1951, 1961, and 1971.

## OCCUPATIONAL INEQUALITY BY ETHNICITY, 1931 TO 2006

Table 12.1 contains indexes of occupational dissimilarity for 16 ethnic groups in 1971 and 17 groups in 2006. These scores summarize results based on just fewer than five hundred occupations in 1971 and just more than five hundred occupations in 2006. Generally, ethnic occupational differentiation is lower in 2006 than in 1971. In 2006, average ethnic dissimilarity among men (23 percent) is 7 points lower than in 1971 (30 percent), while it is 9 points lower among women (18 percent, compared with 27 percent). Exceptions to this pattern of declining index scores occur for men and women of German, Dutch, and Scandinavian origin, and for men of Polish origin. There was no change in the score for men of Ukrainian origin and women of Jewish origin.

Table 12.1 also shows that there is a generally consistent pattern of ethnic occupational differentiation. Groups of North and East European origins exhibit below-average occupational dissimilarity, while, with a few exceptions, groups of South European, Jewish, Asian, Aboriginal, and black origins show above-average dissimilarity. The generally lower levels of ethnic differentiation in 2006 compared with 1971 are consistent with the decreases reported by Lautard and Loree (1984) for 1931 ~~Occupational Dissimilarity~~ uggesting an easing of differentiation. Nevertheless, consider-pational dissimilarity remains among ethnic groups.[3]

Recall that occupational dissimilarity does not necessarily involve occupational stratification. Table 12.2 contains indexes of net difference in occupational status for 1971 and in occupational skill group for 2006 for the ethnic groups discussed previously. In 1971, with the exception of the indexes for men and women of British, Jewish, and South Asian origins, all indexes are negative, indicating the relatively low occupational status of the other groups. Note also that in 1971, both men and women of South European and Aboriginal origin have lower overall occupational status than do the other groups.

**TABLE 12.1** OCCUPATIONAL DISSIMILARITY[a] AMONG SELECTED ETHNIC GROUPS AND THE REST OF THE LABOUR FORCE, BY SEX, CANADA, 1971 AND 2006

| ETHNIC GROUP | MALE | | FEMALE | |
|---|---|---|---|---|
| | 1971 | 2006 | 1971 | 2006 |
| British | 15 | 11 | 16 | 11 |
| French | 14 | 10 | 18 | 11 |
| German | 15 | 19 | 11 | 12 |
| Dutch | 16 | 20 | 15 | 16 |
| Scandinavian | 17 | 22 | 12 | 16 |
| Ukrainian | 15 | 15 | 16 | 12 |
| Polish | 15 | 17 | 14 | 13 |
| Hungarian | 21 | 19 | 20 | 16 |
| Italian | 35 | 20 | 38 | 20 |
| Portuguese | 46 | 27 | 57 | 21 |
| Greek | 48 | 30 | 51 | 22 |
| Yugoslav | 33 | 22 | 35 | 17 |
| Jewish | 51 | 44 | 32 | 32 |
| Chinese | 52 | 34 | 34 | 26 |
| South Asian | 46 | 28 | 31 | 15 |
| Aboriginal | 41[b] | 28 | 32[b] | 21 |
| Black | NI | 26 | NI | 23 |
| Mean ($\overline{x}$) | 30 | 23 | 27 | 18 |
| Number of occupations | (498) | (521) | (464) | (521) |

[a] Each figure in the table indicates the percentage of the ethnic group that would have to have a different occupation for there to be no difference between the occupational distribution of that group and the rest of the labour force.
[b] Does not include Inuit.
NI: Not included.

SOURCE: Statistics Canada. Special tabulations of census data. Reproduced and distributed on an "as is" basis with the permission of Statistics Canada.

In 2006, the indexes of net difference are mainly positive. In 1971, they are mainly negative. This is true for both women and men. We conclude that ethnic stratification was less pronounced in 2006 than in 1971.

**TABLE 12.2** NET DIFFERENCE[a] IN OCCUPATIONAL STATUS (1971) AND OCCUPATIONAL SKILL GROUP (2006) AMONG SELECTED ETHNIC GROUPS AND THE REST OF THE LABOUR FORCE, BY SEX, CANADA

| | MALE | | FEMALE | |
|---|---|---|---|---|
| Ethnic Group | 1971 | 2006 | 1971 | 2006 |
| British | 0.13 | 0.05 | 0.14 | 0.05 |
| French | −0.06 | 0.03 | −0.02 | 0.06 |
| German | −0.08 | 0.02 | −0.09 | 0.00 |
| Dutch | −0.09 | 0.04 | −0.10 | 0.04 |
| Scandinavian | −0.08 | 0.06 | −0.01 | 0.03 |
| Ukrainian | −0.09 | 0.05 | −0.13 | 0.03 |
| Polish | −0.08 | 0.02 | −0.12 | −0.01 |
| Hungarian | −0.06 | 0.06 | −0.13 | 0.02 |
| Italian | −0.22 | 0.02 | −0.35 | 0.02 |
| Portuguese | −0.38 | −0.14 | −0.62 | −0.14 |
| Greek | −0.27 | 0.06 | −0.48 | 0.01 |
| Yugoslav | −0.12 | 0.03 | −0.29 | −0.01 |
| Jewish | 0.36 | 0.32 | 0.24 | 0.25 |
| Chinese | −0.04 | 0.17 | −0.20 | 0.02 |
| South Asian | 0.26 | −0.04 | 0.19 | −0.12 |
| Aboriginal | −0.35[b] | −0.14 | −0.23[b] | −0.09 |
| Black | NI | −0.10 | NI | −0.09 |
| Mean ($|\bar{x}|$) | 0.17 | 0.08 | 0.21 | 0.06 |
| Number of Occupational Ranks/Skill Groups | (498) | (4) | (464) | (4) |

[a] A negative figure indicates relatively lower overall occupational status/skill group, a positive figure relatively higher status/skill group. Zero indicates overall equality of occupational status/skill group. The greater the absolute size of the index, the greater the inequality.

[b] Does not include Inuit.

NI: Not included.

SOURCE: Statistics Canada. Special tabulations of census data. Reproduced and distributed on an "as is" basis with the permission of Statistics Canada.

Note also that the indexes for 2006 exhibit a pattern more or less similar to that noted above for occupational dissimilarity among ethnic groups. Most men and women of North, East, and South European origin, as well as those of Jewish and Chinese origin, tend to be in higher occupational skill groups than people of South Asian, Aboriginal, and black origin.[4]

# FROM VERTICAL MOSAIC TO MULTICULTURALISM?

Has multiculturalism eclipsed the vertical mosaic? Is ethnic inequality, at least as measured by occupational stratification, only a historical curiosity in Canada? Our results show that between 1931 and 2006, a decline in the significance of ethnicity occurred, for both occupational differentiation and stratification. Yet ethnic origin continues to affect occupational inequality.

The trend in occupational dissimilarity indicates a reduction in the ethnic division of labour of about 30 percent for men and 45 percent for women in 70 years (Figure 12.1). Slowly but surely, social differentiation based on ethnicity is eroding. With respect to occupational stratification, there has been a reduction of approximately 50 percent for men and 45 percent for women, although over a shorter span (from 1951 to 2006). From 1971 to 2006, the trend continued. These historical comparisons have the advantage of a 75-year interval of comparison, but such a lengthy interval also makes the specific contrasts cruder than would be ideal.

Do these results imply a "collapse" of the vertical mosaic? No. Between 1971 and 2006, both occupational differentiation and occupational stratification have eroded, but for both women and men, differences persist. Furthermore, these findings are not inconsistent with recent research by Pendakur and Pendakur (2011) that show an increase in the earning gap in the 1990s for both Aboriginal peoples and members of visible minority groups born in Canada, compared

**FIGURE 12.1** MEAN OCCUPATIONAL DISSIMILARITY SCORES, 1931–2006

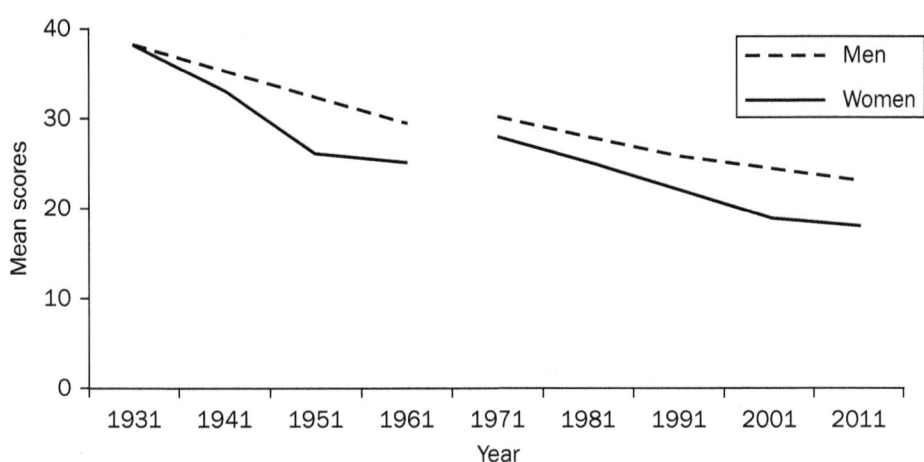

Note: Scores are comparable from 1931 to 1961, using roughly three hundred occupations for women and four hundred for men; between 1971 and 2006, scores increase slightly because more occupations are available for comparison (approximately five hundred for both women and men).

with other Canadian-born labour force participants. Also, work by Hou, Balakrishnan, and Jurdi (2009), shows that recent immigrants to Canada have been faring more poorly than in earlier decades in labour market integration. Based on this research, there is no firm ground on which to conclude that multiculturalism has eliminated the vertical mosaic.

The research design we employed prevents us from investigating which of Porter's two dynamics best explains the continuing level of ethnic inequality: differential immigration or blocked mobility. Our reading of the research literature suggests that differential immigration continues to be the more important factor, especially in terms of visible minorities (Creese and Kambere, 2001; Davies and Guppy, 2010; Sorensen, 1995). That is, ethnicity has less of an effect on inequality for native-born Canadians than it does for immigrants. However, immigration patterns cannot be the sole explanation, because our results are also consistent with research showing that some visible minorities, for example, men of black and South Asian heritage, face earning penalties in the labour market, penalties that are consistent with the blocked mobility thesis (Geschwender and Guppy, 1995; Li, 2000; Pendakur and Pendakur, 2011). Whatever the extent and sources of the vertical mosaic, it coexists with other aspects of ethnic and racial inequality beyond the scope of our analysis, including prejudice, hate, and violence, as well as systematic and systemic discrimination in recruitment, interviewing, hiring, promotion, training, and termination practices.

## NOTES

1. For much of Canada's history, foreign-born workers have had a higher level of education than have native-born Canadians (Légacé, 1968; Boyd, 1985). What this average hides, however, is the tendency for immigrants to be either relatively well educated or relatively poorly educated. Note also that earlier in Canadian history, the credentials of immigrants from the United Kingdom in particular were recognized without question. Now, the credentials of immigrants are frequently not accepted as legitimate professional qualifications for the Canadian labour market (Boyd and Thomas, 2001).

2. In the 1971 and earlier censuses, the census question to determine ethnic origin was: "To which ethnic or cultural group did you or your ancestor (on the male side) belong on coming to this continent?" In 1981, the question was: "To which ethnic or cultural group did you or your ancestors belong on first coming to this continent?" Notice how difficult it is for Aboriginal people especially to answer such a

question accurately. Beginning in 1981, multiple ethnic origins were accepted, and the 2006 question read: "What were the ethnic or cultural origins of this person's ancestors?" Our ethnic categories for 2006 are based on single responses and exclude those reporting multiple ethnic or cultural origins, except for multiple origins involving only constituent groups of certain categories. For example, "British" includes persons who report their origin(s) to be British or any one or more of English, Irish, Scottish, Welsh, and so on, but no non-British origin(s). Scandinavian includes persons who report their origin(s) as Scandinavian or any one or more of Danish, Icelandic, Norwegian, Swedish, and so forth, but no non-Scandinavian origin(s). Although the *2006 Census Guide* still made it clear that ethnic origin did not refer to citizenship, "Canadian" was among the examples listed with the question itself. Our data, however, corroborate Li's (2003: 128) observation that "the growth of people reporting Canadian origin ... did not have a measurable impact on the reporting of ethnic minorities." Finally, given the disbanding of the long-form census, this is likely to be the last time this series can be updated.

3. Just as Lautard and Loree's (1984) average dissimilarity for men in 1961 (29) was about double that reported by Darroch (1979), our 1971 averages for men (30) and women (27) are roughly double Darroch's 1971 average for men and women combined. This shows why trend comparisons are so important; the dissimilarity measure is sensitive to the number of occupations used (Lautard and Loree, 1984: 336). The level of dissimilarity reported by other authors is important as a statement about ethnic differences (i.e., how big or small they might be), but it is comparison over time, using a consistent methodology, that answers questions about how ethnic divisions are changing in Canada.

4. Data for the intervening census years, 1981 and 1991, indicate that the overall decline and pattern in ethnic inequality is comparable to those reported by Lautard and Loree (1984), for the census years studied by Porter (1951 and 1961), as well as for 1971 (Lautard and Guppy, 2004).

## REFERENCES

Agocs, Carol, and Monica Boyd. (1993). "The Canadian Ethnic Mosaic Recast: Theory, Research and Policy Frameworks for the 1990s."

In J. Curtis et al., eds., *Social Inequality in Canada: Patterns, Problems, Policies* (pp. 330–52). Toronto: Prentice-Hall.

Boyd, Monica. (1985). "Immigration and Occupational Attainment." In M. Boyd et al., eds., *Ascription and Attainment: Studies in Mobility and Status Attainment in Canada* (pp. 393–446). Ottawa: Carleton University Press.

Boyd, Monica and Derrick Thomas. (2001). "Match or Mismatch? The Employment of Immigrant Engineers in Canada's Labor Force." *Population Research and Policy Review, 20* (1–2), 107–33.

Creese, Gillian and E. N. Kambere. (2001). "What Colour Is Your English?" *Canadian Review of Sociology and Anthropology, 40* (5), 565–74.

Darroch, Gordon. (1979). "Another Look at Ethnicity, Stratification and Social Mobility in Canada." *Canadian Journal of Sociology, 4* (1), 1–25.

Davies, Scott and Neil Guppy. (2010). *The Schooled Society: An Introduction to the Sociology of Education,* 2nd ed. Toronto: Oxford University Press.

Geschwender, Jim and Neil Guppy. (1995). "Ethnicity, Educational Attainment, and Earned Income among Canadian-Born Men and Women." *Canadian Ethnic Studies, 27* (1), 67–83.

Guppy, N. and K. Lyons. (2012). "Multiculturalism, Education Practices and Colonial Legacies: The Case of Canada." In C. Kassimeris and M. Vryonides, eds., *The Politics of Education: Challenging Multiculturalism* (pp. 114–35). New York: Routledge.

Heath, Anthony and S. Yu. (2005). "Explaining Ethnic Minority Disadvantage." In A. F. Heath, J. Ermish, and D. Gallie, eds., *Understanding Social Change* (pp. 187–224). Oxford, UK: Oxford University Press.

Hou, Feng, T.R. Balakrishnan, and R. Jurdi. (2009). "The Economic Integration of Visible Minorities in Contemporary Canadian Society Revisited." In E. Grabb and N. Guppy, eds., *Social Inequality in Canada: Patterns, Problems, and Policies,* 5th ed. (pp 253–72). Toronto: Pearson Prentice Hall.

Lautard, Hugh and Neil Guppy. (2004). "Multiculturalism or Vertical Mosaic: Occupational Stratification among Canadian Ethnic Groups." In Robert J. Brym, ed., *Society in Question: Sociological Readings for the 21st Century,* 4th ed. (pp. 165–75). Toronto: Nelson.

Lautard, Hugh and Donald Loree. (1984). "Ethnic Stratification in Canada, 1931–1971." *Canadian Journal of Sociology, 9* (3), 333–44.

Légacé, Michael D. (1968). "Educational Attainment in Canada." *Dominion Bureau of Statistics, Special Labour Force Survey No. 7.* Ottawa: Queen's Printer.

Li, Peter. (2000). "Earning Disparities between Immigrants and Native-Born Canadians." *Canadian Review of Sociology and Anthropology, 37* (3), 289–311.

Li, Peter. (2003). *Destination Canada: Immigration Debates and Issues.* Toronto: Oxford University Press.

Nakhaie, M. Reza. (1997). "Vertical Mosaic among the Elites: The New Imagery Revisited." *Canadian Review of Sociology and Anthropology, 34* (1), 1–24.

Ogmundson, Richard and M. Doyle. (2001). "The Rise and Decline of Canadian Labour/1960 to 2000: Elites, Power, Ethnicity and Gender." *Canadian Journal of Sociology, 27* (3), 413–25.

Ogmundson, Richard and J. McLaughlin. (1990). "Trends in the Ethnic Origins of Canadian Elites: The Decline of the BRITS." *Canadian Review of Sociology and Anthropology, 29* (2), 227–42.

Pendakur, Krishna and Ravi Pendakur. (2011). "Colour by Numbers: Minority Earnings in Canada, 1995–2005." *Journal of International Migration and Integration, 12* (3), 305–29.

Pendakur, Ravi. (2002). *Immigrants and the Labour Force: Policy, Regulation, and Impact.* Montreal: McGill-Queen's University Press.

Pineo, Peter and John Porter. (1985). "Ethnic Origin and Occupational Attainment." In M. Boyd et al., eds., *Ascription and Achievement: Studies and Status Attainment in Canada* (pp. 357–92). Ottawa: Carleton University Press.

Porter, John. (1965). *The Vertical Mosaic: An Analysis of Social Class and Power in Canada.* Toronto: University of Toronto Press.

Porter, John. (1985). "Canada: The Social Context of Occupational Allocation." In M. Boyd et al., eds., *Ascription and Achievement: Studies in Mobility and Status Attainment in Canada* (pp. 29–65). Ottawa: Carleton University Press.

Sorensen, Marianne. (1995). "The Match Between Education and Occupation for Immigrant Women in Canada." *Canadian Ethnic Studies, 27* (1): 48–66.

# Gender

Professor Ted Cohen describes an exercise he uses in his gender studies class to demonstrate the significance of gender in the lives of men and women:

*Close your eyes and think carefully about what you believe life must be like for the "opposite sex." Then complete the following statements:*
*"The best thing(s) about being a (male/female) in this society must surely be . . ."*
*"The worst thing(s) about being a (male/female) in this society must surely be . . ."*

Andrew Paterson/Alamy

Professor Cohen has the male students answer the questions about being female and the female students respond to the statements about being male. Following is a summary of the most common responses by his students.

**Women's Views of the Best Things About Being Male**
- Higher pay, access to higher-status positions
- Respect
- Freedom of movement, less fear about safety and the possibility of rape
- No monthly periods, no PMS
- Not having to worry about pregnancy, childbirth, and child care
- Less concern about one's appearance

**Women's Views of the Worst Things About Being Male**
- Need to be stoic and emotionally strong, and tendency to be inexpressive
- Pressure to be the breadwinner or devote oneself to work
- Depleted emotional or physical health: earlier death
- Restricted intimacy

**Men's Views of the Best Things About Being Female**
- Freedom to show feelings, especially vulnerability or affection
- Ability to choose—though within limits—whether to work outside the home or raise children
- Depth of connection felt in relationships
- Giving birth
- Longer life span

**Men's Views of the Worst Things About Being Female**
- Being sexually harassed, assaulted, or objectified
- Being judged and related to so much in terms of one's appearance
- Being underpaid, occupationally segregated, and discriminated against
- Having so much responsibility for children, families, and households

- Having to think so much about one's safety and potential vulnerability
- Being trivialized in conversation and patronized in relationships*

This exercise highlights the significant impact that gender has on our lives. As Professor Cohen explains, gender both constrains and enables us. To further emphasize the impact of "gender," he asks his students one last question:

*Imagine and describe how your life would differ if you had been born and were living as the opposite sex.* (2001:2-3)

Although significant gains have been made in recent years, the responses of Professor Cohen's students clearly demonstrate that gender inequality still exists. As this exercise further demonstrates, this inequality has negative consequences for both men and women. Young men and women continue to live "gendered lives" with societal "scripts" that impose accepted parameters of being male or female. Specific ideas of femininity and masculinity are inescapable products of the society in which we are socialized. Although significant changes have occurred in the last half of the 20th century in terms of work activities, notions of gender remain firmly embedded in social institutions and relationships. Gender is so much a part of who we are that it often goes unexamined. As sociologist Judith Lorber explains, we often take gender and the profound effect it has on our lives for granted:

*From Cohen, Men and Masculinity, 1E. © 2001 Cengage Learning.

*Gender is so much the routine ground of everyday activities that questioning its taken-for-granted assumptions and presuppositions is like thinking about whether the sun will come up. Gender is so pervasive that in our society we assume it is bred into our genes. Most people find it hard to believe that gender is constantly created and re-created out of human interaction, out of social life, and is the texture and order of that social life. Gender, like culture, is a human production that depends on everyone constantly "doing gender."* (2001:19)

In this chapter, we will examine the issue of gender: what it is and how it affects us. Before reading on, test your knowledge about gender inequality by taking the quiz in Box 11.1 on page 306.

## Critical Thinking Questions

1. How would you respond to Professor Cohen's questions? What would you identify as the best and worst aspects of being female or male in today's society?
2. How would you answer Professor Cohen's follow-up question? Describe how your life would differ if you had been born and were living as the opposite sex.
3. What do your answers reveal about gender equality?

| CHAPTER FOCUS QUESTION | What effect does gender inequality have on men and women? |

# LEARNING OBJECTIVES
## AFTER READING THIS CHAPTER, YOU SHOULD BE ABLE TO

**LO-1** Understand how gender is defined and how it differs from "sex."

**LO-2** Explain the significance of gender in our everyday lives.

**LO-3** Discuss how the nature of work affects gender equality in societies

**LO-4** Identify and discuss the primary agents of gender socialization.

**LO-5** Explain the causes of gender inequality in Canada.

**LO-6** Understand how functionalist, conflict, feminist, and interactionist perspectives on gender stratification differ.

BOX 11.1

# SOCIOLOGY AND EVERYDAY LIFE

## How Much Do You Know About Gender Inequality?

| True | False | |
|------|-------|---|
| T | F | 1. The average earnings of employed women are still substantially lower than those of men, even when they are employed full time. |
| T | F | 2. Men continue to outnumber women in Canadian universities. |
| T | F | 3. Most Canadians living in poverty are female. |
| T | F | 4. Men in Canada have a shorter life expectancy than women. |
| T | F | 5. Married couples today who both work full time tend to share the "unpaid labour" fairly equally. |

For answers to the quiz about gender inequality, go to **www.nelson.com/sociologyinourtimes6e.**

## LO-1    UNDERSTANDING GENDER

**gender** The culturally and socially constructed differences between females and males found in the meanings, beliefs, and practices associated with "femininity" and "masculinity."

**Gender** refers to the culturally and socially constructed differences between females and males found in the meanings, beliefs, and practices associated with "femininity" and "masculinity." In contrast, as we will see in Chapter 12, *sex* refers to the biological and anatomical differences between females and males. Although biological differences between women and men are important, most "sex differences" are socially constructed "gender differences." According to sociologists, social and cultural processes—not biological "givens"—are most important in defining what females and males are, what they should do, and what sorts of relations do or should exist between them. Sociologist Judith Lorber summarizes the importance of gender:

> Gender is a human invention, like language, kinship, religion, and technology; like them, gender organizes human social life in culturally patterned ways. Gender organizes social relations in everyday life as well as in the major social structures, such as social class and the hierarchies of bureaucratic organizations. (1994:6)

Virtually everything social in our lives is *gendered:* People continually distinguish between males and females and evaluate them differentially. Gender is an integral part of the daily experiences of both women and men (Mandell, 2001).

A microlevel analysis of gender focuses on how individuals learn gender roles and acquire a gender identity. **Gender role** refers to the attitudes, behaviour, and activities that are socially defined as appropriate for each sex and are learned through the socialization process (Lips, 2007). For example, in Canadian society, males traditionally are expected to demonstrate aggressiveness and toughness, while females are expected to be passive and nurturing. **Gender identity** is a person's perception of the self as female or male. Typically established between 18 months and three years of age, gender identity is a powerful aspect of our self-concept (Lips, 2007). Although this identity is an individual perception, it is developed through interaction with others. As a result, most people form a gender identity that matches their biological sex: Most biological females think of themselves as female and most biological males think of themselves as male.

A macrolevel analysis of gender examines structural features, external to the individual, that perpetuate gender inequality. These structures have been referred to as *gendered institutions,*

**gender role** Attitudes, behaviour, and activities that are socially defined as appropriate for each sex and are learned through the socialization process.

**gender identity** A person's perception of the self as female or male.

meaning that gender is one of the major ways by which social life is organized in all sectors of society. Gender is embedded in the images, ideas, and language of a society and is used as a means to divide up work, allocate resources, and distribute power. For example, every society uses gender to assign certain tasks—ranging from child rearing to warfare—to females and males, and differentially rewards those who perform these duties.

These institutions are reinforced by a *gender belief system* that includes all of the ideas regarding masculine and feminine attributes that are held to be valid in a society. This belief system is legitimated by religion, science, law, and other societal values (Lorber, 2005). For example, gendered belief systems may change over time as gender roles change. Many fathers take care of young children today, and there is a much greater acceptance of this change in roles. However, popular stereotypes about men and women, as well as cultural norms about gender-appropriate appearance and behaviour, serve to reinforce gendered institutions in society.

## LO-2   The Social Significance of Gender

Gender is a social construction with important consequences in everyday life. Just as stereotypes regarding race and ethnicity have built-in notions of superiority and inferiority, gender stereotypes hold that men and women are inherently different in attributes, behaviour, and aspirations. Stereotypes define men as strong, rational, dominant, independent, and less concerned with their appearance. Women are stereotyped as weak, emotional, nurturing, dependent, and anxious about their appearance.

The social significance of gender stereotypes is illustrated by eating problems. The three most common eating problems are anorexia, bulimia, and obesity. With *anorexia,* a person must have lost at least 25 percent of body weight due to a compulsive fear of becoming fat (Ressler, 1998). With *bulimia,* a person binges by consuming large quantities of food and then purges the food by induced vomiting, laxatives, or fasting (Renzetti and Curran, 1992). A relatively new eating disorder—activity bulimia—may become more dangerous than both anorexia and bulimia. *Activity bulimia* is characterized by excessive exercising, usually attached to feelings of guilt about eating. The danger with this eating disorder is that it is virtually impossible to detect until serious health problems arise (Sharell, 1996). With *obesity,* individuals are 20 percent or more above their ideal weight, as established by the medical profession. For a woman 1.7 m (5 ft., 4 in.) tall, that is about 11 kg (25 lbs); for a man 1.8 m  (5 ft., 10 in.) tall, that is about 13.5 kg (30 lbs) (Burros, 1994:1).

Sociologist Becky W. Thompson argues that, based on stereotypes, the primary victims of eating problems are presumed to be white, middle-class, heterosexual women. However, such problems also exist among women of colour, working-class women, lesbians, and some men. According to Thompson, explanations for the relationship between gender and eating problems must take into account a complex array of social factors, including gender socialization and women's responses to problems such as racism and emotional, physical, and sexual abuse (Thompson, 1994; see also Heywood, 1998).

Bodybuilding is another gendered experience. *Bodybuilding* is the process of deliberately cultivating an increase in mass

© Fabio Cardoso/zefa/Corbis

For males, objectification and gender stereotyping may result in excessive bodybuilding.

and strength of the skeletal muscles by means of lifting and pushing weights (Mansfield and McGinn, 1993). In the past, bodybuilding was predominantly a male activity; musculature connoted power, domination, and virility (Klein, 1993). Today, an increasing number of women engage in this activity.

As gendered experiences, eating problems and bodybuilding have more in common than we might think. Women's studies scholar Susan Bordo (2004) has noted that the anorexic body and the muscled body are not opposites but instead are both united against the common enemy of soft, flabby flesh. In other words, the body may be objectified in both compulsive dieting and in compulsive bodybuilding.

## Sexism

> **sexism** The subordination of one sex, usually female, based on the assumed superiority of the other sex.

**Sexism** is the subordination of one sex, usually female, based on the assumed superiority of the other sex. Sexism directed at women has three components: (1) negative attitudes toward women; (2) stereotypical beliefs that reinforce, complement, or justify the prejudice; and (3) discrimination—acts that exclude, distance, or keep women separate (Lott, 1994).

Can men be victims of sexism? Although women are more often the target of sexist remarks and practices, men can be victims of sexist assumptions. According to the social psychologist Hilary M. Lips (2007), an example of sexism directed against men is the mistaken idea that it is more harmful for female soldiers to be killed in battle than male soldiers.

> **patriarchy** A hierarchical system of social organization in which cultural, political, and economic structures are controlled by men.

Like racism, sexism is used to justify discriminatory treatment. When women participate in what is considered gender-inappropriate endeavours in the workplace, at home, or in leisure activities, they often find that they are the targets of prejudice and discrimination. Obvious manifestations of sexism are found in the undervaluing of women's work, in hiring and promotion practices that effectively exclude women from an organization or confine them to the bottom of the organizational hierarchy. Even today, some women who enter nontraditional occupations (such as firefighting and welding) or professions (such as dentistry and architecture) encounter hurdles that men do not face.

> **matriarchy** A hierarchical system of social organization in which cultural, political, and economic structures are controlled by women.

Sexism is interwoven with **patriarchy**—a hierarchical system of social organization in which cultural, political, and economic structures are controlled by men. By contrast, **matriarchy** is a hierarchical system of social organization in which cultural, political, and economic structures are controlled by women; however, few societies have been organized in this manner. Patriarchy is reflected in the way men may think of their position as men as a given, while women may deliberate on what their position in society should be (see Box 11.2 for an example).

## LO-3   WORK AND GENDER INEQUALITY

How do tasks in a society come to be defined as "men's work" or "women's work"? Three factors are important in determining the gendered division of labour in a society: (1) the type of subsistence base, (2) the supply of and demand for labour, and (3) the extent to which women's child-rearing activities are compatible with certain types of work. *Subsistence* refers to the means by which a society gains the basic necessities of life, including food, shelter, and clothing. Based on subsistence, societies are classified as hunting and gathering, horticultural and pastoral, agrarian, industrial, or post-industrial. The first three of these categories are *preindustrial* societies.

### Preindustrial Societies

The earliest known division of labour between women and men is in hunting and gathering societies. While the men hunt for wild game, women gather roots, nuts, seeds and berries. A relatively equitable relationship exists because neither sex has the ability to provide all the food

BOX 11.2   **SOCIOLOGY IN GLOBAL PERSPECTIVE**

## The Rise of Islamic Feminism in the Middle East?

I would like for all of the young Muslim girls to be able to relate to Iman, whether they wear the hijab [head scarf] or not. Boys will also enjoy Iman's adventures because she is one tough, smart girl! Iman gets her super powers from having very strong faith in Allah, or God. She solves many of the problems by explaining certain parts of the Koran that relate to the story.

–Rima Khoreibi, an author from Dubai (United Arab Emirates), explaining that she has written a book about a female Islamic superhero because she would like to dispel a widely held belief that sexism in her culture is deeply rooted in Islam (see theadventuresofiman.com, 2007; Kristof, 2006)

Although Rima Khoreibi and many others who have written fictional and nonfictional accounts of girls and women living in the Middle East typically do not deny that sexism exists in their region or that sexism is deeply interwoven with patriarchy around the world, they dispute the perception that Islam is inherently misogynistic (possessing hatred or strong prejudice toward women). As defined in this chapter, patriarchy is a hierarchical system of social organization in which cultural, political, and economic structures are controlled by men. The influence of religion on patriarchy is a topic of great interest to contemporary scholars, particularly those applying a feminist approach to their explanations of why persistent social inequalities exist between women and men and how these inequalities are greater in some regions of the world than in others.

According to some gender studies specialists, a newer form of feminist thinking is emerging among Muslim women. Often referred to as "feminist Islam" or "Islamic feminism," this approach is based on the belief that greater gender equality may be possible in the Muslim world if the teachings of Islam, as set forth in the Qur'an, the Islamic holy book, are followed more closely. Islamic feminism is based on the principle that Muslim women should retain their allegiance to Islam as

an essential part of their self-determination and identity, but that they should also work to change patriarchal control over the basic Islamic worldview (Wadud, 2002). According to journalist Nicholas D. Kristof, both Islam and evangelical Christianity have been on the rise in recent years because both religions provide "a firm moral code, spiritual reassurance and orderliness to people vexed by chaos and immorality around them, and they offer dignity to the poor" (2006:A22).

Islamic feminists believe that the rise of Islam might contribute to greater, rather than less, equality for women. From this perspective, stories about characters such as Iman may help girls and young women realize that they can maintain their deep religious convictions and their head scarf (hijab) while working for greater equality for women and more opportunities for themselves. In *The Adventures of Iman*, the female hero always wears a pink scarf around her neck and she uses the scarf to cover her hair when she is praying to Allah. Iman quotes the Qur'an when she is explaining to others that Muslims are expected to be tolerant, kind, and righteous. For Iman, religion is a form of empowerment, not an extension of patriarchy.

The focus of Islamic feminism is quite different from what most people view as Western feminism. For example, Islamic feminism puts less emphasis than might be expected on issues such as the wearing of the hijab or the fact that in Saudi Arabia, a woman may own a motor vehicle but cannot legally drive it. As rapid economic development and urbanization affect the lives of many people, however, change is clearly under way in many regions of the Middle East and in other areas of the world.

In light of such differences, consider the following. Why is women's inequality a complex issue to study across nations? What part does culture play in defining the roles of women and men in various societies? How do religious beliefs influence what we think of as "appropriate" or "inappropriate" behaviours for men, women, and children? What do you think?

*Sources:* Kristof, 2006; theadventuresofiman.com, 2007; Wadud, 2002.

necessary for survival. When wild game is nearby, both men and women may hunt. When it is far away, hunting becomes incompatible with child rearing (which women tend to do because they breastfeed their young) and women are placed at a disadvantage in terms of contributing to the food supply (Lorber, 1994). In most hunting and gathering societies, women are full economic partners with men; relations between them tend to be cooperative and relatively egalitarian (Bonvillain, 2001; Chafetz, 1984). Little social stratification of any kind is found because people do not acquire a food surplus.

In horticultural societies, which first developed 10,000 to 12,000 years ago, a steady source of food becomes available. People are able to grow their own food because of hand tools, such as the digging stick and the hoe. Women make an important contribution to food production because cultivation with hoes is compatible with child care. A fairly high degree of gender equality exists because neither sex controls the food supply.

When inadequate moisture in an area makes planting crops impossible, *pastoralism*—the domestication of large animals to provide food—develops. Herding is primarily done by men, and women contribute relatively little to subsistence production in such societies. In some herding societies, women have relatively low status; their primary value is their ability to produce male offspring so that the family lineage can be preserved and enough males will exist to protect the group against attack (Nielsen, 1990). Even so, the relationship between men and women is more equitable than it is in agrarian societies, which first developed about 8000 to 10,000 years ago.

In agrarian societies, gender inequality and male dominance become institutionalized. Agrarian societies rely on agriculture—farming done by animal-drawn or mechanically powered plows and equipment. Because agrarian tasks require more labour and greater physical strength than horticultural ones, men become more involved in food production. It has been suggested that women are excluded from these tasks because they are viewed as too weak for the work and because child-care responsibilities are considered incompatible with the full-time labour that the tasks require (Nielsen, 1990). Most of the world's population currently lives in agrarian societies in various stages of industrialization.

Why does gender inequality increase in agrarian societies? Scholars cannot agree on an answer; however, some suggest that it results from private ownership of property. When people no longer have to move continually in search of food, they can acquire a surplus. Men gain control over the disposition of the surplus and the kinship system, and this control serves men's interests (Lorber, 1994). The importance of producing "legitimate" heirs to inherit the surplus increases significantly, and women's lives become more secluded and restricted as men attempt to ensure the legitimacy of their children. Premarital virginity and marital fidelity are required; indiscretions are punished (Nielsen, 1990). However, some scholars argue that male dominance existed before the private ownership of property (Firestone, 1970; Lerner, 1986).

## Industrial Societies

An *industrial society* is one in which factory or mechanized production has replaced agriculture as the major form of economic activity. As societies industrialize, the status of women tends to decline further. Industrialization in North America created a gap between the nonpaid work performed by women at home and the paid work that was increasingly performed by men and unmarried young women (Krahn and Lowe, 2007).

In Canada, the division of labour between men and women in the middle and upper classes became much more distinct with industrialization. The men were viewed as "breadwinners"; the women were seen as "homemakers." In this new "cult of domesticity" (also referred to as the "cult of true womanhood"), the home became a private, personal sphere in which women created a haven for the family. Those who supported the cult of domesticity argued that women were the natural keepers of the domestic sphere and that children were the mother's responsibility. Meanwhile, the "breadwinner" role placed enormous pressures on men to support their families—providing for them well was considered a sign of manhood. This gendered division of labour increased the economic and political subordination of women.

The cult of true womanhood not only increased white women's dependence on men but also became a source of discrimination against women of colour, based on both their race and the fact that many of them had to work to survive. Employed, working-class white women were similarly stereotyped; they became more economically dependent on their husbands because their wages were so much lower.

## Post-Industrial Societies

Chapter 5 defines *post-industrial societies* as societies in which technology supports a service- and information-based economy. In such societies, the division of labour in paid employment is increasingly based on whether people provide or apply information or are employed in service jobs, such as fast-food restaurant counter help or healthcare workers. For both women and men in the labour force, formal education is increasingly crucial for economic and social success. However, even as some women have moved into entrepreneurial, managerial, and professional occupations, many others have remained in the low-paying service sector, which affords few opportunities for upward advancement.

Will technology change the gendered division of labour in post-industrial societies? Scholars do not agree on the effects of computers, the Internet, cellphones, tablets, and many other newer forms of communications technology on the role of women in society. For example, some feminist writers had a pessimistic view of the impact of computers and monitors on women's health and safety, predicting that women in secretarial and administrative roles would experience an increase in eyestrain, headaches, and problems such as carpal tunnel syndrome. However, some medical experts now believe that such problems extend to both men and women, as computers have become omnipresent in more people's lives. The term *24/7* has come to mean that a person is available 24 hours a day, seven days a week, via cellphone, email, and other means of communication, whether the individual is at the office or a continent away on "vacation."

Although some analysts presumed that technological developments would reduce the boundaries between women's and men's work, researchers have found that the gender stereotyping associated with specific jobs has remained remarkably stable even when the nature of work and the skills required to perform it have been radically transformed. Today, men and women continue to be segregated into different occupations, and this segregation is particularly visible within individual workplaces (as discussed later in the chapter).

How does the division of labour change in families in post-industrial societies? For a variety of reasons, more households are headed by women with no adult male present. This means that women in these households truly have a double burden, both from family responsibilities and from the necessity of holding gainful employment in the labour force. Even in single-person or two-parent households, programming "labour-saving" devices (if they can be afforded) often means that a person must have some leisure time to learn how to do the programming. According to analysts, leisure is deeply divided along gender lines and women have less time to "play in the house" than do men and boys. Some websites seek to appeal to women who have economic resources but are short on time, making it possible for them to shop, gather information, "telebank," and communicate with others at all hours of the day and night.

In post-industrial societies such as Canada, close to 80 percent of adult women are in the labour force. This reality means that despite living in an information- and service-oriented economy, women will continue to bear the heavy burden of finding time to care for children, help aging parents, and meet the demands of the workplace (Marshall, 2011).

How people accept new technologies and the effect these technologies have on gender stratification are related to how people are socialized into gender roles. However, gender-based stratification remains rooted in the larger social structures of society, which individuals have little ability to control.

### TIME TO REVIEW

- How do new technologies influence gender relations in the workplace and the division of labour in the home?
- Is it likely that technology will increase or decrease the divisions between men and women at work and home?

We learn gender-appropriate behaviour through the socialization process. Our parents, teachers, friends, and the media all serve as gendered institutions that communicate to us our earliest, and often most lasting, beliefs about the social meanings of being male or female and thinking and behaving in masculine or feminine ways. Some gender roles have changed dramatically in recent years; others remain largely unchanged over time.

Many parents prefer boys to girls because of stereotypical ideas about the relative importance of males and females to the future of the family and society. Although some parents prefer boys to girls because they believe old myths about the biological inferiority of females, research suggests that social expectations also play a major role in this preference. We are socialized to believe that it is important to have a son, especially as a first or only child. For many years, it was assumed that a male child could support his parents in their later years and carry on the family name.

Across cultures, boys are preferred to girls, especially when the number of children that parents can have is limited by law or economic conditions. For example, in China, which strictly regulates the allowable number of children to one per family, a disproportionate number of female fetuses are aborted. In India, the practice of aborting female fetuses is widespread and female infanticide occurs frequently. As a result, both India and China have a growing surplus of young men who will face a shortage of women their own age. In Canada, sex selection through the use of assisted reproductive technologies has been officially banned since 2004.

### Parents and Gender Socialization

From birth, parents treat children differently on the basis of the child's sex. Baby boys are perceived to be less fragile than girls and tend to be treated more roughly by their parents. Girl babies are thought to be "cute, sweet, and cuddly" and receive more gentle treatment. Parents strongly influence the gender-role development of children by passing on—both overtly and covertly—their own beliefs about gender. When girl babies cry, parents respond to them more quickly, and parents are more prone to talk and sing to girl babies (Wharton, 2004).

The toys that parents select for their children are a significant source of gender socialization. Children's toys reflect their parents' gender expectations. In a study of preschoolers, for example, little boys selected the tool sets over dish sets, indicating that their fathers thought playing with dishes is "bad" (Raag, 1999). Gender-appropriate toys for boys include computer games, trucks and other vehicles, sports equipment, and war toys, such as guns and soldiers. Girls' toys include Barbie dolls, play makeup, and homemaking items.

When children are old enough to help with household chores, boys and girls are often assigned different tasks. Maintenance chores (such as mowing the lawn) are assigned to boys, while domestic chores (such as shopping, cooking, and cleaning the table) are assigned to girls. Chores may also become linked with future occupational choices and personal characteristics. Girls who are responsible for domestic chores, such as caring for younger brothers and sisters, may learn nurturing behaviours that later translate into employment as a nurse or schoolteacher. Boys may learn about computers and other types of technology that lead to different career options.

In the past, most studies of gender socialization focused on white middle-class families and paid little attention to ethnic differences (Raffaelli and Ontai, 2004). According to earlier studies in the United

Are children's toys a reflection of their own preferences and choices? How do toys reflect gender socialization by parents and other adults?

© BananaStock/Thinkstock

States, children from middle- and upper-income families are less likely to be assigned gender-linked chores than children from lower-income backgrounds. In addition, gender-linked chore assignments occur less frequently in African American families, where both sons and daughters tend to be socialized toward independence, employment, and child care (Bardwell, Cochran, and Walker, 1986; Hale-Benson, 1986). Sociologist Patricia Hill Collins (1991) suggests that African American mothers are less likely to socialize their daughters into roles as subordinates; instead, they are likely to teach them a critical posture that allows them to cope with contradictions.

In contrast, a recent study of gender socialization in U.S. Latino/Latina families suggests that adolescent females of Mexican, Puerto Rican, Cuban, or other Central or South American descent receive different gender socialization by their parents than do their male siblings (Raffaelli and Ontai, 2004). Latinas are given more stringent curfews and are allowed less interaction with members of the opposite sex than are the adolescent males in their families. Rules for dating, school activities, and part-time jobs are more stringent for the girls because many parents want to protect their daughters and keep them closer to home.

From an early age, we are encouraged by a number of societal influences to learn gender-appropriate behaviour.

Many parents are aware of the effect that gender socialization has on their children and make a conscientious effort to provide nonsexist experiences for them. Mothers' education and employment have a significant effect on the gender attitudes of their sons and daughters. Many fathers also take an active role in socializing their sons to be thoughtful and caring individuals who do not live by traditional gender stereotypes. However, children's peers often make non-traditional gender socialization much more difficult for parents and their children.

## Peers and Gender Socialization

Peers help children learn prevailing gender role stereotypes, as well as gender-appropriate—and inappropriate—behaviour. During the school years, same-sex peers have a powerful effect on how children see their gender roles; during adolescence, they are often more influential agents of gender socialization than adults (Maccoby and Jacklin, 1987).

Children, especially boys, are more socially acceptable to their peers when they conform to implicit societal norms governing the "appropriate" ways that girls and boys should act in social situations. Male peer groups place more pressure on boys to do "masculine" things than female peer groups place on girls to do "feminine" things. For example, girls wear jeans and other "boy" clothes, play soccer and softball, and engage in other activities traditionally associated with males. But if a boy wears a dress, plays hopscotch with girls, and engages in other activities associated with being female, he will be ridiculed by his peers. This distinction between the relative value of boys' and girls' behaviours strengthens the cultural message that masculine activities and behaviour are more important and more acceptable.

The male bonding that occurs during adolescence is believed to reinforce masculine identity (Gaylin, 1992) and to encourage gender-stereotypical attitudes and behaviour (Huston, 1985; Martin, 1989). For example, male peers have a tendency to ridicule and bully others about their appearance, size, and weight. One woman painfully recalled walking down the halls at school when boys would flatten themselves against the lockers and cry, "Wide load!" At lunchtime, the boys made a production of watching her eat lunch and frequently made sounds like pig grunts or moos (Kolata, 1993). Because peer acceptance is so important for both males and females during their first two decades, such actions can have very harmful consequences for the victims.

As young adults, men and women still receive many gender-related messages from peers. Among university students, for example, peers are organized largely around gender relations and play an important role in career choices and the establishment of long-term, intimate relationships (Holland and Eisenhart, 1990).

Peer pressure is often at its strongest in relation to norms of appearance. As other researchers have shown, peer pressure can strongly influence a person's body consciousness. Women in university often feel pressure to be very thin, as Karen explains:

> "Do you diet?" asked a friend [in my first year of university], as I was stuffing a third homemade chocolate chip cookie in my mouth. "Do you know how many calories there are in that one cookie?"
>
> Stopping to think for a moment as she and two other friends stared at me, probably wanting to ask me the same question, I realized that I really didn't even know what a calorie was . . .
>
> From that moment, I'd taken on a new enemy, one more powerful and destructive than any human can be. One that nearly fought me to the death—my death . . .
>
> I just couldn't eat food anymore. I was so obsessed with it that I thought about it every second . . . In two months, I'd lost thirty pounds . . . Everyone kept telling me I looked great . . .
>
> I really didn't realize that anything was wrong with me . . . There were physical things occurring in my body other than not having my period anymore. My hair was falling out and was getting thinner . . . I would constantly get head rushes every time I stood up . . . When my friends would all go out to dinner or to a party I stayed home quite often, afraid that I might have to eat something, and afraid that my friends would find out that I didn't eat. (Twenhofel, 1993:198)

Feminist scholars have concluded that eating problems are not always psychological "disorders" (as they are referred to by members of the medical profession). Instead, eating (or not eating) may be a strategy for coping with problems, such as unrealistic social pressures about slenderness (see Hesse-Biber, 2006) or social injustices caused by racism, sexism, and classism in society (Thompson, 1994).

## Teachers, Schools, and Gender Socialization

From kindergarten through university, schools operate as gendered institutions. Teachers provide important messages about gender through both the formal content of classroom assignments and informal interaction with students. Sometimes, gender-related messages from teachers and other students reinforce gender roles that have been taught at home; however, teachers may also contradict parental socialization. During the early years of a child's schooling, the teacher's influence is very powerful; many children spend more hours per day with their teachers than they do with their parents.

According to some researchers, the quantity and quality of teacher–student interactions often vary between the education of girls and that of boys (Wellhousen and Yin, 1997). **Gender bias** consists of showing favouritism toward one gender over the other. Gender bias is displayed in a number of different ways in academic settings: through teacher–student interactions, biased or stereotyped resources, and responses to male and female interactions. Although girls are more academically successful than boys, close examination of what goes on in our classrooms shows that girls and boys continue to be socialized in ways that work against gender equality (Chapman, 2003). For example, research indicates that males receive more praise for their contributions and are called on more frequently in class, even when they do not volunteer. Teachers also influence how students treat one another during school hours. Many teachers use sex segregation as a way to organize students, resulting in unnecessary competition between females and males. Competition based on gender often reinforces existing misconceptions about the skills and attributes of boys and girls, and may contribute to overt and subtle discrimination in the classroom and beyond.

**gender bias** Behaviour that shows favouritism toward one gender over the other.

The effect of gender bias is particularly problematic if teachers take a boys-will-be-boys attitude when boys and young men make derogatory remarks or demonstrate aggressive behaviour against girls and young women. When girls complain of **sexual harassment**—unwanted sexual advances, requests for sexual favours, or other verbal or physical conduct of a sexual nature—their concerns are sometimes overlooked or downplayed by teachers and school administrators. Sexual harassment is prohibited by law, and teachers and administrators are obligated to investigate such incidents.

Girls, however, are not alone in experiencing sexual harassment at school. A national U.S survey of more than 2000 public school students in Grades 8 through 11 found that 83 percent of girls and 79 percent of boys reported having experienced sexual harassment at least once, and that one in four of the students surveyed had experienced such harassment often. The same survey found that girls experienced more forms and a higher frequency of harassment than boys (AAUW, 2001). Similar results were reported in Canadian surveys of sexual harassment.

Teachers often use competition between boys and girls because they hope to make a learning activity more interesting. Here, a middle school girl leads other girls against boys in a Spanish translation contest. What are the advantages and disadvantages of gender-based competition in classroom settings?

For example, a 1994 survey of secondary students in Ontario found over 80 percent of female students reported they had been sexually harassed in a school setting. The pervasiveness of sexual harassment in the lives of girls and young women was reconfirmed in a 2002 Canada-wide study of elementary and high school students (Berman, 2002; Mancini, 2012).

Women now constitute a larger proportion of all college and university students. In some academic fields of study, however, women remain a distinct minority and may be more marginalized in classrooms and interpersonal interactions with professors and other students. Men still constitute the majority of majors in architecture, engineering, computer technology, and the physical sciences. Despite such obstacles, women are more likely than men to earn an undergraduate degree, but at the graduate level, the number of women to earn a degree declines dramatically. See Figure 11.1.

> **sexual harassment**
> Unwanted sexual advances, requests for sexual favours, or other verbal or physical conduct of a sexual nature.

## Mass Media and Gender Socialization

The media, including newspapers, magazines, television, movies, and Internet sources, are powerful sources of gender stereotyping. Although some critics argue that the media simply reflect existing gender roles in society, others point out that the media have a unique ability to shape ideas (see Box 11.3 on page 317). Think of the impact that television might have on children if they spend one-third of their waking time watching it, as has been estimated.

From children's cartoons to adult shows, television programs offer more male than female characters. Furthermore, the male characters act in a strikingly different manner from female ones. Male characters in both children's and adult programs are typically aggressive, constructive, and direct, while some female characters defer to others or manipulate them by acting helpless, seductive, or deceitful.

In prime-time television, several significant changes in the past several decades have reduced gender stereotyping; however, men still outnumber women as leading characters, and they are often "in charge" in any setting where both men and women are portrayed. In the popular ABC series *Grey's Anatomy*, for example, the number of women's and men's roles is evenly balanced, but the male characters typically are the top surgeons at the hospital,

FIGURE 11.1     UNIVERSITY DEGREES AWARDED, BY SEX, 2011

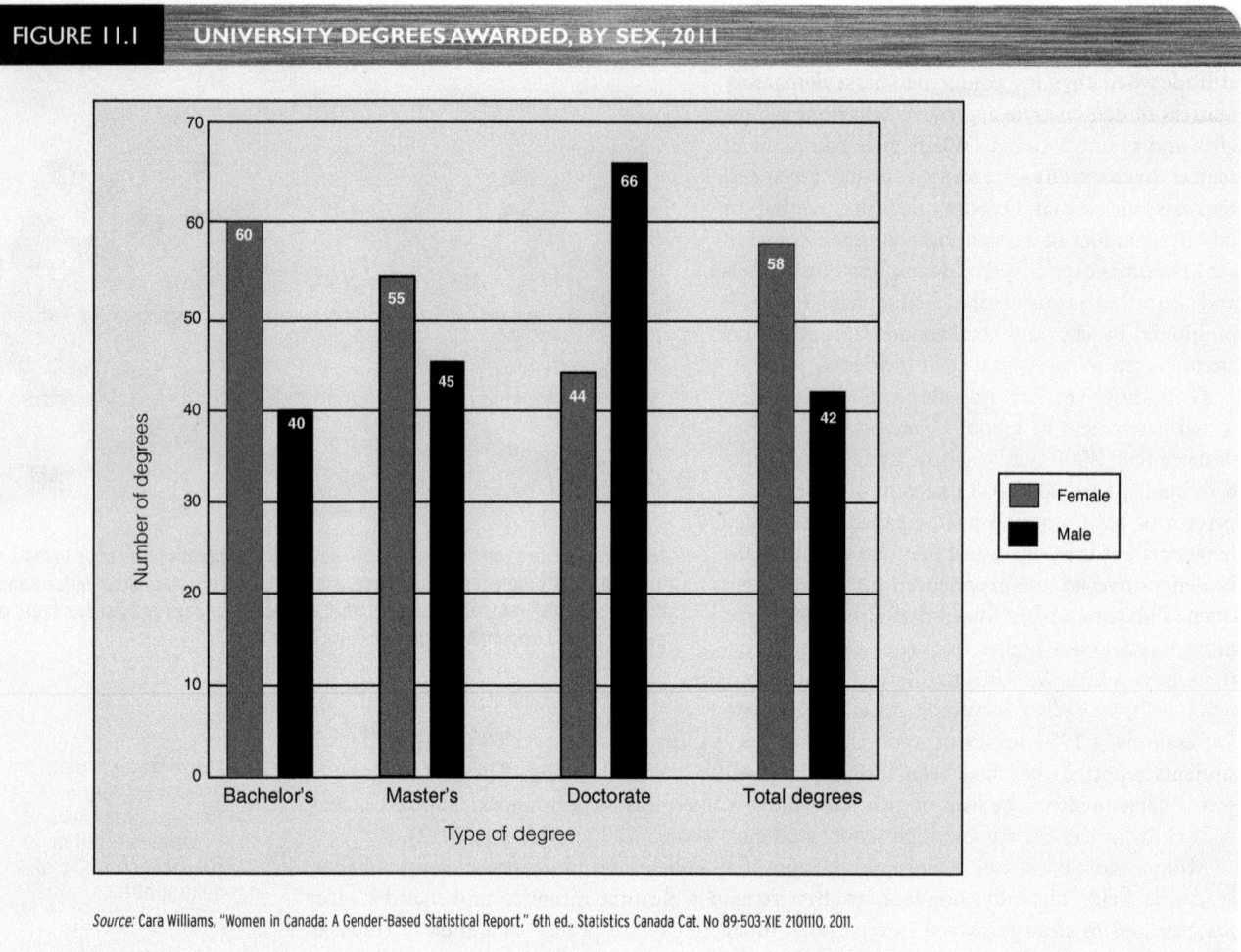

Source: Cara Williams, "Women in Canada: A Gender-Based Statistical Report," 6th ed., Statistics Canada Cat. No 89-503-XIE 2101110, 2011.

whereas the female characters are residents, interns, or nurses. In shows with predominantly female characters, such as *Desperate Housewives or Cougar Town,* the women are typically attractive, thin, and ultimately either hysterical or compliant when dealing with male characters (Stanley, 2004).

Whether on television and billboards or in magazines and newspapers, advertising can send out persuasive messages about gender roles. The intended message is clear to many people: If they embrace traditional notions of masculinity and femininity, their personal and social success is assured; if they purchase the right products and services, they can enhance their appearance and gain power over other people. In commercials, men's roles are typically portrayed differently from women's roles: Men are more likely to be shown working or playing outside the house rather than inside, whereas women are more likely to be doing domestic tasks, such as cooking, cleaning, shopping, or taking care of the children. As such, television commercials may act as agents of socialization, showing children and others what women's and men's designated activities are (Kaufman, 1999).

A study by the sociologist Anthony J. Cortese (2004) found that women—regardless of what they were doing in a particular ad—were frequently shown in advertising as being young, beautiful, and seductive. Although such depictions may sell products, they may also have the effect of influencing how we perceive ourselves and others with regard to issues of power and subordination.

BOX 11.3 **POINT/COUNTERPOINT**

## "You Can Never Be Too Beautiful" and Teen Plastic Surgery

***News Item:* Cosmetic Surgery Is Teenagers' Reward for Passing Exams**

Chinese teenagers are being given cosmetic surgery by their parents as a reward for their hard work in school. Three hospitals in Guangzhou reported that 90 percent of their plastic surgery patients were middle school graduates . . . [whose] parents were paying for the surgery to reward children for passing university entrance exams.

–Ananova News Service, 2005

***News Item:* Teenagers Opt for Cosmetic Surgery**

I'm only a 32B so having a bigger bust would make me feel happier in my clothes . . . I could wear better tops and not have to resort to wearing padded bras to create the illusion of a larger bust.

–Kimberley Brooke, a college student in the United Kingdom, describing why she is interested in having cosmetic surgery (quoted in Atkins, 2005)

***News Item:* For More Teenage Girls, Adult Plastic Surgery**

My family was upset that I was so young. But I explained to them that it was about being confident.

–Nicole Castro of the United States, explaining why she had breast implant surgery (quoted in Boodman, 2004:A1)

Although both men and women seek plastic surgery, the majority of elective cosmetic surgery procedures are performed on women. In the United States and other nations, the number of young women seeking procedures such as rhinoplasty (nose reshaping), breast implants, and liposuction appears to be increasing (Boodman, 2004).

Why do young women want to undergo surgical procedures to make their bodies more "beautiful" or "perfect"? According to some analysts, the pressure to improve one's appearance comes primarily from acquaintances; however, other researchers assert that how the media frame stories about personal appearance influences the way we think about ourselves and the improvements that we may believe our bodies require. If this assertion is correct, media framing plays an important role in the growing phenomenon of young women opting for cosmetic enhancement or change.

For example, television reality shows such as *Extreme Makeover* may encourage people to believe that cosmetic surgery could be the answer to all their problems. These programs are framed in such a manner that the negative attributes of a person's "before" appearance are emphasized and often exaggerated, while the positive aspects of the "after" appearance are carefully highlighted and enhanced for media audiences. This type of framing gives audiences a perception that things were originally worse than they were, that everything afterward is much better than it is, and that surgery is a simple matter. Such stories often have a profound influence on how viewers see themselves and others. And in some cases, media framing even suggests that we should want to look like a celebrity. Consider MTV's *I Want a Famous Face,* where contestants in the second season stated their desire to look like celebrities such as Carmen Electra, Tiffani-Amber Thiessen, Arnold Schwarzenegger, Jennifer Aniston, Britney Spears, Ricky Martin, and Janet Jackson (MTV, 2005).

Before performing cosmetic surgery, physicians are encouraged to carefully evaluate teenagers on factors such as their level of physical and emotional maturity (Canadian Society of Plastic Surgeons, 2009); however, this kind of scrutiny may be overwhelmed by intense media framing of stories that suggests young people are inadequate; by advertising that uses models to sell all kinds of products; and by the advertisements for physical improvements and plastic surgery that are omnipresent in newspapers, magazines, and cable television shows. Magazines for teenage girls, including *Teen Vogue* and *Seventeen,* regularly carry ads for products such as herbal breast enhancement tablets and often have articles about "problems" associated with having small breasts. Music videos make teenagers cognizant of their breast size as they are constantly bombarded with images of scantily clad, generously endowed women (Quart, 2003). Some researchers have found that popular magazines typically describe very tall, very thin women as beautiful and those who are shorter or thicker as plain. As a result of constantly seeing images of tall, thin bodies in the media, many females begin to compare themselves to a body type that is unattainable for 99 percent of all women (Kilbourne, 2000).

Clearly, the media industry is a big business that makes billions of dollars by selling magazines, producing television shows, and reaching audiences through various other avenues; however, it is important for all of us, as media consumers, to ask ourselves if we are being sold ideal images of beauty that are not only unattainable but

*(continued)*

also subject us to procedures, such as cosmetic surgery, that may have adverse consequences. Harvard Medical School psychologist Nancy Etcoff notes that plastic surgery isn't just "someone waving a magic wand and you look better. You're subjecting yourself to potential dangers" (quoted in Kornblum, 2004). Should we be concerned about girls and young women who become so obsessed with their looks that they are willing to pursue risky procedures that may not have the result they so hope to achieve? What do you think?

*Sources:* Ananova News Service, 2005; Atkins, 2005; Boodman, 2004; Canadian Society of Plastic Surgeons, 2009; Kilbourne, 2000; Kornblum, 2004; MTV, 2005; Quart, 2003.

## TIME TO REVIEW

- Consider all of the primary socialization agents considered in this section. Which of these socialization agents have had the greatest impact on your gender identity?

## LO-5    CONTEMPORARY GENDER INEQUALITY

According to feminist scholars, women experience gender inequality as a result of economic, political, and educational discrimination. Women's position in the Canadian workforce reflects their overall subordination in society.

### Gendered Division of Paid Work

The workplace is another example of a gendered institution, and where people are located in the occupational structure of the labour market has a major effect on their earnings. In industrialized countries, most jobs are segregated by gender and by race and ethnicity. Lorber notes that in most workplaces, employees are either gender-segregated or all of the same gender. *Gender-segregated work* refers to the concentration of women and men in different occupations, jobs, and places of work (Reskin and Padavic, 2002). Despite some progress, the majority of employed women continued to work in occupations in which they have been traditionally concentrated. In 2009, 67 percent of all employed women were working in teaching, nursing and related health occupations, clerical or other administrative positions, or sales and service occupations (Ferrao, 2010).

To eliminate gender-segregated jobs in North America, more than half of all men or all women workers would have to change occupations. Moreover, women are severely underrepresented at the top Canadian corporations, at only about 17 percent of the corporate officers in the *Financial Post 500* list (comprising the 500 largest companies in Canada). Of these, only about 6 percent hold the highest corporate officer titles, and only 23 women serve as chief executive officer (Catalyst Canada, 2012). Based on current rates of change, the number of women reaching the top ranks of corporate Canada will not reach an acceptable level of 25 percent until the year 2025. See Table 11.1 for more on gender segregation in occupations.

Although the degree of gender segregation in parts of the professional labour market has declined since the 1970s, racial–ethnic segregation has remained deeply embedded in the social structure. The relationship between visible minority status and occupational status is complex and varies by gender, however. Visible minority males are overrepresented in both lower- and

| TABLE 11.1 | GENDER SEGREGATION BY OCCUPATION |
|---|---|

**PERCENTAGE OF WOMEN IN THE 10 HIGHEST-PAYING OCCUPATIONS**

| | |
|---|---|
| Judges | 25% |
| Specialist physicians | 34% |
| General practitioners and family physicians | 38% |
| Dentists | 31% |
| Senior managers (goods production, utilities, transportation, construction) | 12% |
| Senior managers (financial, communications, other business) | 21% |
| Lawyers | 39% |
| Senior managers (trade, broadcasting, other services) | 19% |
| Engineering managers | 10% |
| Banking, credit, and investment managers | 55% |

**PERCENTAGE OF WOMEN IN THE 10 LOWEST-PAYING OCCUPATIONS**

| | |
|---|---|
| Sewing machine operators | 91% |
| Cashiers | 84% |
| Ironing, pressing, and finishing occupations | 70% |
| Artisans and craftspersons | 52% |
| Bartenders | 55% |
| Harvesting labourers | 54% |
| Service station attendants | 20% |
| Food service attendants and food preparers | 75% |
| Food and beverage servers | 76% |
| Babysitters, nannies, and parents' helpers | 98% |

*Source:* UN Platform for Action Committee, 2005.

higher-status occupations; nonwhite women are heavily overrepresented in lower-paying, low-skilled jobs (Krahn, Lowe, and Hughes, 2007).

*Labour market segmentation*—the division of jobs into categories with distinct working conditions—results in women having separate and unequal jobs (Amott and Matthaei, 1996; Lorber, 2005). The pay gap between men and women is the best documented consequence of gender-segregated work (Reskin and Padavic, 2002). Most women work in lower-paying, less prestigious jobs with little opportunity for advancement. Because many employers assume that men are the breadwinners, men are expected to make more money than women to support their families. For many years, women have been viewed as supplemental wage earners in a male-headed household, regardless of the women's marital status. Consequently, women have not been seen as legitimate workers but mainly as wives and mothers (Lorber, 2005).

Gender-segregated work affects both men and women. Men are often kept out of certain types of jobs. Those who enter female-dominated occupations often have to justify themselves and prove that they are "real men." They have to fight stereotypes (gay, "wimpy," and passive) about why they are interested in such work (Williams, 2004). Even if these assumptions do not push men out of female-dominated occupations, they affect how the men manage their gender identity at work. For example, men in occupations such as nursing emphasize their masculinity, attempt to distance themselves from female colleagues, and try to move quickly into management and supervisory positions (Williams, 2004).

Occupational gender segregation contributes to stratification in society. Job segregation is structural; it does not occur simply because individual workers have different abilities, motivations, and material needs. As a result of gender and racial segregation, employers are able to pay many men of colour and all women less money, promote them less often, and provide fewer benefits. If they demand better working conditions or wages, workers are often reminded of the number of individuals (members of Marx's "reserve army") who would like to have their jobs.

## The Gender Wage Gap

**wage gap** A term used to describe the disparity between women's and men's earnings.

Occupational segregation contributes to a second form of discrimination—the **wage gap**, a term used to describe the disparity between women's and men's earnings. It is calculated by dividing women's earnings by men's to yield a percentage, also known as the *earnings ratio* (Reskin and Padavic, 2002). Today, women who work full time for the whole year still earn just over 70 cents for each dollar earned by their male counterparts (Williams, 2010). One study found that the majority of this wage gap can be explained by fields of study chosen by men and women, the continued overrepresentation of women in low-paying sectors of the economy, and gender differences in the division of time between caregiving and paid employment (Cool, 2010; Drolet, 2011). Marital status has a dramatic impact on the wage gap. The wage gap is smallest between single, never-married men and women (86 percent) and biggest between married men and women (65 percent). As shown in Figure 11.2, the gender wage gap exists for all levels of education. In 2008, women with a bachelor's degree who worked full time for the full year earned 85 cents for every dollar earned by their male counterparts. Once again, this gap is partially attributable to occupational segregation. The majority of female university students enroll in degree programs in education, health professions, fine arts, and the humanities, while males continue to dominate in the fields of science and engineering. Even within occupations that require specialized educational credentials, the wage gap does not disappear—for every dollar earned by men, women earned 65 cents as dentists, 68 cents as lawyers, and 77 cents as university professors (Statistics Canada, 2008k).

## Pay Equity and Employment Equity

A number of strategies have been implemented in an attempt to achieve greater gender equality in the labour market. *Pay equity* attempts to raise the value of the work traditionally performed

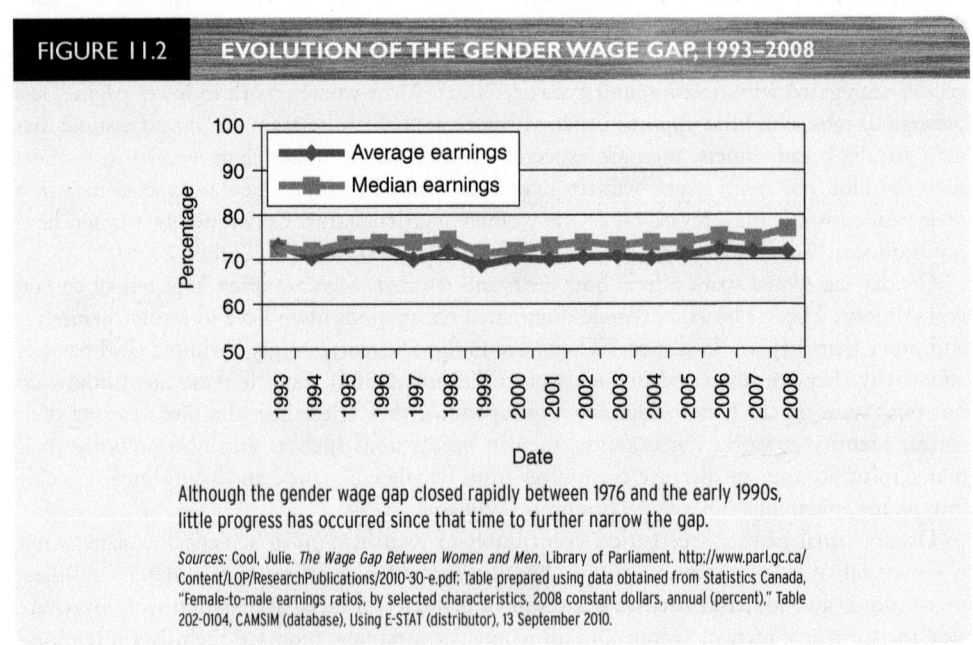

| FIGURE 11.2 | **EVOLUTION OF THE GENDER WAGE GAP, 1993–2008** |

Although the gender wage gap closed rapidly between 1976 and the early 1990s, little progress has occurred since that time to further narrow the gap.

*Sources:* Cool, Julie. *The Wage Gap Between Women and Men.* Library of Parliament. http://www.parl.gc.ca/Content/LOP/ResearchPublications/2010-30-e.pdf; Table prepared using data obtained from Statistics Canada, "Female-to-male earnings ratios, by selected characteristics, 2008 constant dollars, annual (percent)," Table 202-0104, CAMSIM (database), Using E-STAT (distributor), 13 September 2010.

by women. *Employment equity* strategies focus on ways to move women into higher paying jobs traditionally held by men. Since the 1980s, the federal government, some provincial governments, and several private companies have implemented pay equity and employment equity policies (Nelson, 2006).

**Pay equity** (or, as it is sometimes called, **comparable worth**) reflects the belief that wages ought to reflect the worth of a job, not the gender or race of the worker (Kemp, 1994). How can the comparable worth of different kinds of jobs be determined? One way is to compare the work involved in women's and men's jobs and see if there is a disparity in the salaries paid for each. To do this, analysts break a job into components—such as the education, training, and skills required, the extent of responsibility for others' work, and the working conditions—and then allocate points for each (Lorber, 2005). For pay equity to exist, men and women in occupations that receive the same number of points should be paid the same. In short, pay equity promotes the principle of equal pay for work of equal value.

A second strategy for addressing inequality in the workplace is **employment equity**—a strategy to eliminate the effects of discrimination and to make employment opportunities available to groups who have been excluded (Krahn, Lowe, and Hughes, 2007). The target groups for employment equity are visible minorities, persons with disabilities, Aboriginal peoples, and women. In comparison with pay equity, which addresses wage issues only, employment equity covers a range of employment issues, such as recruitment, selection, training, development, and promotion. Employment equity also addresses issues pertaining to conditions of employment, such as compensation, layoffs, and disciplinary action. Critics of employment equity policies have pointed out that the *Employment Equity Act* of 1996 has jurisdiction over a tiny percentage of the population; it covers only federal government employers or companies that have contracts with the federal government. As shown in Figure 11.2 these policies represent a start in the right direction, male resistance and poor regulation and enforcement have resulted in minimal progress toward gendered employment equity (Nelson, 2006). See Figure 11.3.

> **pay equity (comparable worth)** The belief that wages ought to reflect the worth of a job, not the gender or race of the worker.

> **employment equity** A strategy to eliminate the effects of discrimination and to make employment opportunities available to groups who have been excluded.

## Paid Work and Family Work

As previously discussed, the first big change in the relationship between family and work occurred with the Industrial Revolution and the rise of capitalism. The cult of domesticity kept many middle- and upper-class women out of the workforce during this period. Primarily working-class and poor women had to deal with the work/family conflict. Today, however, the issue spans the entire economic spectrum. The typical married woman in Canada combines paid work in the labour force and family work as a homemaker. Although this change has occurred at the societal level, individual women bear the brunt of the problem.

Today, women who work full time for the whole year still earn just over 70 cents for each dollar earned by their male counterparts.

FIGURE 11.3    THE WAGE GAP

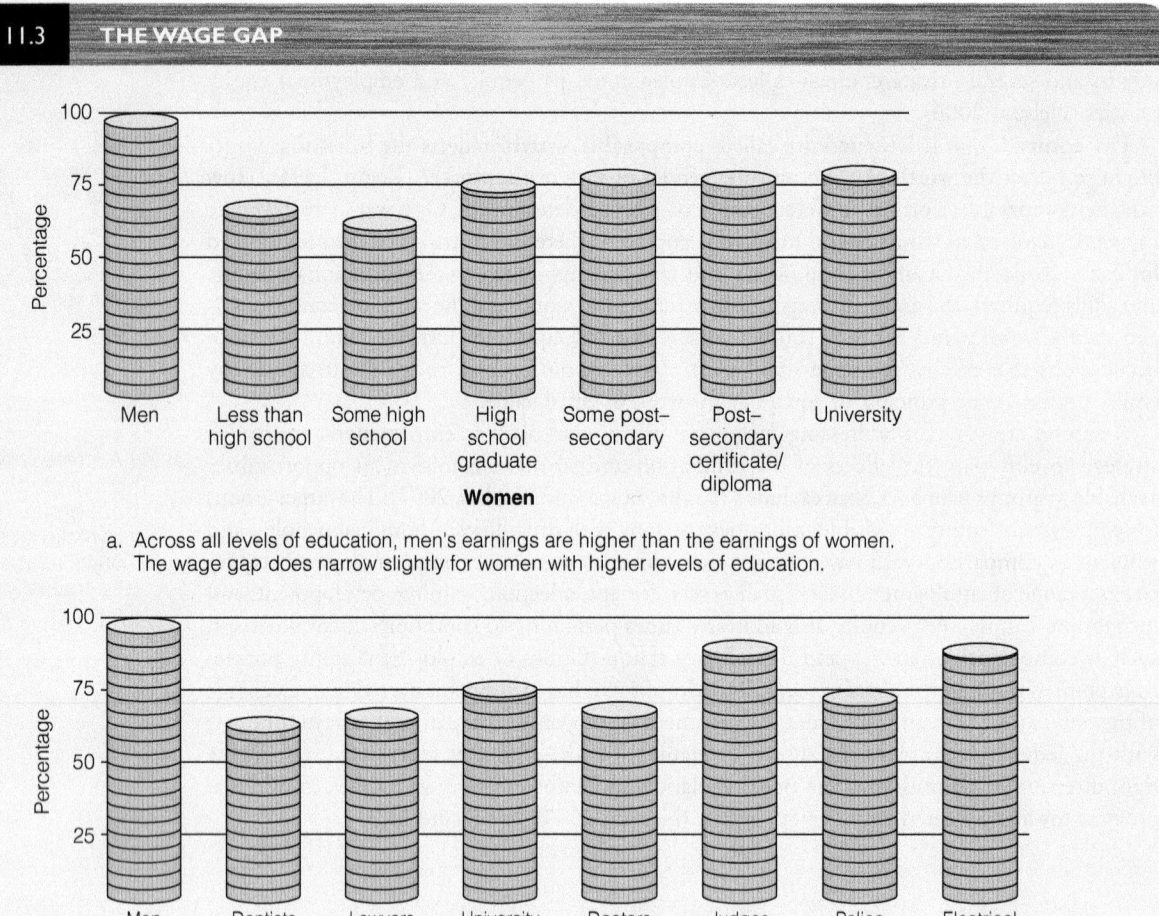

a.  Across all levels of education, men's earnings are higher than the earnings of women.
    The wage gap does narrow slightly for women with higher levels of education.

b.  Regardless of occupation, women on average receive lower wages.

*Sources:* Statistics Canada, 2001f; UN Platform for Action Committee, 2005.

While dramatic changes have occurred in women's participation in the workforce, men's entry into housework has been gradual, prompting some to refer to the latter as a "stalled revolution" (Cooke, 2004, cited in Marshall, 2006:16). Recent time-use surveys have confirmed that the burden of unpaid work continues to rest disproportionately on women. Even when women work full time, most maintain primary responsibility for child care, elder care, housework, shopping, and meal preparation. Among couples, the woman does close to two hours per day more housework than her male partner. Consequently, many women have a "double day" or "second shift" because of their dual responsibilities for paid and unpaid work (Hochschild, 1989, 2003; see also Chapter 13). Working women have less time to spend on housework; if husbands do not help do routine domestic chores, some chores do not get done or get done less often. Although the income that many women earn is essential for the economic survival of their families, they must spend part of their earnings on family maintenance, such as daycare, fast food, and laundry and housecleaning, in an attempt to keep up with their obligations.

NEL

What stereotypes are associated with men in female-oriented occupations? With women in male-oriented occupations? Do you think such stereotypes will change in the near future?

Especially in families with young children, domestic responsibilities consume much time and energy. Although some kinds of housework can be put off, the needs of children often cannot be ignored or delayed. When children are ill or school events cannot be scheduled around work, parents (especially mothers) may experience stressful role conflicts. ("Shall I be a good employee or a good mother?")

Many working women care not only for themselves, their husbands, and their children but also for elderly parents or in-laws. Some analysts refer to these women as "the sandwich generation"—caught between the needs of their young children and elderly relatives. Many women try to solve their time crunch by forgoing leisure time and sleep. When Arlie Hochschild first interviewed working mothers, she found that they talked about sleep "the way a hungry person talks about food" (1989:9). In more recent research, Hochschild (1997) learned that some married women with children found more fulfillment at work and worked longer hours because they liked work better than facing the pressures of home (see Chapter 13).

Although the transition into housework has been slow for men, there is room for optimism as the household–work gender gap slowly narrows. As shown in Figure 13.2 (see page 388), gender differences in the division of labour remain, but they are slowly diminishing. Since 1986, as women have increased their participation in paid work, men have increased their time spent on housework. In particular, men have made significant changes in their participation in core housework, such as meal preparation and cleanup, cleaning, and laundry. For couples with children, there have also been noticeable changes in men's participation in meeting child-care responsibilities and duties (Marshall, 2011). See Figure 11.4.

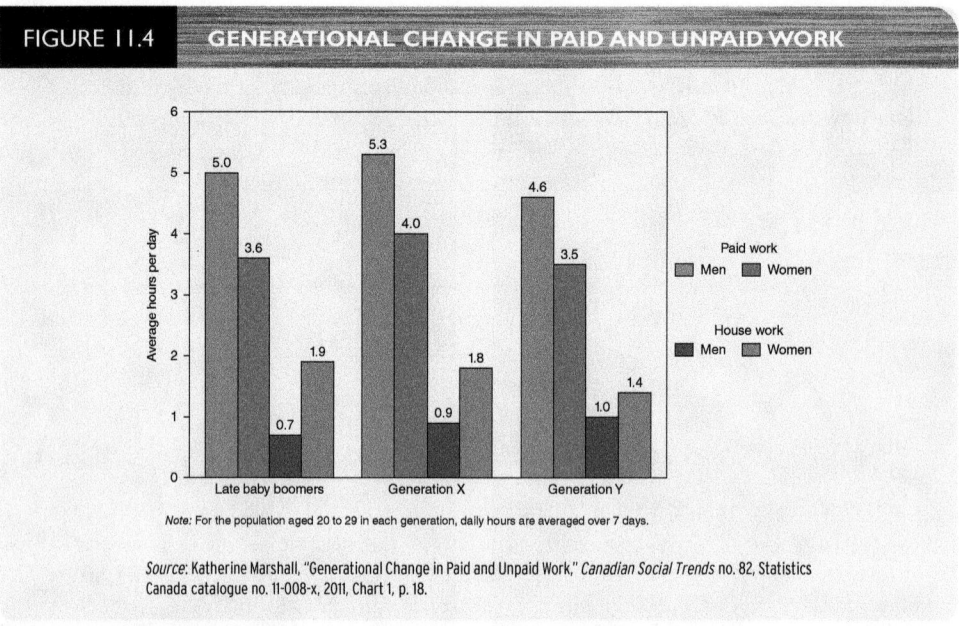

FIGURE 11.4    GENERATIONAL CHANGE IN PAID AND UNPAID WORK

Note: For the population aged 20 to 29 in each generation, daily hours are averaged over 7 days.

Source: Katherine Marshall, "Generational Change in Paid and Unpaid Work," *Canadian Social Trends* no. 82, Statistics Canada catalogue no. 11-008-x, 2011, Chart 1, p. 18.

### TIME TO REVIEW

- Based on your understanding of the gender wage gap, do you think the gap will get larger, smaller, or disappear completely as younger men and women enter the paid workforce? Why or why not?

- Analysts believe that the burden of the "double day" or "second shift" will likely preserve women's inequality at home and in the workplace for another generation. If this is the case, what needs to be done to address the gendered division of unpaid work?

## LO-6    PERSPECTIVES ON GENDER STRATIFICATION

Sociological perspectives on gender stratification vary in their approach to examining gender roles and power relationships in society. Some focus on the roles of women and men in the domestic sphere; others note the inequalities arising from a gendered division of labour in the workplace. Still others attempt to integrate both the public and private spheres into their analyses. The Concept Snapshot on page 330 outlines the key aspects of each sociological perspective on gender stratification.

### Functionalist and Neoclassical Economic Perspectives

As seen earlier, functionalist theory views men and women as having distinct roles that are important for the survival of the family and society. The most basic division of labour is biological: Men are physically stronger, while women are the only ones able to bear and nurse children. Gendered belief systems foster assumptions about appropriate behaviour for men and women and may have an impact on the types of work women and men perform.

**THE IMPORTANCE OF TRADITIONAL GENDER ROLES** According to functional analysts such as Talcott Parsons (1955), women's roles as nurturers and caregivers are even more pronounced in contemporary industrialized societies. While the husband performs the *instrumental* tasks of providing economic support and making decisions, the wife assumes the *expressive* tasks of providing affection and emotional support for the family. This division of family labour ensures that important societal tasks will be fulfilled; it also provides stability for family members.

This view has been adopted by a number of conservative analysts who assert that relationships between men and women are damaged when changes in gender roles occur and that family life suffers as a consequence. From this perspective, the traditional division of labour between men and women is the natural order of the universe.

THE HUMAN CAPITAL MODEL Functionalist explanations of occupational gender segregation are similar to neoclassical economic perspectives, such as the human capital model (Horan, 1978; Kemp, 1994). According to this model, individuals vary widely in the amount of human capital they bring to the labour market. *Human capital* is acquired by education and job training; it is the source of a person's productivity and can be measured in terms of the return on the investment (wages) and the cost (schooling or training) (Kemp, 1994; Stevenson, 1988).

From this perspective, what individuals earn is the result of their own choices (the kinds of training, education, and experience they accumulate, for example) and of the labour market need (demand) for and availability (supply) of certain kinds of workers at specific times. For example, human capital analysts argue that women diminish their human capital when they leave the labour force to engage in childbearing and child-care activities. While women are out of the labour force, their human capital deteriorates from non-use. When they return to work, women earn lower wages than men because they have fewer years of work experience and because their education and training may have become obsolete. They have "atrophied human capital" (Kemp, 1994:70).

Other neoclassical economic models attribute the wage gap to such factors as (1) the different amounts of energy men and women expend on their work (women who spend much energy on their family and household have less to put into their work), (2) the occupational choices women make (choosing female-dominated occupations so that they can spend more time with their families), and (3) the crowding of too many women into some occupations (which suppresses wages because the supply of workers exceeds demand) (Kemp, 1994).

EVALUATION OF FUNCTIONALIST AND NEOCLASSICAL ECONOMIC PERSPECTIVES Although Parsons and other functionalists did not specifically endorse the gendered division of labour, their analysis views it as natural and perhaps inevitable. Critics argue that problems inherent in traditional gender roles, including the strains placed by these roles on both men and women, and the social costs to society, are minimized by this approach. For example, men are assumed to be "money machines" for their families when they might prefer to spend more time in child-rearing activities. Also, the woman's place is assumed to be in the home, an idea that ignores the fact that many women hold jobs out of economic necessity.

Couples & Families CD 79

According to the human capital model, women earn less in the labour market because of their child-rearing responsibilities. What other explanations are offered for the lower wages that women receive?

Another limitation of the functionalist approach is that it does not take a critical look at the structure of society—especially the economic inequalities—that make educational and occupational opportunities more available to some than to others. Furthermore, it fails to examine the underlying power relations between men and women or to consider that the tasks assigned to women and men are unequally valued by society (Kemp, 1994). Similarly, the human capital model is rooted in the premise that individuals are evaluated based on their human capital in an open, competitive market where education, training, and other job-enhancing characteristics are taken into account. From this perspective, those who make less money (often men from visible minority groups and all women) have no one to blame but themselves.

## Conflict Perspectives

According to many conflict analysts, the gendered division of labour within families and in the workplace results from male control of and dominance over women and resources. Differentials between men and women may exist in terms of economic, political, physical, and/or interpersonal power. The importance of a male monopoly in any of these arenas depends on the significance of that type of power in a society (Richardson, 1993). In hunting and gathering and horticultural societies, male dominance over women is limited because all members of the society must work to survive (Collins, 1971; Nielsen, 1990). In agrarian societies, however, male sexual dominance is at its peak. Male heads of household gain a monopoly not only on physical power but also on economic power, and women become sexual property.

Although men's ability to use physical power to control women diminishes in industrial societies, men still remain the household heads and control the property. Men also gain more power through their predominance in the most highly paid and prestigious occupations and the highest elected offices. In contrast, women have the ability to trade their sexual resources, companionship, and emotional support in the marriage market for men's financial support and social status; as a result, however, women as a group remain subordinate to men (Collins, 1971; Nielsen, 1990).

All men are not equally privileged, though. Some analysts argue that women and men in the upper classes are more privileged, because of their economic power, than men in lower-class positions and members of some minority groups (Lorber, 1994). In industrialized societies, persons who occupy elite positions in corporations, universities, the mass media, and government or who have great wealth have the most power (Richardson, 1993). Most, however, are men.

Conflict theorists in the Marxist tradition assert that gender stratification results from private ownership of the means of production; some men not only gain control over property and the distribution of goods but also gain power over women. According to Friedrich Engels and Karl Marx, marriage serves to enforce male dominance. Men of the capitalist class instituted monogamous marriage (a gendered institution) so that they could be certain of the paternity of their offspring, especially sons, whom they wanted to inherit their wealth. Feminist analysts have examined this theory, among others, as they have sought to explain male domination and gender stratification.

## Feminist Perspectives

**feminism** The belief that women and men are equal and that they should be valued equally and have equal rights.

**Feminism**—the belief that women and men are equal and that they should be valued equally and have equal rights—is embraced by many men as well as women. Gender is viewed as a socially constructed concept that has important consequences in the lives of all people (Craig, 1992). According to sociologist Ben Agger (1993), men can be feminists and propose feminist theories; both women and men have much in common as they seek to gain a better understanding of the causes and consequences of gender inequality.

Although all feminist perspectives begin with the assumption that the majority of women occupy a subordinate position to men, they often diverge in terms of their explanations of how and why women are subordinated and the best strategies for achieving true equality for women (Chunn, 2000). Feminist perspectives vary in their analyses of the ways in which norms, roles, institutions, and internalized expectations limit women's behaviour. Taken together, they all seek to demonstrate how women's personal control operates even within the constraints of a relative lack of power (Stewart, 1994).

**LIBERAL FEMINISM**  In liberal feminism, gender equality is equated with equality of opportunity. Liberal feminists assume that women's inequality stems from the denial to them of equal rights (Mandell, 2001). Liberal feminism strives for sex equality through the elimination of laws that differentiate people by gender. Only when these constraints on women's participation are removed will women have the same chance of success as men. This approach notes the importance of gender-role socialization and suggests that changes need to be made in what children learn from their families, teachers, and the media about appropriate masculine and feminine attitudes and behaviour. Liberal feminists fight for better child-care options, a woman's right to choose an abortion, and elimination of sex discrimination in the workplace.

**RADICAL FEMINISM**  According to radical feminists, male domination causes all forms of human oppression, including racism and classism (Tong, 1989). Radical feminists often trace the roots of patriarchy to women's childbearing and child-rearing responsibilities, which make them dependent on men (Chafetz, 1984; Firestone, 1970). In the radical feminist view, men's oppression of women is deliberate, and ideological justification for this subordination is provided by other institutions, such as the media and religion. For women's condition to improve, radical feminists claim, patriarchy must be abolished. If institutions currently are gendered, alternative institutions—such as women's organizations seeking better health care, daycare, and shelters for victims of domestic violence and sexual assault—should be developed to meet women's needs.

**SOCIALIST FEMINISM**  Socialist feminists suggest that the oppression of women results from their dual roles as paid *and* unpaid workers in a capitalist economy. In the workplace, women are exploited by capitalism; at home, they are exploited by patriarchy (Kemp, 1994). Women are easily exploited in both sectors; they are paid low wages and have few economic resources. Gendered job segregation is "the primary mechanism in capitalist society that maintains the superiority of men over women, because it enforces lower wages for women in the labour market" (Hartmann, 1976:139). As a result, women must do domestic labour either to gain a better-paid man's economic support or to stretch their own wages (Lorber, 1994). According to socialist feminists, the only way to achieve gender equality is to eliminate capitalism and develop a socialist economy that would bring equal pay and rights to women.

**MULTICULTURAL FEMINISM**  During the "second wave" of feminism (1970–1990), the mainstream feminist movement was criticized for ignoring the experiences of poor women, women of colour, and women with disabilities. Feminism in its various forms described middle-class white women's experiences as the norm, and other women's experiences were treated as "different" (Cassidy, Lord, and Mandell, 2001). Recently, academics and activists have been attempting to address these criticisms and working to include the experiences of women of colour and Aboriginal women. Antiracist feminist perspectives are based on the belief that women of colour experience a different world than do middle-class white women because of multilayered oppression based on race and ethnicity, gender, and class (Khayatt, 1994). Building on the civil rights and feminist movements of the late 1960s and early 1970s, contemporary feminists have focused on the cultural experiences of marginalized women, such as women of colour, immigrant women, and Aboriginal women. A central assumption of this analysis is that race, class, and gender are forces that simultaneously oppress some women (Hull, Bell-Scott, and Smith, 1982). The effects of these statuses cannot be adequately explained as "double" or "triple" jeopardy (class plus race plus gender) because these ascribed characteristics are not simply added to one another. Instead, they are multiplicative (race times class times gender); different characteristics may be more significant in one situation than another. For example, a wealthy white woman (class) may be in a position of privilege as compared with people of colour (race) and men from lower socioeconomic positions (class), yet be in a subordinate position as compared to a white man (gender) from the capitalist class (Andersen and Collins, 1998). To analyze the complex relationship among these characteristics, the lived experiences of women of colour and other previously "silenced" people must be heard and examined within the context of particular historical and social conditions.

Feminists who analyze race, class, and gender suggest that equality will occur only when all women, regardless of race and ethnicity, class, age, religion, sexual orientation, or ability (or disability), are treated more equitably (Cassidy, Lord, and Mandell, 2001).

**POSTMODERNIST FEMINISM** One of the more recent feminist perspectives to emerge is *postmodernist feminism.* Postmodernist feminists argue that the various feminist theories—liberal, Marxist, radical, and socialist among them—that advocate a single or limited number of causes for women's inequality and oppression are flawed, inadequate, and typically based on suppression of female experiences. In keeping with the assumptions of postmodernist theory, postmodernist feminists resist making generalizations about "all women." Rather, they attempt to acknowledge the individual experiences and perspectives of women of all classes, races, ethnicities, abilities, sexualities, and ages. To postmodernist feminists, a singular feminist theory is impossible because there is no essential "woman." The category *woman* is seen as a social construct that is "a fiction, a non-determinable identity" (Cain, 1993, cited in Nelson, 2006:94).

Given that the category *woman* is regarded as socially constructed, the challenge of postmodernist feminism is to "deconstruct" these notions of the natural or essential woman. For example, the traditional sciences, in particular medicine, have viewed reproduction as a central construct of "woman." As Phoenix and Woolett have argued, "Women continue to be defined in terms of their biological functions" such that "motherhood and particularly childbearing continues to be defined as the supreme route to physical and emotional fulfillment and as essential for all women" (1991:7). Postmodernist feminists challenge the concept of the reproductive woman as essential and highlight the oppressive nature of such so-called scientific knowledge.

Postmodernist feminists strive to deconstruct our traditional understanding of what constitutes being female or male in society today. They argue that nothing is essentially male or female. In fact, they go so far as to challenge the idea of any real biological categories of male or female—suggesting, rather, that our understanding of biological differences between the sexes is of socially constructed categories that have emerged from specific cultural and historical contexts. Some scholars view the distinction between sex and gender as false because it is based on the assumption of biological differences as real. In sum, the categories of male and female, and man and woman, are viewed by postmodernist feminists as fluid, artificial, and malleable (Anderson, 2006:395).

Critics have suggested that this understanding of gender contradicts the fundamental principle of other feminist perspectives—that is, a central focus on women. As one critic asks, "How can it ascribe to be feminist, since feminism is a theory that focuses on the unitary category 'woman'?" (Cain, 1993:76).

**EVALUATION OF CONFLICT AND FEMINIST PERSPECTIVES** Conflict and feminist perspectives provide insights into the structural aspects of gender inequality in society. These approaches emphasize factors external to individuals that contribute to the oppression of women; however, they have been criticized for emphasizing the differences between men and

NEL

women without taking into account their commonalities. Feminist approaches have also been criticized for their emphasis on male dominance without a corresponding analysis of the ways in which some men also may be oppressed by patriarchy and capitalism.

## Symbolic Interactionist Perspectives

In contrast to functionalist, conflict, and feminist theorists, who focus primarily on macrolevel analysis of structural and systemic sources of gender differences and inequities, symbolic interactionists focus on a microlevel analysis that views a person's identity as a product of social interactions. From this perspective, people create, maintain, and modify gender as they go about their everyday lives. Candace West and Don Zimmerman utilized a symbolic interactionist perspective to explain what they refer to as "doing gender." An individual is "doing gender" whenever he or she interacts with another in a way that displays characteristics of a particular gender. This perspective views gender not as fixed in biology or social roles, but rather as something that is "accomplished" through interactions with others. They explain:

> Gender is not a set of traits, nor a variable, nor a role, but the product of social doings of some sort. What then is the social doing of gender? It is more than the continuous creation of the meaning of gender through human actions. We claim that gender itself is constituted through interaction. (1991:16)

In illustrating the concept of "doing gender," West and Zimmerman refer to a case study of Agnes, a transgender raised as a boy until she adopted a female identity at age 17. Although Agnes underwent a sex reassignment operation several years later, she had the challenging task of displaying herself as female even though she had never experienced the everyday interactions that women use to attach meaning to the concept of being female. Agnes had to display herself as a woman while simultaneously learning what it was to be a woman. To make matters more difficult, she was attempting to do so when most people at that age "do gender" virtually without thinking. As West and Zimmerman explain, this does not make Agnes's gender artificial:

> She was not faking what real women do naturally. She was obliged to analyze and figure out how to act within socially constructed circumstances and conceptions of femininity that women born with the appropriate biological credentials take for granted early on . . . As with others who must "pass" . . . Agnes's case makes visible what culture has made invisible—the accomplishment of gender. (1991:18)

Can you think of ways in which you "do gender" in your daily interactions? Using a symbolic interactionist perspective helps us to understand how we create, sustain, or change the gender categories that constitute being a man or a woman in our society. Analysts emphasize that socialization into gender roles is not simply a passive process whereby people internalize others' expectations, but rather people can choose to "do gender" (Messner, 2000, cited in Anderson, 2006). The interactionist perspective has been criticized for failing to address the power differences between men and women, as well as the significant economic and political advantages that exist in the larger social structure (Anderson, 2006).

### TIME TO REVIEW

- Do any of these socialization agents discussed previously provide you with conflicting messages about how you "do gender"?

## CONCEPT SNAPSHOT

| | |
|---|---|
| **FUNCTIONALIST PERSPECTIVES**<br><br>**Key thinker:** Talcott Parsons | According to functionalists, the division of labour into instrumental tasks for men and expressive tasks for women ensures stability in society. |
| **NEOCLASSICAL ECONOMIC PERSPECTIVE** | Human capital analysts argue that women create "atrophied human capital" when they leave the labour force to engage in childbearing and child-care activities. While women are out of the labour force, their human capital deteriorates from nonuse. When they return to work, women earn lower wages than men because they have fewer years of work experience and because their education and training may have become obsolete. |
| **CONFLICT PERSPECTIVES**<br><br>**Key thinkers:** Friedrich Engels, Karl Marx | According to conflict theorists Engels and Marx, marriage serves to enforce male dominance. Men of the capitalist class instituted monogamous marriage (a gendered institution) so that they could be certain of the paternity of their offspring, especially sons, whom they wanted to inherit their wealth. |
| **FEMINIST PERSPECTIVES** | Feminist perspectives vary in their analyses of the ways in which norms, roles, institutions, and internalized expectations limit women's behaviour. Taken together, they all seek to demonstrate how women's personal control operates even within the constraints of a relative lack of power. |
| **SYMBOLIC INTERACTIONIST PERSPECTIVES**<br><br>**Key thinkers:** Candace West, Don Zimmerman | From this perspective, people create, maintain, and modify gender as they go about their everyday lives. Candace West and Don Zimmerman utilized a symbolic interactionist perspective to explain what they refer to as "doing gender" whenever he or she interacts with another in a way that displays characteristics of a particular gender. |

**11**

## LO-1
**Understand how gender is defined and how it differs from "sex."**

*Sex* refers to the biological categories and manifestations of femaleness and maleness; *gender* refers to the socially constructed differences between females and males. In short, sex is what we (generally) are born with; gender is what we acquire through socialization.

*Andrew Paterson/Alamy*

*© Fabio Cardoso/zefa/Corbis*

## LO-2
**Explain the significance of gender in our everyday lives.**

Gender role encompasses the attitudes, behaviours, and activities that are socially assigned to each sex and that are learned through socialization. Gender identity is an individual's perception of self as either female or male. Gendered institutions are those structural features that perpetuate gender inequality.

## LO-3
**Discuss how the nature of work affects gender equality in societies.**

In most hunting and gathering societies, fairly equitable relationships exist because neither sex has the ability to provide all of the food necessary for survival. In horticultural societies, cultivation with hoes is compatible with child care and a fair degree of gender equality exists because neither sex

*© Spencer Grant/PhotoEdit*

controls the food supply. In agrarian societies, male dominance is apparent; agrarian tasks require more labour and physical strength, and women often are excluded from these tasks because they are viewed as too weak or too tied to child-rearing activities. In industrialized societies, a gap exists between nonpaid work performed by women at home and paid work performed by men and women. A wage gap also exists between men and women in the marketplace. In post-industrial societies, the division of labour in paid employment is increasingly based on whether people provide or apply information or are employed in service jobs.

## KEY TERMS

**employment equity** A strategy to eliminate the effects of discrimination and to make employment opportunities available to groups who have been excluded. (p. 321).

**feminism** The belief that women and men are equal and that they should be valued equally and have equal rights (p. 326).

**gender** The culturally and socially constructed differences between females and males found in the meanings, beliefs, and practices associated with "femininity" and "masculinity." (p. 306).

**gender bias** Behaviour that shows favouritism toward one gender over the other (p. 314).

**gender identity** A person's perception of the self as female or male (p. 306).

**gender role** Attitudes, behaviour, and activities that are socially defined as appropriate for each sex and are learned through the socialization process (p. 306).

**matriarchy** A hierarchical system of social organization in which cultural, political, and economic structures are controlled by women (p. 308).

**patriarchy** A hierarchical system of social organization in which cultural, political, and economic structures are controlled by men (p. 308).

**pay equity (comparable worth)** The belief that wages ought to reflect the worth of a job, not the gender or race of the worker (p. 321).

sexism The subordination of one sex, usually female, based on the assumed superiority of the other sex (p. 308).

sexual harassment Unwanted sexual advances, requests for sexual favours, or other verbal or physical conduct of a sexual nature (p. 315).

wage gap A term used to describe the disparity between women's and men's earnings (p. 320).

**LO-4** Identify and discuss the primary agents of gender socialization.

Parents, peers, teachers and schools, sports, and the media are agents of socialization that tend to reinforce stereotypes of gender-appropriate behaviour.

**LO-5** Explain the causes of gender inequality in Canada.

Gender inequality results from economic, political, and educational discrimination against women. In most workplaces, jobs are either gender-segregated or the majority of employees are of the same gender. Although the degree of gender segregation in the professional workplace has declined since the 1970s, racial and ethnic segregation remains deeply embedded.

**LO-6** Understand how functionalist, conflict, feminist, and interactionist perspectives on gender stratification differ.

According to functional analysts, women's roles as caregivers in contemporary industrialized societies are crucial in ensuring that key societal tasks are fulfilled. Whereas the husband performs the instrumental tasks of economic support and decision making, the wife assumes the expressive tasks of providing affection and emotional support to the family. According to conflict analysis, the gendered division of labour within families and the workplace—particularly in agrarian and industrial societies—results from male control and dominance over women and resources.

Although feminist perspectives vary in their analyses of women's subordination, they all advocate social change to eradicate gender inequality. In liberal feminism, gender equality is connected to equality of opportunity. In radical feminism, male dominance is seen as the cause of oppression. According to socialist feminists, women's oppression results from their dual roles as paid and unpaid workers. Antiracist feminists focus on including knowledge and awareness of the lives of marginalized women in the struggle for equality. Postmodernist feminists focus on deconstructing what they see as fluid, artificial notions of the category *woman*. Symbolic interactionists view gender not as fixed in biology or social roles, but rather as something that is "accomplished" through interactions with others. An individual is viewed as "doing gender." whenever he or she interacts with another in a way that displays characteristics of a particular gender.

# APPLICATION QUESTIONS

1. As discussed throughout this chapter, gender may be viewed as a social construction. "Doing gender," whether you are male or female, is something you have learned through a process of socialization. What changes would you have to make in your "gender performance" if you were to wake up one morning as the opposite gender?

2. Do the media reflect societal attitudes on gender, or do the media determine and teach gender behaviour? (As a related activity, watch television for several hours and list the roles women and men play in the shows and the advertisements.)

3. Examine the various academic departments at your university. What is the gender breakdown of the faculty in selected departments? What is the gender breakdown of undergraduates and graduate students in those departments? Are there major differences among various academic areas of teaching and study? What hypotheses can you come up with to explain your observations?

 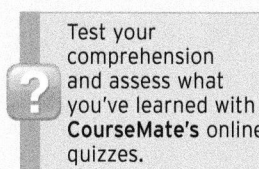 Test your comprehension and assess what you've learned with **CourseMate's** online quizzes.

 For other interesting Lived Experiences, watch the video clips on **CourseMate.**

 Practise what you've learned with flashcards containing key terms and definitions on **CourseMate.**

# 18

## Sex and Gender Through the Prism of Difference

MAXINE BACA ZINN, PIERRETTE HONDAGNEU-SOTELO, AND MICHAEL MESSNER

"Men can't cry." "Women are victims of patriarchal oppression." "After divorces, single mothers are downwardly mobile, often moving into poverty." "Men don't do their share of housework and child care." "Professional women face barriers such as sexual harassment and a 'glass ceiling' that prevent them from competing equally with men for high-status positions and high salaries." "Heterosexual intercourse is an expression of men's power over women." Sometimes, the students in our sociology and gender studies courses balk at these kinds of generalizations. And they are right to do so. After all, some men are more emotionally expressive than some women, some women have more power and success than some men, some men do their share—or more—of housework and child care, and some women experience sex with men as both pleasurable and empowering. Indeed, contemporary gender relations are complex and changing in various directions, and as such, we need to be wary of simplistic, if handy, slogans that seem to sum up the essence of relations between women and men.

On the other hand, we think it is a tremendous mistake to conclude that "all individuals are totally unique and different," and that therefore all generalizations about social groups are impossible or inherently oppressive. In fact, we are convinced that it is this very complexity, this multifaceted nature of contemporary gender relations, that fairly begs for a sociological analysis of gender. We use the image of "the prism of difference" to illustrate our approach to developing this sociological perspective on contemporary gender relations. The *American Heritage Dictionary* defines "prism," in part, as "a homogeneous transparent solid, usually with triangular bases and rectangular sides, used to produce or analyze a continuous spectrum." Imagine a ray of light—which to the naked eye appears to be only one color—refracted through a prism onto a white wall. To the eye, the result is not an infinite, disorganized scatter of individual colors. Rather, the refracted light displays an order, a structure of relationships among the different colors—a rainbow. Similarly, we propose to use the "prism of difference"... to analyze a continuous spectrum of people, in order to show how gender is organized and experienced differently when refracted through the prism of

SOURCE: From Maxine Baca Zinn, Pierrette Hondagneu-Sotelo, and Michael Messner, eds. *Gender through the Prism of Difference* 2nd ed., pp. 1–6. Copyright © 2005. Reprinted by permission of Oxford University Press, Inc.

151

sexual, racial/ethnic, social class, physical abilities, age, and national citizenship differences.

## EARLY WOMEN'S STUDIES: CATEGORICAL VIEWS OF "WOMEN" AND "MEN"

... It is possible to make good generalizations about women and men. But these generalizations should be drawn carefully, by always asking the questions "*which* women?" and "*which* men?" Scholars of sex and gender have not always done this. In the 1960s and 1970s, women's studies focused on the differences *between* women and men rather than *among* women and men. The very concept of gender, women's studies scholars demonstrated, is based on socially defined difference between women and men. From the macro level of social institutions such as the economy, politics, and religion, to the micro level of interpersonal relations, distinctions between women and men structure social relations. Making men and women *different* from one another is the essence of gender. It is also the basis of men's power and domination. Understanding this was profoundly illuminating. Knowing that difference produced domination enabled women to name, analyze, and set about changing their victimization.

In the 1970s, riding the wave of a resurgent feminist movement, colleges and universities began to develop women's studies courses that aimed first and foremost to make women's lives visible. The texts that were developed for these courses tended to stress the things that women shared under patriarchy—having the responsibility for housework and child care, the experience or fear of men's sexual violence, a lack of formal or informal access to education, and exclusion from high-status professional and managerial jobs, political office, and religious leadership positions (Brownmiller, 1975; Kanter, 1977).

The study of women in society offered new ways of seeing the world. But the 1970s approach was limited in several ways. Thinking of gender primarily in terms of differences *between* women and men led scholars to overgeneralize about both. The concept of patriarchy led to a dualistic perspective of male privilege and female subordination. Women and men were cast as opposites. Each was treated as a homogeneous category with common characteristics and experiences. This approach *essentialized* women and men. Essentialism, simply put, is the notion that women's and men's attributes and indeed women and men themselves are categorically different. From this perspective, male control and coercion of women produced conflict between the sexes. The feminist insight originally introduced by Simone De Beauvoir in 1953—that women, as a group, had been socially defined as the "other" and that men had constructed themselves as the subjects of history, while constructing women as their objects—fueled an energizing sense of togetherness among many women. As college students read books such as *Sisterhood Is Powerful* (Morgan, 1970), many of them joined organizations that fought—with some success—for equality and justice for women.

## THE VOICES OF "OTHER" WOMEN

Although this view of women as an oppressed "other" was empowering for certain groups of women, some women began to claim that the feminist view of universal sisterhood ignored and marginalized their major concerns. It soon became apparent that treating women as a group united in its victimization by patriarchy was biased by too narrow a focus on the experiences and perspectives of women from more privileged social groups. "Gender" was treated as a generic category, uncritically applied to women. Ironically, this analysis, which was meant to unify women, instead produced divisions between and among them. The concerns projected as "universal" were removed from the realities of many women's lives. For example, it became a matter of faith in second-wave feminism that women's liberation would be accomplished by breaking down the "gendered public-domestic split." Indeed, the feminist call for women to move out of the kitchen and into the workplace resonated in the experiences of many of the college-educated white women who were inspired by Betty Friedan's 1963 book, *The Feminine Mystique*. But the idea that women's movement into workplaces was itself empowering or liberating seemed absurd or irrelevant to many working-class women and women of color. They were already working for wages, as had many of their mothers and grandmothers, and did not consider access to jobs and public life "liberating." For many of these women, liberation had more to do with organizing in communities and workplaces—often alongside men—for better schools, better pay, decent benefits, and other policies to benefit their neighborhoods, jobs, and families. The feminism of the 1970s did not seem to address these issues.

As more and more women analyzed their own experiences, they began to address the power relations that created differences among women and the part that privileged women played in the oppression of others. For many women of color, working-class women, lesbians, and women in contexts outside the United States (especially women in non-Western societies), the focus on male domination was a distraction from other oppressions. Their lived experiences could support neither a unitary theory of gender nor an ideology of universal sisterhood. As a result, finding common ground in a universal female victimization was never a priority for many groups of women.

Challenges to gender stereotypes soon emerged. Women of varied races, classes, national origins, and sexualities insisted that the concept of gender be broadened to take their differences into account (Baca Zinn et al., 1986; Hartmann, 1976; Rich, 1980; Smith, 1977). Many women began to argue that their lives were affected by their location in a number of different hierarchies: as African Americans, Latinas, Native Americans, or Asian Americans in the race hierarchy; as young or old in the age hierarchy; as heterosexual, lesbian, or bisexual in the sexual orientation hierarchy; and as women outside the Western industrialized nations, in subordinated geopolitical contexts. These arguments made it clear that women were not victimized by gender alone but by the historical and systematic denial of rights and privileges based on other differences as well.

## MEN AS GENDERED BEINGS

As the voices of "other" women in the mid- to late 1970s began to challenge and expand the parameters of women's studies, a new area of scholarly inquiry was beginning to stir—a critical examination of men and masculinity. To be sure, in those early years of gender studies, the major task was to conduct studies and develop courses about the lives of women in order to begin to correct centuries of scholarship that rendered invisible women's lives, problems, and accomplishments. But the core idea of feminism—that "femininity" and women's subordination is a social construction—logically led to an examination of the social construction of "masculinity" and men's power. Many of the first scholars to take on this task were psychologists who were concerned with looking at the social construction of "the male sex role" (e.g., Pleck, 1976). By the late 1980s, there was a growing interdisciplinary collection of studies of men and masculinity, much of it by social scientists (Brod, 1987; Kaufman, 1987; Kimmel, 1987; Kimmel & Messner, 1989).

Reflecting developments in women's studies, the scholarship on men's lives tended to develop three themes: First, what we think of as "masculinity" is not a fixed, biological essence of men, but rather is a social construction that shifts and changes over time as well as between and among various national and cultural contexts. Second, power is central to understanding gender as a relational construct, and the dominant definition of masculinity is largely about expressing difference from—and superiority over—anything considered "feminine." And third, there is no singular "male sex role." Rather, at any given time there are various masculinities. R. W. Connell (1987; 1995; 2002) has been among the most articulate advocates of this perspective. Connell argues that hegemonic masculinity (the dominant form of masculinity at any given moment) is constructed in relation to femininities *as well as* in relation to various subordinated or marginalized masculinities. For example, in the United States, various racialized masculinities (e.g., as represented by African American men, Latino immigrant men, etc.) have been central to the construction of hegemonic (white middle-class) masculinity. This "othering" of racialized masculinities helps to shore up the privileges that have been historically connected to hegemonic masculinity. When viewed this way, we can better understand hegemonic masculinity as part of a system that includes gender as well as racial, class, sexual, and other relations of power.

The new literature on men and masculinities also begins to move us beyond the simplistic, falsely categorical, and pessimistic view of men simply as a privileged sex class. When race, social class, sexual orientation, physical abilities, immigrant, or national status are taken into account, we can see that in some circumstances, "male privilege" is partly—sometimes substantially—muted (Kimmel & Messner, 2004). Although it is unlikely that we will soon see a "men's movement" that aims to undermine the power and privileges that are connected with hegemonic masculinity, when we begin to look at "masculinities" through the prism of difference, we can begin to see similarities and possible points of coalition between and among certain groups of women and men (Messner,

1998). Certain kinds of changes in gender relations—for instance, a national family leave policy for working parents—might serve as a means of uniting particular groups of women and men.

## GENDER IN INTERNATIONAL CONTEXTS

It is an increasingly accepted truism that late twentieth-century increases in transnational trade, international migration, and global systems of production and communication have diminished both the power of nation-states and the significance of national borders. A much more ignored issue is the extent to which gender relations—in the United States and elsewhere in the world—are increasingly linked to patterns of global economic restructuring. Decisions made in corporate headquarters located in Los Angeles, Tokyo, or London may have immediate repercussions on how women and men thousands of miles away organize their work, community, and family lives (Sassen, 1991). It is no longer possible to study gender relations without giving attention to global processes and inequalities....

Around the world, women's paid and unpaid labor is key to global development strategies. Yet it would be a mistake to conclude that gender is molded from the "top down." What happens on a daily basis in families and workplaces simultaneously constitutes and is constrained by structural transnational institutions. For instance, in the second half of the twentieth century young, single women, many of them from poor rural areas, were (and continue to be) recruited for work in export assembly plants along the U.S.-Mexico border, in East and Southeast Asia, in Silicon Valley, in the Caribbean, and in Central America. While the profitability of these multinational factories depends, in part, on management's ability to manipulate the young women's ideologies of gender, the women ... do not respond passively or uniformly, but actively resist, challenge, and accommodate. At the same time, the global dispersion of the assembly line has concentrated corporate facilities in many U.S. cities, making available myriad managerial, administrative, and clerical jobs for college educated women. Women's paid labor is used at various points along this international system of production. Not only employment but also consumption embodies global interdependencies. There is a high probability that the clothing you are wearing and the computer you use originated in multinational corporate headquarters and in assembly plants scattered around third world nations. And if these items were actually manufactured in the United States, they were probably assembled by Latin American and Asian-born women.

Worldwide, international labor migration and refugee movements are creating new types of multiracial societies. While these developments are often discussed and analyzed with respect to racial differences, gender typically remains absent. As several commentators have noted, the white feminist movement in the United States has not addressed issues of immigration and nationality. Gender, however, has been fundamental in shaping immigration policies (Chang,

1994; Hondagneu-Sotelo, 1994). Direct labor recruitment programs generally solicit either male or female labor (e.g., Filipina nurses and Mexican male farm workers), national disenfranchisement has particular repercussions for women and men, and current immigrant laws are based on very gendered notions of what constitutes "family unification." As Chandra Mohanty suggests, "analytically these issues are the contemporary metropolitan counterpart of women's struggles against colonial occupation in the geographical third world" (1991:23). Moreover, immigrant and refugee women's daily lives often challenge familiar feminist paradigms. The occupations in which immigrant and refugee women concentrate—paid domestic work, informal sector street vending, assembly or industrial piece work performed in the home—often blur the ideological distinction between work and family and between public and private spheres (Hondagneu-Sotelo, 2001; Parrenas, 2001).

## FROM PATCHWORK QUILT TO PRISM

All of these developments—the voices of "other" women, the study of men and masculinities, and the examination of gender in transnational contexts—have helped redefine the study of gender. By working to develop knowledge that is inclusive of the experiences of all groups, new insights about gender have begun to emerge. Examining gender in the context of other differences makes it clear that nobody experiences themselves as solely gendered. Instead, gender is configured through cross-cutting forms of difference that carry deep social and economic consequences.

By the mid-1980s, thinking about gender had entered a new stage, which was more carefully grounded in the experiences of diverse groups of women and men. This perspective is a general way of looking at women and men and understanding their relationships to the structure of society. Gender is no longer viewed simply as a matter of two opposite categories of people, males and females, but a range of social relations among differently situated people. Because centering on difference is a radical challenge to the conventional gender framework, it raises several concerns. If we think of all the systems that converge to simultaneously influence the lives of women and men, we can imagine an infinite number of effects these interconnected systems have on different women and men. Does the recognition that gender can be understood only contextually (meaning that there is no singular "gender" per se) make women's studies and men's studies newly vulnerable to critics in the academy? Does the immersion in difference throw us into a whirlwind of "spiraling diversity" (Hewitt, 1992:316) whereby multiple identities and locations shatter the categories "women" and "men"? ...

We take a position directly opposed to an empty pluralism. Although the categories "woman" and "man" have multiple meanings, this does not reduce gender to a "postmodern kaleidoscope of lifestyles. Rather, it points to the *relational* character of gender" (Connell, 1992:736). Not only are masculinity and femininity relational, but different *masculinities* and *femininities* are interconnected through other social structures such as race, class, and nation. The concept of relationality suggests that the lives of different groups are interconnected even without face-to-face relations (Glenn, 2002:14). The meaning of "woman" is defined by the existence of women of different races and classes. Being a white woman in the United States is meaningful only insofar as it is set apart from and in contradistinction to women of color.

Just as masculinity and femininity each depend on the definition of the other to produce domination, differences *among* women and *among* men are also created in the context of structured relationships. Some women derive benefits from their race and class position and from their location in the global economy, while they are simultaneously restricted by gender. In other words, such women are subordinated by patriarchy, yet their relatively privileged positions within hierarchies of race, class, and the global political economy intersect to create for them an expanded range of opportunities, choices, and ways of living. They may even use their race and class advantage to minimize some of the consequences of patriarchy and/or to oppose other women. Similarly, one can become a man in opposition to other men. For example, "the relation between heterosexual and homosexual men is central, carrying heavy symbolic freight. To many people, homosexuality is the *negation* of masculinity…. Given that assumption, antagonism toward homosexual men may be used to define masculinity" (Connell, 1992:736).

In the past decade, viewing gender through the prism of difference has profoundly reoriented the field (Acker, 1999; Glenn, 1999, 2002; Messner, 1996; West & Fenstermaker, 1995). Yet analyzing the multiple constructions of gender does not just mean studying groups of women and groups of men as different. It is clearly time to go beyond what we call the "patchwork quilt" phase in the study of women and men—that is, the phase in which we have acknowledged the importance of examining differences within constructions of gender, but do so largely by collecting together a study here on African American women, a study there on gay men, a study on working-class Chicanas, and so on. This patchwork quilt approach too often amounts to no more than "adding difference and stirring." The result may be a lovely mosaic, but like a patchwork quilt, it still tends to overemphasize boundaries rather than to highlight bridges of inter-dependency. In addition, this approach too often does not explore the ways that social constructions of femininities and masculinities are based on and reproduce relations of power. In short, we think that the substantial quantity of research that has now been done on various groups and subgroups needs to be analyzed within a framework that emphasizes differences and inequalities not as discrete areas of separation, but as interrelated bands of color that together make up a spectrum….

## REFERENCES

Acker, Joan. 1999. "Rewriting Class, Race and Gender: Problems in Feminist Rethinking" Pp. 44–69 in Myra Marx Ferree, Judith Lorber, and Beth B. Hess (eds.), *Revisioning Gender*. Thousand Oaks, CA: Sage Publications.

Baca Zinn, M., L., Weber Cannon, E., Higgenbotham, & B., Thornton Dill. 1986. "The Costs of Exclusionary Practices in Women's Studies," *Signs: Journal of Women in Culture and Society* 11: 290–303.

Brod, Harry (ed.). 1987. *The Making of Masculinities: The New Men's Studies*. Boston: Allen & Unwin.

Brownmiller, Susan. 1975. *Against Our Will: Men, Women, and Rape*. New York: Simon & Schuster.

Chang, Grace. 1994. "Undocumented Latinas: The New 'Employable Mothers.'" Pp. 259–285 in Evelyn Nakano Glenn, Grace Chang, and Linda Rennie Forcey (eds.), *Mothering, Ideology, Experience, and Agency*. New York and London: Routledge.

Connell, R. W. 1987. *Gender and Power*. Stanford, CA: Stanford University Press.

Connell, R. W. 1992. "A Very Straight Gay: Masculinity, Homosexual Experience, and the Dynamics of Gender," *American Sociological Review* 57: 735–751.

Connell, R. W. 1995. *Masculinities*. Berkeley: University of California Press.

Connell, R. W. 2002. *Gender*. Cambridge: Polity.

De Beauvoir, Simone. 1953. *The Second Sex*. New York: Knopf.

Glenn, Evelyn Nakano. 1999. "The Social Construction and Institutionalization of Gender and Race: An Integrative Framework," Pp. 3–43 in Myra Marx Ferree, Judith Lorber, and Beth B. Hess (eds.), *Revisioning Gender*. Thousand Oaks. CA: Sage Publications.

Glenn, Evelyn Nakano. 2002. *Unequal Sisterhood: How Race and Gender Shaped American Citizenship and Labor*. Cambridge, MA: Harvard University Press.

Hartmann, Heidi. 1976. "Capitalism, Patriarchy, and Job Segregation by Sex," *Signs: Journal of Women in Culture and Society* 1(3), part 2, spring: 137–167.

Hewitt, Nancy A. 1992. "Compounding Differences," *Feminist Studies* 18: 313–326.

Hondagneu-Sotelo, Pierrette. 1994. *Gendered Transitions: Mexican Experiences of Immigration*. Berkeley: University of California Press.

Hondagneu-Sotelo, Pierrette. 2001. *Doméstica: Immigrant Workers Cleaning and Caring in the Shadows of Affluence*. Berkeley: University of California Press.

Kanter, Rosabeth Moss. 1977. *Men and Women of the Corporation*. New York: Basic Books.

Kaufman, Michael. 1987. *Beyond Patriarchy: Essays by Men on Pleasure, Power, and Change*. Toronto and New York: Oxford University Press.

Kimmel, Michael S. (ed.). 1987. *Changing Men: New Directions in Research on Men and Masculinity*. Newbury Park, CA: Sage.

Kimmel, Michael S. 1996. *Manhood in America: A Cultural History*. New York: Free Press.

Kimmel, Michael S. & Michael A. Messner (eds.). 1989. *Men's Lives*. New York: Macmillan.

Kimmel, Michael S. & Michael A. Messner (eds.). 2004. *Men's Lives*, 6th ed. Boston: Pearson.

Messner, Michael A. 1996. "Studying Up on Sex," *Sociology of Sport Journal* 13: 221–237.

Messner, Michael A. 1998. *Politics of Masculinities: Men in Movements*. Thousand Oaks, CA: Sage Publications.

Mohanty, Chandra Talpade. 1991. "Cartographies of Struggle: Third World Women and the Politics of Feminism." Pp. 51–80 in Chandra Talpade Mohanty, Ann Russo, and Lourdes Torres, (eds.), *Third World Women and the Politics of Feminism.* Bloomington: Indiana University Press.

Morgan, Robin. 1970. *Sisterhood Is Powerful: An Anthology of Writing from the Women's Liberation Movement.* New York: Vintage Books.

Parrenas, Rhacel Salazar. 2001. *Servants of Globalization: Women, Migration and Domestic Work.* Stanford: Stanford University Press.

Pleck, J. H. 1976. "The Male Sex Role: Definitions, Problems, and Sources of Change," *Journal of Social Issues* 32: 155–164.

Rich, Adrienne. 1980. "Compulsory Heterosexuality and the Lesbian Experience," *Signs: Journal of Women in Culture and Society* 5: 631–660.

Sassen, Saskia. 1991. *The Global City: New York, London, Tokyo.* Princeton: Princeton University Press.

Smith, Barbara. 1977. *Toward a Black Feminist Criticism.* Freedom, CA: Crossing Press.

West, Candace & Sarah Fenstermaker. 1995. "Doing Difference," *Gender & Society* 9: 8–37.

# Sexual Orientation

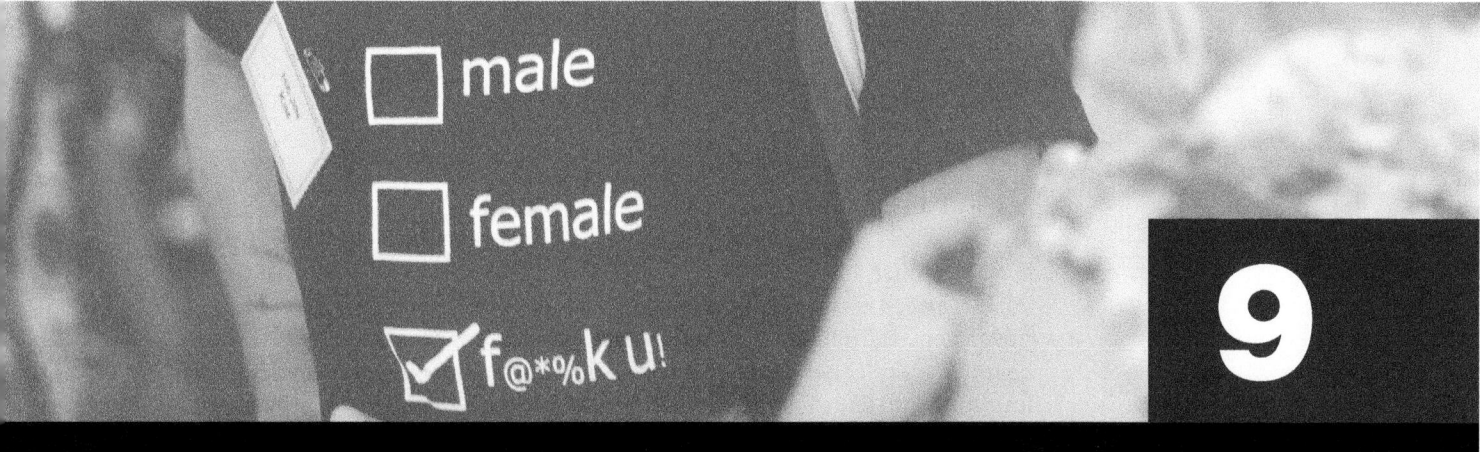

# Sexualities

## Is It True?

**1.** In some countries, same-sex activity is punishable by the death penalty.

**2.** People who believe that gay individuals are born that way tend to be more tolerant of gays than are people who believe that gay individuals choose their sexual orientation.

**3.** Most countries throughout the world have laws that protect gay individuals from discrimination because of sexual orientation.

**4.** Homosexuality is classified as a mental disorder.

**Read more here:** 1 = p. 294, 2 = p. 308, 3 = p. 294, 4 = p. 302

Answers can be found on p. 321.

© AFP/Getty Images

# 9.1 The Canadian Context

On November 17, 2001, 42-year-old Aaron Webster was beaten to death in a vicious attack in a parking lot in Stanley Park, Vancouver, in what is believed to have been British Columbia's first lethal incident of "gay bashing." Webster had been bludgeoned with either a baseball bat or a pool cue by a group of three to four men and left to die. At a memorial service for Webster that drew more than 1500 participants, Vancouver Police Inspector Dave Jones referred to Webster as the victim of a "hate crime, pure and simple" and promised that his department would "do everything in our power" to find the perpetrators and "bring them to justice" (Associated Press 2001; Nagle 2001).

Of the many issues raised by Aaron Webster's death, one was the adequacy of the definition of a "hate crime" under Canada's *Criminal Code* (Bush and Sainz 2001). According to the *Criminal Code* of the time, crimes committed against sexual orientation minorities were not, technically speaking, "hate crimes" (Wetzel 2001). In 1999, Justice Minister Anne McLellan had announced that she would introduce amendments to the Code to protect lesbians and gays from hate crimes, but by 2001 that had not happened (EGALE 2001).

Arising out of Aaron Webster's death, then NDP member of Parliament Svend Robinson tabled a private member's bill, C-250, in the House of Commons in 2003. The bill extended Canada's already existing hate crimes law to include as an "identifiable group" those who experience hate crimes as a result of their perceived sexual orientation—one need not *be* lesbian, transgendered, bisexual, or gay to experience a hate crime. The bill was passed by the Senate in 2004 and received royal assent in spring 2005. Thus, sexual minority groups were included in the ethnic model of multiculturalism that lay the foundations for the rationale of the initial law against hate crimes. Viewing crimes against those perceived to be sexual minorities as hate crimes instead of criminal assaults recognizes that the motivational aspect of prejudice heightens the threat to the general good of Canada's people. In principle, our hate crimes law is intended to protect not only specific groups, but also our national value system of *multiculturalism*. The law sends the message that prejudice is no excuse and that the courts and nation do not agree that some people "deserve a beating" (or worse) because of their skin colour, race, ethnicity, religion, or sexuality. At its foundation, hate crimes are specifically identified as distinct from other forms of crime because they inflict a **"disproportionate harm"** on the victims. Citing the work of Garafolo and Martin (1991), in a report for Canada's department of Justice Julian Roberts (1995) notes three distinct characteristics that separate hate crimes from other crimes. First, hate crimes attack a core feature of the victim's identity, with the implication being that there is nothing the victim can do to prevent being the target of an attack; better locks and avoiding walking alone at night do not solve the problem of prejudice. Second, hate crimes negatively impact entire communities by making other members of a vulnerable group fear for their safety and security:

**disproportionate harm**

Exceeds harm inflicted on individuals; has as its goal to intimidate and/or injure an entire community.

> Hate crimes convey a message of fear to all members of the community to which the specific individual belongs. The seriousness of a hate crime cannot be fully understood without taking this additional element into consideration. The harm lies in the atmosphere of fear and apprehension to which all hate crimes contribute. (Roberts 1995: 3)

Finally, research on the extent of injury in other regions that track hate crimes shows that where a crime is motivated by hate, the injuries and damage inflicted on victims are more severe than in cases of crimes not motivated by particular hatred (Roberts 1995: 4).

In 2004, on April 29, Bill C-250 was granted Royal Assent and became part of Canada's criminal legal code. Bill C-250 was introduced to the House of Commons as a private member's bill by British Columbia MP Svend Robinson. Bill C-250 was initially passed by the House of Commons on September 13, 2003, and adds "sexual orientation" to the text of subsection 318(4) so that gays and lesbians would be included in the "identifiable group" category that had previously included recognition only for colour, race, religion, and ethnic origin.

As of the writing of the current edition of this book, lobby groups and activists are hard at work to have Bill C-389 passed into law. The bill, introduced by NDP MP Bill Siksay, seeks to include both **gender identity** and **gender expression** as prohibited grounds for discrimination, and to make targeted crimes based on gender identity and/or gender expression subject to punishment under Canada's hate crimes law. The bill passed the report stage on December 8, 2010 at the House of Commons level with 143 votes in favour and 131 against (EGALE 2010).

In this chapter we examine prejudice and discrimination toward those who engage in same-sex activity whether male or female, and those who identify as lesbian, gay, transexual, or bisexual. We also address problems of homophobia and transphobia.

It is beyond the scope of this chapter, though, to explore how sexual diversity and its cultural meanings vary throughout the world. Rather, our focus is on Western conceptions of sexual diversity. Sexuality has often been thought of in terms of **"sexual orientation,"** whereby individuals are classified as heterosexual, bisexual, or homosexual, based on their emotional and sexual attractions, relationships, and self-identification. However, current scholarship and activism in the field note that the concept of orientation, while sometimes useful—as in the hate crimes law—does not allow room to think about the ways in which desires, attractions, and practices can vary over our lifetimes; furthermore, it encourages the assumption that all people in a given identity category share identical and unchanging desires and practices. Biologist Anne Fausto-Sterling (2001) has taken her own life history as an example of the shifts and complexities for which a simple use of "orientation" simply cannot account:

> This young girl didn't like dolls, kept pet snakes and frogs, and grew up first with heterosexual interests and later developed homosexual ones. How are we to interpret her life, or any life? Speculating about genes for analytic personalities or homosexuality may make for good party chitchat or provide solace for those eager to explain why someone turned out "that way." But partitioning genes from environment, nature from nurture, is a scientific dead end, a bad way of thinking about human development. Instead, I suggest we heed the words of the philosophers John Dewey and Arthur Bentley, who half a century ago "asserted the right to see together...much that is talked about conventionally as if it were composed of irreconcilable fears." (pp. 234–35)

While some advocate using the term **transgender** to include lesbians, gays, and bisexuals—those whose bodies do not fit neatly into either the

**gender identity**

The gender that a person feels him or herself to be. Sometimes gender identity is concordant with one's assigned sex at birth, and sometimes one's gender identity is more fluid, or can be "opposite" to one's sex of rearing.

**gender expression**

How we express our gender (as masculine, feminine, tomboys or androgynous, as "butch," "straight," etc.).

**sexual orientation**

The identification of individuals as heterosexual, bisexual, or homosexual based on their emotional and sexual attractions, relationships, self-identity, and lifestyle.

**transgendered individuals**

Persons who do not fit neatly into either the male or female category, or whose behaviour is not congruent with the rules and expectations for their sex in the society in which they live.

male or female category, or whose behaviour is incongruous with the roles and expectations for their sex in the society in which they live (Bornstein 1994; Bullough 2000; Gilbert 2000; Herdt 2001)—others observe that such a conceptualization risks collapsing very real political and personal experiences into one falsely homogenized image (Hines 2006; Roen 2001; Sullivan 2003). In common usage, transgender can include transexuals (individuals who have undergone hormone treatment and sex reassignment surgery to achieve a new identity as a member of the biologically opposite sex) and those who choose to assert and claim their non-adherence to standard gender roles.

There is some controversy over how people categorize transgender and transexual persons, and what distinguishes the concepts. In his critical ethnography, David Valentine (2007) seeks to map the manner in which these terms arose, what they describe, who gets to use them, and for what purposes. Valentine explains that the terms "transgender" and "transexual" are politicized categories that have largely been imposed from the outside by juridical interests, social scientists, and health workers. Very importantly, Valentine also situates the distinct conceptualization of transgender, transex/uality, and homosexual/ity as the effect of the twentieth-century medical system, which did the work of separating the previously enmeshed concepts of gender and sexuality. Valentine's account helps to explain why some people who identify as transexual have not had—and do not necessarily wish to have—surgery to effect a movement from one sex to the other; for these people the separation of gender and sexuality as imposed from the outside does not reflect their lives as they experience them. Valentine's analysis reveals that the adoption of transgender and transex has occurred mostly in circles of socio-economic privilege where people are able to use concepts in order to gain access to health benefits, or to political rights lobbying, but that many people who are gender variant find that the subtle overlapping of their experiences of sexuality, gender, class, and race cannot be captured by either term.

Much of the current scholarship and social activism regarding the treatment and political and social agendas of **lesbigays** also includes trans-identified persons; hence, the term **GLBT** is often used to refer collectively to gays, lesbians, bisexuals, and transgendered individuals (Craig 2002; Goldie 2001).

We begin by summarizing the legal status of lesbians and gay men around the world. Then, we review biological and environmental explanations for different sexualities, and apply sociological theories to better understand the social mechanisms that shape the way people understand and respond to various sexualities. The chapter ends with a discussion of strategies to reduce homophobia and discrimination against those who are gender variant. Because the label "homosexual" developed in the nineteenth century as a medical diagnosis of disease (Krafft-Ebing 1965), and tends to refer more to men than to women, we have chosen to use the term same-sex to refer to sexual practices and relationships that take place between persons of the same sex. This choice does not get around the problematic assumption that males and females are somehow "opposite," but it does avoid the language of pathology. We reserve the term homosexual only for historical accuracy when discussing legal and biomedical thinking on same-sex behaviour.

Because contemporary Western societies are largely heteronormative, few people who view themselves as heterosexual ever have to confront their own

**lesbigays**

A collective term sometimes used to refer to lesbians, gays, and bisexuals.

**GLBT**

A term used to refer collectively to gays, lesbians, bisexuals, and transgendered individuals.

■ **Table 9.1**  *The Heterosexual Questionnaire*

1. What do you think caused your heterosexuality?
2. When and how did you decide you were a heterosexual?
3. Is it possible that your heterosexuality is just a phase you may grow out of?
4. Is it possible that your heterosexuality stems from a neurotic fear of others of the same sex?
5. If you have never slept with a person of the same sex, is it possible that all you need is a good gay lover?
6. Do your parents know that you are straight? Do your friends and/or roommate(s) know? How did they react?
7. Why do you insist on flaunting your heterosexuality? Can't you just be who you are and keep it quiet?
8. Why do heterosexuals place so much emphasis on sex?
9. Why do heterosexuals feel compelled to seduce others into their lifestyle?
10. A disproportionate majority of child molesters are heterosexual. Do you consider it safe to expose children to heterosexual teachers?
11. Just what do men and women do in bed together? How can they truly know how to please each other, being so anatomically different?
12. With all the societal support marriage receives, the divorce rate is spiralling. Why are there so few stable relationships among heterosexuals?
13. Statistics show that lesbians have the lowest incidence of sexually transmitted diseases. Is it really safe for a woman to maintain a heterosexual lifestyle and run the risk of disease and pregnancy?
14. How can you become a whole person if you limit yourself to compulsive, exclusive heterosexuality?
15. Considering the menace of overpopulation, how could the human race survive if everyone were heterosexual?
16. Could you trust a heterosexual therapist to be objective? Don't you feel she or he might be inclined to influence you in the direction of his or her own leanings?
17. There seem to be very few happy heterosexuals. Techniques have been developed that might enable you to change if you really want to. Have you considered trying aversion therapy?
18. Would you want your child to be heterosexual, knowing the problems that she or he would face?

SOURCE: Rochlin, M. 1982. "The Heterosexual Questionnaire." *Changing Men* (Spring).

assumptions about why they are heterosexual. Instead, many heterosexuals pose questions to gay, lesbian, and bisexual people that begin with the premise that homosexuality is a problem. The "Heterosexual Questionnaire," featured as Table 9.1, first appeared in 1982 in *Changing Men*. It confronts readers with their own assumptions, forcing them to consider their ideas more carefully. Read the questionnaire for yourself. What do you think about having to provide an explanation for your own desires, whether for the same sex or the "opposite" sex? Have you ever posed these kinds of questions to people you have learned were gay, lesbian, or bisexual?

Throughout this chapter, we consider heteronormative assumptions more carefully and encourage questioning of the idea that people are "naturally" heterosexual and will remain that way unless something "goes wrong."

## 9.2 The Global Context: A World View of Laws Pertaining to Same-Sex Activity

Same-sex behaviour and love relationships have existed throughout human history and in most, perhaps all, human societies (Kirkpatrick 2000). Legal penalties for violating laws that prohibit same-sex sexual acts vary. In 10 countries, individuals found guilty of engaging in same-sex sexual behaviour may receive the death penalty. For example, a Somali lesbian couple were sentenced to death for "exercising unnatural behaviour" ("Jail, Death Sentences in Africa" 2001). Although executions in this region are performed by firing squads, religious tradition dictates that those convicted of homosexuality should either have a wall pushed over onto them or be thrown off a roof or other high place.

In general, countries throughout the world are moving toward increased legal protection of sexual-orientation minorities. Between 1984 and 1995, 86 countries changed their policies regarding sex between men, sex between women, or both, and nearly every change was toward increased liberalization of policies on same-sex sexual behaviour (Frank and McEneaney 1999). According to the International Gay and Lesbian Human Rights Commission (IGLHRC), 86 countries still have laws to prohibit sexual acts carried out in private between consenting adults (IGLHRC 2003). In 1996 South Africa became the first country in the world to include in its constitution a clause banning discrimination based on sexual orientation. Canada, Fiji, and Ecuador also have constitutions that ban discrimination based on sexual orientation ("Constitutional Protection" 1999). In the *Lawrence v. Texas* case, the U.S. Supreme Court settled that state laws prohibiting "homosexual sodomy" were unconstitutional and, therefore, unenforceable; it also ruled that such laws fundamentally violated the right to privacy. In Canada, meanwhile, same-sex sexual activity between consenting adults has been protected as a private matter since the passing of the 1969 Omnibus bill of Pierre Trudeau, who quipped, "The state has no business in the bedrooms of the nation." How law enforcement agencies have interpreted what counts as a private venue has still rendered the GLBT community vulnerable to persecution on occasion—with, for example, the infamous Toronto Bathhouse Raids of 1983 and the 2000 raid on a lesbian club, The Pussy Palace, in Toronto.

In Brazil, a gay, lesbian, bisexual, or transgendered individual is murdered on the average of every two days. However, the brutal gay-bashing murder of Edson Neris da Silva by a gang of about 30 people resulted in what some believe is Brazil's first trial and convictions in an antigay hate crime ("Brazilian Killers Sentenced" 2001). The first two gang members tried for this murder were sentenced to 21 years in prison.

In June 2000, Canada enacted a bill that extends to same-sex couples and unmarried heterosexual couples who have lived together for at least a year all the benefits and obligations of married couples (*LAWbriefs* 2000). (More recent changes are discussed later in this chapter.) In the same month, Brazil extended to same-sex couples the right to inherit each other's pension and social security benefits. The law represents the first time a Latin American country has legally recognized gay relationships (*LAWbriefs* 2000). Also in 2000, the Netherlands enacted a law allowing same-sex marriages. Just after

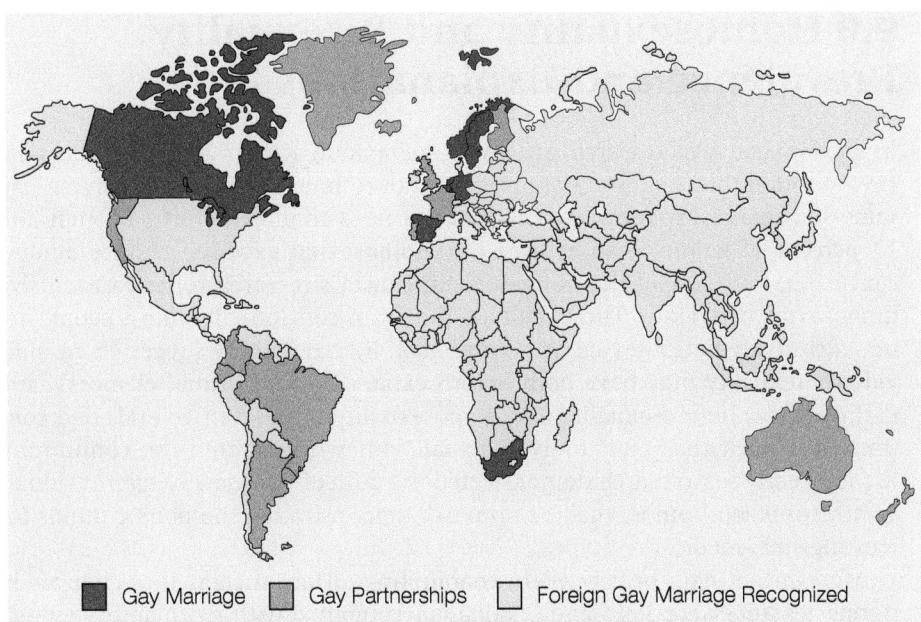

**■ Figure 9.1** *Changing Global Attitudes toward Same-Sex Marriage and Same-Sex Partnerships*

■ Gay Marriage   ■ Gay Partnerships   □ Foreign Gay Marriage Recognized

the stroke of midnight on the day the Dutch law went into effect (April 1, 2001), the world's first fully legal same-sex civil marriages took place in Amsterdam (Drinkwater 2001).

Closer to home, a referendum on the issue of "gay marriage" was part of the 2004 federal election in the United States. All 11 states that included the question voted to ban gay marriage (NCSL 2004). Meanwhile, the Conservative minority government in Canada proposed to reopen the issue of marriages for same-sex couples in the House of Commons with a free vote; in December 2006 the issue did go to a free vote over whether to revisit the constitutionality of same-sex marriage, but was defeated with 175 nays to 123 yeas. As you will see later in this chapter, the road to equal marriage rights has been difficult to travel, with powerful groups intervening to stop the advance of civil rights to same-sex couples along the way. Figure 9.1 provides an at-a-glance view of global attitudes toward marriage and partnerships for same-sex couples.

Clearly, public legitimation of same-sex relations is occurring in the global society. Human rights treaties and transnational social movement organizations have increasingly asserted the rights of persons to engage in same-sex relations. International organizations, such as Amnesty International, which resolved in 1991 to defend those imprisoned for homosexuality, the International Lesbian and Gay Association (founded in 1978), and the International Gay and Lesbian Human Rights Commission (founded in 1990), continue to fight prejudice and discrimination against lesbians and gays. Despite the worldwide movement toward increased acceptance and protection of homosexual individuals, the status and rights of lesbians and gays in Canada continues to be one of the most divisive issues in Canadian society. Shifts in government demonstrate that rights secured through law may also be rescinded through law. In response, many queer theorists and activists question the wisdom of spending effort on legal recognition of gay marriage; they argue that it may be more practical simply to reject marriage rights.

# 9.3 Homosexuality and Bisexuality: Prevalence and Explanations

In their exhaustive research on sexual behaviour, Kinsey and his colleagues (1953) found that a substantial proportion of respondents reported having had same-sex sexual experiences. The data revealed that 37 percent of men and 13 percent of women had at least one homosexual experience since adolescence. Yet, very few of the individuals in Kinsey's research reported exclusive homosexual behaviour. These data led Kinsey to conclude that most people are not exclusively heterosexual or homosexual. Rather, Kinsey suggested an individual's sexuality may have both heterosexual and homosexual elements, and that exclusive heterosexuality and homosexuality represent two ends of a continuum. He felt that most individuals fall somewhere within the continuum. Kinsey's early sex research demonstrated the difficulty of classifying individuals as heterosexual, homosexual, or bisexual, demonstrating the poor grounds for creating such medicalized types.

More recent data bear out Kinsey's findings. They suggest that changes in norms, negative sanctions, and restrictions, combined with more positive sensibilities about what it means to be involved in same-sex relationships, may correlate positively with increases in the percentage of women and men reporting same-sex sexual partnering in the past five years—the percentage increased from 0.2 in 1988 to 2.8 in 1998 (Butler 2000). This research also notes the following:

> These estimates of same-gender sex partnering should not be taken as estimates of the proportion of the population that is gay or lesbian. Some people may engage in same-gender sexual activity and yet identify as heterosexual, whereas other people may identify as gay or lesbian but may not have been sexually active in recent years. (Butler 2000: 342)

### Origins of Sexual-Orientation Diversity: Nature or Nurture?

One of the prevailing questions about homosexuality and bisexuality centres on origin or "cause." Because heterosexuality is considered normative and "natural," causes of heterosexuality are rarely considered. Many researchers now believe that an interaction of biological and environmental forces affects the development of one's sexual orientation (De Cecco and Parker 1995).

**Environmental Explanations of Sexual Orientation** According to Doell (1995), "we all probably develop, from infancy, the capacity to have heterosexual, homosexual, or bisexual relationships" (p. 352). Environmental theories propose that such factors as availability of sexual partners, early sexual experiences, and sexual reinforcement influence subsequent sexual orientation. The degree to which early sexual experiences have been negative or positive has been hypothesized as influencing sexual orientation. Having pleasurable same-sex experiences would likely increase the probability of a homosexual orientation. By the same token, it has been suggested that early traumatic sexual experiences may cause fear of heterosexual activity. However, a study that compared sexual histories of lesbian and heterosexual women found no differences in the incidence of traumatic experiences with men (Brannock and Chapman 1990).

**Biological Origins of Sexual Orientation** Biological explanations of sexual orientation diversity usually focus on genetic or hormonal differences between heterosexuals and homosexuals. In an overview of genetics research on homosexual and heterosexual orientations, Pillard and Bailey (1998) conclude that genes account for at least half of the variance in sexual orientation. Their review of family, twin, and adoptee studies indicates that homosexuality (and thus heterosexuality) runs in families. However, the empirical research on isolating a biological-cause basis for sexuality is less than convincing in its findings.

For example, science has yet to identify a "homosexuality" gene despite the assertion of some researchers, such as Hamer and colleagues (1993), who claim to have discovered *statistical* evidence for its existence. In their examination of 40 pairs of gay brothers, Hamer and colleagues note that a significantly higher number than expected of the pairs (33 out of 40 versus 20 out of 40) shared matching DNA in a region called Xq28 at the tip of the X chromosome, a chromosome males inherit from their biological mothers. The researchers focused on this chromosome after noting in previous research that more gay male relatives appear to be found on the mother's side of the family.

Hamer and his research team did not isolate a specific gene, or even a specific set of genes, existing within that chromosomal region; they only provided the statistics-based suggestion that such genes must be there. Nor do they specifically account for the homosexuality of those brothers who do not possess the matching DNA. Furthermore, they have not examined heterosexual brothers for the existence or nonexistence of matching DNA in the Xq28 region to determine whether heterosexual brothers are similar to or different from homosexual brothers (Peele and DeGrandpre 1995). Consider, as well, the results of a Canadian study (Rice et al. 1999) based on 62 gay male sibling pairs. When the microsatellite markers at position Xq28 were analyzed, Hamer's suggestion of an X-linked gene underlying homosexuality was not supported.

Among the serious methodological problems confronting such research is determining what counts as "homosexuality"; the definitions vary from one study to another and what subjects mean when they say they are homosexual may not be the same from one subject to the next. Is it an issue of desire? of activity? of identity? Nevertheless, researchers continue in the quest to isolate a biological cause for human sexuality. This chapter's *Social Problems Research Up Close* feature highlights one such recent effort.

**Can Homosexuals Change Their Sexual Orientation?** Although "homosexuality" was removed from the *Diagnostic and Statistical Manual-IV* in 1974, some conservative, often Christian organizations claim to be able to "cure" homosexuality through **reparative therapy** or conversion therapy. Some religious organizations, like the U.S.-based Exodus, sponsor ex-gay ministries, which claim to "cure" homosexuals and transform them into heterosexuals through prayer and other forms of "therapy." Critics of ex-gay ministries take a different approach:

**reparative therapy**
Various therapies that are aimed at changing homosexuals' sexual attraction.

## Youth Speak Up about Homophobia and Transphobia

This report discusses the results of a national survey of Canadian high school students undertaken in order to identify the forms and extent of their experiences of homophobic and transphobic incidents at school and the efficacy of measures being taken by schools to combat these common forms of bullying.

Phase One of the study involved surveying almost 1700 students from across Canada through two methods: individual online participation and in-school sessions conducted in four school boards. This report analyzes the data from individual online participation.

Educators and researchers have long been aware that students experience homophobic incidents ranging from hearing "gay" used as a synonym for "stupid" or "worthless" to being insulted or assaulted because of their actual or perceived sexual or transgender identity. However, the lack of a solid Canadian evidence base has been a major impediment faced by educators who need to understand the situation of lesbian, gay, bisexual, transgender, queer, and questioning (LGBTQ) students in order to respond appropriately and to assure the school community that homophobic and transphobic bullying are neither rare nor harmless but major problems that schools need to address.

### Summary of Methods for Data Gathering and Analysis

The survey itself was a 54-item questionnaire made available online and in print, and consisting mostly

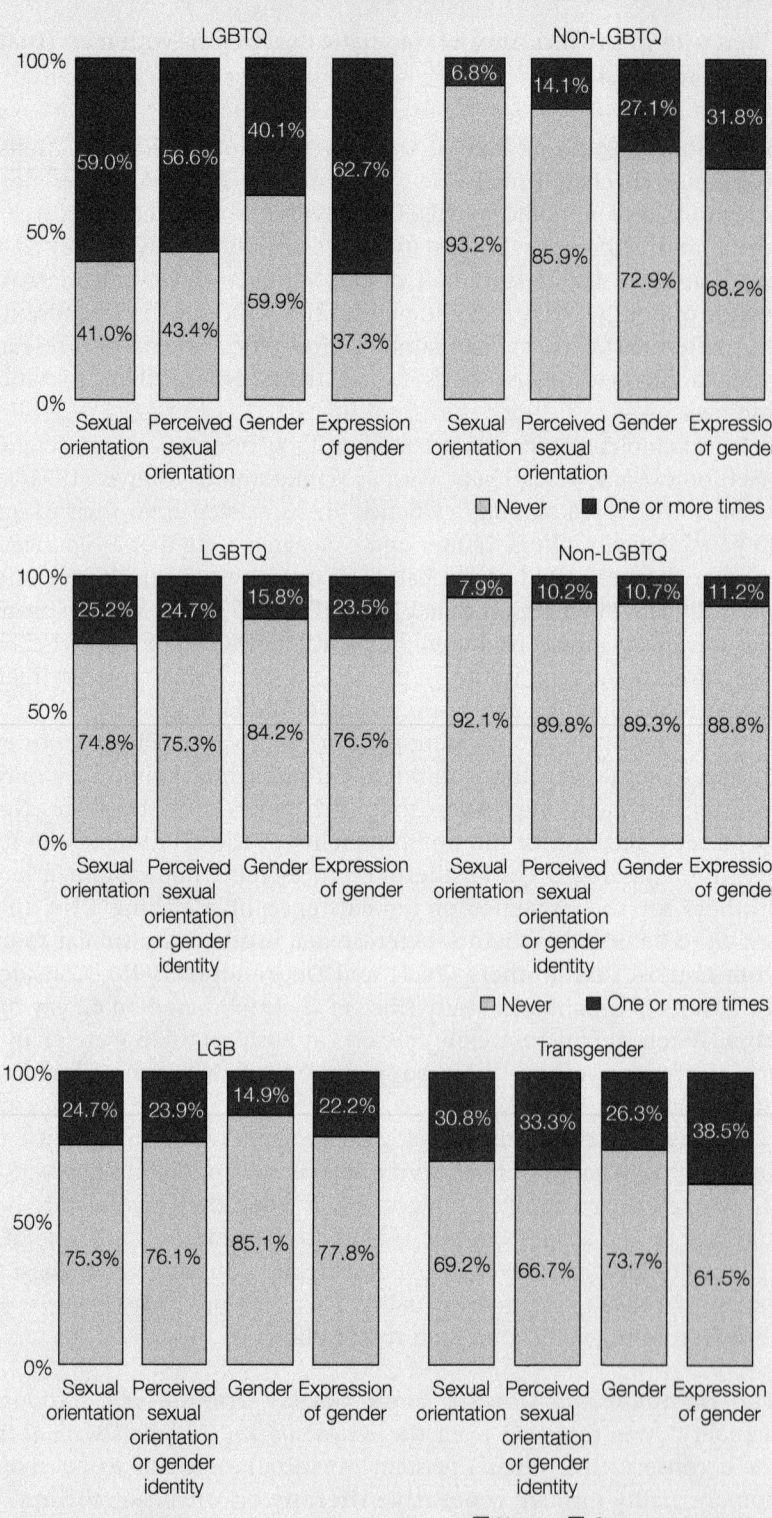

SOURCE: Taylor, Catherine, and Tracey Peter. 2009. "Youth Speak Out About Homophobia and Transphobia: The First National Climate Survey on Homophobia in Canadian Schools." EGALE Canada Human Rights Trust: Winnipeg, Ontario, p. 41. Reprinted with permission.

of multiple-choice questions of three kinds: demographic (e.g., age, province, gender identity, sexual identity), experiences (e.g., hearing the word gay used as an insult, being verbally harassed), and institutional responses (e.g., staff intervention, inclusive safe-school policies). Quantitative data were tested for statistical significance through bivariate analyses that compared the responses of various groups of students (e.g., LGBTQ and non-LGBTQ, LGB and transgender, current versus past).

## Key Findings: Unsafe Spaces

Homophobic comments:

- Current students were even more likely than past students to hear expressions such as "that's so gay" in school.
- Current students were also more likely than past students to hear homophobic comments from other students every day in school.

One sign of progress:

- Current students were significantly less likely than past students to report that school staff never intervened.

## Impacts

- Three-quarters of LGBTQ students and 95 percent of transgender students felt unsafe at school, compared to one-fifth of straight students.
- Over a quarter of LGBTQ students and almost half of transgender students had skipped school because they felt unsafe, compared to fewer than a tenth of non-LGBTQ.
- Many LGBTQ students would not be comfortable talking to their teachers (four in ten), their prin-

cipal (six in ten), or their coach (seven in ten) about LGBTQ issues.
- Only one in five LGBTQ students could talk to a parent very comfortably about LGBTQ issues. Three-quarters could talk to a close friend about these issues.
- Over half of LGBTQ students did not feel accepted at school, and almost half felt they could not be themselves at school, compared to one-fifth of straight students.
- Transgender students (over a third) were twice as likely as LGB students to strongly agree that they sometimes feel very depressed about their school and that they do not belong at their school, and four times as likely as straight students.

Institutional responses:

- Fewer than half of participants knew whether their school had a policy for reporting homophobic incidents.
- Of those participants who did know, only one-third believed there was such a policy.

LGBTQ students who believed their schools have anti-homophobia policies were much more likely than other LGBTQ students . . .

- to feel their school community was supportive (one-half compared to fewer than one-fifth),
- to feel comfortable talking to a counsellor (one-half compared to fewer than one-third), and to feel comfortable talking to classmates (over one-third compared to one-fifth),
- to believe their school was becoming less homophobic,
- to hear fewer homophobic comments and to say that staff intervene more often,

- to report homophobic incidents to staff and their parents, and
- to feel attached to their school.

LGBTQ students who believed their schools have anti-homophobia policies were much less likely than other LGBTQ students...

- to have had lies and rumours spread about them at school or on the internet,
- to have had property stolen or intentionally damaged,
- to feel unsafe at school, and
- to have been verbally or physically harassed.

The results were similar for students who believed that their school districts had such policies.

## Conclusions and Recommendations

This survey confirms what LGBTQ students and their allies have known for some time: that despite Canada's leadership on human rights for LGBTQ people, a great deal of verbal and physical homophobic and transphobic harassment goes on in Canadian schools, that LGBTQ students are more likely to be aware of it than are other students who are not its main targets, and that the institutional response to harassment has more often than not been inadequate.

The survey also shows, however, that the situation is much improved where schools and school divisions have developed safe-schools policies and procedures that explicitly address homophobia and have informed students of their existence. In such schools, LGBTQ students are less likely to hear homophobic comments or to be targeted by verbal or physical harassment, they are more likely to report it to staff and

(continued)

parents when they are, and staff are more likely to intervene. In these schools, LGBTQ students feel safer, more accepted, and more attached to their school.

Developing inclusive safe schools policies and making them known to students is not a complete solution. However, this survey has identified significant differences between schools with and schools without inclusive policies.

### Recommendations

1. That schools develop and implement anti-homophobia and anti-transphobia policies and make these policies well known to students, parents, administration, and all staff as a positive part of their commitment to making schools safe.

2. That schools strongly support the efforts of students to start Gay-Straight Alliances (GSAs).

3. That in schools where students have not come forward, administration should ask teachers to offer to work with students to start a GSA. It is not safe to assume that LGBTQ students would prefer to go through high school isolated from their peers and teachers.

4. That school divisions develop anti-homophobia and anti-transphobia policies to provide leadership for schools. Although our analysis showed that students are less likely to know about division-level policies, it would be helpful for principals to know that their school-level efforts have strong divisional endorsement in the form of official policy at that level.

5. That provincial Ministries of Education advocate the inclusion of anti-homophobia and anti-transphobia measures in safe schools policies and programs, including those of Catholic schools, along with steps for

the implementation of these policies, in order to provide institutional support and motivation to divisional and school staff.

6. That individuals and organizations with expertise in anti-homophobia and anti-transphobia education be consulted in the above developments.

What students have told us in the First National Climate Survey on Homophobia in Canadian Schools is that speaking up works, and that they want the adults in their lives to do their part, too. These students are weary of seeing teachers and principals look the other way. And they are grateful to the many dedicated school staff who have worked to make schools safer for everyone in their care—not everyone but them.

SOURCE: Taylor, Catherine et al. 2009. "Executive Summary." *Youth Speak Up About Homophobia and Transphobia.* EGALE Canada: Winnipeg. Reprinted with permission.

---

The cure for unhappiness is not the "ex-gay" ministries—but coming out with dignity and self-respect. It is not gay men and lesbians who need to change...but negative attitudes and discrimination against gay people that need to be abolished. (Besen 2000: 7)

The Canadian Psychiatric Association, the Canadian Psychological Association, and the Canadian Medical Association agree that sexual orientation cannot be changed, and that efforts to change sexual orientation do not work and may be harmful (Human Rights Campaign 2000a). In addition, close scrutiny of reports of "successful" reparative therapy reveal that (1) many claims come from organizations with an ideological perspective on sexual orientation, rather than from unbiased researchers; (2) the treatments and their outcomes are poorly documented; and (3) the length of time that clients are followed after treatment is too short to evaluate their success or failure (Human Rights Campaign 2000a). In addition, at least 13 ministries of one reparative therapy group, Exodus, have closed because their directors reverted to homosexuality (Fone 2000).

# 9.4 Sociological Theories of Sexual Orientation

Sociological theories do not explain the origin or "cause" of sexual orientation, but help explain societal reactions to and contexts for sexual diversity. The sociology of sexuality can provide insight into shifting meanings in sexual identity and provide critical insight on the overlap of institutions and ideologies (like marriage, sexism, and heterosexism) and the costs of those overlaps as expressed in the form of prejudice, harm, and bias. Sociological inquiry brings a decidedly *social* understanding of the intersection of gender ideologies and sexualities.

## Structural-Functionalist Perspective

Structural-functionalists, focusing on the operations fulfilled through institutions, emphasize the importance of monogamous heterosexual relationships for the reproduction, nurturance, and socialization of children. From a functionalist perspective, sexual relations are defined as "deviant" when they do not fulfill the family institution's main function of producing and rearing children. Clearly, this argument is less salient in a society in which (1) other institutions, most notably schools, have supplemented the traditional functions of the family; (2) a societal goal is to reduce population; and (3) same-sex couples can and do raise children.

Some functionalists argue that antagonisms between heterosexuals and homosexuals may disrupt social equilibrium. Durkheim, however, recognized that deviation from society's norms "may be useful as a prelude to reforms which daily become more necessary" ([1938] 1993: 66). Specifically, the gay rights movement has motivated many people to re-examine their treatment of sexual-orientation minorities; it has also produced a sense of cohesion and solidarity among members of the gay population (although bisexuals and the transgendered have often been excluded from gay and lesbian communities and organizations). Bringing benefit to society as a whole, gay activism has been instrumental in advocating for more research on HIV and AIDS, more and better health services for HIV and AIDS patients, protection of the rights of HIV-infected individuals, and HIV/AIDS public education.

Finally, the structural-functionalist focus on the interconnectedness of society fosters an understanding that urbanization has contributed to the formation of strong social networks of gays and bisexuals. Cities "acted as magnets, drawing in gay migrants who felt isolated and threatened in smaller towns and rural areas" (Button et al. 1997: 15; Goldie 2001). Given the formation of gay communities in large cities, it is not surprising that the gay rights movement first emerged in large urban centres.

Other research has demonstrated that the worldwide rise in liberalized national policies on same-sex relations and the lesbian and gay rights social movement has been influenced by three cultural changes: (1) the rise of individualism that values personal satisfaction, (2) increasing gender equality, and (3) the emergence of a global society in which nations are influenced by international pressures (Frank and McEneaney 1999). Whereas once sex was approved strictly for the purpose of family reproduction, sex increasingly serves to pleasure individualized men and women in society. Individualism "appears to loosen the tie between sex and procreation, allowing more personal modes of sexual expression" (p. 930).

Gender equality involves the breakdown of sharply differentiated sex roles, thereby supporting the varied expressions of male and female sexuality. Globalization permits the international community to influence individual nations. For example, when Zimbabwe President Robert Mugabe pursued antihomosexual policies in 1995, many international organizations and human rights associations joined to protest his actions and to ask that he halt his campaign. The pressure of international opinion led Zimbabwe's Supreme Court to rule in favour of lesbian and gay groups' right to organize.

## Conflict Perspective

Conflict theorists, particularly those who do not emphasize a purely economic perspective, note that the antagonisms between "straight" and GLBT communities represent a basic division in society between those with power and those without power. When one group has control of society's institutions and resources, as in the case of heterosexuals, it has the authority to dominate other groups. Current battles over gay rights form one example of the political struggle between those with power and those without it.

A classic example of the power struggle between gays and "straights" took place in 1973. At that time, the American Psychiatric Association (APA) met to revise its classification scheme of mental disorders. Homosexual activists had been appealing to the APA for years to remove homosexuality from its list of mental illnesses, but with little success. However, in 1973, the APA's board of directors voted to remove homosexuality from its official list of mental disorders. The board's move encountered much resistance from conservative APA members. The issue was put to a referendum, which reaffirmed the board's decision (Bayer 1987).

In recent years, many organizations have recognized that implementing antidiscrimination policies that include sexual orientation is good for the bottom line. Over half (51 percent) of Fortune 500 companies and 82 percent of Fortune 1000 companies have included sexual orientation in their nondiscrimination policies, and employers are increasingly offering benefits to domestic partners of GLBT employees (Human Rights Campaign 2000b). Gay-friendly workplaces help employers maintain a competitive edge in recruiting and a talented and productive workforce.

In some settings, however, the changes have been hard won. Gay rights activists have turned to Canadian courtrooms and human rights tribunals, successfully employing the equality provision of the *Canadian Charter of Rights and Freedoms*. As a result of their activities, some Canadian workplaces have been transformed as "[g]overnments have changed legislation and policies either because courts have ordered them to do so or because of threats of court cases" (Dranoff 2001: 133).

In summary, conflict theory frames the gay rights movement and the opposition to it as a struggle over power, prestige, and economic resources. Recent trends toward increased social acceptance of homosexuality may, in part, reflect the corporate world's competition over the gay and lesbian consumer dollar.

## Symbolic Interactionist Perspective

Symbolic interactionism focuses on the meanings of heterosexuality, homosexuality, and bisexuality and how these meanings are socially constructed. The meanings we associate with same-sex relations are learned from society—from family, peers, religion, and the media. Freedman and D'Emilio (1990: 485) observed: "sexual meanings are subject to the forces of culture. Human beings learn how to express themselves sexually, and the content and outcome of that learning vary widely across cultures and across time."

Historical and cross-cultural research reveals the socially constructed nature of sexuality and its meanings. Although many North Americans assume that same-sex romantic relationships have always been taboo, during the nineteenth century, "romantic friendships" between women were encouraged and regarded as preparation for a successful marriage. President Grover Cleveland's sister Rose, for example, wrote to her friend Evangeline Whipple in 1890: "It makes me heavy with emotion...all my whole being leans out to you.... I dare not think of your arms" (Goode and Wagner 1993: 49).

The symbolic interactionist perspective also points to the effects of labelling on individuals. Once individuals become identified or labelled as lesbian, gay, or bisexual, that label tends to become their **master status**. In other words, the dominant heterosexual community tends to view "gay," "lesbian," and "bisexual" as the most socially significant statuses of individuals identified as such. Esterberg (1997: 377) notes that "unlike heterosexuals, who are defined by their family structures, communities, occupations, or other aspects of their lives, lesbians, gay men, and bisexuals are often defined primarily by what they do in bed. Many lesbians, gay men, and bisexuals, however, view their identity as social and political as well as sexual."

**master status**

The status that is considered the most significant in a person's social identity.

## Feminist Perspectives

Feminist work on sexuality is diverse, a result of highly variable concerns that arise in the attempt to understand sexuality. A foundational point, however, is the clear observation that issues related to sexuality are central to women's lives, not marginal or frivolous. Clearly, for example, women's ability to acquire education and to achieve a measure of financial independence—both very important in a capitalist context—depends on women's ability to control their reproduction, a matter tied in part to sexuality.

Feminist work has also revealed that beliefs about women's sexuality have made them extremely vulnerable to a variety of oppressive forces. Among these is the tendency to "pedestalize" some women for their ability to act appropriately as good mothers and wives, adornments for men of privileged classes; meanwhile, women from marginalized groups may be simultaneously eroticized and vilified as "excessively sexual." This oppositional pairing of women as good and bad is popularly known as the "Madonna/whore dichotomy." Feminists have pointed out that in such a symbolic and structural ordering no woman is free—a problem we take up further throughout this chapter.

It is important to remember that feminist work does not have to be done by women, though it often is. For example, Sander Gilman's historical assessment of racism and sexism in medicine revealed that nineteenth-century "experts" claimed that African women, Jewish women, and European prostitutes and lesbians all shared similarly deviant and *excessively large* genitalia (Gilman 1985).

What makes a work on sexuality feminist if it is not the body of the researcher? A central answer to that question arrives in the principle of **anti-essentialism** developed within feminist scholarship since the 1980s. Anti-essentialist work observes that nothing is guaranteed by the body, most particularly by the sex, of a person. Instead, our social and cultural contexts shape who we are. It is through this **constructionist** position that much contemporary feminist work on sexuality operates. A constructionist approach understands, for example, that "how we classify individuals according to sex [as a matter of law] is a matter of interpretation.... Moreover, what we take sex itself to be [as a biological phenomenon]...is also a question of interpretation" (Warnke 2005: 113). "Sex" then is a matter of perception and a vehicle for controlling how bodies are organized into categories. As Gayle Rubin observed in "The Traffic in Women" (1975), sex and sexuality are the central mechanisms through which societies organize their kinship systems, with those labelled as women bearing the burden of structural inequality that guarantees men the bulk of power.

Finally, feminist scholarship observes that what counts as sexuality and how sex is organized varies around the world; it is not universally identical, even though every society has a sex-based system for organizing its members.

## Queer Theory Perspectives

The most prominent contributors to the sociological application of queer theory to the understanding of sexualities are Michel Foucault and Judith Butler. Their conceptual work has largely shaped the tools and approach we use to critically assess powerful and normative institutions.

Foucault's exhaustive three-volume work on sexuality (1990a, 1990b, 1990c) makes the point that bodies and sexualities came to have meaning only as a result of a variety of interventions and invasions: these label us by sex, by practice, and by general state-of-health assessments that teach us how to see ourselves and to understand our practices and desires by the tools of science, law, and medicine that Foucault labelled as a form of "gaze." A *gaze* is a view that imposes meaning rather than being simply a passive way of looking; it is, instead, a look that can pass judgment, mete out punishments, make assessments, and tell us who we are as much as demand it. For Foucault, the gaze structures the meanings of sexuality, for example, through claims to genetic foundations for predispositions, orientations, desires, and practices. The gaze can structure meanings through the admittance of some forms of marriage but not others, thereby conferring or refusing legitimacy; finally, the gaze requires that we also look back at it to confirm that we accept its conclusions as truths, for example, in popular media claims that

**anti-essentialism**

The refusal of simplistic biological explanations for complex social relations, motivations, behaviours, and identifications.

**constructionist**

The belief that social context provides the mode and meaning for both sexuality and gendered behaviours, roles, and relationships.

overstate the conclusions of biomedicine with regard to what "causes" same-sex desire.

Butler, who began writing on gender and sexuality in the late 1980s, made the powerful observation that as the symbolic basis upon which a variety of social and sexual demands are fixed, gender is not a natural expression of our sex, but a means of conveying and of securing a socially legitimated place for ourselves—a place from which we can be recognized as male or female, and out of which a variety of norms regarding sex(uality) are expressed. In her 1990 book *Gender Trouble*, Butler argued that gender was a performance, something that was unstable, and that all of us have to work at it every day, to make ourselves knowable and recognizable to others. Many people took her statement to suggest that we could simply decide on our gender and then act it out. However, Butler later argued in *Bodies That Matter* (1993) that this was a misreading: our performance could not be freely and individually willed, but was compelled by those around us; those who do not "fit in" to the performance demands are placed at grave risk in a heteronormative and homophobic society.

For the social study of sexualities, the combined observations of feminist and queer theories help us to understand that the way things are is not the way things have to be, that oppressive functions can be challenged, and that claims to "the naturalness" of one form of sexuality operate to the benefit of only a tiny minority of the population, neither providing an accurate description nor an adequate understanding of sex and sexuality. Moreover, such claims place many people, including most women and those who are in some way "queer," in highly vulnerable positions.

# 9.5 Heterosexism, Homophobia, and Biphobia

**Heterosexism** refers to "an ideological system that denies, denigrates, and stigmatizes any nonheterosexual form of behaviour, identity, relationship, or community" (Herek 1990: 316). Heterosexism is based on the belief that heterosexuality is "natural" and, therefore, "normal," that it is superior to homosexuality, and that homosexuality is what happens when something disrupts a presupposed "natural order." Heterosexism lays the foundation for prejudice and discrimination against GLBT persons. Prejudice refers to negative attitudes, whereas discrimination refers to behaviour that denies individuals or groups equality of treatment. Before reading further, you may wish to complete this chapter's *Self and Society* feature, The Homophobia Scale.

**heterosexism**

The belief that heterosexuality is the superior sexual orientation; it results in prejudice and discrimination against homosexuals and bisexuals.

## Homophobia

The term **homophobia** is commonly used to refer to negative attitudes and emotions toward homosexuality and those who engage in it. Other terms that refer to negative attitudes and emotions toward homosexuality include *homonegativity* and *antigay bias*.

**homophobia**

Negative attitudes toward homosexuality.

## The Homophobia Scale

Directions: Indicate the extent to which you agree or disagree with each statement by placing a check mark on the appropriate line.

| | Strongly Agree | Agree | Undecided | Disagree | Strongly Disagree |
|---|---|---|---|---|---|
| 1. Homosexuals contribute positively to society. | ___ | ___ | ___ | ___ | ___ |
| 2. Homosexuality is disgusting. | ___ | ___ | ___ | ___ | ___ |
| 3. Homosexuals are just as moral as heterosexuals are. | ___ | ___ | ___ | ___ | ___ |
| 4. Homosexuals should have equal civil rights. | ___ | ___ | ___ | ___ | ___ |
| 5. Homosexuals corrupt young people. | ___ | ___ | ___ | ___ | ___ |
| 6. Homosexuality is a sin. | ___ | ___ | ___ | ___ | ___ |

### Scoring

Assign scores of 0, 1, 2, 3, and 4 to the five choices respectively ("strongly agree" through "strongly disagree") for items 1, 3, and 4. Assign scores of 0, 1, 2, 3, and 4 to the five choices in reverse order ("strongly disagree" through "strongly agree") for items 2, 5, and 6. All items are summed for the total score. The possible range is 0 to 28; high scores indicate greater homophobia.

### Comparison Data

The Homophobia Scale was administered to 524 students enrolled in introductory psychology courses at the University of Texas. The mean score for men was 15.8; for women, it was 13.8. The difference was statistically significant.

SOURCE: Bouton, Richard A., P. E. Gallagher, P. A. Garlinghouse, T. Leal, et al. 1987. "Scales for Measuring Fear of AIDS and Homophobia." *Journal of Personality Assessment* 67(1): 609. Copyright © Francis and Taylor Group, www.informaworld.com. Used with permission.

Prevailing attitudes can, however, shift; as with most social phenomena, change is always possible. We can identify some of the features that have correlated with large shifts in popular attitudes and perception. People who are younger, more educated, never married, living in the West, living in heavily populated urban areas, and Jewish are least likely to have antigay attitudes (Klassen et al. 1989). Also, positive contact with GLBT people is associated with less homophobia (Simon 1995). The development of attitudes is, however, complex. Sociological studies reveal that issues of class, of education, of family history, of one's gender, and so forth are all influential forces in attitude development.

In a study of undergraduates (101 men, 98 women) attending a Canadian university where most students were of working-class or middle-class families of European descent, Schellenberg and colleagues (1999) found that attitudes toward gay men were more negative than toward lesbians. When compared to science or business students, students in the faculties of arts and social sciences had more positive attitudes toward gay men, and women were more positive than men were. Attitudes toward gay men improved with time spent at university, but only for male students. Although attitudes toward lesbians also improved with time at university, this trend was not associated with students' gender or faculty of enrolment. Schellenberg and colleagues conclude that university education may encourage a reduction in antihomosexual prejudice among young people, particularly among young men. In an effort to reduce homophobia and its consequences, campuses across Canada have set up "Positive Space" programs. These let people know that homophobic and hateful behaviour will not be tolerated, and that GLBT students can find a safe place to think, learn, and live on the campus.

## Cultural Origins of Homophobia

Why is homosexuality viewed so negatively in North America? Antigay bias has its roots in various aspects of our culture.

1. *Religion.* Most individuals who view homosexuality as unacceptable say they object on religious grounds (Rosin and Morin 1999). Although some religious groups accept homosexuality, many religions teach that homosexuality is sinful and prohibited by God. The Roman Catholic Church rejects all homosexual expression and resists any attempt to validate or sanction the homosexual orientation. Some fundamentalist churches have endorsed the death penalty for homosexual people and teach the view that AIDS is God's punishment for engaging in homosexual sex (Nugent and Gramick 1989). In June 1999, a U.S. Baptist preacher from Topeka, Kansas, announced that he and a group of his followers would be leading a demonstration on the steps of the Supreme Court of Canada to protest its decision to extend the definition of "spouse" to same-sex couples. Mr. Phelps, who on previous occasions has picketed gay funerals, same-sex unions, and even Girl Scout meetings brandishing signs that read, "AIDS cures fags," had announced, "We're coming to spread the gospel to you sinners." Phelps referred to Canada as the "sperm bank of Satan" and vowed that he and his supporters would burn Canadian flags in protest. In the end, Mr. Phelps did not appear and his group blamed the unwillingness of Canadian police, "who are as blackhearted as the perverts," to provide him with the level of protection he sought as the reason for the group's absence (Anderssen 1999).

    Some religious groups, such as the Quakers, accept homosexuality, and other groups have made reforms toward increased acceptance of lesbians and gays. In the United States, some Episcopal priests perform "ceremonies of union" between same-sex couples; some Reform Jewish groups sponsor gay synagogues, and the United Church of Christ ordains gay men and women (Fone 2000). The United Church of Canada has ignited conflict by declaring that "all persons, regardless of their sexual orientation, are welcome to become full members of the church and are eligible for ordination as ministers" (in Dawson 1993: 323).

2. *Marital and procreative bias.* Many societies have traditionally condoned sex only when it occurs in a marital context that provides for the possibility of producing and rearing children. However, science continues to challenge the necessity of opposite-sex parents. "Under cell nuclear replacement, scientists replace the nucleus from the egg of a female donor with the nucleus from a sperm cell. The resulting 'male egg,' containing only male DNA, is then fertilized in vitro by sperm from another man" (Honore 2000). Even though already-available assisted reproductive technologies make it possible for gay individuals and couples to have children, many people believe that only heterosexual married couples should use these advances (Franklin 1993).

3. *Concern about HIV and AIDS.* Although transmission rates vary upward and downward for different groups over time and most cases of HIV and AIDS worldwide are attributed to heterosexual transmission, HIV and AIDS in Canada is more prevalent among gay and bisexual men than among other groups. Because of this, many people associate HIV and AIDS with homosexuality and bisexuality. Lesbians, incidentally, have a very low risk for sexually transmitted HIV—a lower risk than heterosexual women do.

4. *Threat to the power of the majority.* Like other minority groups, the gay minority threatens the power of the majority. Fearing loss of power, the majority group stigmatizes gays and lesbians and transgender people as a way of limiting their power.

5. *Rigid gender roles.* Antigay sentiments also stem from rigid gender roles. When Cooper Thompson (1995) was asked to give a guest presentation on male roles at a suburban high school, male students told him that the most humiliating insult was being called a "fag." The boys in this school gave Thompson the impression that they were expected to conform to rigid, narrow standards of masculinity to avoid being labelled in this way.

   From a conflict perspective, heterosexual men's subordination and devaluation of gay men reinforces gender inequality. "By devaluing gay men...heterosexual men devalue the feminine and anything associated with it" (Price and Dalecki 1998: 155–56). Negative views toward lesbians also reinforce the patriarchal system of male dominance. Social disapproval of lesbians is a form of punishment for women who relinquish traditional female sexual and economic dependence on men. Not surprisingly, research findings suggest that individuals with traditional gender role attitudes tend to hold more negative views toward homosexuality (Louderback and Whitley 1997).

6. *Psychiatric labelling.* As noted earlier, before 1973 the APA (American Psychiatric Association) defined homosexuality as a mental disorder, and "treatment" included lobotomies, aversive conditioning, and, in some cases, castration. The APA definition contributed to negative reactions to gays and also created feelings of guilt, low self-esteem, anger, and depression for many gays and lesbians. The psychiatric care system is now busily treating the very conditions it, in part, created.

7. *Myths and negative stereotypes.* Prejudice toward gays and lesbians may also stem from some of the unsupported beliefs and negative stereotypes regarding same-sex sexuality. One such belief is that gays and lesbians lack

"family values," such as monogamy and commitment to relationships. While some do engage in casual sex, as do some heterosexuals, many gay and lesbian couples develop and maintain long-term committed relationships.

Another myth is that, as groups, gay men and lesbians (to a lesser extent perhaps because of the common assumption that women are less sexual than men) are child molesters. Yet, the ratio of heterosexual to gay male child molesters is approximately 11 to 1 (Moser 1992). When a father sexually assaults his daughter, the media do not report that something is wrong with heterosexuality or with traditional families, but when a homosexual is reported to have molested a child, it is viewed as confirmation of "the way homosexuals are" (Mohr 1995: 404).

## Biphobia

Just as the term *homophobia* refers to negative attitudes toward gay men and lesbians, **biphobia** refers to "the parallel set of negative beliefs about and stigmatization of bisexuality and those identified as bisexual" (Paul 1996: 449). Although heterosexuals often reject both homosexual- and bisexual-identified individuals, bisexual-identified women and men also face rejection from many homosexual individuals. Thus, bisexuals experience "double discrimination."

Biphobia includes negative stereotyping of bisexuals; the exclusion of bisexuals from social and political organizations of lesbians and gay men; and fear and distrust of, as well as anger and hostility toward, people who identify themselves as bisexual (Firestein 1996). Individuals who are biphobic often believe that bisexuals are really homosexuals afraid to acknowledge their real identity or homosexuals maintaining heterosexual relationships to avoid rejection by the heterosexual mainstream. Bisexual individuals are sometimes viewed as heterosexuals who are looking for exotic sexual experiences.

Negative attitudes regarding bisexuality and people who identify as bisexual are not the exclusive domain of heterosexual homophobes. Lesbian philosopher Elizabeth Grosz suggested in a conference paper that "bisexuality was a luxury, that bisexuals want to have their cake and eat it" (Angelides 1995: 27). Steven Angelides (1995) holds out this summary of Grosz's position as a statement that exemplifies a not uncommon mistrust of bisexuals by gays and lesbians, but argues that attitudes such as Grosz's rest on ideas about identity that reinforce the notion that someone who is not oppressed based on a given trait (like race, ethnicity, or sexuality) cannot fully commit to anti-oppressive politics. Angelides argues that biphobia discounts the productive and rich political value of bisexuality and avers that our ethical commitments are built on awareness, not identity, and that our political commitments do not have to be bounded and bordered by our personal desires.

## Effects of Homophobia and Heterosexism on Heterosexuals

The homophobic and heterosexist social climate of our society is often viewed in terms of how it victimizes the gay population. However, heterosexuals are also victimized by homophobia and heterosexism. "Hatred, fear, and ignorance are bad for the bigot as well as the victim" (*Homophobia 101* 2000).

**biphobia**

Negative attitudes toward bisexuality and people who identify as bisexual.

Due to the antigay climate, heterosexuals, especially males, are hindered in their own self-expression and intimacy in same-sex friendships. "The threat of victimization (i.e., antigay violence) probably also causes many heterosexuals to conform to gender roles and to restrict their expressions of (nonsexual) physical affection for members of their own sex" (Garnets et al. 1990: 380). Homophobic epithets frighten youth who do not conform to gender role expectations, leading some youth to avoid activities that they might otherwise enjoy and benefit from (arts for boys, athletics for girls, for example) (*Homophobia 101* 2000).

Some sexual assaults are related to homophobia and compulsory heterosexuality. For example, some men who participate in gang rape entice others into the act "by implying that those who do not participate are unmanly or homosexual" (Sanday 1995: 399). Homo-negativity also encourages early sexual activity among adolescent men. Adolescent male virgins are often teased by their peers, who say things like "You mean you don't do it with girls yet? What are you, a fag or something?" Not wanting to be labelled and stigmatized as a "fag," some adolescent boys "prove" their heterosexuality by having sex with girls.

Antigay cultural attitudes also affect family members and friends of homosexuals, who often fear that their lesbian or gay friend or family member will be victimized by antigay prejudice and discrimination. Youth with gay and lesbian family members are often taunted by their peers.

As we have already noted, extreme homophobia can lead to instances of physical violence against homosexuals. But "gay bashings" are crimes of perception because victims of antigay violence may not be homosexual, only perceived as being homosexual. Many heterosexuals have been victims of antigay physical violence because the attacker(s) perceived them to be gay. Antigay harassment has also been a factor in some cases of school violence. One study concluded, "For boys, no other type of harassment provoked as strong a reaction on average; boys in this study would be less upset about physical abuse than they would be if someone called them gay" (Dozetos 2001).

## 9.6 Discrimination against Sexual-Orientation Minorities

Like other minority groups in Canada, GLBT persons have experienced and continue to experience various forms of discrimination. From 1952 to 1977, immigration laws prohibited homosexuals from entering Canada and subjected homosexuals to the threat of deportation if their sexual orientation became known. From 1892 to 1969, Canadian criminal law made certain forms of sexual conduct engaged in by gay men illegal and rendered gay men vulnerable to indefinite incarceration as "dangerous sexual offenders."

Next, we look at sexual-orientation discrimination in the workplace, in family matters, and in violent expressions of hate. This chapter's *Focus on Technology* feature discusses the discriminatory effects of internet filtering and monitoring technology on sexual-orientation minorities.

NEL

## The Impact of Internet Filtering and Monitoring on Sexual-Orientation Minorities

Joan Garry is the executive director of the Gay and Lesbian Alliance Against Defamation (GLAAD) and a mother of three children. When her 10-year-old daughter Sarah approached her for information about COLAGE (Children of Lesbians and Gays Everywhere), a support organization for the children of lesbian and gay parents, they signed on to America Online to look up the website. The COLAGE site was "Web Restricted": Sarah could not access the site because her computer was equipped with AOL's filtering software called Kids Only. When Joan tried to look up various family, youth, and national organization websites with lesbian and gay content, most sites came up "Web Restricted" as well (Garry 1999). For example, the Kids Only software blocked access to several youth-oriented gay and lesbian resource sites, including PFLAG (Parents, Family and Friends of Lesbians and Gays), Family Pride, !OutProud!, GLSEN (Gay, Lesbian and Straight Education Network), and *Oasis Magazine*, a gay and lesbian youth webzine (Javier 1999).

An explosion of filtering technologies to help maintain "decency" and "community standards" on the internet has occurred. Examples of filtering technologies include those that block key words or URLs. For example, the search engine Jayde. com, which marketed itself as being able to filter out pornographic material, decided to block the word "lesbian" in its search engine. The filtering software "CYBERsitter" automatically filters out such words

and phrases as "gay," "lesbian," "gay rights," and "gay community" (Javier 1999). Filtering technologies are promoted as tools to help parents, schools, libraries, and communities prevent children's access to sexually explicit and pornographic material on the internet. However, some filtering software also denies users access to several lesbian, gay, and bisexual youth resource sites.

Schneider (1999) presents the following scenario:

> Imagine a teenager seeking information about his or her sexual orientation whose attempts to go to gay-related Web sites are met with a warning that tells him or her "Bess doesn't want you to go there." In an unfiltered environment...the teen could be expected to privately retrieve all kinds of information in a discreet, nonjudgmental environment. But place a filter on that computer, and...the teen gets the message that he or she is somehow..."inappropriate." (p. 13)

Given the impact of internet filtering on the gay community, some gay rights groups oppose the use of filtering software. Instead, they advocate parental oversight, school supervision, and training of young internet users (Bowes 1999).

Another concern of sexual-orientation minorities is the use of monitoring software. This software allows parents, teachers, and other authority figures to track sites a Web surfer tries to access. The monitoring software industry markets its products by claiming that they allow for parental awareness without censorship and that parental use of monitoring software encourages open family communication. But for youth who are not ready to reveal their sexual orientation to their family, "such software could

potentially 'out' them before they are ready, leading to strained family relations and deeper isolation" (Javier 1999: 8).

In addition, internet service providers may record every click of your mouse, including personal information you exchange in chat rooms, emails, and instant messages.

Say you visit a Web magazine: the time and date of your visit are recorded. You conduct a search for all articles containing the word "gay." Your inquiry is recorded. You click on an article about new AIDS drugs. Your request for that article is recorded. While reading the article, you click on an ad about online dating services, and that choice is recorded.... You decide to enter a gay-oriented chat room and see if you can make any new friends, or even get a date. You chat with a number of people, and finally connect with one special person, with whom you share instant messages, pictures, and perhaps even a virtual date. Depending on the Internet provider in question, that date could have just been recorded (Aravosis 1999: 30).

Websites also record information about your internet usage. When you visit a free news website, you may be required to "subscribe" by giving them your name and email address. After subscribing, you read a few articles. But unbeknownst to you, the news website has put a "cookie," or piece of computer code, on the hard drive of your computer. This cookie contains a unique identifier permitting the news site to recognize you when you return to that site. Cookies can do helpful things, like remember your password for accessing that site, and tailor Web pages for preset preferences. But they can also contain a

(continued)

record of what you did on that site, including what searches you made and what articles you read (Aravosis 1999). According to one study, of the 7500 busiest servers on the Web, 93 percent of the sites collect personal information from consumers, yet only 66 percent post any disclosure about their information practices (Bowes 1999).

Although some websites have strict privacy policies, others sell information about site visitors. One company boasts on its website that it is "the world's oldest and largest mailing list manager and broker for Gay, Lesbian, and HIV-related names, currently managing almost two million names, which we estimate to be about 65 percent of all those commercially available in this segment" (Aravosis 1999: 33). Databases containing the names of gay consumers are valuable because gays are perceived as a "wealthy

and wired market." A 1998 study found that the average household income of lesbians and gay men on the internet was $57 300, slightly higher than the $52 000 for the general internet population (Aravosis 1999).

The internet has been a useful tool for gays, lesbians, and bisexuals. Going online has allowed the gay community to create safe places for support and information. However, internet filtering and monitoring software that has been installed on computers in homes, schools, libraries, and workplaces represents a threat to the gay community. Filtering and monitoring technologies make it impossible or dangerous for a closeted gay or lesbian to seek out support and information about their community.

We live in an age in which the Internet has become an extremely important part of the coming out

process for many gay and lesbian youth. In many cases, it can be a lifeline to those in geographically isolated areas. To deny basic educational and support resources to lesbian and gay youth could seriously endanger their physical and emotional well being. (Appendix A 1999: 46)

SOURCES: Appendix A. 1999. "Frequently Asked Questions." In *Access Denied Version 2.0, The Continuing Threat against Internet Access and Privacy and Its Impact on the Lesbian, Gay, Bisexual and Transgender Community.* New York: Gay and Lesbian Alliance Against Defamation, pp. 45–48; Aravosis, John. 1999. "Privacy: The Impact on Lesbian, Gay, Bisexual and Transgender Community." In *Access Denied Version 2.0*, pp. 30–33; Bowes, John. 1999. "Conclusions." In *Access Denied Version 2.0*, pp. 38–44; Garry, Joan M. 1999. "Introduction: How Access and Privacy Impact the Lesbian, Gay, Bisexual and Transgender Community." In *Access Denied Version 2.0*, pp. 3–5; Javier, Loren. 1999. "The World since Access Denied." In *Access Denied 2.0*, pp. 6–9; Schneider, Karen G. 1999. "Access: The Impact on the Lesbian, Gay, Bisexual and Transgender Community." In *Access Denied Version 2.0*, pp. 10–15.

## Discrimination in the Workplace

In recent years, the percentage of Canadians who express approval of equal employment rights for homosexuals has increased. Nevertheless, many Canadians still feel that homosexuals should not be entitled to the same rights and privileges as others. While support levels for gays working in a variety of different occupations increased between 1988 and 2001, certain occupations are still considered "more suitable" than others. For example, the vast majority of Canadians find it acceptable for gays to work as salespersons (94 percent vs. 72 percent in 1988), members of Parliament (86 percent vs. 62 percent in 1988), members of the Canadian Forces (82 percent vs. 60 percent in 1988), physicians (82 percent vs. 52 percent in 1988), or prison officers (75 percent vs. 44 percent in 1988). However, there is less support for gays working as junior-school teachers (67 percent vs. 45 percent in 1988) or members of the clergy (63 percent vs. 44 percent in 1988) (Bricker and Greenspon 2001: 267–68).

Only a few decades ago, there were few legal protections for gay and lesbian individuals who experienced employment discrimination. In the 1960s, hostility toward gays in the workplace led to more than 8000 gay men being investigated by the RCMP; as a result, approximately 150 gay federal civil servants resigned or were dismissed from their employment positions without just cause. It was only in 1992 that the Canadian armed forces, facing a court challenge, agreed to stop discrimination against gays. At the time of writing, discrimination on the basis of sexual orientation was prohibited everywhere in Canada except for the Northwest Territories and Nunavut. While Alberta's legislation does not state this prohibition specifically, the Supreme Court of Canada declared in the 1998 case of *Vriend v. Alberta* that Alberta's human rights legislation "would be interpreted to include sexual orientation as a prohibited ground—whether or not it is specified in the legislation.... This marked the first time the Supreme Court of Canada amended legislation on constitutional grounds by reading into law new rights that elected politicians had expressly refused to grant" (Dranoff 2001: 134).

## Discrimination in Family Relationships

In addition to discrimination in the workplace, sexual-orientation minorities in Canada have also experienced discrimination in policies on marriage, child custody and visitation, and adoption.

**Same-Sex Marriage** In June of 1999, the Canadian House of Commons voted overwhelmingly in favour of a motion, introduced by Eric Lowther, the Reform Party critic on "Children and Families," opposing same-sex marriages. The motion, which signalled the first time same-sex marriage was the subject of a vote in the House of Commons, affirmed the exclusion of gays and lesbians from the institution of marriage; it also committed Parliament to "take all necessary steps" to preserve legal marriage as an opposite-sex institution. Although passing the motion had no immediate legal impact, it might be presumed that as an official declaration of Parliament's position on the matter, the "necessary steps" could include invoking the "notwithstanding" clause within the Constitution. This clause allows governments to opt out of the *Charter of Rights and Freedoms* and to deny equality to some of their citizens—in this case, lesbians and gay men. In total, 216 members of Parliament (MPs) from all parties voted in favour of the motion, including the overwhelming majority of the Liberal caucus (all but 11), all Reform Party MPs, and a number of those from the New Democratic Party, Bloc Québécois, and Progressive Conservative Party. Only 55 MPs voted against the motion. Although a "free vote"—with MPs able to "vote their conscience" rather than follow a party line—had been expected, in the end the Liberal government adopted a government position that supported the Reform Party (EGALE 1999). By 2005, though, the then minority Liberal government passed legislation to permit same-sex marriages.

In that year, various provincial governments also grappled with the issues presented by same-sex marriages. In May 1999, the Supreme Court of Ontario ruled that an Ontario law that excluded gays and lesbians from a definition of common-law couples was unconstitutional. Shortly after, the Ontario government passed an omnibus bill that amended 67 of its laws to include same-sex couples.

Although the Supreme Court's ruling was binding only on the Ontario government, several other provinces quickly announced plans to make similar changes. For example, in June of that year, when the Quebec National Assembly unanimously passed Bill 32, Quebec became the first Canadian province to ensure that same-sex couples would receive all the benefits and responsibilities of opposite-sex couples. Bill 32 changed the definition of "spouse" within that province and committed the Quebec government to making changes in 39 provincial laws and regulations. A month later, the British Columbia government

# The *Human Side*

## "It's about Love": A Canadian Couple Fighting for Recognition of Same-Sex Unions

*Kevin Bourassa, 44, and Joe Varnell, 32, were one of two Canadian same-sex couples married on July 14, 2001, at Toronto's Metropolitan Community Church. When the provincial government of Ontario refused to grant them a wedding licence, Bourassa and Varnella turned to the courts. In mid-July of 2002, three Ontario Superior Court judges ruled that the federal law that prohibits same-sex couples from marrying was unconstitutional—a ruling that Ottawa is appealing. In the following extract from an interview which originally appeared in Maclean's in August 2002, Bourassa and Varnell, co-authors of Just Married: Gay Marriage and the Expansion of Human Rights, discuss their fight for the right to marry.*

**Were you expecting the federal government to appeal the court's decision?**

Varnell: When we started, we knew there was a strong possibility that a positive decision would be appealed. But because of the overwhelmingly strong wording of the judgment, telling the government its laws were unconstitutional, we were a little surprised.

Bourassa: Various things led us to be hopeful. The polls, the provincial Conservatives saying they wouldn't appeal the ruling, the federal government floating the trial balloon about getting out of the marriage business, fueled our hope that Ottawa would honour the Charter.

**What do you think of the proposal that there should be no more state-sanctioned marriages, just religious ceremonies or civil arrangements?**

Varnell: It's an extremely radical step—far more radical than simply extending

the definition of marriage to include gays and lesbians. But it would be a disappointing option for us because they would be saying that rather than pollute the institution of marriage with same-sex couples, they'd prefer to pick up their toys and go home.

**Why is marriage so important for gay and lesbian couples?**

Bourassa: First, it's about the government being allowed to treat one group that is otherwise protected by the Charter differently. It's important to send a message that gays and lesbians are not second-class citizens. But on a personal level, marriage is about love. We should be able to experience that love in the manner we choose, in a manner available to all Canadians.

**Is marriage something you think other gay couples should do?**

Varnell: Marriage isn't for every couple. Relationships have to be protected in law. But the formalization

introduced the "Definition of Spouse Amendment," which expanded the definition of "spouse" in that province to include "a person who has lived and cohabited with another person, for a period of at least two years immediately before the other person's death, in a 'marriage-like' relationship, including a marriage-like relationship between persons of the same gender." In that province, same-sex couples who meet this definition have the same spousal rights and responsibilities as heterosexual couples, including a right to contract into property and pensions, and to inherit from their partner as a spouse if the partner dies without a will. This chapter's *The Human Side* feature takes a personal look at the fight of Canadian couples to have their unions recognized, and to be allowed to marry.

In 2000, legislation in Nova Scotia revised the definition of "spouse" to include both opposite and same-sex couples who have lived together in a conjugal relationship for at least one year. In that year, "for the first time in the seven years it had been asking the question, less than half of Canadians [48 percent] opposed same-sex marriage" (Bricker and Greenspon 2001: 267).

Advocates of same-sex marriage maintain that as long as same-sex couples cannot be legally married, they will not be viewed as legitimate families by the larger society and will face undue stress as a result. On the other hand, opponents of same-sex marriage do not want their children to learn that

of those relationships has to be an individual choice.

## How has being married affected your personal lives?

Bourassa: Over the past 12 months, I've gone from a banking career to working full time at advocacy. I couldn't do that if it wasn't for Joe. Marriage is like that—it's sharing resources and complementing one another.

## And what have you personally, emotionally, got out of marriage?

Bourassa: It's brought us closer and closer together. If you can work together through stress and you can also find that you're building something together that's bigger than the two of you could do alone, that's great. And I think we're doing that.

## How have people reacted when you tell them you're married?

Bourassa: Most people respond positively. It's usually not confrontational unless you're dealing with a situation such as when we were watching fireworks on a blanket, and a bunch of kids heckled us from a car. People will do it from a distance. It's much more difficult to do to your face....

Varnell: It's fine to have protection in law, but until you have acceptance in your community, the protection in law can be very cold comfort.

## Update

In January of 2011, Bourassa and Varnell celebrated their tenth wedding anniversary by renewing their marriage vows. They shared their renewal along with Anne and Elaine Vatour, who had been the first lesbian couple in Canada to marry, also on January 14, 2001. In an interview that Varnell and Bourassa gave to the *Toronto Star* in 2011, looking back on their wedding day 10 years earlier, Bourassa reported that the day had come with threats against their lives and that they had required police protection for the ceremony:

> We said our goodbye to people, we told them we loved them.... We were told we were under threat. The last words the police officers said to us as we went down the aisle was, "If you hear a shot don't move, somebody will move you, just stand still." (Talaga 2011)

SOURCE: Abridged from *Maclean's*. 2002. "'It's about Love': A Pioneering Gay Couple Defends Same-Sex Unions." August 12, 2002: 46–47. Reprinted by permission of *Maclean's* magazine.

homosexuality is an accepted and acceptable life. Many of them view homosexuality as unnatural, sick, and/or immoral.

The most common argument against same-sex marriage is that it subverts the stability and integrity of the heterosexual family. Sullivan (1997), though, points out that gays and lesbians are already part of heterosexual families:

> [Homosexuals] are sons and daughters, brothers and sisters, even mothers and fathers, of heterosexuals. The distinction between "families" and "homosexuals" is, to begin with, empirically false; and the stability of existing families is closely linked to how homosexuals are treated within them. (p. 147)

According to the 2001 Canadian census, 13 percent of female same-sex couples have children living with them and 3 percent of same-sex male couples are also parenting children (Arnold 2002).

**Child Custody, Visitation, and Reproductive Rights** Another milestone for gay activists was attained in 2001 when, for the first time, a Canadian survey reported majority support for gay adoption (Bricker and Greenspon 2001: 267). In 1995, an Ontario provincial judge ruled that gay and lesbian couples have the right to apply to adopt a child under that province's *Child and Family Services Act*. In 1998, British Columbia passed amendments to its

*Adoption Act* and *Family Relations Act* that provided same-sex couples who cohabit continuously for two years with the same right to apply to adopt a child. In 1999, Alberta joined with these provinces in permitting same-sex couples to adopt.

Little was known until relatively recently about the nature of gay and lesbian family life. Many published accounts were non-empirical and saturated with a heterosexist bias that framed gay and lesbian families as "deviant" and "pathological." Even though research on gay and lesbian families expanded dramatically in the 1990s (e.g., Arnup 1995; Benkov 1994; Stone 1990; Weston 1991), generalizable information still remains sparse due to nonrandom sampling, limited sample sizes, and the diversities of these families occasioned by ethnicity, class, age of parents and offspring, and circumstances leading to family formation. However, in a review of research on family relationships of lesbians and gay men, Patterson (2001) concludes that "the greater majority of children with lesbian or gay parents grow up to identify themselves as heterosexual" and that "concerns about possible difficulties in personal development among children of lesbian and gay parents have not been sustained by the results of research" (p. 279). Patterson (2001) additionally notes that the "home environments provided by lesbian and gay parents are just as likely as those provided by heterosexual parents to enable psychosocial growth among family members" (p. 283).

At least in theory, custody and access orders in Canada are equally available to members of same-sex unions and opposite-sex unions, with decisions made in "the best interests of the child." However, while "[n]othing in Canadian law stops a homosexual parent from applying for custody, the courts will often take judicial notice of the fact that some harm might arise from living with a homosexual parent" (Yogis et al. 1996: 56). Yogis and colleagues note that Canadian case law suggests that "custody is awarded to discreet, non-militant homosexual parents who do not flaunt their sexual orientation" (p. 56).

## Hate Crimes against Sexual-Orientation Minorities

In eighteenth-century North America, where laws against same-sex sexual activity often included the death penalty, violence against gays and lesbians was widespread, and included beatings, burnings, various kinds of torture, and execution (Button et al. 1997). Although such treatment of sexual-orientation minorities is no longer legally condoned, gays, lesbians, and bisexuals continue to be victimized by hate crimes. Surveys indicate that as many as one-fourth of lesbians and gay men report having been victims of physical attacks because of their sexual orientation (Herek 1989). A survey of more than 3000 high-school students found that students who reported having engaged in same-sex relations were more than three times as likely to report not going to school because they felt unsafe and more than twice as likely to report having been threatened or injured with a weapon at school (Faulkner and Cranston 1998). These students were also significantly more likely to report that their property was deliberately damaged or stolen at school.

Hate-motivated violence toward sexual-orientation minorities can be brutal. The following example is given in *Reaching Out: A Report on Lesbian, Gay, and Bisexual Youth Issues in Canada*, prepared for the United Church of Canada by

9.7 Strategies for Action: Reducing Antigay Prejudice and Discrimination **317**

John Fisher (1999), executive director of Equality for Gays and Lesbians Everywhere (EGALE):

> When Christian Hernandez was 14 and a Grade 9 student at Notre Dame College High School in Niagara Falls, Ontario, he screwed up his courage and told his best friend that he was gay. That was his first mistake. "He told me he couldn't accept it," recalls Hernandez. "And he began to spread it around." Over the next two years, Hernandez was teased and harassed almost daily. One day, a group of boys waited for him after school. Their leader had a knife, and, says Hernandez, "He told me he didn't accept faggots, that we brought AIDS into the world." The boy then cut Hernandez on the neck, putting him in the hospital for a week. When Hernandez told his parents about the attack, his father, who has since moved back to his native El Salvador, said he would "rather have a dead son than a queer son."

Next, we highlight some of the strategies for reducing and responding to prejudice and discrimination toward sexual-orientation minorities.

# 9.7 Strategies for Action: Reducing Antigay Prejudice and Discrimination

Many of the efforts to change policies and attitudes regarding sexual-orientation minorities have been spearheaded by organizations. These include the above-mentioned EGALE, Canada's only national equal rights organization advocating for lesbians, gays, and bisexuals, with members in every province and territory; Parents, Family, and Friends of Lesbians and Gays (PFLAG); the Foundation for Equal Families (FFEF); Victoria Youth Pride Society; Pink Triangle Services Youth Group in Ottawa; Lesbian and Gay Health Services in Saskatoon; and the British Columbia Civil Liberties Association.

These organizations are politically active in their efforts to achieve equal rights for gays, lesbians, and bisexuals. For example, the mandate of the FFEF is to achieve equality and recognition of same-sex relationships and associated family rights through legal action and education. In January 1999, the Foundation launched an omnibus challenge of 58 federal laws affecting the rights of lesbian and gay couples. The omnibus challenge affected laws as diverse as the *Income Tax Act*, the *Canadian Pension Plan Act*, the *Criminal Code*, the *Immigration Act*, the *Evidence Act*, the *Judges' Act*, the *Old Age Security Act*, the *Veterans Allowance Act*, and the Royal Canadian Mounted Police's *Superannuation Act*. The gay rights movement is also active in promoting HIV/AIDS research, adequate health care for AIDS victims, and the rights of HIV-infected individuals.

In addition, demonstrative and cultural expressions of gay activism, such as "gay pride" celebrations, marches, demonstrations, or other cultural activities promoting gay rights, are important in organizing gay activists. However, it has been noted that

> Too many people have seen the cultural activity as a substitute for democratic political participation. In too many cases over the past decades we have left the political arena to our most dedicated opponents [of gay rights], whose letter writing, phone calling, and lobbying have easily triumphed over our marching,

demonstrating, and dancing. The most important lesson...is that politics—conventional, boring, but essential politics—will ultimately have a major impact on the extent to which we can rid our lives of prejudice. (Frank 1997: xi)

In Canada, the various political parties have shown different levels of support for gay rights issues. For example, despite its caucus dominance from 1993 to 2005, no Liberal member of Parliament identified himself or herself as gay, lesbian, or bisexual and some, such as Roseanne Stoke and Tom Wappel, consistently referred to homosexuality as "unnatural," "immoral," and a "perversion." In the New Democratic Party, an openly gay former MP, Svend Robinson, consistently demonstrated strong support for lesbian and gay equality, as has the leader of the federal NDP. In contrast, members of the federal Conservative Party and its precursor Alliance and Reform parties nearly invariably voted against bills seeking to advance GLBT rights (EGALE 2001).

Although in the late 1990s Winnipeg elected its first openly gay mayor, Glen Murray, it would seem presumptuous to suppose that the issue of a candidate's sexual orientation is not considered relevant by at least some voters. It seems undeniable that the Christian right, religious and church groups, conservative family groups, and other conservative organizations and their political allies will continue to crusade against gay rights. Nevertheless, opposition groups are up against an increasingly powerful pro–gay rights movement.

### Educational Strategies: Policies and Programs in the Schools

A survey of youths' risk behaviour found that 30 percent of gay teens attempted suicide in the previous year, compared with 7 percent of their straight peers (reported in Platt 2001). Forty percent of gay youth report schoolwork being negatively affected by conflicts around sexual orientation, and over one-quarter of gay youth drop out of school (Chase 2000; *Homophobia 101* 2000). Research conducted in Calgary reports that gay and bisexual males were "almost 14 times more likely to have made a serious suicide attempt at some point in their lives than their heterosexually oriented counterparts" and that lesbian, gay, and bisexual youth of colour were dramatically overrepresented in attempted suicide statistics. According to one of the authors of this research, Pierre Tremblay, "This is the fallout of living with no guidance and no support. It's a problem every teacher knows about, but too often the attitude is, 'we would like to help, but we don't want to promote homosexuality.' It is a total abdication" (in Fisher 1999).

All of these findings suggest that if schools are to promote the health and well-being of all students, they must address the needs of gay, lesbian, and bisexual youth and promote acceptance of sexual-orientation diversity within the school setting (Flowers and Buston 2001; Murphy 2001). One strategy for promoting tolerance for diversity among students involves establishing and enforcing a school policy prohibiting antigay behaviour. Another strategy for addressing the needs of homosexual and bisexual youth is having school-based support groups. Such groups can help students increase self-esteem, overcome their sense of isolation, provide information and resources, and provide a resource for parents. In-service training for teachers and other staff is also important and may include examining the effects of antigay bias, dispelling myths about homosexuality, and brainstorming ways to create a more inclusive environment (Mathison 1998). Most public schools, though, offer little support and education regarding sexual-orientation diversity. Most schools lack support groups or special counselling services for gay and lesbian youth, and the majority of schools do not have any policies prohibiting antigay harassment (Button et al. 1997).

Nevertheless, some progress is being made. For example, in February 1997, the Calgary Board of Education approved an "Action Plan on Gay/Lesbian/ Bisexual Youth and Staff Safety" that requires guidance counsellors to provide "comprehensive information to students" when discussing sexual orientation and to "encourage students to discuss the issue with their parents." In Toronto, the Triangle Program offers gays who have been harassed at school an alternative place to study for up to 18 months and a curriculum that emphasizes the contributions of gays and lesbians in various fields, though as our chapter on education notes, this program is not without limitations. Various Canadian school boards and teaching institutes have adopted policies or initiatives that promote the equal treatment of gays and lesbians. For example, the Vancouver School Board's Statement of Mission and Beliefs states, "We believe in equitable treatment for all individuals, regardless of race, culture, gender, religion, socioeconomic status, sexual orientation or physical or mental ability." In addition, the federal government has launched a national initiative, the "Safe Spaces Project," funded by the federal Department of Health, to help produce educational materials for both heterosexual and lesbian and gay youth on lesbian, gay, and bisexual issues, and to create safe spaces for lesbian, gay, and bisexual youth.

## Campus Policies Regarding Homosexuality

Student groups have been active in the gay liberation movement since the 1960s. Numerous gay student groups are organized in community colleges and universities across Canada.

D'Emilio (1990) suggests that colleges and universities have the ability and the responsibility to promote gay rights and social acceptance of homosexual people:

> For reasons that I cannot quite fathom, I still expect the academy to embrace higher standards of civility, decency, and justice than the society around it. Having been granted the extraordinary privilege of thinking critically as a way of life, we should be astute enough to recognize when a group of people is being systematically mistreated. We have the intelligence to devise solutions to problems that appear in our community. I expect us also to have the courage to lead rather than follow. (p. 18)

In addition to including sexual orientation in discrimination policies, colleges and universities have also taken more proactive measures to support the lesbigay student population. Such measures have included offering gay and lesbian studies programs, social centres, and support groups, and sponsoring events and activities that celebrate diversity. "These programs serve as both a refuge for lesbians and gay men on campus, and common ground from which to launch educational projects that foster respect for difference" (Lambda Legal Defense and Educational Fund 2000: 10).

Strategies for reducing antigay prejudice and discrimination are influenced largely by politicians, religious leaders, courts, and educators, who will continue to make decisions that either promote the well-being of sexual-orientation minorities or hinder it. Ultimately, however, each individual must decide to embrace either an inclusive or an exclusive ideology; collectively, those individual decisions will determine the future treatment of sexual-orientation minorities.

In addition, lesbigay individuals must find their own strategies for living in a homophobic and biphobic society. They may find encouragement in the following:

> If you dream of a world in which you can put your partner's picture on your desk, then put his picture on your desk...and you will live in such a world.
>
> If you dream of a world in which there are more openly gay elected officials, then run for office...and you will live in such a world.
>
> And if you dream of a world in which you can take your partner to the office party...then take her to the party. I do, and now I live in such a world.
>
> Remember, there are two things that keep us oppressed—them and us. We are half of the equation. (Baldwin 2000)

## *Understanding* Sexualities

As both functionalists and conflict theorists note, "alternatives" to heterosexuality are threatening to traditionalists because they require new understandings and arrangements of family, childrearing, and gender roles. The conflict is expressed in economic, social, and legal discrimination by the majority. GLBT individuals are also victimized by hate crimes, and in some countries, same-sex activity is punished with sanctions ranging from fines to imprisonment and even death.

Evidence suggests that sexuality, like handedness, may have a biological component. The debate between biological and social explanations is commonly referred to as the "nature versus nurture" debate. Research indicates that both forces affect sexual orientation, although debate over which is dominant continues. Sociologists are interested in society's response to sexual-orientation diversity and how that response affects the quality of life of society's members. Because individuals' views toward sexuality are related to their beliefs about what "causes" any deviation from sexual norms, the question of the origins of sexual-orientation diversity has sociological significance.

Prejudice and discrimination toward sexual-orientation minorities are rooted in various aspects of culture, such as religious views, rigid gender roles, and negative myths and stereotypes. Hate crimes against homosexuals and bisexuals are blatant examples of the discrimination that sexual-orientation minorities continue to experience.

Attitudes toward lesbians and gays have become more accepting. One explanation for these changing attitudes is that awareness of personal contact with openly gay individuals has increased in recent years as more people come out to family and friends. "This is likely to increase support for gay and lesbian equality because contacts with openly gay individuals reduce negative stereotypes and ignorance" (Wilcox and Wolpert 2000: 414). Another explanation for changing attitudes toward homosexuality is the positive depiction of gays and lesbians in the popular media. In 1992 *Roseanne* and *Melrose Place* had gay and lesbian characters, in 1998 Ellen DeGeneres came out on her sitcom *Ellen*, and by the 2000s, central gay and lesbian characters appeared in many television shows, including

*Dawson's Creek, Will & Grace, Buffy the Vampire Slayer, Friends, ER, Spin City,* and *Normal, Ohio* (Deziel 2000). To these we can add the cable-television series *Six Feet Under* and *The L Word*.

But, as one scholar expressed: "the new confidence and social visibility of homosexuals...have by no means conquered homophobia. Indeed it stands as the last acceptable prejudice" (Fone 2000: 411). Although the gay rights movement has made significant gains in the last few decades, it has also suffered losses and defeat due to opposition groups and politicians. Many strategies for promoting gay rights have been successful and the Canadian public is becoming increasingly supportive of gay rights. But, as Yang (1999) points out, as the antigay minority diminishes in size, "it often becomes more dedicated and impassioned" (p. ii). For those who believe that all Canadians, regardless of sexual orientation, should be treated equally,

> Our task in the coming years is to get...[those] who support our cause to feel as passionately outraged by the injustices we face and to be as strongly motivated to act in support of our rights as our adversaries are in their opposition to our rights. (p.iii)

## Critical Thinking

**1.** What relationship do you see between the legalization of same-sex marriages in Canada and public attitudes toward same-sex couples?

**2.** Sexual-orientation minorities today can readily gain access to support organizations and networks via the internet. How do you see this use of the internet influencing the gay rights movement?

**3.** How are GLBT populations similar to and different from other minority groups?

**4.** Do you think that social acceptance of homosexuality leads to the creation of laws that protect lesbians and gays? Or does the enactment of laws that protect lesbians and gays help to create more social acceptance of gays? Explain.

## "Is It True?" Quiz: Answers

1 = true; 2 = false; 3 = false; 4 = false

# 8

# "Doing It": The Social Construction of S-E-X

TRACEY STEELE

*Sex is a natural, normal, enjoyable activity, right? Not so simple, says Tracey Steele as she shows how humans construct sex. This involves a number of processes and differs across cultures and with motivation of those involved. Steele discusses some of the ways humans view and construct sex to meet various goals: love, money, pleasure, exercise, companionship—the list goes on as do the methods for defining sex.*

*As you read, consider the following questions:*

1. *Why is "sex" complicated to define?*
2. *Which factors should one consider when defining sex?*
3. *Is homosexual sex really sex?*
4. *Why is sex a social construction?*

GLOSSARY **Social construction** Behaviors that are learned and produced within specific cultural contexts. **Deconstructing** Examining the hidden assumptions built into how a situation is defined and understood.

What is sex? And by this question I do not mean the dichotomous morphological division of the species into male and female. Rather, I mean what is "sex," **S–E–X?** Is it the sacred joining of two souls on a spiritual and physical plane? A commodity bought, sold, and traded in the cultural marketplace? A way to sustain the species? A delightful muscle spasm? A conjugal obligation? A weapon used to objectify, humiliate, and subjugate?

Sex is all of these things and many more. Its meanings and functions vary from epoch to epoch, and from culture to culture. It can simultaneously serve a variety of private motives and social aims, which are themselves shaped by the vicissitudes of personal desire and the sexual possibilities articulated through existing social conventions. In short, the meaning of sex is a product of both individual and social factors. What often goes unnoticed, however, is that while the purpose and ultimate significance of our sexual interactions may differ, the underlying sense that we know what sex *is,* generally does not. I may be in it for love, and you may be in it for money, pleasure, revenge, pity, exercise, or countless other reasons, but we both *"know"* what *"it"* is. After all, it's sex, it's natural, and *everybody* knows what sex is.

Source: Steele, Tracey. 2008. Revised version of previously published paper in Steele, Tracey. 2005. *Sex, Self and Society: The Social Context of Sexuality.* Belmont, CA: Wadsworth Publishing.

56

But do we? Curiously, we seem to forget, or wholly disregard, the fact that the road to adulthood is routinely paved with intense insecurity, doubt, and angst concerning that great mystery of mysteries—sex. Playing "doctor" with the next-door-neighbor, furtive scrutiny of purloined pornography, tentative adolescent fumblings, as well as those "mature" jokes told by friends that induced our hesitant laughter, silent confusion, and nervously feigned sophistication all testify to a decided uncertainty and *lack* of knowledge regarding sex. The truth is sex is *not* something innate, something we instinctively know; it is something we learn about as we grow to adulthood.

In fact, like most of our social behaviors, we gain our knowledge about what sex is from others, including key agents of socialization such as parents, peers, and the media. These groups convey cultural constructions—they pass on ideas about what "normal" sex is supposed to be, including who is supposed to be involved, for how long, in what locations, and toward what ends. And because sexual socialization begins quite early, it typically becomes so internalized that by the time we reach adulthood we fail to realize it was something we ever learned at all.

In the following pages I will utilize what is known as the social-constructionist perspective to explore the meaning of sex in contemporary American society. This perspective posits that sex, rather than being natural and instinctual is, in fact, principally a *learned* behavior that is produced within specific cultural contexts. I begin by **deconstructing** the meaning of sex in contemporary American society. Deconstructing sex involves examining the hidden assumptions built into how sex is defined and understood. In addition, the deconstruction of sex will reveal both the possibilities and the limits of existing definitions (Rubin, 1984). It will also bring to light how existing definitions work to privilege some social groups at the expense of others. Together these discussions will show that sex is largely shaped and defined by factors external to the individual and is, fundamentally, a *social* enterprise.

# THE SOCIAL CONSTRUCTIONIST PARADIGM

Modern Western societies are not the first to explore sexuality as a topic of intellectual inquiry. Philosophers, scholars, and clergy of countless generations have pondered its significance and come to radically different conclusions about how best to define, express, circumscribe, and manage libidinal energies and behaviors.

Lynne Segal (1994) has identified three historical intellectual traditions that have dominated Western thinking about sex. These frameworks are the spiritual, the biological, and the social. In pre-industrial Europe, societal views about sexuality were largely shaped by spiritual and religious beliefs. With the emergence of the Industrial Revolution, however, the dominance of these views were supplanted by models grounded in "science" and scientific thinking. In these early stages, modem science was heavily influenced by Darwinian logic; thus, scientific explorations of human behavior tended to be flavored with a decidedly biological bent. It is within this historical moment that the idea that sex is a biological phenomenon became a centrally accepted truism in Western thought (Segal, 1994).

Generally, such *essentialist* approaches to sexuality hold that sex is a matter of biological essence, that it is a product of biological force "seeking expression in ways that are preordained" (Epstein, 1987:15). For essentialists, sexuality is fundamentally a product of organic and biochemical processes, a function of our "nature." Essentialists consider sexual identities to be "cognitive realizations of genuine, underlying differences" (Epstein, 1992:241). For example, essentialists maintain that individuals are *by nature* heterosexual or homosexual. We are *born* a top or a bottom. Men are *naturally* more sexually aggressive and promiscuous than women [ostensibly because they have been biologically programmed to spread their seed and maximize their procreative potential (Buss, 1998)]. All of these claims are grounded in the fundamental notion that sex is a category of human existence dictated by nature that is eternally "unchanging, asocial and transhistorical" (Rubin, 1984:275).

The association of sex with nature in these models is not unintentional. There is great rhetorical power in terminology such as *sexual nature* because it "sounds like something solid and valid, not human-made" (Tiefer, 1995:33). In other words, by invoking nature, the *claims* of scientists regarding the etiology of sex and sexual behavior are consequently elevated to seeming "*facts*" and larger "*truths*" conveniently eluding the role of social forces in their creation.

In recent years, a formidable challenge to essentialist models of sex and sexual behavior has emerged. Though biological models still hold considerable sway in both popular and scientific thinking, new thinking about sex, sexuality, and the erotic assert that each is, in fact, socially constructed and not simply a matter of biological mandates.

Social constructionism is a theoretical perspective which argues that our perception of what is real is defined only by the meaning that we attribute to a given situation (Berger and Luckman, 1967; Blumer, 1969). Things do not have their own intrinsic meaning; we impose meaning upon them. These meanings are created through social interaction that occurs in particular social environments. Simply put, it is through our interaction with others that we learn how to interpret and evaluate the world around us. Constructionists also reveal that social hierarchies play an important role in ascription of meaning; individuals and groups at the top of social hierarchies are those most likely to have their definitions and views imposed and enforced as "reality."

Applied to sexuality this perspective holds that sexuality has no "inherent essence" (Harding, 1998:9). Ideas about sexuality are not hard-wired or "natural"; they arise in particular social–historical contexts (Foucault, 1980). For constructionists, sexuality is an arrangement of cultural norms, values, and expectations, which themselves are fundamentally shaped by hierarchies and matrices of social power relations (Foucault, 1980; Gagnon and Parker, 1995; Harding, 1998; Vance, 1984).

Constructionists argue that if sex and the realm of the sexual *were* natural, we would not have to be taught what sex was and it would take consistent forms across societies (Tiefer, 1995). But, evidence shows that sex is learned, and it does vary. Robert Padgug observes: "The forms, content, and context of sexuality always differ. There is no abstract and universal category of 'the erotic' or 'the sexual' applicable without change to all societies" (1992:54). Sex and the erotic are highly malleable constructs that take innumerable forms across the globe—in fact, we can (and do) attach erotic desires to almost anything. For example, in some cultures, small feet may be considered sexually appealing in women, in another culture it is large earlobes that are particularly "sexy," and in yet another culture it is women's breasts that are supposed to make (heterosexual) men "hot." In one culture the term "sex" might be reserved exclusively for heterosexual intercourse, while in another "sex" might refer to any sexual encounter that produced orgasm in at least one of the participants. The bottom line is—sex varies.

The definition of sex, who can engage in it, at what age, for how long, and from what position are just a few examples of sites of sexual variation. Our culture provides the template upon which our erotic desires are channeled and shaped. Because we share the same cultural sexual indoctrination as other members of society, we generally share the same sexual beliefs, values, and desires as those around us. So, for all intents and purposes, sex *appears* to be invariant and natural when it is not. In fact, because sex *is* culturally constituted, what we regard as "natural" will often be viewed as "unnatural" in other societies.

The implications of this perspective challenge many contemporary notions about sexuality. For example, a constructionist perspective would assert that sexual aggression in men is learned rather than inborn, that women may not "naturally" wish to bear children, and that public nudity, promiscuity, and premarital sex are not "inherently" wrong or sinful. Rather, constructionists contend, ideas and values surrounding sexual "reality" are learned, and they can, and do, change. In the following section, I adopt a constructionist framework to critically examine, identify, explore, and "deconstruct" cultural assumptions about S-E-X that are embedded within contemporary American society. This construct is essential to examine because it serves as a primary focal point for most scientific inquiry and public debate—for most of us, sexuality is primarily about S-E-X. A critical examination of the social construction of S-E-X can therefore provide considerable conceptual entrée into a wider analysis of the sexual realm.

## ISSUES OF DEFINITION

I begin my course on sexuality by having students write their definition of sex down on a small index card. "Let's say someone from Mars came to Earth and asked you to explain what this thing called sex is that s/he keeps hearing about in movies, songs, and barroom conversations," I begin. "What would you say? What is it? What is it for? How do you know when you've had it? How would you explain to this ultimate outsider what this activity 'sex' is all about?"

Quickly they set to the task, most of them confident and eager. A few finish quickly. "The man puts his penis in the woman's vagina." "Intercourse." "It is something adults do when they are in love." "It's the way we reproduce the species." A few take longer to complete the task. Slowly, steadily, frustration grows. Brows wrinkle, heads tilt, lips purse. Many struggle trying to put into words something they believe they "know, " something "natural," something that, as they put pen to paper, suddenly does not seem so simple, or so automatic. Typically, clarification is requested: "Do we need to discuss gay sex?" "Does the Martian know what genitalia are?" "Should I limit it to 'vanilla' sex?" "Sex like in the movies or 'real' sex?" "Should I explain about how men want it all the time?" "The Martian knows NOTHING about sex," I reply. "Start from ground zero." Invariably, someone remarks, "This is hard!"

And indeed it is. When we speak of sex and matters sexual, we may be referring to a single specific act, a group of acts, or something that can encompass an enormously wide variety of thoughts, emotions, and behaviors. Does sex inhere in certain affective states (e.g., love), physiological responses (e.g., excitement, orgasm) specific actors (e.g., males with females), or specific acts (e.g., vaginal penetration by an erect penis)?

The ambiguity inherent in these questions was perhaps best illustrated in 1997 with the eruption of a sexual political scandal involving former President Bill Clinton and White House intern Monica Lewinsky. Amid intense political pressure and media scrutiny, the president made a public address in which he vehemently denied "having sex" with Ms. Lewinsky. However, later, the public learned that the President and the intern *had* been involved in *oral* sex. While many members of the general public may have felt understandably deceived, the President was by no means alone in making this kind of categorical distinction.

Several recent studies indicate that the American public does differentiate between oral sex and what it considers "real" sex (Bogart, Cecil, Wagstaff, Pinkerton, and Abramson, 2000; Bogart, Pinkerton, Myaskovsky, Wagstaff, and Abramson, 1999; Sanders and Reinish, 1999). The work of Bogart et al. (2000), for example, indicates that while a vast majority of the college students they sampled (97%) considered heterosexual vaginal intercourse to be "sex," slightly fewer (93%) were willing to label anal heterosexual sex as "sex," and less than half (44%) considered that oral sex constituted real "sex."

Similar findings have been echoed in national opinion surveys. Of particular interest are reports that youth may be engaging in significantly higher rates of oral sex and other sexual behaviors, believing that by doing so they have not "had sex." Further, many indicate that by engaging in this particular form of erotic expression they have not "technically" lost their virginity (Sanders and Reinisch, 1999; Indigo, 2000) In short, despite the existence of a wide variety of socially identified sexual behaviors, in modern American society, the designation of having "had sex" is typically limited to a quite narrow range of erotic expression.

A critical examination of S-E-X reveals that the term represents a particularized constellation of socially determined sexual norms and expectations. In other words, sex, *real* sex, means something very specific in this culture, but the content of that meaning lies cloaked beneath layers of taken-for-granted assumptions that are so embedded in our cultural framework that they are rendered conceptually invisible. So, what *is* the content of S-E-X? What exactly *does* S-E-X mean? I raise this and subsequent questions not in search of definitive answers or solutions, but rather, in order to stimulate awareness and provoke discovery—to peel back the ornate and intricate layers of the social fabric to expose both the limits and possibilities of human sexual interaction.

## SO, S-E-X IS...

To discern the basic assumptions that go into defining sex in this culture, it is useful to strip away rhetoric and focus on the basics. Though there are several ways to do this, let's try pantomimes. Take a moment and, using only your hands, make a gesture for sex. Go ahead; it won't work nearly as well if you don't play along. C'mon—it won't hurt, really. Great! Now, repeat this gesture and pay close attention as you do it. This simple exercise goes a long way toward capturing many of the essential elements that constitute the modern conceptualization of S-E-X. What did you notice about your gesture? Think about the shapes you formed, the movements you utilized and how these are meant to represent S-E-X. For example, did your gesture involve one hand or finger actively breaching the boundaries of the other in a mock penetrative motion? This, and other gestures for sex, reveals many of the unspoken requisite components of S-E-X that will be described in the paragraphs below.

### Penetration and Male Agency

As symbolized in the exercise above, active penile penetration is one of the most essential components of the social construction of S-E-X in our culture. Its centrality is well illustrated in the research

conducted by Bogart and her colleagues described above (Bogart et al., 2000). In both of the cases involving penile penetration (anal and vaginal sex), a majority of the respondents concluded that the activities involved constituted "sex." This was not the case for the non-penetrative activity described in the scenarios (i.e., oral sex). Similar findings were echoed in Sanders and Reinisch's 1999 study, which indicated that 99.5% of their Midwestern college student sample defined penile–vaginal intercourse as sex, while somewhat fewer (81%) reported that penile–anal intercourse would qualify. However, only about 40% of the respondents indicated that oral sex constituted "having sex" (1999).

These findings point to the cultural privileging of sex as penile penetration, revealing a conceptualization of sexuality that is tacitly connected to male agency. Sex in America is a male purview; women *can* have sex but to be a "real man," men *must* have "real," aggressive, penetrative sex (Stoltenberg, 1990). In our culture's hegemonic articulation of sex, it is men who are defined as the sexual actors, as those who seek sex, as those around whom notions of sexuality are constructed, and to which active female agency is the notable (though increasing) exception. It is also significant that, in this construction, all qualitative aspects of penetration are rendered irrelevant. The question is not, for example, the depth, frequency, or duration of penetration, but whether or not penile penetration has occurred at all.

### Heterosexuality

Another important assumption built into our cultural system is that S-E-X is a *heterosexual* activity—it is penetrative, male agentic, and it takes place between a man and a woman. But, *must* sex involve a man and a woman? If so, are we asserting that gay men and lesbians do not have sex? Why, then, all the concern about homosexuality if we don't really count same-sex sexual activities as "real" sex? What *would* we call these activities? Near-sex? Pseudo-sex? Sex-like? And what of bisexuals? Does it only count as sex when a bisexual participates in penetrative, male agentic sexual activity with someone of the "opposite" sex?

Do we consider mutual digital genital stimulation between two lesbians "sex"? If so, then why would we not consider this same activity performed between a man and a woman to qualify as "sex"? In grade-school vernacular this is merely "third base," clearly short of making it "home" or "all the way." How can we say Veronica had sex with Betty but Archie "only got to third" if they engaged in identical sexual practices?

Continuing in this same vein, we might ask if there is a need to call gay male sexual activities something entirely different than lesbian sexual activities. After all, gay men have penises: they can engage in penile penetrative activity. But herein lies the problem of constructing a definition of sex as contingent on the relative genitalia of the actors involved; identical acts may be evaluated differently depending upon the biological sex of the participants. For example, it is typically considered to be sex when a man penetrates a woman anally with his penis [93% believed as much in Bogart et al.'s (2000) research and 81% in Sanders and Reinisch's (1999)]. Would as many people consider that this same act counted as sex if it were conducted by a man upon a man? However, even if we consider expanding Americans' tacitly heterosexist definitional criterion to include same-sex sexual expression, we are still excluding valid and important alternative conceptualizations. For example, must the erotic activities involve two people? What about masturbation? Is this sex? Multiple partners? Non-human partners?

It is also important to note that our culture gives us important cues as to the culturally legitimated forms of sex. The presence of a qualifier or hyphen differentiates subordinated forms from the hegemonic: hence the denotations of *lesbian sex* and *gay-male sex* rather than simply "*sex.*" Linguistic devices such as these signal that the qualified forms are different from, and inferior to, the presumed norm. These linguistic devices operate in a similar manner as when they are used to qualify occupations in gendered ways such as "male nurse," "female firefighter," and the "**W**"NBA.

## Orifice Specification

Another essential component of the hegemonic construction of sex in contemporary American society follows logically from the three preceding presumptive elements—if sex is constituted as a penetrative heterosexual male activity, what, we may ask, is the site of this activity? Where is all this effort supposed to be directed? To answer this, we can again gain considerable insight by looking at the linguistic cues; take, for example, anal sex and oral sex. Both are sex acts that specify the orifice or bodily site of sexual expression. Both modify the presumptive case. What orifice is involved in plainole "vanilla" S-E-X? What is the presumed site of erotic expression when we say he, she, or they had "sex"? The answer is the vagina. The vagina disappears from view linguistically because its presence is presupposed in much the same way that the heterosexuality of the participants in S-E-X remains unacknowledged.

Why such a focused concern surrounding the penetration of a vagina by a penis? Modem constructions of S-E-X are derivate of historical constructions which held that sex was an activity directed toward procreation (Seidman, 1996) In other words, our understanding of what sex is has evolved over time from definitions of sex which were tied to human reproduction. *Real* sex was what could get you pregnant—historically this has necessitated vaginal penile penetration. However, the majority of Americans today do not have sex for procreative purposes. Most typically, sex is a recreational activity pursued with an eye toward pleasure rather than procreation (Seidman, 1996; Vance, 1984). In fact, great pains are typically taken to *avoid* pregnancy. This shift away from reproductively oriented constructions of sex renders the heterosexual imperative embedded in contemporary constructions particularly anachronistic.

Further, medical technology has now made it possible for the human species to reproduce without any direct contact between male and female generative parts. In fact, technology has so far removed procreation from sex that a woman can give birth to a child harvested from another woman's eggs that have been fertilized with a complete stranger's sperm. There is no *sex* (as we define it) in this reproductive equation. The issue of human cloning moves the reproduction of the species even further into the laboratory and away from the embodied and imperfect process of human sexual intercourse.

## Orgasm, Pleasure, and Love

Another issue that is closely tied to the issue of reproduction is orgasm. What is the role of orgasm in S-E-X? Typically, orgasm is viewed as the culmination of a sexual encounter. However, not all orgasms are created equal. Male orgasm in heterosexual coital relations is the event that is most closely associated with human reproduction (Laumann, Gagnon, Michael, and Michaels, 1994; Masters and Johnson, 1966) and *both* males and females indicate that it is chiefly *male* orgasms which signal whether or not a particular sexual interaction qualifies as sex (Segal, 1994; Bogart et al., 2000). And, although many females are capable of multiple orgasms, it is typically the number of male climaxes that heterosexual partners count when describing how many "times" they have had sex. So accustomed are we to conceiving of sex in this manner that it is difficult to imagine alternate conceptualizations. Consider Marilyn Frye's discussion of the "number of times" question for lesbians:

> Some might have counted a two- or three-cycle evening as one "time" they "had sex"; some might have counted it as two or three "times." Some may have counted as "times" only the times both partners had orgasms; some may have counted as "times" occasions on which at least one had an orgasm; those who do not have orgasms or have them far more rarely than they "have sex" may not have figured orgasms into the calculations; perhaps some counted as a "time" every episode in which both touched the other's vulva more than fleetingly and not for something like a health examination. For some, to count every reciprocal touch of the vulva would have made them count as "having sex" more than most people with a job or

work would dream of having time for; how do we suppose those individuals counted "times"? Is there any good reason why they should *not* count all those as "times"? Does it depend on how fulfilling it was? Was anybody else counting by occasions of fulfillment? (1990:308)

What of fulfillment? What about love? Unlike the factors mentioned previously, neither of these concepts is intrinsically bound up in prevailing constructions of sex. Though often desired, neither is generally considered to be a conditional prerequisite of the claim of having had "sex." It may be the cultural ideal, and the most culturally *legitimated* form, but sex that occurs between two people who are in love is by no means the *hegemonic* norm. S-E-X is about physical pleasure, and is measured (male) orgasm by (male) orgasm.

A few considerations remain. For example, what do we call cases where there is orgasm between two people who have no actual physical contact? Is that sex? Is, for example, phone sex "sex"? Is cyber sex "sex"? If the informal student polls I have taken in my sexuality courses are any indication, then it appears the answer is "not really"—S-E-X is, apparently, a contact sport.

Ironically, however, when these same students are asked if these activities should be considered "cheating" if engaged in by someone in a committed relationship with someone outside of that relationship, most say yes. While these acts will not typically qualify as S-E-X, for many, they still feel like sexual betrayal. Structurally, S-E-X and romantic love may be defined as separate and distinct categories of human activity, but at the interpersonal level such normative distinctions appear to dissolve quite readily.

## Consent

Finally, we must address the issue of consent. Even in cases that fit all of the criteria tacitly embedded in our cultural construction of S-E-X, one would hope that most Americans would be loathe to consider that a forced sexual assault could be construed as sex. It's likely most survivors of sexual assault don't. However, even though S-E-X is generally constructed as a pleasurable pursuit, sexual pleasure is more strongly associated with its male participants. Because sexual agency is ascribed to males in contemporary conceptualizations, S-E-X does not necessarily require enjoyment or consent on the part of the sexual "recipient" (be they male or female). Further, not only are issues of power, domination, and force not precluded, but some authorities contend that contemporary definitions of sexuality proceed from a foundation of male domination and aggression. From this perspective; S-E-X *is* violence within patriarchal regimes. (Dworkin, 1981; MacKinnon, 1987; Stoltenberg, 1990).

The dangers inherent in contemporary constructions of S-E-X begin to emerge quite clearly here. S-E-X is something one "gets," something (or some*one*) one "has"; the subjective needs and desires of the "object of affection" are largely irrelevant. Nor is this the only example of how the social construction of S-E-X manifests and propagates social inequality. The examples discussed above demonstrate quite clearly that our culture privileges some forms of sexuality (e.g., penetrative, male agentic, heterosexual) while simultaneously marginalizing others (e.g., non-penetrative, female-agentic, gay, lesbian, transgendered). From this we can begin to discern not only the benefits that accrue to those members of society whose beliefs and activities fall within prescribed expectations, but also the costs of our sexual constructions for subordinated groups—those whose sexual values and practices fall outside normative boundaries. Vance notes:

> Our ability to think about sexual difference is limited ... by a cultural system that organizes sexual differences in a hierarchy in which some acts and partners are privileged

and others are punished. Privileged forms of sexuality ... are protected and rewarded by the state and subsidized through social and economic incentives. Those engaging in privileged acts, or pretending to do so, enjoy good name and good fortune. Less privileged forms of sexuality are regulated and interdicted by the state, religion, medicine, and public opinion. Those practicing less privileged forms of sexuality ... suffer from stigma and invisibility although they also resist. (1984:19)

The benefits of conformity are as enriching as the price of nonconformity is costly. Yet, as Vance notes, many do resist the confines of social strictures and normative boundaries. And, it is in resistance, struggle, and defiance that we find the avenues to social change. Social constructions are far from static: As ideological silhouettes they shift and change, ebb and flow, remaining ever-powerful, yet as historically ephemeral as the social structures they serve.

The examination I have presented here is by no means meant to be perceived as exhaustive; there are many more aspects of S-E-X that remain for analysis. We could, for example, discuss the construction of S-E-X as shameful, S-E-X as sin, S-E-X as signifier of adulthood, and so on, as well as the social inequalities that each of these categorizations engenders. Nonetheless, it is my hope that this brief analysis has demonstrated the importance of critically examining the hidden assumptions and varying functions of sex that are deeply rooted within our cultural framework, and has fostered an appreciation of how an examination of alternate understandings of sex and sexual behaviors across a diversity of cultural contexts may help us better understand our own.

# REFERENCES

Berger, Peter, and Thomas Luckman. 1967. *The Social Construction of Reality: A Treatise in the* *Sociology of Knowledge*. Garden City, NY: Anchor Books.

Blumer, Herbert. 1969. *Studies in Symbolic Interaction*. Englewood Cliffs, NJ: Prentice Hall.

Bogart, Laura M., Heather Cecil, David A. Wagstaff, Steven D. Pinkerton, and Paul R. Abramson. 2000. "Is It 'Sex'?: College Students' Interpretations of Sexual Behavior Terminology," *Journal of Sex Research* 37(2).

Bogart, L. M., S. D. Pinkerton, H. Cecil, L. Myaskovsky, D. A. Wagstaff, and P. R. Abramson. 1999. "Attitudes Toward and Definitions of Having Sex" [Letter], *Journal of the American Medical Association* 282:1917–1918.

Buss, D. M. 1998. "Sexual Strategies Theory: Historical Origins and Current Status," *Journal of Sex Research* 35(1).

Dworkin, Andrea. 1981. *Pornography: Men Possessing Women*. London: Women's Press.

Epstein, Steven. 1987. "Gay Politics, Ethnic Identity: The Limits of Social Constructionism," *Socialist Review* 93/94.

Epstein, Steven. 1992. "Gay Politics, Ethnic Identity: The Limits of Social Constructionism," in Edward Stein (ed.), *Forms of Desire: Sexual Orientation and the Social Constructionist Controversy*. New York: Routledge.

Foucault, Michel. 1980. *The History of Sexuality. Volume I: An introduction*. New York: Vintage Books.

Frye, Marilyn. 1990. "Lesbian 'Sex,'," in Jeffner Allen (ed.), *Lesbian Philosophies*. Albany NY: Statue University of New York Press.

Gagnon, John H., and Richard G. Parker, 1995. "Conceiving Sexuality," in Richard G. Parker and John H. Gagnon (eds.), *Conceiving Sexuality. Approaches to Sex Research in a Postmodern World*. New York: Routledge.

Harding, Jennifer. 1998. *Sex Acts: Practices of Femininity and Masculinity*. London: Sage.

Indigo, Susannah. 2000. "Blow Jobs and Other Boring Stuff," xxxxx. Published December 14, 2000. Accessed January 6, 2001.

Laumann, E. J. Gagnon, R. Michael, and S. Michaels. 1994. *The Social Organization of Sexuality*. Chicago: University of Chicago Press.

MacKinnon, Catherine. 1987. *Feminism Unmodified*: Discourses on Life and Law. Cambridge, MA: Harvard University Press.

Masters, W. H., and V. E. Johnson. 1966. *Human Sexual Response*. Boston: Little, Brown.

Padgug, Robert. 1992. "Sexual Matters: On Conceptualizing Sexuality in History," in Edward Stein (ed.), *Forms of Desire: Sexual Orientation and the Social Constructionist Controversy*. New York: Routledge.

Rubin, Gayle S. 1984. "Thinking Sex: Notes for a Radical Theory of the Politics of Sexuality," in Carole Vance (ed.), *Pleasure and Danger: Exploring Female Sexuality*. Boston: Routledge & Kegan Paul.

Sanders, S. A., and J. M. Reinisch. 1999. "Would You Say You 'Had Sex' if…?", *Journal of the American Medical Association* 281(2).

Segal, Lynne. 1994. *Straight Sex: The Politics of Pleasure*. London: Virago.

Seidman, Steven. 1996. "The Sexualization of Love," in Steven Seidman (ed.), *Queer Theory/Sociology*. Cambridge, MA: Blackwell.

Stoltenberg, John. 1990. "How Men Have (a) Sex," in *Refusing to Be a Man*. Meridian Books.

Tiefer, Lenore. 1995. *Sex Is Not a Natural Act and Other Essays*. Boulder, CO: Westview Press.

Vance, Carole. 1984. *Pleasure and Danger: Exploring Female Sexuality*. Boston MA and London: Routledge and Kegan Paul.

# Deviance & Crime

# MODULE

# (3.1) Defining Deviance

## Objective

You will learn how sociologists define deviance and how almost any behavior or appearance can be defined as deviant depending on context.

When you think of military homecomings, do you think of two women engaged to be married greeting each other with a kiss and embrace?

The U.S. Navy released this photograph on December 21, 2011. This kiss attracted national, even global, attention because it signaled a historical shift in military policy ushered in by the repeal of "Don't Ask, Don't Tell" (DADT) signed into law on December 22, 2010. The law allowed the military some time to adjust. On September 20, 2011, the military indicated that gays could now openly serve in the military without fear of discharge. The United States joined 25 countries that explicitly allow gays to serve in the military (Frank 2010; see Figure 3.1a). The repeal of DADT reveals an important fact about the nature of deviance: what is considered deviant at one time and place may not be considered deviant at another time or place.

100  **SEEING SOCIOLOGY**

370

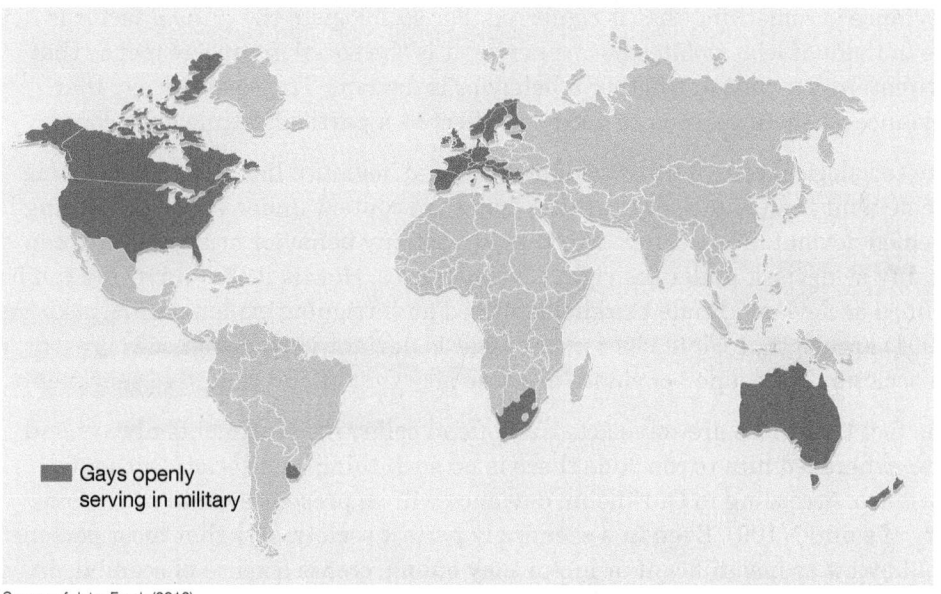

Figure 3.1a: **Countries In Which Gays Can Join the Military and Be Open about Their Sexual Orientation**

The countries highlighted on this map explicitly allow gays to serve openly in the military. The United States officially joined this group September 20, 2011. Something that the U.S. military once formally punished is now no longer subject to disciplinary action. One should not conclude that the countries highlighted are uniform in their treatment of gays. As examples, Estonia has never had a ban on gays serving in the military; Germany removed its ban in 2001; and while the Slovenian military does not ban homosexuality, its medical community labels homosexuality a psychiatric disease.

Gays openly serving in military

Source of data: Frank (2010)

# Defining Deviance

**Deviance** is any behavior or physical appearance that is socially challenged and/or condemned because it departs from the norms and expectations of some group. **Norms** are rules and expectations for the way people are supposed to behave, feel, and appear in a particular social situation. Norms exist for virtually every kind of situation, including how many times a day to eat, how to greet a friend, what to wear to school, how to handle the American flag, and when to use a gun.

Norms can vary according to whom they apply to and whether people (1) know they exist, (2) accept them, (3) enforce them uniformly, (4) think them important, (5) back them up with the force of law, and (6) adhere to them in their public *and* private lives (Gibbs 1965). Consider speed limits, which are backed by the force of law. Most people know the speed limits from observing posted signs but, depending on the setting, do not find it important to follow them to the letter of the law. In fact, most drivers exceed posted limits by 10 or 15 miles per hour without fear of getting caught and, even when caught, are not always cited for the exact number of miles they were driving over that limit. Norms vary by group. Some people, depending on the groups with which they identify, celebrate tattoos as a normal or expected rite of passage; others treat tattoos as a broad indicator of some character flaw.

Some norms exist for seemingly valid reasons—for example, to prevent harm to self and/or others. But there are just as many examples of norms in place for which there seems to be no valid reason. People often overlook behavior that is objectively deviant, such as corporate crime, but take sharp notice of behavior

**DEVIANCE, CONFORMITY, AND SOCIAL CONTROL** 101

that is for all practical purposes harmless, such as a certain appearance, way of dressing, or way of expressing sexuality (K. Erikson 1966).

## The Sociological Perspective

The definition of deviance given earlier suggests that what makes something deviant is the presence of a social audience that regards a behavior or appearance as deviant and takes some kind of action to discourage it. Deviance is not inherent to a specific behavior. Marrying a first cousin, for example, is not in itself deviant; if so, that behavior would be deviant everywhere in the world. Deviance is something that is conferred. For sociologists the critical factor is not the individual who violates norms per se; it is the social group's response that ultimately determines whether a behavior is deviant. Thus, we can say that deviance exists in relation to norms in effect at a particular time and place.

The sociological contribution to understanding deviance lies not with studying the deviant individuals, but with studying the context under which something is deemed deviant. Sociologists note that almost any behavior or appearance can qualify as deviant under the right circumstances. How is it that anything can be defined as deviant? Émile Durkheim offered an intriguing explanation. Durkheim (1901) argued that while ideas about what is deviant vary, deviance is present in all societies. He defined deviance as those acts that offend collective sentiments.

The fact that there are some acts that offend collective sentiments always and everywhere led him to conclude there is no such thing as a society without deviance. According to Durkheim, deviance will be present even in a "community of saints" (100). Even in a seemingly perfect society, acts that most persons would view as insignificant or minor may offend, create a sense of scandal, or be treated as crimes. To explain this, Durkheim (1901) drew an analogy to the "perfect and upright" person.

Just as "perfect and upright" people judge their own smallest failings with a severity that others reserve for the most serious offenses, so too do those who belong to groups considered exemplary. In such societies, some act will offend, simply because "it is impossible for everyone to be alike if only because each of us cannot stand in the same spot" (100). Thus, what makes an act or appearance deviant, even criminal, is not so much the act itself or its consequences, but rather the fact that the group has defined it as something dangerous or threatening to its well-being.

➤ The military represents a setting in which acts that most people would view as minor offenses, if that, are treated as crimes. Facial hair or a chin strap slightly off angle takes on critical significance for new military recruits in basic training.

U.S. Army

Durkheim argued that the ritual of identifying and exposing a wrongdoing, determining a punishment, and/or carrying it out is an emotional experience that binds together the members of a group and establishes a sense of order and community. Durkheim maintained that a group that went too long without noticing deviance or doing something about it would lose its identity as a group.

## Who Defines What Is Deviant?

In answering the question "Who defines what is deviant?" sociologists focus on the ways in which specific groups (such as undocumented workers), behaviors (such as child abuse), conditions (such as teenage pregnancy, infertility, or pollution), or artifacts (such as song lyrics, guns, art, or tattoos) become defined as problems. In particular, sociologists examine claims makers and claims-making activities.

**Claims makers** are those who articulate and promote claims and who tend to gain in some way if the targeted audience accepts their claims as true. Claims makers include government officials, advertisers, scientists, professors, and other stakeholders. Claims-making activities are actions taken to draw attention to a claim—actions such as "demanding services, filling out forms, lodging complaints, filing lawsuits, calling press conferences, writing letters of protest" (Spector and Kitsuse 1977, 79). Studying claims-making activities can help us understand why smoking in public places has been largely banned in the United States. Before 1980, people could freely smoke in public. In fact, professors and students smoked during class without eliciting a raised eyebrow. Today, such behavior would be unthinkable.

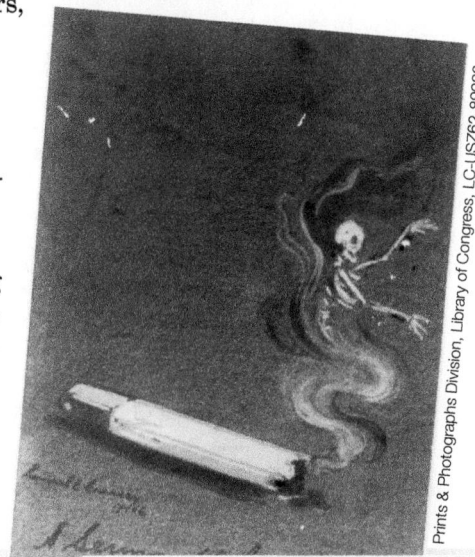

Prints & Photographs Division, Library of Congress, LC-USZ62-89928

➤ Negative health effects of smoking were claimed as early as 1900, as evidenced by this poster (top) showing a skeleton rising from the smoke of a burning cigarette. However, other claims makers (bottom) argued successfully for decades that because even doctors smoke, it must be safe.

Apic/Getty Images

The success of a claims-making campaign depends on a number of factors: claims makers' access to the media; available resources; position in society; and skill at fund-raising, promotion, and organization. When sociologists study the process by which a group or behavior is defined as deviant, they focus on who makes claims, whose claims are heard, and how audiences respond to them (Best 1989).

Sociologists also pay attention to any labels that claims makers apply because they tend to evoke a specific cause, consequence, and/or solution to a problem (Best 1989). For example, labeling an

**DEVIANCE, CONFORMITY, AND SOCIAL CONTROL** 103

addiction—whether it be to gambling, credit card use, prescription drugs, or alcohol—as a medical problem is to locate the cause in the biological workings of the body or mind and to suggest that the solution rests with a drug, a vaccine, or surgery. Labeling an addiction as a personal failing, on the other hand, is to locate the cause in the character of the person, such as an inability to delay gratification or a lack of discipline.

## (Write a Caption)

Write a caption that relates this "reserved for drunk driving victim" display to the concept of claims making.

Rachel Ponder

## Hints: In writing this caption

* review the concept of claims making, and
* consider the labels employed to bring attention to the problem of drunk driving.

## Critical Thinking

Describe something that your parents claim was deviant in their lifetime but is no longer the case today, or something that is deviant today but was not considered so in the past.

## Key Terms

claims makers                 deviance                        norms

© CP/Ryan Remiorz

Maurice "Mom" Boucher was the most powerful Hells Angels leader in Canada. President of the Quebec Nomads chapter, Boucher was consolidating his power over organized crime in Quebec. In 1997, he decided to go to war against the justice system. His first act in this war was to order the killing of some prison guards. Stéphane "Godasse" Gagné was ordered to do the killings. Gagné was a member of the Rockers, a Hells Angels' puppet gang that did much of the Angels' dirty work. For several years, he enforced drug debts, served as a bodyguard, and did other jobs for the Hells Angels.

On two separate operations, Gagné and another gang member killed guards Diane Lavigne and Pierre Rondeau. Gagné was eventually arrested and confessed to the murders. In exchange for some minor concessions, he also agreed to testify against Mom Boucher for ordering the murders.

In 1998, Boucher was acquitted, but the Crown successfully appealed and Boucher was convicted at a second trial in 2002 and is currently serving a life sentence. At Boucher's first trial, Gagné testified about Boucher's role in the murders. In his cross-examination, Boucher's lawyer, Jacques Larochelle, tried to discredit Gagné's testimony by highlighting his criminal past. Gagné's responses illustrate the brutality of organized crime:

> "During this entire time, you evidently had no respect for authority?"
> "No."
> "No respect for other people's property."
> "No."
> "No respect for the truth?"
> "No."

*Source:* Excerpted from *The Road to Hell: How the Biker Gangs are Conquering Canada* by Julian Sher and William Marsden. Copyright © 2003 Journalismnet Enterprises Inc. and William Marsden. Reprinted by permission of Knopf Canada.

Larochelle then tried to show Gagné's readiness to do anything he thought would please the Hells Angels. He recalled a hunger strike at Sorel prison that Mom ordered because he was sick of eating shepherd's pie. One inmate broke ranks and ate the meal.

> "And without anyone asking you to do it," Larochelle asked, "you went over and beat him up?"
> "Yes."
> "In fact you courageously waited until he was asleep and you went to attack him in his bed, is that correct?"
> "Yes."
> "You hit him so hard with your fist that the bone came out his nose—all so that you would be noticed, is that correct?"
> "Yes."

Larochelle also elicited the sordid details of Gagné's attempted murder of the drug dealer Christian Bellemare. He showed how Gagné acted alone, deciding to kill him because he owed him money.

> "The first two bullets hit Bellemare in the throat or in that area. But the other bullets didn't fire, and Bellemare was still alive?" Larochelle said, taking the jurors back to the scene of the crime.
>
> "Yes," Gagné agreed.
>
> "You went running up to Bellemare and you put your fingers around his neck, your two hands around his neck, and squeezed?"
>
> "Yes."
>
> "He tries to talk, is that correct?" Larochelle pushed. "You have a good idea of what he is trying to tell you, I imagine?"
>
> "Yes."
>
> "Don't kill me, or something like that?" the lawyer suggested.
>
> "Something like that, yes," said Gagné.
>
> "That didn't impress you?"
>
> "I had a job to do," he admitted. (Sher and Marsden, 2003:147-148)

*Source:* Excerpted from *The Road to Hell: How the Biker Gangs are Conquering Canada* by Julian Sher and William Marsden. Copyright © 2003 Journalismnet Enterprises Inc. and William Marsden. Reprinted by permission of Knopf Canada.

Despite the attempts of the Hells Angels to convince the public that they are just a social club, supporting the community through events such as toy runs, they are one of Canada's most powerful criminal organizations. The violence of Godasse Gagné is typical of the methods used by organized criminals and explains why nearly one in every five Canadian homicides—94 killings in 2010—is gang-related (Mahony, 2011).

Organized crime is one of a wide range of behaviours that society has defined as deviant and/or criminal. For many years, crime and deviance have been of special interest to sociologists. Many of the issues they have examined remain important today: What is deviant behaviour, and how does it differ from criminal behaviour? Why are some people considered to be "deviants" or "criminals" while others are not? How should society deal with those who break the rules? Before reading on, take the quiz on crime and organized crime in Box 7.1 on page 175.

### Critical Thinking Questions

1. The violence perpetrated by the Hells Angels and other organized crime groups is fed by the huge amounts of money made by selling illegal drugs. Many of the people who buy these drugs are otherwise respectable lawyers, electricians, and even students. How do you think these people justify sustaining organized crime?

2. In the *Safe Streets and Communities Act*, passed in 2012, the federal government imposed mandatory minimum penalties for some relatively minor drug offences, including growing six marijuana plants and selling or sharing the crop. Do you think these mandatory penalties will help reduce drug crime in Canada?

3. Should so-called victimless crimes such as recreational drug use and prostitution be decriminalized? What do you think would be the positive and negative effects of decriminalization?

---

**CHAPTER FOCUS QUESTION**  What are the causes and consequences of crime in Canada?

## LEARNING OBJECTIVES
### AFTER READING THIS CHAPTER, YOU SHOULD BE ABLE TO

**LO-1** Explain the meanings of the terms *crime* and *deviance*.

**LO-2** Understand the way in which crime and deviance are explained by functionalist, conflict, interactionist, feminist, and postmodern theories.

**LO-3** Describe how sociologists count and classify crimes.

**LO-4** Understand how age, gender, class, and race are related to deviance and crime.

**LO-5** Describe how the criminal justice system deals with crime.

Outlaw motorcycle gangs such as the Hells Angels are highly profitable criminal organizations.

## LO-1    WHAT IS DEVIANCE?

How do societies determine what behaviour is acceptable and what is unacceptable? All societies have norms that govern acceptable behaviour. If we are to live and to work with others, these rules are necessary. We must also have a reasonable expectation that other people will obey the rules. Think of the chaos that would result if each driver decided which side of the road she would drive on each day or which stop sign he would decide to obey. Most of us usually conform to the norms our group prescribes. Of course, not all members of the group obey all the time. All of us have broken many rules, sometimes even important ones. These violations are dealt with through various mechanisms of **social control**—systematic practices developed by social groups to encourage conformity and discourage deviance. One form of social control takes place through the process of socialization, whereby individuals *internalize* societal norms and values. A second form of social control is the use of *negative sanctions* to punish rule-breakers and nonconforming acts. Later in this chapter, you will read about the legal system, which is a *formal* means of social control

Although the purpose of social control is to ensure some level of conformity, all societies have some degree of **deviance**—any behaviour, belief, or condition that violates cultural norms in the society or group in which it occurs (Adler and Adler, 1994).

**social control** Systematic practices developed by social groups to encourage conformity and discourage deviance.

**deviance** Any behaviour, belief, or condition that violates cultural norms in the society or group in which it occurs.

## Defining Deviance

According to sociologists, deviance is *relative*—that is, an act becomes deviant when it is socially defined as such. Definitions of deviance vary widely from place to place, from time to time, and from group to group. For example, you may have played the Pick 3 lottery. To win, you must pick a three-digit number matching the one drawn by the government lottery agency. Television commercials encourage us to risk our money on this game from which the government profits. Several years ago, the same game was called the numbers racket and was the most popular form of gambling in many low-income neighbourhoods. The two main differences between now and then are that the game used to be run by organized criminals, and those criminals paid the winners a higher share of the take than the government now does. While the profits now go to social services rather than into the pockets of criminals, the example illustrates the point that the way societies define behaviour can be more important than the harm caused by that behaviour, as legalized gambling involves far more people suffering losses than was the case when gambling was illegal.

Definitions of deviance are continually changing. Several hundred thousand "witches" were executed in Europe during the Middle Ages; now the crime of witchcraft doesn't exist. Racist comments used to be socially acceptable; now they are not. Tattoos and piercings are now common among students, but 30 years ago they were almost unknown.

Deviance can be difficult to define. Good and evil are not two distinct categories. The two overlap, and the line between deviant and nondeviant can be *ambiguous*. For example, how do we decide if someone is mentally ill? What if your brother begins to behave in a strange fashion? He occasionally yells at people for no apparent reason and keeps changing topics when you talk to him. He begins to wear clothes that don't match and phones you in the middle of the night to talk about people who are threatening him. How would you respond to this change in

## BOX 7.1    SOCIOLOGY AND EVERYDAY LIFE

### How Much Do You Know About Crime and Organized Crime?

| True | False | |
| --- | --- | --- |
| T | F | 1. Official statistics accurately reflect the amount of crime in Canada. |
| T | F | 2. Most organized criminals are affiliated with the Italian Mafia. |
| T | F | 3. Organized crime exists largely to provide goods and services demanded by "respectable" members of the community. |
| T | F | 4. Rates of murder and other violent crimes have been steadily rising for the past 20 years. |
| T | F | 5. Gang-related killings have been declining at about the same rate as other types of homicides in Canada. |

For answers to the quiz about crime and organized crime, go to **www.nelson.com/sociologyinourtimes6e.**

behaviour? Would it make any difference if you knew that your brother was drinking heavily at the time or was under a lot of stress at work? Would it make a difference if he behaved this way once a year or twice a week? When would you decide that he had a problem and should seek help? What is the difference between someone who is eccentric and someone who is mentally ill? These questions reflect the difficulty we have in defining deviance.

Deviant behaviour also varies in seriousness, ranging from mild transgressions to quite serious violations of the law. Have you kept a library book past its due date or cut classes? If so, you have broken the rules. Others probably view your infraction as relatively minor; at most, you might have to pay a fine. Violations of other university regulations—such as cheating on an examination—are viewed as more serious infractions and are punishable by stronger sanctions, such as academic probation or expulsion. Some forms of deviant behaviour are defined as crimes. A **crime** is an act that violates criminal law and is punishable with fines, jail terms, and other sanctions. Crimes range from minor—running an illegal bingo game or disorderly conduct—to major offences such as sexual assault and murder.

Sociologists study the behaviours that are defined as deviant, who does the defining, how and why people become deviants, and how society deals with deviants (Schur, 1983). In this chapter, we present several sociological explanations of deviance. These theories are quite different from one another, but each contributes in its own way to our understanding of deviance. No one perspective provides a comprehensive explanation of all deviance. In many respects, the theories presented in this chapter can be considered complementary.

> **crime** An act that violates criminal law and is punishable with fines, jail terms, and other sanctions.

## SOCIOLOGICAL PERSPECTIVES ON CRIME AND DEVIANCE    LO-2

### Functionalist Perspectives on Crime and Deviance

**STRAIN THEORY: GOALS AND THE MEANS TO ACHIEVE THEM** According to Robert Merton (1938, 1968), in a smoothly functioning society, deviance will be limited because most people share common cultural goals and agree upon the appropriate means for reaching them.

However, societies that do not provide sufficient avenues to reach these goals may also lack agreement about how people may achieve their aspirations. Deviance may be common in such societies because people may be willing to use whatever means they can to achieve their goals. According to **strain theory**, people feel strain when they are exposed to cultural goals that they are unable to obtain because they do not have access to culturally approved means of achieving these goals. The goals may be material possessions and money; the approved means may include an education and jobs. When denied legitimate access to these goals, some people seek access through deviant means.

Typically, strain theory has been used to explain the deviance of the lower classes. Denied legitimate access to the material goods that are such an important part of North American culture, some individuals may turn to illegal activities to achieve their goals. However, not only the poor turn to illegal ways of achieving their goals. Some sociologists feel that strain theory can help explain upper-class deviance as well. In 2007, Conrad Black, one of Canada's wealthiest and most influential businessmen (and as Lord Black of Crossharbour, also a member of the British House of Lords), was convicted of fraud and obstruction of justice  and sentenced to three and a half years in prison. Despite his wealth, Black took money from the Hollinger company that rightfully belonged to shareholders. A committee established to investigate Black's activities concluded that "Black and [his partner] Radler were motivated by a ravenous appetite for cash . . . and Hollinger International, under their reign 'lost any sense of corporate purpose, competitive drive or internal ethical concerns' as the two executives looked for ways to 'suck cash' out of the company" (McNish and Stewart, 2004:288).

**strain theory** The proposition that people feel strain when they are exposed to cultural goals that they are unable to obtain because they do not have access to culturally approved means of achieving these goals.

**OPPORTUNITY THEORY: ACCESS TO ILLEGITIMATE OPPORTUNITIES** Expanding on Merton's strain theory, Richard Cloward and Lloyd Ohlin (1960) suggested that for deviance to occur, people must have access to **illegitimate opportunity structures**—circumstances that provide an opportunity for people to acquire through illegitimate activities what they cannot achieve through legitimate channels. For example, members of some communities may have insufficient legitimate means to achieve conventional goals of status and wealth but have much greater access to illegitimate opportunity structures—such as theft, drug dealing, or robbery—through which they can achieve these goals.

According to Cloward and Ohlin (1960), three different forms of delinquent subcultures—criminal, conflict, and retreatist—emerge based on the type of illegitimate opportunities available in a specific area. The criminal subculture focuses on economic gain and includes acts such as theft, extortion, and drug dealing. Elijah Anderson (1990) suggested that the "drug economy [is an] employment agency superimposed on the existing gang network" for many young men who lack other opportunities. For young men who grow up in a gang subculture, running drug houses and selling drugs on street corners provides illegitimate opportunities. Using the money from these "jobs," they can support themselves and their families, as well as purchase material possessions to impress others. When illegitimate economic opportunities are not available, gangs may become conflict subcultures that fight over turf (territory) and adopt a value system of toughness, courage, and similar status-enhancing qualities. Those who lack the opportunity or ability to join one of these gangs may turn to retreatist forms of deviance, such as drinking and drug use.

Opportunity theory expands strain theory by pointing out the relationship between deviance and the availability of illegitimate opportunity structures. Some studies of gangs have supported this premise by pointing out that gang membership provides some women and men in low-income central-city areas with an illegitimate means to acquire money, entertainment, refuge, and physical protection (Esbensen and Huizinga, 1993; Jankowski, 1991).

**illegitimate opportunity structures** Circumstances that provide an opportunity for people to acquire through illegitimate activities what they cannot achieve through legitimate channels.

**CONTROL THEORY: SOCIAL BONDING** Early social control theories explained how some types of social structures led to high rates of deviance. Communities characterized by poverty, physical deterioration, and internal conflict were too disorganized to exert effective control over residents' behaviour. These communities often had high rates of suicide, mental illness, substance abuse, and crime.

Although most of the research documenting the correlation between community disorganization and crime has been done in large, urban areas, Linda Deutschmann (2002) has applied the theory to frontier areas as well. Many small Canadian communities were created solely to develop an economic resource. Such towns have grown up around mines, railroads, pulp mills, and hydro dams. These towns may be lasting or short-lived depending on the nature of the project or the life of the resource. Deutschmann notes that in these towns' early stages, the absence of controls, such as families and churches, means that deviant behaviour, such as fighting and alcohol abuse, may be common. In later stages of development, the strains of a booming town may also facilitate deviance.

While work in this tradition continues, most of the recent work on control theory has focused on the individual rather than on the community. In doing so, it has posed the fundamental question about causes of deviance in a new way. Most theories of deviance ask this question: Why do they do it? Control theorists reverse this question. They ask: Why don't we *all* do it? Or, put another way, they wonder: Why do some people *not* engage in deviant behaviour? In answer to this question, Travis Hirschi (1969) suggested that deviant behaviour is minimized when people have strong bonds that bind them to families, school, peers, churches, and other social institutions.

**Social bond theory** holds that the likelihood of deviant behaviour increases when a person's ties to society are weakened or broken. According to Hirschi, social bonding consists of (1) *attachment* to other people; (2) *commitment* to conventional lines of behaviour, such as schooling and job success; (3) *involvement* in conventional activities; and (4) *belief* in the legitimacy of conventional values and norms. The variables of attachment and commitment are much more strongly related to delinquency than involvement and belief. Although Hirschi did not include females in his study, others who have replicated it with both females and males have found that the theory explains the delinquency of both (Linden and Fillmore, 1981).

While Hirschi's theory did not differentiate between bonds to conventional and to deviant others, several researchers have modified the theory and suggested that the probability of crime or delinquency increases when a person's social bonds are weak and when peers promote antisocial values and deviant behaviour (Linden and Fillmore, 1981). Gang members may bond with one another rather than with persons who subscribe to dominant cultural values. As one gang member explains:

> Before I joined the gang, I could see that you could count on your boys to help in times of need and that meant a lot to me. And when I needed money, sure enough they gave it to me. Nobody else would have given it to me; my parents didn't have it, and there was no other place to go. The gang was just like they said they would be, and they'll continue to be there when I need them. (Jankowski, 1991:42)

## Symbolic Interactionist Perspectives on Crime and Deviance

According to symbolic interactionists, deviance is learned in the same way as conformity— through interaction with others. Differential association and labelling theory are two interactionist theories of deviance.

**DIFFERENTIAL ASSOCIATION THEORY** Edwin Sutherland (1939) developed a theory to explain how people learn deviance through social interaction. **Differential association theory** states that individuals have a greater tendency to deviate from societal norms when they frequently

**social bond theory**
The proposition that the likelihood of deviant behaviour increases when a person's ties to society are weakened or broken.

**differential association theory**
The proposition that individuals have a greater tendency to deviate from societal norms when they frequently associate with persons who favour deviance over conformity.

associate with persons who favour deviance over conformity. According to Sutherland, people learn the necessary techniques and the motives, drives, rationalizations, and attitudes of deviant behaviour from people with whom they associate.

Misha Glenny described the transition of a "whitehat" computer hacker named Max Vision into a criminal "blackhat" hacker named Iceman. Vision had been working for the U.S. government searching for vulnerabilities in their website security. For reasons that were unclear, Vision left a U.S. Air Force website vulnerable to later attack and was sentenced to prison. After his release, Vision decided to change his life:

> Abandoned by his wife for another man, forsaken by his erstwhile friends in the FBI, Max Vision tumbled down the abyss, at the bottom of which lay a deep depression. Here he landed next to a fellow inmate, one Jeffrey Normington, who extended a hand of friendship when nobody else would.
>
> On his release from prison, Vision was unable to find regular work that paid more than the minimum wage. He . . . was offered senior positions in security companies abroad, but as he was on parole, he was not eligible for a passport. In Silicon Valley, nobody wanted to employ someone whose CV included an indelible conviction for computer crime.
>
> His debts mounted as his despair deepened. Then one day friend Normington reappeared, promising a path out of the abyss and back into California's sunshine . . . Normington promised him a top-of-the-line Alienware laptop, a must-have but expensive accessory for hackers. That was just for starters. He said he'd find Vision an apartment and pay for it. Normington would arrange everything.
>
> In exchange for a few favors.
>
> Crime was not Vision's sole option. There were other avenues to explore. He could have gone to friends and family. But he was tired, he felt abandoned and Normington was convincing . . .
>
> Max Vision, all-round good guy, was discarded back into an abyss. In his place, Iceman emerged—all-round bad guy. . . . (2011:102)

Vision is now in prison, serving a 13-year sentence for credit card hacking that cost consumers over $85 million.

Differential association is most likely to result in deviant activity when a person has extensive interaction with rule-breakers. Ties to other deviants can be particularly important in organized crime, where the willingness of peers to stand up for one another is a response to violent competitors. Daniel Wolf, an anthropologist who rode with an Edmonton biker gang, describes this solidarity:

> For an outlaw biker, the greatest fear is not of the police; rather, it is of a slight variation of his own mirror image: the patch holder [full-fledged member] of another club. Under slightly different circumstances those men would call each other "brother." But when turf is at stake, inter-club rivalry and warfare completely override any considerations of the common bonds of being a biker—and brother kills brother. None of the outlaws that I rode with enjoyed the prospect of having to break the bones of another biker. Nor did they look forward to having to live with the hate–fear syndrome that dominates a conflict in which there are no rules . . .
>
> When a patch holder defends his colours, he defends his personal identity, his community, his lifestyle. When a war is on, loyalty to the club and one another arises out of the midst of danger, out of apprehension of possible injury, mutilation, or worse. Whether one considers this process as desperate, heroic, or just outlandishly foolish and banal does not really matter. What matters is that, for patch holders, the brotherhood emerges as a necessary feature of their continued existence as individuals and as a group. (1996:11)

Group ties are not only important in organized crime groups such as motorcycle gangs. Think of the different subcultural groups that are involved in deviant activities in many Canadian high schools. Whether the focus of the group is graffiti, using drugs, or fighting, the encouragement and support of peers is vital to recruiting and teaching new members and to sustaining the group.

Differential association theory contributes to our knowledge of how deviant behaviour reflects the individual's learned techniques, values, attitudes, motives, and rationalizations. However, critics question why many individuals who have had extensive contact with people who violate the law still conform most of the time. They also assert that the theory does not adequately assess possible linkages between social inequality and criminal behaviour.

**LABELLING THEORY** Two complementary processes are involved in the definition of deviance. First, some people act (or are believed to act) in a manner contrary to the expectations of others. Second, others disapprove of and try to control this contrary behaviour. Part of this social control process involves labelling people as deviants. A very important contribution to the study of deviance was made by sociologists who asked this question: Why are some people labelled as deviants while others are not? **Labelling theory** suggests that deviants are those people who have been successfully labelled as such by others. The process of labelling is directly related to the power and status of those persons who do the labelling and those who are being labelled. To the labelling theorist, behaviour is not deviant in and of itself; it is defined as such by a social audience (Erikson, 1962). Labels are applied most easily to those who lack the power to resist them.

William Chambliss (1973) witnessed the labelling process when he observed members of two groups of high school boys: the Saints and the Roughnecks. Both groups were "constantly occupied with truancy, drinking, wild parties, petty theft, and vandalism." The Saints committed more offences than the Roughnecks, but the Roughnecks were labelled as troublemakers by school and law enforcement officials, while the Saints were seen as being likely to succeed. Unlike the Roughnecks, none of the Saints was ever arrested.

Chambliss attributed this contradictory response by authorities to the fact that the Saints came from "good families," did well in school, and thus were forgiven for their "boys will be boys"–type behaviour. By contrast, the Roughnecks came from lower-income families, did poorly in school, and generally were viewed negatively. Although both groups engaged in similar behaviour, only the Roughnecks were stigmatized by a deviant label.

The concept of secondary deviance is important to labelling theory because it suggests that when people accept a negative label or stigma that has been applied to them, the label may contribute to the type of behaviour it was initially meant to control (see Figure 7.1). According to Lemert (1951), **primary deviance** is the initial act of rule breaking. **Secondary deviance** occurs when a person who has been labelled deviant accepts that new identity and continues the deviant behaviour. For example, a person may shoplift, not be labelled deviant, and subsequently decide to forgo such acts in the future. Secondary deviance occurs if the person steals from a store, is labelled a "shoplifter," accepts that label, and then continues to steal.

Labelling theorists have made an important contribution to our understanding of the process by which society defines behaviours and individuals as deviant and of the consequences of that definition. Let us first look at the impact of labelling on a person who is defined as deviant.

Robert Scott (1969) conducted a fascinating study that examined the effects of two different ways of treating blind people. One agency defined the blind as helpless, dependent people and developed programs to accommodate them. Their clients were driven to the agency's offices, where they worked in sheltered workshops and ate food that had been cut before being served.

**labelling theory** The proposition that deviants are those people who have been successfully labelled as such by others.

**primary deviance** A term used to describe the initial act of rule breaking.

**secondary deviance** A term used to describe the process whereby a person who has been labelled deviant accepts that new identity and continues the deviant behaviour.

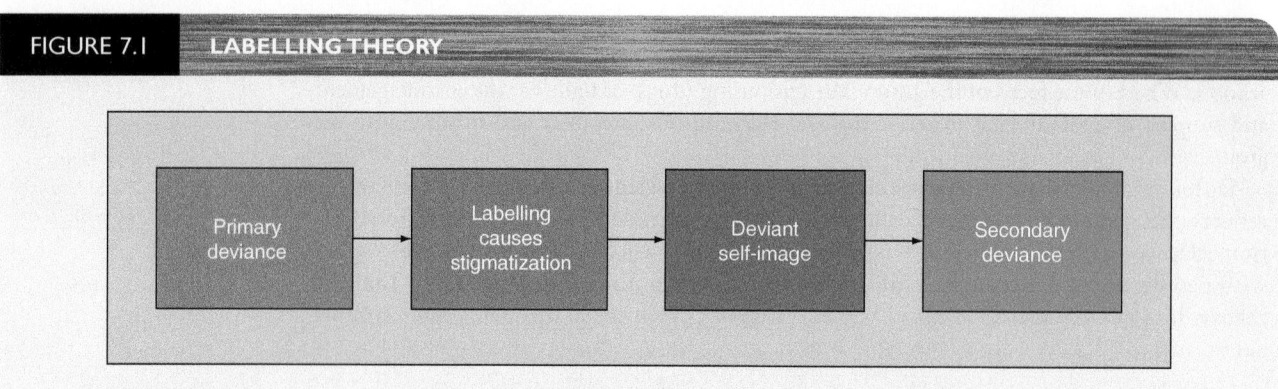

FIGURE 7.1    LABELLING THEORY

When an act is labelled as deviant, the label may cause the behaviour it was intended to control. The individual may find that others now respond differently to him or her because of the stigmatization of being labelled as deviant. While some individuals may successfully resist the label, others may develop a deviant self-image and subsequently get involved in secondary deviance.

Not surprisingly, the clients had trouble adapting to life outside the agency. Another agency, which dealt mainly with Vietnam War veterans, used a different approach. Their goal was to reintegrate clients into the community. Instead of being driven places, they were trained to take public transit. They were given confidence training and encouraged to live on their own and work in normal job settings. Scott concluded that these different approaches, with different labels for the visually impaired clients, had a significant impact on the self-image and social adjustment of the blind clients.

Think of the impact that labels can have on a person's self-concept and life chances. Being labelled a drug addict can lead to serious difficulties in getting a job even after successful treatment. If the label prevents the former addict from reintegrating into the conventional community, that person may accept this deviant status and return to his or her friends in the drug world. Similar problems come with other deviant labels. The impact of the label "mentally ill" is described by Tom, an ex-patient:

> Having been diagnosed as a psychiatric patient with psychotic tendencies is the worst thing that has ever happened to me. It's shitty to be mentally ill; it's not something to be proud of. It makes you realize just how different you are from everybody else—they're normal and you're not. Things are easy for them; things are hard for you. Life's a ball for them; life's a bitch for you. I'm like a mental cripple! I'm a failure for life! (Herman, 1996:310)

Not everyone passively submits to the labelling process—some people successfully resist the imposition of a label. This can be done individually or by working with others. The leader of one Ontario group of former psychiatric patients described the aims of his group:

> Simply put, we're tired of being pushed around. We reject everything society says about us, because it's just not accurate . . . We don't like the meaning of the words [people] use to describe us—"mentals" and "nuts." We see ourselves differently, just as good and worthy as everybody out there. In our newsletter, we're trying to get across the idea that we're not the stereotypical mental patient you see in movies. We're real people who want to be treated equally under the Charter of Rights. We're not sitting back, we're fighting back! (Herman, 1996:323)

The view that deviance is socially defined draws our attention to the question of why particular behaviours are defined as deviant and others are not. One of the answers highlights the role of **moral entrepreneurs**—people or groups who take an active role in trying to have particular behaviours defined as deviant (Becker, 1963). Think of the role that groups such as Mothers Against Drunk Driving (MADD) have played in getting governments to increase the penalties for drunk driving and in educating the public about the dangers of this behaviour. Similarly, in recent years, health advocates have stigmatized cigarette smoking and many of our communities have passed legislation banning smoking in most public places. A few decades ago, there was little opposition to smoking; people smoked on buses, in airplanes, in classrooms, in offices, and in virtually all other public places. Because of the health risks of smoking, the antismoking movement was able to overcome tobacco company lobbying and convince governments to impose restrictions on smoking. Not only is smoking banned in public places, but many people now define smokers as deviants who threaten public health (Tuggle and Holmes, 2000). Thus, smoking has moved from a normative behaviour to a stigmatized behaviour over a period of about 30 years.

> **moral entrepreneurs** People or groups who take an active role in trying to have particular behaviours defined as deviant.

Moral entrepreneurs often create **moral crusades**—public and media awareness campaigns that help generate public and political support for their causes. In recent years, we have seen moral crusades against abortion providers, wife abusers, squeegee kids, panhandlers, prostitutes, and a wide variety of other real or perceived threats to society. Some crusades have been more successful than others. The campaign by women's groups for zero-tolerance policies mandating arrest in domestic violence cases has been successful. However, anti-abortion groups have drawn attention to their cause but have been unable to bring about changes in the law.

> **moral crusades** Public and media awareness campaigns that help generate public and political support for moral entrepreneurs' causes.

Some groups succeed in changing perceptions and laws and others do not. A major reason for the difference is the distribution of power and resources in society. Those who control the levers of power are much more likely to be able to impose their definitions of what is right and wrong on the rest of society.

Labelling theory has had an important impact on the justice system. It has led to an increased use of diversion for minor offences so a formal label would not be applied. Critics argue that this theory neither explains what causes the original acts that make up primary deviance nor provides insight into why some people accept deviant labels and others do not (Cavender, 1995).

## Conflict Perspectives on Crime and Deviance

Who determines what behaviours are deviant or criminal? Conflict theorists feel that people in positions of power maintain their advantage by using the law to protect their own interests. Conflict theorists suggest that lifestyles considered deviant by political and economic elites are often defined as illegal. The activities of poor and lower-income individuals are more likely to be defined as criminal than those of persons from middle- and upper-income backgrounds. For example, those who commit welfare fraud are more likely to face criminal charges than are professionals whose misconduct is generally dealt with by disciplinary committees of their peers rather than by the criminal courts. The relative social harm caused by either of these groups seems to have little relevance in the determination of who is defined as criminal; what matters more is the power of some groups to resist sanctions.

**THE CONFLICT APPROACH** Although Karl Marx wrote very little about deviance and crime, many of his ideas influenced a critical approach that is based on the assumption that the criminal justice system protects the power and privilege of the capitalist class.

As you learned in Chapter 1, Marx based his critique of capitalism on the inherent conflict that he believed existed between the capitalists and the working class. According to Marx, social institutions (such as law, politics, and education) make up a superstructure that legitimizes the class structure and maintains the capitalists' dominant position in it. Crime is an expression of the individual's struggle against the unjust social conditions and inequality produced by capitalism.

According to Quinney (1980), people with economic and political power define as criminal any behaviour that threatens their own interests. For example, drug laws enacted early in the 20th century were passed and enforced in an effort to control immigrant workers, particularly Chinese workers, who were more inclined than most other residents of Canada to smoke opium. The laws were motivated by racism more than by a real concern with drug use (Cook, 1969). By contrast, while the Canadian government passed anti-combines legislation in 1889 in response to concerns expressed by labour and small-business people about the growing power of monopoly capitalists, the law had no impact. Large companies still engaged in price fixing and other means of limiting competition. Having symbolic anti-combines laws on the books merely made the government appear responsive to public concerns about big business (Smandych, 1985).

Why do people commit crimes? Some conflict theorists believe that the affluent commit crimes because they are greedy and want more than they have. Corporate and white-collar crimes, such as stock market manipulation, land speculation, and price fixing, often involve huge sums of money and harm many people. By contrast, street crimes, such as robbery and aggravated assault, generally involve small sums of money and cause harm to limited numbers of victims (Bonger, 1969). According to conflict theorists, the poor commit street crimes to survive; they cannot afford the necessary essentials, such as food, clothing, and shelter. Thus, some crime represents a rational response by the poor to the unequal distribution of resources in society (Gordon, 1973). Further, living in poverty may lead to violent crime and victimization *of the poor by the poor.* For example, violent gang activity may be a collective response of young people to seemingly hopeless poverty (Quinney, 1979).

In sum, the conflict approach argues that the law protects the interests of the affluent and powerful. The way laws are written and enforced benefits the capitalist class by ensuring that individuals at the bottom of the class structure do not take the property or threaten the safety of those at the top (Reiman, 1984). However, this theory explains some types of laws but not others. People of all classes share a consensus about the criminality of certain acts. For example, laws that prohibit murder, rape, and armed robbery protect not only middle- and upper-income people but also low-income people, who are frequently the victims of such violent crimes (Klockars, 1979). While some laws do protect the rich and powerful, others reflect the interests of all citizens.

## Feminist Perspectives on Crime and Deviance

The few early studies that were conducted on "women's crimes" focused almost exclusively on prostitution and attributed the cause of this crime to women's biological or psychological "inferiority." As late as the 1980s, researchers were still looking for unique predisposing factors that led women to

This British Columbia accident killed 3 farm workers and injured 14 when their employer transported 17 people in a 10-passenger van with wooden benches and no seat belts. While the RCMP recommended 33 criminal charges, none were laid and the driver was only fined $2000.

© CP PHOTO/Don MacKinnon

NEL

commit crime, which was often seen as individual psychopathology rather than as a response to their social environment. These theories, which reinforce existing female stereotypes, have had a negative impact on our understanding and treatment of female offenders.

A new interest in women and deviance developed in 1975 when two books—Freda Adler's *Sisters in Crime* and Rita James Simons's *Women and Crime*—declared that women's crime rates were going to increase significantly as a result of the women's liberation movement. Although this so-called emancipation theory of female crime has been strongly criticized by subsequent analysts (Comack, 2012), Adler's and Simons's works encouraged feminist scholars to examine the relationship between gender, deviance, and crime more closely.

Feminist scholars have concluded that the roots of female criminality lie in a social structure that is "characterized by inequalities of class, race, and gender" (Comack, 2012:173). Women's deviance and crime is seen as a rational response to gender discrimination experienced in work, marriage, and interpersonal relationships. Some female crimes are attributed to women's lack of job opportunities and to stereotypical expectations about appropriate roles for women. Other theorists feel that women are exploited by capitalism and patriarchy. Because most females have had relatively low-wage jobs and few economic resources, minor crimes, such as prostitution, shoplifting, and passing bad cheques, were means to earn money or acquire consumer products. Increases in women's criminality during the 1970s and 1980s reflect the fact that the number of single female parents living in poverty grew significantly during this period.

Some of the most interesting work on female criminality has focused on the simultaneous effects of race, class, and gender on deviant behaviour. Arnold (1990) attributes many of the women's offences to living in families in which sexual abuse, incest, and other violence left them few choices except deviance. Economic marginality and racism also contributed to their victimization.

These conclusions are reinforced by the work of Elizabeth Comack, who examined the relationship between women's victimization and their subsequent involvement in Manitoba's criminal justice system. The incidence of prior victimization was pervasive among the 24 women she interviewed while they were incarcerated in a provincial jail. The abuse suffered by the women was connected to their criminal behaviour in several ways. Some women turned to crime as a means of coping with their abuse. "Meredith" had been sexually abused by her father since the age of four or five. She was in jail for fraud and had been involved in drug use and prostitution:

> Some people are violent, some people take it out in other ways, but that was my only way to release it. It was like, it's almost orgasmic, you know, you'd write the cheques, and you'd get home and you'd go through all these things and it's like, "There's so much there. I have all these new things to keep my mind off. I don't have to deal with the old issues." And so you do it. And it becomes an escape. (1996b:86)

Others broke the law while resisting abuse. "Janice" had been raped as a teenager and turned to alcohol as a way to cope. Serving time for manslaughter, she recounts the offence:

> Well I was at a party, and this guy, older, older guy, came, came on to me. He tried telling me, "Why don't you go to bed with me. I'm getting some money, you know." And I said, "No." And then he started hitting me and then he raped me and then [pause] I lost it. Like I just, I went, I got very angry and I snapped. And I started hitting him. I threw a coffee table on top of his head and then I stabbed him, and then I left. (1996b:96)

While abuse was strongly related to the women's law violations, Comack also found that race and class were factors contributing to their criminal behaviour—most were Aboriginal and poor.

Feminist theorists feel that women who violate the law are not "criminal women" but "criminalized women" (Laberge, 1991). This means that they commit crimes and acts of deviance because they have been forced into difficult situations that are not of their own making. The women interviewed by Comack faced many social pressures caused by race, class, and gender, and had few options for escaping their situations and improving their lives.

Feminist scholars have also focused attention on violence against women. Much of this violence was hidden, as sexual assault and domestic violence were rarely reported and were not taken seriously by the justice system. Several studies focusing on how rapes were dealt with by the justice system, including an important work by Clark and Lewis (1977), led to new sexual assault legislation in 1983 that changed some of the worst parts of the old law, including a section that gave husbands the right to rape their wives (Comack, 2012).

Feminist research has also helped to change the way domestic violence is dealt with by the justice system. Until the 1970s, little was known about this crime. In 1980, the Canadian Council on the Status of Women released a report showing that wife abuse was a major problem (MacLeod, 1980). Attitudes toward domestic violence at that time were illustrated by the fact that when these findings were released in the male-dominated House of Commons, parliamentarians responded with laughter. Despite this response, some legislators did take the issue seriously and recognized that the police response to domestic violence was inadequate. As a result, many provinces implemented mandatory charging policies for domestic violence complaints. This dramatically increased the number of charges laid for this offence (Ursel, 1996).

## Postmodern Perspectives on Crime and Deviance

How do postmodernists view deviance and social control? In his book *Discipline and Punish* (1979), Michel Foucault analyzed the intertwining nature of power, knowledge, and social control. In his study of prisons from the mid-1800s to the early 1900s, Foucault found that many penal institutions stopped torturing prisoners who disobeyed the rules and began using new surveillance techniques to maintain social control. Although the prisons appeared to be more humane in the post-torture era, Foucault contends that the new means of surveillance impinged more on prisoners and brought greater power to prison officials. Foucault described the *Panopticon*—a structure that gives prison officials the possibility of complete observation of inmates at all times. The Panopticon might be a tower in the centre of a circular prison from which guards can see all the cells. The prisoners know they can be observed at any time but do not know precisely when their behaviour is being scrutinized. As a result, prison officials are able to use their knowledge as a form of power over inmates. Eventually, the guards would not even have to be present all the time because prisoners would believe that they were under constant scrutiny by officials in the observation post.

How does Foucault's perspective explain social control in the larger society? Technologies such as the Panopticon make widespread surveillance and disciplinary power possible in many settings, including the police network, factories, schools, and hospitals. And current technology has the potential to expand surveillance far more broadly than Foucault could have imagined. The computer can act as a modern Panopticon that gives workplace supervisors virtually unlimited capabilities for surveillance. Technological developments have broadened the capacity of governments and corporations to control our behaviour. The Japanese have designed a toilet that companies can use to determine whether employees have recently used illegal drugs (Newham, 2004). Many people who were responsible for the 2010 Stanley Cup riots in Vancouver were identified and arrested because of facial recognition software that was used to analyze digital photos of the riots, and the police in many cities have licence plate recognition cameras that can identify wanted drivers and track stolen vehicles.

These technologies can be valuable tools in improving public safety. Closed-circuit television cameras in the subway were used to identify the people who carried out the July 2005 bombings that took more than 50 lives in London. Licence number recognition cameras have helped the police to get many auto thieves and suspended drivers off the road. DNA technology has freed many people who had been unjustly convicted of serious crimes and has enabled the justice system to imprison others who have committed crimes, such as sexual assault and murder. A system that would allow us to log on to our computers by scanning the iris of our eyes or our fingerprints would eliminate the confusing number of security passwords that each of us must remember.

However, these technologies raise important issues of privacy and individual rights, and society will have to decide whether greater protection is worth our loss of personal privacy. What are your views on this issue? Where should the balance lie between collective security and individual rights?

We have examined functionalist, interactionist, conflict, feminist, and postmodern perspectives on deviance and crime (see the Concept Snapshot). These explanations help us understand the causes and consequences of certain kinds of behaviour and provide us with guidance about how we might reduce crime and deviance. However, they also make us aware of how limited our knowledge of deviance and crime really is.

## CONCEPT SNAPSHOT

| FUNCTIONALIST PERSPECTIVES | In a smoothly functioning society, deviance will be limited because most people will share common culture goals and agree upon the appropriate means for reaching them. However, societies that do not provide sufficient avenues to reach these goals may also lack agreement about how people may achieve their aspirations. Deviance may be common in such societies because people may feel free to use whatever means they can to achieve their goals. |
|---|---|
| **Key thinkers:** Robert Merton, Richard Cloward, Lloyd Ohlin | |
| **INTERACTIONIST PERPECTIVES** **Key thinkers:** Edwin Sutherland, Howard Becker, Edwin Lemert | Deviance is learned in the same way as conformity—through interaction with others. A person becomes deviant when exposure to law-breaking attitudes is more meaningful to them than exposure to law-abiding attitudes. Societal reaction to someone who has been labelled as deviant may also cause people to develop a deviant self-concept. |
| **CONFLICT PERSPECTIVES** **Key thinkers:** Karl Marx, Richard Quinney | The powerful use law and the criminal justice system to protect their own class interests. The way laws are written and enforced benefits the capitalist class by ensuring that individuals at the bottom of the class structure do not take the property or threaten the safety of those at the top. The poor may also be forced to commit crimes to survive. |
| **FEMINIST PERSPECTIVES** **Key thinker:** Elizabeth Comack | The structured inequalities of race, class, and gender lead to the criminalization of women. Women's deviance and crime is seen as a rational response to gender discrimination experienced in work, marriage, and interpersonal relationships. Some female crimes are attributed to women's lack of job opportunities and to stereotypical expectations about appropriate roles for women. Other theorists feel that women are exploited by capitalism and patriarchy. |
| **POSTMODERN PERSPECTIVES** **Key thinker:** Michel Foucault | Power, knowledge and social control are intertwined. In prisons, for example, new means of surveillance make prisoners think they are being watched all the time. This gives prison officials power over the inmates. Modern technologies make widespread surveillance and disciplinary power possible in many settings, including the police network, factories, schools, and hospitals. |

## TIME TO REVIEW

- Discuss how crime differs from deviance.
- Describe how functionalist theorists explain the causes of crime and deviance. How do strain theories differ from control theories of deviance?
- Explain the two interactionist theories described in the text—differential association theory and labelling theory.
- Describe how conflict theorists critically assess the justice system and blame capitalism for causing crime.
- How do feminist theorists link women's criminality with inequalities of class, race, and gender?
- Explain how postmodern theorists such as Foucault view deviance and social control.

## LO-3 CRIME CLASSIFICATION AND STATISTICS

There are many different types of crimes. To study them, sociologists have put them into broader categories.

### How Sociologists Classify Crime

Sociologists categorize crimes based on how they are committed and how society views the offences. We will examine four types: (1) street crime; (2) occupational, or white-collar, and corporate crime; (3) organized crime; and (4) political crime. There is also a box on the relatively new category of **cybercrime**—offences where a computer is the object of a crime or the tool used to commit a crime (see Box 7.2 at **www.nelson.com/sociologyinourtimes6e**). As you read about these types of crime, ask yourself how you feel about them. Should each be a crime? How severe should the sanctions be against each type?

**cybercrime** Offences where a computer is the object of a crime or the tool used to commit a crime.

**street crime** All violent crime, certain property crimes, and certain morals crimes.

**STREET CRIME** When people think of crime, they most commonly think of **street crime**, which includes all violent crime, certain property crimes, and certain morals crimes. Examples are robbery,

Computers are increasingly being used as a means of committing a wide variety of crimes ranging from the distribution of child pornography to industrial espionage and identity theft.

NEL

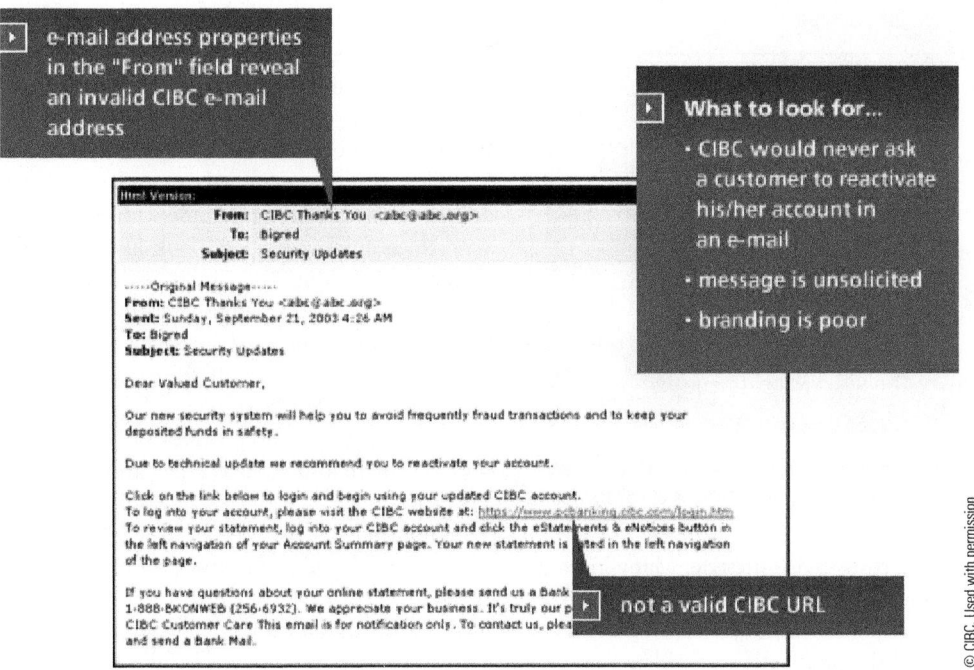

© CIBC. Used with permission

For some people, the "information superhighway" is a new avenue of illegitimate opportunity. Computer mischief and crime demonstrate how new opportunity structures can elicit new forms of deviance. This is an attempt by CIBC to educate its banking customers to avoid Internet fraud.

assault, and break and enter. These crimes occupy most of the criminal justice system's time. All street crime does not occur on the street; it frequently occurs in the home, workplace, and other locations.

*Violent crime* involves force or the threat of force against others, including murder, sexual assault, robbery, and aggravated assault. Violent crimes are probably the most anxiety-provoking of all criminal behaviour. Victims are often physically injured or even lose their lives, and the psychological trauma may last for years (Parker, 1995). Violent crime receives the most sustained attention from law enforcement officials and the media. While much attention may be given to the violent stranger, the vast majority of violent crime victims are injured by someone they know: family members, friends, neighbours, or co-workers (Silverman and Kennedy, 1993).

*Property crimes* include break and enter, theft, motor vehicle theft, and arson. While violent crime receives the most publicity, property crime is much more common. In most property crimes, the primary motive is to obtain money or some other valuable.

*Morals crimes* involve an illegal action voluntarily engaged in by the participants, such as prostitution, illegal gambling, the use of illegal drugs, and illegal pornography. Many people assert that such conduct should not be labelled as a crime. These offences are often referred to as "victimless crimes" because they involve exchanges of illegal goods or services among willing adults (Schur, 1965).

**OCCUPATIONAL AND CORPORATE CRIME Occupational, or white-collar, crime** consists of illegal activities committed by people in the course of their employment or in dealing with their financial affairs. Much of white-collar crime involves the violation of positions of trust. These activities include employee theft of company property or profits, soliciting bribes or kickbacks, and embezzling. Some white-collar criminals set up businesses for the sole purpose of victimizing the general public, engaging in activities such as land swindles, securities thefts, and consumer fraud.

In addition to acting for their own profit, some white-collar offenders become involved in criminal conspiracies designed to improve the profitability of their companies. This is known as **corporate crime**—illegal acts committed by corporate employees on behalf of the corporation and with its support. Examples include antitrust violations; false advertising; infringements on patents, copyrights, and trademarks; price fixing; and financial fraud. These crimes involve deliberate decisions made by corporate personnel to enhance profits at the expense of competitors, consumers, and the general public.

**occupational or white-collar, crime** A term used to describe illegal activities committed by people in the course of their employment or in dealing with their financial affairs.

**corporate crime** An illegal act committed by corporate employees on behalf of the corporation and with its support.

Conrad Black, one of Canada's most influential businessmen, has now completed a three-and-a half-year sentence in a Florida prison for misappropriating millions of dollars from shareholders of his newspaper chain.

The cost of white-collar and corporate crimes far exceeds that of street crime. Tax evasion costs Canadians billions of dollars a year. In one of the world's biggest white-collar crimes, investors in Calgary's Bre-X gold-mining company lost about $5 billion when it was learned that geologist Michael de Guzman had salted core samples with gold to make a worthless mining property look like the world's biggest gold find. In 2011, investors discovered that Sino-Forest, a Canadian-listed company that claimed to control vast amounts of Chinese forests, may have issued fraudulent reports. If these accusations are true, the losses may exceed those of Bre-X.

At the individual level, while few bank robbers get away with more than a few thousand dollars, Earl Jones, a Montreal investment adviser, defrauded clients of more than $50 million to support his lavish lifestyle. Many investors trusted Jones with their life savings and were financially devastated by his actions (Sutherland, 2009).

Corporate crimes can also be costly in terms of lives lost and injury. Laureen Snider (1988) found that occupational accidents and illnesses were the third leading cause of death in Canada. She attributes at least half of these deaths to unsafe and illegal working conditions. Working conditions in the mining industry, for example, have been especially dangerous. Decades ago, large numbers of Canadian miners died because their employers failed to protect them from mine hazards. Coal miners died of black lung, a condition caused by inhaling coal dust, and fluorspar miners died from the effects of inhaling silica dust in unventilated mineshafts. Not only did the mine owners fail to provide safe working conditions, but company doctors were also told not to advise the miners of the seriousness of their illnesses (Leyton, 1997).

One reason why many employers have been reluctant to implement required safety measures is because the penalties for violating workplace health and safety laws are so light. Typically, companies have been fined only a few thousand dollars even when employees died because of their employers' negligence.

Although people who commit occupational and corporate crimes can be arrested, fined, and sent to prison, many people do not regard such behaviour as "criminal." In Canada, punishment for such offences is usually a fine or a relatively brief prison sentence at a minimum-security facility; in the United States, however, penalties have become much more severe.

The concept of white-collar crime also fits some people who wear blue collars. Thus, *occupational crime* may be a more accurate term. Many tradespeople defraud the government by doing work "off the books" in order to avoid sales taxes, and some blue-collar businesses, such as auto repair, have bad records of consumer fraud.

**ORGANIZED CRIME Organized crime** is a business operation that supplies illegal goods and/ or services for profit. Organized crime includes drug trafficking, prostitution, liquor and cigarette smuggling, loan sharking, money laundering, and large-scale theft, such as truck hijacking (Simon and Eitzen, 1993). No single organization controls all organized crime, but many groups operate at all levels of society. Organized crime thrives because there is great demand for illegal goods and services. This public demand has produced illicit supply systems with global connections. These activities are highly profitable, since groups that have a monopoly over goods and services the public strongly desires can set their own price. Legitimate competitors are excluded because of the illegality; illegitimate competitors are controlled by force.

Gang-related killings have been increasing in Canada. The deadly nature of organized crime has been shown in Metro Vancouver. In early 2009, there were 16 gang-related shootings, seven of them fatal, in less than a month. Many of the shootings took place in public places, including

**organized crime** A business operation that supplies illegal goods and/or services for profit.

streets and mall parking lots. In one incident, a woman was fatally shot one morning while driving her car with a four-year-old child in the back seat. Arrests in such incidents are rare.

Along with their illegal enterprises, organized crime groups have infiltrated the world of legitimate business. Linkages with organized crime exist in many businesses, including immigration consulting, real estate, garbage collection, vending machines, construction, and trucking.

POLITICAL CRIMES **Political crime** involves illegal or unethical acts involving the misuse of power by government officials, or illegal or unethical acts perpetrated against a government by outsiders seeking to make a political statement or to undermine or overthrow the government. Government officials may use their authority unethically or illegally for material gain or political power. They may engage in graft (taking advantage of political position to gain money or property) through bribery, kickbacks, or "insider" deals that financially benefit them. While Canadian governments have a better record than those of most other countries, there have been a number of scandals. In the late 1990s, several members of former premier Grant Devine's Saskatchewan government were charged with fraud and many—including the former deputy premier—received prison sentences for misusing government funds. The 2005 Gomery Inquiry exposed serious wrongdoing by some members of Prime Minister Jean Chrétien's Liberal government who illegally funnelled millions of dollars to Quebec advertising agencies in exchange for their political support.

> **political crime** Illegal or unethical acts involving the usurpation of power by government officials, or illegal or unethical acts perpetrated against a government by outsiders seeking to make a political statement or to undermine or overthrow the government.

## Crime Statistics

It is difficult to measure crime. While citizens, police, and policymakers all wish to know how much crime there is and what forms this crime takes, those who commit crimes normally try to conceal their actions. Thus our information about crime will always be incomplete and we can never be certain of its accuracy. Our main sources of information about crime are police statistics and victimization surveys.

OFFICIAL STATISTICS Our most important source of crime data is the Canadian Uniform Crime Reports (CUCR) system, which summarizes crimes reported to all Canadian police departments. Most of our public information about crime comes from the CUCR. When we read that the homicide rate in British Columbia is higher than the national average, or that in 2010 more than 2.2 million offences were reported to the police, the information is usually based on CUCR data. Figure 7.2 shows trends in violent and property crimes, and Figure 7.3 shows Canada's homicide rates. These figures show that crime has declined significantly over the past two decades. The decline is particularly significant in the case of homicide, where rates are now the lowest they have been in more than 30 years.

Crime figures should be interpreted cautiously. While one can have confidence in homicide and auto theft statistics, the accuracy of other crime statistics is less certain. Since many policy decisions by governments, as well as decisions by individuals about their personal safety, are based on CUCR statistics, it is important to recognize their limitations.

The major weakness of the CUCR is that police statistics always underreport the actual amount of crime. The vast majority of offences reported in the CUCR come to the attention of the police from the reports of victims of crime, and victims do not report all crimes. Official crime rates are the result of a criminal act, a complaint by a victim or witness, and a response by the criminal justice system. A change in any of these will lead to an increase or decrease in crime rates. As a result, it can be difficult to analyze crime patterns and trends.

For example, Figure 7.2 shows that rates of reported violent crimes increased significantly in Canada during the late 1980s and early 1990s, almost doubling between 1980 and 1990. We know that at least part of the increase in reported crime was because violence against women was more likely to be reported rather than because violence actually increased (Linden, 1994). In the mid-1980s, many provincial governments directed police to lay charges in all suspected cases of domestic violence. These zero-tolerance policies have been made progressively more effective since they were first implemented. This visible support of the justice system may have encouraged more victims to report spousal assaults. The impact of these changes was seen in

FIGURE 7.2    CANADIAN CRIME RATES, 1962–2011

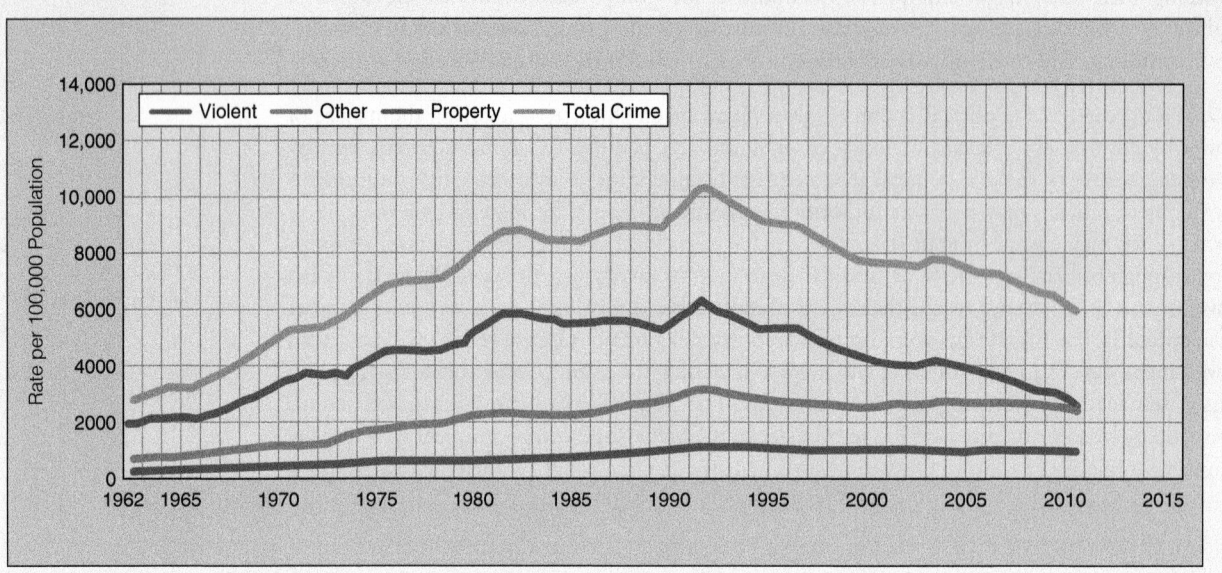

*Sources:* Adapted from Statistics Canada, *Crime Statistics in Canada 2007*, Cat. no. 85-002-X, Vol. 28 no. 7, 2008; Brennan, Shannon, *Police-reported Crime Statistics in Canada, 2011*, Statistics Canada, Cat. no 85-002-X, 2012.

FIGURE 7.3    CANADIAN HOMICIDE RATES, 1961–2011

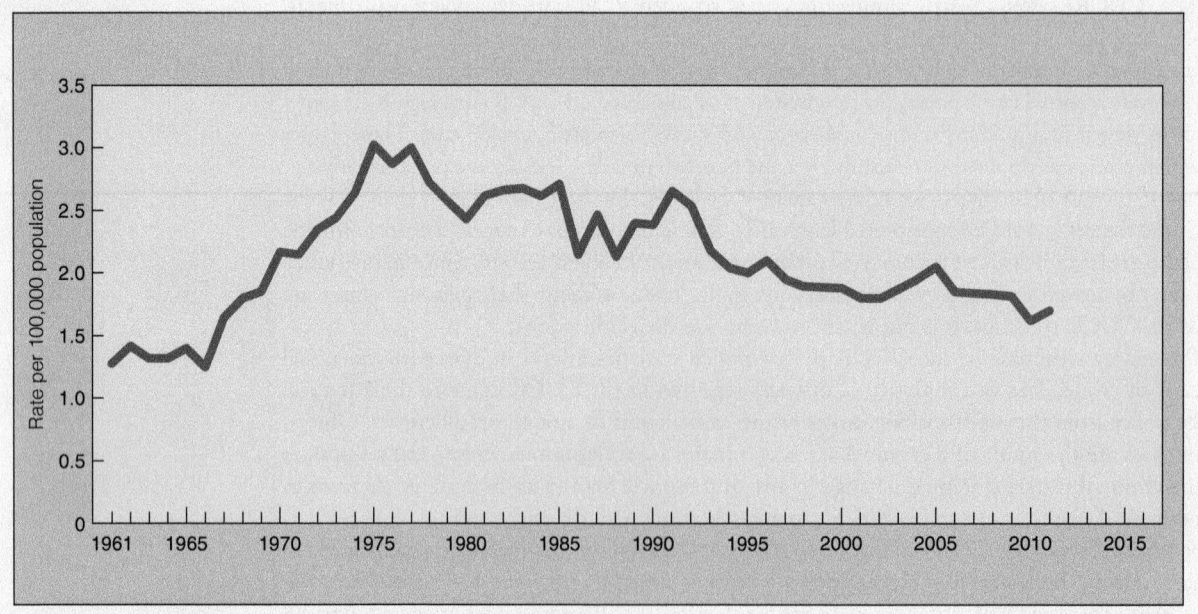

As of 1971, population estimates were adjusted to reflect new methods of calculation.

*Sources:* Statistics Canada, *Crime Statistics in Canada 2007*, Cat. no. 85-002-X, Vol. 28 no. 7, 2008; Brennan, Shannon, *Police-reported Crime Statistics in Canada, 2011*, Statistics Canada, Cat. no 85-002-X, 2012.

Winnipeg, where the police instituted a mandatory charging policy and where the province set up a special family violence court for spouse abuse cases. The number of domestic violence cases dealt with by this court rose from 1444 in 1990, the first year of the court's operation, to 3387 three years later (Ursel, 1996). This increase was likely due to changes in the reporting and recording of domestic assaults rather than to any increase in family violence.

Another weakness of official statistics is that many crimes committed by persons of higher socio-economic status are routinely handled by administrative bodies or by civil courts. To avoid negative publicity, many companies prefer to deal privately with offences like embezzlement committed by their employees, and these cases may not be reported to the police. As a result, many elite crimes are never classified as "crimes," nor are the businesspeople who commit them labelled as "criminals."

**VICTIMIZATION SURVEYS**    The weaknesses of the CUCR have led to the development of the *victimization survey.* Because many people do not report their victimization to police, governments conduct surveys in which members of the public are directly asked if they have been victims of crime. In the latest Canadian survey, only 31 percent of the victimizations reported by respondents had been reported to the police (Perreault and Brennan, 2010). Thus, reported crimes are only the tip of the iceberg. People reported that they did not report a crime because they considered the incident too minor, because they felt it was a personal matter, because they preferred to deal with the problem in another way, or because they did not feel the police could do anything about the crime.

Victimization surveys provide us with information about crimes that have not been officially reported. The additional information that they provide has helped to confirm that the rise in violent crime during the 1980s and early 1990s was due to an increase in the reporting and recording of domestic assaults. Assaults did not likely increase during this period—we just did a better job of counting them.

These surveys, however, also have weaknesses: People may not remember minor types of victimization; they may not report honestly to the interviewer; and they do not provide any information about "victimless crimes," such as drug use and illegal gambling. Despite these flaws, victimization surveys have shed new light on the extent of criminal behaviour. They are a valuable complement to other ways of counting crimes.

## WHO COMMITS CRIMES: CHARACTERISTICS OF OFFENDERS    LO-4

Given the limitations of official statistics, is it possible to determine who commits crimes? Age, gender, class, and race are important *correlates of crime.* That is, they are factors associated with criminal activity. One method of testing theories of crime is to see how well they explain these correlates.

## Age and Crime

The offender's age is one of the most significant factors associated with crime and most other kinds of deviance. Arrests increase from early adolescence, peak in young adulthood, and steadily decline with age. There is some variation in this pattern—for example, violent crimes peak at a later age than property crimes—but the general pattern is almost always the same. Crime is a young person's game, with rates peaking between the ages of 15 and 18.

The relationship between age and criminality exists in every society for which we have data (Hirschi and Gottfredson, 1983). This is also true for most other types of high-risk behaviours, some of which are considered to be deviant. Adolescence and early adulthood are the peak times for both offending and victimization. Possible explanations for the decline in crime and deviance rates after early adulthood are the physical effects of aging, which make some criminal activity more difficult, and the realization by older chronic offenders that further arrests will result in very long jail sentences. Perhaps the best explanation for maturational reform, though, is related to the different social positions of youth and adults. Adolescents are between childhood and adult life. They have few responsibilities and no clear social role. Adolescence is also a time when young people are breaking away from the controls of their parents and others and preparing to live on their own. As we age, we begin to acquire commitments and obligations that limit our freedom to choose a lifestyle that includes crime and other forms of deviance.

## Gender and Crime

Another consistent correlate of crime is gender. Most crimes are committed by males. Females are more likely to be victims than offenders. As with age and crime, this relationship has existed in almost all times and cultures. However, while the age distribution is remarkably stable, there is considerably more variation in male/female crime ratios in different places, at different times, and for different types of crime.

Men make up more than 80 percent of those charged with crimes in Canada. As Figure 7.4 shows, the degree of involvement of males and females varies substantially for different crimes. The most important gender differences in arrest rates are reflected in the proportionately greater involvement of men in violent crimes and major property offences.

The difference between male and female involvement in crime has narrowed over the past three decades. Hartnagel (2004) found that the percentage of *Criminal Code* offences committed by females nearly doubled, from 9 percent to 17 percent, between 1968 and 2000. While there was virtually no change in the percentage of homicides committed by women (11 percent versus 10 percent), women's involvement in serious theft (9 percent versus 23 percent), fraud (11 percent versus 30 percent), and minor theft (22 percent versus 28 percent) increased substantially.

| FIGURE 7.4 | PERCENTAGE OF CHARGES IN ADULT CRIMINAL COURTS, BY GENDER, 2010–11 (SELECTED CRIMINAL OFFENCES) |

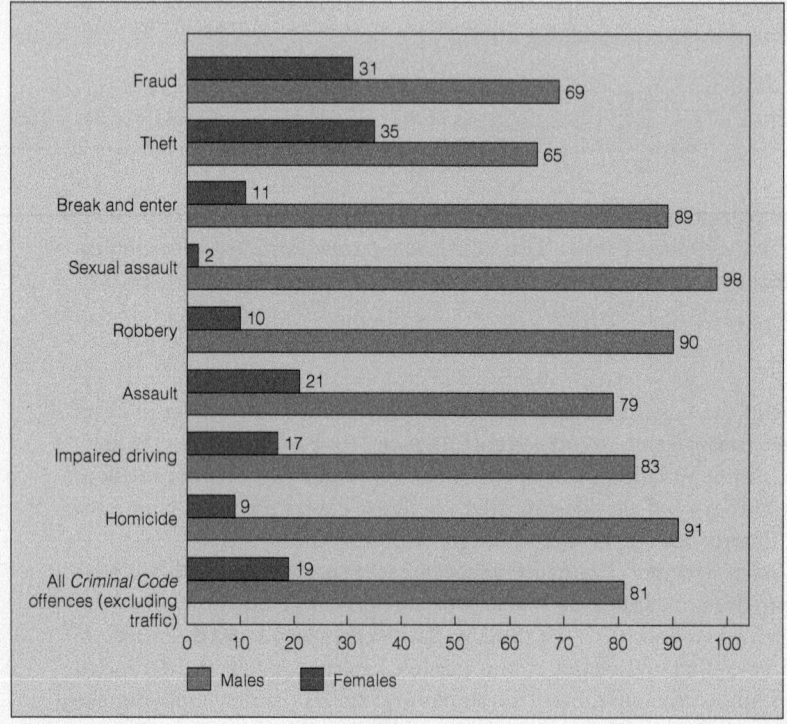

*Source:* Statistics Canada, CANSIM Table 252-0053. Integrated Criminal Court Survey.

What has caused this change in the sex distribution of crime? One clue comes from cross-cultural data showing very large differences in sex ratios of criminal involvement in different parts of the world. We know from comparisons of different countries that women's rates of crime are lowest in countries having the greatest differences between the roles of men and women. Where women follow traditional roles in which their lives are centred exclusively on the home, their crime rates are low. On the other hand, where women's lives are more similar to men's, their crime rates will be higher. This finding is consistent with the change in women's crime rates over the past several decades in Canada, where the role of women has come to resemble that of men.

While role convergence may explain some of the reduction in the gap between male and female crime rates, the convergence in crime rates had almost stopped over two decades ago, and it does not seem likely that women will ever become as involved in crime as men or that they will adopt male patterns of crime, particularly for violent crime. The increase in female crime has been greatest for property crimes, such as theft and fraud. These two categories include offences such as shoplifting, credit card fraud, and passing bad cheques, which are among the least serious property offences. Comack (2009) has concluded that this reflects the feminization of poverty rather than any convergence of gender roles. Thus, much of the increase in female crime may reflect the increased economic marginalization of poor women.

While female crime rates have increased more rapidly than male crime rates, it is important to remember that the numbers seem more dramatic than they are because the percentage changes are based on very low numbers of female crimes in earlier decades. Women have a long way to go to reach equality in crime with men, and the increases in female crime have now levelled off.

## Social Class and Crime

Many theories assume that crime is economically motivated and that poverty will lead to criminal behaviour. However, the evidence concerning the impact of economic factors on crime is mixed. We know that persons from lower socioeconomic backgrounds are more likely to be arrested for violent and property crimes. However, we also know that these crimes are more likely to come to the attention of the police than are the white-collar crimes that are more likely to be committed by members of the upper class. Because the vast majority of white-collar crimes are never reported; we lack the data to fully assess the relationship between class and crime.

Before looking at some of the data on social class and crime, let us consider several other economic variables. Does crime increase during times of high unemployment? Do poor cities, provinces, and countries have higher crime rates than richer communities? The answer to both these questions is no. Historically, crime rates are at least as likely to rise during periods of prosperity as during recessionary times. We are also as likely to find high crime rates in rich countries as in poor ones. Within Canada, the poorer provinces of Quebec and New Brunswick have crime rates far lower than the wealthier provinces of British Columbia and Alberta (see Map 7.1 on page 197). Hartnagel (2012) has concluded that the *degree of inequality*—poverty amid affluence—is a better predictor of crime than is the amount of poverty.

We know that lower-class people are overrepresented in arrest and prison admission statistics; however, we do not know if lower-class people commit more crimes or if the justice system treats them more harshly. To get closer to actual behaviour, researchers developed self-report surveys in which respondents were asked to report the number of deviant acts they had committed during a specified time. There is some disagreement about the conclusions that should be drawn from this research, most of which has used adolescent subjects. However, the most likely conclusion is that for the vast majority of people, class and crime or delinquency are not related. However, the most frequent and serious offenders are most likely to come from the bottom of the class ladder—from an underclass that is severely disadvantaged economically, educationally, and socially. There is also some evidence that other forms of deviance, such as suicide, alcoholism, mental illness, and drug addiction, are also more common among the underclass.

A unique victimization survey reinforces this conclusion. More than 12,000 Canadian women were interviewed for the national Violence Against Women Survey (Johnson, 1996). Several findings supported the view that violence is greatest at the very bottom of the class ladder. First, men with high school educations assaulted their wives at twice the rate of men with university degrees. Second, men who were out of work committed assaults at twice the rate of men who were employed. Third, men in the lowest income category (less than $15,000 a year) assaulted their wives at twice the rate of men with higher incomes. Above this $15,000 level, however, there was no relationship between income and crime. This again suggests that the highest crime rates can be found at the bottom of the economic ladder, but that above this level there is no relationship.

## Race and Ethnicity and Crime

In societies with culturally heterogeneous populations, some ethnic and racial groups will have higher crime rates than others. For example, in the United States, African Americans and Hispanics are overrepresented in arrest data. However, because Statistics Canada does not routinely collect data about racial and ethnic correlates of crime, we know relatively little about the situation in Canada.

In addition to data about Aboriginal Canadians, which will be discussed later, there have been several Canadian studies dealing with minorities and crime. The first of these examined race and ethnicity in the federal prison system. Offenders from non-Aboriginal visible ethnic minorities were *underrepresented* in the federal correctional system's population (Thomas, 1992). Specifically, the study found that in 1989, 5.2 percent of the federal corrections population were members of ethnic minority groups, while these groups made up more than 6.3 percent of the general population. The second study, which examined provincial youth and adult correctional centres in British Columbia, arrived at similar findings. Only 8.2 percent of the prison population were members of non-Aboriginal visible ethnic minorities, yet these groups made up 13.5 percent of the province's population. Contrary to the common view that immigrants have high crime rates, only 11 percent of B.C. inmates were not born in Canada, compared with 22 percent of the population of the province. The Commission on Systemic Racism in the Ontario Criminal Justice System (1995) reported that the rate of imprisonment for black adults in Ontario was five times higher than the rate for white adults. Black adults were also more likely to be imprisoned while awaiting trial, particularly for discretionary charges, such as drug possession and drug trafficking. Most recently, the *Toronto Star* used Canada's criminal records database to show that 16.7 percent of people with a criminal record in Canada were "non-white" (Rankin and Powell, 2008). This is below the percentage of visible minorities and Aboriginal people in the Canadian population, which is about 20 percent.

While statistics on other minorities are limited, there are extensive data on Aboriginal peoples because of special inquiries held to find out whether the justice system has discriminated against Aboriginal people. Many studies have demonstrated the overinvolvement of Aboriginal people (Hartnagel, 2009). For example, while Aboriginal people made up about 4 percent of the population in 2006, they made up about 24 percent of admissions to provincial prisons and 18 percent of admissions to federal prisons (Landry and Sinha, 2008). They also made up 23 percent of those accused of homicide between 1997 and 2004 (Brzozowski, Taylor-Butts, and Johnson, 2006). It is important to note that there is much variation in Aboriginal crime rates among different communities and different parts of the country (Wood and Griffiths, 1996).

What is the reason for these racial and ethnic differences in crime rates? One answer is that there has often been discrimination against minority groups. The treatment of blacks in South Africa and in the Southern United States are obvious examples. Discrimination against

BOX 7.3

# POINT/COUNTERPOINT

## "If It Bleeds, It Leads": Fear of Crime and the Media

Most Canadians learn about crime through the media, which shape our views about crime and criminals. However, the media do not simply "report" the news. Editors and reporters select the crime news and construct the way this news is presented to us (McKnight, 2012).

Unfortunately, the picture of crime we receive from the media is distorted. For example, while most crime is property crime, most media stories deal with violent crime. Gabor (1994) reviewed all the crime-related stories reported over two months in an Ottawa newspaper. More than half the stories focused on violent crimes, particularly murders. However, violent crimes made up only 7 percent of reported crimes in Ottawa, and the city averaged just six murders per year. While violent crimes were overreported, property crimes rarely received much attention.

The portrayal of crime in the fictional media is even more distorted. Video games, television programs, and movies are often extremely violent. Consider the partial list of the 221 violent acts depicted in *South Park: Bigger, Longer & Uncut*, the R-rated movie based on the animated series *South Park*, and ask whether the list reflects the reality of life in your community:

> 130 weapons fired (with multiple killings), 18 electric shocks, 10 blows to the body, 8 blood spatterings, 3 burnings, 3 hanging-body scenes, 1 breaking of body in half, 1 assault with a chainsaw, 1 attempted electrocution, and 1 dog attack. (Media Index, 1999)

Why do the media misrepresent crime? The primary goal of the media is to make profits by selling advertising. Stories about violent crime will boost ratings and circulation, even if these stories give people a false picture of crime. The informal media rule "If it bleeds, it leads" reflects the public fascination with sensationalized, bloody stories, such as those of mass murders. Commenting on his experience with the media, the executive director of a provincial legal society said, "If there's no blood and gore, or there's no sex, it's not newsworthy. And if it falls into the category of being newsworthy, then they have to show the dead body. They've got to show the corpse" (McCormick, 1995:182). Some parts of the media also have an ideological agenda, as they favour "tough on crime" policies that are more likely to be supported by members of the public who fear being victimized by violent crime.

The media's crime coverage is selective in other ways. Some have blamed the media for failing to cover the story of large numbers of missing women in Vancouver until Robert Pickton was charged with 26 murders. While a missing child from a middle-class home will generate an avalanche of publicity, the stories of dozens of missing lower-class women—many of whom were sex trade workers—were not seen as important. Robert Pickton's trial generated international coverage, but the media focused on the gruesome crimes and did not consider larger social issues such as legal policies that endanger sex trade workers, the structural reasons why so many of the victims were Aboriginal, and the role of the state in producing socially impoverished neighbourhoods such as Vancouver's Downtown Eastside, where Pickton found most of his victims (Hugill, 2010). What is the impact of the media's misrepresentation of crime? First, Canadians greatly overestimate the amount of violent crime and have a fear of crime that is higher than the risk of victimization justifies (McKnight, 2012). Meanwhile, global coverage of violence means that violent crimes, such as school shootings in Europe or Australia, are reported as immediately and as thoroughly as if they had happened in our own communities.

The media also provide a distorted stereotype of offenders. Violent crimes are most often committed by relatives, friends, and acquaintances, not by the anonymous stranger so many of us fear. Corporate and white-collar criminals are responsible for a great deal of social harm, but except for the most dramatic cases—such as Conrad Black in Canada and Bernie Madoff in the United States—their activities rarely receive much attention in the media. Reporting of these cases is typically limited to the business section rather than the headlines.

Members of the media pursue a vehicle containing convicted murderer Karla Homolka following a court hearing.

Aboriginal people in Canada, Australia, and New Zealand has also been well documented by commissions of inquiry. Members of minority groups, who tend to be poor, may go to prison for minor offences if they are unable to pay fines. While this type of discrimination may be unintentional, it is nonetheless real. The justice system also tends to focus its efforts on the types of crimes that are committed by low-income people rather than on white-collar crimes, so members of poor minority groups may be overrepresented in crime statistics. Discrimination accounts for some, but not all, of the high rates of criminality of some minority groups.

To provide a further explanation, consider the case of Canada's Aboriginal people. Their situation is unique, but the same kinds of factors may apply in other racial contexts. While a number of theories have been advanced to explain Aboriginal overinvolvement (Hartnagel, 2004; Wood and Griffiths, 2000), consider the following explanation, which has been drawn from conflict and social control theories. Canada's Aboriginal people have far less power and fewer resources than other Canadians. They must cope with systems of education and religion that have been imposed on them from outside their cultural communities and that are incompatible with their customs and traditions. In the past, forced attendance at residential schools and forced adoption outside the community weakened family ties. Crippling rates of unemployment in many areas mean no job ties, and school curricula that are irrelevant to the lives of Aboriginal students mean that children do not become attached to their schools. Under these conditions, strong social bonds are difficult to develop and high rates of crime can be predicted. Manitoba's Aboriginal Justice Inquiry concluded: "We believe that the relatively high rates of crime among Aboriginal people are a result of the despair, dependency, anger, frustration and sense of injustice prevalent in Aboriginal communities, stemming from the cultural and community breakdown that has occurred over the past century" (Hamilton and Sinclair, 1991:91).

### TIME TO REVIEW

- Compare the different categories used by sociologists to classify different types of crime.
- Discuss some of the different types of cybercrime.
- What are the strengths and weaknesses of official crime statistics, self-reported crime statistics, and victimization surveys?
- Explain how and why age, gender, class, and race are correlated with crime.

## LO-5    THE CRIMINAL JUSTICE SYSTEM

The criminal justice system includes the police, the courts, and prisons. However, the term criminal justice *system* is misleading because these institutions do not work together and each has considerable autonomy.

### The Police

Most people think that the main function of the police is to enforce the law. That is indeed one of their functions, but there are several others, including order maintenance and the provision of social services. *Order maintenance* refers to keeping the peace and includes things like stopping arguments, controlling the areas where skid-row alcoholics drink, and making a group of

| MAP 7.1 | 2011 CRIME RATES PER 100,000 POPULATION (*CRIMINAL CODE* EXCLUDING TRAFFIC OFFENCES) |

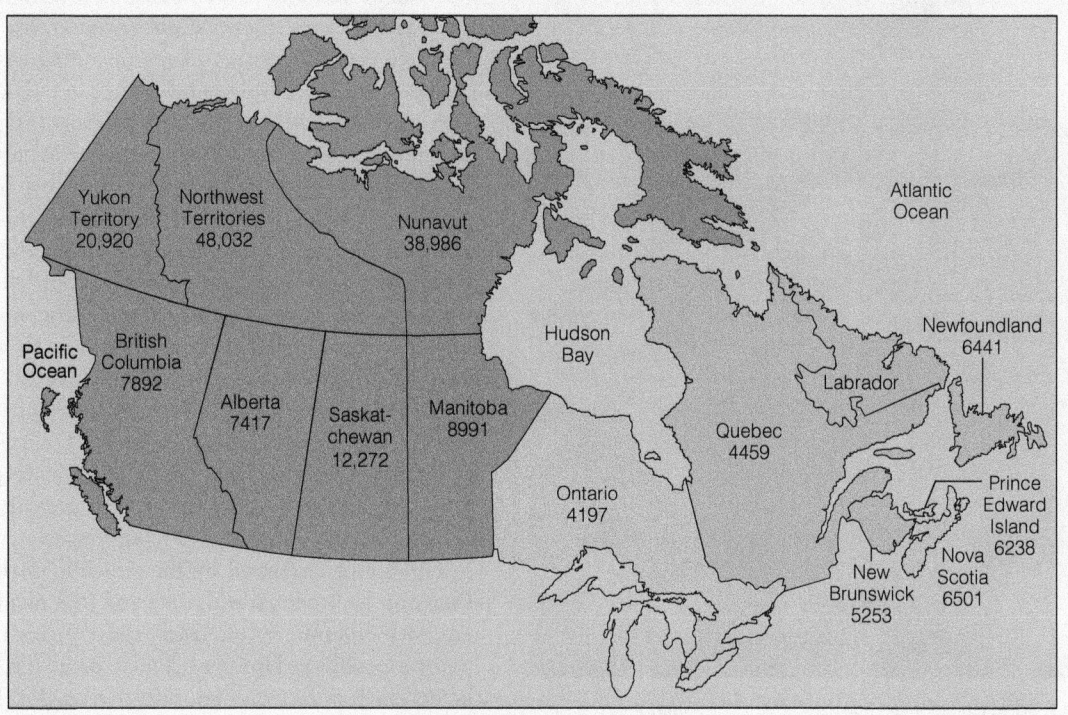

There are major regional differences in crime rates within Canada. Crime rates are highest in the West and the North, and lowest in Central Canada.

*Source:* Statistics Canada, "Police-Reported Crime Statistics in Canada, 2011," Catalogue no. 85-002-X, p. 27.

boisterous teenagers move away from the parking lot of a convenience store. While the main concern in law enforcement is arresting a suspect, the main concern in order maintenance is restoring peace in the community. The service role, also important, consists of many different activities, including finding lost children, counselling crime victims, and notifying next of kin in fatal accidents.

Two questions you might ask are these: Why do the police have such a broad range of responsibilities? What ties these diverse activities together? In answer to the first question, there are several reasons why the police have the broad responsibilities they do:

1. The police are one of the few public agencies open 24 hours a day.
2. In many cases, the police are serving clients that other agencies may not be interested in. The poor, the homeless, and the mentally ill may become police clients almost by default. If no other agency will look after intoxicated people who pass out on downtown streets, the police must do it.
3. The police may not know about, or have access to, other agencies that could handle some of their cases.

The second question—What ties these diverse activities together?—is best answered by looking at two dimensions of the police role. First, the police have the *authority* (and often the duty) to intervene in situations where something must be done immediately. This authority is the same whether the incident is an armed robbery in progress, a naked man standing on a busy street

A Nova Scotia Board of Inquiry found that a member of the Halifax Police Service discriminated against boxer Kirk Johnson when Mr. Johnson was stopped, ticketed, and had his car impounded despite having committed no offenses.

screaming at people, or a complaint that someone's pet boa constrictor has just appeared in someone else's apartment. Second, the authority is backed up by *non-negotiable force.* If someone refuses to obey a police officer, the officer can use force (usually arrest) to back up his or her demands. Even professional caregivers may resort to calling the police when clients refuse to cooperate with them. Egon Bittner has summed up the patrol officer's role: "What policemen do appears to consist of rushing to the scene of any crisis whatever, judging its needs in accordance with canons of common sense reasoning, and imposing solutions upon it without regard to resistance or opposition" (1980:137).

The police have a high degree of discretion in that they often have to decide which rules to apply and how to apply them. For example, if a police officer stops a driver for speeding and the driver has alcohol on his or her breath, several outcomes are possible. The police officer may warn the person and tell her or him to go straight home, write a speeding ticket, or administer a Breathalyzer and lay charges of impaired driving.

The use of discretion by the police is unavoidable. If discretion is dispensed equitably and in a manner consistent with community standards and the rule of law, this is not a problem. However, if it is based on extra-legal factors, such as race or class, or if it is used to favour certain individuals over others, it can be considered *discriminatory.* Issues of racial discrimination have generated the most discussion in Canada in recent years, as inquiries have been held in many provinces following police shootings of minority group members.

Earlier in this chapter, we discussed some of the ways in which the justice system discriminates against Aboriginal people. Similar conclusions may also apply to other groups. Many blacks, particularly young people, feel that they are harassed by the police and that they are stopped and questioned because of their race. Carl James interviewed a number of black youth in several Ontario cities about their experiences with the police. Their comments show that they do not feel they have been treated equitably by the police:

> You can't win. As long as you're Black you are a target.

> They drive by. They don't glimpse your clothes, they glimpse your colour. That's the first thing they look at. If they judge the clothes so much why don't they go and stop those white boys that are wearing those same things like us?

> No matter what the situation that you're in, what your dress is like . . . they will find a negative way of thinking about you, because you're Black, and secondly because you're Somali, and thirdly because you're an immigrant and you speak a different language. (1998:165–168)

A survey conducted for the Commission on Systemic Racism in the Ontario Criminal Justice System (1995) also found that black respondents were much more likely than white and Chinese respondents to report that they had been stopped by the police and were more likely to report feeling that the police had treated them unfairly. These perceptions of racial profiling have been supported by research done in Toronto (Wortley and Tanner, 2003) and Kingston (CTV, 2005) showing that black drivers are more likely to be stopped by the police than drivers of other races. While not all researchers agree that these studies demonstrate racial profiling (see Melchers, 2003), there is little doubt that being more frequently stopped does contribute to the perception of police harassment felt by many black people.

Most recently, Peter Carrington and Robin Fitzgerald also reported that minority youth were more likely than white youth to be questioned by the police. This difference could not be explained by the extent of differential involvement in crime by minority youth. They conclude that the evidence suggests that the "disproportionate minority youth contact with the police in Canada is at least partly a result of racially discriminatory policing practices" (2012:195).

## The Courts

Criminal courts decide the guilt or innocence of those accused of committing a crime. In theory, justice is determined in an adversarial process in which the prosecutor (a lawyer representing the state) argues that the accused is guilty and the defence lawyer asserts that the accused is innocent. Proponents of the adversarial system feel this system best provides a just decision about guilt or innocence.

The essence of the adversarial system can be seen in the defence lawyer's role, which is to defend the accused. This role was described by Lord Brougham, the defence lawyer in an 1821 case that could have had disastrous consequences for the British government had his defence been successful:

> An advocate, in the discharge of his duty, knows but one person in all the world, and that person is his client. To save that client by all means and expedients, and at all hazards and costs to their persons, and amongst them, to himself, is his first and only duty; and in performing this duty he must not regard the alarm, the torments, the destruction which he may bring upon others. Separating the duty of a patriot from that of an advocate, he must go on reckless of the consequences, though it should be his unhappy fate to involve his country in confusion. (cited in Greenspan, 1982:201)

We can add that in an adversarial system, the defence lawyer is obliged to fulfill this duty to the client without concern for the client's guilt or innocence.

Most of those working in the courts view the adversarial system as one of the cornerstones of a free and democratic society. Many of the procedures that seem to restrict the ability of the court to get at the "truth," such as the rule that accused persons cannot be forced to testify against themselves, were adopted to prevent the arbitrary use of state power against the accused. However, some critics feel that our system does not deal adequately with crime because it places more emphasis on winning than on doing what is best for the accused, for the victim, and for society.

Not all Western countries use the adversarial court system. Several European countries use systems in which the judge takes a much more active role in ensuring that justice is done. At the trial, the judge leads the questioning and there is much more concern with getting at the truth and less on legal constraints of the kind that exist in our system. The holistic, restorative approach to justice advocated by many Aboriginal people is another alternative to our current system. This approach tries to take into account the needs of the victim, the accused, and the community, rather than simply applying formal legal rules and procedures.

## Restorative Justice

For many years, we have relied on the formal justice system to deal with crime. Community members have been discouraged from participating in their own protection and have had little say in the services they received. After the victim called the police, the police would arrive to take care of the problem, and if an arrest was made, processing the case was left in the hands of the formal justice system. Some of those found guilty by the court were removed from the community and sent away to jail. Professionals controlled each step in the system, and victims and other community members had little involvement.

While most people have come to accept this as the proper way of dealing with crime, some feel the system has failed them. Victims feel left out, as their injury is forgotten and they are relegated to the role of witnesses. Offenders are also dealt with impersonally and are rarely reminded of the personal harm they have done. The public is often dissatisfied with a justice system that does not respond to their concerns.

Many critics have proposed an alternative system that is intended to restore social relationships rather than simply to punish (Church Council on Justice and Corrections, 1996). Advocates of *restorative justice* seek a system that will repair the harm that has been done to the victim and to the community. A key element is the involvement of the victim and other members of the community as active participants in the process in order to reconcile offenders with those they have harmed and to help communities reintegrate victims and offenders.

Restorative justice has its roots in traditional societies where the restoration of order was crucial to society's survival. In Canada, Aboriginal communities are leading the way in the return to restorative justice practices. They have used a variety of different methods, including *sentencing circles,* which bring an offender together with the victims and other community members, to resolve disputes. Two of the most widespread contemporary restorative justice methods are *victim–offender reconciliation* and *family group conferencing*.

*Victim–offender reconciliation* was devised in Elmira, Ontario, as an initiative to persuade a judge to deal in a positive fashion with two youths who had vandalized property belonging to 22 different victims. Mediators worked with the victims and the offenders to reach an acceptable resolution. As a result, the youths had to deal personally with each of their victims and to make restitution for the damage they had caused. The restorative process gave victims a say in what happened and gave offenders the chance to make amends.

*Family group conferencing* is similar to sentencing circles. It typically applies to young offenders and normally involves the victim, the offender, and as many of their family and friends as possible. All parties speak and then discuss how to repair the harm done to the victim. Negotiation continues until a plan is agreed on and written down. The coordinator then establishes mechanisms for enforcing the plan. The family and friends of both the victim and the offender are encouraged to offer continuing help to ensure that the resolution arrived at during the conference is carried out in the community.

While there have been concerns about issues such as the potential for net-widening through including offenders who might otherwise be screened out and dealt with in less formal ways, restorative justice programs provide us with a valuable alternative to the formal justice system.

## Prisons

The incarceration rate in Canada in 2008 was 116 per 100,000 people. This rate is lower than the rates in the United States (756) and England and Wales (153), but higher than the rates in many other countries, including Italy (92), Germany (89), and Denmark (63) (Public Safety Canada, 2010). And prisons are very expensive—it costs $110,000 a year to keep an inmate in a federal penitentiary.

Why do we send people to jail? We deprive people of their liberty for several reasons:

1. *Retribution.* We send people to jail to punish them for their crimes.
2. *Incapacitation.* We imprison offenders so they cannot commit further crimes.
3. *Rehabilitation.* We seek to return offenders to the community as law-abiding citizens.
4. *Deterrence.* We try to reduce criminal activity by instilling a fear of punishment.

You can see that these goals may conflict. Those who focus on retribution and deterrence may want to make the prison experience as punitive and harsh as possible. This conflicts with rehabilitation, however, because this goal is best accomplished by providing inmates with the skills to get jobs following release, by helping them deal with the issues that led them into crime, and by carefully reintegrating them into their communities.

While prisons are very costly, we do not know as much as we should about their effectiveness. The research you learn about in Box 7.4 shows that longer prison sentences are not effective

BOX 7.4 **POINT/COUNTERPOINT**

## Do Tougher Prison Sentences Reduce Crime?

The law clearly deters. Most people do not deliberately park where they know their car will be towed away and do not speed if they see a police car behind them. However, the more important question concerns the limits of deterrence. How can we change the system to make it more effective?

The Canadian government has decided to "crack down" on crime, and since 2006, Parliament has passed several pieces of legislation designed to put more people in jail for longer periods of time. Prisons are expensive—the cost of keeping someone in a federal penitentiary is $110,000 per year (Public Safety Canada, 2010)—so it is important to know whether this policy of sending more people to jail for longer periods reduces crime rates or whether other crime reduction strategies would keep Canadians safer.

The research tells us that longer sentences do *not* reduce crime rates. Steven Durlauf and Daniel Nagin reviewed the evidence on the deterrent effect of imprisonment and conclude that long prison sentences "are difficult to justify on a deterrence-based, crime prevention basis" (2011:38). Some of the research they reviewed suggests that imprisonment may actually *increase* an individual's likelihood of future criminal behaviour.

The most conclusive studies reviewed by Durlauf and Nagin are the evaluations of laws requiring mandatory minimum prison sentences for particular offences or for offenders with significant prior records. Mandatory minimum sentences have become widely used—they are part of many of Canada's new laws—and there has been much debate about their effectiveness.

The harshest mandatory sentencing law in any Western country is California's three-strikes law. This law provides a mandatory sentence of 25 years in prison for a third felony conviction following two earlier convictions for serious felonies (a category that includes residential burglary). This has resulted in some bizarre sentences, including cases where two men will spend 25 years in prison, one for stealing a slice of pizza and the other for shoplifting a small package of meat.

The three-strikes law has been costly. The California State Auditor (2010) calculated that the cost of three-strikes sentences was $20 billion more than if the inmates had been sentenced for the crimes they committed rather than for the "strikes" against them. California can no longer afford its prison system and in 2012 the U.S. Supreme Court ordered the state to release 32,000 inmates because of severe overcrowding. Mandatory minimum sentences also significantly increase court costs because individuals facing long mandatory penalties are more likely to insist on a trial rather than pleading guilty. The law is also very hard on the offenders and their families.

The high social and financial costs of mandatory minimum sentences might be worthwhile if they reduced crime rates. However, they do not. Michael Tonry concluded: "Mandatory penalties are a bad idea. They often result in injustice to individual offenders . . . And the clear weight of the evidence is, and for nearly 40 years has been, that there is insufficient credible evidence to conclude that mandatory penalties have significant deterrent effects" (2009:100).

Tonry bases this conclusion in part on a series of evaluations of California's three-strikes laws. While California's crime rate has declined since the passage of three strikes in 1994, this decline was not a result of the three-strikes laws. Only one of 15 studies reviewed by Tonry concluded that the legislation reduced crime rates. Several studies, including those by Marvell and Moody (2001) and Chen (2008), showed that crime rates in California did not decline faster than in other states even though the penalties in California were far more severe than in any other state. Zimring (2012) found that crime rates in New York City dropped far more than in Los Angeles and San Diego between 1990 and 2009 despite the fact that incarceration actually declined substantially in New York as it climbed in California.

Why don't severe penalties such as mandatory sentences deter crime? One reason is because offenders may not feel they are at risk of receiving those penalties. And potential offenders are actually correct in believing that their next crime is unlikely to lead to punishment. Most crimes are not reported, most reported offences do not result in arrests, most arrests do not lead to convictions, and most convictions do not result in imprisonment. Nearly 2.2 million crimes were reported to Canadian police in 2009 (Dauvergne and Turner, 2010). Vicitmization surveys have shown that less than one-third of all crimes are reported to the police, so there are likely over seven million crimes each year in Canada. Despite this huge number of offences, only about 5000 people were sentenced to federal penitentiaries (all sentences of two years or more) and 80,000 to provincial custody each year (Public Safety Canada, 2011). Thus, the likelihood of being arrested, convicted, and punished for any offence is so low that tinkering with the level of punishment makes no difference. Governments promise

*(continued)*

to "crack down" on crime, but this promise is kept so rarely that it is ignored by potential offenders, who know from their own experience (and from that of their peers) that the odds of getting away with a crime are in their favour. This means that a harsh system like California's is really one of randomized severity in which some offenders receive very harsh sentences while many others with similar patterns of offending remain on the streets.

Evaluations show that techniques such as improving the lives of high-risk youth and policing targeted toward high-crime locations and high-rate offenders can be very effective at reducing crime (Linden, 2012) . Why do you think the Canadian government has chosen to pursue a prison-based strategy they know will not work?

Canada's latest mandatory minimum sentences require a mandatory sentence of at least six months in prison for growing as few as six marijuana plants if the grower is involved in marijuana trafficking. Do you think this will have any impact on marijuana use in your community?

*Source:* Rick Linden, *Criminology: A Canadian Perspective* (7th ed.), Toronto: Nelson, 2012.

deterrents. Research on rehabilitation has shown that prison programs can reduce recidivism (getting in trouble again) if three principles are followed (Smith, Gendreau, and Swartz, 2009):

1. *The risk principle.* Rehabilitation programs should be based on the offender's risk of reoffending.
2. *The needs principle.* Interventions should address the offender's individual needs.
3. *The responsivity principle.* This means that programs should be "based on cognitive, behavioral, and social learning theories" (2009:154) and offenders should be matched with treatments and with particular treatment staff.

While these principles are well established, prison managers seldom explicitly utilize them in dealing with inmates. While virtually all inmates are released back into the community, governments have not made effective rehabilitation a priority.

## Community Corrections

Our relatively high incarceration rate has led some to suggest that Canada should rely more heavily on community corrections. These dispositions include programs such as community probation, community service orders, intensive probation supervision, and bail supervision.

The movement toward community-based sanctions has been driven by three major concerns. First, these programs are much cheaper. It costs $30,000 for community supervision, which is about one-quarter the cost of imprisonment (Public Safety Canada, 2010). The second concern is humanitarian. Prison life is unpleasant and it can be unfair to send people to jail for relatively minor offences. Finally, an offender may benefit from maintaining ties with family and community, which may make subsequent involvement in crime less likely.

### TIME TO REVIEW

- Explain why the police have such a broad range of responsibilities.
- Discuss the use of discretion in the criminal justice system.
- How does the adversarial system affect the way our court system operates?
- Explain how the restorative approach to justice differs from the normal operation of our criminal justice system.
- Explain why our society sends some convicted criminals to jail. What are some of the alternatives to this practice?

**LO-1** Explain the meanings of the terms *crime* and *deviance*.

Deviant behaviour is any act that violates established norms. Deviance varies from culture to culture and in degree of seriousness. Crime is seriously deviant behaviour that violates written laws and that is punishable by fines, incarceration, or other sanctions.

**LO-2** Understand the way in which crime and deviance are explained by functionalist, conflict, interactionist, feminist, and postmodern theories.

There are many different ways of explaining crime and deviance. Strain theory says that if people are denied legitimate access to cultural goals, some will engage in illegal behaviour to achieve these goals. Social control theory says that our social bonds help to keep us from crime and deviance, while differential association theory focuses on ties to deviant peers. The emphasis of labelling theory is on those who apply a deviant label to people who break the rules, because that label may lead to subsequent deviance. Conflict theories examine the impact of social inequality. Those with power exploit the lower classes and the legal order protects people at the top. Feminist theorists conclude that women's deviance and crime is a response to gender discrimination experienced in work, marriage, and interpersonal relationships. Postmodern theorists have focused on social control and discipline based on the use of knowledge, power, and technology.

**LO-3** Describe how sociologists count and classify crimes.

Official crime statistics are taken from the Canadian Uniform Crime Reports survey, which lists crimes reported to the police. We also use victimization surveys that interview households to determine the incidence of crimes, including those not reported to police.

## KEY TERMS

**corporate crime** An illegal act committed by corporate employees on behalf of the corporation and with its support (p. 187).

**crime** An act that violates criminal law and is punishable by fines, jail terms, and other sanctions (p. 175).

**cybercrime** Offences where a computer is the object of a crime or the tool used to commit a crime (p. 186).

**deviance** Any behaviour, belief, or condition that violates cultural norms in the society or group in which it occurs (p. 174).

**differential association theory** The proposition that individuals have a greater tendency to deviate from societal norms when they frequently associate with persons who favour deviance over conformity (p. 177).

**illegitimate opportunity structures** Circumstances that provide an opportunity for people to acquire through illegitimate activities what they cannot achieve through legitimate channels (p. 176).

**labelling theory** The proposition that deviants are those people who have been successfully labelled as such by others (p. 179).

**moral crusades** Public and media awareness campaigns that help generate public and political support for moral entrepreneurs' causes (p. 181).

**moral entrepreneurs** People or groups who take an active role in trying to have particular behaviours defined as deviant (p. 181).

occupational 'or white collar' crime A term used to describe illegal activities committed by people in the course of their employment or in dealing with their financial affairs (p. 187).

organized crime A business operation that supplies illegal goods and/or services for profit (p. 188).

political crime Illegal or unethical acts involving the usurpation of power by government officials, or illegal or unethical acts perpetrated against a government by outsiders seeking to make a political statement or to undermine or overthrow the government (p. 189).

primary deviance A term used to describe the initial act of rule breaking (p. 179).

secondary deviance A term used to describe the process whereby a person who has been labelled deviant accepts that new identity and continues the deviant behaviour (p. 179).

social bond theory The proposition that the likelihood of deviant behaviour increases when a person's ties to society are weakened or broken (p. 177).

social control Systematic practices developed by social groups to encourage conformity and discourage deviance. (p. 174).

strain theory The proposition that people feel strain when they are exposed to cultural goals that they are unable to obtain because they do not have access to culturally approved means of achieving these goals (p. 176).

street crime All violent crime, certain property crimes, and certain morals crimes (p. 186).

**LO-4** Understand how age, gender, class, and race are related to deviance and crime.

Persons under the age of 25 have the highest rates of crime. Persons arrested for assault and homicide and white-collar criminals are generally older. Women have much lower rates of crime than men. Persons from lower socioeconomic backgrounds are more likely to be arrested for violent and property crimes, while corporate crime is more likely to occur among upper socioeconomic classes.

**LO-5** Describe how the criminal justice system deals with crime.

The criminal justice system includes the police, the courts, and prisons. These agencies often have considerable discretion in dealing with offenders. The police often use discretion in deciding whether to act on a situation. Prosecutors and judges use discretion in deciding which cases to pursue and how to handle them.

# KEY FIGURES

**Robert Merton (1910-2003)** Merton was one of the most important figures in the development of sociology in the United States. His work in criminology was important because it placed the sources of crime in the social structure rather than in individual psychopathology.

**Edwin Sutherland (1883-1950)** Sutherland was also a key figure in criminological theory. He is best known for his differential association theory and identification of white-collar crime as a serious problem.

## KEY FIGURES

**Michel Foucault (1926-1984)** Foucault's work spanned a wide variety of areas in the field of social theory. He was also one of the first to recognize the potential of new surveillance technologies on all members of society.

© Jean Pierre FOUCHET/RAPHO/Gamma-Rapho/Getty

**Elizabeth Comack (b. 1952)** Comack's work has focused on the intersections of gender, race, and crime and on the sociology of law. Her most recent research has been on inner-city crime and on racialized policing.

Courtesy of Elizabeth Comack

## APPLICATION QUESTIONS

1. As a sociologist armed with a sociological imagination, how would you propose to deal with the problem of crime in Canada? What programs would you suggest enhancing? What programs would you reduce?

2. Do you ever feel afraid of being a crime victim? How do you think that people like you can best reduce their likelihood of being victimized?

3. Legalized gambling provides Canadian governments with billions of dollars in revenue each year. Some provinces now even allow online gambling. What are the positive and negative consequences of this gambling? Do you think that gambling laws should be liberalized, or should gambling be restricted? Why?

4. Look at today's paper or an online media site. What sorts of crimes are in the headlines? How well do these media reports reflect the reality of crime in your community?

5. Legislation passed by the federal government in 2012 provided mandatory penalties for some marijuana offences that were as long or longer than sentences for sexually abusing children. Do you think these mandatory minimum sentences reflect society's attitudes toward these offences? Why do you think the government passed such harsh laws against growing marijuana?

**CourseMate**

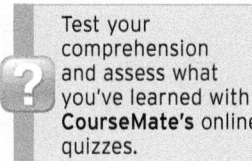Test your comprehension and assess what you've learned with **CourseMate's** online quizzes.

For other interesting Lived Experiences, watch the video clips on **CourseMate.**

Practise what you've learned with flashcards containing key terms and definitions on **CourseMate.**

## CREDITS FOR VOLUME 1 and VOLUME 2 of COMMIT SOCIOLOGY

This page constitutes an extension of the copyright page. We have made every effort to trace the ownership of all copyrighted material and to secure permission from copyright holders. In the event of any question arising as to the use of any material, we will be pleased to make the necessary corrections in future printings. Thanks are due to the following authors, publishers, and agents for permission to use the material indicated.

Religion: The Comeback
Bibby, Reginald. Beyond the Gods and Back: Religion's Demise and Rise and Why it Matters. Lethbridge: Project Canada Books, 2011. Reprinted with permission of Project Canada Books.

Definition of Family Correctional Services Canada
Private Family Visiting http://www.csc-scc.gc.ca/family/003004-1000-eng.shtml
Correctional Services Canada, 2012 Reproduced with the permission of the Minister of Public Works and Government Services Canada, 2013

The Changing Face of Matrimony: Same-Sex Civil Marriage in the Twenty-First Century by Adam Green
Reprinted by permission of the author.

McJobs: McDonaldization and its Relationship to the Labour Process
Republished with permission of SAGE Publications, from McDonaldization: The Reader, George Ritzer, Thousand Oaks: Pine Forge Press, 2002; permission conveyed through Copyright Clearance Center, Inc.

Be Thin: Contradictions Within the Social Construction of Beauty and Happiness
Roberts, Sharon. "Be Thin: Contradictions Within the Social Construction of Beauty and Happiness." Unpublished Manuscript, 2011. Reproduced with permission of the author.

Meanwhile Backstage: Behavior in Public Bathrooms
Spencer Cahill, William Distler, Cynthia Lachowetz, Andrea Meaney, Robyn Tarallo, and Teena Willard, "Meanwhile Backstage: Public Bathrooms and the Interaction Order," Journal of Contemporary Ethnography (formerly Urban Life), 14(1), pp. 33–34, 38–49, 56. Copyright © 1985 by SAGE Publications. Reprinted by Permission of SAGE Publications.